Gothic Nightmares

Gothic Nightmares

Fuseli, Blake and the Romantic Imagination

Martin Myrone

With essays by
Christopher Frayling and Marina Warner
and additional catalogue contributions by
Christopher Frayling and Mervyn Heard

Tate Publishing

First published 2006 by order of the Tate Trustees by Tate Publishing, a division of Tate Enterprises Ltd, Millbank, London SW1P 4RG
www.tate.org.uk/publishing

on the occasion of the exhibition
Gothic Nightmares: Fuseli, Blake and the Romantic Imagination
at Tate Britain 15 February – 1 May 2006

British Library Cataloguing in Publication Data
A catalogue record for this book is available from the British Library

ISBN-13: 978-185437-582-2
ISBN-10: 1-85437-582-7

Distributed in the United States and Canada by Harry N. Abrams, Inc., New York

Library of Congress Cataloguing in Publication Data
Library of Congress Control Number 2005933811

Designed by bc, mh (www.bcmh.co.uk)
Printed in Italy by Conti Tipocolor, Florence

Cover: Henry Fuseli, *The Nightmare* exh. RA 1782 (detail, no.1)

Measurements are given in centimetres, height before width. Dimensions refer to the support size, with the exception of prints, where they refer to plate mark, unless otherwise stated.

'exh. RA' indicates that the work was first exhibited at the Royal Academy of Arts, London.

All biblical references are to the Authorised (King James) edition.

Contents

Foreword

At the core of this exhibition lies the art of Henry Fuseli (1741–1825), the Swiss-born artist who settled in London and is remembered above all for his distinctively expressive and often disturbing visual interpretations of literary subject matter. It is over thirty years since his works were last seen in depth in a British exhibition – the great Tate Gallery show of 1975, curated by the pre-eminent Fuseli scholar Gert Schiff (1926–90), which gave a strong sense of the range and complexity of his art. Now, Tate Britain offers a new vision of his achievement, placing a selection of the finest of his paintings and drawings firmly in the context of the art of the late eighteenth century and the wider cultural phenomenon of the Gothic.

Since 1975 much has changed in the way we are able to think about Fuseli and his times. The publication of his English letters (1982) and the catalogue raisonné of his prints (1994), both by the eminent scholar David H. Weinglass, has helped transform our understanding of his art. Taken together with the extensive commentary available in the contemporary press of the late eighteenth century – a resource inaccessible to Schiff but now, through the great efforts of staff at the Courtauld Institute of Art and the Paul Mellon Centre for Studies in British Art, more accessible than ever – these materials have made it possible to redate or date more precisely many of Fuseli's most important canvases. The present publication makes much of this new information available for the first time. There have, additionally, been a number of significant rediscoveries, unknown to Schiff in 1975, including such imposing canvases as *Satan Starting from the Touch of Ithuriel's Lance* (no.37), *Queen Katherine's Dream* (no.100) and *The Night-hag Visiting Lapland Witches* (no.91).

At the same time, our understanding of the period in which Fuseli lived and worked has been greatly altered by the research of historians of art, literature and society. Fuseli's divided identity has perplexed commentators, who have tended to see in him a split between the public and the private, the 'Neoclassical' and the 'Romantic', the enlightened and the irrational. He has often been considered an eccentric, driven by his personal idiosyncrasies and obsessions. The present exhibition draws out further facets of an art which spans the divide – or imagined divide – between 'high' and 'low' culture, the high-minded and the sensational. This puts Fuseli in the context of the major institutional and social developments in the London art world of the late eighteenth century – the emergence, from the 1760s, of annual exhibitions of contemporary art, the rise of press criticism and publicity, the growth of the art market and the changing social make-up of the audience for art and literature. These altered forever the way in which art was understood, appreciated and valued, laying the foundations for what we know as a peculiarly modern kind of art world.

In order to explore Fuseli's role within this changing art world, and the influence of further historical factors in what was an age of often traumatic social and political change, we have chosen to present his art in relation to that of some of his contemporaries. The work of William Blake (1757–1827) draws from and develops Fuseli's art in highly original ways; as friends, and sometimes mutual-supporters, the lives of these two men were closely intertwined. The satirical art of James Gillray (1756–1815) offers another take on the 'Fuselian'. These three artists, working in quite different ways but each powerfully original and visionary, lie at the heart of the exhibition. Further works by George Romney, Joseph Wright of Derby (whose art may appear so unlike Fuseli's, but who was linked to him by a shared circle of patrons), Richard and Maria Cosway, and many others, enrich the selection. Through their work we see the taste for the Gothic – the weird, supernatural and romantic – transformed and revised from many different angles.

This survey of the visual dimensions of the Gothic would have been impossible without the generous support of our lenders from around the world. My sincere thanks to them all, but I would like to give particular acknowledgement to the Kunsthaus, Zurich, which has lent an important group of drawings, prints and paintings from their unrivalled collection of Fuseli's art. Indeed, our project was developed as a complement to their monographic exhibition, *Füssli: The Wild Swiss* (14 October 2005 – 8 January 2006). We have worked closely with the Director of the Kunsthaus, Christoph Becker, and his colleagues, and I would like to thank them warmly for their co-operation. The exhibition at Tate Britain has been generously supported by The Horace W. Goldsmith Foundation, with additional support from Aroldo Zevi and Ivor Braka.

The making of this exhibition has been predominantly the work of Dr Martin Myrone, Tate Britain's Curator of eighteenth- and nineteenth-century art. He proposed it, conceived it, selected it, wrote much of its catalogue, and organised and led the whole project in all its practical aspects as well. That he should operate so confidently across so many areas of museum expertise is remarkable enough, but to do so in parallel with contributing to several other exhibition and academic projects at Tate, and indeed beyond, is extraordinary. He has worked closely alongside Professor Sir Christopher Frayling, from the outset a key member of the curatorial team whose advice, ideas and energy has helped to shape the exhibition in decisive ways. I would like to thank Chris, and also Professor Marina Warner, for their excellent contributions to this catalogue. Martin's own acknowledgements refer to the vital support he has received in addition from many staff across Tate, to whom I am also indebted.

Stephen Deuchar
Director, Tate Britain

Acknowledgements

I have been singularly fortunate to have as a partner in this endeavour Christopher Frayling. His brilliant, wide-ranging explorations of art, cinema and cultural history are an enduring inspiration, and his role on this project, as consultant curator, extends far beyond the essay and catalogue contributions appearing here. The exhibition as a whole has benefited enormously from the wholehearted commitment of his energy, judgement and intellect. Marina Warner has generously brought her acute understanding of folklore, fantasy and the imagination to bear, in conversation, by example, and in her thoughtful contribution to the present publication. Mervyn Heard has been a further crucial member of the core team, and has advised and assisted in the re-creation of a 'Phantasmagoria' show; he is the co-author of the essay on the topic appearing here. The exhibition's designers are Richard Cottrell and Brian Vermeulen, of Cottrell & Vermeulen Architecture. They have worked closely with the graphic design team of Ben Chatfield and Mark Hopkins, of bc, mh, and have together brought their characteristic combination of verve and subtlety to the installation. At the Kunsthaus, Zurich I would like to thank particularly Christoph Becker, Franziska Lentzsch and Eveline Schmid, for their kind co-operation and assistance.

Within the Tate, Ben Tufnell has assisted and advised on every aspect of the exhibition project, and has taken particular responsibility for the complex audio-visual aspects of the installation. His energy and judgment have been vital ingredients in shaping this show. The interpretation was overseen by Richard Humphreys, with important input from Christina Bagatavicius and Sarah Hyde. Loic Tallon helped research some of the interpretative materials, and Mareike Doleschal generously assisted on several aspects of the preparation of the show. The exciting and varied programme of events around this exhibition has been organised by Rebecca Heald and her colleagues. The installation was overseen by Andy Shiel, and implemented, with their characteristic professionalism, by Mikei Hall and his team; Anna Nesbit, AV Manager, has had a critical role in realising the Phantasmagoria. Gillian Buttimer has expertly managed the loan arrangements. Tate's superbly dedicated team of registrars, conservators and technicians have prepared works for display. As always, Stephen Deuchar, Director of Tate Britain, and Judith Nesbitt, Head of Exhibitions and Display, have been a decisive source of inspiration and direction.

As the Director notes, we have been heartened by the very great generosity of lenders from around the world, both public institutions and private collectors. First among these is the Kunsthaus, Zurich, who have made available to us a wonderful selection of works from the outstanding collections there, and the Department of Prints and Drawings at the British Museum who have made an especially generous loan. But we are grateful to all our lenders. In this respect, I would additionally like to thank, for their support, assistance and advice, MaryAnne Stevens and Nick Savage of the Royal Academy, Antony Griffiths, Kim Sloan, Sheila O'Connell, and Charlie Collinson at the British Museum, Mary Kisler of Auckland Art Gallery Toi o Tāmaki, Suzanna Folds McCullagh, Art Institute of Chicago, Sarah Allard, Keeper, Derby Art Gallery, David Fraser, Valerie Hunter at the National Gallery of Scotland, John Fisher, Librarian, Guildhall Library, Alex Kidson of The Walker, Liverpool, Katy Baldwin, Ted Gott, National Gallery of Victoria, Roberta Waddell, Curator of Prints, New York Public Library, Erin Blake, Curator of Art & Special Collections, Folger Shakespeare Library, Aroldo Zevi, Andrew Edmunds, John Sargent, Westminster Archives, Ivor Braka, Richard and Nona Barrett, Luba Mittelman, Caroline Bacon of the Cecil Higgins Art Gallery, Ron Clarke of the Herbert, Coventry, Robert N. Essick, Sir Robert Goff, Anne Crookshank, Claire Bradley, Paul Norris, Fylde Borough Council, Margaret O'Sullivan, County and Diocesan Archivist, Derbyshire Record Office, Michael Burden and Maggie Davies, New College, Oxford, Andrew Wyld and Susan Sloman of W/S Fine Art, and Timothy A. Riggs of Ackland Art Museum. Max Browne has been generous in his help and advice with regards to the works by Theodor von Holst included in the exhibition, and has made material contributions to the catalogue entries. The realisation of the Phantasmagoria would have been impossible without the support of Thomas Wynants, Martin Gilbert, Jorgen From Andersen, Hauch's Physiske Cabinet, Soro, and Jaana Tegelberg, Cabinet of Physics, Helsinki University Museum. There are many more individuals who have, directly or indirectly, shaped this project. Foremost among these are David Bindman and David Solkin, whose researches and publications on late eighteenth-century art have been a guiding influence. Further ideas, comments and inspiration have been drawn from Mark Hallett, Bronwyn Gardner, Fintan Cullen, John Barrell, Michael Rosenthal, Karen Junod, Ludmilla Jordanova, Luisa Calè, Wendy Bird, Simon Wilson, the late Richard Godfrey, Rosie Dias, Ann Bermingham and, of course, Felicity Kerr.

I know that my fellow-contributors would like to join me in thanking most warmly Judith Severne of Tate Publishing, who has overseen the production of this volume with supreme skill. Judith has had additional support from Rebecca Fortey and freelance copy-editor Johanna Stephenson. The production has benefited enormously from the acute eye and dedication of Sophie Lawrence, Production Manager at Tate Publishing. Ben Chatfield and Mark Hopkins of bc, mh have designed the catalogue with meticulous attention to every detail.

The idea for the present exhibition has grown out of doctoral research (completed at the Courtauld Institute in 1998) and the subsequent book, *Bodybuilding: Reforming Masculinities in British Art* (Yale University Press 2005). None of these endeavours would have been possible without the support of my parents, Tony and Jo, to whom I say 'thank you'.

Martin Myrone

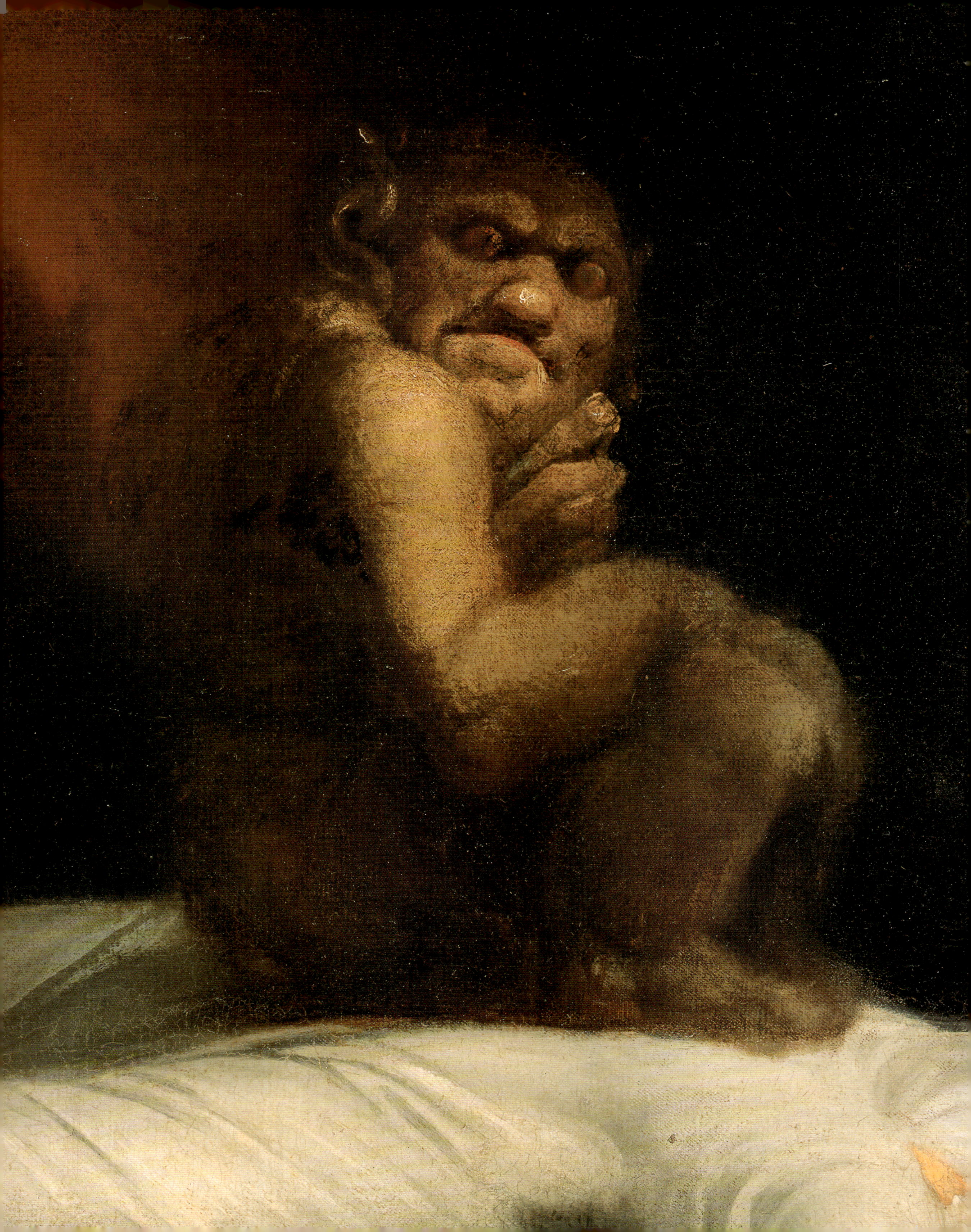

Fuseli's *The Nightmare*: Somewhere between the Sublime and the Ridiculous

Christopher Frayling

The Royal Academy summer show of 1782, the third to take place in its new purpose-built exhibition galleries at Somerset House, ran from Monday 29 April until Monday 3 June. During this five-week period, the show was visited by 55,357 people – an increase of 12,533 on the previous year.[1] There was an entrance fee of one shilling 'to prevent the Rooms being filled by improper Persons'. One visitor wrote of the social atmosphere on a busy day:

> People Flock in a forenoon to saunter about gazing at each other as at any other kind of Route [gathering], and now and then perhaps look with admiration on an *Outré* Piece, that on account of its staring colours and sharp unnatural Angles would *attrappe* their notice sooner than the most chaste and classical piece …[2]

Johann Heinrich Ramberg (1763–1840) – who, as it happens, exhibited one of his satirical drawings in the 1782 show – five years later inspired a well-known engraving of the overcrowding and social game-playing at the Royal Academy exhibition (fig.1), which could almost be an illustration of these words: the fashionably dressed visitors, a sample of London high society, are indeed 'gazing at each other' rather than at the paintings; one male figure is pretending to pay close attention to a work of art when in fact he is eyeing up a beautiful woman who seems to take no notice; another is trying hard to seem a connoisseur by looking at nothing in particular through an eyeglass; George, Prince of Wales, meanwhile, poses portrait-style next to Joshua Reynolds in the centre of the picture – the subject of much more concentration than any of the pictures, many of which are hung like washing above the line and beyond anyone's field of vision. Beneath the engraving, in Greek, was the motto – the same as the one above the entrance door of the Great Room – 'Let no Stranger to the Muses enter' (which was more usually translated in the 1780s as 'Let none but Men of Taste presume to enter here').

The motto, in the context of the engraving, has become ironic. It refers in part to the debate among artists and connoisseurs about how best to reconcile the new pressures of the marketplace and of 'a fashionable Rage' – recently brought into sharp focus by surprisingly large attendances at the Academy – with high-minded ideas about classical models, a space for public enlightenment rather than private business and the primacy of history painting.

Joshua Reynolds had observed in the most recently delivered of his *Discourses on Art* that it was the role of artists rather than connoisseurs to 'raise the thoughts and extend the views of the spectator'; and it was the mission of artists (no longer just called painters) to elevate the public's visual standards as well.[3] The purest version of this ideal held that, where possible, artists should choose sublime subject matter representing a key moment from ancient history or the Bible – 'sublime' in the sense of noble and intending to 'raise thoughts' and encourage virtue in the viewer. But since the mid-1770s, there had been the beginnings of pressure from some younger artists to emphasise the *experience* of a work of art rather than necessarily its wholesome influence. The painter James Barry (1741–1806), for example, in a pamphlet of 1775, had argued that 'the Sublime' had recently become too associated with good manners: 'We affect such nice feelings and so much sensibility, as not to be able to bear the sight of pictures where the action turns upon any circumstance of distress'.[4]

'Nice feelings' did not automatically produce great art; extremes of feeling, or 'terror' – another definition of that slippery term 'the Sublime' – could sometimes do so, through extreme expressions, unnerving compositions and subject matter that shocked.

One trouble was that despite all the talk about a space for moral instruction and edification – or even for sublime feelings of terror – most of the paintings shown at the Academy still tended to be portraits, landscapes, still lifes and genre studies: indeed, it has been estimated that in the years 1781–5 the proportion of history paintings never rose to more than 20 per cent of the works on show; portraits and landscapes on the other hand – admittedly smaller in scale – accounted for about 70 per cent.[5] And despite the President's injunctions to bestow 'refinement of taste', and the newly fashionable emphasis on 'circumstances of distress', many artists seemed to be using the Academy show – and

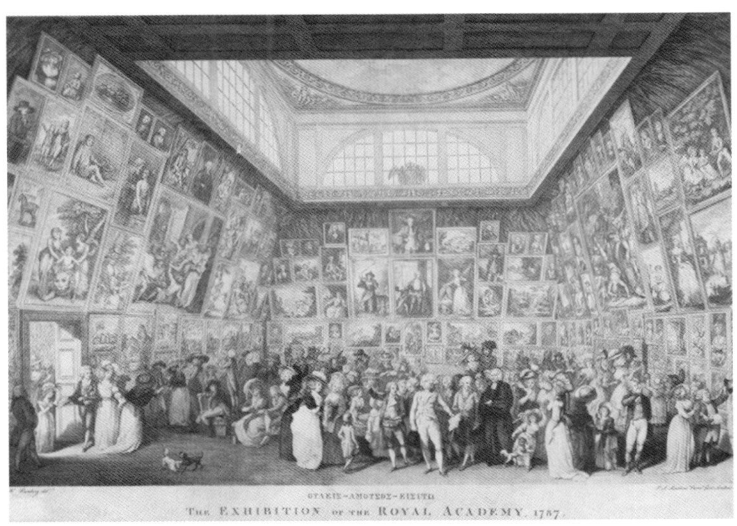

fig.1 Johann Heinrich Ramberg (1763–1840), *Exhibition of the Royal Academy, 1787*, pub. A.C. de Poggi, 1 July 1787. Engraving and etching. Courtauld Institute of Art, London

Detail from Henry Fuseli, *The Nightmare* exh. RA 1782 (no.1)

gossipy coverage of it in the journals – as ways of stimulating private commissions and editions of prints.

The 1782 exhibition fitted the pattern of previous years. Since the titles and descriptions in the catalogue were approximate at best, it is sometimes difficult to match them to surviving paintings. But between catalogue numbers 46 and 85 – the pictures were numbered consecutively as located in the Great Room, first number over the entrance, so most of these would probably have been hung on the wall opposite the door – it is possible to identify the Dublin-born George Barret's painting *A Wood Scene with a Group of Beech Trees in Norbury Park* or *The Drive, Norbury Park* (no.46, now in Norwich Castle Museum and Art Gallery), Johan Zoffany's *A Conversation, John Wilkes and his Daughter* (no.53, now in the National Portrait Gallery, London), Thomas Gainsborough's *Portrait of an Officer, Major St Leger* (no.58, Royal Collection), Dominic Serres's *The British Fleet under the Command of Rear Admiral Hyde Parker … St Lucia, 25th of March 1780* (no.58, now in Melford Hall, Suffolk), George Stubbs's *Portrait of a Young Lady in the Character of Una, from Spencer's Fairy Queen* (no.70, now in the Lady Lever collection, National Museums, Liverpool) and the same artist's enamel on ceramic *Portrait of a Young Gentleman out Shooting* (no.79, now in the Tate), and Joshua Reynolds's *Children* or *The Infant Academy* (no.72, now at Kenwood). Among all these paintings, considerably smaller than most of them, next to T. Gooch's *Portraits of Horses and Dogs Belonging to the Hon. Mr Pitt* (no.63) and one of Philippe Jacques de Loutherbourg's landscapes with cattle (no.65) was Fuseli's *The Nightmare* (no.64, here no.1). Horace Walpole wrote one word beside the entry in his catalogue: 'shocking'.[6]

Fuseli already knew how to draw attention to himself and his work, amid all these seductions. As someone who was not yet an Associate of the Royal Academy (he was elected in November 1788) – even though he was in his forty-second year – he was fortunate to have his entry for 1782 hung so close to the works of such well-known artists. Reynolds had fifteen paintings in the exhibition, Gainsborough eleven, Stubbs seven, de Loutherbourg six, Zoffany and West three each, and Fuseli just the one.

Fuseli had no formal art education – he was always insecure about his technical limitations, one reason perhaps why he went on so much about Phidias and Michelangelo – he had no network of aristocratic patrons, and although he liked to refer to himself as 'a gentleman' not everyone was convinced. He was also a late starter. He did, however, have a good classical education – which gave him an advantage over most of his fellows, who only aspired to one – and he was a born showman with an interesting Zurich accent, a short fuse and plenty of well-rehearsed eccentricities. He had also been aware for some time 'that I am approaching the period which commonly decides a man's life with regard to fame and infamy …'[7]

In August 1780, Fuseli wrote a letter to the banker Sir Robert Smyth, his patron and a contact from his stay in Rome – in which he requested 'a Supply of Some money – being nearly left without any' – describing a fateful visit to 'Sir Joshua, whom I Spent lately a whole day with, [and who] is busy with a *Dido* again – the Same in every respect as the first but less promising in point of execution; he himself begins to think that he has failed'.[8] This was *The Death of Dido* (Royal Collection), a large-scale painting in the grand baroque manner based on the pivotal moment in Virgil's *Aeneid*. Fuseli immediately seized the opportunity to aim at something greater – or at least more extreme and distinctively designed – and exhibit it at the Academy, preferably in a location where visitors could directly compare it with the President's effort.

As competition? As a challenge? As flattery? Fuseli certainly admired, and sometimes copied, Reynolds as a theorist. Whatever his motives, Fuseli's vertical version of *The Death of Dido* (or *Dido on the Funeral Pyre* 1780; fig.2) attracted more attention in the journals than his earlier Shakespearean entries to the Academy and this time the consensus was that a terrible beauty had been born. A week after his letter to Smyth about *Dido*, Fuseli had written again – reminding his patron that 'my Stock of Subsistence is litteraly exhausted', and mentioning that a commission called 'Queen Catherine' was keeping him busy and 'do so still'.[9] This was *The Vision of Queen Katherine* or *Queen Katherine's Dream* (from Shakespeare's *Henry VIII*), which was also exhibited in the Academy show of 1781, possibly as a pendant for *The Death of Dido*. It (no.100) depicted Queen Katherine of Aragon reclining on a chaise longue the night before her death, and having a vision of a procession of ghosts dressed in white crowning her with garlands: although this time it was an angelic vision – the nude figures, like Roman *bacchanti*, float in an elegant arc – the painting had the same sort of hallucinatory drama as Fuseli's earlier entries *The Death of Cardinal Beaufort* (exh. 1774; The Walker, Liverpool) and the painting of *The Witches Show Macbeth the Descendants of Banquo* (exh. 1777; see no.33). He was finding a distinctively visual idiom in which to express his strange readings of Shakespeare's plays, and had by now made his name as a 'painter of Shakespeare': the mixture of classical stories, British folklore and big performances was to him irresistible.

Fuseli's *The Death of Dido* and *The Vision of Queen Katherine* showed that he was capable of taking on morally elevating subjects from well-known classical or quite well-known literary texts, and at the same time of drawing attention to himself by being more extreme and 'poetical' in his treatment of them than the pillars of the artistic establishment, especially Reynolds and Benjamin West. The result was sometimes to

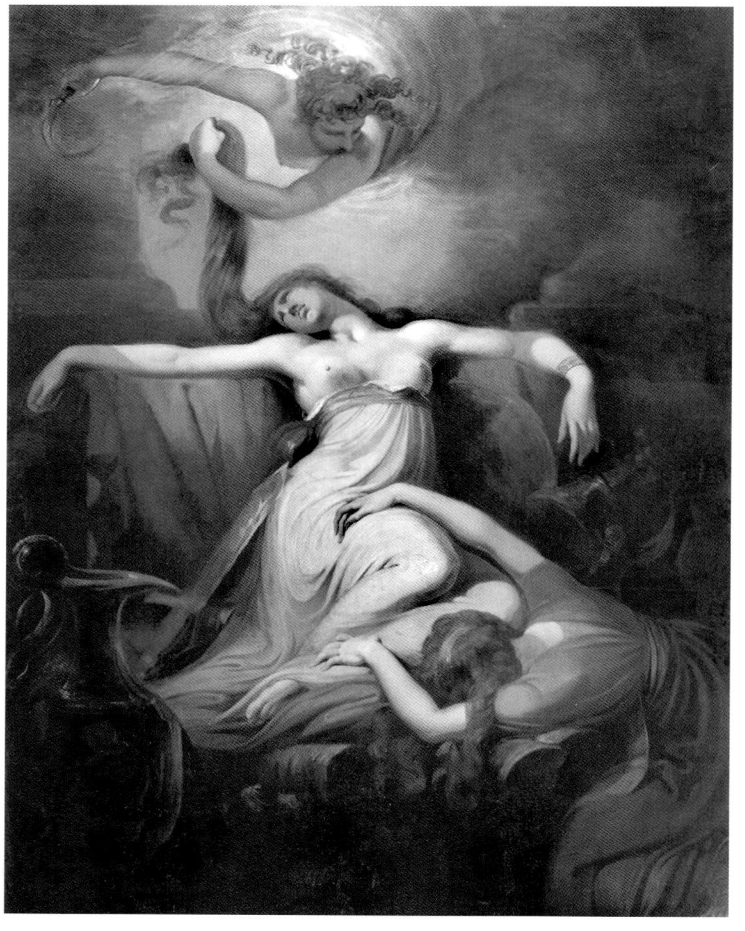

fig.2 Henry Fuseli (1741–1825), *The Death of Dido*, exh. R.A. 1781, oil on canvas 244.3 x 183.4 cm. Paul Mellon Collection, Yale Center for British Art

become popular, although Fuseli claimed he would never knowingly lower his standards to 'the charm-struck crowd'. He had produced storytelling pictures which featured idealised figures doing extreme things at a 'middle moment' against neutral backgrounds, and the critics had almost convinced themselves that the stories embodied lofty ideas as well. Almost.

Then came *The Nightmare*, exhibited the following year, another painting of a vision or hallucination which Fuseli may have started preparing as early as March 1781. He may even have been drawing *The Nightmare* around the time he first saw Reynolds's *Dido* on the easel. Fuseli had been working in parallel on *The Changeling* (drawn March 1780; cat. no. 2). *The Nightmare* was a small painting, 101 x 127 cm, and a relatively simple composition: young girl sleeping on her back, incubus or *mara* squatting on her abdomen while staring at the viewer, spectral horse's head with white orbs for eyes staring blankly though a dark red curtain, bed with pink and yellow coverlet or shawl, wooden dressing-table at the girl's feet with jars and a mirror on it, all surrounded by darkness.

The *Morning Chronicle* of Tuesday 30 April 1782,[10] the second day of the exhibition, had – not surprisingly – made no mention of Fuseli, preferring to focus on the much-publicised rivalry between Gainsborough and Reynolds, and the talents of West, de Loutherbourg, Zoffany and Stubbs. The *Morning Post* of the same day provided some helpful 'rules that have been laid down as essential in assisting the judgement to form a correct opinion of a painting': these included 'the expression must be proper to the subject', 'the drawing must be just', 'the colouring ... must be natural, beautiful and clear' and 'NATURE must be the foundation that must be seen at the bottom; but nature must be raised and improved in the painter's mind'. For an artist such as Fuseli who liked to assert 'Damn Nature! she always puts me out', and who preferred 'the judicious adoption of figures in art', to build rather than design, these previews were not at all promising. 'Puzzlepate' of the *Morning Herald* was the first to write a proper review on Wednesday 8 May:

> There is a wildness of conception in Mr Fuseli's picture of the Night Shade at the Royal Academy, which teems with that usual concomitant of genius, inaccuracy. He has introduced a mare's head into the piece, to characterise his subject. Now the personification of that disorder, which attacks the human frame in sleep, is borrowed from a word of northern origin; Mair or Mêre, a witch or sorceress. Shakespeare's Mad Tom [in *King Lear*, Act III, scene 4] mentions her in that character from some legendary ballad, not unknown, perhaps, to the ingenious compiler [Thomas Percy] of the reliques of our ancient English poetry.
>
> 'St Withold footed thrice the wold,
> He met the Night Mare and her nine-fold;
> Bid her alight and her troth plight
> And aroynt thee, witch, aroynt thee!'

So, according to this critic of *The Nightmare* – the first – Fuseli had confused a witch's visit with a horse. The review quoted Mad Tom's song on the heath (with the eighteenth-century variant of 'wold' for 'old'), which in turn may have been suggested by Dr Johnson's *Dictionary* (1755), where there was another alternative reading ('her nine-fold' became 'her name told'). Johnson was still the authority, and could be depended on to cite interesting literary references as usage:

> NIGHTMARE [*night*, and according to Temple, *mara*, a spirit that, in the northern mythology, was related to torment or suffocate sleepers]. A morbid oppression in the night, resembling the pressure of weight upon the breast.
>
> 'Saint Withold footed thrice the wold
> He met the *nightmare*, and her name be told;
> Bid her alight, and her troth plight ...'
>
> MARE, on the other hand, was 'the female of a horse'.[11]

The Nightmare, unusually for Fuseli, did not make explicit reference to a particular literary or mythological source. The critics were accustomed to paintings of specific dreams experienced by Old Testament sages, Trojan warriors, Renaissance artists or Shakespearean kings – but a generic nightmare perhaps set in the present day was something new. Surely, given Fuseli's reputation up to now, this had a Shakespearean meaning – maybe to do with *King Lear*? The *Morning Chronicle*, of the following day, acknowledged that *The Nightmare* was a virtuoso performance but was more turned off by the subject matter:

> *The Nightmare*, by Mr Fuseli like all his productions has strong marks of genius about it; but hag-riding is too unpleasant a thought to be agreeable to anyone, and is unfit for furniture [i.e. as decoration] or reflection – *Qui bono*? ... Yet surely a disagreeable subject, well executed, is preferable to the most engaging one ill described.

Fuseli was to tackle the night-hag as a subject in 1794–6 (no.91).'Hag-riding' in the review may be another reference to Mad Tom's song, or even to *Paradise Lost*. Under 'Nighthag', Dr Johnson had written:

> Witch supposed to wander in the night.
> 'Nor uglier follows the night-hag, when called
> In secret, riding through the air she comes
> Lur'd with the smell of infant-blood, to dance
> With Lapland witches'
> (Milton's *Paradise Lost* 6 II)

So maybe *The Nightmare* contained a reference to Milton? On the other hand, it could perhaps refer to Queen Mab. Under 'Mare', Dr Johnson had continued:

> [From *mara*, the name of a spirit imagined by the nations of the north to torment sleepers]. A kind of torpor or stagnation, which seems to press the stomach with a weight; the night hag.
> 'Mab, his merry queen by night,
> Bestrides young folks that lie upright,
> In elder times the *mare* that hight,
> Which plagues them out of measure.'
> (Drayton's *Nymphiad*)

If *The Nightmare*, with its elf-ape, *was* about Queen Mab, then by extension maybe Mercutio's speech from Act I, scene 4 of *Romeo and Juliet* was hidden in there somewhere as well:

> And in this state she gallops night by night
> Through lovers' brains, and then they dream of love;
> ...This is the hag, when maids lie on their backs,
> That presses them and learns them first to bear,
> Making them women of good carriage

The debate in the journals of 8 and 9 May – which created an aura of mystery around 'a disagreeable subject, well executed' – may well have stimulated public interest in *The Nightmare*. On Thursday 9 May, 2,713 people were recorded as visiting the Academy exhibition – the highest figure for a single day of the entire run (apart from the last) and even higher than that for the first opening day of the Academy on Friday 2 June 1780, which was 2,680. The average so far in 1782 had been 1,962 people a day. Only on Monday 3 June, when the exhibition was about to close, were more people crammed into the Great Room: an astonishing 5,085 last-minuters on a single insufferable day.[12]

Monday 3 June was a few days after the *Public Advertiser* had judged the subject matter of *The Nightmare* to be more acceptable:

> The Exhibition of the Royal Academy consists (like all others) of good, bad and indifferent, and some capital ... The few capital may possibly be confined to the *Night Mare* of Fuseli, the view of *St Vincent's Rocks by Moon Light*, with the *Aeolus* and *Cynthia* [nos 17 and 78] of that sublime genius Maria Cosway.

Horace Walpole, meanwhile, deemed the Cosway *Eolus raising a Storm* 'execrable'. *The Gazetteer* of Saturday 1 June, two days before the exhibition closed, concluded that *The Nightmare* did conform, after all, to the canons of good taste. It was more than just an *outré* piece:

> Any artist who *personifies an idea upon canvas*, has at least the merit of imagination. The present picture seems to be not only well conceived, but well executed ... The whole produces the effect very powerfully, and the foreshortening of the head, neck and arms, seem to be given in the true style of drawing.

Over six and a half thousand people could have seen *The Nightmare* on Saturday 1 June and Monday 3 June, and probably did. But so far the debate about the painting had concerned its 'wildness', whether the subject matter was 'disagreeable' or acceptable, and possible sources of inspiration in Shakespeare. The critics seemed to agree that Fuseli had personified an idea. The question was, what exactly *was* the idea? Where paintings of visions were concerned, the critics seemed much more comfortable describing the visual conventions than they were at explaining what all this might *mean*. It took a Church of England vicar, Rev. Robert Anthony Bromley, Rector of St Mildred's in the Poultry, to be the first to suggest that *The Nightmare* might after all be about sex. In the first volume of his *Philosophical and Critical History of the Fine Arts – Painting, Sculpture and Architecture* (1793), Bromley included in his chapter on 'the qualifications essential in the constitution of moral painting' a longwinded sideswipe at Fuseli's picture[13]. He did not mention the artist by name but he did not need to:

> the dignity of moral instruction is degraded, whenever the pencil is employed on frivolous, whimsical, and unmeaning subjects ... *The Night-mare* [no.1], *Little Red Riding Hood* [exhibited by Maria Cosway at the Royal Academy in 1783], *The Shepherd's Dream* [no.101] or any dream that is not marked in authentic history as combined with the inspiring dispensations of Providence, and many other pieces of a visionary and fanciful nature, are speculations ... If it be right to follow Nature, there is nothing of her here, all that is presented to us is a *reverie* of the brain ... mere waking dreams, as wild as the conceits of a madman. [A recent commentator] very properly calls these persons 'libertines of painting': as there are libertines of religion, who have no other law but the vehemence of their own inclinations ...

In strongly implying that Fuseli was among the 'libertines of painting', Bromley was breaking new ground. Maybe *The Nightmare* was an example of the kind of libertine art which had been exhibited in recent Paris salons, or was known to be collected for private consumption by well-heeled connoisseurs. *The Philosophical and Critical History* continued – at great and ponderous length – to enunciate the principles that 'whatever is outré and extravagant can never be beautiful', and 'whatever is empty or poor of sentiment cannot instruct any persons'. Fuseli was furious. He took bitter offence at Bromley's attack on *The Nightmare*. It was one thing to encourage a public reputation for eccentricity and even for being 'Painter in ordinary to the Devil' – Fuseli did that whenever the opportunity arose, and on one occasion said of his diabolic reputation 'Aye, he has sat for me many times' – it was quite another to be publicly accused of being a libertine, especially to someone who was desperate to be accepted by the artistic establishment. So Fuseli wrote an ill-tempered notice of Bromley's book in the *Analytical Review* (July 1793):

> the whole [of Bromley's book] is delivered in the style and with the somnific loquacity of a drowsy homily ... the reader will forgive us if we refuse to enter into a more circumstantial analysis of a work which to us appears to have hardly any other title to grave consideration than its size ...[14]

Not content with this (the 'size' reference may have been an echo of criticisms made of himself), Fuseli then took part in a debate at Somerset House which resulted in the Royal Academy cancelling its subscription to the second volume of Bromley's *History*. This debate took place on 20 February 1794, and during the course of a heated discussion (which resulted in a vote seventeen to four in favour of cancellation), Fuseli's friend the painter Joseph Farington (1747–1821) helped to swing it by stating that 'a man who had written with so little delicacy on the works of living artists already' might well traduce 'in his future volumes the professional characters of the very persons then assembled'.[15] The vicar responded to these 'few men, acting in an Academic capacity' – and to Fuseli's 'shallow and contemptible objections' – in a series of seven letters published in the *Morning Herald*. His sixth letter, dated 17 April 1794 and reprinted at length in the equally angry Preface to volume two of the *History*, after extolling 'the instructive purposes of the Art' again, returned with heavy-handed irony to the question of what was the good of *The Nightmare*:

> Has not [Fuseli's] pencil always instructed? Was there not instruction in *Little Red Riding-Hood*? Yes; for old women teach the story to children; *pull the string, my dear, and the latch will come up*; it is the first lesson by which they learn to move to and fro. Was there not instruction in the *NightMare*? Certainly, the very next in progress after the former; for, next to teaching infants how to move about, is the teaching them how to lie in their beds: *Don't lie on your back, my dear, and no harm will come to you* ... But what have we not to expect ... for grown people? I anticipate it all ... the allegorical display of *Shakespeare's Spider Entangled in His Own Web*![16]

Bromley's point about the moral content and even narrative sense of 'any dream that is not marked in authentic history' chimed with another contemporary question which Fuseli's career as an exhibiting painter had already raised. If viewers could not share a story they already knew, where did the nobility of the painting reside? What was to prevent the transaction becoming 'as wild as the conceits of a madman'? When the large painting *The Witches Show Macbeth the Descendants of Banquo* (see no.33) was first shown in 1777, critics had complained that 'such a scene never existed in nature'. Fuseli had followed *The Witches* in 1780 with the painting *Ezzelin Musing over the Body of his Wife Meduna* (fig.16 on p.33) which, despite its pseudo-authentic title, had told a made-up story. A connection between invented stories with visionary themes, and commercial success, was implied by the artist in a letter to his Liverpool patron William Roscoe (1753–1831) of 22 October 1791:

> Your Approbation of my proposal for painting Small pictures to make the Large ones go on, gives me much pleasure ... such Situations as I have myself Combined Such as Ezelin, [Percival Delivering] Belisane [no.41] &c; Philosophical Ideas made intuitive, or sentiment personified, suit in my opinion, Small Canvases eminently – Want You want anything you will let me know ... my object is to enable myself to go on.[17]

So 'such Situations as I have myself combined' – the '&c' includes *The Nightmare* – suit a smaller, less epic scale, and as small canvases they are useful in promoting historical subjects on a grander scale. They are like trailers for the main feature. Fuseli was to be less pragmatic when he later devoted a whole Academy lecture to the theme of invention and invented subjects – which he again associated with visionary themes. After arguing the difference between invention and creation, he discussed the connections between the 'fancies' of the ancients and contemporary art – 'their furies and our witches': the differences between them were less about essence than about 'local, temporary, social modifications'. Fuseli then posed the question '*whether it be within the artist's province or not, to find or to combine a subject from himself, without having recourse to tradition or the stories of history and poetry?*'. His answer was an unequivocal yes:

> Why not, if the subject be within the limits of art and the combinations of nature, though it should have escaped observation? Shall the immediate avenues of the mind, open to all its observers, from the poet to the novelist, be shut only to the artist ... For if these images so pursue us when our minds are ... in a kind of waking dream ... and all this with an air of reality, why should we not turn to use this vice of the mind.[18]

The reference to a 'waking dream' suggests that Fuseli may still have been smarting from Rev. Bromley's attack, some eight years after it was first delivered. His third *Lecture on Painting* also related closely – more closely than has been noted by art historians up to now – to the artist's often-quoted aphorism (no.231) about dreams: 'one of the most unexplored regions of art are dreams, and what may be called the personification of sentiment'.[19] This aphorism has been treated as the one and only time that Fuseli touched on 'the mysteries of the dream world' in his theoretical writings, revealing that he had 'very little to say about them'. In fact, the aphorism is about the validity of invented subjects, 'sentiment personified', and a cluster of issues about making things up which Fuseli often wrote and spoke about. It is also indirectly about his intention in painting *The Nightmare*. The aphorism is famously ungrammatical, which perhaps made the Revd Bromley smile.

John Knowles concludes his discussion of the subjects Fuseli invented with some thoughts about how far the artist should go: in carrying the terrible to its utmost limits, I know of no subject from his pencil calculated to create horror or disgust'.[20] It was fine to create extremes of feeling, or 'terror': after all, Edmund Burke (1729–97) had placed 'terror' at the pinnacle of the Sublime. But it was unacceptable to create 'horror or disgust'. This was more than a moral issue. Horror was already associated with popular taste, as evidenced by the heated debate about explicit horror and implied terror which had recently been stimulated by developments in the Gothic novel. Since Fuseli was known to have rejected the redemptive or religious function of art – not least in his quarrel with Revd Bromley – he was at pains to make it clear, on many occasions, that he did not mean by this that he was opening the door to the popular taste for horror, or indeed to the popular taste for anything. 'The truth is', Fuseli wrote in a review article signed 'R.R.' in the *Analytical Review* for October 1792, 'that horror and loathsomeness in all its branches are equally banished from the painter's and the poet's province. Terror, as the chief ingredient of the Sublime, composes in all instances, and in the utmost extent of the word, fit material for both.'[21]

He was not arguing for 'tame antiquaries and tame painters', he continued. But there was all the difference in the world between a butcher's dream and a poet's. When Horace Walpole called *The Nightmare* 'shocking', he was saying that Fuseli had overstepped this mark, even though Walpole himself had launched the whole Gothic fashion in literature with a huge, plumed metal helmet and a giant figure clanking around a picture gallery in *The Castle of Otranto* some twenty years before. But *The Castle of Otranto* was about 'an ancient castle', dynastic squabbles, esoteric magic spells and interior design – its nightmare was safely distanced way back in the Middle Ages. There was an immediacy about *The Nightmare* which was indeed 'shocking'. Fuseli's ex-student Benjamin Robert Haydon (1786–1846), writing about the popular success of the original version of *The Nightmare*, concluded that it was this painting more than any other which had muddled the issue:

> Amongst all classes he was considered a painter of horrors; whereas his genius was essentially one of terror, a very different sentiment ... Not being advanced enough in art to make this distinction, is one reason why Fuzeli got a reputation, which legitimately may be called a *bloody* reputation[22]

The Nightmare had spread '[Fuzeli's] name over the earth', well beyond the elite of connoisseurs who knew all about literary sources – even the obscurer ones – for whom he claimed to be painting. Knowles called *The Nightmare* 'his most popular picture ... considered to be unequalled for originality of conception': the engraved version by Thomas Burke [no.4] proved so popular ... that the publisher acknowledged to have gained upwards of five hundred pounds by the sale of the prints, although vended at a small price'.[23] This turned it from a painting into a popular image.

The Nightmare started public life on the wall of the Royal Academy. Then the authorised stipple engraving went on sale at the end of January 1783, price five shillings, with four lines from Erasmus Darwin's *The Botanic Garden* (1791) underneath it. If Smith did make more than five hundred pounds on the deal, then over two thousand printings must have been made from the original plate.[24] Already a pirate edition had been issued in Paris, dated 1782. A version of one or the other was seen by Goethe's patron at the Leipzig Print Fair, also on 30 January 1783: Duke Carl August of Weimar wrote 'I have not seen anything for a long time which has intrigued me so much'. There were subsequent authorised editions of the Burke up to 1802, but there were also countless copies and variants. Fuseli himself, realising that Smith had driven too hard a bargain, produced variant versions of *The Nightmare* for various printsellers and *still* felt he was not making enough money until he began to employ his own engraver from 1803 onwards. All these prints distributed the image across Europe and America until it became *the* way of visualising bad dreams, *the* design for depicting monsters of the night – still the most celebrated (and most often travestied) image of terror, apart possibly from Munch's *The Scream* (1893), in the visual lexicon. It was one of the great ironies of Fuseli's life: the man who often wrote that art should only be accessible to a self-selected elite of connoisseurs and practitioners – as Knowles confirmed, 'he gloried in never having made his pencil pander to the public taste' – had become indelibly associated with a popular image which had spread well beyond the confines of the art world and into mass culture. So well-known was the painting – so embedded in the bloodstream

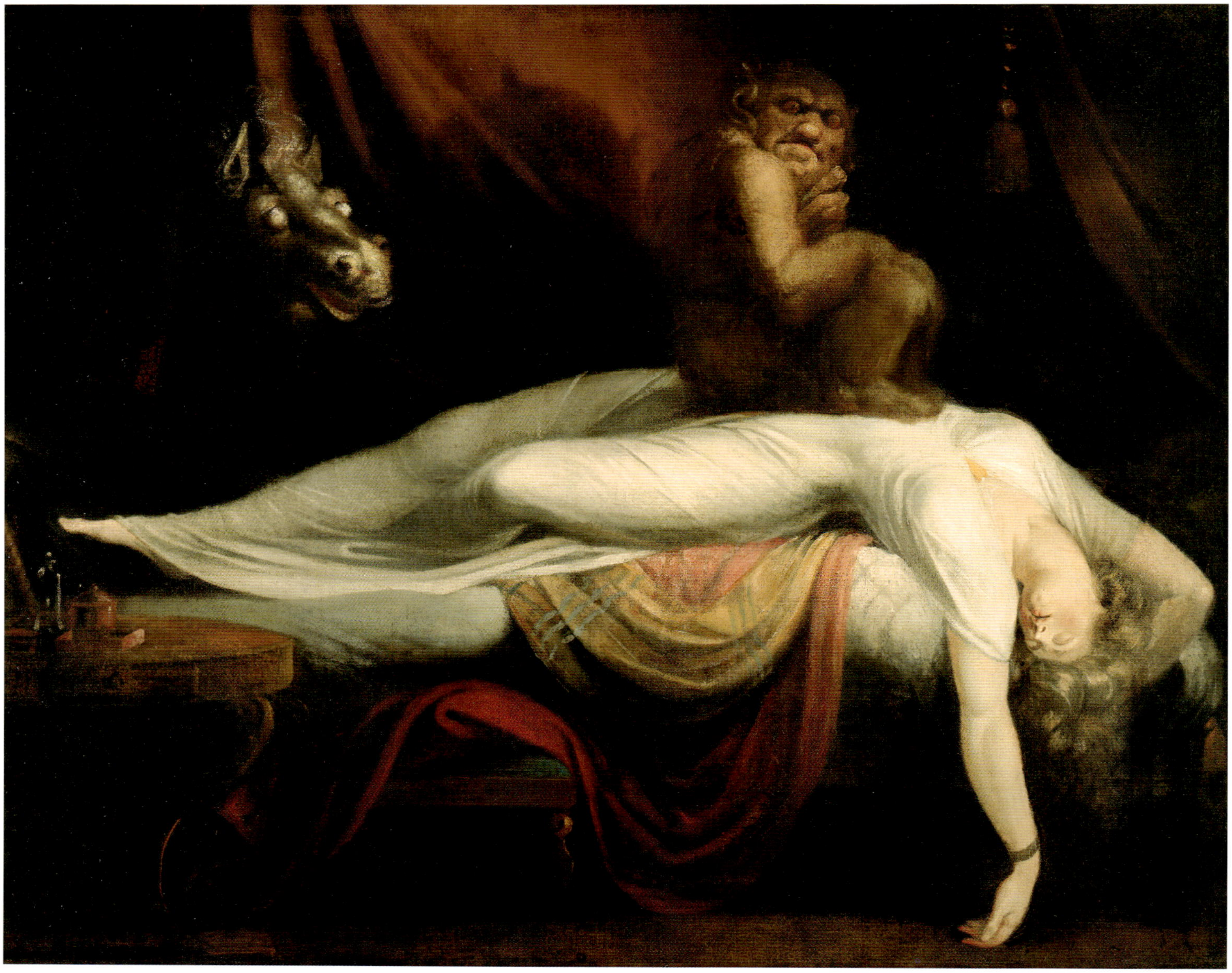

fig.3 Henry Fuseli, *The Nightmare* exh. RA 1782 (no.1)

HORSE
(then attributed to) **Phidias, *The Horse Tamers* in the Piazza Quirinale, Rome**
Leonardo da Vinci, *Battle of Anghiari*
Hans Baldung, *Wild Horses* (1534, woodcut)
Veronese, *Venus and Mars* (1570; Metropolitan Museum of Art, New York)
Salvator Rosa, *Saul and the Witch of Endor* (1668; Louvre, Paris)

MARA
A fertility fetish or stone gargoyle
Greek vases depicting Marsyas, a satyr; Etruscan vases depicting a Gorgon-figure
Hellenistic versions of 'the hunch-backed beggar'
Roman carvings of Bacchus' drinking friend Silenus, crouching
Roman mosaic comic mask (first century AD)
Roman relief sculpture of satyr in Bacchanalian scene
Pan and Hermaphrodite (Pompeii, House of Castor and Pollux), and other satyrs
Tibaldi, fresco in Castel Sant'Angelo, with two monkeys squatting

SLEEPING GIRL
Vatican sculpture, *Sleeping Ariadne*
Marcantanio Raimondi's engraving then called *The Dream of Raphael* (c.1507)
Giulio Romano, *Sleeping Psyche* (1528)
Romano, *The Dream of Hecuba* (1538–9)
Agostino Veneziano engraving after Romano, *Il stregozzo* (1520s)
Parody of Joshua Reynolds, *The Death of Dido*

OVERALL DESIGN
Bacchanalian scene with reclining Maenad on a second-century AD marble sarcophagus (then in Rome, now in Naples)
Hellenistic *Dying Amazon* in Naples
Salvator Rosa, *Saul and the Witch of Endor* (1668; Louvre)
Jean-Honoré Fragonard's paintings on the theme of the fainting sultana
Fragonard, *Coresus Sacrificing himself to Save Callirhoe* (1765; Louvre)
Erotic scenes based on classical mythology from the Paris Salon of 1779
Parody of Benjamin West, *Nature Attired by the Graces* 1779–80, on the ceiling of the Royal Academy Council Chamber

FURNITURE
Pompeii or Herculaneum
Simplified rococo, fashionable in Germany in the 1770s

of the reading and viewing public – that it became the first ever contemporary work to form the basis of an entire sub-genre of 'mock Sublime' in English political caricature, from 1792 in French caricature too. David H. Weinglass lists fifteen *direct* transcriptions, between 1783 and 1823, in England associating the nightmare with revolution, in France with fear of revolution. One of Fuseli's last ever productions was a new version of *The Nightmare* with fairies on the dressing-table and a horned owl, which in turn became a posthumous engraving in 1827 (no.152).

As *The Nightmare* was transformed from painting into image, interest in its esoteric visual provenance melted into the air.[25] In the process, from the 1830s onwards the painting disappeared from the radar of serious British art historians to be consigned to the annals of 'Teutonic hobgoblinry'.[26] But, following the Fuseli revival of the 1920s – with the fashion for surrealism, the Blake renaissance and at the same time the promotion of Swiss tourism – successive generations of historians attempted to trace the visual sources of the painting, for the first time since the late eighteenth century. By that stage, the best way into Fuseli was thought to be by treating him as a collagist of visual quotations, a painter who thought he was creating homogeneous compositions through 'the judicious adoption of figures in art' but who sometimes created visual disjointedness instead; a builder rather than a designer. Where *The Nightmare* is concerned, the 'figures in art' have since included the contenders listed opposite (favourites in bold), all of which could have been/were seen by Fuseli on his travels, or could have been/were in his own collection of prints.[27]

This source-spotting has related *The Nightmare* to classical sculpture, Italian Mannerist painting, the rococo 'moment of terror', sado-mannerism, contemporary libertine work, Pompeian *and* late eighteenth-century furniture; to sculptures the artist saw in Rome or Naples; to contemporary art politics. Others have preferred to interpret Fuseli's painting as a 'neoclassic horrific' illustration of sections of the so-called handbook of witchcraft *Malleus Maleficarum* (1487); a visualisation of Erasmus Darwin's lines on the nightmare in his poem *The Loves of the Plants* (not fully published until 1789, but written earlier; the two men probably met in 1781 and Darwin may possibly have suggested adding the horse to Fuseli's original drawing); an image of the 'eroticised female'/Sadean woman in the last stages of abandon and orgasm; or, on the other hand, an image of dark, male desire that the viewer is forced to share; a visual debate about physiognomy in the context of Johann Caspar Lavater's writings on the subject; an externalisation of the semantic confusion between female horse and bad dream; and, a favourite interpretation, an autobiographical painting about Fuseli's unrequited passion of two years before for Lavater's niece, Anna Landolt of Zurich, who was already engaged to be married.[28]

There is an unfinished portrait of a provocative young woman on the back of *The Nightmare* (1782 version; fig.4), and she may be Anna Landolt or she may not: Fuseli confessed – in language self-consciously modelled on Rousseau and Goethe – to being madly in love with at least three women between 1778 and 1780. The sleeping girl in the painting may resemble the unfinished portrait on the back or it may not. The *mara* may resemble Fuseli himself – in which case the painting is an act of fantasy retribution – or it may not. Still others have since linked *The Nightmare* to Shakespearean subjects again – such as Queen Mab and *A Midsummer Night's Dream* (the incubus does in some ways resemble some of Fuseli's more malevolent elves).[29]

But apart from 'figures in art', or indeed figures in life, there are some specific intellectual contexts which help to clarify the contemporary meaning of *The Nightmare* – the ways in which the painting could have been 'read' at the time of its first reception. Fuseli was fascinated by visions and dreams, play-acting and orating, larger-than-life superheroes and curvaceous heroines, and painterly gloom, but in a quieter, more private way he was almost equally fascinated by aspects of applied science and medicine. He was well informed about entomology and liked to study it over breakfast; he wrote a number of articles about insects for the *Analytical Review* (usually over the signature 'R.R.'); he made a surprising number of drawings of entomological subjects which he called 'his favourite study and amusement'; and he tended to lose himself in the close analysis of butterflies and moths when he was feeling particularly depressed.[30] He also knew a great deal about the Linnaean system of classifying plants, insects and animals, and how 'his divisions and subdivisions are crumbling every hour to dust', especially when viewed through the latest microscopes. Ever since he first arrived in London in the mid-1760s, Fuseli had particularly enjoyed mixing in medical circles. On one occasion he surprised Farington when the conversation turned to the subject of madness. Instead of waxing lyrical about Lady Macbeth and King Lear, he talked statistics:

> Fuseli mentioned that a Medical man who attended Bedlam had said that the greatest number of these who were confined were *Woemen in love*, and the next class in respect of number was *Hackney* and *Stage Coachmen*, caused it was supposed by the constant shaking exercise to which they are subject which affects the *pineal gland*.[31]

One of Fuseli's closest friendships in London was with Dr John Armstrong (1709–79) – notoriously waspish medical practitioner, poet and friend of John Wilkes (1725–98) – of whom the painter 'always entertained a high opinion', and who returned the compliment by 'praising him in the

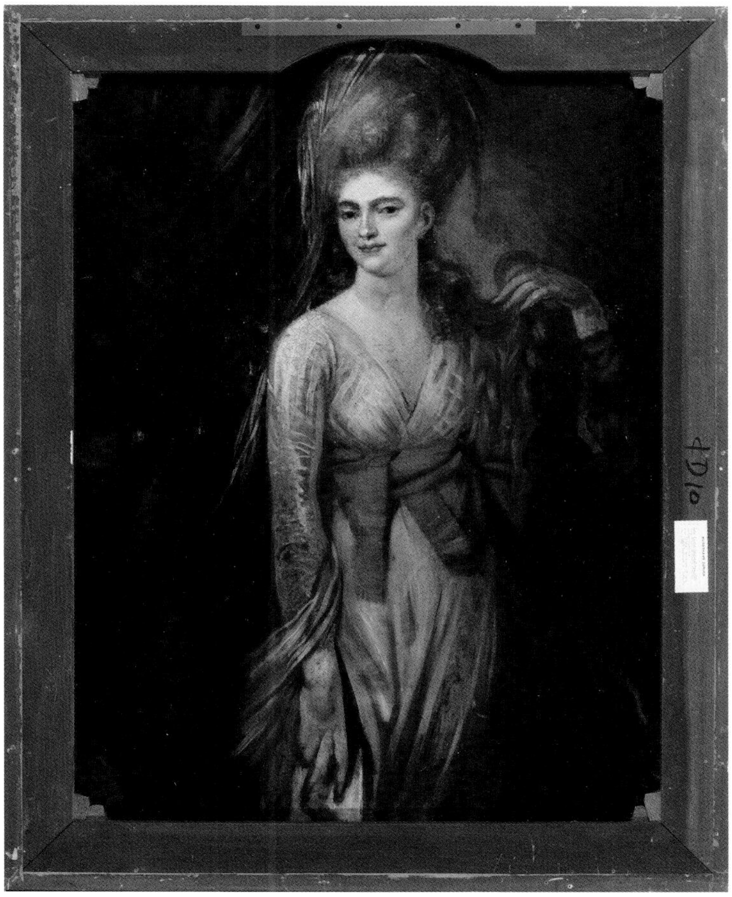

fig.4 Henry Fuseli (1741–1825), *Portrait of a Lady* (verso of *The Nightmare* exh.1782), oil on canvas 101.6 x 127 cm. Detroit Institute of Arts. Founders Society Purchase with funds from Mr and Mrs Bert L. Smokler and Mr and Mrs Lawrence A. Fleischman (55.5B).

Journals'. In 1744 Armstrong had published his best-known poem, *The Art of Preserving Health* (it was often reprinted), a polemic in favour of regular exercise, moderation in all things, fresh air, honest toil, thinking pure thoughts and eating sensibly.[32] In the long section devoted to 'Exercise' (Book III), Armstrong wrote of nightmares:

> Oppress not nature sinking down to rest
> With feasts too late, too solid, or too full ...
> Not all a monarch's luxury the woes
> Can counterpoise, of that most wretched man,
> Whose nights are shaken with the frantic fits
> Of wild Orestes; whose delirious brain,
> Stung by the furies, works with poisoned thought:
> While pale and monstrous painting shocks the soul;
> And mangled consciousness bemoans itself
> For ever torn; and chaos floating round

Ways of avoiding nightmares, Armstrong went on, included going to bed early, avoiding rich food, engaging in 'pleasing talk' just before going to bed and as a very last resort reading Homer aloud. 'Sickly musing', 'hideous fictions' and nasty paintings, especially when alone, were not recommended. As part of the 'Diet' section of *The Art of Preserving Health* (Book II), when discussing how 'the keen appetite will feast beyond/ what nature well can bear', Armstrong cited the researches of Dr John Bond who was soon to publish a full-length *Essay on the Incubus, or Night-mare* (1753).[33] In this essay Bond contrasted the old folkloric and moral explanations of the nightmare with the new medical ones. He began by dismissing superstitions 'that did not appear serious or probable', and explaining why he would confine himself instead 'the laws of animal economy'.

> I have therefore omitted an inquiry into the origins of many odd epithets and quaint names commonly given to this Disorder; such as Hag-riding, Wizard-pressing, Mare-riding, Witch-dancing &c ... In our language it is generally known by the name of the Night-mare; which strange term probably arose from superstitious notions which the British had, and perhaps still have, of it[34]

The popular confusion between 'mare' (female horse) and 'night-mare' (bad dream) was, apparently, part of this superstition. Bond also excluded the thesis that 'the Night-mare is an imaginary Disease, and proceeds from the idea of some demon, which existed in the mind the day before'. Instead, he carefully listed the symptoms – people lying on their backs, having bad dreams, breathing with difficulty, experiencing a violent oppression on the breast and losing voluntary motion – and explained them all as relating to blockages in the circulation of the blood. In particular, he noted, nightmares occurred when the head was lower than the legs, when the victim had turned onto the left side, and when too much blood was flowing into the brain. So each of the folkloric explanations was 'really internal'. For Dr Bond, the kinds of people who were susceptible to nightmares were relatively easy to classify: 'Young persons of gross full habits, the luxurious, the drunken and they who sup late, are most subject to the night-mare. Also Women who are obstructed; girls of full, lax habits before the eruption of the Menses'[35].

The sensation of a 'great, heavy Man stretching himself upon [a woman]' was as a matter of medical fact about the 'accumulation of blood' just before menses. Hag-riding and Wizard-pressing were really preludes to heavy periods, and the explanations were medical rather than moral. Within this same frame of reference, Bond's thesis about blood circulation was to be explicitly challenged by another Lockean, Dr Robert Whytt (1714–66), in his *Observations on the Nature, Causes and Cure of those Disorders which Have Been Commonly Called Nervous* (1765, reprinted 1777). Whytt reckoned that Bond's conclusions were 'far from being satisfactory' – they begged many more questions than they answered – and proposed instead that the causes of nightmares lay not in the blood but in the stomach: indigestion, wind, excessive phlegm, eating too late, 'certain medicines or poisons' including nervous medicines, in short 'strange ideas excited in the mind in consequence of the disordered state of the stomach, not then corrected by the external senses as they are when we are awake'. Whytt agreed with Bond's list of symptoms – and his thoughts about 'a suppression of the menses in women' – but: 'neither a horizontal posture, sleep, nor heavy suppers, do ever produce the night-mare, at least in any considerable degree, unless the person be predisposed to it from the particular condition of the nerves of the stomach'.[36]

Armstrong died in September 1779, shortly before Fuseli started work on *The Nightmare*. The painting refers in many detailed ways to the contemporary debate about the causes of nightmares (today the technical term would be 'sleep paralysis'), and – in parallel – includes most of the folkloric explanations as well. The victim is sleeping on her back, turned to her left side, with her head below her legs and with a pressure on her stomach. On the bedside table is a jar of liquid, maybe a 'nervous medicine'. But the sightless horse and the *mara* are there as well – the superstitious notions, as Bond had written, 'which the British had, and perhaps still have, of it'.

Like so many aspects of *The Nightmare*, this medical debate even found its way into Fuseli's reputation. In the year he became a full Academician, the *Public Advertiser* started a rumour that the artist's imagination did not spring from refinement of taste but from 'an animal process, and is brought about after regular intervals by Mr. Fuseli's eating raw pork for supper' (*Public Advertiser*, 31 May 1790). This rumour was evidently still in the ether when Allan Cunningham issued an edition of his biography in 1830, three years after after Fuseli's death; he felt the need to refute it: 'The story of his having supped on raw pork chops that he might dream his picture of the nightmare has no foundation'. On the contrary, wrote Cunningham, Fuseli ate two frugal meals a day (the Armstrong diet) and always avoided supper if he could.[37]

The contemporary debate about nightmares was part of a wider project in the mid to late eighteenth century to reduce popular superstitions to 'natural causes' – classifying the medical symptoms and then hoping to explain them away. There was a parallel literature – involving some of the authorities cited by Bond and Whytt – about the epidemics of vampirism which seemed to have spread across Eastern Europe in the early eighteenth century.[38] This was a mode of argument which Jean-Jacques Rousseau (1712–78) had famously questioned in his open letter to Christophe de Beaumont, Archbishop of Paris (1703–81), as part of *Emile* (1762), when he discussed miracles and vampires in the same breath: both required obscurantist dogma to explain them, both were more to do with belief and metaphor than medicine, neither was fully explicable by reductive medics. Fuseli was well aware of Rousseau's letter. In his *Remarks on the writings and Conduct of Jean-Jacques Rousseau* (published 23 April 1767; fig.5), among several references to the Beaumont letter he referred to 'what [Rousseau] dared *not to conclude* from his anatomy of miracles', and added that 'God might rather have created fifty individuals than recalled one from the grave'. He continued, in his analysis of *Emile*, with a rant about popular superstitions surrounding child-rearing during the Middle Ages 'in the fogs of popery':

> whatever boy or girl proved haggard, 'twas a changeling, an abortion, substituted by an incubus; and sometimes a tender religious mother would carry her offspring to the next bridge, to know whether it was

> a goblin she was going to suckle, or her own child. In the first case, the little monster, whistled at by the legion in the water, would jump out of the basket, and plunge to join his brethren; in the other, the child would cross himself. It may, and with charity too, be presumed that the number of devil-brats somewhat exceeded that of babies.[39]

The feeble light of reason and information, he concluded, could only 'make the darkness more visible'. It could not explain the darkness away. That Fuseli was still very interested in Rousseau's ideas fifteen years later, in the 1780s – notably in the cult of sensibility and the corruption of modern civilisation – is confirmed by William Godwin (1756–1836):

> A young man embraces entire the opinions of a favourite writer, and Mr Fuseli has not had leisure to bring the opinion of his youth to a revision. Smitten with Rousseau's conception of the perfectness of the savage state, and the essential abortiveness of all civilization, Mr Fuseli looks at all our little attempts at improvement, with a spirit that borders perhaps too much upon contempt and indifference[40]

Fuseli's *Remarks* had indeed centred on 'Rousseau's conception of the perfectness of the savage state' as contained in the *Discourse on Inequality* (1755), and how the *Discourse* 'known to all, read by few, understood by less' should be read as a 'triumph of conjecture' about contemporary life rather than a literal plea for a return to the state of nature.[41] Most of the *Remarks* are about public misunderstandings of Rousseau's work. The liveliest passages are a series of all-stops-out attacks on Voltaire – under the name of 'Pansophe' – who had recently written in his satirical *Lettre au Docteur Pansophe* (1765) that Rousseau wanted to encourage the citizens of London to return to nature, get down on all fours and eat grass in Hyde Park. 'No four legs! No state of nature! No acorns!', replied Fuseli, over and over again, in his *Remarks*. Fuseli's engraved frontispiece to the *Remarks* also refers to the contemporary public debate about Rousseau's supposed primitivism. It represents Voltaire in a riding habit with spurs and a whip, straddling the naked figure of *'l'homme sauvage'* who is on all fours, wearing a bridle like a horse; next to Voltaire is the noble figure of Jean-Jacques Rousseau in his Armenian outfit – as recently depicted (March 1766) in a portrait by Allan Ramsay (1713–84). This Fuseli engraving was itself a visual reply to another polemical print, published in January 1767 and called *The Savage Man*: the *Remarks* ask Rousseau 'if the print-shops exhibit ye but for a savage'. *The Savage Man*, based on a journalistic sketch by James Boswell (1740–95), represents Rousseau as a hairy wildman with a beard who is throwing coins at David Hume, while behind him sit three apes – one of which is saying 'The Inequality of Mankind'. On the right of the image, Voltaire is dressed as a schoolboy straddling a hobby-horse while whipping Rousseau with a cloth.[42]

Both prints reflect public understanding, or rather misunderstanding, of the controversy about the *Discourse*, and they also reflect – in caricatured form – Rousseau's radical conjectures in that essay about the evolution of the human species and about the serious possibility that the species was not after all distinctly created. The creature Rousseau described in the *Discourse* as an 'orang-utan' (or 'man of the woods') could even conceivably be a human being like the rest of us. 'Orang-utan' society in the state of nature was perhaps a precursor of human society, even though the two still coexisted in the contemporary world. The botanist Carl Linnaeus (1707–78) and the naturalist Georges Buffon (1707–88) had asserted that humans were the most noble of species separated from all the rest – that *Homo* and *Simia* were distinct categories – in part because there could surely be no hybrid offspring from the sexual union of a woman with any beast. For Rousseau, this assertion had yet to be proved: there ought perhaps to be experiments to establish whether matings between human beings and orang-utans (who had constitutions similar to our own) could possibly prove fruitful.[43]

It is possible that the mara figure in *The Nightmare* was intended to be an 'Orang-outan' or a reference to one, and that the *real* sexual nightmare was about cross-breeding, the idea that the human species was not specially created, and the union of a woman and a beast. The *mara* bears a certain family resemblance to the illustrations of the orang-utan or 'Le Jocko' in the 1766 edition of Buffon's *Histoire naturelle* (fig.6); also to the depiction of the large ape, after a drawing by William Cowper, in the 1699 edition of Edward Tyson's (1650–1708) classic description in *Orang-Outang*.[44] But there had been a much more recent reference to cross-breeding in the news, and in London too. Eberhard Zimmermann's (1743–1815) study of *Der aufrechte Gang des Menschen* (The upright walk of human beings, 1778), after summarising Tyson's and Buffon's conclusions about the closeness of orang-utans to humans – where physique, behaviour and mannerisms were concerned – and their assumptions about the nobility of human beings, went on to elaborate:

> it is not entirely improbable that an Orang-outang could breed with a human being, to produce a kind of middle-species in between. It has

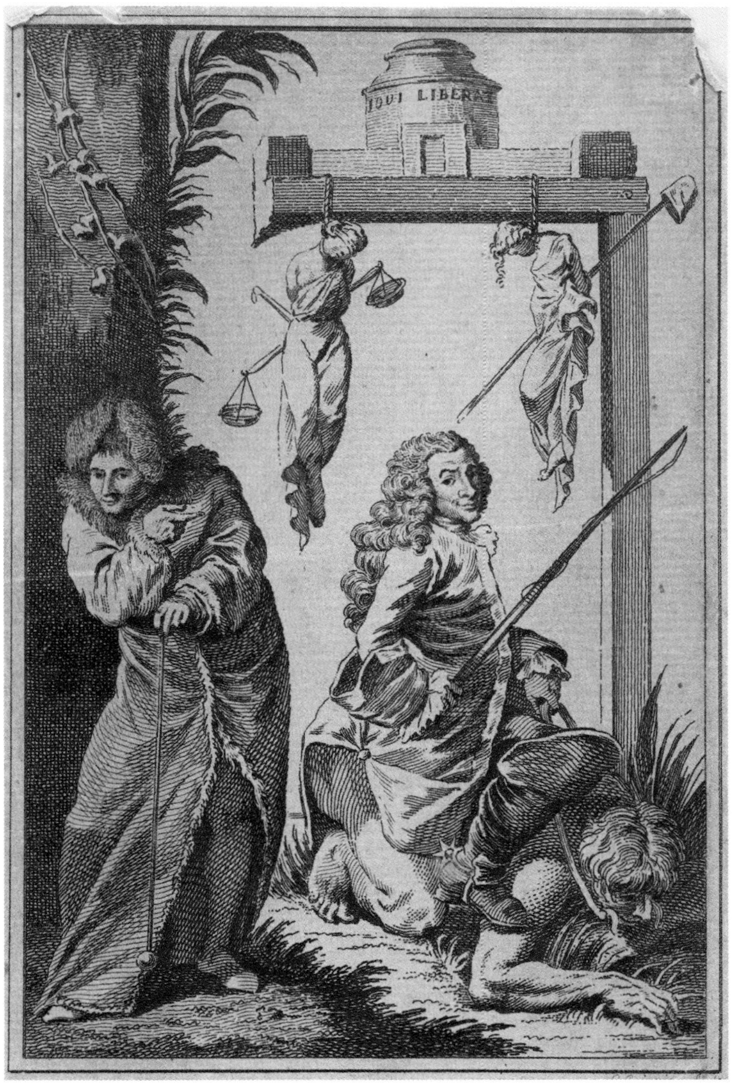

fig.5 Charles Grignion (1721–1810) after Henry Fuseli (1741–1825), engraved frontispiece to Henry Fuseli, *Remarks on the Writings and Conduct of J.J. Rousseau*, London 1767. The British Museum, London

come to my attention that recently in London such an attempt was made. A male Orang was offered to a female prostitute who was paid for it; but, as far as I know, this attempt was completely fruitless. The attempt was not condemned or banned on moral grounds, but failed on physical grounds – because an equally bad result would in all probability have happened if a human being had tried to mate with such a female. In addition, one knows how very excitable monkeys can become during intercourse, which suggests a premature ejaculation and this may in fact have been the case. So if this experiment were to stand any chance of success, it would have to involve a male human with a female Orang ... Whether this should ever happen, though, I leave to the moralists to decide.[45]

Rousseau's reference in the *Discourse* to cross-breeding and evolution had not only been satirised in prints. Voltaire, too, had referred to them in chapter sixteen of *Candide* (1759), where in the land of the savage Oreillons, two naked girls are chased by two monkeys 'nibbling their buttocks', until Candide shoots the creatures – only to discover that he has inadvertently killed the girls' lovers. *Candide* was a book Fuseli knew well. This strange interlude may also relate to Gulliver's adventures in the land of the Houyhnhnms (1726), where after encountering the hairy, mute, yahoos who walk on all fours and behave 'after the manner of monkeys', Lemuel Gulliver reflects with understandable confusion 'that by copulating with one of the yahoo species, I had become a parent of more.'[46] When *The Nightmare* was first exhibited, some commentators – including Fuseli's friend Erasmus Darwin, who himself was beginning to speculate on evolution and epigenesis – referred to the *mara* as a 'Demon-Ape' with leathern ears: 'On her fair bosom sits the Demon-Ape/Erect, and balances his bloated shape'.

Among the many possible sources for *The Nightmare*, as we have seen, Frederick Antal suggested a detail from Pellegrino Tibaldi's grisaille fresco at Castel Sant'Angelo in Rome, which shows two baboons sitting in the foreground and sharing a bunch of grapes: the right-hand baboon is squatting in a way which certainly resembles Fuseli's *mara*. But in Fuseli's later works the figure which most closely resembles the mara is not in his nightmare or fairy or even dream images: it is his design for Caliban – an equally simian and libidinous figure – in an engraving of 1803 (after Fuseli) for *The Tempest*; Caliban squats on a rock, his arms folded like the *mara*'s, licking his thumb; he is staring at a very provocative sleeping Miranda with big hair, while an heroic Prospero waves his magic staff. This thing of darkness I acknowledge mine. The association implies a racial, as well as a biological or anthropological, meaning – another kind of nightmare in 1782 London. For Cunningham, Fuseli's Caliban was 'a connecting link between man and brute'.[47]

Recent art historians have had difficulty making up their minds about who or what the *mara* might resemble. A creature from English folk superstition? A Gorgon? A Faunus or Pan? A goblin? An elf? A cliché of libertine painting? A thoughtful penis? A self-portrait?

Perhaps its most enduring legacy within *popular* culture – one which has been experienced by more people than can possibly have seen a reproduction of *The Nightmare*, even if they do not realise it – was in Mary Shelley's novel *Frankenstein*, first published in 1818. And progeny. There were many biographical and literary connections between Fuseli and Mary Shelley (1797–1851), and she was certainly familiar with *The Nightmare*. In 1810 Percy Shelley (1792–1822) had written a horror tale (now lost) called *The Nightmare* which he said he would have liked Fuseli to illustrate. At the same time he wrote a barnstorming Gothic ballad called *Ghasta; or the Avenging Demon*, which ends with:

> At last came night, ah! horrid hour,
> Ah! chilling time that wakes the dead
> When demons ride the clouds that lower
> The phantom sat upon my bed[48]

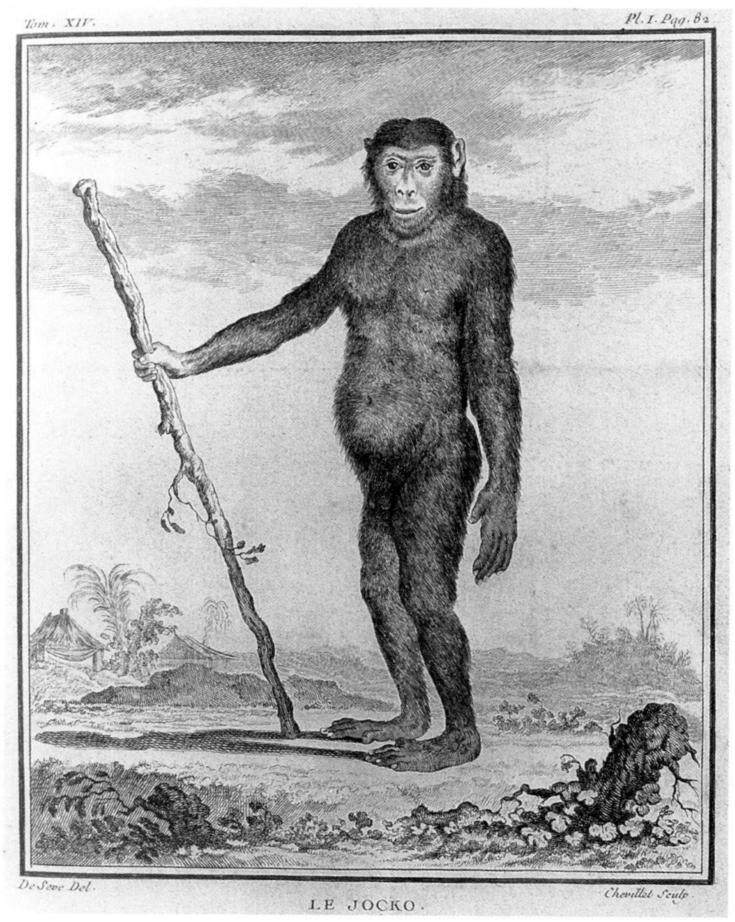

fig.6 'Le Jocko', engraved illustration from Georges Louis Leclerc Buffon, *Histoire naturelle, générale et particulière*, Paris 1766. The Wellcome Library, London

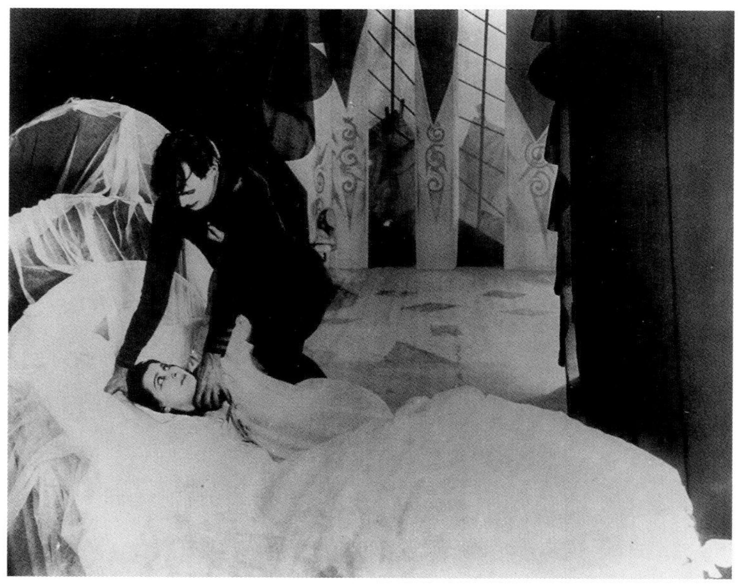

fig.7. Still from *Cabinet of Dr Caligari* (dir. Robert Wiene, Germany 1919)

Lord Byron (1788–1824) became interested in Fuseli's *Ezzelin* in March 1814, and wanted to research the story – only to discover it had been made up by the artist.[49] And so in Mary Shelley's *Frankenstein* (volume 3, chapter VI of the 1818 edition) she may well have based the chilling scene of the creature fulfilling his prophecy 'I shall be with you on your wedding-night' directly on the design of Fuseli's most famous painting (see no.156). Subsequent references in film – from German Expressionism to Hollywood horror to recent costume dramas – have 'democratised' Fuseli's most famous painting to the point where it has long since gone well beyond visual cliché (fig.7; see below, pp.207–12). In a similar vein, superhero comics – of all unlikely places – have consigned Fuseli's exaggerated gods and heroes to an even stranger and more proletarian fate. *The Nightmare* itself, for example, has explicitly appeared in two issues written by Alan Moore (b.1953) of the graphic novel *Swamp Thing*, in both cases hanging as a painting above a bed where the heroine has bad dreams: 'framed upon the wall … an incubus … squats upon … a sleeping woman's chest … and leers knowingly'.[51] Given Fuseli's written and spoken views on the intended audience for his work, this trajectory would no doubt have given him nightmares. The artist's reputation since the 1920s has even – with the usual post-Freudian elision of life and work – reinforced the more outlandish legends of his own lifetime. Benjamin Robert Haydon had some of these legends whirring in his head, plus a letter from his father saying 'God speed you with the terrible Fuzeli', when he first visited the artist's studio in 1805, fresh from Devonshire. Perhaps Fuzeli would be as tall as his own Satan; perhaps he stood seven feet![52]

> At last, whilst I was wondering what metamorphosis I was to undergo, the door slowly opened, and I saw a little hand come slowly round the edge of it, which did not look very gigantic, or belonged to a very powerful figure, and round came a little white-faced lion-headed man, dressed in an old flannel dressing-gown, tied by a rope, and the bottom of Mrs. Fuseli's work-basket on his head for a cap. I was perfectly amazed … was this the painter himself?

A less charitable contemporary, Leigh Hunt (1784–1859), wrote that Fuseli painted horrible pictures as a child tells horrible stories, and that in reality he was terrified of his own shadow. Hazlitt reckoned that the painter's *foreignness* tended to be confused with strangeness, and that his paintings would always 'lie like a nightmare on the breast of our native art'.[53] Whatever the relationship of artist to artefact, Fuseli's *The Nightmare* has continued for over two centuries – as the saying goes – to sputter gloriously like a smoky candle at a black mass.

Notes

1 Royal Academy Archive 471A, Exhibition Daily Receipts 1781-6.
2 Cited in Myrone 2001a, p.79. See also Hofmann 1975, pp.35-6. On the Academy at this time see Solkin 1993, pp.247-76; Brewer 1997, pp.228-43, 278-9.
3 Cited in Brewer 1997, p.293.
4 Cited in Martineau 2003, pp.61-3.
5 Brewer 1997, pp.246-7.
6 Note in the Royal Academy catalogue of 1782, formerly in the collection of the Dowager Countess Rosebery (photo in Courtauld Institute). Thanks to Norma Watt of Norwich Castle Museum for helping to identify the Barret. RA catalogues are in Royal Academy Archive, 29F.
7 See Weinglass 1982, letter of 27 April 1771, p.13.
8 Letter to Robert Smyth of 27 August 1780, in Weinglass 1982, pp.19-20.
9 Letter to Robert Smyth of 3 September 1780, in Weinglass 1982, p.20. On *Queen Katherine*, see also Martineau 2003, pp.76-7.
10 Reviews of the RA exhibition of 1782: *Morning Chronicle*, 30 April 1782; *Morning Post*, 30 April 1782; *Morning Herald*, 8 May 1782; *Morning Chronicle*, 9 May 1782; *Public Advertiser*, 28 May 1782 and *Gazeteer*, 1 June 1782.
11 Johnson 1755.
12 Royal Academy Archive 471A, Exhibition Daily Receipts 1781-6.
13 See Bromley 1793, pp.36-7, 56-61. Bromley's book was distributed by the Royal Academy's printer, Thomas Cadell in the Strand.
14 Cited in Mason 1951, pp.278-9.
15 See Farington 1978-98, I, p.165.
16 Bromley 1793-5, Preface, pp.i-xxvii. See also *Morning Herald*, 17 April 1794 in Weinglass 1982, pp.109-12.
17 Letter to William Roscoe, 22 October 1791, in Weinglass 1982, pp.74-5.
18 Knowles 1831, III, pp.140-5 (Lecture III, 'On Invention'); see also I, pp.403-4.
19 Ibid., II, pp.145-6, 'Aphorisms'.
20 Ibid., I, pp.404-5.
21 Cited in Mason 1951, p.218. For variations on this theme, see Cunningham 1830-3, II, p.292, and Mason 1951, pp.215-19.
22 Haydon 1844-6, II, lecture VIII on 'Fuzeli', pp.8-10.
23 Knowles 1831, I, pp 64-5.
24 On the history of *The Nightmare* as a print see D'Oench 1999, pp.81-5 and Weinglass 1994, pp.55-72. See also Tomory 1972, pp.201-3 and Powell 1973, pp.80-96.
25 See also Cunningham 1830-3, II, pp.289-90.
26 On Victorian criticism of Fuseli see Mason 1951, pp.76-8.
27 This chart of possible visual sources for *The Nightmare* has been compiled from Powell 1973, pp.37-75; Antal 1958, pp.92-3, 102-4; Schiff 1973; Schiff 1975, pp.122-38; Tomory 1972, pp.92-3; Chappell 1986; Andrus 1995; and Schiff and Viotto 1977.
28 For *Malleus Maleficarum* see Moffatt 1990; on Fuseli and Erasmus Darwin see Haut 2004; on the 'eroticized female' see Allentuck 1973; on semantic confusion see Starobinski 1974; and for the Anna Landolt thesis see Tomory 1972, pp.31, 92-3; Mason 1951, pp.149-56; Powell 1973, pp.60-3; and Antal 1956, pp.92-3.
29 Kalman 1971.
30 On Fuseli and entomology see Mason 1951, pp.332-6 and Todd 1946, pp.72-3.
31 Farington, 1978-98, VI, p.2288, entry for 2 April 1804.
32 Armstrong 1744, Book III, pp.84-6, Book IV, pp.108-9. On Fuseli and Armstrong, see Knowles 1831, I, pp.58-9; Cunningham 1830-3, II, pp.276-80 and Mason 1951, p.127.
33 Armstrong 1744, Book II, pp.38-9. See also, in prose, Armstrong 1773, pp.22-30, and Bond 1753, pp.1-83. Bond claimed this was the first-ever full-length work on the subject. It was not.
34 Bond 1753, pp.2-5, 24, 46-7, 79-82.
35 Ibid., pp.46-51. For much more recent medical analyses which refer to the painting, see Broughton 1968 and Schenck 1969.
36 Whytt 1765, pp.315-18.
37 Cunningham 1830-3, II, pp.338-9; Tomory 1972, pp.181-4.
38 Frayling 1991, pp.19-36, 85-103.
39 Fuseli 1960, pp.34-50 on *Emile*, esp. pp.37-8, 40, 44-6. On the 'changeling' reference see Mason 1951, pp.173-4.
40 Godwin 1927, pp.56-65, 128-31, 182-7; also Knowles 1831, I, pp.160-70; Cunningham 1830-3, II, pp.297-9; and Tomory 1972, p.40, 173-5.
41 Fuseli 1960, pp.20-33. On Fuseli and Rousseau in general, see Mason 1951, pp.121-136, though he seriously downplays Rousseau's continuing influence on the artist.
42 Taylor 1992; also Mason 1951, pp.130-6.
43 See Frayling and Wokler 1982, pp.109-15, 121. For Rousseau on the 'orang-utan' see his 'Lettre à Philopolis' of 1756 (Rousseau 1964, III, pp.234-5); the 'Discourse on Inequality', esp. note 10 (Rousseau 1964, III, pp.209-11, also p. 137n.) and Rousseau's letter to David Hume, 29 March 1766 (Leigh 1965, XXIX, p.66) in which Rousseau suggests that monkeys can in fact speak but have decided not to, for fear they might otherwise be made to work!
44 See also Rawson 2001.
45 Footnote to subsection on 'Man' in Zimmerman 1778, I, Pt.I, pp.117-29.
46 Voltaire 1974, pp.68-72; Swift 1996, pp.213-31: 'A Voyage to the Country of the Houyhnhnms'.
47 Cunningham 1830-3, II, p.293; Powell, 1973, p.57; Schiff 1975, pp.58-73.
48 Holmes 1974, pp.31, 35. See also Ward 2000, pp.20-31.
49 Marchand 1973-81, III, pp.252-3; IV, p.160. For the history of *Ezzelin* as a print see Weinglass 1994, pp.53-4.
50 Shelley 1974, pp.193-4. For the 'visual progeny' of *Frankenstein*, see Levine and Knoepflmacher 1979, pp.243-315.
51 Moore 1990, II, p.183; Moore 2002, IV, p.22.
52 Haydon 1844-6, II, pp.10-12; also Todd 1946, pp.70-1.
53 Mason 1951, pp.72-74.

Thanks to Martin Myrone, who helped find some obscure sources; to Mark Pomeroy of the Royal Academy archive; and to the late Angela Carter, with whom I visited the 1975 *Henry Fuseli* exhibition at the Tate Gallery and who shared my enthusiasm for his darker works.

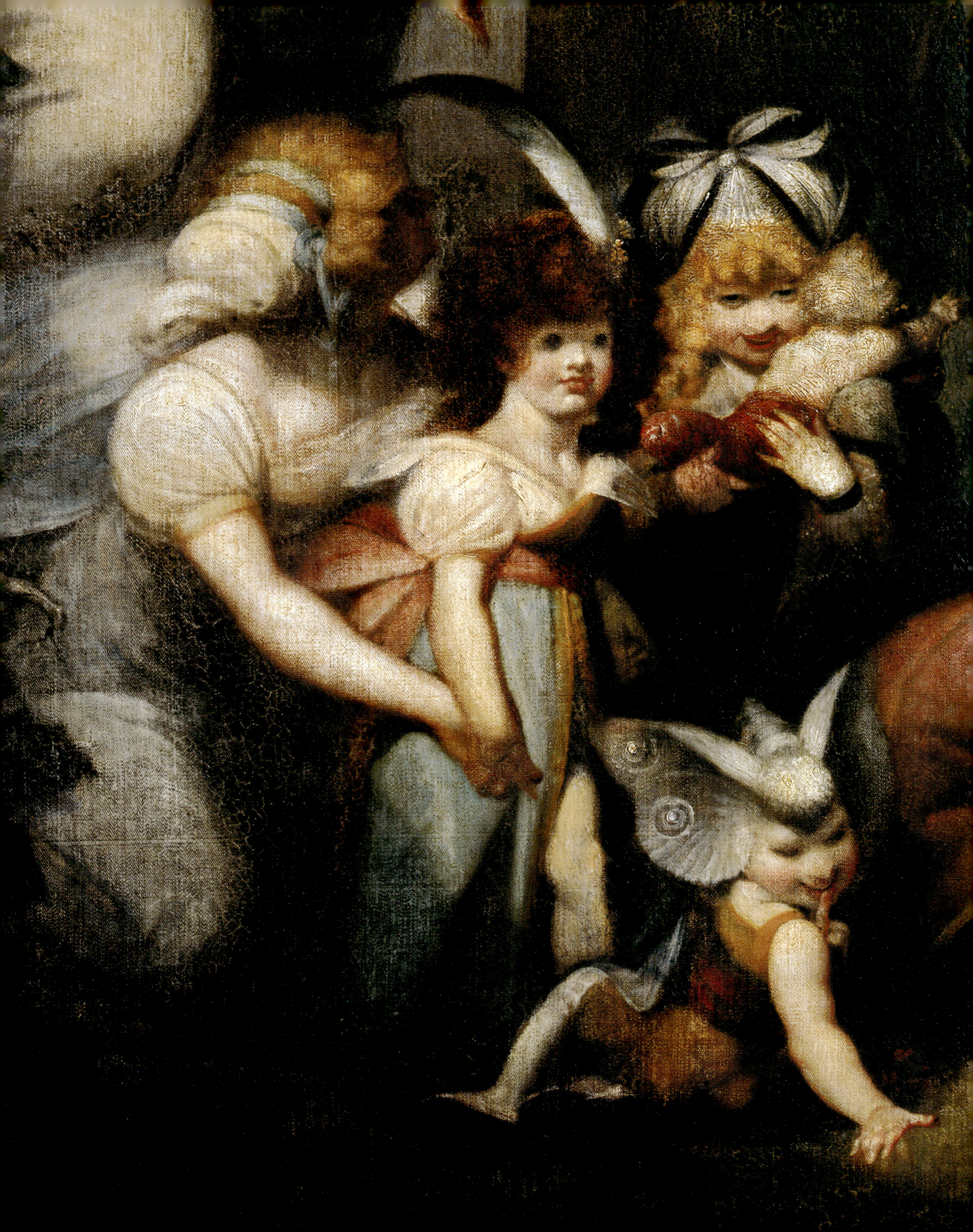

Invented Plots: The Enchanted Puppets and Fairy Doubles of Henry Fuseli

Marina Warner

Beneath the surface of the visible world exists a 'secret commonwealth'; there, our 'fetches', our doppelgängers or 'co-walkers', lead another life, eating and drinking, marrying and partying in the company of 'all sorts of spirits which assume light aery bodies'. These elves and fairies are waited on at their revels by 'pleasant children like inchanted puppets'; they exercise a range of weird and terrible powers over human lives, abducting mothers to nurse their fairy children, leaving behind a phantom nurse ('like their reflexion in the mirror') and substituting a changeling in the cradle, who is doomed soon to die.

These were the deeds of the fairies, as reported by the Scottish pastor Robert Kirk (1644–1697), an antiquarian and scholar of some distinction, in his book about fairyland, *The Secret Common-Wealth of Elves, Fauns and Fairies* (1691).[1] A great deal of similar lore can be found in earlier, Elizabethan poetry and drama: Shakespeare's fairies Moth, Mustardseed, Cobweb, and of course Puck or Robin Goodfellow, are entirely recognisable from the descriptions Kirk gives here. So are Robert Herrick's trooping mischief-makers from 'Oberon's Feast' and 'Oberon's Palace'.[2] But the straight, near-scientific language of the ethnographer reporting from the field gives Kirk's work an enhanced strangeness: he was collecting the beliefs of his parishioners.

He discusses the fairies' eating habits, the services they perform for humans – mending shoes and sweeping house and other activities – which led to the naming of the Brownies' section of the Girl Guides. He describes the gift of Second Sight – which allows one to see fairies – surprisingly he says that men are mostly endowed with this power, women rarely so. The fairies' social arrangements amongst themselves, as well as their attendance at ours, then busies his pen, and he comes back again and again to those weird doubles, evoking how everyone might have a fairy counterpart,

> every way like the man, as a Twin-brother and Companion, haunting him as his shadow and is oft seen and known among men (resembling the Originall) both befor and after the Originall is dead ... This copy, Eccho, or living picture, goes at last to his own herd. It accompanied that person so long and frequently, for ends best known to itselfe, whither to guard him from the secret assaults of som of its own folks, or only as a sportful Ape to counterfeit all his actions [sic].[3]

Kirk does not condemn his flock for thinking these things happen; even more startlingly, he explicitly allowed such beliefs in an enchanted other world to co-exist with his own and his followers' Christian faith. Oddly, his treatise strikes the contemporary reader as a far stranger document, being a report of matters held to be fact, than the fanciful fairy plays and poetry of his predecessors: *A Midsummer Night's Dream* opens with the quarrel between Titania and Oberon over her 'changeling Indian boy', whom she has adopted after his mother died and Oberon stole him; Puck, when challenged to identify himself by a passing Fairy, boasts merrily about his tricks and turns, his shape-shifting and mischief, all of them part of the popular belief in the antics of brownies and goodies and boggarts and imps; Titania, commanding her fairy troop to give Bottom every care, recommends a grotesque recipe of bugs and moths and worms – the kind of creepy-crawlies associated with nocturnal business, and so with witchcraft (Act III, scene 1):

> The honey-bags steal from the humble-bees,
> And for night-tapers crop their waxen thighs,
> And light them at the fiery glow-worm's eyes,
> To have my love to bed and to arise;
> And pluck the wings from painted butterflies,
> To fan the moonbeams from his sleeping eyes.

This speech is often cut in school productions, and the associations of Titania's name overlooked in the interests of light comedy. Yet Shakespeare named her after the goddess of the moon in her most imposing form, who, as Hecate in Macbeth, presides over the weird sisters.

Like his younger contemporary William Blake, Fuseli was steeped in reading, especially Shakespeare and Milton, and he obsessively arrays his fairies in insect forms, with butterfly wings, antennae, probosces, bulging eyes, and attenuated limbs; he also respects the extreme contrasts of scale that Shakespeare and his contemporaries suggest when, for example, 'dainty Ariel' in *The Tempest* sings (Act V, scene 1):

> Where the bee sucks, there suck I,
> In a cowslip's bell I lie;
> There I couch when owls do cry.
> On the bat's back I do fly ...
> Merrily, merrily shall I live now.

Numerous scenes devised by Fuseli picture the enchanted population in their miniature dimension, with bats and owls and bees for bedfellows and steeds; the contrast with Bottom's colossal limbs, for example, compounds the weaver's 'mortal grossness' and sharpens the strangeness of the 'little people' and their frenzied dancing and ogling, their 'nods and becks and wreathéd smiles'.

The fantastical hybrid 'grylli' contrived by medieval illuminators and Hieronymus Bosch might appear to be the forerunners of these sinister visions of faerie; it is however absolutely characteristic of Fuseli, who was a full citizen of the continental Enlightenment, that his

Detail from Henry Fuseli, *Titania and Bottom with the Ass's Head* 1788–9 (no.105)

creatures are not surrealist confections, but real species, painted 'with great care and fidelity,' commented a contemporary, '[which] when taken with the subject ... made them frequently incongruous'. Fuseli's passion for entomology inspired him to collect and raise special species of moths – one called *Sphinx atropos* (Fatal Sphinx), no less.[4]

Thirty years after Fuseli's death, Richard Dadd returned to Shakespeare's fairy folk, casting eerie moonlight on rings of dancing fairies round an elfin baby Puck, and then, in the bizarre and obsessional details of *The Fairy Feller's Master-Stroke* 1855–64 (fig.8), queering the traditional vision of an enchanting, secret, natural world teeming with fairy creatures.

Elizabethan fairylands now seem to us light-hearted products of fancy, designed to charm audiences with their magic, not command our belief – or our fear. Though fairies continue to look like Fuseli's interpretations of Shakespeare, they have shed the unsettling, brooding, uncanny atmosphere he established, and have turned whimsical. We can take easy pleasure in Oberon and Titania's quarrel, in Puck's mischief-making, and in the night riding of Queen Mab, as a consequence of Victorian and Edwardian stagecraft, the pretty conjurings of Cecily Mary Barker's flower fairies, J.M. Barrie's Tinkerbell, and the sprites photographed dancing in the glen at Cottingley in the 1920s. But the vision of Henry Fuseli predates this taming of fairy dangers; his avidity for tales of spells and horror, magic and enthrallment, drew on the lore of Britain and Germany through their national literature, and his illustrations of Shakespeare, for example, responded to the deep strain of supernatural terror in all the plays – comedies, tragedies, histories, and romances.

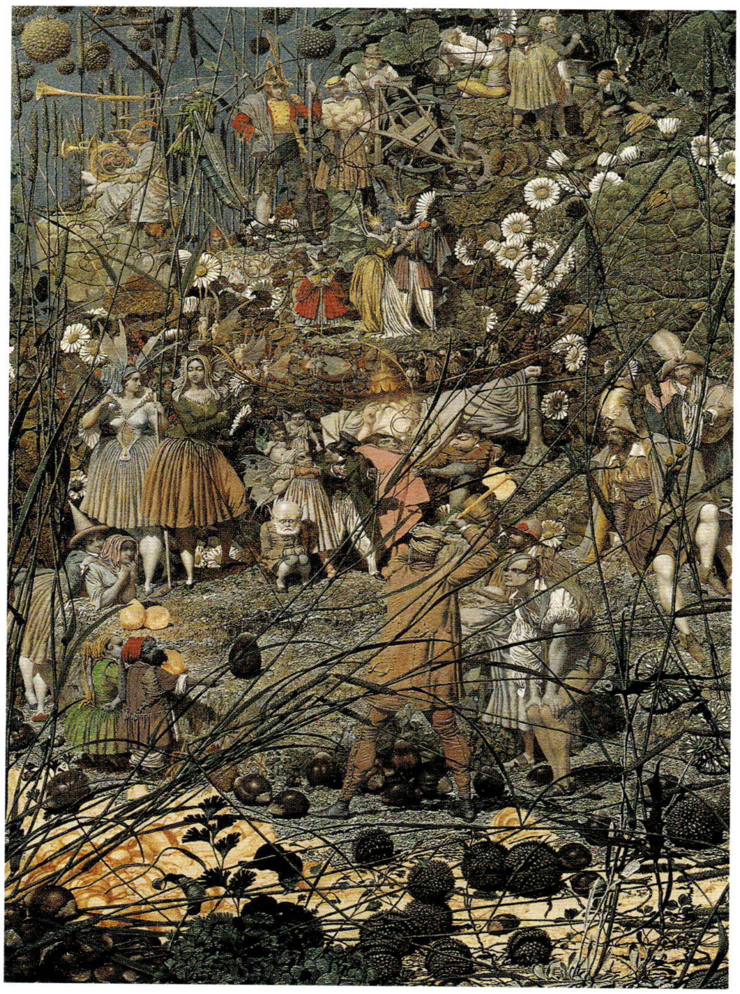

fig.8 Richard Dadd (1817–86), *The Fairy Feller's Master-Stroke* 1855–64, oil on canvas 54 x 39.4 cm. Tate. Presented by Siegfried Sassoon in memory of his friend and fellow officer Julian Dadd, a great-nephew of the artist, and of his two brothers who gave their lives in the First World War 1963

Fuseli transmogrified his sources according to his own sensibility, a sensibility with a taste for excitement, morbidity, and turbulence, for a constant rhythm of stimulus and arousal. This led him to fashion his own Shakespeare as a proto-Gothic master of horror and hallucination, a kind of Caligari working behind the scenes, and to perform similar horrid metamorphoses on many of his other literary sources and their materials.

Besides fairies, Fuseli raised nightmares and spectres – from the obvious plays (*Macbeth*, *Hamlet*) and also from lesser known scenes of vision and conjuring – the dream of Queen Katherine, from *Henry VIII*, for example, inspired him to several compositions (see no.100), and he even surrounds Perdita in her rustic exile with a bevy of imps, including several of his signature fairies in huge mob caps, while a *jeu d'esprit*, 'The Nursery of Shakespeare', gives the infant bard a train of accompanying goblins and genies, including the Spirit of Comedy who, dressed as one of Fuseli's super-fashionable fairy seductresses looks out of the image, dimpling at us complicitly.[5] Crucially, Fuseli also pictures the dispute between Harry Hotspur and Owen Glendower, when the Welsh bard boasts: 'I can call spirits from the vasty deep.' To which Harry retorts, 'Why, so can I, and so can any man, / But will they come when you do call for them? (*Henry IV Part 1*, Act III, scene 1) (no.42). Later in the same scene, Harry rails against Glendower's 'skimble-skamble stuff', and scorns the way he was 'reckoning up the several devils' names that were his lackeys'. Surprisingly, this chimes with Fuseli's views far more closely than the Welsh wizard's supernatural claims: this supreme artist of hauntings and dream states was a declared and ferocious votary of Reason, and proclaimed unwavering allegiance to scepticism. He has become a supreme painter of the turn to the uncanny, which has now come to seem involved with magic and the supernatural. But at the end of the eighteenth century, the territory was mapped onto the study of the psyche, and dark subterranean realms metamorphosed into the realm of the unconscious.[6] 'It is not by the accumulation of infernal or magic machinery', wrote Fuseli in one of his celebrated lectures, 'that Macbeth can be made an object of terror, – to render him so you must place him on a ridge, his downdashed eye absorbed by the murky abyss; surround the horrid vision with darkness, exclude its limits, and shear its light into glimpses.'[7]

This sable cast of imagination obviously inhabits the shadows, although Fuseli can radiate a quality of heightened excitement through his use of colour at times. But, like the creators of spooky terrors by staged projections – Philippe Jacques de Loutherbourg with his *Eidophusikon* (1782) and Paul de Philipsthal and Etienne-Gaspard Robertson with the Phantasmagoria (see p.146) – chiaroscuro, dark depths and gloamings, flickering shadows and sudden flashes of light predominate among Fuseli's favourite effects. Also like those pioneering illusionists, who proclaimed that through their magical arts they exposed the fallacy and deception governing all such terrors, in order to illuminate the public and steer them away from the terrors of superstition and credulity, so Fuseli seized hold of the potential that spectral delusions offered to his fantasy. This non-believing, often blaspheming, self-styled revolutionary *artiste maudit* summons all kinds of terrifying spirits for his audience and creates a mood of supernatural sublime without restraint of taste or deference to opinion, in order to stir in his viewers that ambiguous pleasure, the aesthetic state famously defined by Coleridge, of the suspension of disbelief.

Boydell's Shakespeare Gallery did not succeed commercially as the publisher – and his artists – had hoped, yet Fuseli's compositions – Hamlet's father's ghost, Titania's fairy court, the Witches appearing to Macbeth, and Caliban as a monstrous faun (fig.9) – have been lastingly influential on stage design, and, above all, on the reception of Shakespeare in the mind's eye of readers. For example, Edward Said recalls in his memoir, *Out of Place* (1999), how when he was young and growing up in Cairo, his mother and he read aloud from a copy of Shakespeare: 'its handsome red morocco leather binding and delicate onion-skin paper embodying for me all that was luxurious and exciting in a book. Its opulence was heightened by the ... drawings illustrating the dramas, *Hamlet*'s being an exceptionally taut tableau by Henry Fuseli of the Prince of Denmark, Horatio, and the Ghost.'[8]

The Swiss pedagogue and theorist Johann Jakob Bodmer (see no.27) was Fuseli's mentor, and, as a important early influence on *Sturm und Drang* and continental Romanticism, also shaped Coleridge's theories of creativity. Bodmer advocated the unfettered play of the imagination, the rejection of classical harmony and tranquillity, the mining of native, popular sources, and storytelling in art – *ut pictura poesis*. Many of the early German Romantic writers were collectors too, working as ethnographers as well as poets and storytellers – Clemens Brentano (1778–1842) explored traditional songs and legends with the famous cycle, later set to music, of *Des Knaben Wunderhorn*, and Adelbert von Chamisso (1781–1838) in *Peter Schlemihl* (1814; fig.10) drew on Jewish legends circulating in the salons of the Schlegel brothers and others in Jena and Berlin, to create the eerie story of a man who sells his shadow to a passing enchanter and finds he has forfeited his soul.[9] Even more resoundingly, the Grimm Brothers strove to retrieve popular, oral stories and the voices of the *Volk* with their edition of *Children's and Household Tales*, first published in 1812 and subsequently reissued in expanded editions to huge international interest and acclaim.

Fuseli extended these writers' innovative approach from literature to art: he too was a voracious anthologist, gathering up stories and more stories from all the different cultures and languages he acquired with such protean facility: his sources come from Germany, France, Italy, as well as the Celtic lore of his adopted British Isles, and from every era and level of literature, without prejudice. Indeed, he displays an insistent eclecticism, choosing to illustrate material set in the distant Orient or the local churchyard, in remote times past or menacing present circumstances, in historical settings or fantastic wonderlands. He belonged to the same enthusiastic revival of national bodies of bardic and magic literature that brought the supposed Celtic epic, *Ossian*, to the height of fame and eventually inspired poets and musicians to retrieve and recast legends and fairytales, previously despised as the superstitions and literature of the common people; this tendency was to expand into Richard Wagner's music theatre and the mythology of *The Ring* (1848). The work of Fuseli shares some qualities with these Romantics: the cruelty and the harshness, the occasionally cloudy bombast, the obsession with female power and sexual perversity.

It is not quite the case, however, that Fuseli told stories in the same way as his scholar-writer contemporaries, such as Bettina von Arnim (1785–1859), Ludwig Tieck (1773–1853) and the painter Philipp Otto Runge (1777–1810, the source of 'The Juniper Tree'), who retold German fairy tales about incest and infanticide. Fuseli himself began as a writer, but gradually realised that he did not have the direct eloquence of a storyteller. Around 1768 Joshua Reynolds recommended he concentrate instead on the visual arts. But his pictures (and they are very much pictures – scenes, images of events and characters, illustrations of stories) do not convey what is happening at all clearly, as he well realised, even if the viewer knows the material. Somehow, adding long, explanatory titles only exacerbated the problem, turning many of his depictions confused and pedantic at the same time. He was well aware of this difficulty, declaring very clearly, 'we turn our eye discontented from a picture or a statue whose meaning ... must be fetched from a book'.

Yet if he was so alive to the tendencies of his own bookishness, why did he illustrate stories so intensively? As the critic Werner Hofmann asked, is Fuseli 'simply playing a masquerade with us?' Does the parade of learned allusions disguise something else?[10]

An intense self-portrait throws light on this question (fig.11[11]): Fuseli is hunched down over his folded arms, leaning on a book of engravings; he is gazing intently out of the frame, his domed forehead thrust towards the picture plane, his brows arched into Gothic points, the

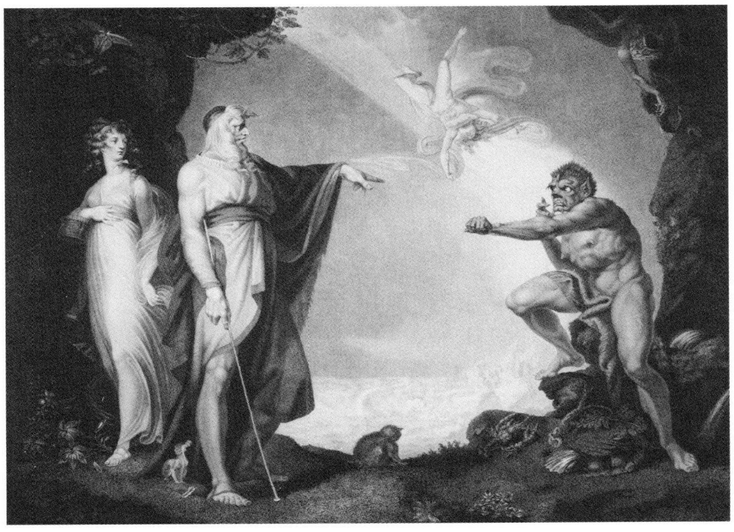

fig.9 Jean-Pierre Simon (1764?–c.1810) after Henry Fuseli (1741–1825), *Prospero, Miranda, Caliban and Ariel*, pub. John and Josiah Boydell, 29 September 1797, stipple engraving 43.6 x 58.5 cm. The British Museum, London

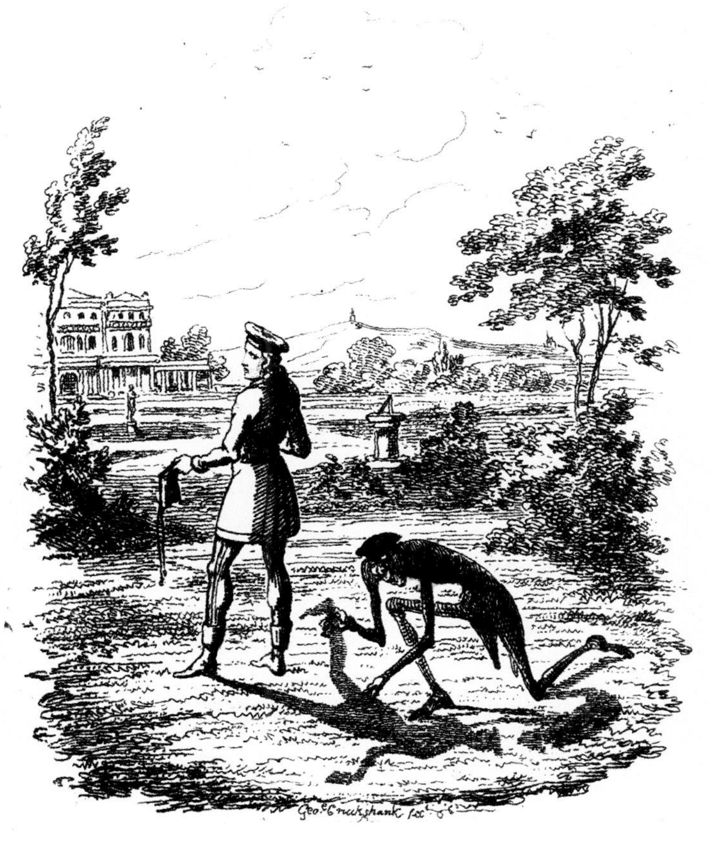

fig.10 George Cruikshank (1792–1878), engraved illustration to Adelbert von Chamisso, *Peter Schlemihl* ('from the German of La Motte Fouqué'), trans. J. Bowring, London 1824. The British Library, London

iris of both eyes rolled upwards so that the white shows, while the left eye is slightly wandering and shadowed. This whole mien corresponds to the exalted analyses of his friend and fellow student in Zurich, the physiognomist Johann Casper Lavater (1741–1801), who analysed character through facial expressions, the relative set of features and the cranial construction.[12] Of foreheads, Lavater declared, 'The form, height, arching, proportion, obliquity, and position of the skull, or bone of the forehead, show the propensity, degree of thought, and sensibility of man'; on the eyebrows: 'Angular, strong, interrupted eyebrows ever denote fire, and productive activity', and, finally, on the relation of eye to lid: 'I have seen no eye, where the eyelid formed a horizontal line over the pupil, that did not appertain to a very acute, able, subtle man … of great penetration and simulation.'[13] And so on and so forth.

Quite apart from Fuseli's self-presentation according to the most favourable diagnoses of personality pronounced by Lavater, the intense self-scrutiny of the portrait drawing meets a central tenet of the artist's vision of what History painting can do: transcend narrative through expression. He shows himself literally looking up from an image in a book, in order to focus all his concentration on the face and the meanings – the personal inscape which physical features can project. 'The exhibition of character', he wrote, 'in the conflict of passions with the rights, the rules, the prejudices of society, is the legitimate sphere of dramatic invention. It inspires, it agitates us by reflected self-love, with pity, terror, hope and fear.'[14]

As a working concept here, 'reflected self-love' corresponds to Aristotelian catharsis: when Fuseli seizes on certain key scenes and creates memorable, if often lurid, scenes of turbulence and conflict, they are not altogether attached to their original works, but rather become syntheses of certain states of passionate loss, turmoil, and crisis – illuminating human experiences far beyond the precise remoteness of their extreme plots with which we can identify, and fear for ourselves. 'Whatever connects [the individual]', he added, 'with [the species], or tears it from the species, may become an organ of pathos'.[15]

Indeed, Fuseli sometimes aimed so single-mindedly at dramatising the pathos of a distressed and torn human psyche rather than the dynamics of a story, that he invented his own primal material: for example, when asked by an interested Lord Byron about the origin of the image *Ezzelin Musing over Meduna, Slain by him, for Disloyalty, during his Absence in the Holy Land* (fig.16 on p.33), Fuseli admitted he had 'combined' various elements to create the picture. (In Italian, one of Fuseli's many languages, the popular verb '*combinare*' is used to convey not so much combining as plotting – using cunning stratagems and devices.) This image shows the murderer sitting sunk in gloom on the floor beside the bed on which his wife lies supine: a rhetorical composition, structured on dramatic frontal axes, in which Ezzelin resembles the artist himself, and the dead woman the spellbound and morbid females of numerous other images in his repertory. Several illustrations featuring Belisane and Percival with the enchantress Urma also derive from an 'orphan' original[16] (no.41).

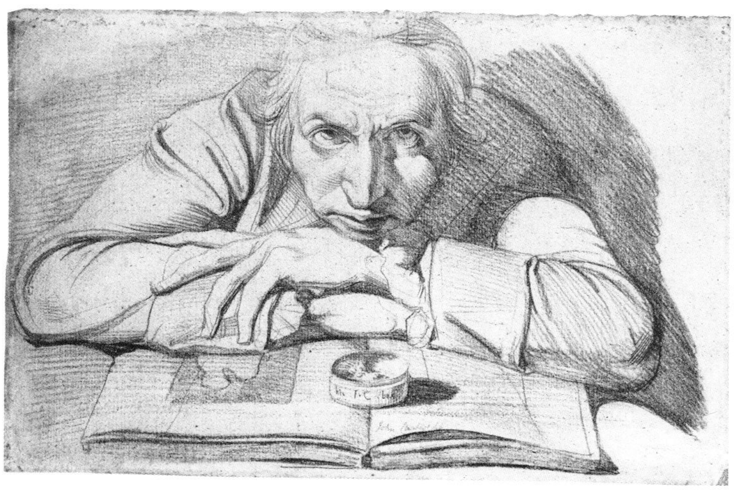

fig.11. Henry Fuseli (1741–1825), *Self-Portrait* c.1778–9 [sometimes identified as a portrait of John Cartwright], black chalk on paper 32.4 x 50.2 cm. National Portrait Gallery, London

As if in a Borgesian short story, Fuseli's ferocious narratives – autobiographical, authorial, imaginary – are nested inside one another, generating their own persuasive reality for his viewers.

Other minds become Fuseli's dominant subject. Supernatural powers and fairy enchantments communicate psychological conditions in material form; airy sprites and hobgoblins, spectre-smitten protagonists and haunted heroines, materialise states of mind and degrees of passion beyond the reach of bodily eyes.[17] Shakespeare already suggests as much when Mercutio, teasing Romeo about Queen Mab, deftly sums up what can now be read as a theory of the unconscious (*Romeo and Juliet*, Act I, scene 4) :

> … she gallops night by night
> Through lovers' brains, and then they dream of love;
> … O'er ladies' lips, who straight on kisses dream …
> This is the hag, when maids lie on their backs
> That presses them …

Fuseli embodies emanations: rather in the same manner as Blake's *Ghost of a Flea* (no.154) incarnates the insect's inner nature as a monster of great vigour and malevolence, the trooping sprites, butterfly-winged elves, dark scowling brownies and lumpen goblins of Fuseli's cast of characters function as inner diagnoses of his protagonists' minds, or, to take the same thought in fairy terms, they figure other co-walkers, our doubles, the self's spirit forms.

To gain access to them, Fuseli marshalled all his powers of theatrical gesture and expression, and seized on bodies as the vehicles of his fantasy, making them anatomically, by assembling – copying – from sources such as engravings after Michelangelo and later baroque masters. But the flexed and clenched musculature of his figures, their soaring or tumbling intertwinings and writhing limbs do not represent a possible physical reality: they express emotions. When he chooses episodes to illustrate, for example from de la Motte Fouqué's novel *Undine* (1811), inspired by a cluster of legends about selkies marrying humans, Fuseli does not depict the heroine's mermaid-like origins, but selects moments of trauma and thralldom, conveyed through the drooping, prostrate, starkly staring and smitten bodies of the characters.[18]

In a letter, the artist explained:

> My observations have been directed not to the countenance of nations only, being convinced … that the general form of the human body, its attitude, and manner, the sunken or raised position of the head, between or above the shoulders, the firm, the tottering, the hasty, or slow walk, may frequently be less deceitful signs of this or that character than the countenance separately considered.[19]

Fuseli, never one for not going to extremes, extends the Lavater system, and offers the whole body as a seismograph of the volcanic eruptions surging inside. He also echoes his friend's work in the focus of his interests, because Lavater commented on aspects of character that are connected above all to feelings and temperament, and to mental powers; likewise, Fuseli observes human propensities and moods at their most pent up and vehement: rage in all its forms – fury, grief, jealousy, madness – sexual desire, again polymorphously, and, above all, terror, convulse his subjects. He also advocated 'philosophical ideas made intuitive, or sentiments personified', and from the figures' tensed toes to their bristling and shaking locks, Fuseli does personify sentiments, exploring the impact of human passions on the heroic, or suffering body. He seems to be striving, through a tireless visual record of stories and their physical sensations, to gain – and pass on – an *Encyclopédie*-like inventory of every shade and extreme of human experience – beyond reason, beyond intellectual analysis. (This is the manner Edgar Allan Poe, himself a follower of Fuseli in tales of terror and dread, was making fun of through the character Signora Psyche Zenobia, who, wanting to make a career as a writer, is advised: 'Sensations are the great things, after all. Should you ever be drowned or hung, be sure and make a note of your sensations – they will be worth to you ten guineas a sheet.'[20])

Does Fuseli gain this knowledge of the passions? Does he manage to transmit it to us? And if he does, what are its principal elements? Many of his interests have special resonance for the twenty-first century and its vision of human psychology – or rather pathology. The House of Death or Lazar House from Milton's *Paradise Lost* inspires him (no.125):

> Numbers of all diseas'd, all maladies …
> Demoniac frenzy, moping melancholy
> And moon-struck madness, pining atrophy …[21]

He shows keen interest in – and sympathy with – madness. Rare excursions into first person testimony take him to hospitals and asylums: he drew a patient in the Santo Spirito in Rome whom he had seen struggling to escape monks who were trying to administer the last rites. He was crying out that he rejected all religion; Fuseli portrays him in frenzy as the brothers tear at his clothes to restrain him. The artist also penned a vivid pencil sketch of a woman with staring eyes and avid mouth, and labelled it 'Mary Anne' after the disturbed sister of Charles Lamb, who in 1796, in a fit of madness, had killed her mother.[22]

As anyone who comes to Fuseli knows, the crazed subjects of his chief curiosity are female: sometimes raving bacchantes or swooning maidens, prostrated in a fit or a stupor, sometimes possessed, sometimes simply driven out of their wits, like 'Mad Kate' from a poem, *The Task* (1785), by William Cowper, who himself suffered from mental trouble (no.71). When it comes to the products of the Greeks' irrationality and fantasies about women, the rational philosopher and Romantic loner becomes a fervent classicist. Maenads, gorgons, furies, harpies, sirens haunt his art. Spellbinders of different sorts – Medusa and Circe – catch his interest, as do several mothers and murderers, or both combined – Medea. His narratives of the psyche – those ideas intuited and sentiments personified – feature women performing myriad permutations of the unconscious and its powers: they faint, they fall into trance, they dream, they sleepwalk, they ride incubi into the night and are themselves ridden, they conjure demons, cast spells, and pursue their victims – sometimes their assailants – like Furies.

When Fuseli took for his inspiration Virgil's lines about the gates of dream in the Underworld, he does not show our hero 'pius Aeneas' taking the way of false dreams and passing through the gate of ivory, as Virgil relates, but stages instead a hyperbolic masturbatory scene, with a phallic elephant goblin poised on the floor, a herm erect and aghast with a finger to his lips, and a butterfly hovering near the groin of the dreamer in question – who is, of course, a swooning, naked, and female (fig.12).[23]

However, unlike most of their predecessors in Renaissance iconography, or their counterparts in Gothic and Romantic fantasy, many of Fuseli's fairies, demons, and sorceresses are dressed in the height of London fashion of his own day, from the trimmings on their extravagant bonnets to the turn of the kitten heels on their boots and the lapdogs they walk on silken leashes (these often as not manikins, bearded and pot-bellied). In his paintings, it is as if Titania's throng of fairies had been to Bath with Sir Walter Elliott to look over pattern books of the latest imported silks, gloves, hats, and ribbons, from France (it comes as a shock – a revealing shock – to realise that Mrs Fuseli would have been the same age as Jane Austen (1775–1817), and that Fuseli and Austen lived in the same time in the same country). The artist's curious flouting of traditional unities, using modern dress for fantastic denizens of a remote once upon a time, produces the particular frisson of Fuseli's own imagination as he invites us, through the mediums of his female characters, into states of heightened emotional tension.

Fuseli's women – inspired again and again by Sophia Rawlins, Mrs Fuseli, of the foxy look and the full overbite – enact the range of his extreme imaginings, often in explicit sado-masochistic scenarios that remove the Gothic visions of his contemporaries from the doomed medieval castle or enchanted palace to a bedroom in London, W1. It is pertinent that Byron provoked the artist's admiration, but none of the Gothic fantasists did – they practised supernatural arts in a manner he scorned. Whereas Horace Walpole (1717–97) safely removed his crazed and depraved protagonist Manfred to far distant Otranto and some indistinct medieval time, and William Beckford (1760–1844) fantasticated far pavilions and Oriental scenery for the wild debaucheries of the Sultan Vathek, Fuseli often stages sexual perversity with women who, while being exceptionally coiffed and arrayed, would have struck anyone of his contemporaries as belonging to the world of the here and now.

In many ways, Fuseli's fetishism, expressed through the obsession with hair-styling, is simply fetishism, his own proclivities set down in pencil and paint, his images of sexual pleasure pictures of his own tastes. (Magdalena Schweizer-Hess, a married woman for whom he entertained a brief passion before he came to London, may be responsible at least for his fixation: among her other eccentricities – she was also a dowser and could sense earthquakes – she would fall into trance while having her hair combed.) The late eighteenth century 'invented' pornography as part of rational modernity, as some literary historians have argued; a taste for erotica belonging alongside other enthusiasms of the Age of Reason: flying, for example.[24] This ancient, deep metaphor for bodily bliss found material realisation for the first time, when a new craze for 'aerostatics' or ballooning took hold. At one level, the learned

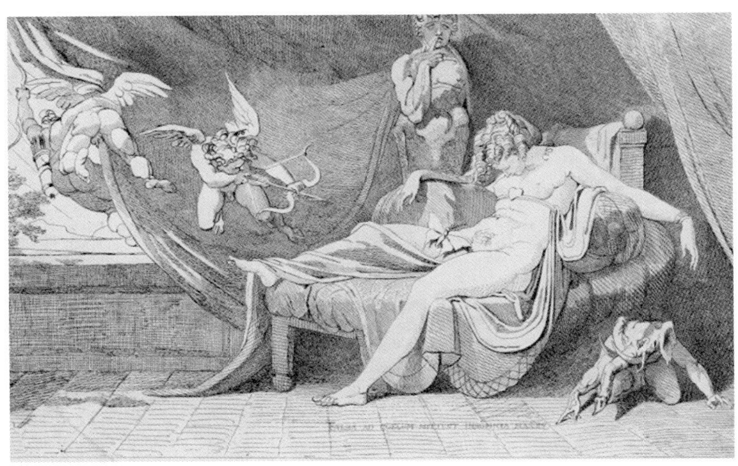

fig.12 William Blake (1757–1827) after Henry Fuseli (1741–1825), *Allegory of a Dream of Love* c.1790, etching 22 x 35 cm. The British Museum, London

Erasmus Darwin (1731–1802) rhapsodised in verse about the hitherto inaccessible views from above the clouds, while at another, the imaginary voyages dreamed up by John Elliott in 1778 included a visit to the 'Powerful Kingdom of Luxo-Volupto', where flying prostitutes in crinolines swoop down and carry off their prey (fig.13).[25] Like these dreams of sexual transport, Fuseli's objects of desire frequently wear wings, soar and tread the upper air as a native element, and he gives his wife's beckoning looks to many of his fantastic inventions.

However, apart from these acute, personal connections, Fuseli's painted women perform another part when they float and fly, swoon and conjure, dance and dimple, or perform their sexual ministry and torment their victims. For the femaleness of Fuseli's phantoms of desire embodies his inner drives according to an eighteenth-century tradition that is not primarily sexual, surprisingly. The convention was still vigorous in his own time and would have been assumed by the artist's contemporaries, but it has become far less visible to us today than, say, the trope of the swooning maiden or the sexual dominatrix. For William Blake, above all, but also for Edward Young (1683–1765) in the poem 'Night Thoughts' (1747), and for many others, female bodies conveyed the inner life of an individual because soul, psyche, happens to be feminine in gender. The inner self correspondingly takes a female form in language and then in image. This idea of the spirit body extends on the one hand to perceived identification of women with mad states and on the other to the incarnation of angels, who rarely appear virile. When Blake created his image of Milton's Satan 'in his original glory' (no.139), the beautiful angel, spreading wings of light and scattering fairy-like sprites from his radiant limbs, seems androgynous to say the least, with small breasts and no genitals.

When Blake conjured up Milton's hero, he was projecting his visions of ideal beauty onto a far horizon of metaphysics; but Fuseli looked through his wife's bandbox and into the mirror of her toilette, an item of furniture that actually became known in the early eighteenth century as '*une psyché*'.

Actresses were the new woman of Regency society (the mistress of the Regent, Mrs Jordan, for one).[26] Mrs Fuseli was not on the stage – in so far as the stage did not serve as her favoured theatre. But the masquerade of the actress was part of her persona, as her husband has captured her in images: the actress's necessary use of artifice, her performance on and off stage, her spectral life as a figment or invented character, lent her to Fuseli's artistic concerns with theatricality and psychological expression. Of course not every one of Fuseli's fairy queens and demonic mistresses is dressed to promenade for quizzing in the streets – some are flimsily draped as classical nymphs – yet most are not in fantastic or mythological attire at all, but look like you and me, if you and I had led fashionable lives under the Regency. We no longer wear the periwigs and flounces so extravagantly assembled by Mrs Fuseli: it is only time that has rendered her accoutrements unfamiliar as well as excessive.

In this sense, Fuseli is an artist of modern life, however odd that may seem; he foreshadows Baudelaire's dandified urban perversity, combining into the figure of the desiring and powerful woman a similar decadent concoction of vice, cosmetics, revolution and misogyny. His ladies of the night are his antagonists, who contend with his heroes to produce images of agitation and animation and expression – his ideal of dramatic aesthetic. They act as his 'pleasant children and inchanted puppets', enigmatic Doppelgängers who embody permitted passions on behalf of the male artist. His own descendants in this role are many, including Dr Coppelius, the invention of his contemporary E.T.A. Hoffmann (1776–1822) in *The Sandman* (1814) and, more recently, the maker of the marionette Lady Purple who, in one of Angela Carter's savage fairy tales, undresses and dresses his dolls:

> Then he tenderly took off her penitential wig and clucked his tongue to see how defencelessly bald she was beneath it. His arms cracked under the weight of her immense chignon and he had to stretch up on tiptoe to set it in place because, since she was as large as life, she was rather taller than he …
>
> Now she was dressed and decorated, it seemed her dry wood had all at once put out an entire springtime of blossoms … She could have acted as the model for the most beautiful of women, the image of that woman whom only a man's memory and imagination can devise …

But this image-doll awakens, rises out of her box, sucks the breath out of puppet-master, and then: 'even if she could not perceive it, she could not escape the tautological paradox … had the marionette all the time parodied the living or was she, now living, to parody her own performance…?'[27]

Unexpectedly, perhaps even counter-intuitively, the perverse enchantresses in Fuseli's fairy paintings, epic history scenes, and boudoir erotica, are fulfilling his ambitions for art, to depict alluring states of excitement and perform the passions that affect the human mind.

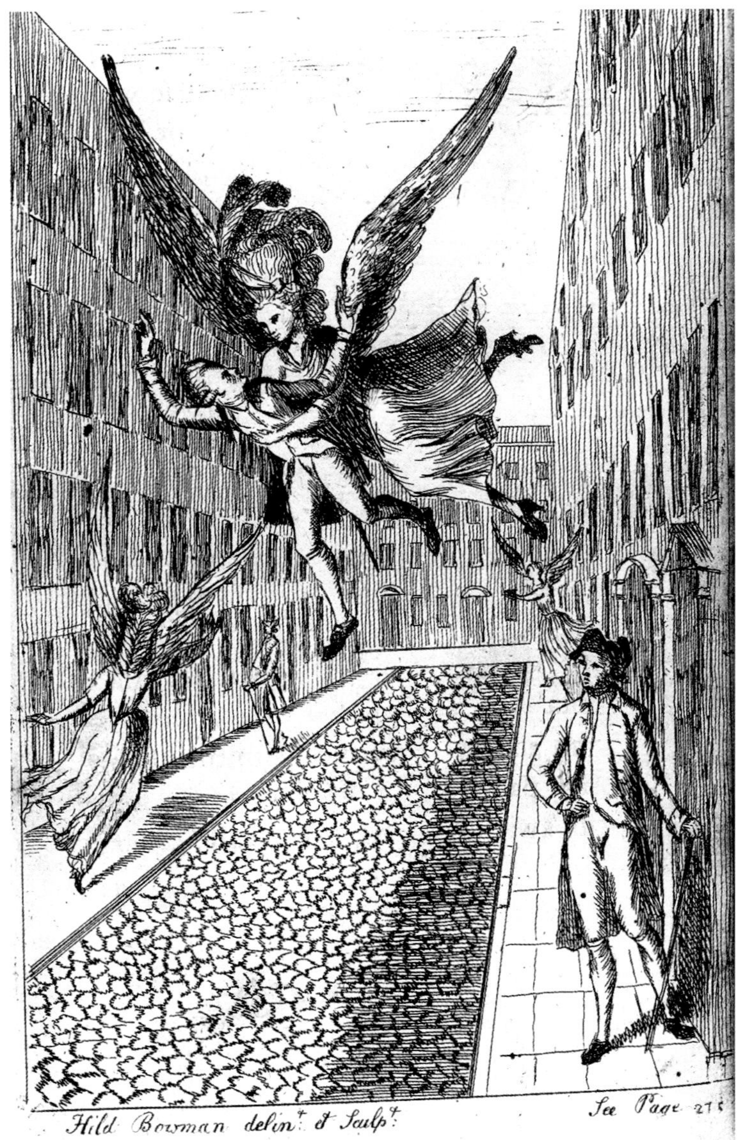

fig.13 Engraved illustration to John Elliott, *The Travels of Hildebrand Bowman, Esquire, into Carnovirria, Taupiniera, Olfactaria, and Audidatne, in New Zealand*, London 1778
The British Library, London

Notes

1 Kirk 1975, pp.49–71: esp. pp.49, 53–4; see also Hunter 2001; for more on British fairies, see Keightley 1910; Briggs 2002; and for an excellent recent study, Bown 2001.
2 Herrick 1915, pp.119–20, 165–9.
3 Kirk 1975, pp.52–3.
4 He even taught himself Dutch (his sixth or seventh language), in order to read a leading work on the entomology. See Knowles 1831, I, p.361.
5 The original painting *The Nursery of Shakespeare* 1810, survives only in fragments (Courtauld Institute, London), or so it is reported in Weinglass 1994, pp 331–2.
6 See Castle 1995 and Warner 1998, pp.254–61.
7 Knowles 1831, II, pp.225–6.
8 Said 1999, p.51.
9 Von Chamisso 1824. This edition mistakenly gives the book to La Motte Fouqué as author, but contains compelling illustrations; another 1851 edition in the British Library (Adelbert von Chamisso, *The Wonderful History of Peter Schlemihl*, trans. and ed. Falck Lebahn) attributes it correctly.
10 Hofmann 1975, p.29.
11 This drawing is identified as a portrait of John Cartwright, a friend of Fuseli, in the National Portrait Gallery, London. However, the pose and intensity of the gaze conveys self-contemplation in a mirror, while the face itself looks identical to other portraits of Fuseli. I am grateful to Martin Myrone for these observations.
12 See J.C. Lavater, *Essays on Physiognomy* (1775–8), trans. Thomas Holcroft, London c.1844, p.353, quoted by Ross Woodrow, http://newcastle.edu.au/discipline/fine-art/pus/lavater/lav-p56A.htm. Lavater died in 1801, when he was bayoneted in Zurich by a soldier in one of the French occupying forces.
13 Ibid., pp.379–97.
14 Knowles 1831, II, p.195.
15 Ibid., p.225–6.
16 Weinglass 1994, nos.56, 65, 70, 70a, 103, pp.44–5, 53–4, 73–4, 81, 110–11. Several images featuring Belisane and Percival and an enchantress called Urma, also derive from a 'ghost' original.
17 See Warren 1999, pp.215–41 for a terrific short story published in 1831, highly concerned with the states that Fuseli explores.
18 F.H.C. de La Motte Fouqué, *Undine, eine Erzählung. Vom Verfasser des Todesbundes*, Berlin 1811), first translated into English in 1818 as *Undine*.
19 Henry Fuseli, 'Letter dated at St Petersburg', in Lavater trans. Holcroft c.1844, p.353 (as at n.12 above).
20 Edgar Allan Poe, 'How to Write a Blackwood Article', in Poe 1978, II, p.340; see Baldick 1999, p.xiv.
21 Milton 1993, Book XI, ll.480–6, p.272.
22 Schiff 1975, no.193, p.134.
23 *Allegory of a Dream of Love*, also known as '*Falsa ad coelum*' from the line from Virgil Book VI inscribed on the floor, was etched by Blake; the elephant-goblin may be suggested by association with ivory, the same word in Greek. See Weinglass 1994, no.112, pp.121–2.
24 Hunt 1993.
25 A celebrated and very mischievous literary hoax, *The Travels of Hildebrand Bowman, Esquire, into Carnovirria, Taupiniera, Olfactaria, and Audidatne, in New Zealand etc.*, London 1778, was identified in 1994 as the work of John Elliott, a midshipman on *The Endeavour* under Captain Cook. See Horden House 2002, no.56.
26 See Tomalin 1994.
27 Angela Carter, 'The Loves of Lady Purple', from Angela Carter, 'Fireworks' (1974), in Carter 1995, pp.49–51.

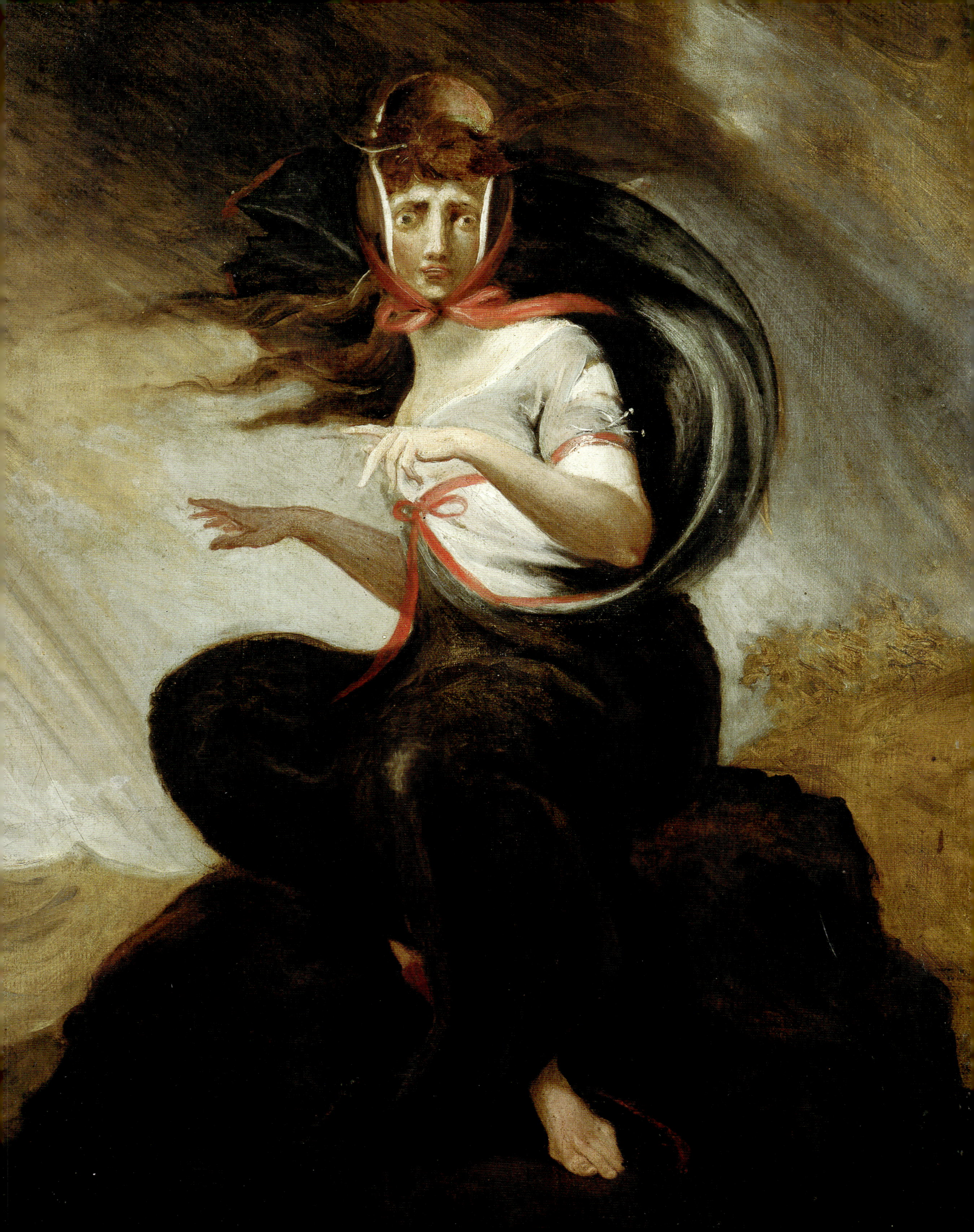

Fuseli to Frankenstein: The Visual Arts in the Context of the Gothic

You think Fuseli is not a Great Painter. Im Glad!
This is one of the best compliments he ever had.

Blake on Fuseli, couplet of around 1809, from his 'Notebook'[1]

Fuseli called on me last night and sat till 12 o'clock. He mentioned Blake, the Engraver, whose genius and invention have been much spoken of. Fuseli has known him a great many years, and thinks He has a great deal of invention, but that 'Fancy is the end, and not the means in his designs'. He does not employ it to give novelty and decoration to regular conceptions; but the whole of his aim is to produce singular shapes and odd combinations … Fuseli says Blake has something of madness abt. him.

Fuseli on Blake, recorded in the diary of Joseph Farington, 1796[2]

Your kind inquiry how ye work goes on encourages me very much & what gives one hopes that some part of my designs are taken up upon right grounds, is ye exact agreement of your Ideas with mine respecting Fuselli <& ye use to be made of him> – ~~depend I am convinced how very necessary~~ his ~~Mock Sublime is "Mad Taste"~~.

Gillray on Fuseli, in a letter to John Sneyd, 1800[3]

Detail from Henry Fuseli, *Mad Kate* c.1806–7 (no.71)

Martin Myrone

Introduction: 'the maddest people that the maddest times were ever plagued with'

On the night of Tuesday 6 June 1780, all hell seemed to break loose in the City of London. The ruffianly anti-Catholic mob which had for the previous days terrorised Westminster now congregated in the east, with the aim of breaking into Newgate Prison. Their intentions were quickly fulfilled (fig.14). Onlookers were horrified by the fervour of the attacking crowd, and the swiftness with which they broke open this notoriously severe and bleak edifice:

> The wild gestures of the mob without, and the shrieks of the prisoners within, expecting an instantaneous death from the flames; the thundering descent of huge pieces of building; the deafening clangor of red hot iron bars, striking in terrible concussion the pavement below; and the loud triumphant yells and shouts of the demoniac assailants on each new success, formed an awful and terrific scene. At length, the work of ruin was accomplished, and while the gaolers and turnkeys were either flying or begging for their lives, forth came the prisoners, blaspheming, and jumping in their chains.[4]

Worse still was to come. On 7 and 8 June private properties were destroyed, a huge, explosive fire started in Holborn, and the crowd even threatened to attack the Bank of England, the prime symbol of the modern, commercial nation, of Britain's status as the pre-eminent world power. Troops were called out in numbers in to dispel the crowds, which task they pursued with extreme prejudice. A veritable bloodbath ensued.

Historians may have called into question the traditional image of the riots of June 1780 as simply hysterical and uncontrolled, relating these events instead to issues of social protest and political dissent.[5] But the sight of up to sixty thousand men and women swarming through the streets of the capital, armed and angry, the extent of the bloodshed, the scale of destruction by fire and force, the sheer ferocity of the passions that motivated this violence, can hardly be dismissed. Witnesses to the riots certainly felt that demonic influences had been at work in London over those summer nights, exciting the crowd to insane destructiveness. Ignatius Sancho (1729–80) called the mob 'the maddest people that the maddest times were ever plagued with', while Susan Burney (1755–1800) wrote that the rioters, 'wth. the flames glaring upon them & the fires between them & us, seemed like to many *Infernals*' and the women in the crowd were 'like the Furies'.[6] Meanwhile, the leader of the anti-Catholic movement, Lord George Gordon (1751–93), was termed 'The monster, that conjured up the tempest'.[7] At the end of the six days of riots, 210 people had died in the streets; a further seventy-five were to perish as a result of their injuries. All these deaths were the result of the brutal oppression of the crowds: there is no single documented case of the rioters themselves causing a fatality. Of the 450 people arrested, sixty-two were sentenced to death, and twenty-five were eventually hanged, including young apprentices and women (one of whom, notably, was black – a sign of London's status as an imperial capital). The grand total of deaths amounts, then, to at least three hundred and ten, arising from a few days of riot and terror that had caused ten times more damage to the fabric of the Metropolis than was perpetrated against Paris in the French Revolution a decade later.[8]

The riots of June 1780 – known as the Gordon Riots – were a central event in the life of late eighteenth century London and in British history more generally. This outburst of ugly violence makes briefly and literally visible the deepest anxieties of the era, anxieties that helped shape and motivate the literature and painting of the time which so frequently pivot around the proximity of order and disorder, of bourgeois authority and primal rebellion, the themes of confinement and bodily violence, extravagance and repression, madness, revolution, revelation and apocalypse. Perhaps most importantly, our brief consideration of the Gordon Riots might remind us of the vitally important – but so often overlooked – role of sectarian strife in eighteenth-century British culture.

The events of that month were the culmination of a year and a half of agitation and action in response to the Catholic Relief Act of 1778. The Act had introduced some – really rather moderate – reforms to allow Catholics some share of the dignity and liberty enjoyed by those who conformed to the Anglican Church. Yet even this gesture in the direction of liberalisation stirred up deeply entrenched prejudices among a wide sector of the British public; among the petitions raised in 1779–80, London's included some forty-four thousand signatures. In June 1780 this general feeling of disquiet erupted, in a manner unknown within living memory. The Riots made it apparent that under the gilded surface of the present 'age of reason' were unpredictable and unmanageable powers, that under the facade of level-headed Anglicanism were passions and prejudices as inflammable as those conventionally attributed to Catholics. The historian – and convert to Rome – Edward Gibbon (1737–94) tellingly called the rioters 'Puritans such as they might be in the time of Cromwell ... started out of their graves', and remarked in horror on 'a dark and diabolical fanaticism, which I had supposed to be extinct'.[9] Such comments suggest that the disturbances were the result of a supernatural resurrection of the brute forces of destruction upon which modern British state institutions had been formed: Reformation, the demolition and robbery of the abbeys and cathedrals, the ruination and outlawing of the Catholic faith. In an era of assumed social and economic progress and self-confidence (ideas given authoritative form in the new modes of town planning or grand edifices such as Somerset House – opened that same year; fig.15) the riots drew attention instead to the imminence of paranoia and doubt. Was this modern, commercial state truly legitimate, relatively infant as it was? Could its claims to reasonableness, rationality and empiricism be upheld?

There were everywhere, and never more than after 1780, signs that this was not the case. The dominant self-image of the Hanoverian state as moderate, reasoning and liberal seemed undermined; whether fatally or not was yet to be determined. It was such threatening cracks in the polished edifice of Georgian culture that defined and gave power to the Gothic as a literary form, and to the visual art considered in this present exhibition, for each exposed the greater horrors suspected by this age of enlightenment.[10]

Three careers: art, caricature and the visionary

On June 1780 three artists prominent in this present exhibition were at work around London. Senior, and most established among them, was the Swiss-born painter Henry Fuseli (1741–1825). He was by then settled back in London, having been in Italy through most of the 1770s and in Switzerland again in 1778–9. By the summer of 1780 had exhausted most of the commissions he had received from the short visit he had made to his native country, though he was probably still at work on his heroically conceived canvas of *The Oath on the Rütli* (no.39). He had, accordingly, made a special effort in his contributions to the annual exhibition at the Royal Academy. In 1780 Fuseli had exhibited his small but powerful painting of an invented romance subject, *Ezzelin Musing over Meduna, Slain by him, for Disloyalty, during his Absence in the Holy Land* (fig.16) the mammoth *Satan Starting from the Touch of Ithuriel's Lance* (no.37)

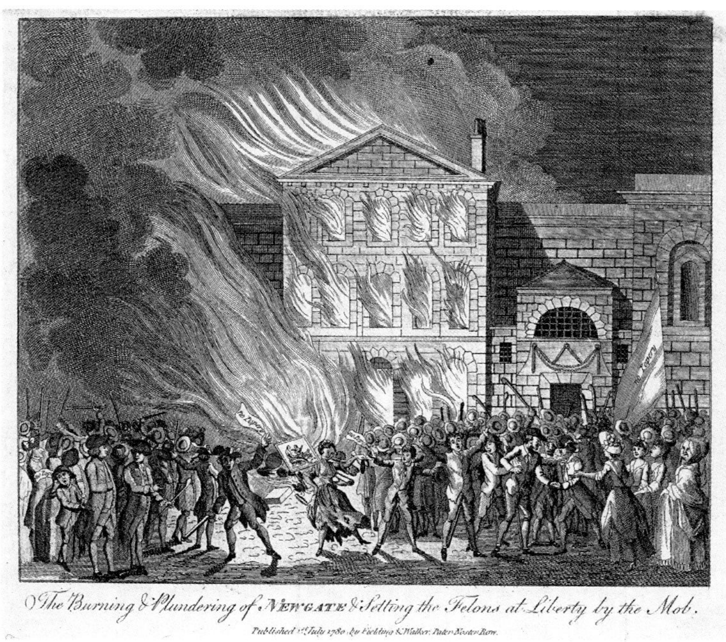

fig.14 Anonymous, *The Burning and Plundering of Newgate*, pub. Fielding and Walker, 1 July 1780, engraving. The Guildhall Library, Corporation of London

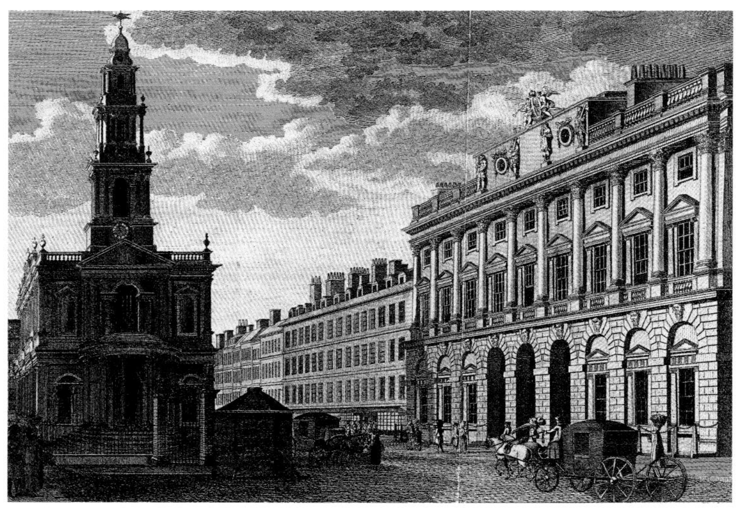

fig.15 William Walker (fl.1775–92) after Paul Sandby (1730/1–1809), *Perspective View of the Royal Academy of Arts, at Somerset House on the Strand*, pub. c.1780, engraving. The Guildhall Library, Corporation of London

and a classical subject, *Jason Appearing before Pelias* (now lost). According to his biographer, John Knowles, 'These paintings raised him, in the opinion of the best judges, to the highest rank in the art; and the President, Sir Joshua Reynolds, considered that they possessed so much merit, that he had them placed in prominent situations in the Exhibition'.[11]

This was the first year in which the annual Academy exhibition was held in the specially designed Great Room of Somerset House. Established only in 1768, the Academy had given the stamp of authority to a self-elected band of artists based in London and headed by the leading portrait and subject painter Joshua Reynolds (1723–92). The art world had long been organised upon decidedly informal, decentralised and arguably democratic lines; now, these new Academicians were claiming authority over their peers, aligning themselves with the grand pictorial traditions of seventeenth-century France and renaissance Italy to back up their claims. Though British artists had in the past only rarely had the opportunity to create the grand narrative works which these traditions placed at the head of the arts, now, with the personal backing of George III and the promise of vast new sources of national wealth in industry, empire and commercial enterprise, some artists believed that such productions could be rewardingly pursued. Fuseli was pre-eminent among those artists whose aspirations had been sharpened by these developments, believing that he could become the greatest painter of the age, but our other artists felt the influence of such ideas as well.

According to his Victorian biographer, Alexander Gilchrist (1829–62), who worked from reliable sources, Fuseli's erstwhile protégé, the young William Blake (1757–1827), directly experienced the action of 6 June. 'That evening', Gilchrist wrote, 'the artist happened to be walking in a route chosen by one of the mobs at large' coursing towards Newgate. Unwillingly, he was caught up in the crowd, and made to witness the breaking open of the prison.[12] Arguably Blake was more readily involved in the riot than his Victorian biographer allowed, and the sight of revolutionary action in the capital certainly haunted the imagery of his work – in written form and, increasingly from this point, in his original graphic works.[13] According to the 'Advertisement' attached to his first collection of writings, the *Poetical Sketches* printed privately in 1783, he had been active as a poet in his teenage years, but at this time his energy was 'wholly directed at the attainment of excellence in his profession'.[14] Still enrolled as a student at the drawing schools of the Royal Academy, and only recently released from his apprenticeship with the reproductive engraver James Basire (1730–1802), Blake was like so many of his generation ambitious to establish a reputation as a painter of historical themes in an academic mode. He had exhibited in the Academy show of 1780 a watercolour of the *Death of Earl Goodwin* (fig.17 is either that design or a related study) in a conventional style, which drew favourable notice in print from his friend George Cumberland (1754–1847).[15]

If we are reliably informed that Blake was caught up in the riot, and if from his current home in St Martin's Lane Fuseli could hardly have avoided the sight and sound of the vast crowds swelling around the streets of Westminster during June 1780, neither has left a direct record. It is left to Blake's close contemporary and peer at the Academy schools James Gillray (1756–1815) to provide a supposed eyewitness image. His *No Popery or Newgate Reformer* (fig.18) shows vividly the animalistic, irrational character projected onto the insurgents, with an inscription that makes the still-disputed claim that the motivations of the crowd were merely criminal, rather than religious. Gillray, like Blake, had been apprenticed to an engraver and had enrolled at the Academy, which experience had helped fuel a desire for better things. In his case this meant the pursuit of elevated engravings, but in this field he was never a success. Through these years he pieced together a living making illustrations and caricatures – often of a pornographic or otherwise disreputable character – which remained unsigned. *No Popery* exhibits a brutal deployment of the etching technique, well fitted to the subject but far from the delicacy and sophistication that was shortly to characterise his work.

The ambitions, expectations and desires of these three artists diverged over the years, though their lives were closely entwined at various points. Both Blake and Gillray were employed as reproductive engravers of Fuseli's work, the former frequently and with the painter's encouragement, the latter only once.[16] But as a satirical artist, Gillray found many more opportunities to use Fuseli's compositions and to adopt a 'Caricatura-Sublime' manner (the term Gillray used in dedicating his *Wierd-Sisters* to the painter; see no.81). Blake and Fuseli were personal associates, oftentimes friends, sometimes mutual advocates, and a full account of their long and complex relationship is beyond the scope of the present exhibition.[17] In contrast, Blake and Gillray were

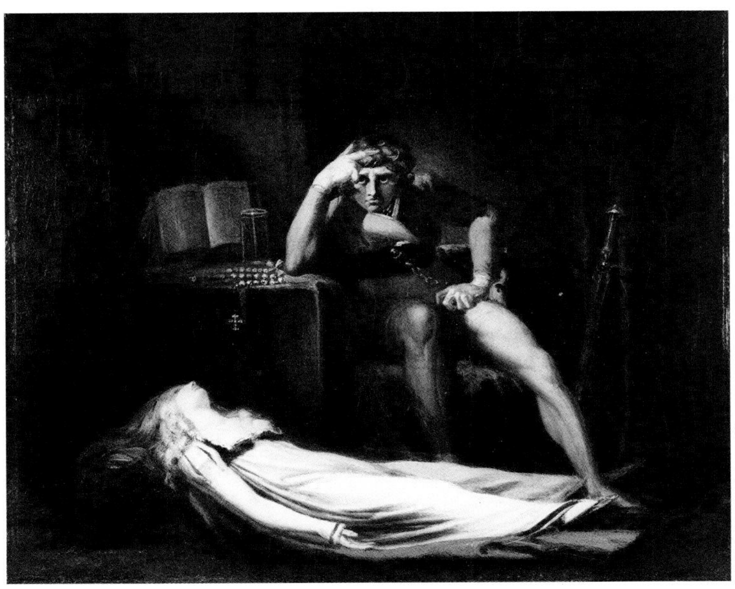

fig.16 Henry Fuseli (1741–1825), *Ezzelin Musing over Meduna, Slain by him, for Disloyalty, during his Absence in the Holy Land* exh. RA 1780, oil on canvas 45.7 x 50.8 cm. Sir John Soane's Museum, London

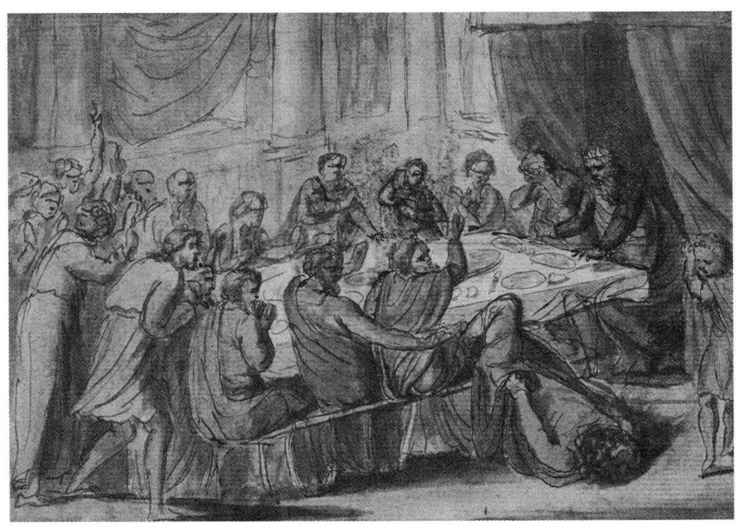

fig.17 William Blake (1757-1827), *The Death of Earl Goodwin* c.1779, pen and watercolour on paper 12.7 x 18 cm.The British Museum, London

contemporaries at the Academy and shared a trade, but are not otherwise linked as far as we know. However, as David Bindman has noted, they share 'a sense of the unremitting corruption of the world' and Blake, arguably, learnt much from the satirist's techniques.[18]

All three artists came from backgrounds that placed them in a somewhat oblique relationship with the metropolitan social establishment. The two engravers came from relatively lowly backgrounds, and were nurtured in the artisanal context of the reproductive engraving trade: Fuseli was Swiss, educated to the highest level and an ordained Zwinglian priest. While the English artists were allowed to socialise to some degree with their superiors, albeit without obtaining high social distinction themselves, the Swiss made a rather theatrical display of his personal alienation from regular society, even as his cause was taken up by some well-placed figures.

Although all three enjoyed a reputation, and varying levels of material success, each was also to become notorious for personal eccentricity. Still, Fuseli eventually became a pillar of the establishment and, by virtue of his posts as Professor of Painting (from 1799) and Keeper of the Royal Academy (from 1804), the dominant figure in the British art world for decades, overseeing the basic art education of a whole generation of artists including such seemingly unlikely figures as John Constable (1776–1837), David Wilkie (1785–1841), J.M.W. Turner (1775–1851) and Edwin Landseer (1802–73). He was admired and collected, but often seen as a figure of fun and, by the end of his life, a curiosity, an anachronistic hangover from an earlier, misguidedly heroic, era of art. Blake, by a combination of political paranoia directed against him and his

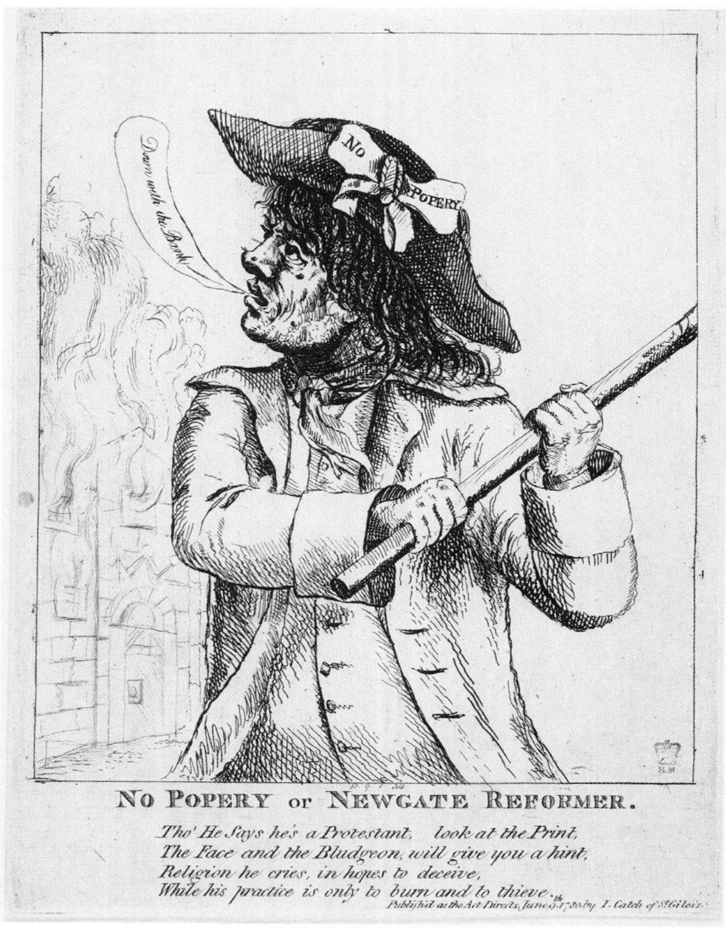

fig.18 James Gillray (1756–1815), *No Popery or Newgate Reformer*, published 9 June 1780. Etching 22.9 x 19.7 cm. The British Museum, London

own technical innovation and iconographic originality, became an isolated, marginalised figure supported by only a tiny circle of friends. Gillray, too wilful and difficult to make a success of his reproductive engravings, became a brilliant caricaturist, the first to be named and acclaimed as such, though his end, in literal madness, is the saddest of all.

In often surprising ways, the work of these three artists connects, interacts, and pursues complimentary or common strategies. That there are 'Queer exchanges and borrowings' between the three artists was, indeed, noted at the very beginning of modern scholarship into these artists.[19] Contemporary commentators, too, had explored the potential connections between high art, caricature and the visionary, in the context of art criticism and biography. Gillray's witty pictorial and literary references and the sheer sophistication of his draughtsmanship brought his works to a level, in the eyes of many, of high art; because of the distortions and extravagances which characterised the productions of Fuseli and Blake, they were correspondingly dismissed as caricaturists, whose productions should not be dignified with the title of 'art'.

How could this be? What wider set of circumstances could make these volatile synergies possible? As much as the social world was in trauma during these years, the realm of the aesthetic and of art were in turmoil too. The year 1780 may have seen the Academy move into authoritative new premises on the Strand, but we should not imagine that its power over the realm of taste was accepted without contest. On the contrary, since the 1760s the reformation of taste had been apparent in the widest variety of contexts, in private and in public, in philosophical criticism and essayistic reflection, in unregulated press commentaries, around the print market, and in alternative spaces of artistic display, formal and informal. More importantly, the means of accounting for taste had themselves become radically destabilised. The ideas of the 'Sublime' and the 'imagination', of 'originality' and 'genius' had been invigorated to become powerful tools in cultural discourse, enabling, restricting and directing artists in unexpected and unpredictable ways.[20]

The ascent of these unstable and destabilising ideas is an element in what we may call the rise of cultural modernity – a kind of modernity that elevates specifically bourgeois values and which anticipates the technological and much of the economic transformation that would establish the modern world as we know it.[21] Part of the fascination of Fuseli, Blake and Gillray is that they occupy the characteristic faultlines within this ascendant modernity, along which values can be radically transformed – where art may become trash, enlightenment mutate into exploitation, the popular be exclusive, and, in every case, vice versa; or, to speak more specifically of artistic matters, where high art may turn into caricature, the classical body may become grotesque, and narrative be vacuously spectacular, a hollow spectacle.[22] A culture which valued so highly and so often qualities in art and literature that exceeded regular judgement (and belonged instead to the realm of 'genius' and the Sublime) did not, perhaps, really know quite *what* to think.

This was far from being an affair of dry scholarly discussion or rarefied aesthetic reflection. These possibilities emerged from and helped to shape a wholly socialised world of art, where values and ideas were formed by active social interaction rather than the formal diktats of any kind of institution. The Royal Academy exhibitions from 1780 were the focus of a cultural calendar busier and more accessible than ever. From around this date, art journalism as a recognisable genre emerged as a force in public opinion. The market for reproductive prints and caricatures, growing healthier since the 1760s, exploded. Despite the economic and political travails of the modern age, with Atlantic war and unrest at home, there appeared to contemporaries to be a greater problem in the superfluity of printed opinion and of luxury goods that alienated Britons from their roots in the simpler rural economy of old. A new breed of art patrons came to the fore – doctors and lawyers and businessmen whose roots and homes were in the newly enriched Midlands or North rather than in the Metropolis, and whose wealth was drawn directly or indirectly from the world of international business where the exchange of goods – including, we should always remember, people, in the form of slaves – created untold fortunes. The Academy, for all its splendour and apparent authority, promulgated a deeply compromised vision, which allowed for the rise of these sources of patronage and critical support – hence Reynolds's advocacy of portraiture as a valid artistic form, and his ultimate admission of Thomas Gainsborough (1727–88), a profoundly anti-academic painter, into the canon of art.[23]

Significantly, these years saw the emergence of distinctly modern forms of literature, intended, for commercial reasons, to appeal to this socially diverse audience: romances, sentimental novels, and, most importantly, Gothic novels, poems and plays focusing on themes of terror, adventure and the supernatural, often in a medieval setting. Parallel to, and sometimes preceding, this literary phenomenon, is the art considered in the present exhibition.

There is nothing new in claiming some degree of correspondence between Fuseli's art and the Gothic.[24] But as much as this exhibition is concerned with identifying comparable themes in the visual arts, it argues that what brings the perverse, strange and supernatural art of Fuseli, Blake, Gillray and their contemporaries into meaningful association with the Gothic in literature is also that they share the same range of new strategic possibilities regarding audiences, marketing and the power of sensation. Which is not to say that they directly emulated Gothic writers, or would have wanted to be seen doing so. While Gothic authors often aspired to a Shakespearean tone to dignify their efforts and lend the thrill of high culture to their productions, painters were much more literally Shakespearean. Very few treated modern Gothic subjects in an illustrative manner; but the art in this exhibition demonstrates how many turned to the most sensational and Gothic themes in the classics, national history, Dante and Elizabethan and Jacobean literature – and how thoroughly they did so. Dignified and legitimate as these sources were, viewed from the perspective of academic art theory, in the hands of Fuseli and his fellows they are transformed into a repository of Gothic horror, visionary excess and kinky eroticism. So if Gothic literature, even at its most tawdry and perishable, claimed some gloss of cultural value, so visual artists drew close to the Gothic in their treatment of ostensibly noble and ennobling themes. If Gillray and other graphic satirists borrowed from, or lampooned, high art, so the exaggerated characterisations and dynamic compositions of many elevated canvases could appear like caricatures. Thus it is that while Fuseli, Blake and Gillray have their own, complex (and overlapping) histories, they can productively be considered together and in relation to the phenomenon of the Gothic.

Gothic, romance and the tales of wonder

In 1783 Horace Walpole (1717–97), the disgruntled son of the late prime minister and a leading connoisseur, penned a note in a blank space in his copy of the catalogue of that year's Royal Academy exhibition: 'Of late, Barry, Romney, Fuseli, Mrs Cosway & others have attempted to paint Deities, Visions, Witchcraft &c, but have only been bombast & extravagant, without true dignity.' Walpole must have had in mind pictures like Fuseli's *Queen Katherine's Dream* (no.100) and *The Nightmare* (no.1), which had been on show in the previous two years, his *Three Witches* (no.80) and *Percival Delivering Belisane* (no.41) on show in the 1783 exhibition, George Romney's (1734–1802) 'cartoons' of horrific classical themes (nos.17, 77), James Barry's (1741–1806) *Medea Contemplating* (exhibited in 1772, now lost) and his gigantic vision of Heaven and Hell for the Great Room of the Society of Arts (1777–84), Maria Cosway's (1760–1838) efforts in the realm of gigantic mythical painting, or John Downman's (1750–1824) *Ghost of Clytemnestra* (no.84). This was not an isolated concern. In 1785, when Fuseli presented his *The Mandrake: A Charm* (no.82) at the Academy, the critic writing for *The Universal Daily Register* (2 May 1785) complained that 'Gypsies, Witches, and flying Devils seem to have engrossed the attention of many artists'. Walpole's further scribbled comments next to the catalogue entries referring to Royal Academy exhibits by Fuseli, Cosway and Downman over the succeeding years are unambiguous: 'shocking ... extravagant ... very mad ... shockingly mad ... strange ... madder than ever ... quite mad'.[25]

Such opinions might appear ripe, given Walpole's established role as the godfather of the Gothic, on the basis of his novel *The Castle of Otranto* (1764), usually taken as the first Gothic text, his rather less read incest-play *The Mysterious Mother* (1768) and what is usually seen as his notorious masterpiece of camp, the papier-mâché extravaganza of Strawberry Hill.[26] But Gothic writing itself did not really gather steam until this latter period, with the ascent of Gothic romances and supernatural tales in the 1780s, theatre productions, private theatricals and masques. The times had changed dramatically, as Walpole knew. He wrote of his book in 1784: 'It was fit for nothing but the age it which it was written, and age in which much was known; that required only to be amused, nor cared whether its amusements were conformable to truth and the models of good sense'. In the same letter, Walpole complained again that 'The exhibitions at Somerset House are crowded with Brobdingnag [i.e. gigantic] ghosts'.[27] *Otranto* had appeared when Britain was riding high after a vast and ultimately successful imperial war with France and her allies. The Seven Years War (1756–63) had established Britain as a virtually unchallenged world power with commercial and military interests stretching across the known continents. By the time Walpole complained about the 'bombast & extravagant' nature of contemporary art, the British Empire had been transformed. The American Revolution had divided opinion at home, caused enormous bloodshed and soul-searching, and, with the arrival of France and Spain to the American cause, dragged on to a now inevitable and (to many) shameful peace settlement (1782). Economic depression, demilitarisation and public unrest combined to lower a cloud of gloom. With America lost, Britain increasingly was to turn its attention to the exploitation and exploration of the East – India in particular, though the morality of this effort was ever in question, and the long drawn-out trial of Warren Hastings (1732–1818) from 1788 exposed the vile abuses that threatened always to accompany imperial conquest. The dream of Britain as a new Athens or Renaissance Rome, its people bathed in a golden haze of enlightenment and its palaces and streets adorned with elegance and splendour, had turned sour, overtaken by a nightmare of corruption, venal passions and violence, brute, ugly art and cheaply sensationalist tastes. The spectres of religious prejudice, the seemingly perverse allure of Catholicism with its rich heritage and cultural achievements, the impossibility of real heroism in an era of commercial enterprise and cynical imperial adventure, the sense of imminent social collapse or revolution, were all invidious, creeping influences on a cultural life outwardly splendid.

In this context, Gothic fantasy served multiple, complex, and sometimes contradictory functions quite beyond anything Walpole might have imagined in the 1760s. The heroes of romance represented a better model of manhood than Britain's actual soldiers, who had failed in conflict and who in more domestic duties at home and abroad were suspected of corruption and brutality. The fainting maidens of Gothic tales were better, too, as models than the viragos and whores and vapid fashion victims who were thought to populate the social world. So, for many conservative writers in the 1780s, Gothic fantasy and medieval romance offered a resource for re-establishing a patriotic myth of Anglo-Saxon heroism and gender norms. But, freed from the weight of expectations that accompanied classical narrative (drummed into Britain's upper class from schooldays), the Gothic was available as a pool of stock images and ideas for writers and readers less attached to the status quo as well. Middle-class dissenters (who were well represented in the circles that supported Fuseli and Blake) could turn to Gothic Romance as a source of heroic and exciting narratives that were more immediately accessible and relevant than the creaking Classics. Then again, the sensationalist aspects of Gothic tales – sex and horror, dungeons and ghouls – reached out to the most immediately gruesome or salacious tastes. This last came most forcibly to the fore in the 1790s, when a new kind of shockingly graphic Gothic tale was imported in translation from Germany and imitated and emulated in a vast upsurge of publication (represented most famously by M.G. 'Monk' Lewis [1775–1818] and in a more measured fashion by Ann Radcliffe [1764–1823]). Lampooned by Jane Austen (1775–1817), it was such lurid tales that were evoked in 1816 when Mary Godwin (later Shelley) (1797–1851) and Percy Bysshe Shelley (1792–1822), John Polidori (1795–1821) and Lord Byron (1788–1824) gathered by Lake Geneva on a stormy night to tell each other ghost stories, the event that famously (following Mary Shelley's account of the event in 1831) spawned *Frankenstein* (1818), Polidori's *The Vampyr* (1819) and further generic transformations that saw modern science fiction and horror erupt from the chest of eighteenth-century Gothic.[28]

As a historical context for these phenomena, we can further note that it was the period of the Gothic that witnessed the removal from most people's lives of the direct encounter with physical horror and death that had been common even in their parents' generation. The public executions at Tyburn, which had been such a rumbunctuous event in previous decades, came to an end in 1783; from that date, they took place at Newgate in a more brutally efficient atmosphere.[29] The last battles on British soil had taken place in 1745; the threats of Irish and French invasion which arose in 1779 and the 1790s were exactly that: threats. While Britain's professional armies and navy grew vast the experience of armed conflict grew more distant for everyone else. The American and French wars were fought in far-off seas and fields, and did not necessarily interrupt life in the quiet parsonage or the country-house drawing room. Then we might consider the introduction of anaesthetic, the great moves to prison reform headed by John Howard (1726–90; see no.128), the rise of a kind of animal rights movement with complaints against vivisection and the mistreatment of bears or dogs for sport, the improvement of roads, the straight new streets of Edinburgh after 1767, the refined grandeur of the Royal Crescent in Bath (1767–74), the mass production of classy Wedgwood classical wares, of buttons, belt-clasps and snuff-boxes. Umbrellas, still a fashionable novelty and a bit of an affectation in the 1760s and 1770s, became a commonplace in the 1780s.[30] When Robert Southey (1774–1843), writing gently mocking *Letters from England* (1807) in the character of 'Don Manuel Alvarez Esprilla', commented on 'Comfort – Curious Conveniences', he catalogued a 'Patent Compound Concave Corkscrew', a mechanical candle-snuffer and a 'machine for slicing cucumbers', separate kinds of knives for fish, butter and cheese, for cutting pens and clipping nails, pocket toasting-forks and a portable fireguard, a wildly expensive set of extra-lightweight fire-irons, and, to cap it all, 'the hunting razor, with which you may shave yourself while riding full gallop'.[31] The taste for the horrid in art and literature grew most rapidly among a generation less aware than ever before of the terrible fate of the body in war and disease, more comfortable, pampered and perfumed than their forebears, more culturally ambitious and needier – not least perhaps because the temporal self-consciousness which assured modern Britons that they had reached the apex of civilisation simultaneously warned them of their precarious position in history.[32]

The Gothic was never so much just a genre as a vast and diffuse practical exploration into the nature and value of art in an emerging modern, bourgeois and capitalist society whose primary, structuring values were as yet still not quite formed. In particular, the decisive distinctions between high culture and low, between the grand and the simply grandiose, the tacky and the tasteful, were in a decidedly volatile state. Gothic writers could be deliberately, even pretentiously Shakespearean even as they were evoking rotting heads and gruesome filth, or scenes of ludicrously unlikely heroic action. Then again, writers and artists of self-conscious distinction (and Fuseli is the prime case here) exposed themselves to accusations of crassness and stupidity in their pursuit of startling effects. Still further, there was the question of historical and moral truthfulness, of the powers and limits of cultural representation. The medieval settings of so many Gothic tales might be simple backdrops; or they might claim to give their stories a foundation in real history, or at least in real moral values which did exist in that historical past. When Revd Bromley sought to belittle Fuseli in his *Philosophical and Critical History of the Fine Arts* of 1793, it was by pitching him against Benjamin West (1739–1820). Where West sought out subjects from 'real history' and depicted them with close attention to historical details, Fuseli was a mere fantasist, and in this like the purveyors of cheap literature.[33] As another writer in the fashionable magazine *La Belle Assemblée* (May 1811) quipped: 'The pictures of Fuseli, like the heroes and dwarfs in the old romances, stir up and agitate the mind without impressing the feelings'.

Madness, genius, sickness

There are few today who would have sympathy with the Revd Bromley, and who would prefer the stolid productions of West to the imaginative excesses of Fuseli. But he had a point, nonetheless. What good were such visions? Were these pictures serviceable, meaningful, useful to society? Many thought not, and in facing materials that appeared to defy accepted standards of taste, mobilised the only concepts that were available to deal with such confrontational, dissident materials – imagination, genius, madness and sickness. But this was uncertain critical ground. Again and again we find Fuseli's art praised or damned in almost identical terms. Because 'the peculiar, but too often caricatured vigour of Mr Fuseli's poetical pencil, is a vigour beyond the law of art', so, it appears, it cannot be judged, assessed, classified in regular terms.[34] This comment from the later 1780s is typical:

> It is a difficult task to estimate the merits of this artist's work, by any rule or criterion by which we judge of others. Pictures are, or ought to be, a representation of natural objects, delineated with taste and precision. Mr *Fuseli* gives us the human figure, from the recollection of its form, and not from the form itself; he seems to be painting every thing from fancy, which renders his work almost incomprehensible, and leaves no criterion to judge of them by, but the imagination. (*Public Advertiser*, 22 May 1786)

In the 1790s rumours circulated that he would eat raw pork before going to bed to fuel the nightmarish visions that were the basis of his art, or take opium to induce the imagination to greater excesses: his 'light-headed compositions' could be put down to 'an indigestion of genius'.[35] He was repeatedly termed a 'mad professor' or 'magician', and biographical accounts and anecdotes tirelessly focused on his strange accent, propensity to swear outlandishly, and curious personal demeanour.[36]

Fuseli's reputation threw a shadow over Blake's: if there was a single artist more eccentric than Fuseli, it was this strange young engraver. The painter Thomas Stothard (1755–1834) said of Blake's designs that they 'were like the conceits of a drunken fellow or a Madman'.[37] Such a judgement became standard. Even Fuseli had remarked that 'Blake has something of madness abt. him'.[38] But if accusations of madness were with that artist essentially metaphorical – and Fuseli held down a proper job at the Academy and had a nice big house in Fitzrovia if anyone doubted otherwise – with Blake, living on the margins of London's society, it came dangerously close to being simply true, with the threat of his being stigmatised as a lunatic and excluded from regular society. The debate still continues as to whether his visionary works, particularly those created with the encouragement – perhaps guidance – of John Varley (1778–1842) in 1819–25 (see nos.153–4) were genuinely inspired, the result of mental disturbance, or incorporated an element of clowning, of playing up to his reputation.

Gillray's madness was, though, beyond doubt. His mental collapse after 1810 is sadly all too evident in the strange, mutilated scrawls that he produced at the end of his life, and documented in his suicide attempt of 1811. Yet whether his earlier visionary works, teeming with monstrosity and effervescent with acid temper, were motivated by mental illness will remain disputable. Can a wholly sane man be the author of such vivid imaginings, such furious, obsessive scrawls as his drawings (such as no.143a)?

These three artists' works and public personalities were caught in the midst of contemporary debates about artistic propriety, taste and cultural value that were reshaping the cultural field in dramatic ways, as artistic institutions, critics of various political shades and social sympathies, the ruling class, new patrons and the great mass of public opinion and market forces conflicted and coincided to transform the lives and career paths of individual painters. In these contexts, the physical and mental health of the artist came to the fore as an endlessly debatable index of quality. What was imagination to one commentator was madness to the next; genius to this, sickness to that.

Life, death and the undead

If the tropes of sickness and disease were refracted through the anecdotal biographies that arose around Fuseli, Blake and Gillray, their treatment of the human form made such themes graphically evident. The study of the human figure was central to the theory and practice of art since these had been formalised by the Continental art writers and academies of the sixteenth and seventeenth centuries. The concept of 'istoria' (history painting, the bodily expressed grand narrative) underpinned the whole universe of values surrounding the visual, as this was re-established in vernacular contexts from the end of the seventeenth century in Britain. The male body, measurable, delimited, stripped of the idiosyncrasies and blemishes of the living form, was the fundamental vehicle of artistic ideas, the test and emblem of expertise.

That was the theory, at least. In practice, artists working in Britain had only rare occasions for portraying the nude figure for profit. Landscape and portrait painting were always more rewarding, the former hardly requiring knowledge of the human form, the latter hardly requiring mastery of the idealised body as a prerequisite to practice. London's major drawing school before the Royal Academy, that established at St Martin's Lane, notably employed both female and male models, and cultivated a more naturalistic and sensual approach to the human form that was latterly fully elaborated into theory by William Hogarth (1697–1764). In his treatise *The Analysis of Beauty* (1753), Hogarth held that the highest aesthetic pleasure was to be derived from the representation of normal life, as famously demonstrated in his advocating a spontaneous preference for the flesh of 'living women' over the chilly idealism of the 'Grecian Venus', in which proposal is to be found a recommendation to naturalistic attention to the peculiarities of the human form quite incompatible with academic precepts.[39]

Hogarth's ideas were not well received, and there were alternatives available. But the legacy of Hogarthian naturalism continued to inform artistic practice, even with the establishment of the more formal, hierarchal and controlling art schools of the Royal Academy (a development that Hogarth, who dreaded the prospect, did not live to see). While students were directed to slow, careful study progressing stage by stage from ancient fragments to sculpted figures to the living model (fig.19), and dissuaded (and officially barred) from painting or working in stone or marble, they were also provided with both male and female models: indeed, Reynolds's important lectures on art as President recommended a more dedicated and attentive study of nature than was perhaps to be expected in an academic setting. Reynolds was concerned above all with recommending care and slowness, knowing that the marketplace and the unprecedented opportunities for the public display of art was encouraging young artists to take short cuts to greatness, by turning to flashy pictorial effects and startling subject matter.

Reynolds was fighting a losing battle. What we find among the more ambitious young artists in the decade after the foundation of the Royal Academy is that, buoyed by the promise of patronage from the old sources of the monarchy and social elite and developing support from the new sources of the ascendant middle-ranks of society and (via print publication and commercial exhibitions) from the public at large, they began formulating pictorial manners that were far from cautious in either their means or their effects. The lead was taken by James Barry, John Hamilton Mortimer, Henry Fuseli and John and Alexander Runciman; Maria Cosway, James Jefferys and George Romney took up their example; James Gillray and William Blake were among the younger generation for whom the highly linear, expressive use of drawing was a basic vocabulary for visual art, by this time given a degree of institutional sanction.

The resulting representational bodies veered toward the qualities of the literary Gothic in their spatial conception and narrative associations: compressed, stretched, distorted, thrown into vast spaces or squeezed into suffocating hollows, they were disassembled, damaged, by turn incomprehensible and vivid, over-stated and extravagant. These are impossible bodies, corporeal conundrums which provide less a reference point for social performance (offering models of deportment or physical type) than artificial tools of rhetorical expression inhabiting a world quite of their own. The essence of this bodily aesthetic lay in the five-point games played by Fuseli in Rome (see no.14), translated into public art: 'with such incomprehensible sublimity are his subjects sometimes

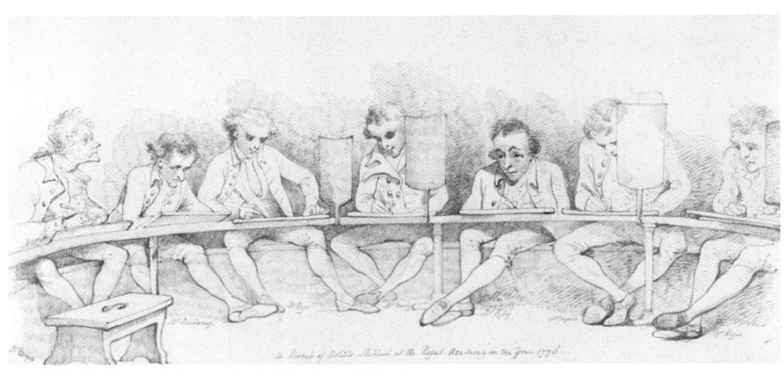

fig.19 Thomas Rowlandson (1756–1827), *A Bench of Artists* 1776, pen and ink and pencil on paper 27.2 x 54.8 cm. Tate. Purchased as part of the Oppé Collection with assistance from the National Lottery through the Heritage Lottery Fund 1996

handled' that a work was reputedly hung upside down at the academy.[40] A female figure in a classical scene was 'Handy dandy!' prompting the inquiry, 'which is the top of her back and which is the bottom!' (*Morning Chronicle*, 15 May 1784). The body's forms appeared to be put out of their ordained order and made mutable (quite in defiance of the more conservative art theory that Fuseli was to develop as Professor at the Academy). The result was a deathly image – with bodies stripped of flesh, living and undead: 'His figures are meagre and poor, and the articulations of the joints are so hardly marked, as to appear without flesh on them';[41] 'the muscles are rigidly marked, and seem more like iron than flesh' (*New Monthly Magazine*, 1 June 1818). Fuseli's bodies are 'extranatural', anatomised yet active: 'his men', wrote Haydon, 'looked like surgical preparations which had burst, skinned as they are, out of bottles in Surgeons' Hall'.[42] Such comments are legion: 'Fuseli would have some pretensions to a twig of the historic laurel, if he could ever paint a figure without breaking his limbs' (*Morning Post*, 6 June 1788), while his *Dido* (fig.2 on p.10) had suffered a '*double* Death' (*Public Advertiser*, 3 May 1781). This is a Frankenstein vision of the body, monstrous, transgressive, confounding the boundaries between life and death, the upper and the lower, the normal and the diseased, the regular and the aberrant, around which culture's values may be structured.[43]

A more modest proposal would be to link these comments back to the abiding problem of making narrative art meaningful once it is displaced from the political and religious contexts in which its standards and aims had been formulated; the conventions of academic art were, after all, forged in the determinedly Catholic contexts of renaissance Italy and of the totalitarian France of Louis XIV. The problem facing aesthetic writers and theorists in eighteenth-century Britain was creating a Hanoverian, Protestant tradition, a task which required considerable ingenuity, leading to innovations such as the modern-life genre painting.[44] The other route was hedonism – the hedonistic acceptance of the irrelevance and absurdity of high art in the context of modern Britain.[45] The deathly qualities which haunt the work of these artists in criticism and commentary registers a sense of distance from an imagined heritage of supremely effective creativity, a lost past of heroic art. Their half-living, tortured figures are the revenants of the ideal figures of classical art, left flailing and purposeless.

Conclusion: art, trash and exploitation

In an essay on cinematic excess, the film theorist and historian Linda Williams has proposed the category of 'body genres' as a critical tool. Starting from observations about the 'gross' – excessive images of sex, violence, emotion – Williams argues that such qualities are 'fundamental elements of the sensational effects' of pornography, horror and melodrama. These 'body genres' work in defiance of the techniques and effects of classical cinema, which is about 'efficient action-centered, goal-oriented linear narratives driven by the desire of a single protagonist, involving one or two lines of action, and leading to a definitive closure'. Body genres focus instead on 'the spectacle of a body caught in the grip of intense sensation or emotion ... the ecstatic body, the body beside itself' and pivots on 'an apparent lack of proper aesthetic distance, a sense of over-involvement in sensation and emotion'.[46]

The parallel with Fuseli's art is suggestive. Would it help to think of his melodramatic, erotic and horrific art in comparable terms? This is an open question. But if the concepts and interpretative strategies developed in relation to cinematic body genres can be used effectively in relation to visual Gothic of the late eighteenth century, this is at least in part because the genres both of contemporary pornography and horror and of eighteenth-century Gothic occupy a similar critical space in relation to the dominant culture (a culture characterised by a certain, important degree of continuity over the intervening centuries). But pursuing this possibility might invite scepticism. The very assumption that work on pornography or the contemporary horror film is irrelevant to discussing Fuseli and Blake is to invest their work with certain values. The protocols of art history have dictated that we should consider their work in relation to pictorial tradition and grand intellectual movements, moments or tendencies. We might accept that Fuseli's art anticipates Joan Miró or Francis Bacon, or even Salvador Dalí, but acknowledging instead the possible relationship with such determinedly exploitative film-makers as Lucio Fulci or Jess Franco might be more risky. What if those Greek inscriptions on Fuseli's dodgiest drawings are just a veil of pretension? What if such designs were literal aids to masturbation, rather than 'erotic' explorations of some profound or dark dimension of humanity? Is it possible to imagine that they could be *both*? Can art history bear to apprehend the possibility of actual physical arousal? Or outright disgust? And is it simply sacrilegious to compare Foster Damon's classic work of reference, *A Blake Dictionary* (1965), to the *Official Handbook of the Marvel Universe*?[47]

There are further historical and sociological issues here. The disciplines of film and cultural studies which would make such comparisons possible have developed out of socially specific circumstances. They are the visible consequence of that productive societal discord which has permitted men and women without an inherited entitlement to educational and cultural capital to negotiate positions of a certain intellectual authority, who are able to make capital of their avowed 'outsider' status, productively engaging with both high and low culture. Such approaches, and the social values arising from these strategies, remain contested.[48]

The art of Fuseli, Blake and Gillray has undergone massive revaluations over the two centuries that have passed since these artists were active. Fuseli's reputation as a painter, always questionable during his lifetime, plummeted after his death. While his drawings were sought after by certain collectors, his paintings fell into obscurity. Many important canvases were destroyed or remain hidden. His life became the stuff of anecdote and whimsy, rather than serious consideration, and he assumed the role of one of the great late Georgian eccentrics rather than of a master. The visionary and perverse dimensions of his art attracted the interest of a few writers and artists in Britain in the 1930s and 1940s.[49] Meanwhile, many of his paintings and drawings were being bought by Swiss collectors, laying the foundations for the unparalleled collection of this artist's work at the Kunsthaus, Zurich. Accordingly, the scholarly documentation of Fuseli's work was advanced most greatly in the German-speaking world, culminating in Gert Schiff's indispensable, Teutonically-proportioned catalogue raisonné (1973). Blake's reappraisal started more quickly: William Michael Rossetti (1829–1919) catalogued his works in the Victorian era; the Tate Gallery collected and exhibited them early in the twentieth century.[50] He is now established (for the right or wrong reasons) as a British 'Old Master'. Gillray's status as a documenter of the characters, whims and political events of his time secured his memory, and he was rewarded with several nineteenth-century studies. It was, though, only recently that his vivid, technically brilliant art has been incorporated as a central component of late eighteenth-century art history, rather than as merely an amusing sidepath or as a source for social history.[51]

Arguably, we are now peculiarly well positioned to consider these artists together, and on different terms. The social and political dimensions of late eighteenth-century British culture have been researched and analysed extensively. The institutions, practices and ideologies of art in this period have been revealed in ever-greater detail and complexity.

But there may be less obvious factors as well. If, as Angela Carter (1940–92) asserted, 'We live in Gothic times',[52] this has meant that distinctions between the grotesque and the beautiful, between good and bad taste, are all the more mutable. Cultural historians of today may be more reckless with regard to the hierarchies of taste and restrictive sense of propriety that has sometimes guided and shaped the art histories of the past. This is not to suggest that they are freed from the cycles of cultural distinction, but that these may be renegotiated to make possible new social positions less dependent upon the always-already existing values of established taste and the social and economic capital which corresponds, in partly obscured ways, to that taste. We are left, as much as ever, with questions, though the social consequences of addressing these may be more unpredictable, perhaps greater, than before.

There is a case to be made that the Gothic tendencies apparent in the art included in this exhibition represent a suppressed dimension of British culture, more true and vital than the legitimately ordained heritage. Our present sense of communal cultural identity, fabricated in the Thatcherite era, tended to emphasise the quaint and restrained, and dismiss – as the Anti-Jacobins did in the 1790s – the excessive, violent, abstract or visionary as vile and foreign. Other stories are possible. Within the realm of the visual this option has been perhaps most energetically explored in relation to cinema, where a concerted effort towards gleeful revisionism has emerged in the last few years. As Matthew Sweet recently noted, 'British cinema tends to be characterised through its most decorous traditions. Our native cinema might be as easily characterised by its savagery, its enduring and energetic commitment to violence, sadism, nihilism and despair'.[53] As Sweet appreciates, this is not just a matter of bringing some extra works into a canon of the legitimate, but accepting that our own standards of taste might be tested and extended to encompass kinds of visual production which were deliberately popular, sensational, exploitational.

Could we imagine the same happening with regard to the 'fine' arts? It is in the nature of museums and the activities which they host and generate to secure values rather than undermine them; art museums are expected to be committed, above all, to preserving and enhancing *aesthetic* quality. Blake knew, in writing his scathing response to Robert Hunt's determinedly bourgeois assessment quoted at the head of this essay, that Fuseli's works may often be found wanting by that measure.[54] His art still provides something of an affront to good taste, eliciting uneasy sniggers as much as admiration. As Marina Warner notes above (p.25), the art historian Werner Hofmann was prompted to ask in relation to the landmark Fuseli exhibition of 1975 whether his art was just a masquerade - could this 'great' artist be just a fraud? Perhaps, despite everything else that has changed in the intervening three decades, this remains the most vital question to ask, if only rhetorically. The art of Fuseli and his contemporaries can be absurd, even laughable, and pretentious in the extreme; it is, perhaps, all the more valuable historically because of that, potentially exposing, rather than helping to mask, the fatal emptiness at the heart of bourgeois modernity.

Notes

1 'To H' in *William Blake's Writings*, Blake 1978, II, p.938. 'H' is presumed to be Robert Hunt, the art critic who fumed against Blake and Fuseli in the pages of *The Examiner*. See Bentley 2004, pp.282–6.
2 Farington 1978–98, II, pp.588–9 (24 June 1796).
3 British Library, Add MS 27, 337, f.69, quoted (with variations) in Hill 1965, p.90.
4 Reynolds 1826, I, p.127.
5 For documentation and contrasting views of the riots see Rudé 1970, pp.268–92; Nicholson 1985; Rogers 1990; Haydon1993, pp.204–44.
6 Sancho 1994, p.230; Susan Burney's comments were accessed through the on-line version of the *Susan Burney Letters Project* http://www.nottingham.ac.uk/hrc/projects/burney/letters/gordon.phtml.
7 Lewis 1937–83, XXV, p.62
8 See Porter 1982, p.116.
9 Gibbon 1956, II, pp.243–5.
10 The literature on the Gothic, even in its most restrictive definition, is vast, but among the most important for the formation of the arguments articulated here are: Paulson 1983, pp.215–47; Monleón 1990; Guest 1992; Charlesworth 1994; Clery 1995; Castle 1995; Watt 1999; Miles 2002; Gibbons 2004 and the compilations, Clery and Miles 2000; Norton 2000; Charlesworth 2002. More widely based cultural studies which are pertinent include: Edmundson 1997; Hawkins 2000; Gelder 2000; Punter 2000; Silver and Ursini 2000.
11 Knowles 1831, I, p.63.
12 Alexander Gilchrist, *Life of William Blake* (1863), quoted in Bentley 2004, p.22.
13 See Ward 1999.
14 Blake 1978, II, p.749.
15 *The Morning Chronicle*, 27 May 1780, in Bentley 2004, p.21.
16 Blake's sixteen engravings are catalogued in Weinglass 1994; see also Bentley 2004 for references, and Essick 1991.Gillray's sole signed reproduction of a Fuseli design was included in the English edition of Lavater's *Essays on Physiognomy* (1789–98); Weinglass 1994, no.100.
17 See Hall 1980, also Heppner 1995.
18 Bindman 1982, pp.25–6.
19 See Erdman 1949.
20 For some pertinent commentaries, see: Hipple 1957; Monk 1960; Rubel 1978; Simonsuuri 1979; de Bolla 1989; Ferguson 1992; Furniss 1993; Clery 1996; Moore 2003.
21 On the modernity of the eighteenth century see particularly Ogborn 1998, pp.1–38.
22 On faultlines see Sinfield 1992.
23 See Rosenthal and Myrone 2002, pp.22–4.
24 See, notably, Todd 1946, p.62; also, Sitwell 1943, p.224n; Friedman 1961, p.285.
25 Comments taken from manuscript additions by Horace Walpole to copies of the Royal Academy exhibition catalogues, formerly in the collection of Lord Rosebery (photographic record at the Witt Library, Courtauld Institute of Art).
26 On Walpole see Brownell 2001.
27 Lewis 1937–83, XXXI, p.221–2.
28 The literature on *Frankenstein* is considerable, but of especial interest are: Baldick 1987; Botting 1991; Bann 1994; Picart 2003.
29 See Gatrell 1994, p.96 and pp.602–4.
30 For this example and a telling discussion, see Crowley 2001, pp.141–70.
31 Southey 1951, pp.95–6.
32 See Monleón 1990, pp.43–4.
33 Bromley 1793–5, I, pp.36–7.
34 Robert Hunt in *The Examiner*, vol.9 (8 May 1808), p.300.
35 Simond 1817, II, p.189. The rumour about Fuseli's opium use was reported in Farington 1978–98, III, p.660 (11 September 1796). Fuseli did later admit to using the drug to aliveate the depression arising from problems with his monumental Milton Gallery; see Farington 1978–98, IV, p.1299 (7 November 1799). The story about raw pork appears to originate with *The Public Advertiser*, 31 May 1790, though this report claims to be copied from a 'morning paper'. It was still being denied on Fuseli's behalf more than half a century later (Balmanno 1858, p.204). On the role of ideas about digestion in relation to theories and ideals of imagination in this period, see Ford 1998, pp.13–32.
36 See Mason 1951, pp.67–84 for a sample of views; see also Myrone 2005, pp.165–6 and pp.227–51.
37 Farington 1978–98, III, pp.745–6 (12 January 1797).
38 Ibid., II, pp.588–9 (24 June 1796). See also the numerous indexed references in Bentley 2004.
39 Quoted here, Hogarth 1997, p.59. On modulations to the hierarchy of the genres see Gibson-Wood 2000, esp. pp.143–178, and Paulson 1996.
40 *Letters from an Irish Student in England to his Father in Ireland* (London 1809), quoted in Bentley 2004, p.264.
41 Pasquin 1796, p.116; Dayes 1805, pp.326–7. See Michel 2001, pp.88–109 for a discussion of this '*Bodybuilding post mortem*'.
42 Haydon 1960–3, III, p.200 (28 May 1827).
43 See Bakhtin 1984; Douglas 1966; Stallybrass and White 1986.
44 See Paulson 1991–3, esp. I, pp.124–34, and Paulson 1996.
45 This theme is explored more fully in Myrone 2005.
46 Williams 1999.
47 Whitlark 1988, p.50.
48 The debate around cultural studies, high and low culture, social capital and hierarchy is wide-ranging and ongoing; particularly pertinent, for this author, are discussions around the 'double-access' academic. Among the contributions consulted are Gripsund 1989; Donald 1989; Sconce 1995; Watson 1997. For a powerful critique of the socially invested nature of academic time see Bourdieu, 2000.
49 See notably, Sitwell 1943; Todd 1946; Ayrton 1946; Piper 1947; Grigson 1950. Frederick Antal's remarkable, Marxist interpretation of Fuseli's work, published posthumously as *Fuseli Studies*, constitutes a rare, thoroughly critical and analytical, contribution from this earlier period of scholarship; see Antal 1956.
50 See Cieszkowski 1990.
51 See Godfrey 2001.
52 Carter 1995, p.460.
53 Sweet 2005, p.255. See also Pirie 1973, Rigby 2004, pp.12–14 and Chibnall and Petley 2002.
54 On Hunt's criticism as 'bourgeois' see Eaves 1992, pp.167–8.

The Nightmare: Fuseli and the Art of Horror

Ever since it was first exhibited to the public in 1782, Henry Fuseli's *The Nightmare* has been an icon of horror. Showing a woman supine in her boudoir or bedroom, oppressed by a foul imp while a ferocious-looking horse glares on, the painting seems to draw on folklore and popular culture, medicine, concepts of imagination, and classical art to create a new kind of sexually charged horror image. Plagiarised and satirised constantly in the two centuries since its creation, *The Nightmare* has become one of the most familiar images in western art.

Although we may all respond to *The Nightmare* in highly personal ways, it also raises a range of broader historical questions that are pertinent to the period as a whole. It may lead us to think about the public and private status of art, the influence of the market place on the ways artists create their works, the relationship between academic tradition, the common culture and personal innovation, and the representation of sexual desire.

Erasmus Darwin, The Loves of the Plants, (1789), ll.51–78

So on his Night-Mare, through the evening fog,
Flits the squab Fiend o'er fen, and lake, and bog,
Seeks some love-wilder'd Maid with sleep oppress'd,
Alights, and grinning sits upon her breast.
– Such as of late amid the murky sky
Was mark'd by FUSSELI'S poetic eye;
Whose daring tints, with SHAKESPEAR'S happiest grace,
Gave to the airy phantom form and place –
Back o'er her pillow sinks her blushing head,
Her snow-white limbs hang helpless from the bed;
While with quick sighs, and suffocative breath,
Her interrupted heart-pulse swims in death.
– Then shrieks of captured towns, and widows' tears,
Pale lovers stretch'd upon their blood-stain'd biers,
The Headlong precipice that thwarts her flight,
The trackless desert, the cold starless night,
And stern-ey'd Murderer with his knife behind,
In dread succession agonize her mind.
O'er her fair limbs convulsive tremors fleet,
Start in her hands, and struggle in her feet;
In vain to scream with quivering lips she tries,
And strains in palsy'd lids her tremulous eyes;
In vain she wills to run, fly, swim, walk, creep;
The WILL presides not in the bower of SLEEP.
– On her fair bosom sits the Demon-Ape
Erect, and balances his bloated shape;
Rolls in their marble orbs his Gorgon-eyes,
And drinks with leathern ears her tender cries.

(Darwin 1791, pp.93–5)

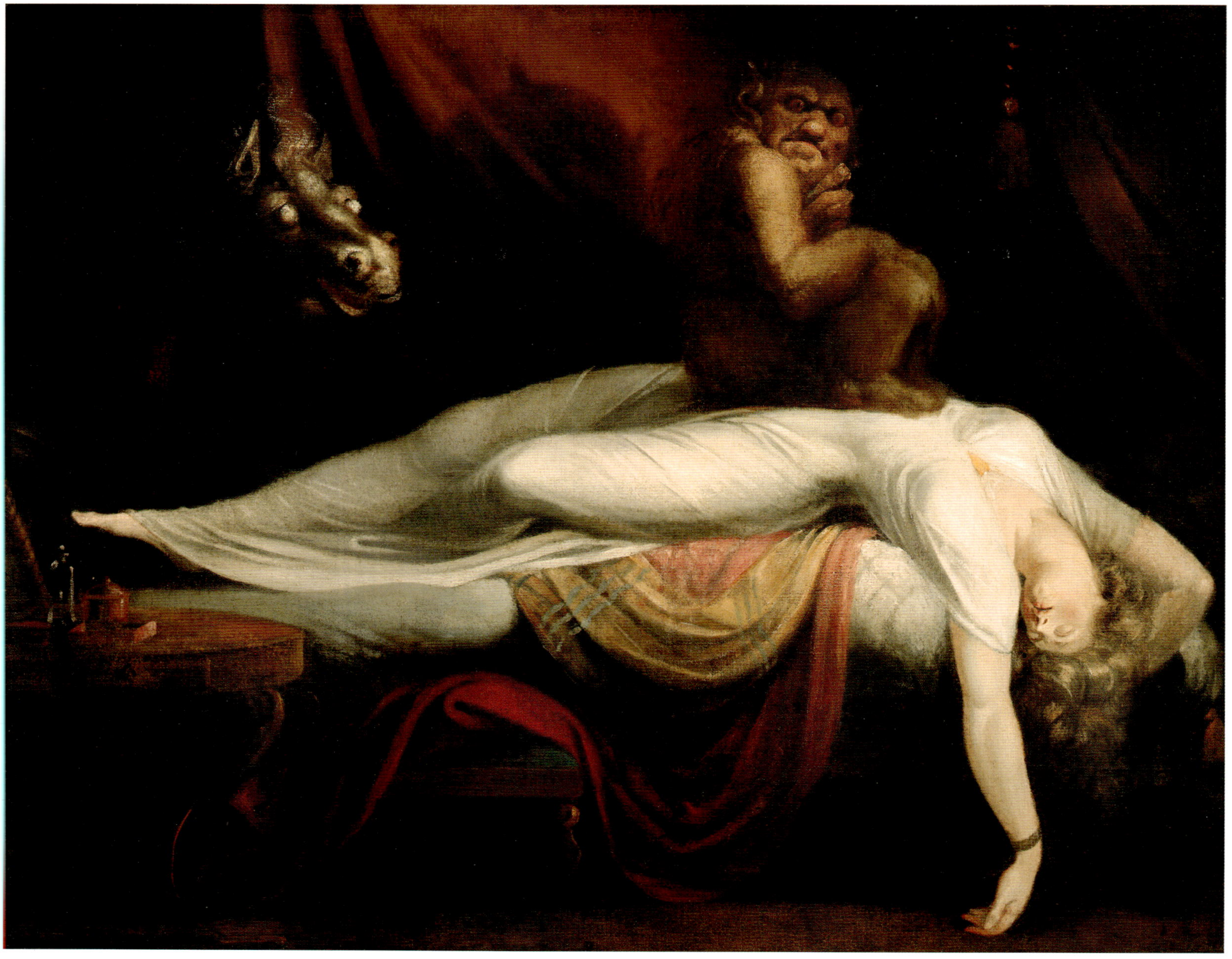

1

Henry Fuseli 1741–1825
The Nightmare exh. RA 1782
Oil on canvas 101.6 x 126.7 cm
Detroit Institute of Arts. Founders Society Purchase with funds from Mr and Mrs Bert L. Smokler and Mr and Mrs Lawrence A. Fleischman (55.5A)

This painting was the sole exhibit included by Fuseli in the Royal Academy exhibition of 1782. After several years of showing groups of sometimes large works, which had garnered considerable public attention and no small degree of controversy, this single painting was calculated by Fuseli to consolidate his reputation as a painter of the strange, perverse and supernatural. It was caricatured, emulated and copied throughout the nineteenth century and resurfaced in the art, satire and cinema of the twentieth. Early in the twenty-first century, there is no reason yet to believe that the composition's possibilities have been exhausted.

Given the intense and often highly personal interpretations of this work over the last two centuries, it may be hard to see this picture afresh. The image has drawn comment from poets and painters, psychologists and historians of science, as well as art historians (Schiff 1973, no.757 and Powell 1973 remain the first points of reference).

Psychological interpretations have focused on the painting as an expression of Fuseli's sexual desires and frustrations. The verso shows the unfinished portrait of a woman, associated by a number of commentators with Anna Landolt, the object of Fuseli's unrequited love during his visit to Switzerland in 1779 (fig.4 on p.15). This has led to the reading of the picture in wholly personal terms, as an expression of sexual revenge or frustration, and the imp's features have been taken as resembling Fuseli's own. Such speculation aside, the sexual dimensions of this image can hardly be overlooked. The young woman's clinging nightclothes, the abandon of her pose, and her full figure, invite erotic attention. The intimation of sexual penetration found in the horse's head protruding through the fleshy curtains to the left cannot, either, be ignored.

As Christopher Frayling explores in depth above (pp.9–20), the folkloric and literary allusions of the image are manifold, and there is the possibility of scientific allusions, either in reference to then current understanding of sleep paralysis or to the effects of narcotics, stimulants and diet. The painting's presentation of sex and horror may suggest some kind of kinship with the Gothic novel, only beginning to gain definition as a genre in the 1780s. More precisely, the picture's foregrounding of female fantasy and desire, and its ambiguous narrative status, parallels certain structural features of the Gothic; as Margaret Anne Doody has written, 'the "real world" for characters in a Gothic novel is one of nightmare. There is no longer a common-sense order against which dream briefly flickers; rather, the world of rational order briefly flickers in and out of the dreamlike. There is no ordinary world to wake up in' (Doody 1977, p.553).

There is the further, distinct possibility that Fuseli had in mind a specific literary source. Thomas Middleton's (1580–1627) *The Witch*, written around 1614–16 but first published from a manuscript only in 1778, includes a reference to the foul, incestuous imp Firestone heading out with his 'Nightmare' 'to overlay a fat parson's daughter'. This reference is important in suggesting that the 'Nightmare' was identified as a horse as early as the seventeenth century, although there was no etymological foundation for this. There is a record in the nineteenth century of a copy of the book inscribed to Fuseli by the editor, George Steevens (1736–1800), and it was certainly in the painter's library at his death (Esche 1993, pp.13–14; for the catalogue of Fuseli's library see Weinglass 1982, p.590).

For art historians, this picture has, with a slightly earlier drawing by the artist (here, no.10) represented iconically the shift from 'neoclassical' restraint to 'romantic' emotional violence. It certainly constitutes a watershed, marking a change in the function and status of art, the character of the audiences who have access to visual culture, the social personality of the artist, and the means by which relations between 'high' and 'low' culture are regulated. As so often with Fuseli, art historians have enjoyed the opportunities this picture presents for pedantic source-spotting. Then, also, there is in a broader sense the use this painting makes of a tradition of paintings of women in bed, implicitly or more explicitly in sexual reverie or actively masturbating. In the previous decade, Matthew William Peters (1742–1814; latterly Reverend) had presented a number of such subjects at the Academy (fig.20) and the genre was prevalent at the French Salon and in reproductive prints. Consider the suggestive relation between this painting and Jean-Baptiste Le Prince's (1734–81) *Fear* (fig.21), shown at the Salon in 1777 and engraved in 1781 or 1782, where a provocatively underdressed young woman is distressed by the departure of her lover (a figure implied by the presence of two coffee-cups, and made visible in a second version of the engraving issued in 1784). The sickly glitter of Fuseli's painting itself suggests a perverse or ironic reworking of such fancy images, with the intimate, dishevelled boudoir interior typical of such confections transformed into a clammy and claustrophobic setting, the theme of frivolous erotic play with a romantic hero displaced by an act of monstrous sexual violation.

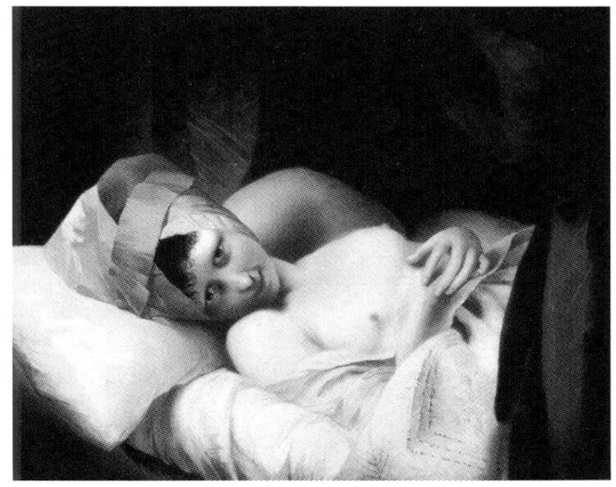

fig.20 Revd Matthew William Peters (1742–1814), *Lydia* c.1777, oil on canvas 64.2 x 77 cm. Tate. Purchased 1986

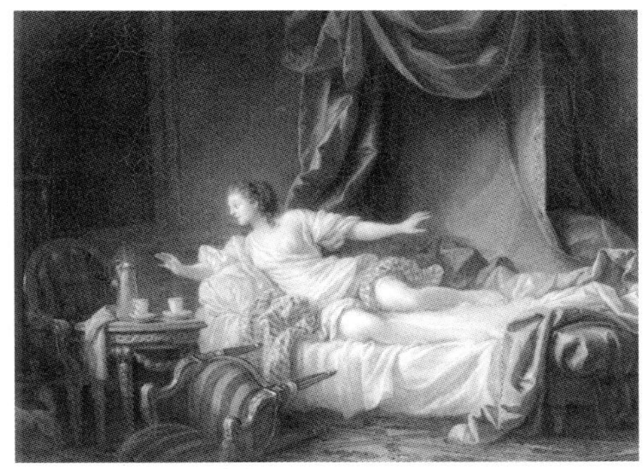

fig.21 Jean-Baptiste Le Prince (1734–81), *Fear* 1769, oil on canvas 50 x 64 cm. The Toledo Museum of Art. Purchased with Funds from the Libbey Endowment, Gift of Edward Drummond Libbey

Gervase of Tilbury, Otia Imperialia: Recreation for an Emperor (c.1200), Bk I.17

Apuleius, however, in his book On Spirits Consecrated to God, says that between the moon and the earth there dwell unclean spirits which are called incubi, from their oppression (incubatio) of the mind; for they afflict people's minds in their sleep, making them believe they are falling from a height or suffocating. They have partly the nature of human beings and partly that of angels, and when they wish they assume human form and sleep with women. Merlin is said to have been fathered by one of these, for he was born, according to the History of the Britons, of a woman but had no human father. And they say that the Antichrist will be begotten in this way, and will claim on this account to be the son of a virgin. We know that many things are seen every day relating to these phenomena. We have actually observed that some demons love women with such passion that they break into unheard-of acts of lewdness, and when they come to bed with them they bear down upon them with extraordinary pressure, and yet are seen by no one else.

(Gervase of Tilbury 2002, p.97)

Thomas Middleton, The Witch, 1614–16, first published 1778
Act I, scene 2, ll.95–106

FIRESTONE. ... *Mother, I pray, give me leave to ramble abroad tonight with the Nightmare, for I have great mind to overlay a fat parson's daughter.*
HECATE. *And who shall lie with me then?*
FIRESTONE. *The great cat.*
For one night, mother, 'tis but a night.
Make shift with him for once.
HECATE. *You're a kind son!*
But 'tis the nature of you, I see that.
You had rather hunt after strange women still
Than lie with your own mothers. Get thee gone!
Sweat thy six ounces about the vessel
And thou shalt play at midnight. The Nightmare
Shall call thee when it walks.
FIRESTONE. *Thanks, most sweet mother.*

(Esche 1993, pp.104–5)

2

Henry Fuseli 1741–1825
The Changeling 1780
Black chalk, grey wash and watercolour, heightened with white, on paper 48 x 53.5 cm
Kunsthaus, Zurich, Grafische Sammlung

A child is shown being stolen from its crib by a witch who disappears into the moonlight through a window. While the bent and elderly nurse sleeps on, the child's mother recoils at the discovery of her child's monstrous replacement.

Like *The Nightmare* (no.1), this design (Schiff 1973, no.240) draws on folklore and literature in a rich and complex way. The idea of a swapped baby is a deeply entrenched tale, from ancient folklore through to modern tabloid stories and horror movies. It featured in German folklore from the ninth century and entered English literature in the sixteenth, with Shakespeare making several references to changelings and Thomas Middleton and William Rowley's play *The Changeling* (1622) making great use of the themes of sexual duplicity and confusion associated with the myth (Kiessling 1977). Shakespeare's references are rather slight and could not suggest the narrative conception apparent here; the later play, while featuring some ripe witchcraft-loaded language, is non-supernatural. A specific literary reference may be found instead in Edmund Spenser's *The Faerie Queene* (1590), Book I, Canto X, Stanza 65, where a brief allusion is made to the fairy roots of the legendary Britons:

> From thence a Faerie thee vnweeting reft,
> There as thou slepst in tender swaddling band,
> And her base Elfin brood there for thee left.
> Such men do Chaungelings call, so chaunged
> by Faeries theft.
> (Spenser 1977, p.142)

Additionally, one of the 'Hags' in Ben Jonson's (1572–1637) *The Masque of Queens* (1609) boasts of having stolen a child's breath in the night. Fuseli used this source for a slightly later witchcraft scene (no.82). He had written of the folklore of the changeling in his *Remarks on Rousseau* (1767; see above, pp.16–17). The motif of the changeling appears in the right-hand corner of his first painting of *The Midsummer Night's Dream* (no.105), where a stooped hag presses on the head of such a child (rather in defiance of Shakespeare's text, which would have the Indian changeling as a beautiful infant). Changeling mythology is also bound into that which underpins *The Nightmare* (no.1), for some tales would tell of witches stealing away the progeny of the unnatural nightly couplings between a human mother and a demon lover (Grudin 1987, pp.7–8). The date of no.2 (inscribed as 'March 1780') would mean that he was thinking about this subject at the same time as *The Nightmare*, and we must wonder whether Fuseli had in mind this subject for a painting as well.

A second version of this drawing is in the Art Institute of Chicago, inscribed with the title given here. Although this was dismissed by Gert Schiff as a copy by another artist (correspondence on file at the Institute), it appears precisely contemporary and is more likely to be simply a further, close version of the design.

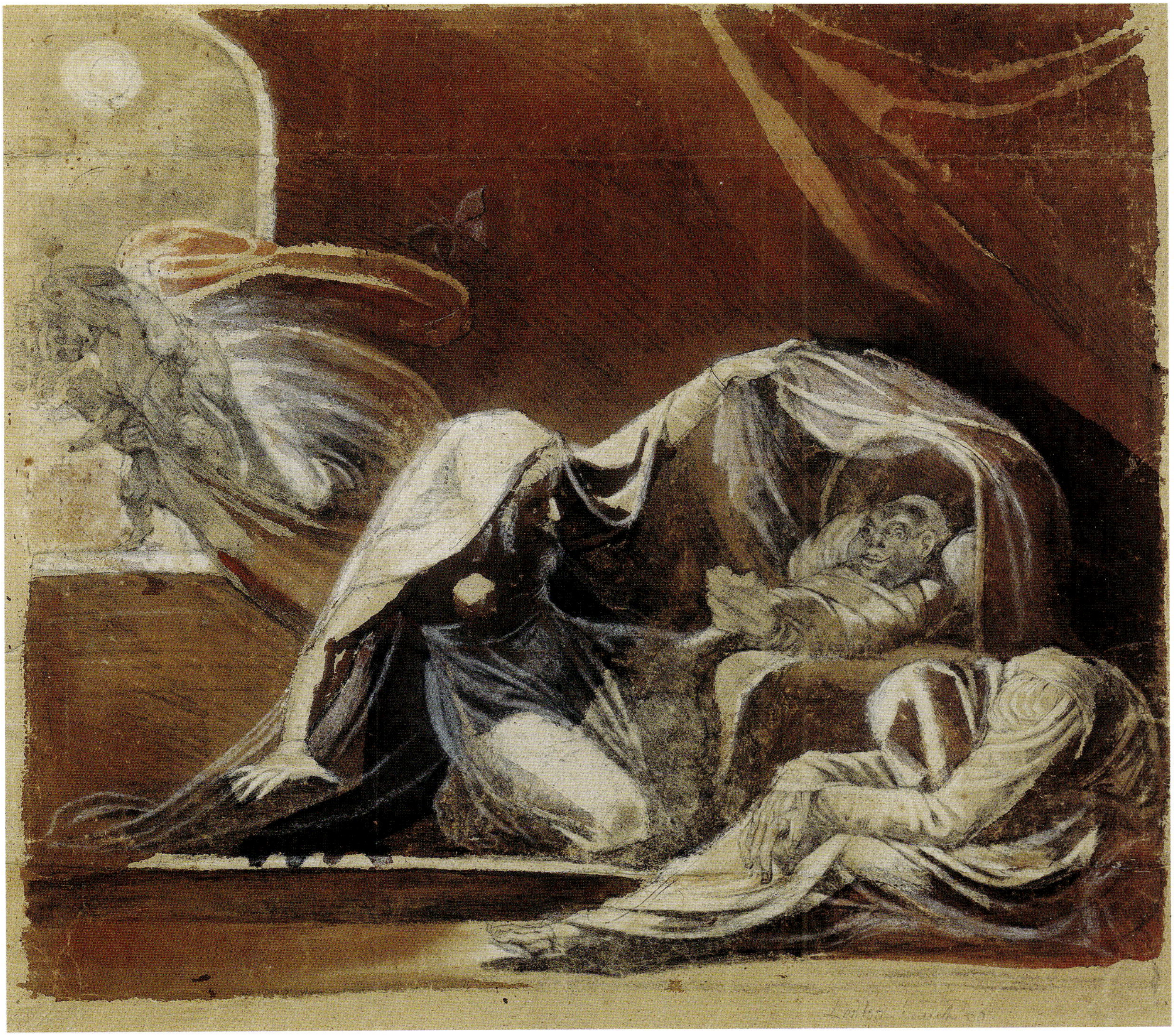

3

Henry Fuseli 1741–1825
The Incubus Leaving Two Sleeping Women
1810
Pencil, wash and watercolour on paper
31.5 x 40.8 cm
Kunsthaus, Zurich, Grafische Sammlung

An incubus has visited two women and is shown departing on a demonic horse through the open window. While this energetic little person speeds into the moonlight – or more probably the first rays of dawn – one of the women stretches as she wakes, her face suggesting she has been troubled (or at least exhausted) by the night's activities.

In some, uncertain, sense the design (Schiff 1973, no.1445) unlocks or elaborates the original *Nightmare* (no.1), and must allude to the same range of sources. The function of the horse as a vehicle for the incubus is stated clearly here, and the sexual implications of the night visit reinforced by the kinky near-nudity of his victims (both wear pretty little night bonnets). The composition also suggests a kind of addled fairy tale, with the sleeping beauties awakened by the departure of the beast, evoking the themes of erotic arousal and sexual initiation that underlie many classic stories: 'The idea of awakening, sometimes erotic but not exclusively, goes to the heart of fairy tale's function' (Warner 1994, p.417).

The design is a variant of a painting of around 1794 (Schiff 1973, no.929) showing the two women clothed, although the nightdress of the waking girl had conveniently slipped down to reveal her breasts. In the present drawing, even this little modesty has been abandoned, proffering titillating intimations of lesbian intimacy.

In its folkloric dimension, the drawing might evoke the tales associated with Robin Goodfellow (the 'cousine' of Incubus) whose shenanigans included pulling the bedclothes from naked sleeping women, as in *The Mad Merry Pranks of Robin Good-Fellow*.

> When house or hath doth sluttish lye,
> I pinch the maidens blacke and blue;
> The bed-clothes from the bed pull I,
> And lay them naked all to view.
> 'Twixt sleepe and wake,
> I do them take,
> And on the key-cold floor them throw.
> If out they cry,
> Then forth I fly,
> And loudly laugh out, ho, ho, ho!
> (Percy 1765, III, p.204; also Ritson 1783, II, p.162)

Then there is the speech of the unsubtly monikered 'Little Pricke' in *The Maydes Metamorphosis* of c.1600:

> When I feele a girle a sleepe
> Underneath her frock I peep.
> There to sport, and there I play,
> Then I byte her like a flea;
> And about I skip.
> (Bullen 1882–5, I, p.128)

The Greek inscription at the bottom left was identified by Schiff as coming from Homer's *Iliad*, Book X, ll.496–7: 'as he breathed hard, for like to an evil dream there stood above his head that night' (Murray 1924, I, p.473). The context of these lines is the fantastically bloody night-time raid by the Greek heroes Ulysses and Diomedes (son of Tydeus), on the camp of the Thracian king, Rhesus. The heroes slaughter numerous of their enemy, wade through their blood and guts, kill the sleeping prince and run away with his famous horses. The lines excerpted by Fuseli refer to the vision sent by the goddess Minerva to Rhesus. In the translation of the *Iliad* by William Cowper (1731–1800) that Fuseli had advised on, the scene had been rendered thus (as Book X, ll.585–8):

> But when the son of Tydeus found the King,
> Him also panting forth his last, last breath,
> He added to the twelve; for at his dead
> An evil dream that night had stood, the form
> Of Diomede, by Pallas art devised.
> (Cowper 1791, I, p.262)

Perhaps more pertinent is the way that the passage had been interpreted by Alexander Pope (1688–1744), as Book X, ll.578–81:

> Just then a dreadful Dream *Minerva* sent;
> A warlike Form appear'd before his Tent,
> Whose visionary Steel his Bosom tore:
> So dream'd the Monarch, and awake'd
> no more.
> (Pope 1967, II, p.28)

Pope had commented:

> This Image is very natural, for a Man in this condition awakes no further than to see confusedly what environs him, and to think it not a reality, but a Vision.
> (Pope 1967, II, p.28n).

Thus, Fuseli's citation of this passage knowingly imports into this erotic scene associations of brute physical violence and banditry, of death and awakening, and, to follow Pope's suggestion, sensory confusion.

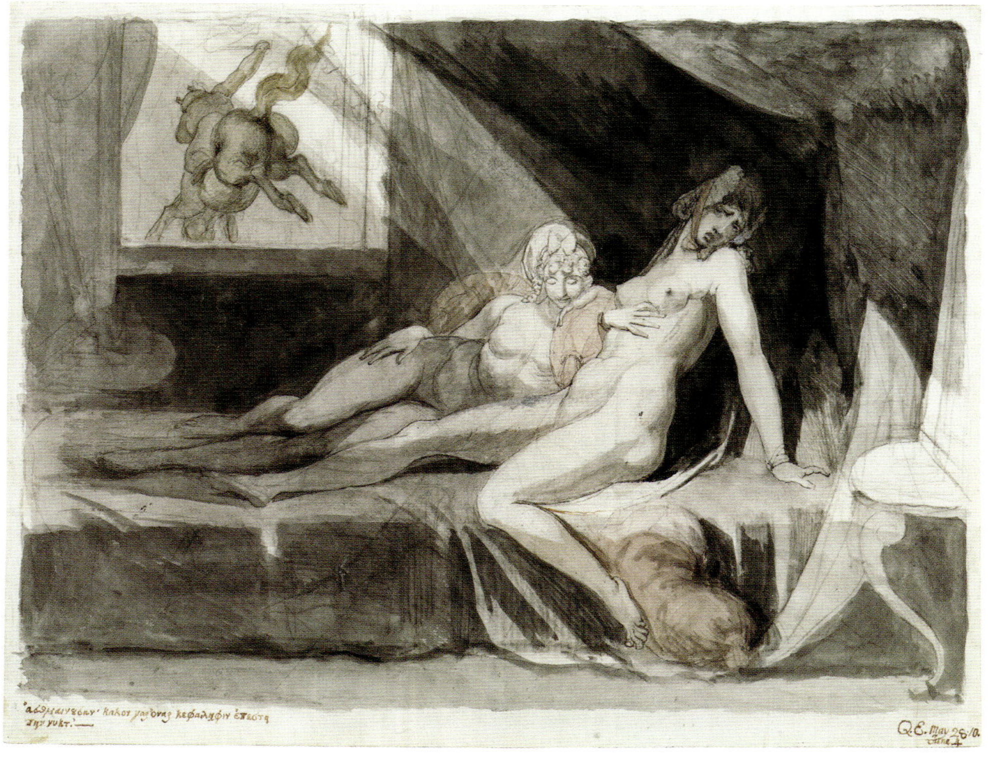

4

Thomas Burke 1749–1815 after Henry Fuseli 1714–1825
The Nightmare published by John Raphael Smith, 30 January 1783
Stipple engraving 22.5 x 25 cm
The British Museum, London
(1870-5-14-1610)

5a

Thomas Rowlandson 1756–1827
A Covent Garden Night Mare 1784
Pencil on paper 18.8 x 27.5 cm
City of Westminster Archive Centre

5b

Thomas Rowlandson 1756–1827
A Covent Garden Night Mare published by William Humphrey, 1784
Handcoloured etching 22.2 x 33.1 cm
City of Westminster Archive Centre

6

James Gillray 1756–1815
Duke William's Ghost published by Hannah Humphrey, 7 May 1799
Handcoloured etching and aquatint 14.4 x 25.7cm
The British Museum, London
(1851-9-1-979)

7

William Blake 1757–1827
Plate 33 from Jerusalem (written c.1804–20), copy A, printed c.1820
Relief etching, uncoloured 22.4 x 16.1 cm
The British Museum, London
(1847-03-18-93 [33])

8

Unidentified artist ('M.G.')
Fatal Effects of Gluttony: A Lord Mayor's Day Night Mare published by Thomas McLean, 4 November 1830
Handcoloured lithograph 23.5 x 33.5 cm
The Guildhall Library, London

4

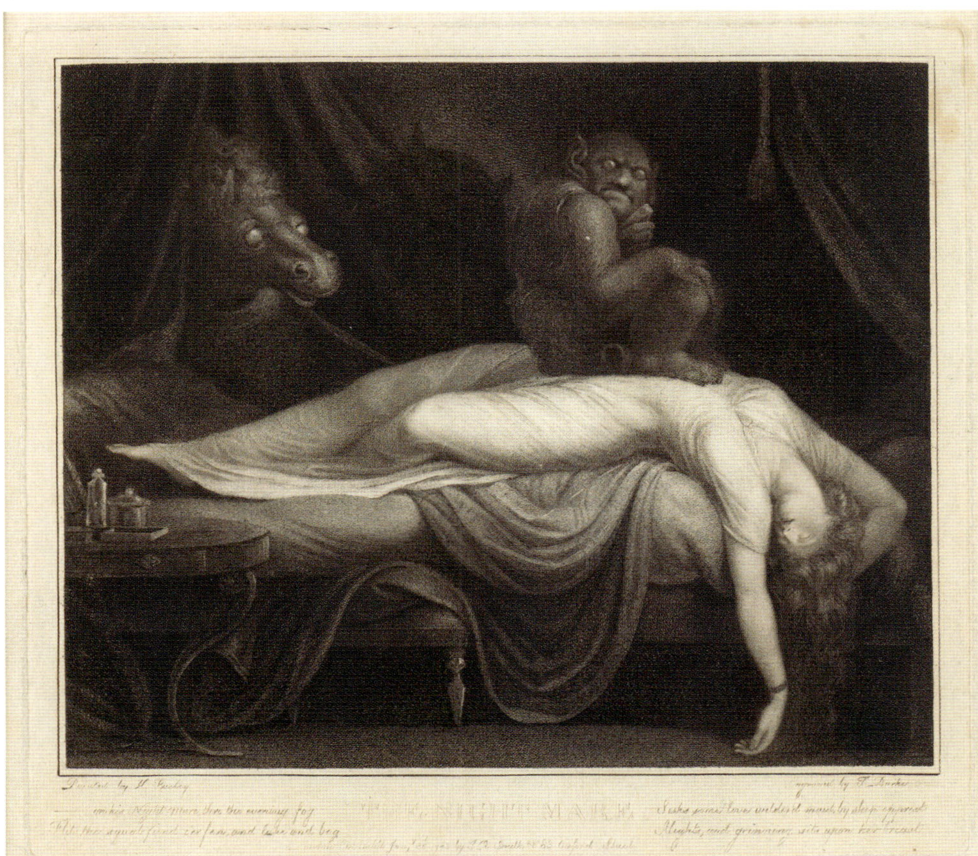

No.4 is the official engraving of Fuseli's *Nightmare*, published within a year of the original exhibition of the painting at the Royal Academy. The painter was paid twenty guineas, although the publisher, John Raphael Smith (1752–1812), 'acknowledged to have gained upwards of five hundred pounds for the sale of the prints' (Knowles 1831, I, p.64; see Weinglass 1994, no.67 and D'Oench 1999, pp.82–5). The choice of the new and fashionable stipple technique – notable for its delicate effects – may seem odd. Its use in this context may conceivably be ironic or parodic, for the medium carried none of the weighty intellectual overtones associated with line engraving, nor of the velvety gloomth of mezzotint associated with Gothic subjects (see no.54), but was generally instead reserved for romantic or pastoral subjects, in which Thomas Burke was a specialist. The first four lines from the section of Erasmus Darwin's (1731–1802) *The Loves of the Plants* quoted above (p.43) appear at the bottom of the print, although that source was not published until 1789, indicating that the poet and the painter were in dialogue about the subject, perhaps even at the conception of this celebrated composition.

Pirated prints of the design – for which the artist would not have been paid – are dated (perhaps fallaciously) as early as 1782 and 1783, and Burke's stipple engraving was reissued in 1802 (Weinglass 1994, no.67A–C). The long history of the use of *The Nightmare* in graphic satire began almost as quickly (see Powell 1973; Weinglass 1994, nos.68A–69DD). Rowlandson's *Night Mare* (nos.5a and 5b was among the earliest. The famously portly and dissolute Whig politician Charles James Fox (1749–1806) takes the role of Fuseli's maiden, here in a sleep troubled by his gambling debts and the forthcoming Westminster election referenced in the title (Deutsch 1996, pp.653–6). No.5a is the original drawing by Rowlandson, which would have been traced or copied onto the copperplate to produce the print, no.5b.

In no.6 the Prince of Wales lies in a drunken, sweaty stupor. William Augustus, Duke of York (1721–65) appears as an unpleasantly nude spectre, shown, mercifully, from the rear (George 1935–54, no.9381). His presence is intended to offer a warning about the evil effects of drink and an excessive diet, for which the Prince, and the Duke formerly, were notorious. Although Gillray's immediate compositional source was Reynolds's painting of the death of Cardinal Beaufort (1789; National Trust, Petworth) – a painting Gillray was careful to satirise on several occasions – the pose of the Prince is lifted directly from *The Nightmare*, or, rather,

Rowlandson's previous lampooning of that image. Gillray used Fuseli's compositions at least half a dozen times through his career (for further examples see nos.81,87), and he may be the author of a version of a rather schematic version of *The Nightmare* from as early as January 1784 (Donald 1996, p.70; McCreevy 1993, pp.178–9).

Although *The Nightmare* was continually recycled in often quite nuanced political contexts, the more straightforward comic possibilities of the image were hardly neglected. In no.8 a rich city merchant is beset by the effects of his indulgence in rich food and booze (Weinglass 1994, no.69Q). The list on his side-table reveals the extent of his carnivorous greed: 'Turtle & fresh Cod / Roast beef & a la mode / Veal and Mutton / Pork and Venison / Pheasants & Pigeons / Lobster & Sturgeon / Turkey & Capon / Goose and Salmon / Turbot & Ducks / Shrimps in Pots / Frogs a la Crapodine / Anguille & a la diabletine'. The effects of diet on the imagination were the source of considerable medical and critical speculation in this period (Ford 1992, pp.13–32). Fuseli was subject to a recurring rumour that he would eat raw pork before going to bed to stimulate his dark dreams.

No.7 shows the motif of *The Nightmare* being stretched and reinterpreted in the most radical and complex way. It is a plate taken from the original 'illuminated' version of Blake's poem *Jerusalem* (written around 1804–20, first printed around 1820) (Paley 1991). This vast and intricate work represents the most complete expression of Blake's personal mythological vision. The upper section of the design shows Albion – Blake's personification of the spirit of England – collapsing into the arms of Christ, between a palm tree (symbol of Christ's triumph) and an oak (symbol of the crucifixion). The lower scene presents the female figure of Jerusalem lying flat, with the 'insane and most deform'd' Spectre evoked by the text hovering over her. It has been proposed that the bat is derived from Blake's illustration of a 'spectre' or vampire bat from Guiana included in John Stedman's *Suriman* (1796) (Bogan 1976; Keynes 1979; Mills 1980). However, this frontal treatment of a bat-thing with outstretched wings had already featured in witchcraft scenes by Alexander Runciman (1736–85) and Fuseli (see nos.75, 82).

Taken as a group, nos.4–8 offer an overview of the range of reproductive technologies that were available in this period (Godfrey 1978; Alexander and Godfrey 1980; Clayton 1997). Nos.4–6 are examples of different 'intaglio' techniques, where a copper plate is incised with lines and marks, that, charged with ink, will convey the design in reverse onto paper when passed together through a press. The most traditional and esteemed form of intaglio printmaking was line engraving, which relied upon the exclusive use of directly cut lines to create the full range of tonal and textural effects. A variety of rather less demanding techniques were used for the generality of prints in the eighteenth century. Stipple, seen in no.4, used dots and lozenges instead of lines. These were slightly easier to execute, and created softer tonal effects. Accordingly, stipple engraving was seen as a more 'feminine' technique. Etching, seen in nos.5b and 6 is an intaglio method where the plate is covered with wax, into which the printmaker draws with a pointed tool. When the plate is treated in acid, the copperplate is 'bitten' where the wax has been removed. This allows for more fluent, personal kinds of mark-making, as the printmaker is drawing into a soft material rather than into metal. Further processes, such as the sugar-lift aquatint in no.6 allow for more subtle tones and textures. Most caricature prints from the later eighteenth century deploy the relatively fast and expressive method of etching, as evinced by the works by Gillray and Newton in the present exhibition. It was perfectly suited to such original designs, while being quite insufficient in itself as a means of reproducing the tones and textures of painting. A further important intaglio technique was mezzotint, discussed below under no.54. For all these methods, a drawn study like no.5a would normally be prepared, for tracing or transfer onto the copper plate.

In the nineteenth century, a number of new techniques came into use which made possible a vast expansion of print and made the illustration of books and magazines much easier. Lithography, used in no.8, was among the most important. Here, the printmaker draws onto a specially prepared stone; when ink is wiped onto the stone it catches on the drawn lines, and it is these that are printed. This was a fast and efficient method that represented directly the intentions of the draughtsman. In this case, as with the intaglio prints shown here, additional colour has been added in the form of watercolour, presumably by assistants working for the publisher, following a model set by the printmaker.

The technical, economic and aesthetic range of these different printmaking methods were the source of much debate among artists and cultural commentators, and must feature in our interpretation and appreciation of such productions (Eaves 1992). There were critics who complained that modern techniques were degrading the art, and that the severe and time-consuming methods of line engraving were the only legitimate way of making prints. Artists themselves might become concerned about how their works were reproduced: Henry Fuseli

5a

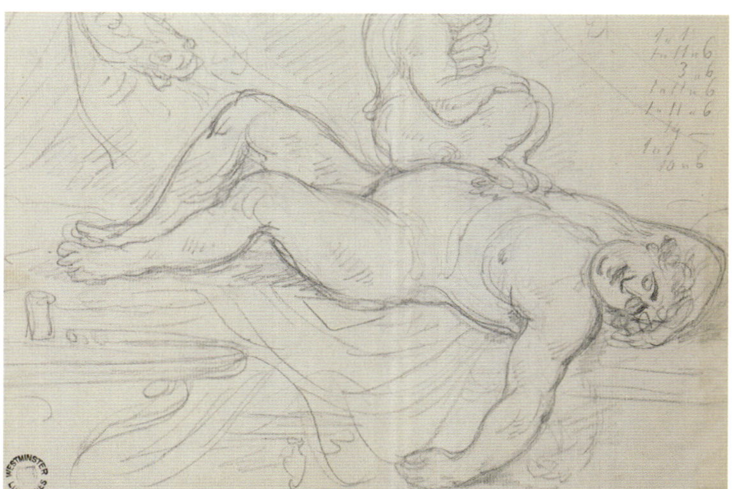

5b

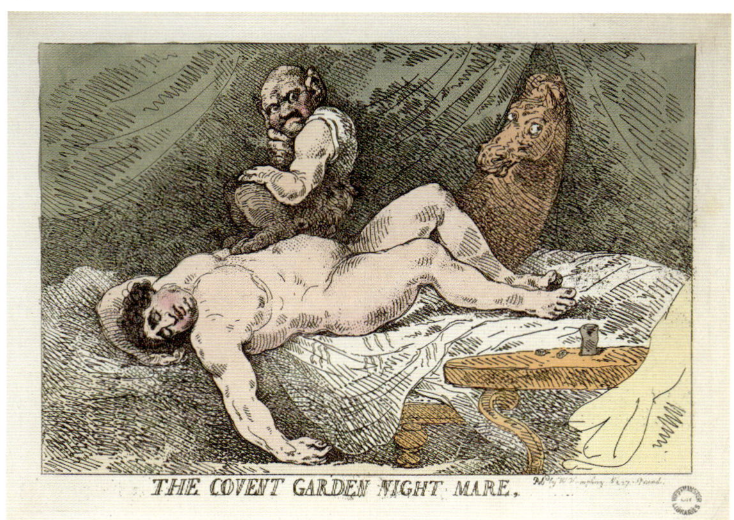

was often unhappy with the way his compositions were engraved, and eventually employed his own, trusted engraver, Moses Haughton (c.1772– after 1848), to make prints of his works. The most famous reproductive engravers could be paid much more than the artist of the original image, and this caused controversy as well. At the same time, engravers were officially excluded from membership of the Royal Academy, and the profession of reproductive engraver was viewed as somewhat lowly and craftsmanlike. The growth of the printmaker seemed to be benefiting the publisher and a few select engravers rather than the art as a whole – a point made against the greatest entrepreneur of the age, John Boydell (1719–1804; see no.87).

It is in this context that William Blake made his highly personal innovations in printmaking technique. He developed a form of 'relief' etching – where the raised part of the plate is printed rather than the incised, as in intaglio – and experimented extensively with the combination of text and image, and the use of colour, notably with the twelve 'large colour prints' produced around 1795 (see no.45). We need to remember that no.7 was originally part of an 'illuminated' book, and the stray word 'His' at the right was a 'catchword' leading on to the next page.

7

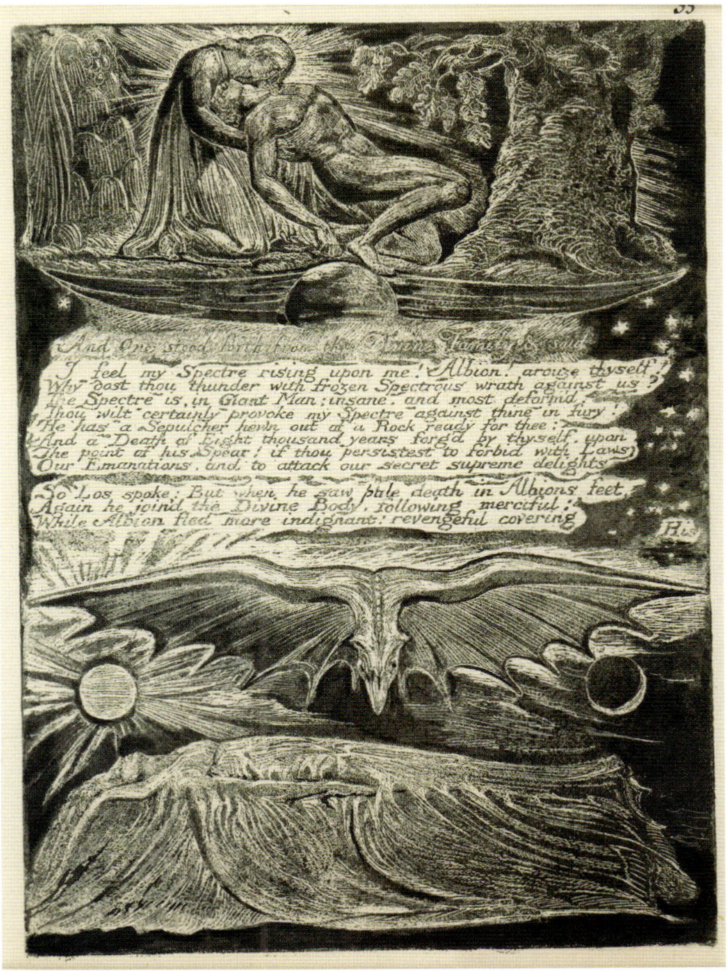

6

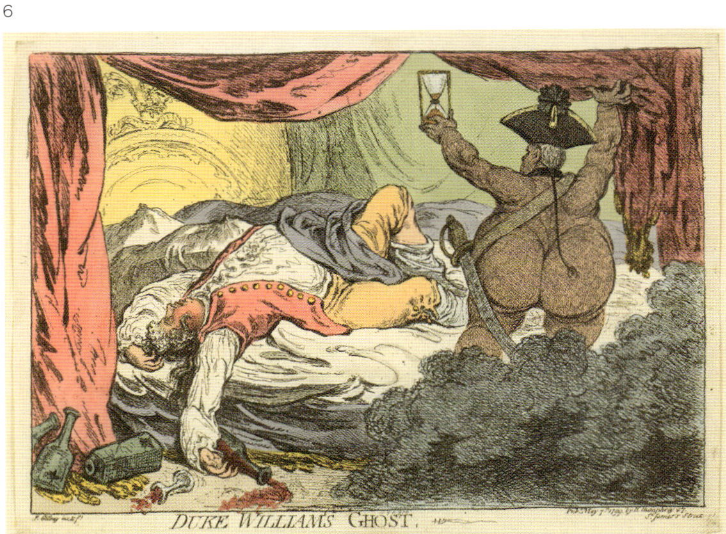

8

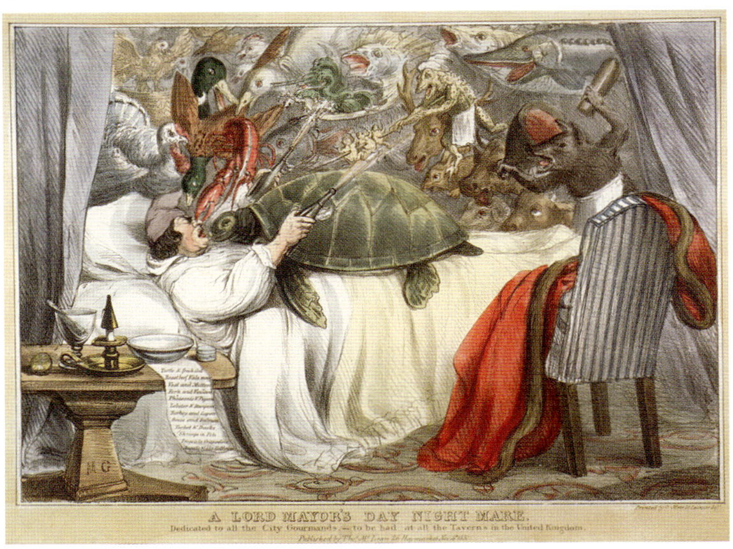

Perverse Classicism

The works in this section introduce the basic visual vocabulary that was used by artists treating 'Gothic' themes in the late eighteenth century. The selection focuses on the shocking, confrontational use of bodily horror and violence by Fuseli and the artists associated with him from the 1770s, and looks in particular at how the theme of confinement and heroic struggle came to embody an idea of artistic genius.

The heroic male body was established as the basic unit of high art in Renaissance art theory. For succeeding artists, critics and teachers, the representation of the masculine form, perfected in its physique and conveying in its movements and gestures an elevated narrative, was the ultimate test of artistic expertise and an emblem of professional triumph. In Britain very few artists had the opportunity to undertake paintings or sculptures of this kind until the last third of the eighteenth century. Around 1770, inspired by the establishment of the Royal Academy of Arts in London, the promised patronage of King George III and other eminent figures and new ideals of artistic creativity and genius, a whole generation of artists turned to such themes. Many travelled to Rome, traditionally the training-ground of high-minded artists, where they could encounter the exemplars of the ancient world and the Renaissance and, more practically, make contact with the aristocratic Grand Tourists who increasingly promised the best opportunities for patronage. In this decade in Rome, Fuseli emerged as the central figure in an international community of artists whose treatment of classical themes and physical forms both conformed to conventional ideas of high art, and exploded those ideals by matching the more expressive and extravagant forms of expression associated with novel concepts of the Sublime and 'original genius' (Pressly 1979; Myrone 2005). More particularly, the representation of extreme physical suffering, often in sadomasochistic contexts, was an important Gothic motif, asserting an extreme and potentially transgressive understanding of sexuality and gender (Bruhm 1994; Gardiner-Scott 1997).

These characteristics were exemplified in the frequently treated theme of Prometheus. The story originates in two accounts from the Greek writer Hesiod (see Brunel 1992). In *Theogony* (ll.507–16) Prometheus, the son of the Titan Iapetus and the Oceanid Clymene, decides to deceive Zeus by dividing in two an ox offered to that god in sacrifice, and tricking Zeus into accepting the inferior portion. By way of revenge, Zeus refuses to give fire to mankind. Prometheus then steals fire, for which sin he is chained to a pillar where his liver is in perpetuity picked at by an eagle, while Hephaestus fashions the likeness of a woman and sends this to earth to punish mankind. In *Works and Days* (ll.42–105) the story is told in greater detail.

As told by Hesiod, there is no doubt but that Prometheus is at fault in causing man's downfall, but the narrative was reworked in important ways by the Greek playwright Aeschylus in a trilogy of plays. The central, surviving portion, *Prometheus Bound*, cast the Titan as a martyr, the victim of unjust power, whose transgressive actions were the foundation of civilisation and the arts. The text was known to most British readers only through secondary accounts until Robert Potter's English translation was published in 1777. Greek theatre was still little appreciated, being viewed as rather offensive to modern taste. The developing tendency to primitivism in cultural criticism opened the way to a more positive understanding of Aeschylus' text, and of the rebellious Titan as a character.

Prometheus had been used as a metaphor for artistic creativity since the fifteenth century. Anthony Ashley Cooper, Third Earl of Shaftesbury (1671–1713), had referred to it in his *Soliloquy or Advice to An Author* (1711), one of the founding texts of elevated English art theory (Shaftesbury 1999, p.93). However, Shaftesbury proposed Prometheus as a model because of his ability to emulate God in his creativity and his inspired fire, not for his rebelliousness as such. The daring, dangerous associations of the figure came back to the fore in the last third of the eighteenth century, potentially also taking on associations with sexual virility. So the distinctly dodgy London sex-doctor John Graham wrote in his *A Lecture on Generation* (1780): 'in the critical efforts of the male, his soul seems, PROMETHEUS like, to spring up to heaven! to snatch life to animate the little embryo!' (quoted in Otto 2004, p.212). For poets and writers – including Mary Shelley (1797–1851), whose *Frankenstein* (1818) is subtitled 'The Modern Prometheus' – the Titan served as a symbol of dangerous, heroic imagination. For Goethe (1749–1832) (who was keenly interested in Fuseli's work, though this was not reciprocated), Prometheus represented the essentially revolutionary nature of the artist, who was able to challenge the authority of the gods. His play fragment and hymn on the theme (of c.1773–4, though only the latter was published in his lifetime) crystallised the idea of the rebel artist at the opening of what we know as the age of 'Romanticism' (Tille 1898; Wutrich 1995, pp.110–31).

Henry Fuseli, 'Aphorisms on Art', c.1788–1818

It is the lot of genius to be opposed, and to be invigorated by opposition.

(Knowles 1831, III, p.65)

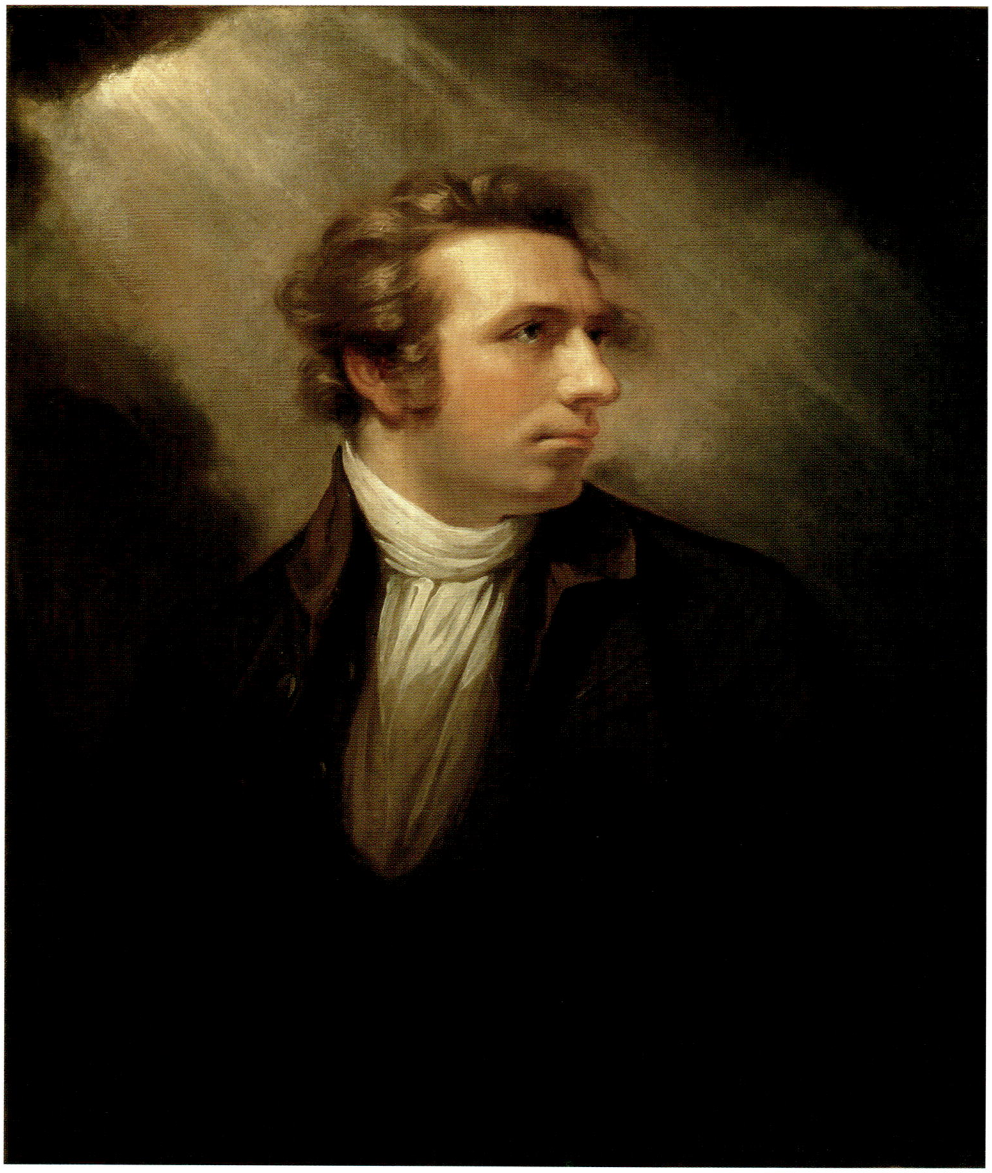

9

James Northcote 1746-1841
Portrait of Henry Fuseli c.1778
Oil on canvas 77.8 x 64.5 cm
National Portrait Gallery, London

Fuseli is shown here as a young man, on the point of returning to England from a period of eight years in Italy (spent almost entirely in Rome) which made his reputation among connoisseurs and fellow artists. The painter of the portrait, James Northcote, was just at the beginning of his stay abroad.

Fuseli's activities in Rome established his persona as a new kind of artist - daring, emotional, confrontational, as rebellious as Prometheus and as ambitious as Michelangelo. In September 1778 he wrote a letter to Northcote warning him about the dangers of the art world, with an accompanying drawing (Kunsthaus, Zurich), which features Fuseli as a gigantic striding heroic figure straddling a map of Europe: England is full of artistic 'mice'; Italy is where his dreams and desires are headed; Switzerland is best used as a lavatory (Weinglass 1982, pp.17-19). Northcote's portrait, with its windswept protagonist glaring forcefully into the gloom, makes much the same point but in a subtler fashion. Paradoxically, this emotional vision of the artist, and his pouting physiognomy, may also suggest a rather feminine quality.

John Knowles, The Life and Writings of Henry Fuseli (1831)

He was rather short in stature, about five feet two inches in height, his limbs were well proportioned, his shoulders broad, and his chest capacious. His complexion was fair; his forehead broad; his eyes were large, blue, and peculiarly expressive and penetrating; his nose large, and somewhat aquiline; his mouth was rather wide; and although his features were not strictly regular, yet his countenance was, in the highest degree, intelligent and energetic; the expression of his face varied in a remarkable manner with the quick impressions of his mind. He was clean and neat in his person and dress, and very particular with his hair, which was carefully dressed every day with powder.

(Knowles 1831, I, pp.350–1)

Johann Casper Lavater, Essays on Physiognomy (1781–6), trans. Henry Hunter (1789–98)

The curve which describes the profile in whole is obviously one of the most remarkable; it indicates an energetic character, which spurns at the idea of trammels. The forehead by its contours and position is more suited to the Poet than the Thinker; I perceive in it more force than gentleness, the fire of imagination, rather than the coolness of reason. The nose seems to be the seat of an intrepid genius. The mouth promises a spirit of application and precision – and yet costs the Original the greatest effort to give the finishing touch to the smallest piece. His extreme vivacity gets the better of that portion of attention and exactness which Nature endowed him, and which is still distinguishable in the detail of all his works. You will even sometimes find in them a degree of finishing almost over curious, and which for this reason forms a contrast with the boldness of the whole ...

Fury and force, an energy uniformly supported, and ever active – this is what distinguishes most of the figures and compositions of this masculine genius. Spectres, Demons, and madmen; fantoms, exterminating angels; murders and acts of violence – such are his favourite subjects; and yet, I repeat it, no one loves with more tenderness. The sentiment of love is painted in his look – but the form and bony system of his face characterize in him a taste for terrible scenes, and the energy which they require.

(Lavater 1789–98, II, pt.2, pp.280–1, 288)

10

Henry Fuseli 1741–1825
Drawing of a Figure Seated before Gigantic Antique Fragments c.1778–80
Red chalk and brown wash on paper
42 x 35.2 cm
Kunsthaus, Zurich, Grafische Sammlung

A figure is slumped, despairingly, next to the gigantic fragments of the left foot and right hand of the ancient Colossus of Constantine, then in the courtyard of the Capitoline Museums in Rome (now in the Palazzo dei Conservatori, Rome). The slight indications of the inscription on the base of these works allude to the overwhelming achievements of the Romans.

The title usually applied to this drawing, 'The Artist in Despair before the Magnitude of the Fragments of Ancient Art', is, we must remember, in its various permutations a modern invention attached to this work in the 1960s. The common identification of the figure as a representation of Fuseli himself is entirely speculative. The purpose of this title is to secure to this design the interpretation of it as (to use an earlier designation) an 'Allegory of Antiquity'. For David Irwin, the drawing 'seems to epitomize the extent to which the young artist has been overwhelmed by the power and influence of the antique', a judgement which remains standard (Irwin 1966, p.47; cf. Nochlin 1994, pp.7–8; Siegel 2000, pp.28–39; Klein 2005, p.72).

Though the image has therefore been taken as an emblem of a shift from 'neoclassical' calm to 'romantic' emotionalism specific to the late eighteenth-century, it represents an overawed response to the lost grandeur of the Antique which was conventional. For poets and travel writers, the sensitive traveller would naturally be moved by the sight of the fragments; for Protestant visitors to Rome, particularly, the sight of these fragments in the context of a Catholic and therefore supposedly depraved and degenerate society would prompt feelings of sadness (see Wrigley 1996; Chard 1999). The sentiment had been expressed in visual form in the architectural prints of Giovanni Battista Piranesi (1720–78), and by Giovanni Francesco Grimaldi (1606–80) in a drawing of a man standing next to a gigantic Antique foot and a similar etching featuring enormous sculpted heads (Turner 1999, no.144 [13]; see also Barkan 1999, pp.119–20). The drawing appears in an album that was put together in Rome by 1701 and was in a British collection by 1775 or 1795, so it is possible that Fuseli knew of the original design. Still, a further, more personal allusion has been ingeniously spotted as well, for '*Füssli*' (the painter's birth-name) means 'little foot' in Swiss dialect (Lindsay 1986).

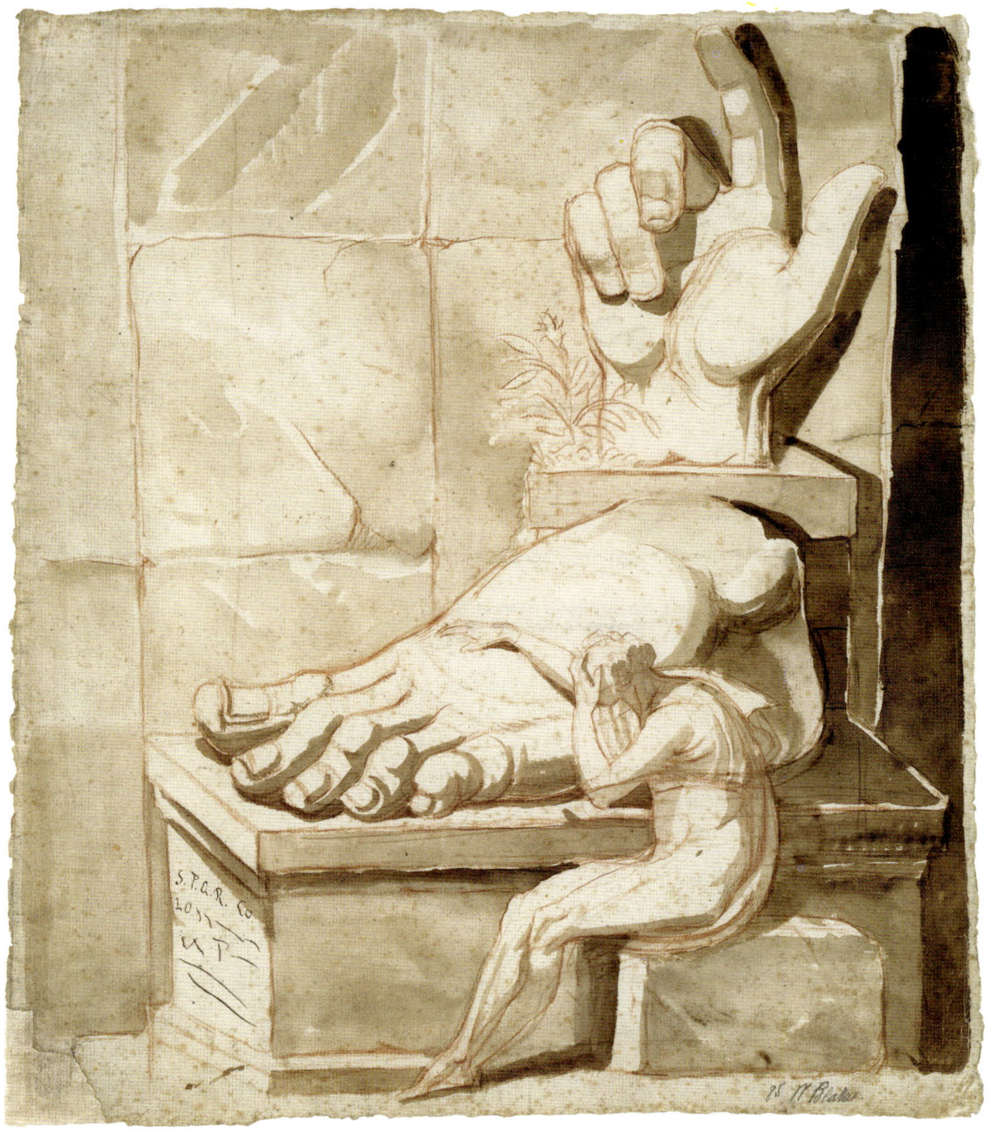

11

John Runciman 1744–1768
The Fall of Phaeton c.1767–8
Red and black chalk on paper 19.1 x 24.5 cm
The National Gallery of Scotland, Edinburgh

In ancient myth Phaeton was the handsome child of the sun god Phoebus and Clymene who, growing vain, claimed from his father the right to drive his chariot for a day:

> Phoebus represented the impropriety of such a request, and the dangers to which it would expose him; but in vain ... His explicit directions were forgotten, or little attended to, and no sooner had Phaeton received the reins from his father, than he betrayed his ignorance and ... The flying horses became sensible of the confusion of their driver, and immediately departed from the usual track. Phaeton repented too late of his rashness, and already heaven and earth were threatened with a universal conflagration, when Jupiter, who had perceived the disorder of the horses of the sun, struck the rider with one of his thunder bolts, and hurled him headlong from heaven into the river. (Lempriere 1792)

Runciman probably took the subject from Ovid's *Metamorphoses*, an important source of subject matter for artists, translated and adapted many times into English.

Compositionally, the figure recalls the fallen figure of Hector in Gavin Hamilton's (1723–98) heroically proportioned composition completed in 1767 (lost; known from an engraving), which in turn summoned the precedent of a whole class of collapsed warriors found on antique reliefs. The Scottish-born Hamilton was the best-established and most widely respected history painter at work in Rome at this time, and was the immediate model for the younger British artists who came to Italy with ambitions in this field (Irwin 1962). The apparently rapid, even slapdash virtuosity of Runciman's drawings strikes a note unlike that established by his older compatriot. Whereas his work was admired for its highly considered absorption of Antique and Renaissance pictorial models, its use of archaeological detail and its display of restraint and self-possession, the younger artist's design speaks of a hasty, violent manner more in tune with emerging ideals of original genius.

'The Story of Phaeton' from Ovid's <u>Metamorphoses</u>, Book II, trans. Joseph Addison (1704), ll.355–80

Jove call'd to witness ev'ry Power above,
And even the God, whose Son the Chariot drove,
That what he acts he is compell'd to do,
Or universal ruine must ensue.
Strait he ascends the high Ethereal throne,
From whence he us'd to dart his thunder down,
From whence his showers and storms he us'd to pour.
But now could meet with neither storm nor shower.
Then, aiming at the youth, with lifted hand,
Full at his head he hurl'd the forky brand,
In dreadful thund'rings. Thus the Almighty Sire
Suppress'd the raging of the fires with fire.

At once from life, and from the chariot driven,
Th' ambitious boy fell thunder-struck from heaven.
The horses started with a sudden bound,
And flung the reins and chariot to the ground:
The studded harness from their necks they broke,
Here fell a wheel, and here a silver spoke,
Here were the beam and axle torn away;
And, scatter'd o'er the earth, the shining
fragments lay.
The breathless Phaeton, *with flaming hair,*
Shot from the chariot, like a falling star,
That in a summer's evening from the top
Of heaven drops down, or seems at least to drop;
'Till on the Po his blasted corps was hurl'd,
Far from his country, in the western world.

(Addison 1914, pp.76–7)

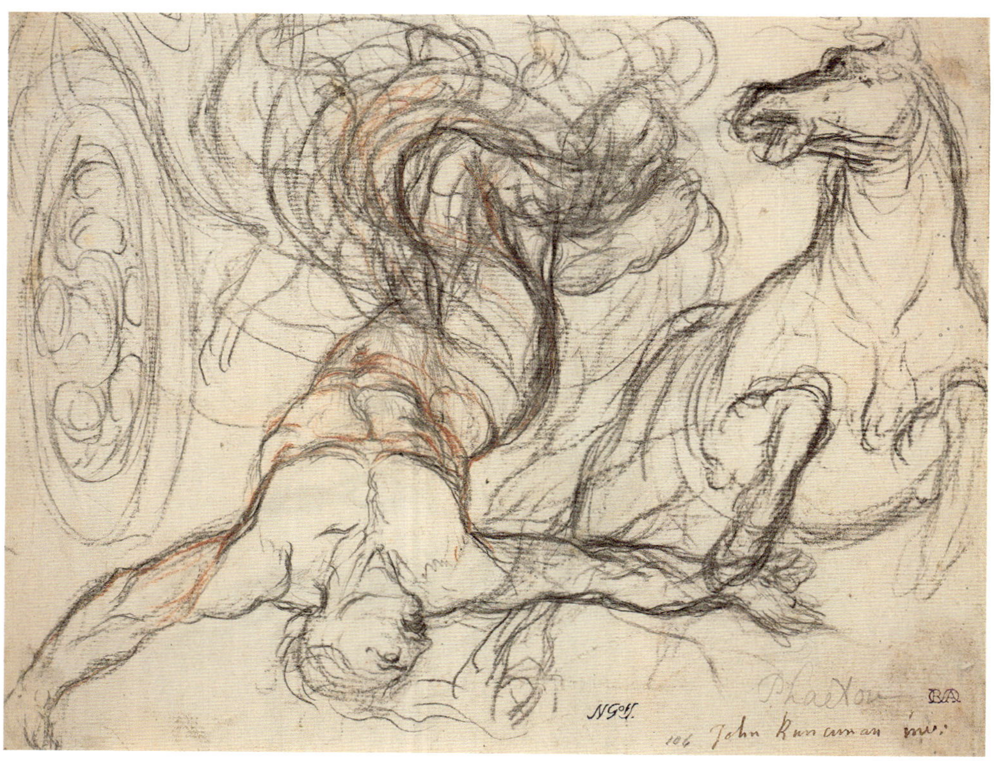

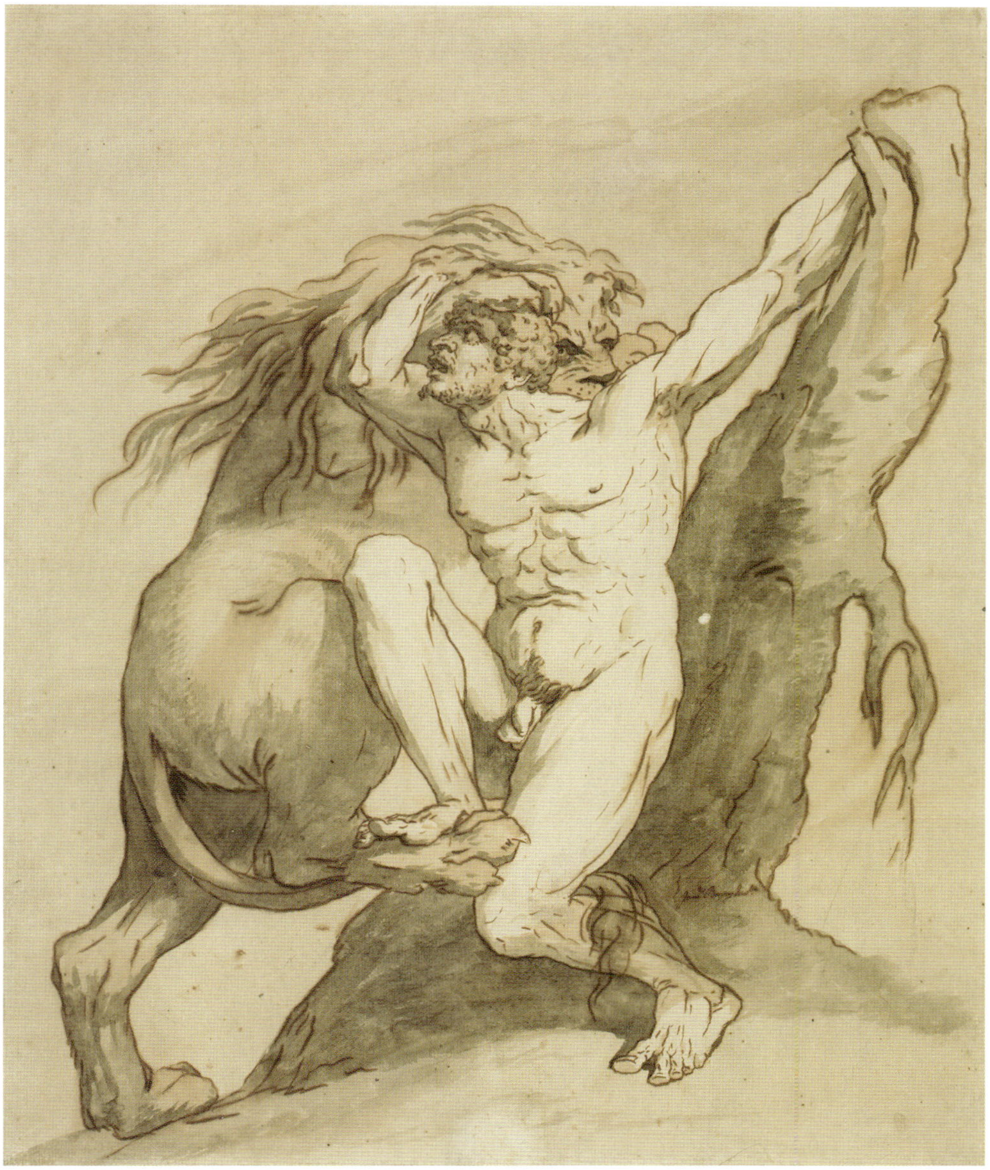

12

James Barry 1741–1806
Milo of Crotona c.1765–6
Pencil, pen and brown ink and brown and grey wash on paper 47.2 x 38.7 cm
The British Museum, London
(1852-2-14-411)

Milo was 'a celebrated athlete of Crotona in Italy ... He early accustomed himself to carry the greatest burden, and by degrees became a monster in strength'. A champion many times, his downfall came because of his pride, like Phaeton and Prometheus:

> In his old age, Milo attempted to pull up a tree by the roots and break it. He partly effected it, but his strength being gradually exhausted, the tree when half cleft reunited, and his hands remained pinched in the body of the tree. He was, then alone, and being unable to disentangle himself he was eaten up by the wild beasts of the place, about 500 years before the Christian era. (Lempriere 1792)

With John and Alexander Runciman and John Hamilton Mortimer, Barry was a founding figure in the development of the new forms of severe and expressive draughtsmanship which dominated narrative art in the last third of the eighteenth century. The recent writings of artistic reformers such as Johann Joachim Winckelmann (1717–68) and François Hemsterhuis (1721–90), as well as the new aesthetic theories promoted by Edmund Burke (1729–97) and others, prompted young artists to experiment, and in particular to explore the expressive and formal possibilities of a linear style (Rosenblum 1967).

Barry's economical treatment of the theme, concentrating on the tightly knit relationship between Milo and the lion, is emphatically sculptural. The theme had been treated by Pierre Puget (1620–94) in a celebrated over-lifesize marble (1671–82; Louvre, Paris), and Barry's restrained treatment of the facial features of Milo derive closely from that example. In its overall compact conception and in the treatment of the lion, Barry's design comes closest to Etienne-Maurice Falconet's (1716–91) smaller marble of 1754 (Louvre, Paris), although the French sculptor had placed his foolhardy hero in a horizontal position and had supplied him with an open, screaming mouth. Barry referred to the Falconet sculpture in his observations on the art he had seen in Paris in 1765–6, and noted the names of Falconet and Puget among those of the French sculptors whose work he admired, above that of the painters of France (Fryer 1809, I, pp.33–4 and 40, and II, p.9). He later referred to the 'famous Milo' of Puget in one of his lectures, delivered as the Professor of Painting at the Royal Academy (1782–99) (see Fryer 1809, I, p.508). The Swedish sculptor Johann Tobias Sergel (1740–1814) had modelled this subject in Rome around 1766, and Barry may also have known this work. As William Pressly has noted (Pressly 1981, p.246), the rather heavy-handed linearity of this design is unusual, and it is likely to be an early study dating to 1765–70. A much smaller, but somewhat more fluently executed version of this design is in a private collection, and has been dated to within Barry's Roman period (1767–70) (Dunne 2005, no.DR38). Given their dependence on the sculptures mentioned here, it would seem reasonable to date these drawings more precisely to 1765–6.

13

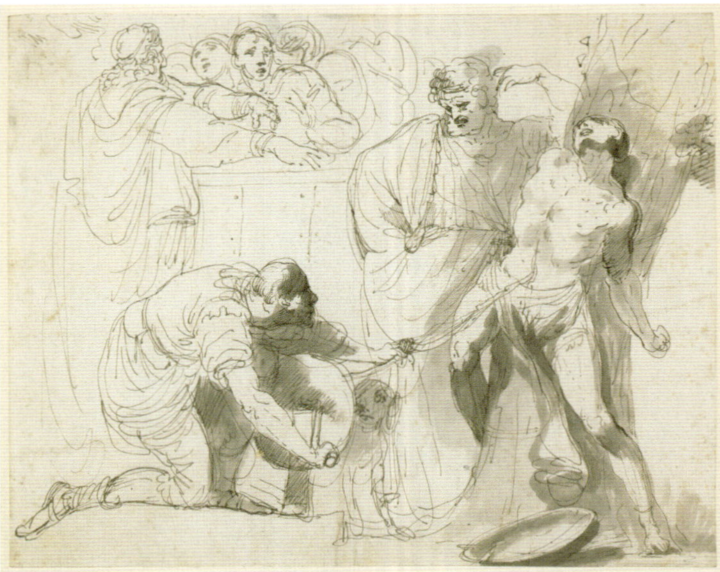

14

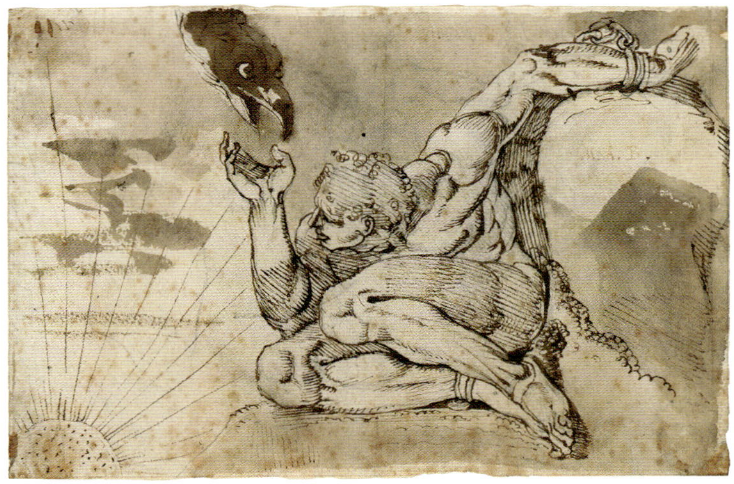

13

John Hamilton Mortimer 1740–1779
The Martyrdom of St Erasmus c.1770–5
Pen and grey ink with grey wash on paper
22.5 x 27.8 cm
The British Museum, London
(1978 U 1591 [2])

This drawing shows the martyrdom believed by tradition to have been suffered around the year AD 300 by St Erasmus (also known as St Elmo), bishop of Formiæ in the Campagna, Italy. According to legend he was killed by having his intestines wound upon a windlass. Nothing is known of his historical life and deeds, and the story of his martyrdom was an invention of the Middle Ages, based on a misunderstanding of his traditional depiction holding a length of rope and a windlass, attributes of his role as the patron saint of sailors. The supposed form of his martyrdom led to his also being taken up as the patron saint of those who suffer from stomach conditions (Butler 1981, II, pp.453–4).

The theme of St Erasmus's martyrdom appeared quite frequently in sixteenth- and seventeenth-century art, particularly in Northern Europe, and was the subject of an altarpiece for St Peter's in Rome by Nicolas Poussin (1629). Mortimer might have had in mind the gruesome depiction of the theme in an etching of c.1630 by Pietro Testa (1611–50). Although compositionally quite different, the scratchy, expressive draughtsmanship, the posture of the saint and the sparse but effective use of sinuous areas of shading are comparable. Testa's print had been reworked as a satire in *The Conduct, of the two B*****rs* (engraving, 1749; fig.22) by George Bickham, Jr, who introduced a white horse of Hanover licking up the blood spilt from the victim's guts (see Hallett 1999, pp.230–2). The dog drawn by Mortimer perhaps threatens to so the same, although this is, more obviously, a reference to the gory detail of a canine eating a human heart in Hogarth's famous anatomy scene from *The Four Stages of Cruelty* (1751). The expressive graphic style of Testa, together with the example of Salvator Rosa (1615–73), were decisive points of reference for Mortimer. Both were seen as artists who had brilliant talent but who also exceeded the bounds of good taste and artistic propriety, a reputation that attached itself to the English artist in turn (see Sunderland 1986, esp. pp.54–6).

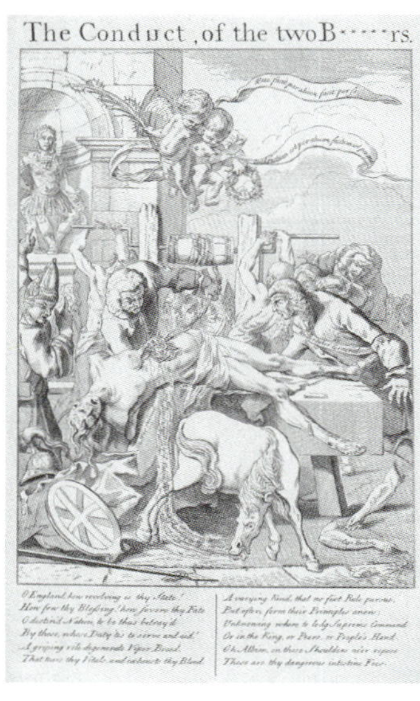

fig.22 George Bickham, Jr (1684–1758) after Pietro Testa (1612–50), *The Conduct, of the Two B*****rs* 1749, engraving 26 x 18.4 cm. The British Museum, London

14

Henry Fuseli 1741–1825
Prometheus c.1770–1
Pencil and brown ink and brown wash on paper
15 x 22.2 cm
Kunstmuseum Basel, Kupferstichkabinett

While in Rome, Fuseli, with Thomas Banks, would play 'five-point' games, which involved placing dots in a random pattern on a sheet and joining these with the head and extremities of a drawn figure. As a means of formulating poses, the games tellingly disregarded the inductive methods of traditional academic draughtsmanship. By being organised by an arbitrary pattern rather than narrative motivation, the resulting poses were extravagant and strange, suggesting violence and perversity (see Hofmann 1975, p.37; Klein 1991, pp.231, 269–70). The essence of the game was speed and facility, rather than plodding observation – the body conceived immediately as a whole rather than built up through the massing of fragments, each observed as carefully as the next – matching the daring, reckless, unconventional forms of creativity associated with the Prometheus myth. As Piranesi, apocryphally, exclaimed on seeing Fuseli's drawings in Rome: 'This is not called *designing*, but *building* a man' (Hoare 1801, p.7).

There are several such designs by Fuseli (Schiff 1973, nos.618–29). Here he has elaborated the figure with the addition of the vulture and chain into the thematically appropriate subject of Prometheus. The inscription on the rock is taken to allude to Fuseli's idol, Michelangelo Buonarroti (1475–1564).

15

Henry Fuseli 1741–1825
The Thieves' Punishment 1772
Pencil, in places reworked with black and brown ink, in places brown wash, heightened with opaque white, on paper 46 x 61.2 cm
Kunsthaus, Zurich, Grafische Sammlung

A subject drawn from Dante's (1265–1321) *Inferno*, Canto 24, from *The Divine Comedy* (c.1319–21, first published 1472). The poet, led by his guide Virgil, encounters a scene of unfathomable horror in the seventh section of Hell (see Schiff 1973, no.424; Gizzi 1985, no.3). Thieves are attacked by snakes and are themselves transformed into serpents, then back again, in a huge, writhing, mutable mass of human and serpentine flesh. The theme of metamorphosis is borrowed from classical authors and the repeated transformations and mutations, like some sort of extended special-effects sequence, are meant to challenge and surpass them in sheer spectacle and invention. Fuseli has made the most of this opportunity for the spectacular display of the grotesquely muscular body which, by virtue of its conjunction of human and serpentine flesh in struggle, must perforce recall the canonical work of ancient art, *The Laocoon* (Louvre, Paris).

The emotional and violent subject matter of Dante was taken up by a number of artists from this point. Reynolds's *Ugolino* (see no.54) was the most famous, but Fuseli turned to his themes repeatedly (see also no.36). William Blake undertook a huge series of illustrations in the last decade of his life, including versions of this subject (see no.29). The recovery of Dante's reputation in Britain has been put down to the prevalence of such 'Gothic' motifs, although the extent to which this played a part is disputed (Sayer 1965; Tinkler-Villani 1989, pp.37–58). Horace Walpole dismissed Dante as 'extravagant, absurd, disgusting, in short a Methodist parson in Bedlam' (Lewis 1937–83, XXXIV, p.256). We may suspect that it was precisely because of these qualities that Fuseli turned to the Italian poet for subject matter.

Fuseli would have known the story, apparently originating in Giovanni Bottari's 1759 edition of Vasari's *Lives*, which claimed that Michelangelo had illustrated a copy of the *Divine Comedy* with 'an infinite number of the most excellent naked figures, in the most striking attitudes' (*Annual Register*, vol.7, 1764, p.272; see Sumner 1938). A later writer commented that 'I wish Mr Fuseli could be prevailed on to supply the loss of the marginal drawings which Michael Angelo drew in his Dante. There is, perhaps, no artist living better qualified to wield the mighty pencil of that wonderful painter' (*Monthly Magazine*, vol.16, August 1803, p.8) and another claimed that he worked 'under the mingled inspiration of Dante, Michael Angelo, and his great Original' (Mathias 1798, II, p.442).

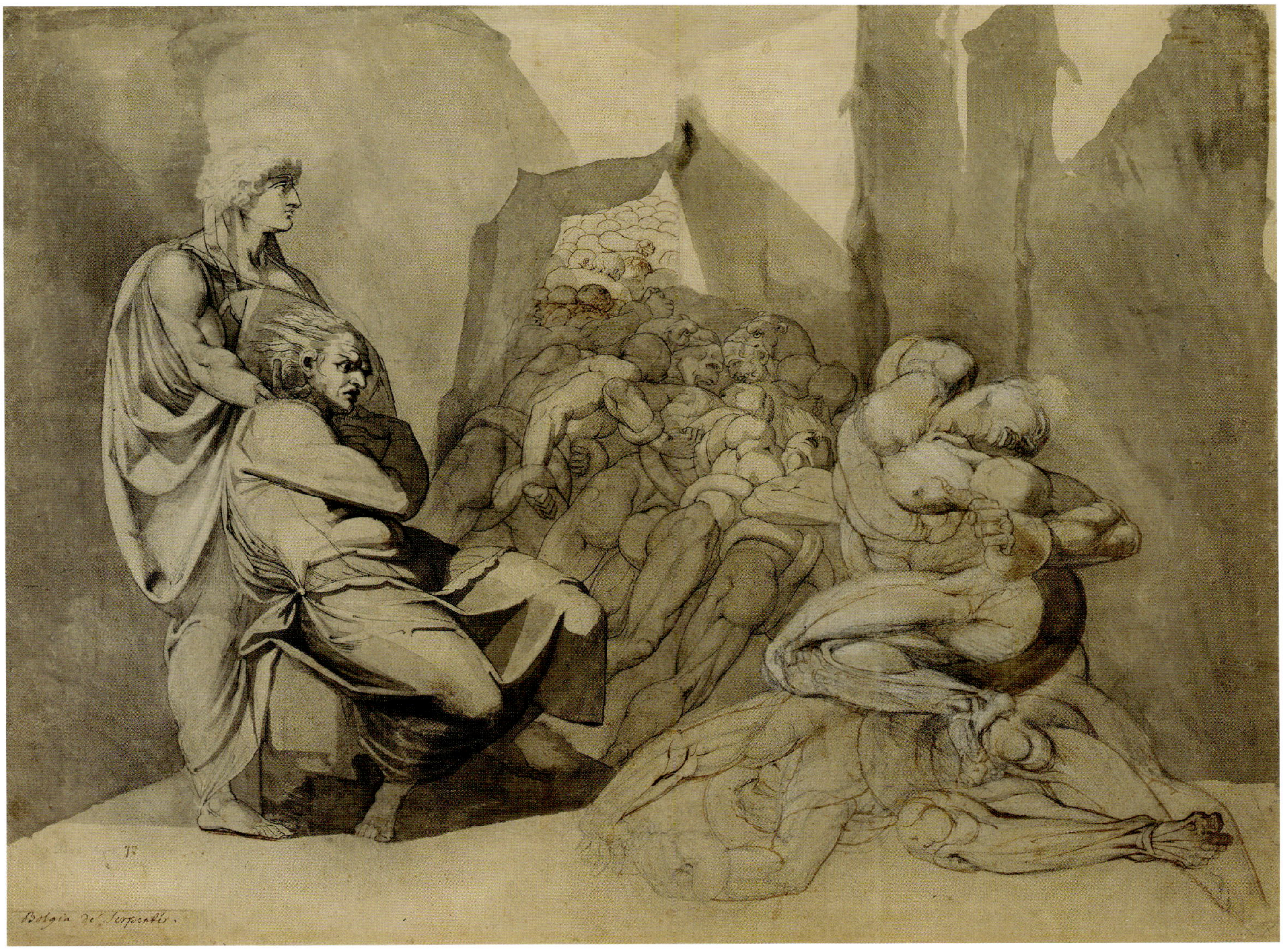

16

Unidentified artist, sometimes identified as James Jefferys 1751–1784
Drawing of a prison scene c.1779
Pen and black ink and grey washes on paper
37.4 x 56.3 cm
Ashmolean Museum, Oxford

Eight male figures are variously bound, by their wrists or arms, chests, waists and heads, in a gloomy dungeon. Most struggle and twist: one, to the bottom right, appears already dead; another, in the centre, looks out of the blackness with eyes whose strained, open brightness may suggest the arrival of madness.

It has been suggested that the subject may be intended as Ugolino and his sons in prison, from Dante's *Inferno*, for which see no.54. But as David Brown has pointed out, there are far too many figures crammed into this composition to make this likely (Brown 1982, no.868). Instead, the scene would appear to be an imagined vision of prison horrors. As such, it invites speculation about the imaginative treatment of the theme of confinement in the eighteenth century, from Tobias Smollett's *Ferdinand, Count Fathom* (1753) through to emotive accounts of the contemporary slave trade.

The drawing comes from a group of works on paper exhibited at the London gallery Roland, Browse and Delbanco in 1949 and subsequently broken up. These were produced by someone working in Rome c.1779, who, on the basis of the draughtsmanship and prevalence of grotesque subject matter, must have known the work of Fuseli. Because of the gigantesque treatment of the figures, the unknown author was named 'The Master of the Giants'.

The identity of this artist remains disputed. These works were long associated with Prince Hoare (1755–1834), the son of the successful Bath portraitist William Hoare (c.1703–92). He was part of Fuseli's circle and his known drawings have a broad clumsiness which fits with these designs. Nancy Pressly has proposed James Jefferys, a skilled draughtsman who was sent to Rome by the Royal Academy. He disappeared from sight at the end of the 1770s, and it is assumed he suffered mental illness (Pressly 1977; Pressly 1979, pp.82–95). A further suggestion may be Maria Cosway, who was certainly in Rome at the right time and by her own admission was enchanted by the work of Fuseli (see no.19). The gigantic treatment of these forms and the predilection for bizarre subject matter fits well with her known work of the 1780s. However, without further supporting evidence, such claims will be moot: it is interesting to observe how designs in this style invite interpretation, apparently equally valid, as the works of a cack-handed semi-amateur, a mentally deranged but skilful professional and an over-enthusiastic youth.

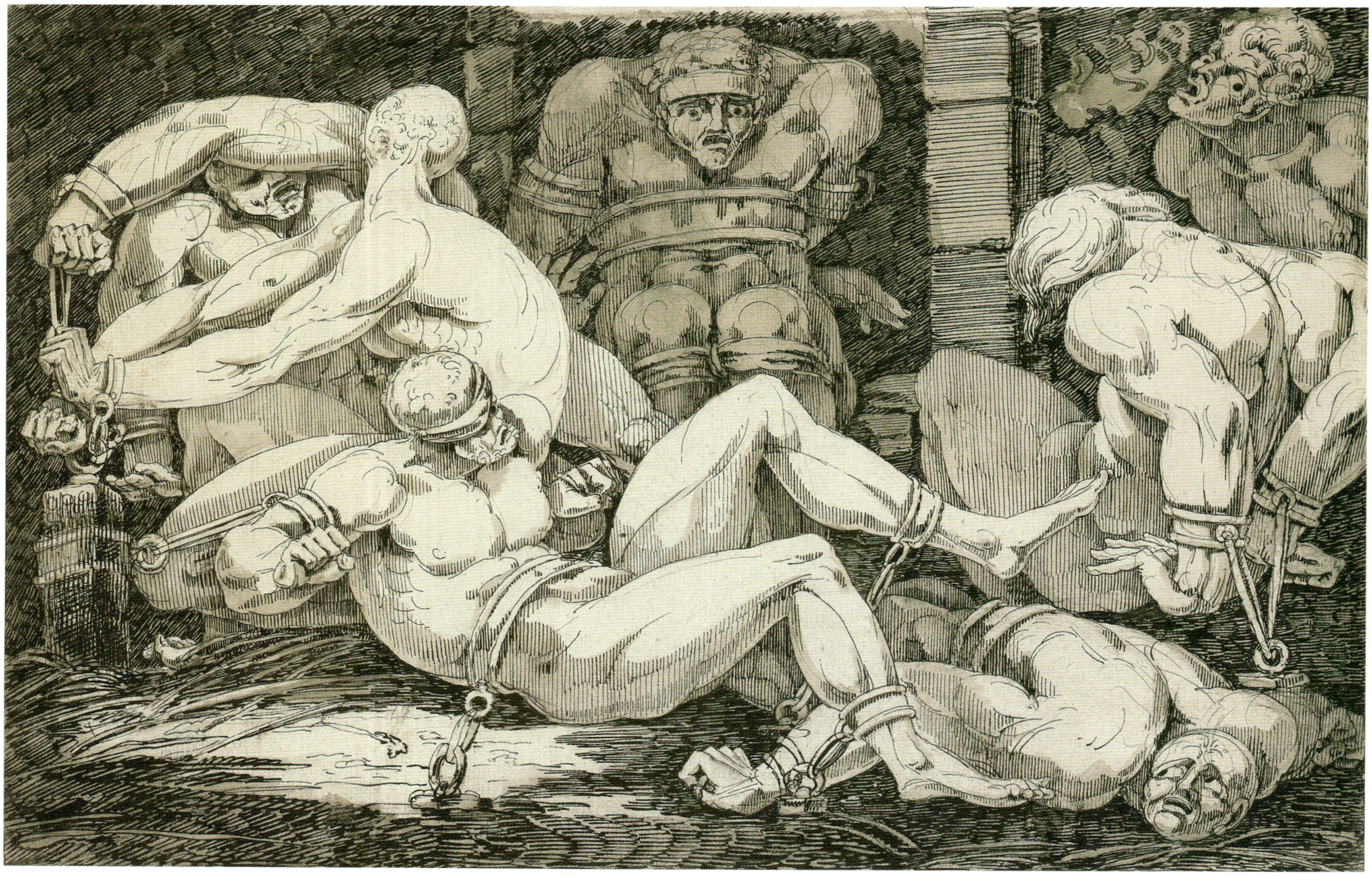

17

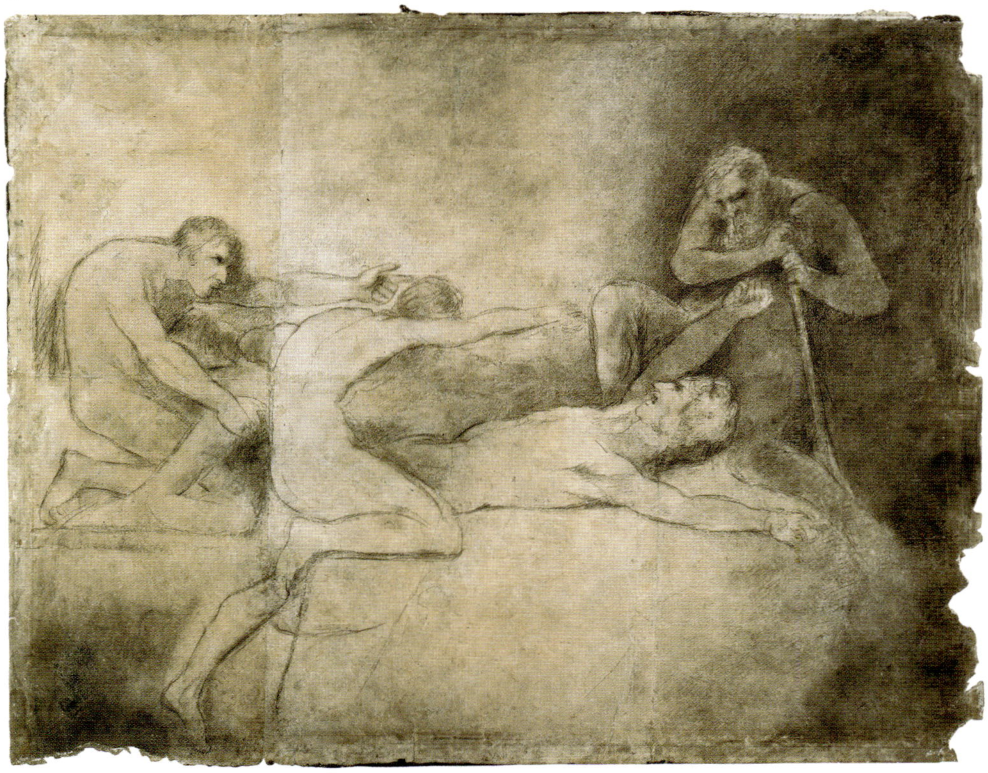

18

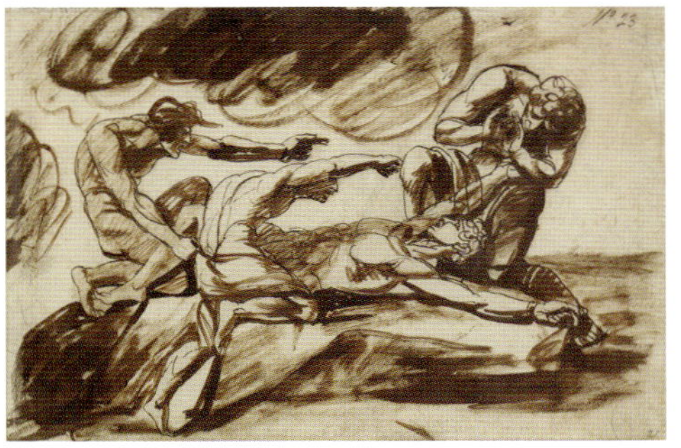

17

George Romney 1734–1802
Prometheus Bound c.1779–80
Black chalk on six sheets of laid paper
100.5 x 126 cm
National Museums Liverpool, The Walker

18

George Romney 1734–1802
Prometheus Bound c.1779–80
Pencil, ink and wash on paper 28 x 41 cm
Private collection, courtesy of Andrew Wyld

The allegorical figures of Force (Bia, the female) and Strength (Crato) tie the rebel Titan, Prometheus, to a rock on Jupiter's orders.

The subject is taken from Aeschylus's *Prometheus Bound*. The full text was first published in English by Robert Potter in 1777. That translator argued that the Greek plays could be a powerful resource for painters, and had noted that Romney had already started designs based on this text prompted by his meeting Potter (see also no.77): 'there indeed the poet has given free scope to this unbounded imagination, and exerted the strength and ardor of his genius with a wild and terrible magnificence' (Potter 1777, p.xix). This represented a turn in the fate of this horrific subject. Father Brumoy, whose commentary on Aesychlus had previously offered English readers access to the play, had complained that 'every circumstance of the punishment is so strongly marked, that the representation must have inspired the utmost horror' (Brumoy 1759, II, p.130). But by the 1770s the time was ripe for a reappraisal of the theme, now with a sense of the rebellious nature of the true artist and a willingness to take aesthetic pleasure in those scenes of horror and violence that could be called Sublime.

The large drawing comes from a series of 'cartoons' produced on the same format by Romney shortly after he had returned from a period of study and work in Rome (Kidson 2002, nos.59–76). These unusual y large graphic compositions are executed on a composite sheet of paper, in black chalk. Concentrating on horrific and supernatural sιbjects, the series was a sustained effort by Romney to create a body of work that would represent him as a Sublime artist. They were known and admired by Romney's supporters, including John Flaxman (1755–1826), who recommended that Blake engrave them (Bentley 2004, p.177). However, Romney was largely taken up with his practice as a fashionable portrait painter, and his ambitions in this field were frustrated.

In its formal qualities and format this drawing extends the thematic ambitions of the composition. The unusιally large scale and direct, vigorous technicue represent an unconventional approach to draughtsmanship. Although the present composition is understood to have been reworked at a later date by the painter's son John Romney (1758–1832) and the condition of the sheets is poor, the manifest faults (if we can call them that) in the figure drawing are apparent also in the freely executed smaller drawing (no.18). The violence done to the figure within the narrative is matched, indexically, by the violence of the drawing itself. Arguably, the Sublime nature of the subject gives latitude for such freedom from the rules of anatomy and disregard for timidly correct designing. As Fuseli put it: 'Negligence is the shade of energy; where there is neither, expect mediocrity' (Knowles 1831, III, p.68).

19

Maria Cosway 1760–1838
Unidentified Scene c.1780–90
Pen and ink and wash on paper 28.3 x 35.6 cm
Victoria and Albert Museum, London

20

Richard Cosway 1742–1821
Prometheus c.1790–1800
Pen and brown ink on paper 22.5 x 18.4 cm
Print Collection, Miriam and Ira D. Wallach Division of Art, Prints and Photographs, The New York Public Library, Astor, Lenox and Tildden Foundations

No.19 is an unidentified subject. Although we might speculate that this is intended to represent some specific classical or early Christian martyrdom, the sadomasochistic content of the image is more dominant and really obviates the need to identify a specific literary source.

Maria Cosway's debt to the work of Fuseli was remarked upon frequently in the 1780s, when she was represented at the Royal Academy exhibitions with visionary and Sublime subjects. In a letter written towards the end of her life, she remarked on her youthful enthusiasm for the artist's work, when she noted of her period as a teenager in Italy: 'Fusely, with his extraordinary Visions, struck my fancy' (Maria Cosway to Sir William Cosway, 24 May 1830, in Barnett 1995, p.260).

Maria had married the fashionable painter Richard Cosway in 1782. Both pursued some fairly strange and perverse subjects in their drawings (see nos.63–5). The posture of the tormenter in this drawing is identical to a figure of a cupid wrestling a lion drawn by Richard, suggesting a shared pictorial source (Lipponi 1998, illustrated after p.192).

Richard Cosway's own treatment of the theme of torture, with his *Prometheus* (no.20), exemplifies his highly refined approach to draughtsmanship and a rather more muted approach to violence and masculine anatomy. This closely worked technique of hatching and making dots and lozenges derives from printmaking, rather than the more expressive methods characteristic of so many drawings of Sublime subjects. Arguably, this technique is rather at odds with the theme, and we might note that he was primarily active as a portrait miniaturist, a profession which demanded close attention to detail and refined technique. Maria Cosway's dedication to Sublime and horrific subjects, and her husband's fashionable pursuit of the delicate medium of the miniature, offered rich materials to contemporary satirists (see Walker 1986; Lloyd 1995, pp.45–51).

19

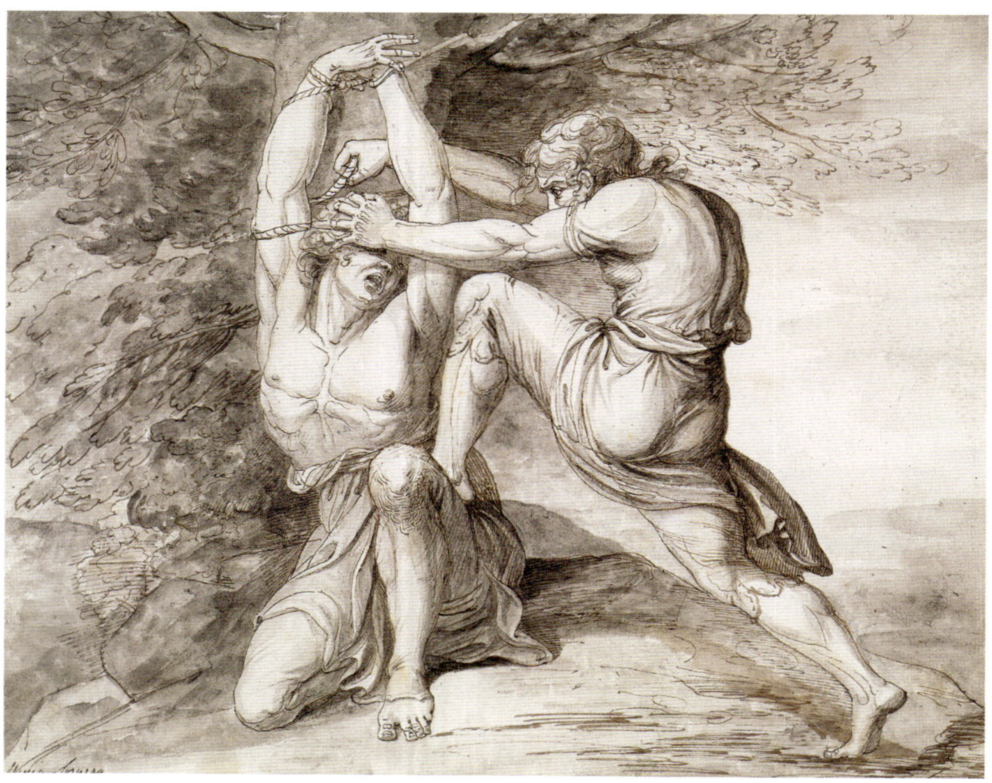

20

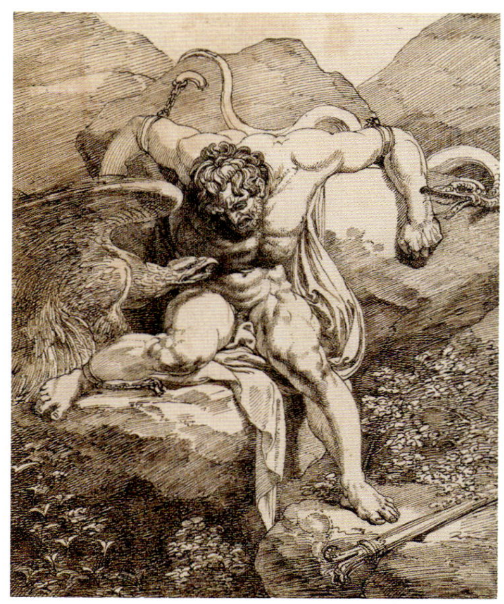

21

Thomas Banks 1735–1805
Falling Titan 1785–6
Marble 83.8 x 90.2 x 52.4 cm
Royal Academy of Arts, London

22

Thomas Banks 1735–1805
Falling Titan c.1785–95
Etching 37.5 x 27.8 cm
The British Museum, London
(1847-7-23-74)

Cast from the heavens, a rebellious Titan crashes through rocks while a satyr flees for his life. According to classical mythology, the giant Titans had sought to overthrow heaven but their revolution failed and they were hurled to earth to make way for Zeus and his family.

No.21 was created by Banks as a Diploma Work when he was elected to the Royal Academy of Arts, and as such the work served to demonstrate the extreme refinement of the sculptor's technical skills and his imaginative capacities. The piece can be placed in the tradition of academic sculpture, most prevalent in France, where the carving of an ideal masculine body in an awkward pose was the ultimate test and proof of abilities. Banks had been trained in the more modest traditions of ornamental and architectural sculpture, but his ambitions had been transformed by early successes in art competitions run by the Society for the Encouragement of Arts, Manufactures and Commerce and the Royal Academy. He had been sent to Rome by the Academy, and there refined his skills and extended the imaginative scope of his art (Myrone 2005, pp.176–82).

Banks was the particular friend of Fuseli in Rome, and together they undertook 'five point drawings' which tested their ability to draw the human body in extremely contorted positions (see no.14). The form of this sculpture has always been understood to relate to such exercises. Furthermore, the introduction of the diminutive humanoid figure and goat creates an extraordinary distortion of scale, which brings this piece closer to the irrational and gigantic efforts of Fuseli than to the academic tradition.

These qualities were enhanced when Banks etched the composition (no.22). The print evokes the pictorial precedents of Salvator Rosa (1615–73) and of Hendricks Goltzius (1558–1617) – eccentric and mannered designers who produced famous images of such flying figures – rather than the more level-headed traditions of classical design.

Once again, the chosen theme of rebellion is telling in the wider context of artistic production and patronage. Opportunities to create such idealistic works of art were extremely rare in Britain, and Banks found his ambitions in this field frustrated. *The Falling Titan* was greatly admired by contemporaries, but seemed to be to them a tragic symbol of a wasted talent. The greater part of Banks's career was taken up with producing portraits and funerary monuments, and his professional reputation may have suffered further setbacks because of his known radical political sympathies (Bell 1938; Bryant 2005).

21

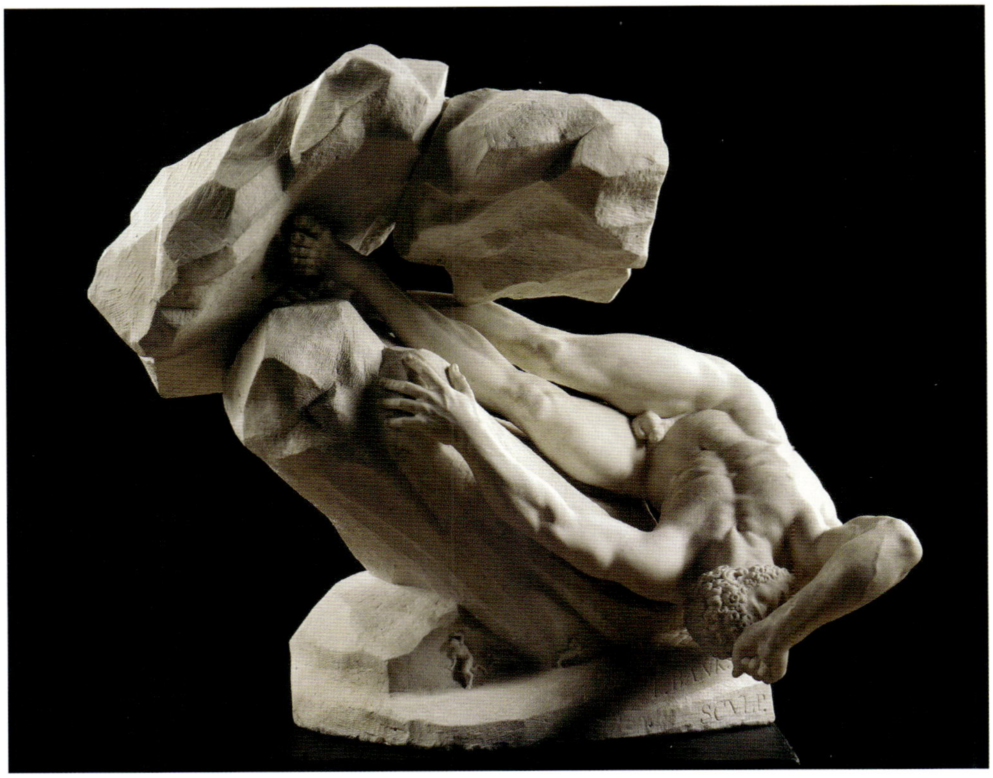

22

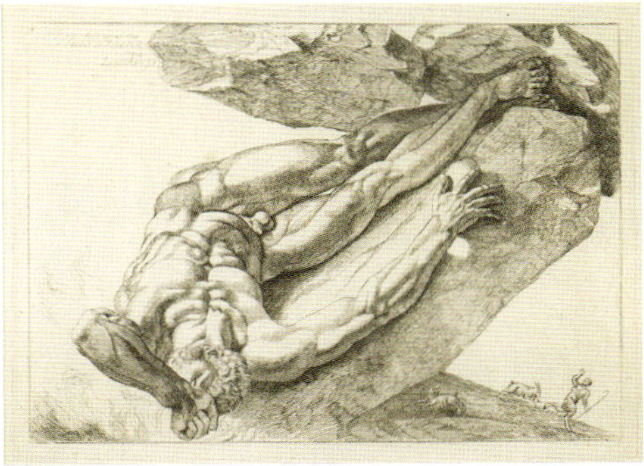

23

John Flaxman 1755–1826
Prometheus Bound 1794
Pen and ink over pencil on paper
27.5 x 36.3 cm
Royal Academy of Arts, London

24

John Flaxman 1755–1826
The Storm 1794
Design for plate 2 from *Tragedies of Aeschylus*, first published 1795
Pen and ink over pencil on paper
24.5 x 28.6 cm
Royal Academy of Arts, London

These two subjects are from *Prometheus Bound* by Aeschylus. In no.23 Prometheus is tied down in punishment for his rebelliousness (as in nos. 17–18). No.24 refers to the lines describing Prometheus on the rock being assailed by Jove: 'Th'impetuous storm / Rolls all its terrible fury on my head' (see Tomory 1979, no.66).

These two designs come from a series of drawings illustrating the tragic plays of Aeschylus. These were commissioned in 1794 from Flaxman while he was based in Rome, by Georgiana, dowager Countess Spencer (1736–1814). Flaxman had already produced two series of similar drawings illustrating Homer's *Iliad* and *Odyssey*, which had been printed as engravings by Thomas Piroli (1752–1824). These had attracted enormous acclaim. In the event, only no.24 was engraved as part of the published series, issued simultaneously in Rome and in London in 1795; the other design was rejected. The engraver was, again, Piroli, but whereas with the earlier series Flaxman released the copyright of the designs meaning that he was given little financial reward despite the success of the prints, with the *Tragedies* Flaxman retained his rights over the images (Bentley 1964).

The line engravings of Flaxman's designs for Homer and Aeschylus exerted a profound influence over artists across Europe (Symmons 1984; Bindman 1979). His use of almost unmodulated line and rejection of tonal and textural effects represented to contemporaries the most complete expression of classical purity. These series also involved Flaxman returning to themes and scenes that had been the stock-in-trade of idealistic British artists over the previous three decades. Of the thirty published plates of the *Tragedies of Aeschylus* about a quarter are concerned with the theme of Prometheus, helping to further demonstrate the importance of this theme for artists of the late eighteenth century.

Flaxman himself saw these designs as preparatory studies rather than necessarily an end in themselves. Arguably, their attenuated technique looks rather bloodless compared to the work of Fuseli and Romney, or Maria Cosway. Certainly his style was readily adapted for decorative uses in ornament design and illustration, a fate which is hard to imagine for these artists.

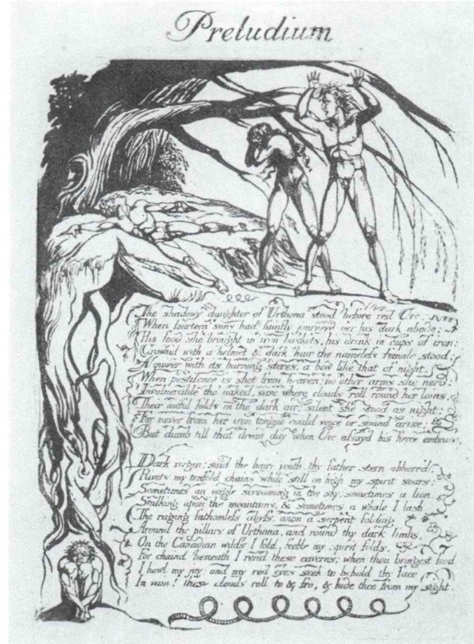

fig.23 William Blake (1757–1827), 'Preludium', plate from *America: A Prophecy* 1793, relief etching, plate size 23 x 17 cm. The British Museum, London

23

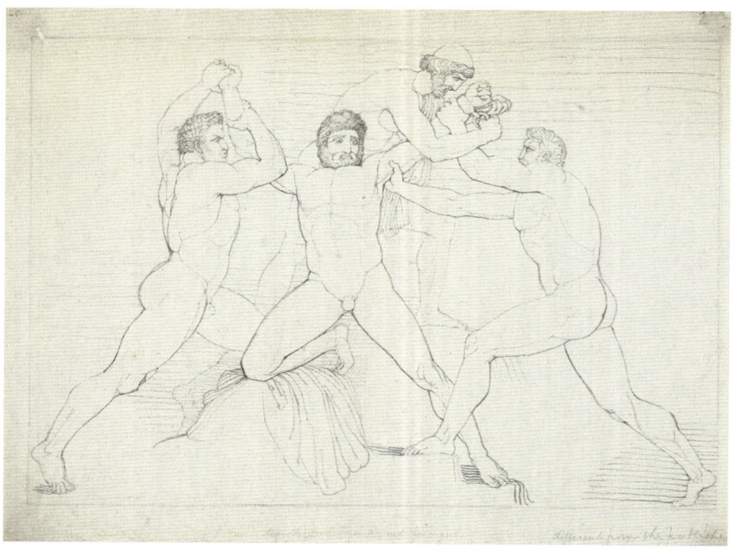

24

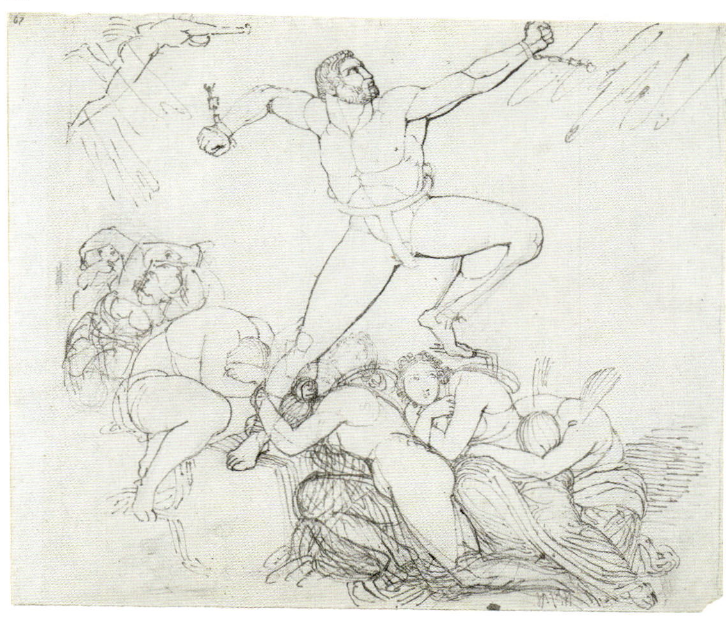

25

William Blake 1757–1827
Los and Orc c.1790–4
Pen and ink and watercolour on paper
21.7 x 29.5 cm
Tate. Presented by Mrs Jane Samuel in memory of her husband 1962

An allegorical scene, which can be interpreted through Blake's invented iconography: Orc, the embodiment of energy and the powers of revolution, is shown chained to a rock in a blasted, bleak landscape, while a second figure, who can be identified as his punitively minded father Los, laments their situation.

The theme of the chaining of Orc by his parents is a key element in Blake's personal mythos. This is a version of a design which appears on the 'Preludium' plate of Blake's illuminated book *America: A Prophecy* (dated 1793, but produced 1791–3; fig.23). The dating of the present work proceeds from the assumption that the watercolour must post-date the realisation of that printed design, although a slightly earlier date for the present sheet is conceivable (see Butlin 1990, no.13; Viscomi 1994, p.54). That printed design accompanies a poetic account – which may stand aside from the main text of *America* – of the youthful Orc being chained by his father Urthona. The pictorial element includes both a male and a female figure lamenting Orc's fate. The iconography of the present watercolour is further linked to Blake's poem *Vala or the Four Zoas* (c.1795–7), where Orc is chained by his parents, now named – as would become standard with Blake – Los instead of Urthona, and Enitharmon. A scene of Orc being chained by his parents also appeared in a separate relief-etched plate by Blake, of 1812.

The chaining of Orc is generally interpreted as representing the restraint of natural energy and the powers of revolution: he is, emphatically, a Prometheus-like figure. Los represents a dimension of the artist, who guides and controls the forces of revolution. In the context of *America: A Prophecy*, Orc seems to represent the young nation of America, while his father Urthona is a more tyrannical figure to be associated with George III (Behrendt 1986).

Blake's invented world of characters continues to resist ready delineation: the function and nature of his different figures shifts in different contexts. However, his visual debt to Fuseli, and the extent to which his formal and thematic interests were shared with other contemporaries, is greatly apparent in designs such as this one.

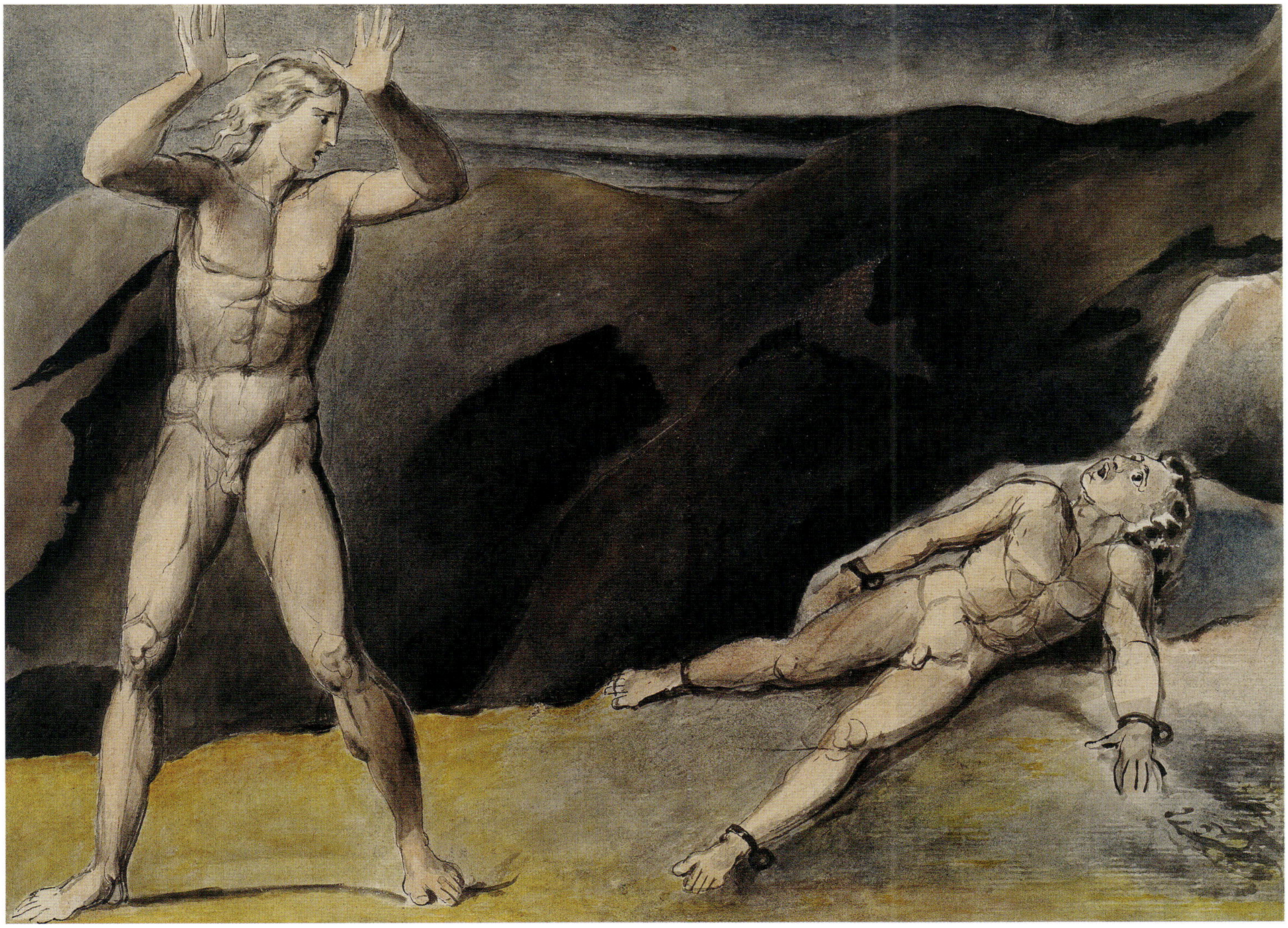

26

William Blake 1757–1827
The Blasphemer c.1800
Pen and watercolour on paper 38.4 x 34 cm
Tate. Bequeathed by Miss Alice G.E. Carthew 1940

A rather slight biblical reference is transformed by Blake into a scene of fantastic, grotesque physical drama. The source is thought to be the story of Moses condemning to death the blasphemous son of an Israelite woman, from Leviticus 24:10–25 (Butlin 1990, no.40). This identification appeared on the old mount for this drawing, in an inscription that is understood to derive from Blake himself. The authority of these inscriptions has been subject to some discussion, and accordingly it has also been suggested that the subject is, instead, the stoning of Achan from Joshua 7:18–25 (see Taylor 1968, pp.63–7). Having confessed to sinfully coveting rich clothes, gold and silver, Achan is condemned to death by stoning and his worldly goods burned and stoned, on the orders of Joshua. If the horribly contorted victim here was Achan, this would explain the plumes of dark smoke that occupy the centre of the composition.

Either subject might be interpreted as a condemnation of the brutality of the laws laid down by the Old Testament prophets, although the culpable materialism of Achan might complicate the meaning of the story if he is actually the victim. As Mary Lynn Johnson has noted, such designs may extend Blake's comments that 'the Divinity of the books in the Bible' consists 'in the Sentiments & Examples which whether true or Parabolic are Equally useful as Examples given to us of the perverseness of some & its consequent evil & the honesty of others and its consequent good' (see Johnson 1983, pp.44–5).

This is one of over 135 watercolour and painted illustrations to the Bible paid for by Thomas Butts (1757–1845), Blake's most constant patron in the middle part of his career (see Butlin 1981, pp.335–6 and nos.433–56). For further examples, see nos.134, 138–42. He had already commissioned tempera paintings on biblical themes from the artist in 1799 – Blake mentioned as many as fifty in a letter of the time, although not nearly that many survive. In 1800 a second series, of watercolours, was requested. It remains uncertain how far Blake considered the series as a sustained exploration of biblical themes, whether he considered them all in relation to closely related groups, or whether he progressed individual designs quite independently. Blake's complex and interpretive relationship with scripture may further complicate our understanding of him as an 'illustrator' of the Bible (see Heppner 1995, pp.170–206). Furthermore, the dating of individual works remains open to discussion, although Blake appears to have finished work on the series by 1806.

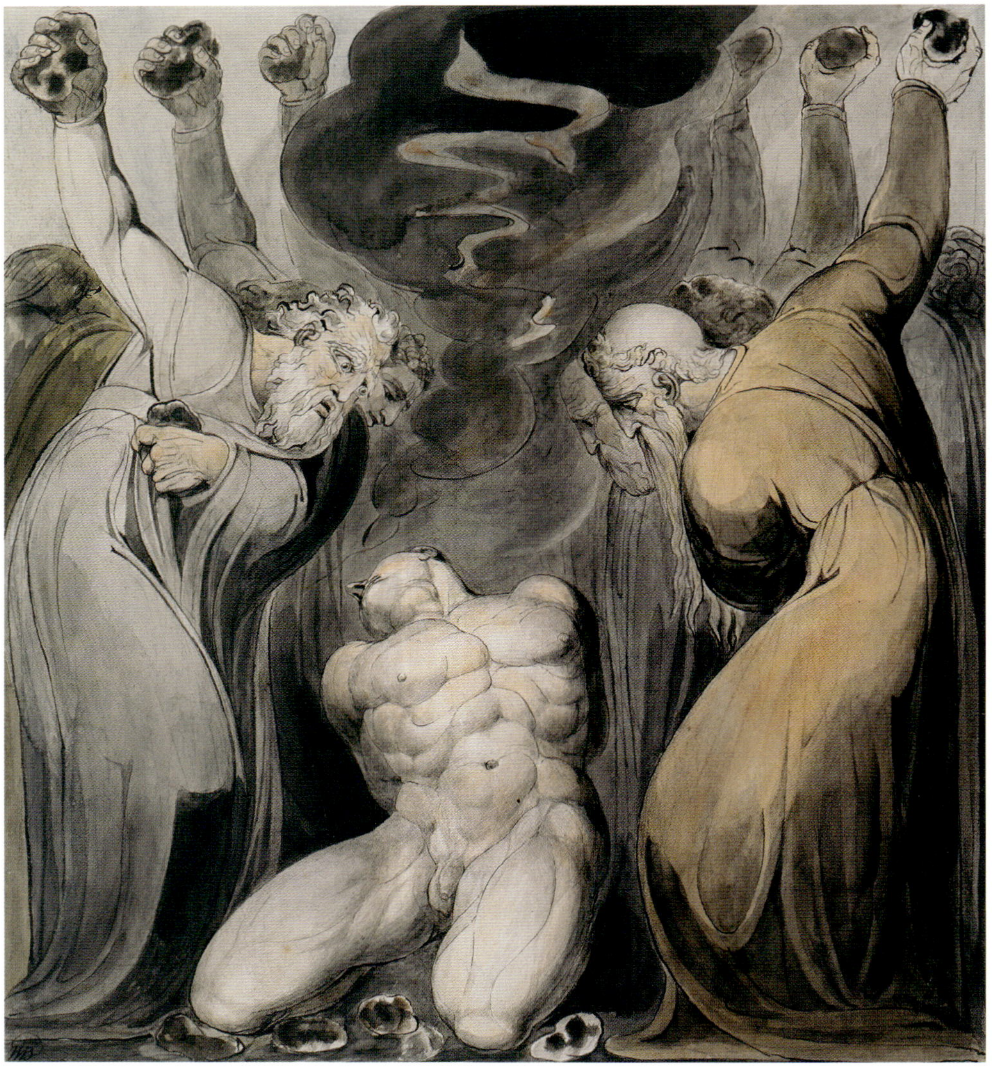

Leviticus 24:16, 23

And he that blasphemeth the name of the LORD, he shall surely be put to death, and all the congregation shall certainly stone him: as well as the stranger, as he that is born in the land, when he blasphemeth the name of the LORD, shall be put to death …
And Moses spake to the children of Israel, that they should bring forth him that had cursed out of the camp, and stone him with stones. And the children of Israel did as the LORD commanded Moses.

Joshua 8:24–5

And Joshua, and all Israel with him, took Achan the son of Serah, and the silver, and the garment, and the wedge of gold, and his sons, and his daughters, and his oxen, and his asses, and his sheep, and his tent, and all that he had, and they brought them unto the valley of Achor.
And Joshua said, Why hast thou troubled us? the Lord shall trouble thee this day. And all Israel stoned him with stones, and burned them with fire, after they had stoned them with stones.

27

Henry Fuseli 1741–1825
Brunhild Watching Gunther Suspended from the Ceiling on their Wedding Night 1807
Pencil, ink and wash on paper 48.3 x 31.7 cm
Nottingham City Museums and Galleries
[Illustrated on p.68]

Marital problems of the most severe kind, from the German medieval epic the *Nibelungenlied*, are depicted here. The Burgundian king, Gunther, has just celebrated his marriage to the icily sexy Brunhild – whose hand has been hard-won only through the interventions of the hero Siegfried – but while he expected a night of passion the new queen wrestles him into submission, binds his hands and feet and leaves him hanging from the ceiling so she can sleep undisturbed (see Schiff 1973, no.1381).

Fuseli was at the forefront of knowledge about the *Nibelungenlied* (see Klemm 2005). His teacher at Zurich, Johann Jakob Bodmer (1698–1783), had been the first to publish a portion of a manuscript of the epic in 1755; the first full German edition was Christoph Heinrich Myller's (1782), which we know that Fuseli owned. In around 1805–7 Fuseli drew a series of scenes from the *Nibelungen* narrative (see also nos.49–50). The artist also wrote a number of original poetic pieces on themes taken from this work. He would have been one of the very few in England to know much about this source, at least at first hand; it was not translated into English until well into the nineteenth century. His interpretation drew out the abrasive sexual politics of the original, with potent women, graceful heroes, and themes of erotic frustration and allure prevailing.

The Nibelungenlied (c.1200), trans. A.T. Hatto (1965)

His attendants, both man and woman, had left him. The chamber was quickly barred, and he imagined that he was soon to enjoy her lovely body: but the time when Brunhild would become his wife was certainly not at hand! She went to the bed in a shift of fine white linen, and the noble knight thought to himself: 'Now I have everything here that I ever wished for'. And indeed there was great cause why her beauty should gratify him deeply. He dimmed the lights one after another with his own royal hands, and then, dauntless warrior, he went to the lady. He laid himself close beside her, and with a great rush of joy took the adorable woman in his arms.

He would have lavished caresses and endearments, had the Queen suffered him to do so, but she flew into a rage that deeply shocked him — he had hoped to meet with 'friend', yet what he met was 'foe'!

'Sir', she said, 'you must give up the thing you have set your hopes on, for it will not come to pass. Take good note of this: I intend to stay a maiden till I have learned the truth about Siegfried.'

Gunther grew very angry with her. He tried to win her by force, and tumbled her shift for her, at which the haughty girl reached for the girdle of stout silk cord that she wore about her waist, and subjected him to great suffering and shame; for in return for being baulked of her sleep, she bound him hand and foot, carried him to a nail, and hung him on the wall. She had put a stop to his love-making! As to him, he had all but died, such strength had she exerted.

And now he who had thought to be master began to entreat her, 'Loose my bonds, most noble Queen. I do not fancy I shall ever subdue you, lovely woman, and I shall never again lie to close to you.'

She did not care at all how he fared, since she was lying very snug. He had to stay hanging there the whole night through to dawn, when the bright morning shone through the windows. If Gunther had ever possessed of any strength, it had dwindled to nothing now.

(Hatto 1969, pp.87–8)

28

Henry Fuseli 1741–1825
Hephaestus, Bia and Crato Securing Prometheus on Mount Caucasus c.1800–1810
Pencil and grey wash on paper 35.9 x 30.2 cm
Auckland Art Gallery Toi o Tāmaki. Purchased 1965
[Illustrated on p.69]

Illustrating the opening scene of Aeschylus's *Prometheus Bound*, the rebel Titan is bound foot, arm and chest to a mountaintop; Crato ('Strength') holding down Prometheus's right arm, commands Hephaestus, the god of fire, to drive a spike through his heart. Crato's sister Bia ('Force') holds the spike to his chest in preparation. Zeus and the vulture await in the upper right-hand corner (see Schiff 1973, no.1790; Tomory 1979, no.24).

Fuseli returned to the theme of Prometheus on a number of occasions (Schiff 1973, nos.711, 1791). This, the most elaborate, offers a scene of intensely sexualised torture, simultaneously tender and perverse. The dominant position of Hephaestus and the emphasis on his exposed buttocks, and the yet more explicit posture of the naked Prometheus, suggest an act of sexual violence even while their bodies barely touch. On the other hand, Bia, the personification of violence, leans down towards Prometheus's face in an intimate fashion, her hands gently but firmly grasping the phallically erect spike sitting upon his exposed chest. Prometheus's pose had appeared in a frankly sexual drawing by Fuseli in the 1770s, which features a woman crouching and manipulating the figure's erect penis just as Bia here handles the spike. In both cases, Fuseli's source for the dramatic foreshortening of the male figure is the radically foreshortened figures that appear in early Renaissance prints by Albrecht Altdorfer (c.1480–1538) and Hans Baldung Grien (1484/5–1545), particularly his famously weird print *The Bewitched Groom* (1544) (see Weinglass 1991, p.300). This radical perspective effects an inversion of the normal organisation of the body, with the 'lowly' anus and genitals gaining visual priority over the 'elevated' head and brain. The sexual submissiveness and degradation implied by this treatment had been exposed in a startlingly scatological woodcut by Peter Flötner (1485/6–1546), *The Human Sundial* (c.1535–40) (see the illustrations and discussion in Koerner 1993, p.441). This image may also have been in Fuseli's recollection in composing the present design.

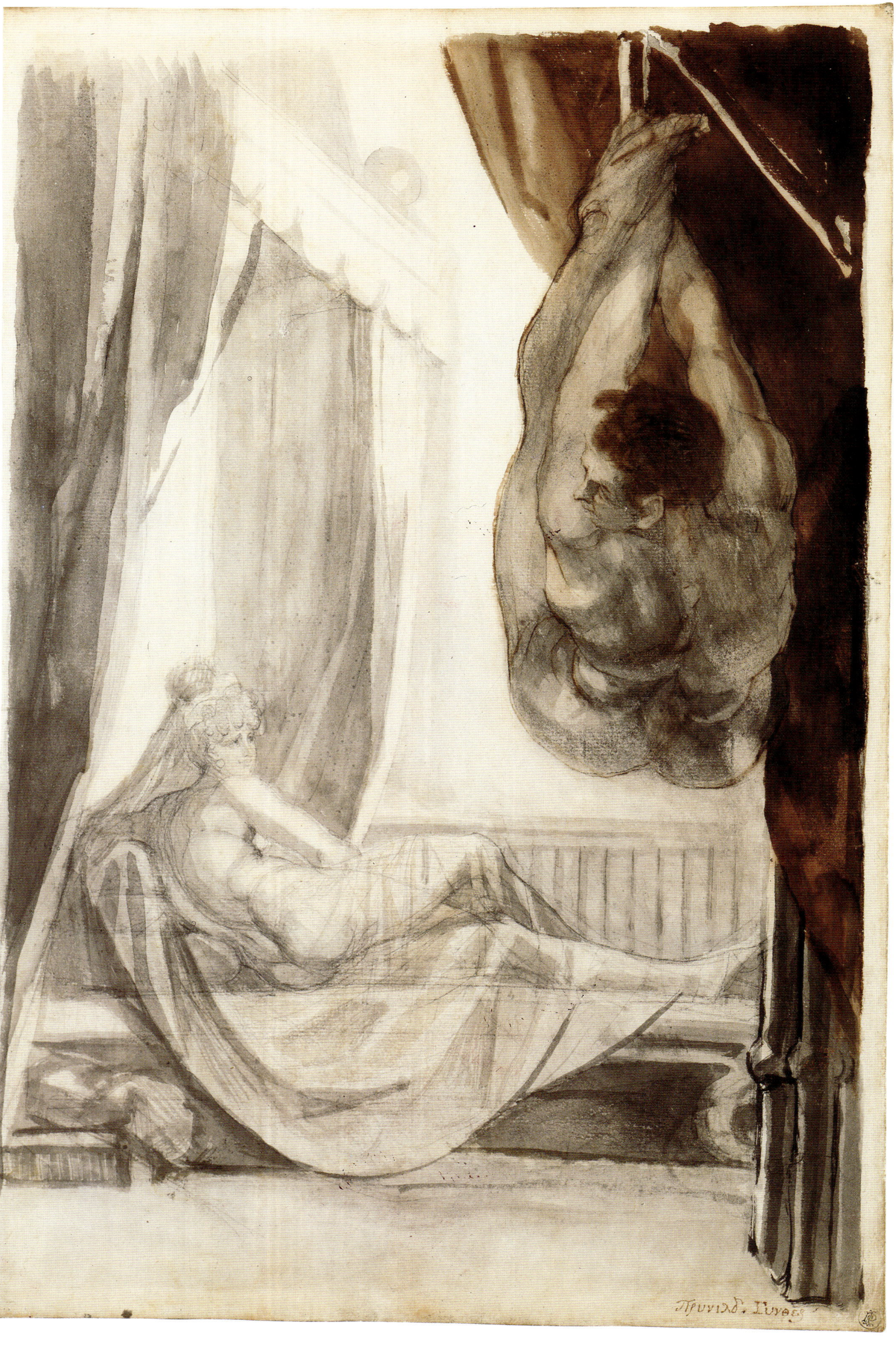

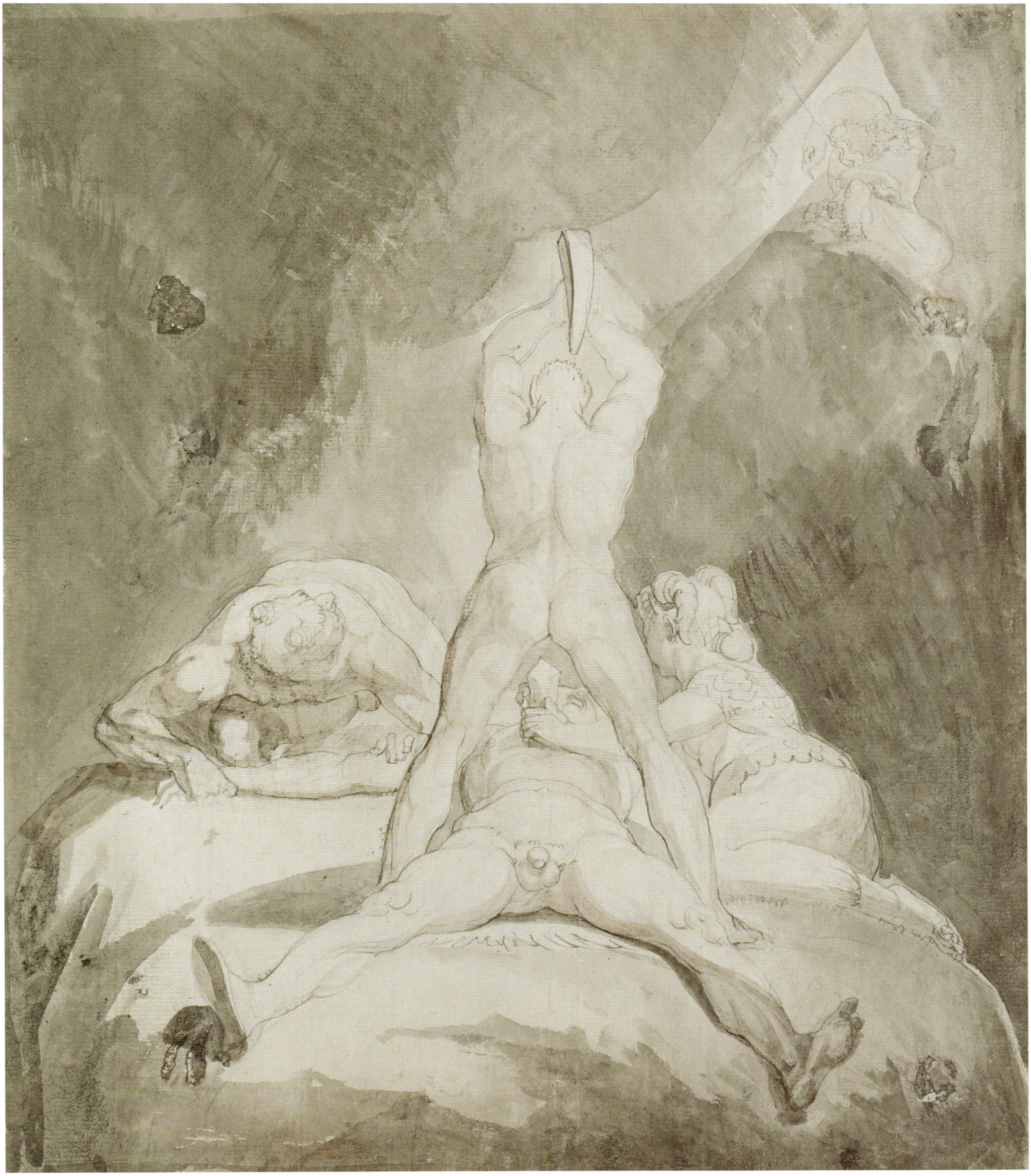

29

William Blake 1757–1827
The Punishment of the Thieves c.1824–7
Black chalk, pen and ink, and watercolour on paper 37.2 x 52.7 cm
Tate. Purchased with the assistance of a special grant from the National Gallery and donations from the National Art Collections Fund, Lord Duveen and others, and presented through the National Art Collections Fund 1919

A writhing mass of statuesque bodies are locked together beside a pool or lake in a compressed composition. It is assumed that this represents the 'Punishment of the Thieves' that Dante and Virgil witness in the eighth circle of Hell, described in Cantos 24 and 25 of *Inferno*, where the punished are attacked by snakes and transformed into monstrous serpents (Butlin 1990, no.150). As with Fuseli's design from a half-century earlier (no.15), it may be difficult to pin this design to a specific line or scene, and rather makes the most of the possibilities for grotesque spectacle offered by Dante.

Blake undertook an extended series of watercolours illustrating Dante in the last three years of his life (Roe 1953; Klonsky 1980; Butlin 1990, pp.202–3). Commissioned by John Linnell (1793–1882), one of the younger generation of artists who gathered around Blake in his final years, the series eventually included 102 designs, finished to varying degrees. Just seven of these were engraved by Blake and printed in proof form before he died.

The relationship between Blake's designs and Dante's text remains debatable (Fuller 1988; Baine 1987). The individual designs have tended to be interpreted in relation to Blake's idiosyncratic mythology and ideas, rather than as direct and deliberate illustrations of the original text. Certainly, Blake's recorded views of the Italian poet's approach to morality and punishment tend to be quite negative (Moskal 1991). This drawing provides some kind of test case. Roe, who saw in this design seven female figures, suggests that it relates to Dante's text only in a rather general way, serving instead as an illustration of Blake's principle 'that the attempt of the Female Will to dominate ultimately brings disaster upon itself' (Roe 1953, p.200). However, the figures do appear to be of both sexes. Klonsky, who could see only five figures, although of both sexes, relates this more closely to Dante's text (Klonsky 1980, p.118). Morton Paley has connected this scene more closely still with Canto 24 (Paley 2003, p.137). Whichever may be the case, the image resonates with a full half-century of grotesque and fantastic imagery, combining the heroic conception of the body defined by Fuseli and his contemporaries in Rome in the 1770s with simultaneously horrifying and enticing Gothic sexuality, apparent in the suggestive presence of snakes crawling between and over the figures' legs.

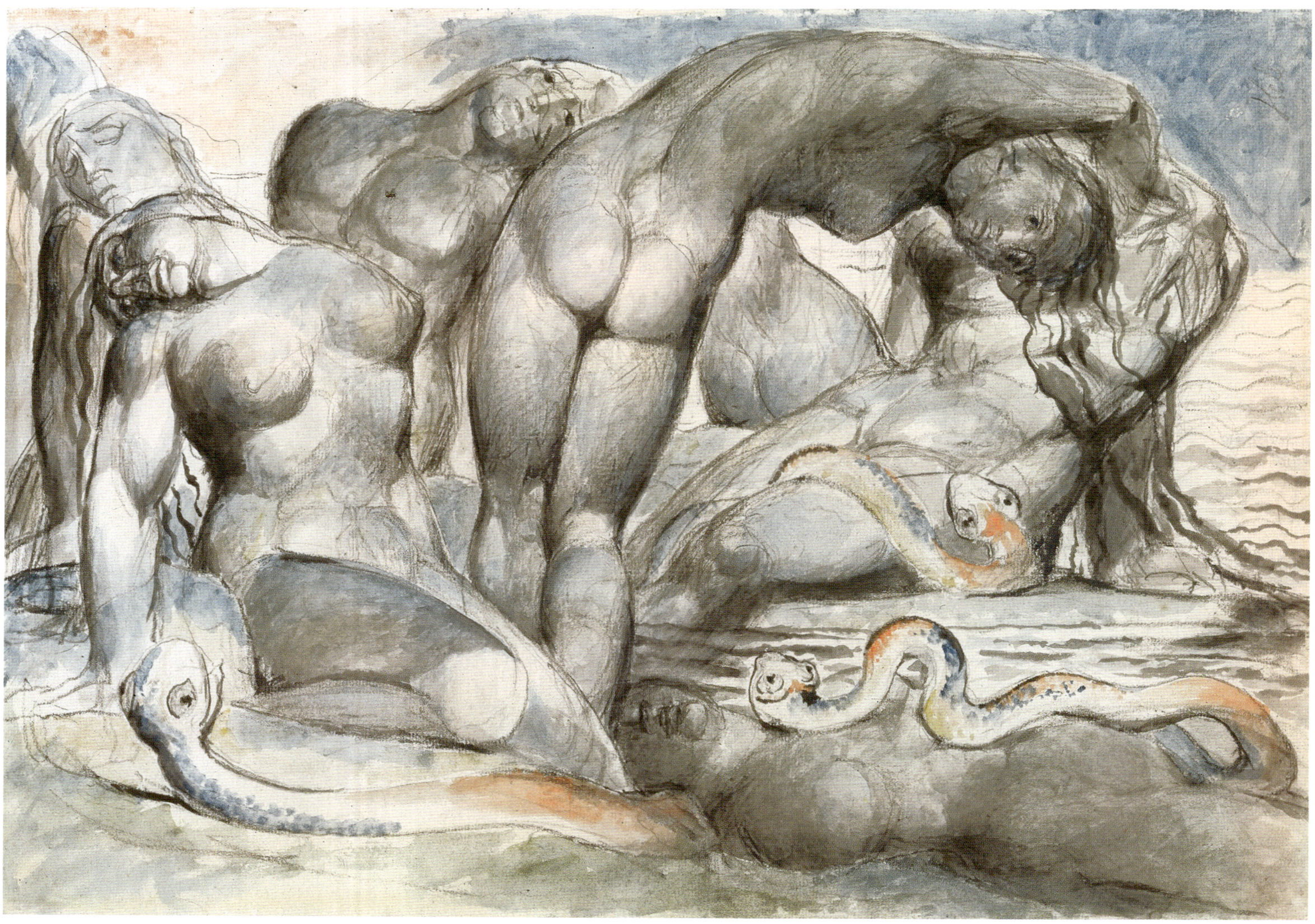

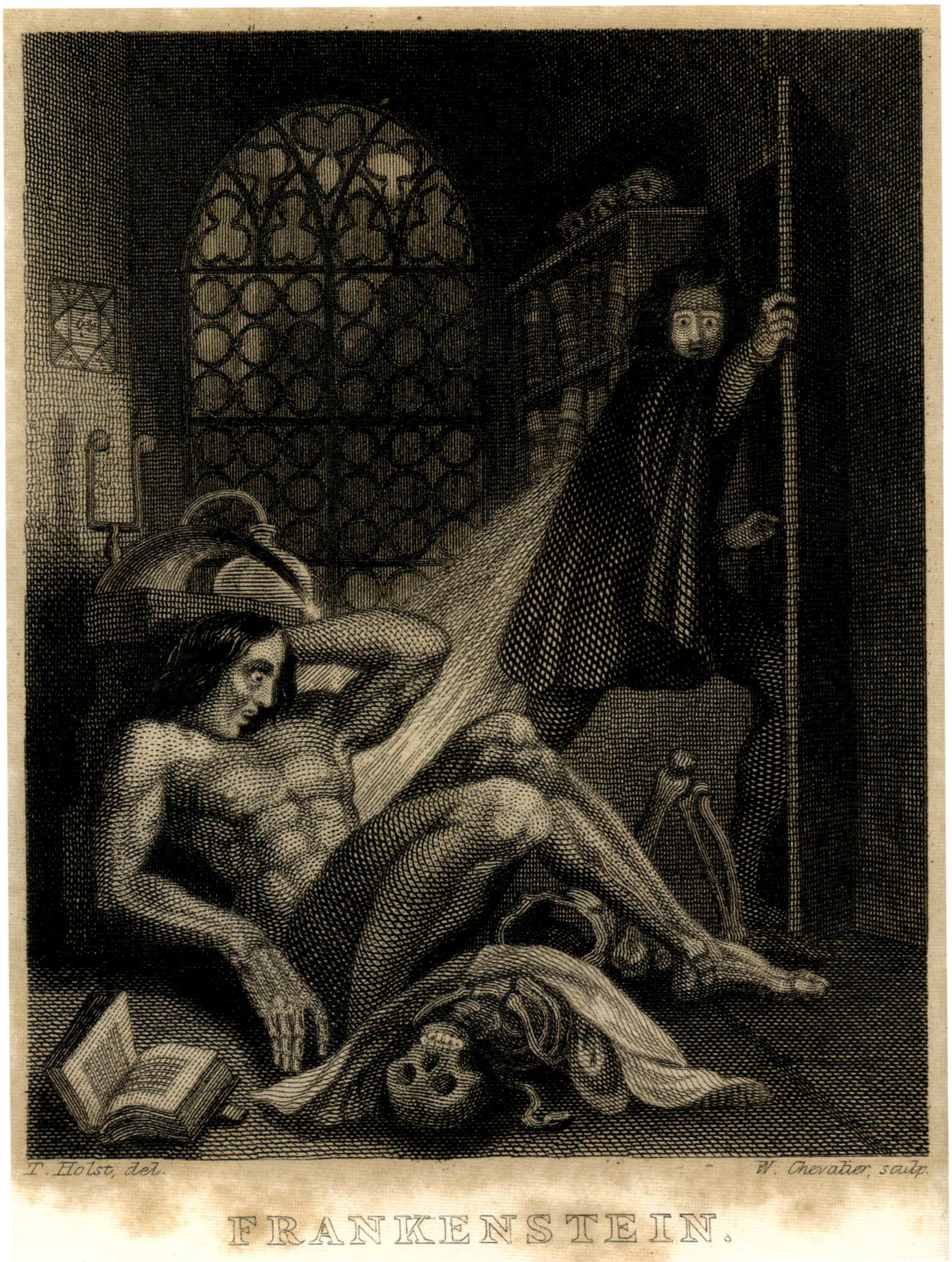

30

W. Chevalier after Theodor von Holst
1810–1844
Frontispiece to Mary Shelley, *Frankenstein*, published by Colburn and Bentley, London 1831
Steel engraving 9.3 x 7.1 cm
Private collection, Bath

This is the first illustrated edition of Mary Shelley's *Frankenstein* (1818). The novel had first been published anonymously. This new pocket-sized edition was intended to reach out to the popular market, and included revisions and a new preface by the author. Here, she acknowledged her authorship and dramatised the circumstances of its creation, evoking the night of story-telling by Lake Geneva in June 1816 with Lord Byron, Mary Shelley and John Polidori as a full-blooded Gothic event, with storms and passions raging (see Shelley 2003, pp.353–9).

Von Holst's frontispiece plays to such Gothic trappings, setting the scene in a medieval chamber, strewn with skulls and a skeleton and illuminated by a weird lunar efflorescence. The theatrical effect of Frankenstein's up-lit features and dynamic posture reflect the taste for melodrama that was apparent in the theatre and literature that von Holst, a self-consciously 'romantic' artist, admired and drew from (see Browne 1994). The monster is, though, weirdly classical, even heroic in physique, matching Shelley's description:

> How can I describe my emotions at this catastrophe, or how delineate the wretch whom with such infinite pains and care I had endeavoured to form? His limbs were in proportion, and I had selected his features as beautiful. Beautiful! Great God! His yellow skin scarcely covered the work of muscles and arteries beneath; his hair was of a lustrous black, and flowing; his teeth of a pearly whiteness; but these luxuriances only formed a more horrid contrast with his watery eyes, that seemed almost of the same colour as the dun-white sockets in which they were set, his shrivelled complexion and straight black lips ... unable to endure the aspect of the being I had created, I rushed out of the room.
> (Shelley 2003, p.85)

Shelley was conscious of the mythic dimension to her narrative, subtitling her novel 'The Modern Prometheus'. In the present context, von Holst's heavy-limbed monster evokes the previous half-century of perverted classicism, emanating in large part from the influence of Fuseli and the Promethean ambitions of the artists and poets of the later eighteenth century. We can trace the original of such a confined, heroic figure in the drawings of Fuseli and his circle created in Rome in the 1770s (for example, nos.14–16 here). The young von Holst admired the old painter passionately, to the extent of copying and pastiching his works (see no.119).

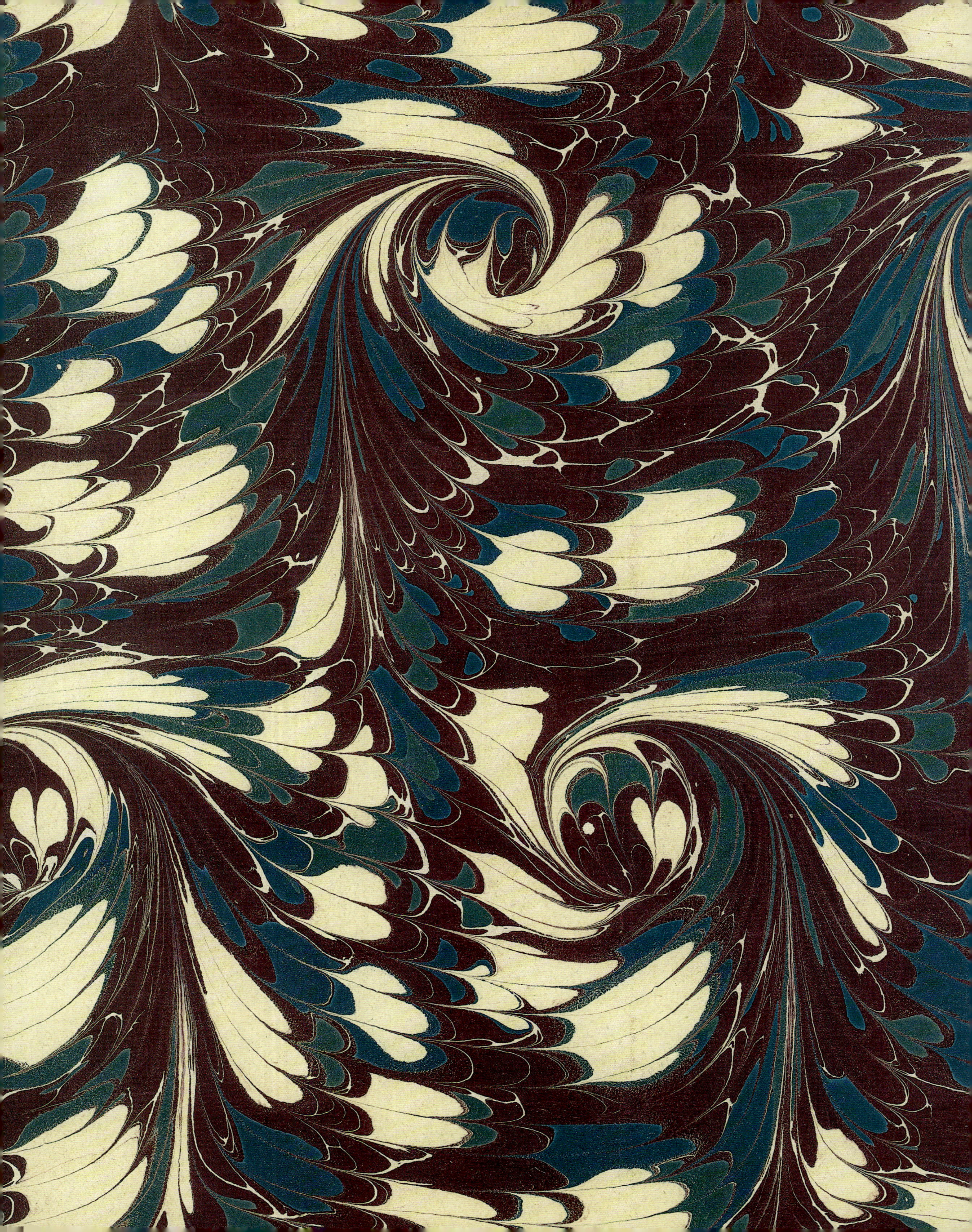

Superheroes

The paintings and drawings in this section show how the dynamic conception of the body introduced by artists in Rome in the late 1760s and 1770s was assimilated into narrative art produced in Britain. The selection makes evident the tendency to extravagant physicality and fantastic action that appeared in the later eighteenth century, and the emergence of distinctly 'Gothic' types of superhero drawn from literature and history.

According to theorists, the most elevated forms of art should exemplify strenuous intellectual and moral aspirations, as embodied in the figure of the ideal hero. For the high-minded art writers of the early eighteenth century such ideal heroes were the role-models for an exclusive elite of men, who could identify with and emulate such figures. To ensure that was the case, such images had to be based on a narrowly defined canon of Latin and Greek texts or ancient history, and be presented in the socially restricted spaces of the palace or grand house. The common people could neither have access to nor properly appreciate such rarefied expressions of heroism, it was claimed. Alternatively, a more moderate and realistic model of heroism could be found in the literature and social commentary actually consumed by a large sector of the populace. Orientated to the middle-rank of society, this ideal of masculine virtue did not require elevated pictorial representation. (For discussions of the hero in eighteenth-century British culture see Hägin 1964; Wardropper 1976; Folkenflik 1982; de Bruyn 1987. For the visual arts see Solkin 1993; Myrone 2005.)

Traditionally, British artists had only very rarely had the opportunity – and perhaps the desire – to actually produce such images. But the 1760s were a turning point, and with the encouragement of the new Royal Academy of Arts and the promise of new sources of patronage, many artists began to pursue such themes. But the images that resulted undermined as much as they secured the image of the ideal hero, and were orientated to the tastes and needs of a cultural public more socially diversified than had ever previously been imagined. Bounding, leaping, flying, extravagantly proportioned, super-virile and ultra-violent, the heroes that appeared were inevitably improbable and irrational, and required a decided suspension of disbelief to be enjoyed. Instead of providing role-models of equitable behaviour and ethical nobility, they were supremely, sometimes vacuously, spectacular. Nor can the sexual dimension of these figures be overlooked, exemplifying the forms of ecstatic fulfilment associated with the Sublime, providing flattering self-images for male spectators, but also, perhaps uneasily, playing on the eroticisation of the male body in ways that might subvert the heterosexist norms of the dominant sectors of society.

After the 1760s, artists, critics and writers expanded and revised ideals of heroism, exploring the possibility of thinking about heroic action in relation to the concepts of the Sublime and Gothic. The primitive, savage, even antisocial forms of heroic physicality associated with the ancient world were reappraised. Homer's brutal and irrational hero Achilles was thought about afresh. New heroes joined the canon, drawn now from real and invented medieval legend, epic and romance, from a reinvigorated interpretation of Spenser, Milton and Shakespeare and from the bleak world of Ossian, the ancient Gaelic Bard, elaborated by James Macpherson. The visual characterisation of such heroes enhanced the sense of improbability attached to these figures. Fuseli, in particular, specialised in producing images of extreme physicality, attenuating and stylising the bodies of his heroes. Their development demonstrated the willingness of the new cultural public to embrace forms of imagery that discarded with the ponderous worthiness of elite culture, the hollow distinctions between legitimate 'high culture' and the guilty pleasures – traditionally associated with children and the lower class – of 'low' adventure and romance.

Tellingly, the images included here may seem more reminiscent of modern comic books than the grand traditions of European high art. The often supremely crafted designs of superhero comic strips and graphic novels play on the same rejection of spatial logic, gravity and anatomical restraint that we find here. More generally, the power of the superhero as a cultural figure persists, as manifested in the phenomenon of protestors for father's rights in our own time dressing up as such characters. Their activities reveal the deep-seated desires that underpin fantasies of modern masculinity – desires whose open expression may be knowingly ridiculous (fig.24). The very absurdity of such activity may emphasise a poignant sense of alienation from masculine archetypes, an understanding that the pursuit of the physical and moral perfection and stoical heroism expected of men may be foolish, frustrated, even impossible.

Henry Fuseli to Salomon Dälliker, letter of November 1765

The Englishman eats roastbeef and plumpudding, drinks port and claret; therefore, if you will read him, you must open the portals of Hell with the hand of Milton, convulse his ear or his sides with Shakespeare's buskin or sock, raise him above the stars with Dryden's Cecilia or sink him to the melancholy of the grave with Gray. Intermediate tones, though they were as sweet as honey, as lovely as the flush of dawn, send him to sleep.

(Mason 1951, pp.110–11)

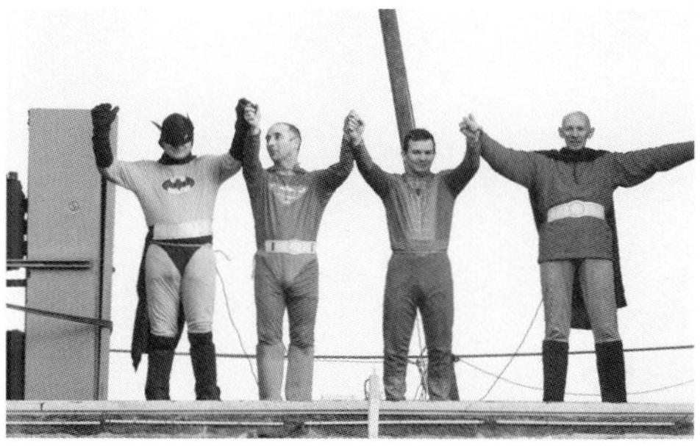

fig.24 Protesting fathers' rights, campaigners dress as superheroes, London

31

Henry Fuseli 1741–1825
King Lear Supported by Kent and the Fool Meeting Edgar on the Heath c.1772
Pen and wash on paper 61 x 97.5 cm
Birmingham City Museums & Art Gallery. Supported by the National Art Collections Fund, Heritage Lottery Fund, and the MGC/V&A Purchase Grant Fund, the Rowlands Trust, the Public Picture Gallery Fund and donations from John Kenrick and Pinsent Curtis

In a scene from Shakespeare's *King Lear* (Act III, scene 4), Edgar, son of the Earl of Gloucester, disguised as 'poor Tom', confronts an increasingly deranged Lear on the stormy heath. Despairing, the king discards his clothes while struggling with his supporters, the Earl of Kent and the Fool.

The amplitude of physique and gesture is matched in this instance by the scale of the drawing. Fuseli's experiments on this large scale coincide with efforts by other artists to create works on paper on an unusually large format. In England, Thomas Gainsborough was at this point creating large-scale drawings intended to have the substance and durability of paintings. Fuseli's contemporaries in Rome, James Jefferys and George Romney, created large-scale drawings of a similar type to this (see no.17). It does not appear that these drawings acted simply as studio preparations, as sometimes suggested (cf. Licht, Pizzetti and Weinglass 1997, no.43). Such experiments challenged academic distinctions between the finished and the unfinished, the public and the more personal and expressive (see Rosenthal 1997, pp.249–74).

King Lear and Shakespeare's other tragedies emerged as Fuseli's preoccupation in his drawings of the 1770s, and remained a central source of subject matter throughout his career. Shakespeare's work had been painted by artists before, although it tended always to be presented as staged enactments of a play rather than being taken as a literary source. The rise of Shakespearean painting with Fuseli and his circle is a complex phenomenon (Boase 1947; Merchant 1959; Pape and Burwick 1996). It registers how Shakespeare began to be appreciated as a literary writer on his own terms, how literature and art might now be assessed by the subjective measures of the Sublime and original genius. It also reflects the widening social character of the market for art, encompassing patrons and consumers of images who were more likely to be familiar with the texts of Shakespeare (either as readers or as theatre-goers) than with the Greek and Latin texts that were the backbone of the classical education of the landowning elite. The plays themselves contained emotive, violent and supernatural material that was perfectly attuned to contemporary tastes. Furthermore, the rising cultural nationalism encouraged a reappraisal of writers who, judged by the stricter rules of composition and propriety enforced by literary theory, might be otherwise found wanting.

William Shakespeare, King Lear (c.1605), Act III, scene 4, ll.79–109

FOOL. *This cold night will turn us all to fools and madmen.*
EDGAR. *Take heed o' th' foul fiend. Obey thy parents, keep thy word's justice; swear not, commit not with man's sworn spouse, set not thy sweet heart on proud array. Tom's a-cold.*
LEAR. *What hast thou been?*
EDGAR. *A serving man! Proud in heart and mind; that curl'd my hair; wore gloves in my cap; serv'd the lust of my mistress' heart, and did the act of darkness with her; swore as many oaths as I spake words, and broke them in the sweet face of heaven: one that slept in the contriving of lust, and wak'd to do it. Wine loved I deeply, dice dearly; and in woman out-paramour'd the Turk. False of heart, light of ear, bloody of hand; hog in sloth, fox in stealth, wolf in greediness, dog in madness, lion in prey. Let not the creaking of shoes nor the rustling of silks betray thy poor heart to woman. Keep thy foot out of brothels, thy hand out of plackets, thy pen from lenders' books, and defy the foul fiend. Still through the hawthorn blows the cold wind: says suum, mun, ha, no, nonny. Dolphin my boy, boy, sessa! let him trot by.*

Storm still

LEAR. *Why, thou wert better in a grave than to answer with thy uncover'd body this extremity of the skies. Is man no more than this? Consider him well. Thou owest the worm no silk, the beast no hide, the sheep no wool, the cat no perfume. Ha? here's three on's are sophisticated! Thou art the thing itself: unaccommodated man is no more but such a poor, bare, fork'd animal as thou art. Off, off, you lendings! Come unbutton here.*

Tearing off his clothes

(Shakespeare 1997, pp.1324–5)

32

Henry Fuseli 1741–1825
King David Being Warned by the Prophet Nathan c.1772
Black chalk and grey wash over pencil on paper 61.6 x 91.8 cm
Private collection, courtesy of Aroldo Zevi Limited, London

An angry encounter between the prophet Nathan and King David, from 2 Samuel 12. Nathan has been sent by God to confront David with his sins of murder and adultery. Having kindled David's anger against the rich by use of an allegory of a man who stole a lamb from a poor person, Nathan throws the accusation back at David – 'Thou art the man' – and tells him of his punishment, that 'the child also that is born unto thee shall surely die'.

Nathan is represented by Fuseli as a bent old man, but David is an enormously muscular figure, more Herculean than monarchical. The role of the younger armed man to the right is not clear; he does, though, serve to underscore the material splendour and power of King David.

Gert Schiff, working from a photograph, suggested that it should be dated to the 1790s (Schiff 1973, no.1766). However, the style would suggest that it dates from the 1770s and the inscription, to the right, can be interpreted as 'Roma 1772' or 'Roma 1778'. The former seems more likely, not least because the scale of the design and treatment of the subject would bear comparison with no.31.

31

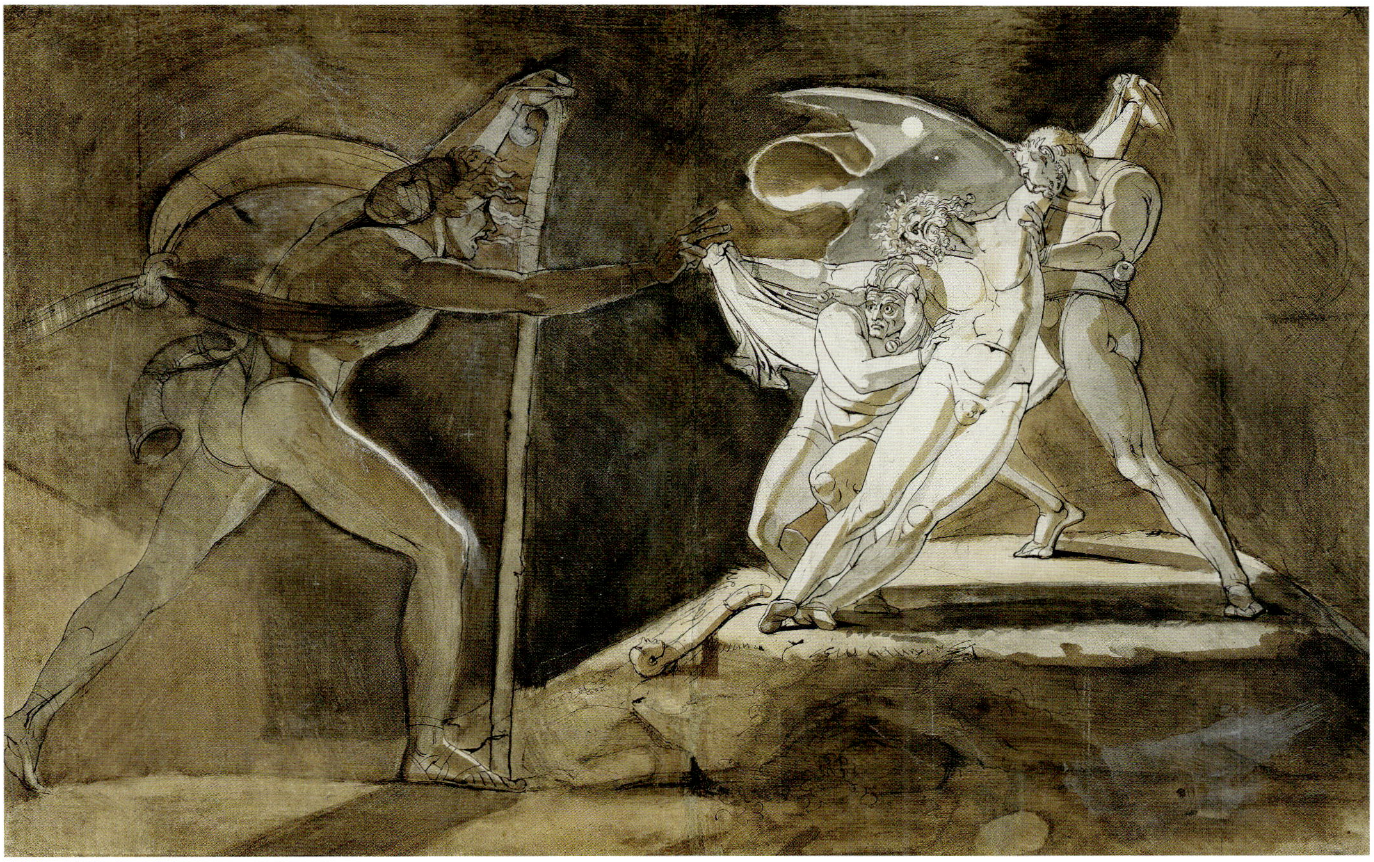

32

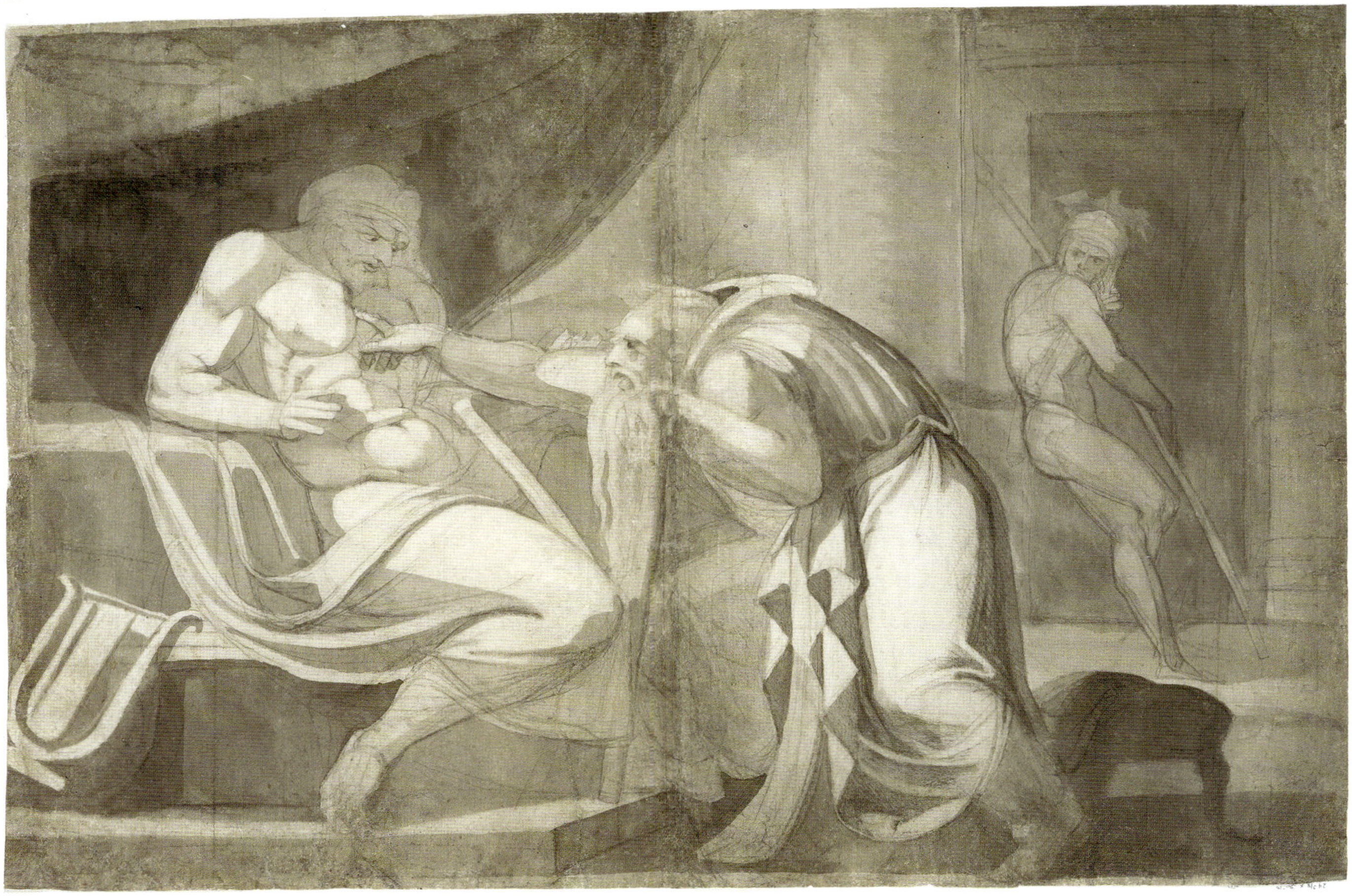

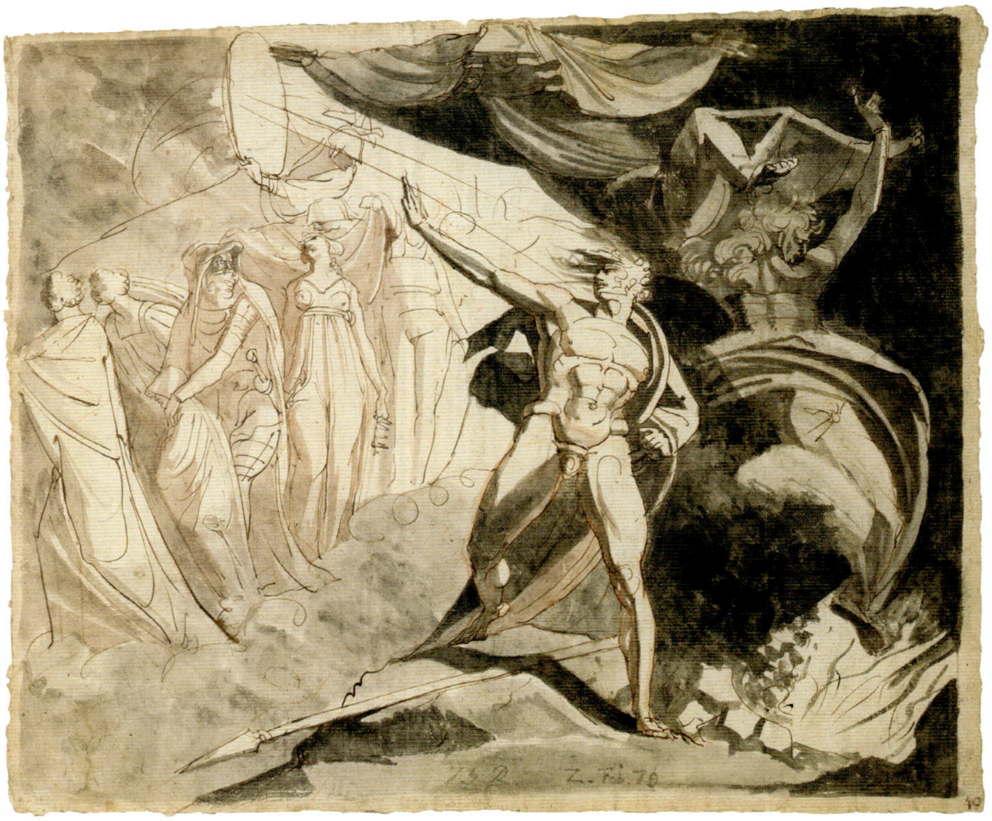

33

Henry Fuseli 1741-1825
The Witches Show Macbeth the Descendants of Banquo dated Rome 1773 and Zurich 1779
Pen and ink and wash on paper 36 x 42 cm
Kunsthaus, Zurich, Grafische Sammlung

Shakespeare's Macbeth is shown a vision of the future that he dreads by the three witches: a procession of the eight kings who will descend from his rival Banquo, the last holding up a mirror that throws light into Macbeth's eyes. This vision has been preceded by the conjured spectre of the armed head (nos. 75,90) and of two children, whose predictions had given Macbeth false hope. Now, crushed and furious, he is taunted by the witches with a dance.

This design was created in 1773 and reworked (perhaps only with the addition of wash) while the artist was briefly revisiting his home town of Zurich in 1779 (Schiff 1973, no.458). It exemplifies Fuseli's approach to Shakespearean themes. The figure of Macbeth is closely based on the classical *Dioscuri* (horsetamers) of Monte Cavallo, Rome, from whose gigantic, stylised physique Fuseli drew directly and incorporated into compositions many times during his time in Rome. The draughtsmanship, combining fine outlines and contours with loose washes, recalls Luca Cambiaso (1527-1585) and Pietro Testa (1611-1650). The supernatural subject matter is also typical of Fuseli's work from this point onwards. The formal effects - raising the figure of Macbeth above eye level and the decorative treatment of the stacked figures of the witches - accentuate the disorientating structure of the composition.

From contemporary press comments and other documentary sources it seems likely that this drawing provided the compositional basis for the huge, over life-size painting of *Macbeth* that Fuseli sent to the Royal Academy exhibition in London in 1777 (Myrone 2001b, pp.30-1). This picture, now lost, was the first opportunity that the British art-going public had to see Fuseli's imagination in full flight.

Shakespeare was Fuseli's abiding source of subject matter. According to his patron, the banker Thomas Coutts (1735-1822), the painter 'had Shakespeare's work so completely in His memory as to be able to recollect any passage alluded to' (Farington 1978-98, IX, p.3407, 24 February 1809).

William Shakespeare, Macbeth (1606), Act IV, scene 1, ll.100–24

MACBETH. – *Yet my heart*
Throbs to know one thing: tell me, if your art
Can tell so much, shall Banquo's issue ever
Reign in this kingdom?
ALL. *Seek to know no more.*
MACBETH. *I will be satisfied. Deny me this,*
And an eternal curse fall on you! Let me know.
Why sinks that cauldron? and what noise is this?

Hoboys

1 WITCH. *Show!*
2 WITCH. *Show!*
3 WITCH. *Show!*
ALL. *Show his eyes, and grieve his heart;*
Come like shadows, so depart!

A show of Eight KINGS, the eigth with
a glass in his hand, and BANQUO last

MACBETH.
Thou art too like the spirit of Banquo; down!
Thy crown does sear mine eye-balls. And thy hair,
Thou other gold-bound brow, is like the first.
A third is like the former. Filthy hags,
Why do you show me this? A fourth? Start, eyes!

Another yet? A seventh? I'll see no more.
And yet the eight appears, who bears a glass
Which shows me many more; and some I see
That two fold balls and treble scepters carry.
Horrible sight! Now, I see 'tis true;
For the blood-bolter'd Banquo smiles upon me,
And points at them for his.

Apparitions vanish

What? is this so?

(Shakespeare 1997, p.1378)

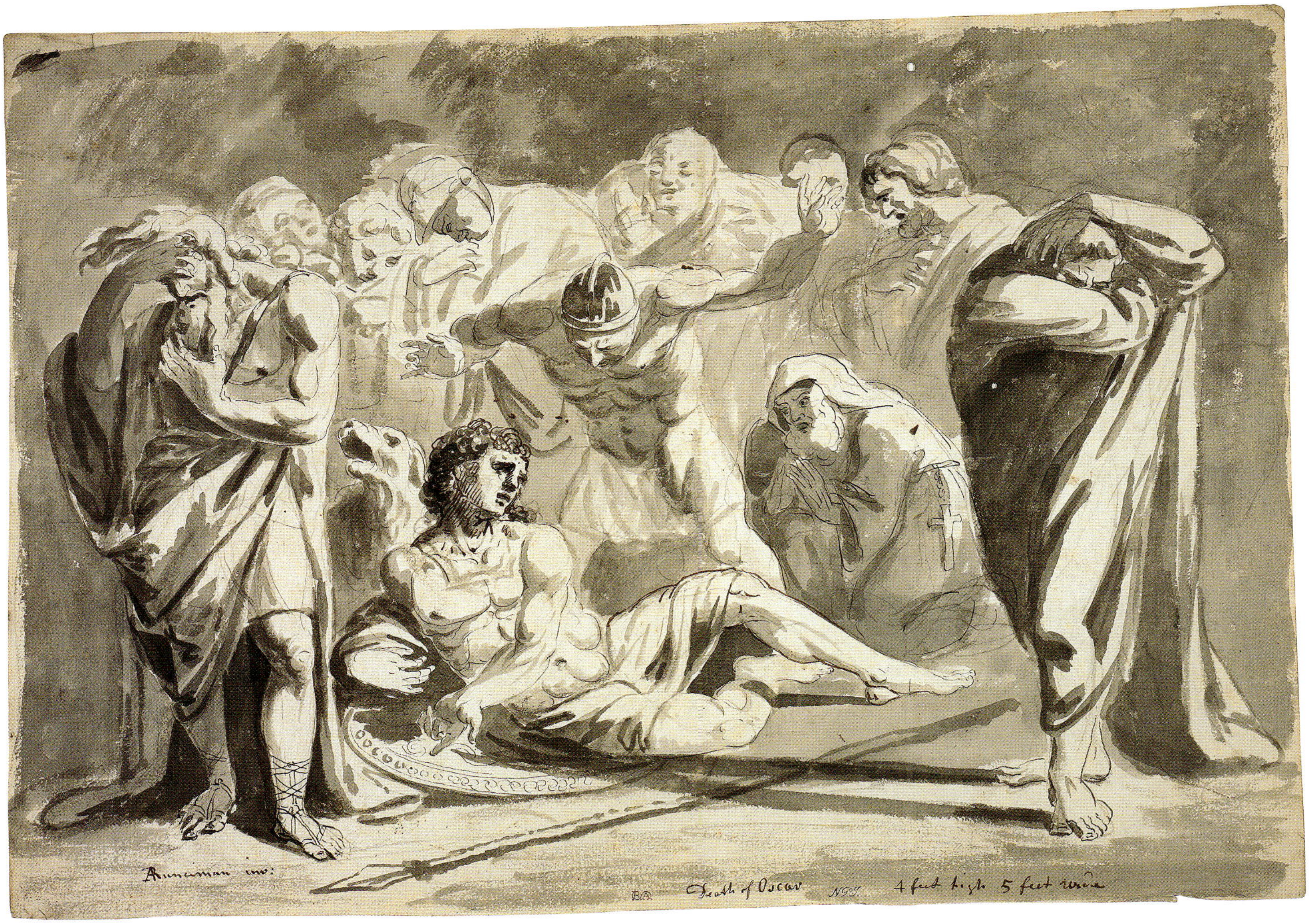

34

Alexander Runciman 1736–1785
The Death of Oscar c.1772–3
Pencil, pen and wash on paper
34.3 x 49.2 cm
National Gallery of Scotland, Edinburgh

Oscar, the ancient Gaelic hero, has fallen in battle, as evoked in James Macpherson's 'Temora, An Ancient Poem' (1763), claimed to be a translation of the third-century Gaelic bard Ossian:

> We saw Oscar on his shield. We saw his blood around. Silence darkened every face. Each turned his face and wept. The King strove to hide his tears. His grey beard whistled in the wind. He bent his head above his son. His words were mixed with sighs. (Macpherson 1996, p.230)

This drawing was prepared in connection with the painted scheme Runciman created for Penicuik Hall, near Edinburgh, on his return from Italy in 1773 (Macmillan 1978). The ceiling of the hall on the first floor was painted with scenes and figures from the works of Ossian. The scheme was destroyed by fire at the end of the nineteenth century. A published account of the scheme by Runciman's friend Walter Ross describes the finished painting:

> This piece seems to be executed in the spirit of the poet; Oscar lyes upon his shield, where he has thrown himself to save it from the enemy, and his favourite dog Bran howls at his feet; his friends are crowding around; Ossian the father has covered his head in an agony of grief; Fingal is distinguished by the grandeur of his deportment. The expression is noble, and suits the elevation of his character; 'He strives to hide his tears'. Before Oscar stands a *Culdee* ['the first Christians in Scotland'], who seems to view him with a mixture of pity and horror at his expiring in infidelity. A soldier behind, stands astonished to see his leader on the ground. Oscar seems to have forgot himself, and feels for his friends. The 'melting of the soul' is pathetically expressed, and forms altogether a most affecting, and deeply tragic scene.
> (Ross 1773, pp.28–9)

The works of Ossian, published by James Macpherson in the early 1760s, were claimed as translations in poetry and prose of an ancient Celtic bard writing before even Homer, historically the original epic writer and the standard of heroic literature. Epic, emotive and fragmentary, sometimes violent, sometimes melancholic, but always sublime and expressive, these writings conformed to the new ideals of primitive purity and masculine energy promoted by reforming writers and critics, particularly those in Scotland who saw such poetry being a means of reforming society and re-establishing national pride (Stafford 1988; Gaskill 1991; Trumpener 1997; Moore 2003). Runciman's ambitious, though awkward, conceptions seemed to his supporters to be a close visual equivalent for such values.

35

Henry Fuseli 1741–1825
Study of a Figure c.1774
Pen and ink and pencil on paper
37.4 x 35.4cm
The British Museum, London
(1885-3-14-235)

36

Henry Fuseli 1741–1825
The Soul of Buonconte da Montefeltro Is Carried up to Heaven by an Angel, his Body Is Cast into Hell by a Devil c.1774
Pen and ink and wash on paper
47.5 x 35.3 cm
The British Museum, London
(1885-3-14-262)

A scene of spiritual conflict from Dante's *Purgatory* (V, ll.85–129) is rendered by Fuseli as a grandiose physical drama atop a rushing waterfall. Buonconte da Montefeltro was an historical figure, born around 1250, the son of the famous Ghibelline captain Guido da Montefeltro. At the battle of Campaldino on 11 June 1289 Buonconte was chased, fatally wounded, from the battlefield. He appears in *Purgatory* among those whose souls were saved by a final act of repentance. In Dante's account he dies, bleeding heavily, with the Virgin's name upon his lips. Good and evil angels vie for his body briefly, but his soul is saved because of one final tear of repentance. As his salved soul ascends, the devil, spitefully, drags his body down to Hell (Schiff 1973, no.429; Gizzi 1985, no.4).

No.36 is a traced version of a drawing in the Kunsthaus, Zurich (dated 1774; Schiff 1973, no.429), which uses rather heavier washes at the expense of the clarity of the design. Although it has been suggested that the present drawing is a copy by another hand, tracing was prominent among the repository of Fuseli's techniques, facilitating the exploration of different textural and tonal effects around an already established design, rather than implying primacy or secondary status.

The large compositional detail, no.35, is relatively unusual for Fuseli, and we cannot be certain whether this was done in preparation for the Zurich or London drawings, after or between them, or even quite separately. The last seems a possibility, as it is almost impossible to tell which way up the design should be viewed. The existing British Museum mount suggests (quite reasonably) that no.36 depicts the figures struggling laterally across a horizontal landscape, and that no.35 should be viewed as if the figure were reaching up. We may be reminded of an early comment on Fuseli's compositions which supposedly exhibited 'such incomprehensible sublimity' that a work of his was meant to have been hung upside down at the Academy (*Letters from an Irish Student in England to his Father in Ireland* [1809], quoted in Bentley 2004, p.264).

35

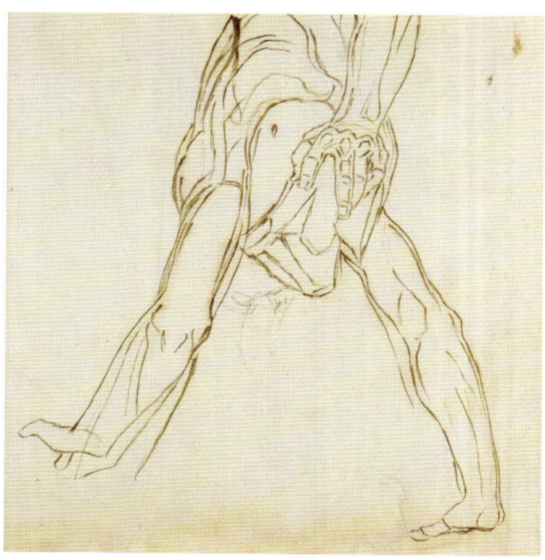

36

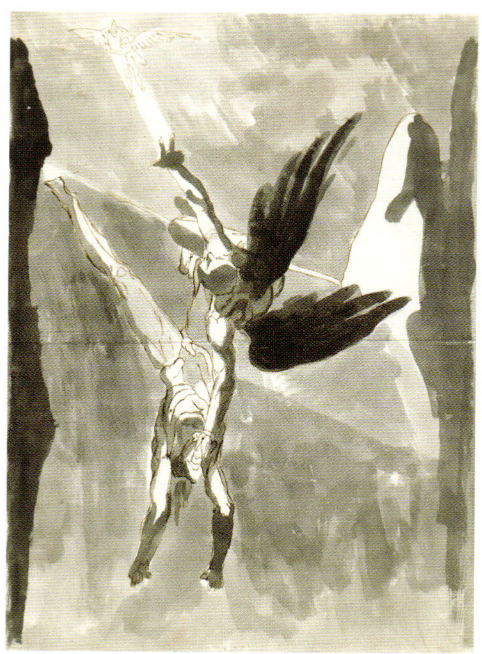

37

Henry Fuseli 1741–1825
Satan Starting at the Touch of Ithuriel's Lance
exh. RA 1780
Oil on canvas 230 x 276 cm
Staatsgalerie, Stuttgart

In a subject from Milton's *Paradise Lost* (Book IV, ll.810–14) the archangels Ithurial and Zephon hover over the sleeping figures of Adam and Eve, guarding these innocents from the influence of Satan. Having crept up on them in the guise of a toad, Satan is discovered and here leaps back from the slightest contact with Ithuriel's spear.

Fuseli was an admirer of John Milton (1608–74) from his youth. His teacher in Zurich, Johann Jakob Bodmer (1698–1783), had translated *Paradise Lost* as early as 1732, and the poet was admired for his sublime effects and his association with what were understood as distinctly British traditions of liberty (see Becker 1997). The treatment of Satan in this picture reflects a critical tradition of seeing Milton's fallen angel as an heroic figure rather than monstrous, the embodiment of an extravagant, libertarian instinct rather than of pure evil. In the context of the riots, revolution and political repressions of the last third of the eighteenth century, this motif was to become ever more pointed.

This large canvas was one of the group of ambitious paintings that Fuseli exhibited in London after his return from Italy. These established his reputation, although critics were divided about the qualities of his art. A pamphlet reviewer ironically noted the positioning of this canvas between John Singleton Copley's portrait of Major Hugh Montgomerie as a ferocious Highland soldier (Los Angeles County Museum of Art) and Thomas Gainsborough's picture of the notoriously bigoted English newspaper editor Henry Bate (Lord Burton; on loan to Tate): 'We have more reasons than one to fancy that there was a little playful spark of satire in the arrangement of the pictures; it could not trust the *Devil*, between any but the *Highlander* and *Mr Bate*' (See Whitley 1915, pp.168–9). This writer, like many others, noted the imbalance between the artist's powers of imagination and his technical abilities. The *Public Advertiser* (2 May 1780) was typical in its comments:

> This is a most admirable Composition, and shews the artist to be a Man of real Genius and elevated Ideas: If the *Execution* of this Piece were equal to the *Conception*, it would be a *Chief d'Oeuvre*. The Groupe of Adam and Eve asleep in each others Arms, is

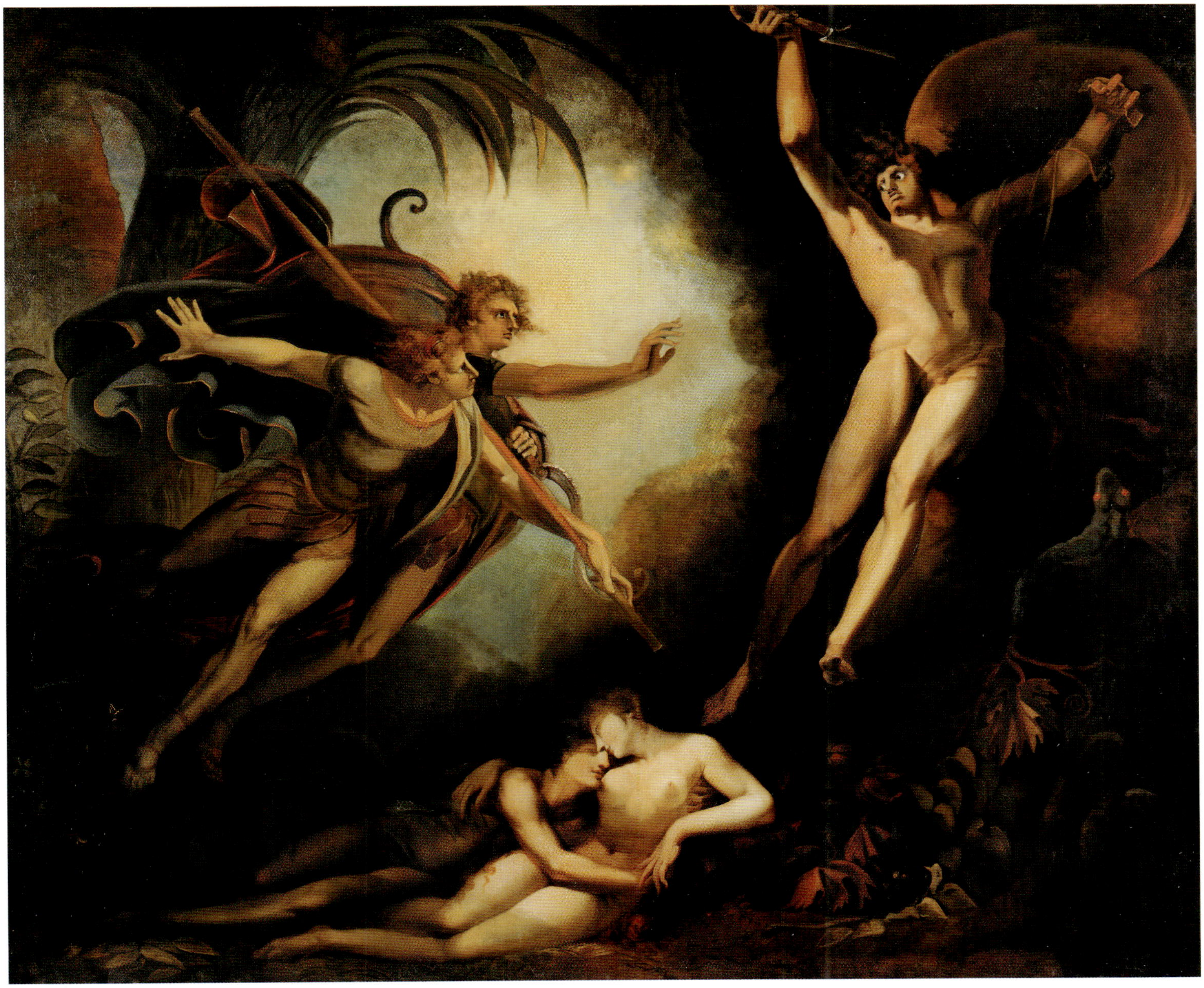

charmingly composed, and is one of the most beautiful Groupes that can be imagined.

Another writer, in the *London Courant* (12 May 1780) made a satirical and political point by connecting Fuseli's character of Satan with another picture in the exhibition, the portrait of the American wax modeller Patience Wright (1725-86) working on the 'bleeding head' of Charles I (see Hoock 2003, p.161). Horace Walpole (1717-97), always succinct in his opinion of the artist, dismissed it as 'extravagant & ridiculous' (marginal manuscript note in 1780 exhibition catalogue, photographic record at Witt Library, London).

This painting, like no.100, was one of the important canvases commissioned from Fuseli by Sir Robert Smyth, Bart. (1744-1802) of Berechurch Hall, Essex. The two had met in Rome in 1778 (see Weinglass 1982, pp.575-6). This picture is closely based on drawings by Fuseli dated to 1776 (Schiff 1973, nos.482-3), which Smyth could have seen while they were in Italy together. The finished picture descended to Smyth's grandson, and appeared in sales in London in 1878 and 1907, before it disappeared. It was considered lost by Schiff (see Schiff 1973, lost works no.18), but re-emerged in a private collection in St Moritz in 1988 when it was bought by the dancer Rudolf Nureyev. The painting was purchased from his collection by the Staatsgalerie, Stuttgart (see Christie's, New York, 13 January 1995, lot N146).

John Milton, Paradise Lost (1667; rev. ed. 1674), Book IV, ll.810–19

Him thus intent Ithuriel with his Spear
Touch'd lightly; for no falsehood can endure
Touch of Celestial temper, but returns
Of force to its own likeness: up he starts
Discoverd and surpriz'd. As when a spark
Lights on a heap of nitrous Powder, laid
Fit for the Tun some Magazin to store
Against a rumord Warr, the Smuttie graine
With sudden blaze diffus'd, inflames the Aire:
So started up in his own shape the Fiend.

(Milton 1998, p.467)

38

John Hamilton Mortimer 1740–1779
Sir Artegall, the Knight of Justice, with Talus, the Iron Man exh. RA 1778
Oil on canvas 242.6 x 146 cm
Tate. Puchased 1976

Sir Artegall (or Arthegall) is the personification of Justice and central protagonist in Book V of Spenser's vast Protestant allegory *The Faerie Queene* (1590). He is accompanied here by his sidekick Talus, who is armoured from head to toe in invulnerable iron.

This painting (Sunderland 1986, p.76 and no.136) was exhibited at the Royal Academy in 1778. For years Mortimer had been more closely associated with the rival Society of Artists, and this painting appears to be a calculated effort in the 'Grand Style' promoted by Reynolds. As John Sunderland has noted, it is 'like some *bandito* version' of Reynolds's grandiose male portraiture. But Mortimer's picture does not represent the likeness of a known person, nor does it really illustrate a narrative. Rather, it presents a rather bald image of a fantasy hero and his companion, emphasising their physical attributes and the details of their costume and armouring. Mortimer had received criticism over the years for his inability to communicate narrative effectively which, in combination with his preference for criminal subject matter, lent his work a morally ambivalent quality. Here, rather than try to convey a story, he depends upon the impressive physique of his Sir Artegall to win the viewer's attention and, we might suppose, admiration. The painter has been especially attentive to the particularities of the different materials represented here, the juxtaposition of beaten metal, stiff leather, folded fabric, flesh and hair. The dramatic foreshortening of Sir Artegall's left foot is a striking detail, further enhancing the impression of technical virtuosity.

Mortimer's early death in 1779 was seen by many of his contemporaries as a particular tragedy, given the profound talents that he had exhibited in his short life. His designs of 'banditti' and soldiers were published in good numbers, and were imitated directly by a number of artists. Most important, though, was the way his work illustrated the possibility of presenting a rather exaggerated, anti-heroic image of the hero. Though Sir Artegall and Talus are intended to be among the 'good guys', their treatment by Mortimer suggests a more ambiguous morality – one subsumed to a generalised macho image. Rather tellingly, this picture may have been sold in the early nineteenth century as 'A bandit chief, with another figure standing at the entrance to a Cavern'. Sir Artegall was characterised by Spenser as a reformed brute – originally 'Salvagesse sans finesse' (Book IV, Canto IV, Stanza 39) – while Talus, as his association with iron would suggest, represents the most unyielding kind of physical force exerted in the sectarian cause. Spenser, as a poet, had been considered typical of a rather primitive period in English literature, and was only recently rehabilitated according to the relativist standards of the emerging literary history and ascendant primitivist tastes (Radcliffe 1996, pp.52–82).

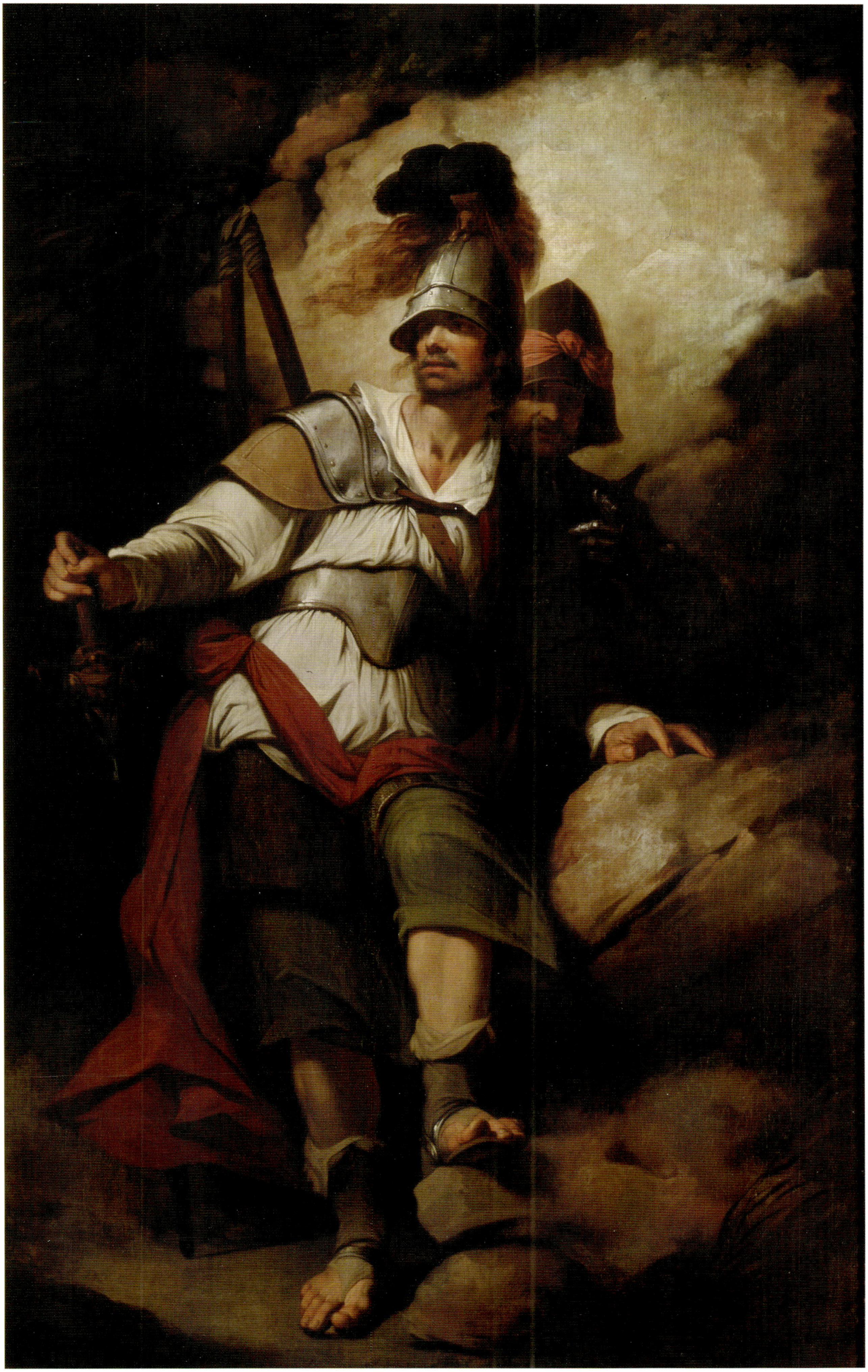

39

Henry Fuseli 1741–1825
The Oath on the Rütli 1780
Oil on canvas 267 x 178 cm
Kunsthaus, Zurich. Deposited by the Canton of Zurich, 1989

This was the key legendary episode in Swiss medieval history: representatives of the three original cantons meet at the Rütli (a meadow on the western shore of Lake Lucerne) to swear their mutual allegiance and their combined will to overthrow the now tyrannical rule of the Austrian Empire and assert their democratic rights. Walter Fürst of Uri is at the centre, accompanied by Arnold von Melchtal of Underwalden and Werner Stauffacher of Schweiz. The revolution took place in 1307/8. Fuseli painted this work on commission, for the Town Hall in Zurich.

There are several sketched studies for this composition, one of which is dated 'Roma May 78' and another 'Zurico 79'; a painted sketch is dated to 1779 or 1780 (Schiff 1973, nos.1739, 412; Feinberg and Wolff 1996, pp.220–6). The present painting (Schiff 1973, no.359) is dated 1780, so it was presumably completed which Fuseli was back in London. He wrote to his friend Johann Caspar Lavater (1741–1801) in October 1781: 'I spent a large part of the summer on it and spared nothing in order to make it worthy of the place where it is to hang, of the men whom it represents, of the impression it is to make of you and me.' As a large-scale commissioned painting on a virtuous theme, destined for public display, the picture represents precisely the kind of opportunity to create a meaningful public art that was so rare in the late eighteenth century.

Fuseli's great achievement here is his translation of a historical subject into dynamically physical terms. Yet the resulting stylisation of these heroic figures may articulate a sense of historical distance: for such virile men were generally seen to belong to an earlier phase of history, before commerce, luxury and modern empire. Fuseli himself remarked frequently on the sad decline of the contemporary world, which he, following Rousseau, attributed to the rise of bourgeois social conformity. Of Switzerland he had written: 'Honour has given way to interest, virtue to expediency, religion to charlatanism and craziness, and what is worst of all, to the meanest, most bourgeois and stinking varieties of all these pests' (Fuseli to Lavater, 6 December 1765, in Mason 1951, pp.105–6).

Switzerland was admired in Britain for its wild landscapes and its history of Protestantism and political independence. But it was only at this moment that British authors began writing extensively on these themes. As Katherine Turner has explored, William Coxe's *Sketches of the Natural, Civil and Political State of Swisserland* (1779) was particularly important, 'constructing Switzerland as a parallel inheritor, with Britain, of ancient Roman virtues which are overlaid on a native tradition of insular integrity guaranteed by Britain's literal insularity, and Switzerland's mountainous encirclement' (Turner 2001, p.33). These associations of liberty, virility and cultural reform with the Swiss national character are important in helping to understand Fuseli's personal ascent in London.

William Coxe, Sketches of the Natural, Civil, and Political State of Swisserland, (1779)

Rhudolph, some time after his accession to the throne of the empire, listened to the ambitious schemes of his son Albert duke of Austria, who was desirous to form Helvetia into a dutchy. For this purpose the emperor purchased the domains of several abbeys, and other considerable fiefs in Swisserland, as well in the canton of Schweitz as in the neighbouring territories. The great increase in power, which the emperor gained by this acquisition, induced the three cantons to renew their alliance, and to demand a confirmation of their privileges: and their demands were granted. Upon the death of Rudolph, Adolphus of Nassau succeeded him, from whom they obtained the same confirmation. But when Albert was afterwards chosen emperor, he refused to ratify it: and, in order totally to subdue the people, he placed over them two governors, who were guilty of many flagitious acts of tyranny and oppression.

Under these circumstances Werner de Staffach of Schweitz, Walthar Furst of Uri, and Arnold de Meltchall of Underwalden, planned the famous revolution, which took place January 13, 1308, and restored liberty to the three cantons.

(Coxe 1779, pp.141–2)

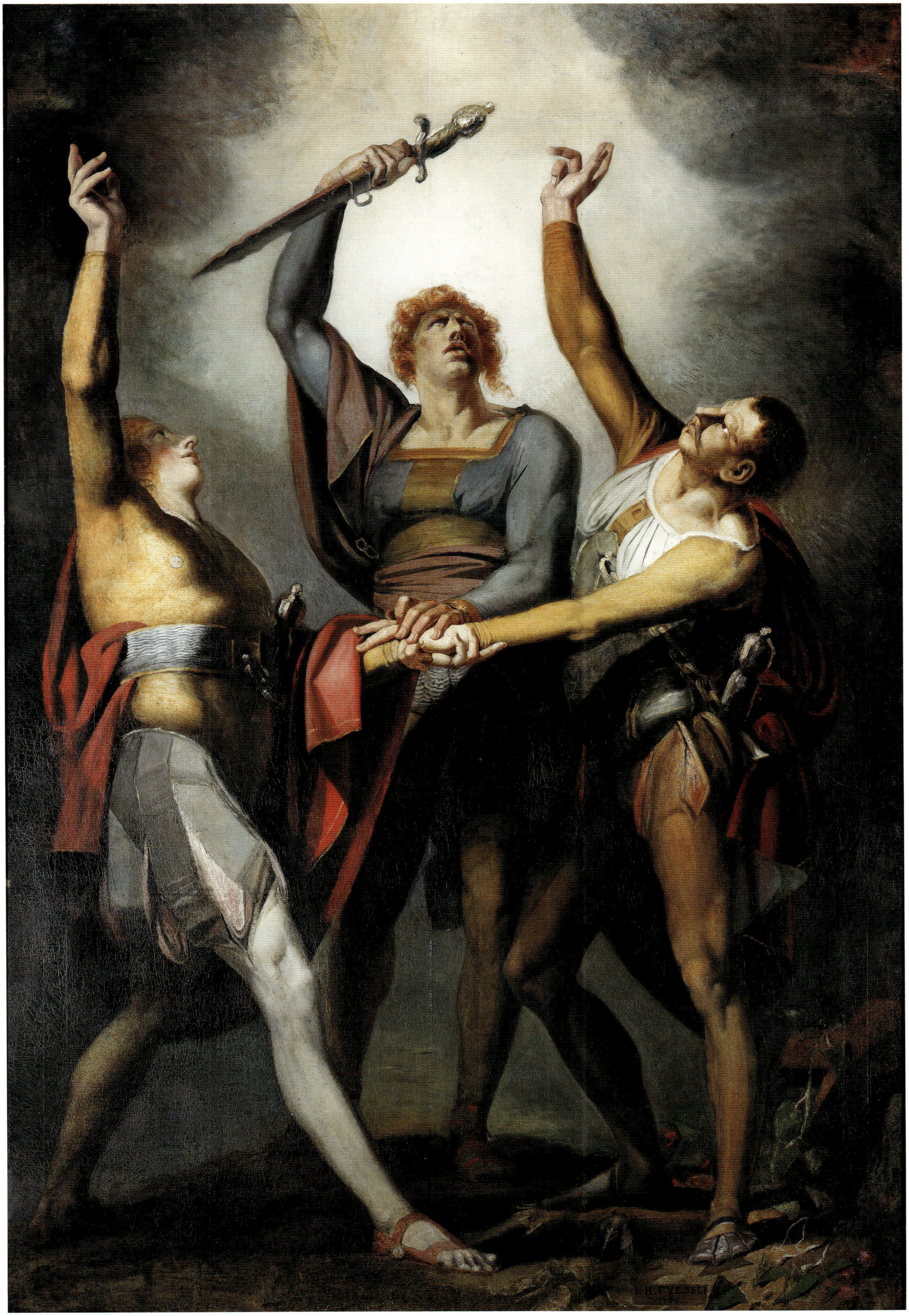

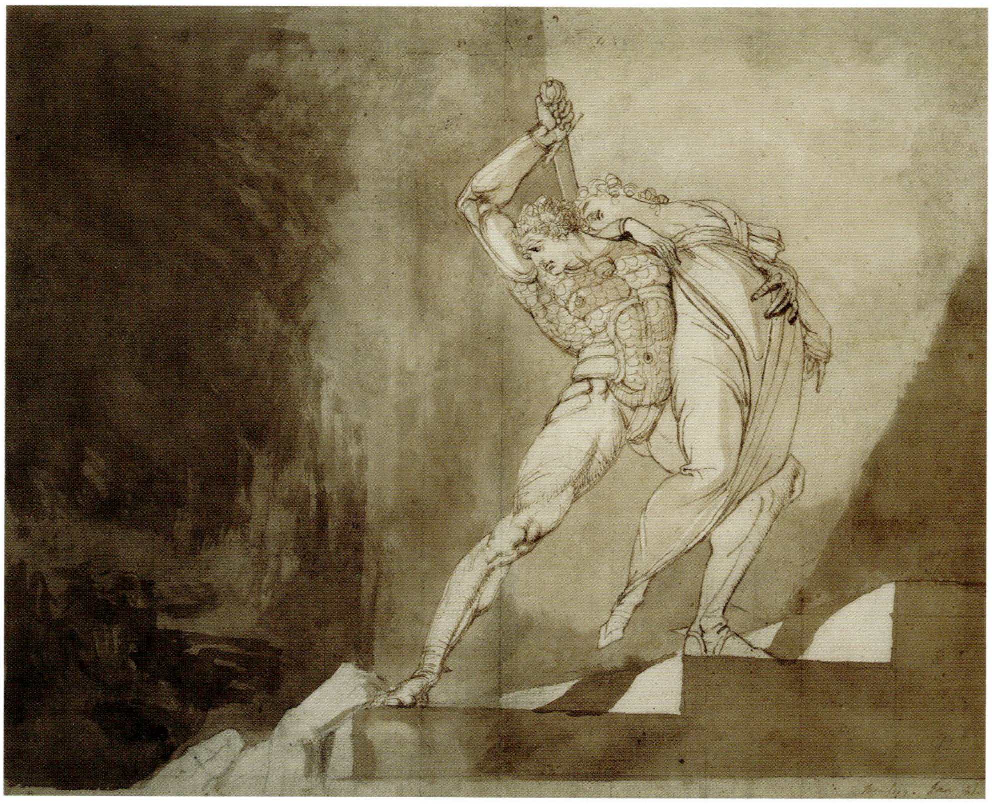

Saxo Grammaticus, The History of the Danes (c.1200)

... he ransacked the depths of the mountain in order to track down the girl, discovered her, slew the giant and led her away with him. The creature in his attentions had bound back her hair into a tight knot so that the bunch of curls was held in a twisted mass, a tangled cluster which no one could unloose except with a knife. Again using various incentives Othar attempted to make the girl look at him, but when he had long tried to attract her drooping eyes and nothing happened according to his wishes, he abandoned his scheme. He could not bring himself to use the girl lustfully, for he was unwilling to stain with disreputable intercourse a daughter of noble parentage.

(Davidson and Fisher 1979–80, I, p.208)

40

Henry Fuseli 1741–1825
Othar Rescuing Siritha from the Giant 1781
Pen and brown ink with brown-grey wash on paper 27 x 30.4 cm
Cecil Higgins Art Gallery, Bedford

A hero saves a maiden from the clutches of a giant; the monster is represented only by an enormous hand clutching at the edge of the step. Minimally suggested, the setting would appear to be a cavernous dungeon or vast castle interior.

Bert Winther has suggested that the drawing might represent the story of Othar and Siritha (or Ottar and Sigrid) from Book Seven of the *Historiae Danicae* (History of the Danes) by Saxo Grammaticus (c.1200) (Winther 1989). Fuseli owned the 1524 edition of this book (see the sale catalogue of his library, in Weinglass 1982, p.594). In this characteristically convoluted romantic tale, when Othar hears that King Siwald's modest daughter (who refuses to look at any of her courtiers in the eye) has been captured by a giant who 'carried her off to his narrow den on a mountain ledge', the self-assured hero goes in hot pursuit, rescues his maiden and kills the monster. The evidently rather careless Siritha is captured by another giant, and is once more rescued by Othar. She then, finally, succumbs to his advances, and they live happily ever after.

The abrupt narrative turns and non-sequesters in the source material (which may suggest historical losses) hardly make for the sort of coherent, comprehensible moral tale that ambitious artists were supposed to represent. Saxo's name was known to most eighteenth-century readers only as the ultimate source for the story of King Amleth, the basis of Shakespeare's *Hamlet*, and almost no one would have read Saxo's original text, as the *History* was not translated into English until 1894. As Winther notes, it is the Shakespearean connection that may lend some meaning to the fragments of text on the back of this design, where the words 'In these deep' and 'To be or not to be that is the question / whether tis better in the mind to suffer' are visible in mirror writing. The very obscurity of this subject, together perhaps with the erotically charged account of Siritha's hair being bound, may have been of the greater interest to the artist.

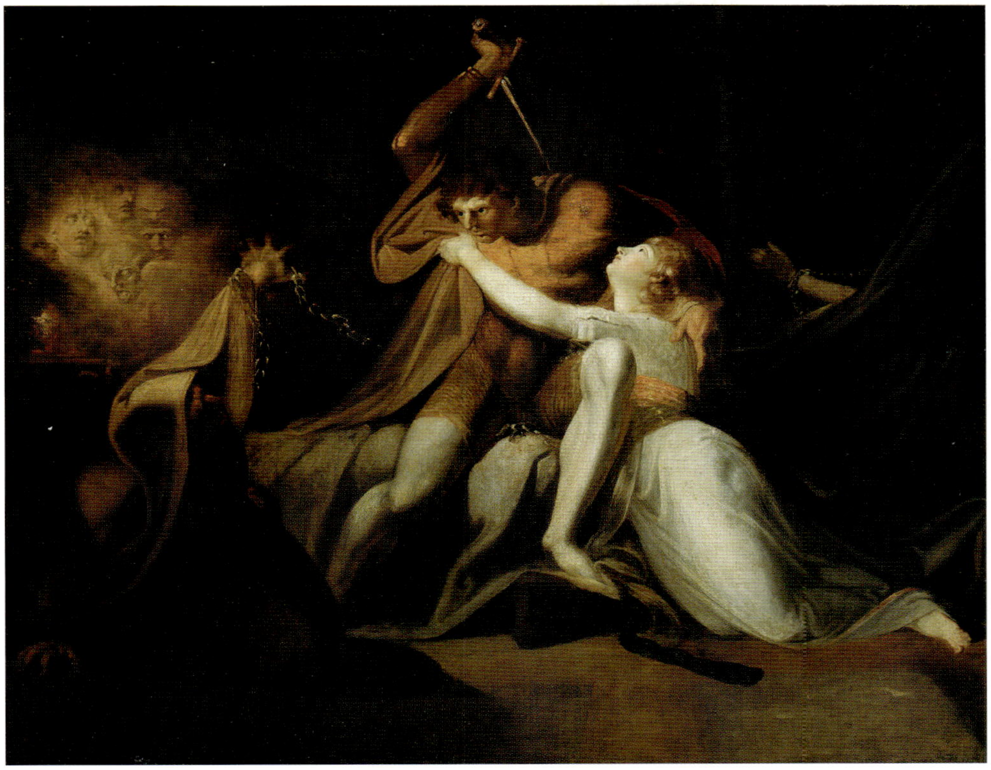

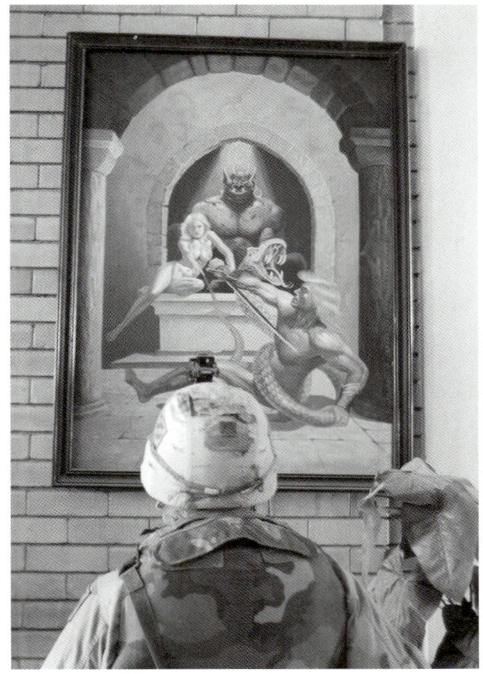

fig.25 American soldiers examine the art found at one of Saddam Hussein's palaces in Baghdad, 2003

41

Henry Fuseli 1741–1825
Percival Delivering Belisane from the Enchantments of Urma exh. RA 1783
Oil on canvas 99.1 x 125.7 cm
Tate. Presented by the National Art Collections Fund 1941

This scene is from a Gothic narrative of Fuseli's invention. The virile hero, waking from his enchanted sleep, raises his sword to attack the wizard, clasping a chained maiden by his side. The ghostly heads to the left are presumably lost or trapped souls, with the manacled hand of a woman hidden to the right belonging to another victim of Urma. The preceding scene was represented in a lost painting by Fuseli, already published as a mezzotint in 1782 (no.60).

In the print and in the catalogue of the 1783 exhibition Fuseli claims that the source of his subject was the 'Provencal Tales of Kyot'. This text was identified by Wolfram Von Eschenbach (c.1170–1220) as the source of his Arthurian romance, *Parzival*, a classic of early German literature written in the early thirteenth century but first published in 1477 (Stevens 1999). But there is no documented Kyot, and no real literary work authored by or even attributed to him: it seems that the source was an invention of Wolfram. And there is a further layer of deceit, for Wolfram claimed that Kyot's text was itself a translation from an Arabic manuscript discovered in Toledo. So in claiming the source of his 'Urma' pictures Fuseli proposes that his picture shows a subject taken from a text which never existed, which was in turn supposed to be a translation of a further non-existent text.

Fuseli's picture combines elements of Spenser as well as Wolfram (Tomory 1972, pp.95, 110; Gizzi 1985, no.1). The names of the characters are generic rather than drawing on any specific source; Percival was a common name for romance heroes, Belisane evokes 'Belisent' and several other maidens from Arthurian legend and chivalry, and 'Urma' is a generically wizardly moniker. Such licence may reflect what Fuseli was to develop into an element of his artistic theory – the idea that by pursuing the representation of elemental or essential qualities, proper names are almost irrelevant (Heppner 1995, pp.79–81). But there was also an already existing sanction implicit in contemporary literary practice. Fuseli is doing only what Gothic writers were inclined to do: claiming, almost never with malicious intent, to be working from ancient manuscripts or absent sources. Walpole's *Castle of Otranto* (1764) was claimed on its first anonymous publication to be the translation of a previously unknown sixteenth-century Italian book, 'found in the library of an ancient Catholic family in the north of England'. Furthermore, the Provençal tale was well established enough as a genre: exactly contemporary with Fuseli's painting, John Pinkerton (1758–1826) proposed that his 'The Ghost of Azo' was 'In the Style of Provenzal Heroic Romance' (Pinkerton 1782).

Like the Gothic, Fuseli's painting may, arguably, descend into the infantile, and precipitates the whole genre of modern 'fantasy art', damned as debased and juvenile (Manlove 1990). Compare this image with, for instance, the paintings discovered in Sadam Hussein's private quarters (fig.25) and taken, in that context, as evidence of that dictator's moral and aesthetic depravity (see Jonathan Jones, *Guardian*, 15 April 2003, G2, p.5). Fuseli has an important, and still under-explored, role as a precursor of such fantasy art, whose own history is only beginning to be written (see Westfahl, Slusser and Plummer 2002).

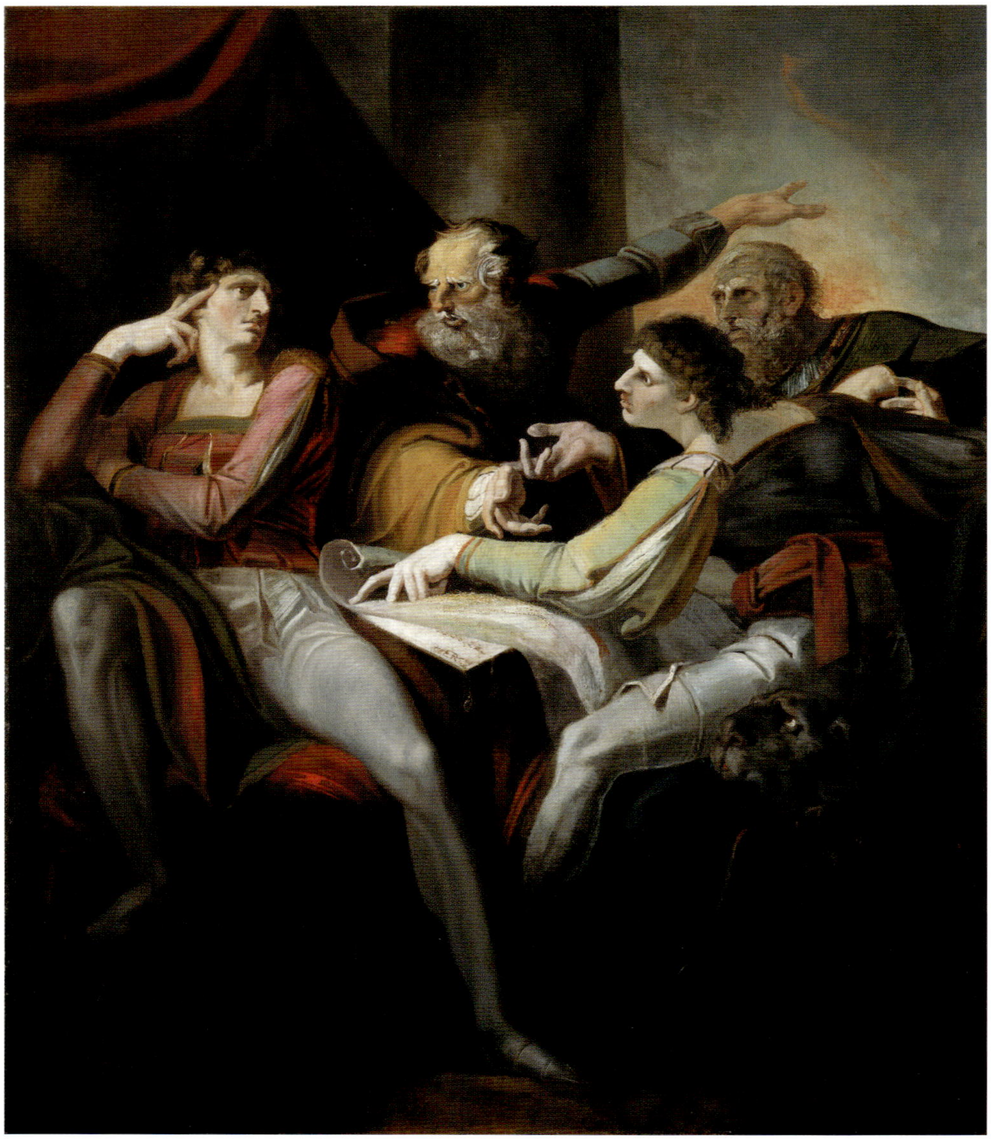

Fuseli renders a lengthy verbal exchange as a monumentally physical composition. Our eye is forcibly directed along the impossibly long legs of Hotspur to his flaming, arrogant visage, and across to the hirsute Glendower, his left arm thrown back into space. Antal (1956, p.100) drew attention to Fuseli's stylistic and compositional debt to a canvas by Joachim Anthonisz Uytewael (c.1566–1638), though he distinguished the 'effeminate and more precious' effects of the Dutch artist from the 'deliberately heroic vigour' of Fuseli. Certainly, Fuseli's painting can be interpreted as distilling current, heavily gendered notions of original genius and expression into bodily form – the massive limbs of his protagonists expressing, as in *The Oath on the Rütli* (no.39) – not just a particular historical idea of nobility but also a sense of the artist's own massive ambition.

The painting (Schiff 1973, no.723) was sent to Liverpool in 1784 to be exhibited in an art exhibition organised by a circle of collectors and art enthusiasts headed by William Roscoe (1753–1831). This Liverpool lawyer, businessman and man of letters was Fuseli's most important patron; this painting was sold to one of Roscoe's friends, Daniel Daulby (1746–98), apparently for forty guineas – a knock-down price for a canvas of this size (see Weinglass 1982, p.24).

42

Henry Fuseli 1741–1825
Hotspur, Glendower, Mortimer and Worcester Disputing the Division of England exh. with the Society for Promoting Painting and Design, Liverpool 1784
Oil on canvas 211 x 180 cm
Birmingham City Museums & Art Gallery. Presented by Sir Alec and Lady Martin through the National Art Collections Fund 1947

A scene from Shakespeare's *Henry IV Part 1* (c.1596–7) (Act III, scene 1): in 1403 the fate of England is vigorously debated by a group of rebellious noblemen. Writing of this picture in August 1784, Fuseli stated that: 'as near as I can now recollect my intention, when I painted it, it was meant to express the Clashing of Hotspur's and Glendower's temper about turning Trent and the Conciliatory exertions of Mortimer and Worcester' (letter to William Roscoe, 18 August 1784, in Weinglass 1982, p.24). Hotspur (Henry Percy, son of the Earl of Northumberland) is the generously limbed figure seated and leaning back with his fingers to his brow. The Welsh lord and wizard Owen Glendower directs him to look again at the map, and points out into the landscape. Edmund Mortimer, Earl of March and Thomas Percy, Earl of Worcester are on the right.

Shakespeare's scene builds a series of bad-tempered exchanges between the 'gallant' but hot-headed Hotspur and boastful, prickly Glendower, climaxing in this argument prompted by Hotspur's deliberately provocative claim that the bend of the river means that the Welsh lord will unjustly received more territory:

> See how this river comes me cranking in,
> And cuts me from the best of all my land.
> A huge half-moon, a monstrous cantle out.
> (Shakespeare 1997, p.907)

43

John Francis Rigaud 1742–1810
Samson Breaking his Bonds 1784
Oil on canvas 129.6 x 163.2 cm
Royal Academy of Arts, London

The biblical hero breaks his bonds, as Delilah and the Philistines look on alarmed (Judges 15:14).

This was Rigaud's Diploma Work, the representative work of art presented by a newly-elected Academician to the Royal Academy of Arts. It was presented to them in 1784.

The painting shows the French-Italian Rigaud returning to the type of subject that he had executed immediately prior to his arrival in Britain: the heroic male nude. William Pressly has termed the work 'an inflated academy study' developed, ultimately, from the painted studies undertaken at the Accademia Clementia in Bologna (Rigaud 1984, pp.13, 31 n.31). At this point in the narrative, neither the treacherous woman who stands beside him, nor the feeble bonds around his wrists and ankles, nor even the Philistines visible to the right, present any challenge to the hero. As an embodiment of a fantasy of superheroic strength, Rigaud's Samson seems complete.

Rigaud's Diploma Work was unusual in that it received a considerable amount of press attention when it was first on show in the Council Room during the Academy's exhibition of 1785; generally, Diploma Works were overlooked completely in favour of the pictures on show in the Great Room. According to Rigaud's son it was kept in the Council Room where 'for many years it was annually seen by the public at the time of the exhibition' (Rigaud 1984, p.71). One piece of criticism even suggests a reading of the image as a heroic allegory of the creative act: 'Mr *Rigaud's* picture of *Sampson*, has over-come all the rival pieces in the Council room. His brother artists may *rail* on, but they will not equal him in power, altho' some of them are furnished with the *jaw-bone* of an *ass*!' (*Morning Herald*, 4 June 1785). Thus as Samson overcomes the Philistines, Rigaud overcomes his opponents, who have only words, through the performance of his art.

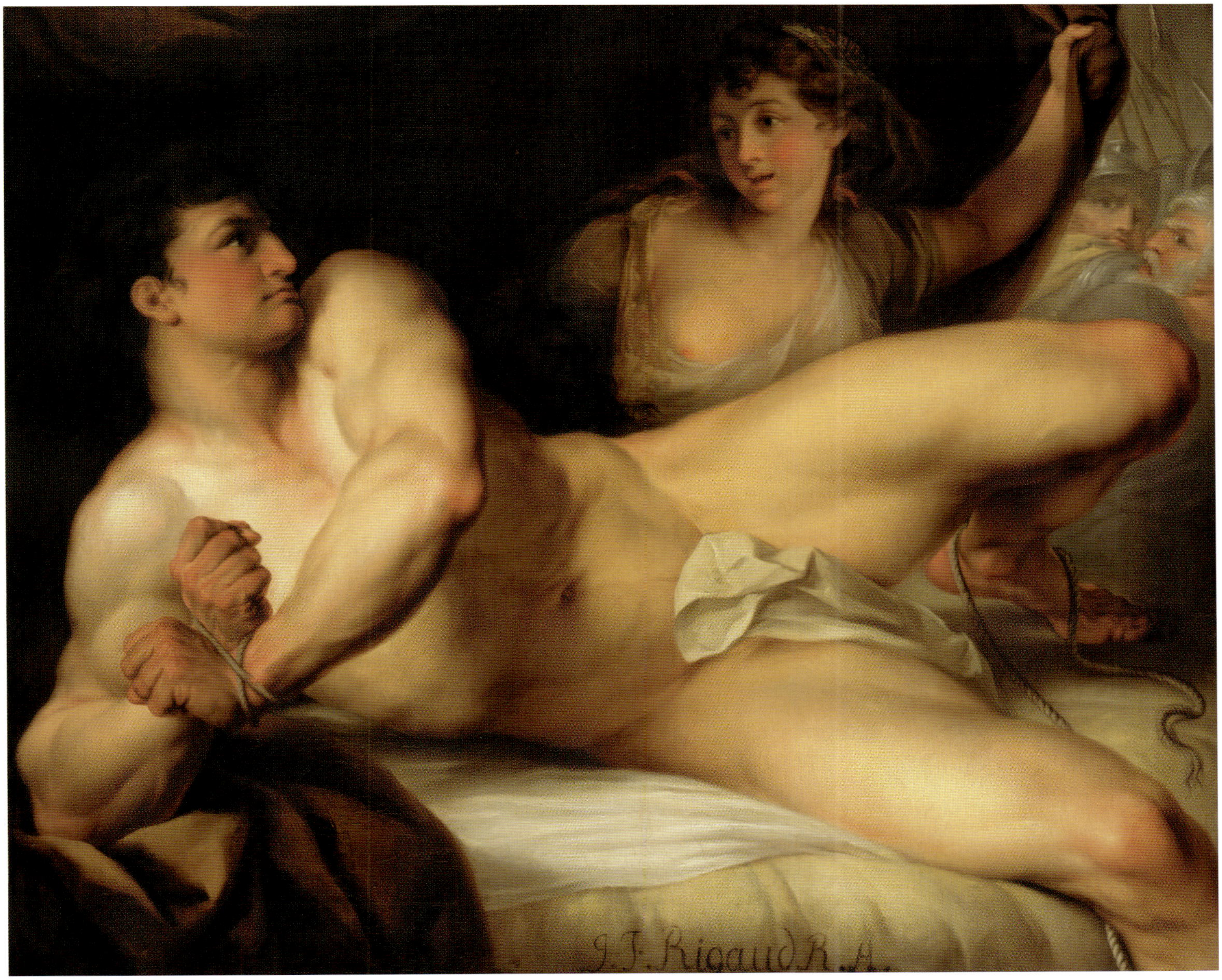

44

Henry Fuseli 1741-1825
Thor Battering the Midgard Serpent 1790
Oil on canvas 131 x 91 cm
Royal Academy of Arts, London

The Icelandic hero Thor raises his weapon to strike at the monstrous Mitgard Serpent, whom he has fished from the churning black sea. Thor stands in the boat of the giant Eymer, who has been tricked into this expedition and who cowers in fear. The diminutive elderly figure at the top of the canvas is the god Odin.

Fuseli's source was Thomas Percy's translation of Paul Henri Mallet's *Introduction à l'Histoire de Dannemarc* (1755), published as *Northern Antiquities* in 1770, which includes a translation of the prose version of the ancient Icelandic mythic cycle, the *Edda* (Omberg 1976; Boyer 1994). Fables 23 to 27 tell of how Thor – 'the strongest and bravest of Gods and Men' – is defeated by magic and deceit in a series of challenges from the giants of Utgard, resulting in his banishment from the city (Mallet 1770, II, p.65). As an act of revenge in the twenty-seventh Fable, the hero attacks the Midgard Serpent, the female monster that had participated in one of the giants' epic challenges. At the crucial moment Eymer cuts the line that holds it fast to the boat. We can note that in Fuseli's picture there is not the slightest indication that Thor will do anything but strike the serpent successfully: in fact the outcome of the battle is uncertain, according to alternative versions of the myth (see Sørensen 2002).

This painting was Fuseli's Diploma Work, created for presentation to the Royal Academy of Arts on his election as a full Academician in 1790. By painting a heroic male nude in action, Fuseli was attending to the most conservative stipulations regarding academic artistic practice, which gave priority to skills in the treatment of such figures. Yet he breaks the basic rules of draughtsmanship – conveniently hiding some of the joints whose convincing representation might be the greater technical challenge – and is drawing not on an established literary source with high-minded moral content, but a strange, sensational tale of magic, violence and fantasy. The caricature quality of the cowering giant and of Odin may, as Schiff suggests (Schiff 1973, p.137), register some element of parody in the treatment of the subject, though Fuseli was personally interested in Norse poetry, and translated examples himself as well as writing on the subject (Ross 1998).

The revaluation of ancient literary sources like the *Edda* was part of the cult of primitivism, as this found popular expression in the 1760s and 1770s, where the obscurity and mystery associated with such stories were appreciated as authenticating characteristics, revelatory of a primal state of freedom that a modern reader could hardly appreciate except at a knowing distance. Like Ossian and Homer, the *Edda* thus enjoyed associations with an ideal of political liberty that was historically estranged from modern society, unrealisable, even undesirable, in real terms. Fuseli's Thor has, further, been interpreted as an allegory of the revolutionary forces in contemporary events in France (Hofmann 1980, no.437; Bindman 1989, p.159).

Paul Henri Mallet, trans. Thomas Percy, Northern Antiquities (1770)

Thor went up to a herd of cattle which belonged to the Giant, and seizing one of the oxen, tore off his head with his own hands; then returning to the bark where Eymer was, they sate down together. Thor placed himself in the middle of the bark, and plied with both his oars at once: Eymer, who rowed also at the prow, saw with surprize how swiftly Thor drove the boat forward, and told him, that by the land-marks on the coast, he discovered that they were come to the most proper place to angle for flat fish. But Thor assured him that they had better go a good way further: accordingly they continued to row on, till at length Eymer told him if they did not stop, they would be in danger from the great serpent of Midgard. Notwithstanding this, Thor persisted in rowing further, and in spite of the giant, was a great while before he would lay down his oars. Then taking out a fishing line extremely strong, he fixed it to the ox's head, unwound it, and cast it into the sea. The bait reached the bottom, the Serpent greedily devoured the head, and the hook stuck fast in his palate. Immediately the pain made him move with such violence that Thor was obliged to hold fast with both his hands by the pegs which bear against the oars: but the strong effort he was obliged to make with his whole body caused his feet to force their way through the boat and they went down to the bottom of the sea; whilst with his hands, he violently drew up the Serpent to the side of the vessel. It is impossible to express the dreadful looks that the God darted at the Serpent, whilst the monster, raising his head, spouted out venom upon him: in the meantime the Giant Eymer seeing, with affright, the water enter his bark on all sides, cut with his knife the string of the fishing-line, just as Thor was going to strike the Serpent with his mace.

(Mallett 1770, II, pp.135–6)

Henry Fuseli, 'Aphorisms on Art', (1788–1818), no.194

The forms of virtue are erect, the forms of pleasure undulate.

(Knowles 1831, III, p.135)

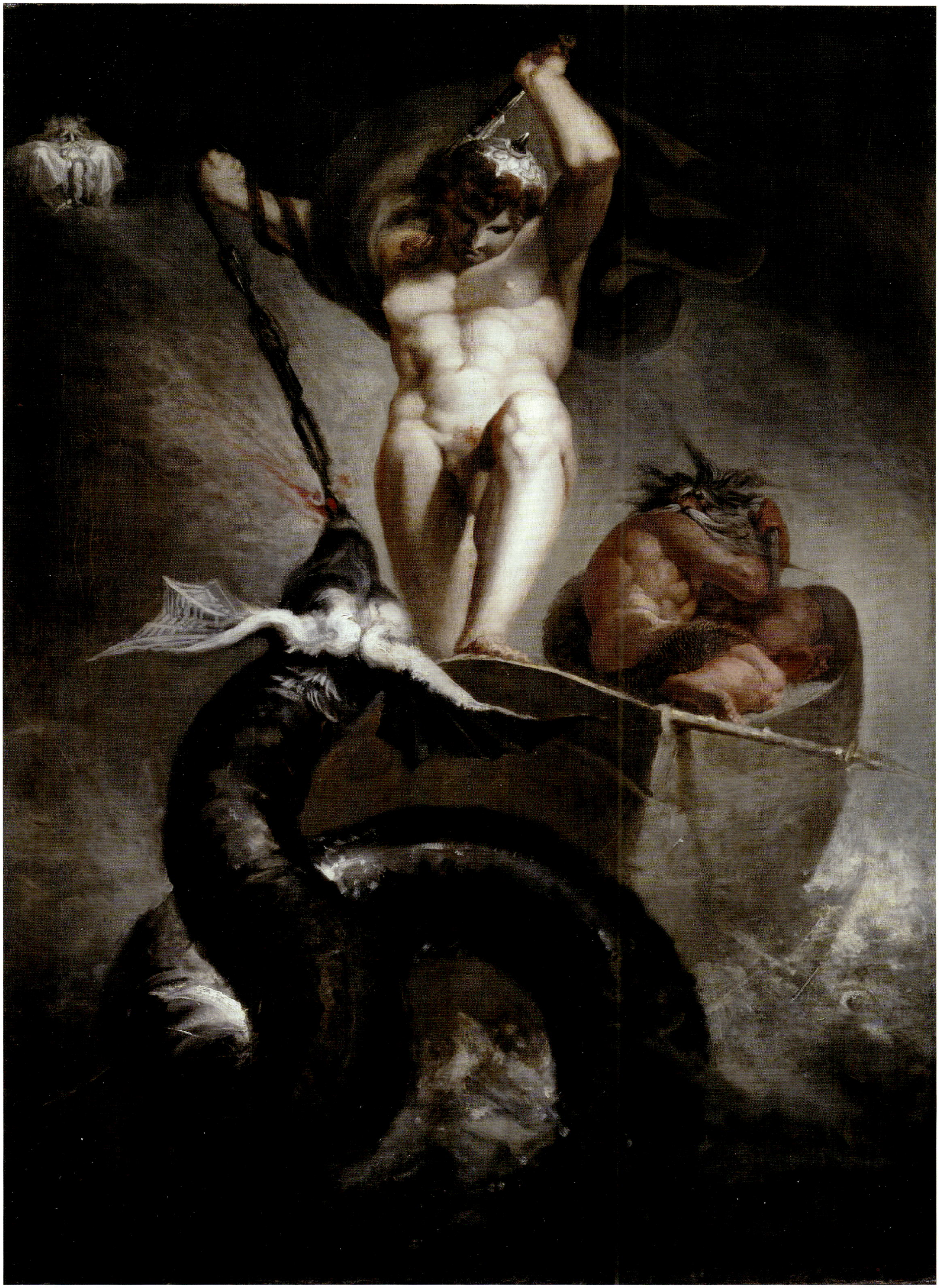

45a

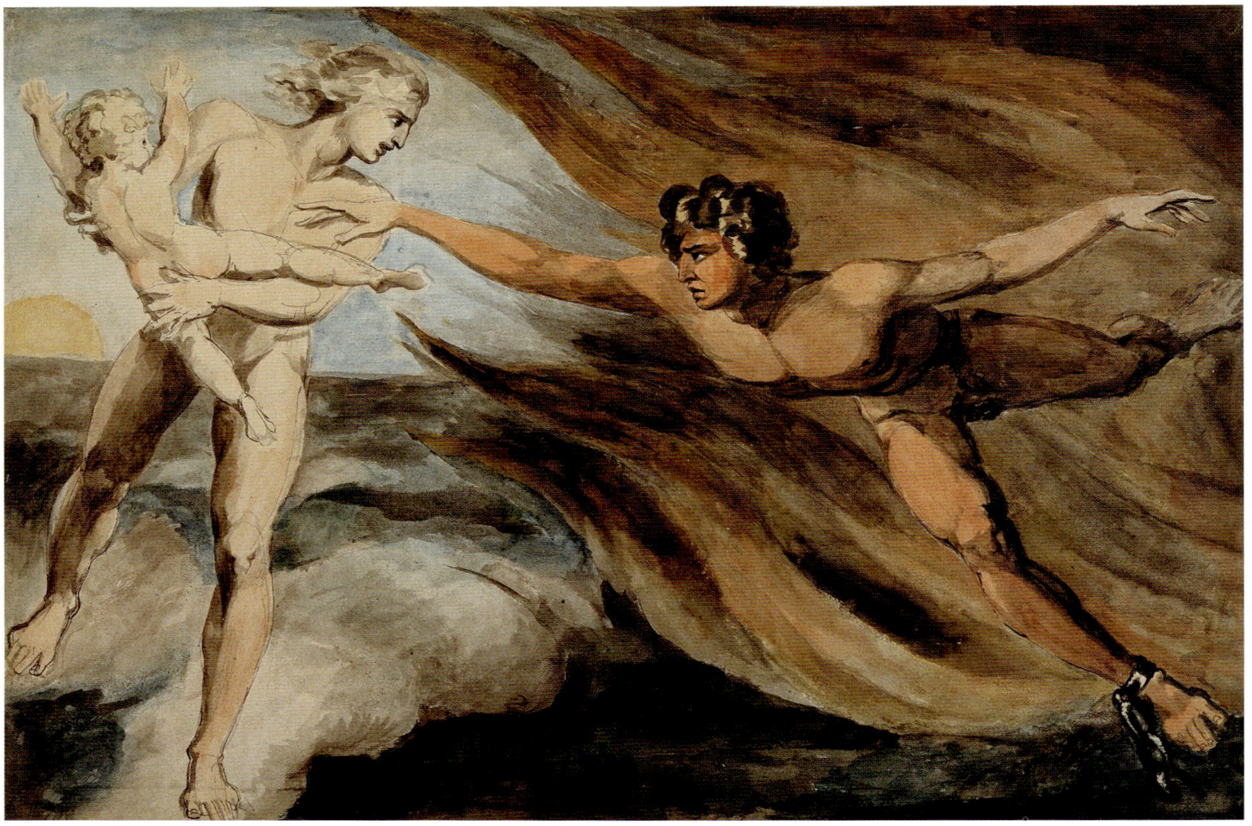

45b

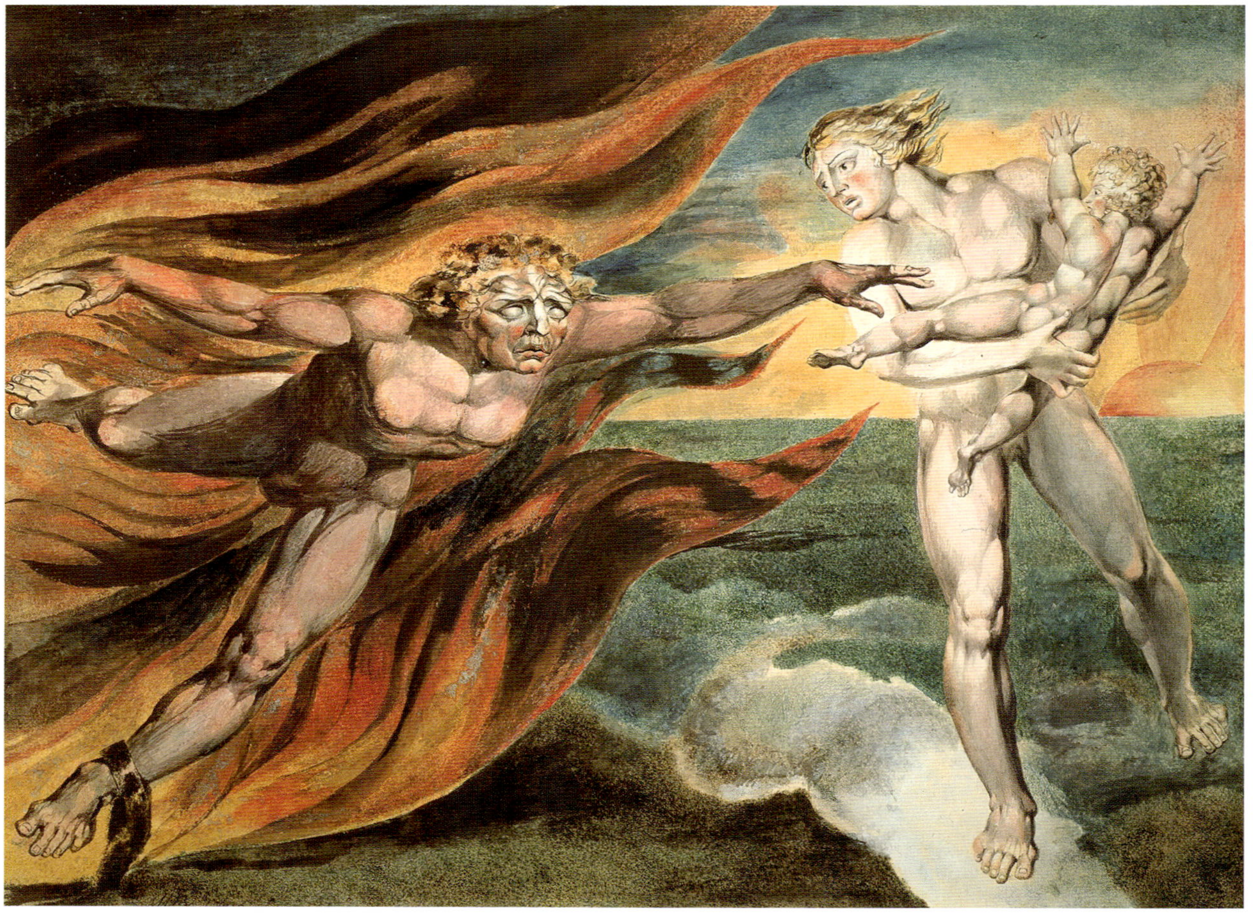

45a

William Blake 1757–1827
The Good and Evil Angels c.1790–4
Pen and watercolour on paper 29.5 x 44.2 cm
The Trustees of the Cecil Higgins Art Gallery, Bedford

45b

William Blake 1757–1827
The Good and Evil Angels 1795/c.1805?
Colour print finished in ink and watercolour on paper 44.5 x 59.4 cm
Tate. Presented by W. Graham Robertson 1939

This watercolour and print represent an allegory of Blake's invention. Two heroically proportioned flying figures struggle over a child in a vast, almost abstract landscape. One is dark-skinned and surrounded by flames, his foot in chains. The other is paler, with golden hair. He clutches a child, perhaps pulling him (or her) to safety and away from the clutches of the dark figure, perhaps not. The interpretation of the image remains disputed, and different emphases and implications can be detected between the watercolour and the print, and even between the different copies of the print.

The watercolour has been dated to around 1790–1 or 1793–4, both dates proceeding from the assumption that it must post-date the appearance of the composition on plate 4 of Blake's illuminated book, *The Marriage of Heaven and Hell* (1790–3) (see Butlin 1981, no.257; Joll 2002, p.30; Viscomi 1994, p.49). Here, a disrupted family seems to represent the 'Errors' elaborated by the text – the separation of energy and reason, and of body and soul. However, we cannot be certain that the watercolour follows this design, or even the conception of the text, or that it is necessarily to be interpreted in relation to the poem.

No.45b shows the design of the watercolour reversed and reworked as a coloured print. This is inscribed, apparently by Blake himself, with the title 'The Good and Evil Angels', now used also for the watercolour. It comes from a group of twelve 'large colour prints' that Blake produced in 1795 (Butlin 1981, pp.156–8 and nos.289–329). The present print was purchased by Blake's benefactor Thomas Butts (1757–1845) in 1805, and may have actually been printed and coloured at that later date (see Butlin 1990, no.33). Aside from the obvious reversal of the composition, the large print differs in some subtler, but suggestive, respects from the watercolour. The physiques of the two adult figures are hardened and made more sculptural; the Good Angel is more expressive, and the Evil Angel more monstrous. The hand of the Evil Angel appears, arguably, more distant from the child's leg, making it less clear that he is clutching at the infant. His apparent blindness reinforces this impression.

In the printed version, the tethered figure can be identified as an older version of Blake's character Orc, the embodiment of revolutionary energy (see no.25) and the other figure as Los, symbolic of the more controlling side of the creative imagination. However, the presence of a conflicting title given by the artist himself confounds this interpretation. In a more general thematic sense the image also recalls the struggles between good and evil that determined the fate of those souls sent to Purgatory, for instance Dante's account of *Buonconte da Montefeltro*, as depicted by Fuseli (no.36). But while Fuseli has rendered narrative in stridently physical terms, Blake's conflation or confusion of allegorical elements and narrative results in a resolutely unreadable image, as Christopher Heppner has detected, noting in particular the curious illegibility of the Evil Angel's gesture (Heppner 1995, pp.131–8).

While printmaking was conventionally a means of mechanically reproducing and mass-producing images, Blake's 'large colour prints' include unique colouring, and each of the very few impressions made of each image offers nuances of difference. Their interpretation remains disputed, and even the appropriate methodology is in question. Are the meanings of these images to be determined in relation to specific texts by Blake or allusions to historic literature and scripture, or are they more open-ended? The possible relationships between individual images open up further questions. The twelve large colour prints are usually considered to be a series, and often in pairs within that series, although the degree to which this is appropriate is disputed. Certainly Blake was prepared to sell the prints individually, suggesting that he could hardly have thought of them as a unity in a very strict sense (see Heppner 1995, pp.105–6).

William Blake, Marriage of Heaven and Hell (1790–3), pl.4

The voice of the Devil
All Bibles or sacred codes. have been the causes of the following Errors.

1. *That Man has two real existing principles Viz: a Body & a Soul.*
2. *That Energy. calld Evil. is alone from the Body. & that Reason. calld Good. is alone from the Soul.*
3. *That God will torment Man in Eternity for following his Energies.*

But the following Contraries to these are True

1. *Man has no Body distinct from his Soul for that calld Body is a portion of Soul discernd by the five Senses. the chief inlets of Soul in this age*
2. *Energy is the only life and is from the Body and Reason is The bound or outward circumference of Energy.*
3. *Energy is Eternal Delight*

(Blake 1978, pp.77–8)

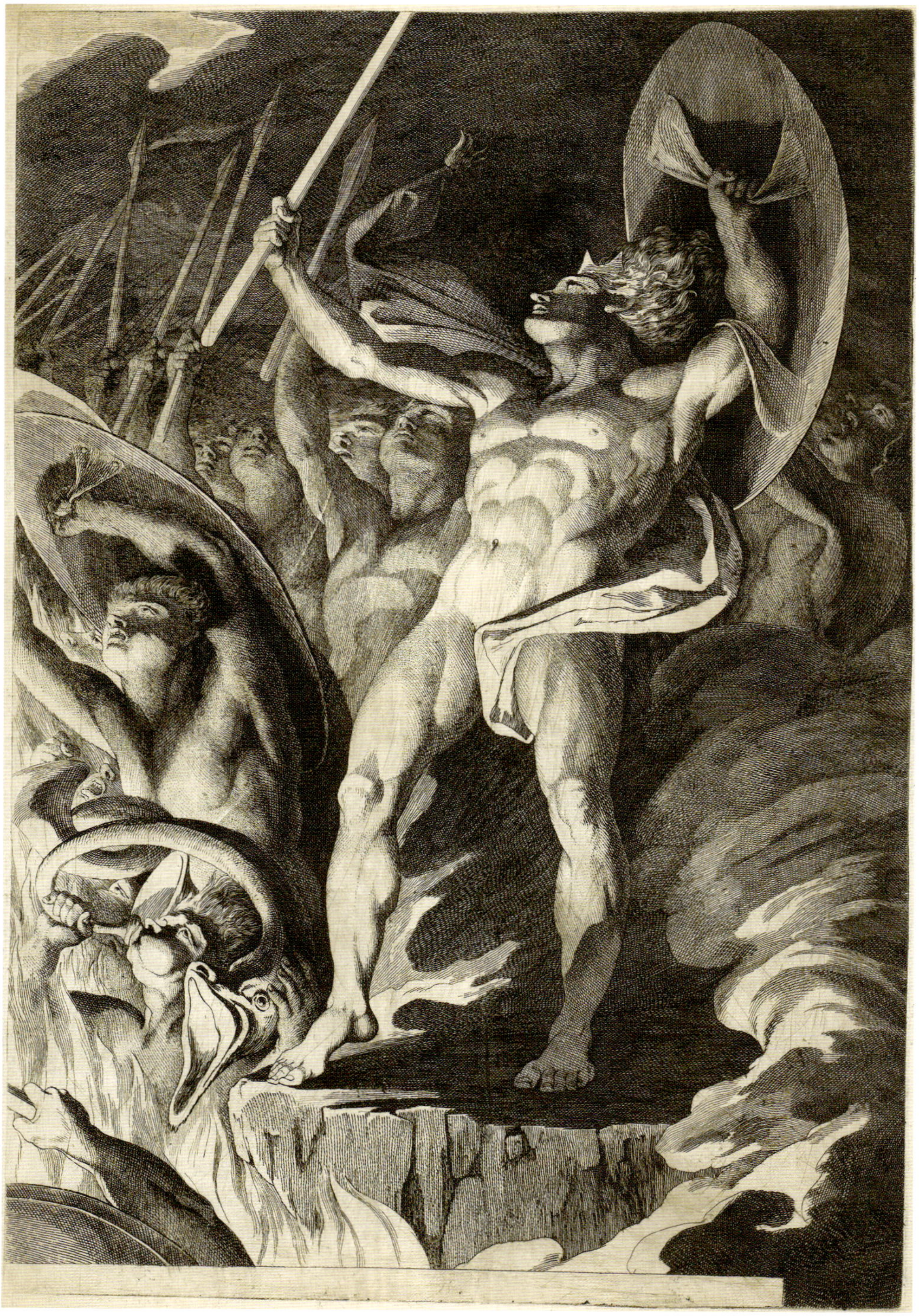

46

James Barry 1741–1806
Satan and his Legions Hurling Defiance toward the Vault of Heaven c.1792–5
Etching 74.6 x 50.4 cm
The British Museum, London
(1848-11-25-583)

Here James Barry depicts John Milton's superheroic Satan, from Milton's *Paradise Lost*. Satan and his troops, having been expelled from heaven for their rebellious nature, glare back from hell and rage against God. In the 1790s Barry embarked on a series of images based on *Paradise Lost* (Pressly 1981, pp.151–69; Dunne 2005, pp.156–63). Although not as systematic, the Irish painter's prints and drawings parallel Fuseli's Milton Gallery in seeking to explore the epic and sublime potential of the poem (see no.47). It is an exercise in the Michelangeloesque, with the gigantic form of Satan enhanced by a low viewpoint.

The heroic – even Promethean – ideal of Satan had been current since John Dryden's elevation of Milton to the canon of great literature in his commentary of 1697 (see Lewis 1992, pp.55–61). For the poets, critics and painters of the revolutionary era of the 1790s, Milton's Satan was reinvigorated as an emblem of the righteous spirit of rebellion (Newlyn 1993, esp. pp.38–40; Meller 1996; Kitson 2001, pp.474–7). However, we should remember how far Milton's work has been reconciled to mainstream political culture, and the degree to which the more radical elements of his writings have been downplayed by generations of anthologisation and extraction (see Simpson 1993, pp.132–4). While there can be little doubt that a politically conscious artist like Barry would have known and played to the radical associations of the theme of Satan, we should not imagine that such a move was immediately and unequivocally legible.

Aside from its imagery, this print is remarkable in its technique. Barry was an innovative and volatile printmaker: he freely combined techniques to create unconventionally rugged effects (Pressly 1981, pp.23–32; Pressly 2001; Phillips 2005). As a contemporary noted of his graphic works, 'They are not calculated for *Fan mounts*' (*Morning Chronicle*, 29 May 1792): in other words, they were not to be considered among the refined graphic luxuries which dominated the market. Here, the inking is so heavy that the print takes on a textured, almost sculptural quality (the effect is, of course, completely lost in photographic reproduction). Such graphic innovation represents in its very facture (the texture of its crafted surface) a sense of Promethean daring.

John Milton, Paradise Lost (1667; rev. ed. 1674), Book 1, ll.663–9

He spake: and to confirm his words, out flew
Millions of flaming swords, drawn from the thighs
Of mighty Cherubim; the sudden blaze
Far round illumin'd hell: highly they raged
Against the Highest, and fierce with grasped Arms
Clash'd on their sounding Shields the din of war,
Hurling defiance toward the Vault of Heav'n

(Milton 1998, p.374)

William Godwin, An Enquiry Concerning Political Justice (1793)
Book IV, appendix I

... poetical readers have commonly remarked Milton's devil to be a being of considerable virtue. It must be admitted that his energies centred too much in personal regards. But why did he rebel against his maker? It was, as he himself informs us, because he saw no sufficient reason for that extreme inequality of rank and power which the creator assumed. It was because prescription and precedent form an adequate ground for implicit faith. After his fall, why did he still cherish the spirit of opposition? From a persuasion that was hardly and injuriously treated. He was not discouraged by the apparent inequality of the contest: because a sense of reason and justice was stronger in his mind, than a sense of brute force: because he had much of the feeling of an Epictetus or a Cato, and little of those of a slave. He bore his torments with fortitude, because he disdained to be subdued by despotic power. He sought revenge, because he could not think with tameness of the unexpostulating authority that assumed to dispose of him. How beneficial and illustrious might the temper from which these qualities flowed have proved with a small diversity of situation!

(Shawcross 1972, p.372)

William Blake, The Marriage of Heaven and Hell (1793)

The reason Milton wrote in fetters when he wrote of Angels & God, and at liberty when of Devils & Hell, is because he was a true Poet and of the Devil's party without knowing it.

(Blake 1978, I, p.80)

47

James Neagle 1765–1822 after Henry Fuseli 1741–1825
'Awake, arise, or be forever fall'n!' (Satan Summoning his Legions) (engraved illustration from John Milton, *Paradise Lost*, 2 vols, London 1802, I, facing p.3) published by F.I. Du Roveray, 1 July 1802
Engraving 11.4 x 8.7 cm
Private collection

Here, Milton's Satan, driven out of heaven for his rebelliousness, summons his demonic army.

In association with his ill-fated 'Milton Gallery', a one-man exhibition of Miltonic subjects opened in 1799–1800, Fuseli had at one time intended to illustrate a luxurious new edition of *Paradise Lost*, to be published by Joseph Johnson (1738–1809) and edited by William Cowper (1731–1800). In the event, Cowper's mental illness and market conditions meant that this was abandoned, and even the independent prints after paintings in the Milton Gallery appeared only sporadically. A more comprehensive opportunity to illustrate the epic poem came, however, in 1801, when the publisher F.I. Du Roveray (1751–1801) commissioned a series of paintings from the artist to be used as illustrations to a two-volume edition (Weinglass 1994, nos.165–70). This modest publication eventually featured six tiny engravings based on the painter's compositions,

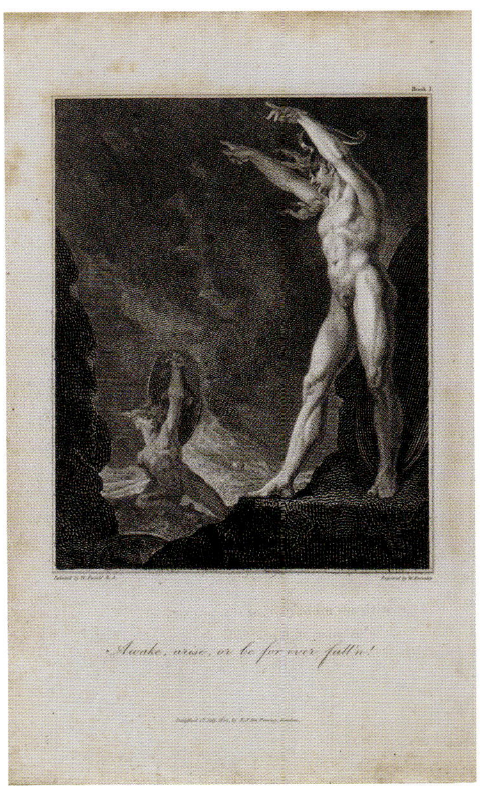

with the other designs being provided by William Hamilton (1751–1801). Fuseli was painfully aware of the irony apparent in such diminutive realisations of his ambitious ideas, a consequence of economics and his unstable reputation as an artist.

The new edition of Milton reflected the revival of critical interest in the poet at the end of the eighteenth century (see Shawcross 1972; Griffin 1986; Newlyn 1993). Milton's concern with grand themes of destiny, his epic imagination and overblown effects represented a canonical achievement in literature; his political radicalism and spirituality deepened the respect of the new generation of poets and painters. However, Milton never achieved the same kind of popular success as Shakespeare, his only near rival in the canon. His poetry seemed rather more earnest, or challenging, as Samuel Johnson noted in his *Lives of the Poets* (1779–81) when he wrote that 'we read Milton for instruction, retire harassed and overburdened, and look elsewhere for recreation'. Fuseli's biographer noted that the artist was prompted by this passage to scrawl an emphatic 'I DO NOT' in the margin (see Knowles 1831, I, pp.198–9).

48

Henry Tresham c.1750–1814
The Earl of Warwick's Vow before the Battle of Towton exh. RA 1797
Oil on canvas 44 x 35.8 cm
Manchester Art Gallery

Before the battle of Towton on 29 March 1461, Richard Neville, Earl of Warwick (1428–71) and the leader of the Edward IV's Yorkist army, kills his own horse and vows that he will face the superior enemy force on the same terms as the common foot soldier.

Part of the War of the Roses, the Battle of Towton was 'arguably the biggest, longest and bloodiest military engagement on British soil' (Boardman 2000, p.xi). The story of Warwick's vow was probably apocryphal (Hicks 1998, p.219). His role in securing Edward IV's triumph and the later ingratitude of the king were the stuff of legend, illustrating the dependent nature of the English monarchy and offering a warning against tyranny. These dimensions of Warwick's story were brought to the fore in a French play by Jean-François de la Harpe (1739–1803), which was adapted by Paul Hiffernan (1719–77) in 1763 and performed at Covent Garden; it was then translated afresh by Thomas Francklin (1721–84) and put into performance in 1792 and 1797. George Colman's 'Prologue' for the latter production referred to 'fierce Warwick ... That setter-up and puller-down of kings'. Tresham focuses instead on Warwick's heroic leadership.

This composition was commissioned from Tresham by Robert Bowyer (1758–1834) for his Historic Gallery, and engraved in 1795 (see Boase 1963 and Hutton 1992, esp. III, pp.581–6). Bowyer, whose scheme was modelled on John Boydell's Shakespeare Gallery and Thomas Macklin's Bible and Poet's Gallery (see no.87), was to publish a luxury edition of David Hume's popular *History of England* (1754–63), illustrated with engravings after specially commissioned paintings by leading British artists. Proposals and a prospectus were issued in the winter of 1791–2 and a series of large canvases commissioned, but financial difficulties meant that Bowyer went on to commission a larger number of rather small, 'cabinet size' pictures like this. Tresham was well employed in this endeavour, along with Robert Smirke (1752–1845) and Thomas Stothard (1755–1834). These smaller pictures were not initially exhibited at Bowyer's premises, like the larger paintings, and Tresham seems to have taken it upon himself to exhibit this work at the Royal Academy in 1797 in order to promote his reputation.

By that time, with war against revolutionary France raging, the demotic and patriotic sentiments represented by the tale of Warwick's vow took on new significance. In a contemporary guide to the exhibition, it was said the incident provided 'strong proof of the fierce character of that war-like noble' (*A Guide to the Exhibition of the Royal Academy of 1797*, London 1797, p.22). Notably, the purpose of this pamphlet was not to provide critical comments on the style and achievements of the artists, but was aimed at 'those visitors whose time may not have been spent in the acquirement of extensive Historical Knowledge'. A compilation of excerpted texts available for sixpence, the pamphlet offered a short-cut into greater cultural comprehension for the more socially variegated middle-rank of professionals, businessmen and craftsmen (and women) who now populated the Academy's annual exhibitions. Arguably, the extreme physicality of Tresham's conception of the subject – ostentatiously indebted to Fuseli – was in itself an aid to such an extension of the cultural franchise, conveying the theme with a visual dynamism that did not depend upon extensive historical foreknowledge for its effect. Or it may be, more simply, shocking: the present picture has been described as 'a truly Fuselian piece discarding any attempt at accuracy for horrific nudity' (Boase 1963, p.174).

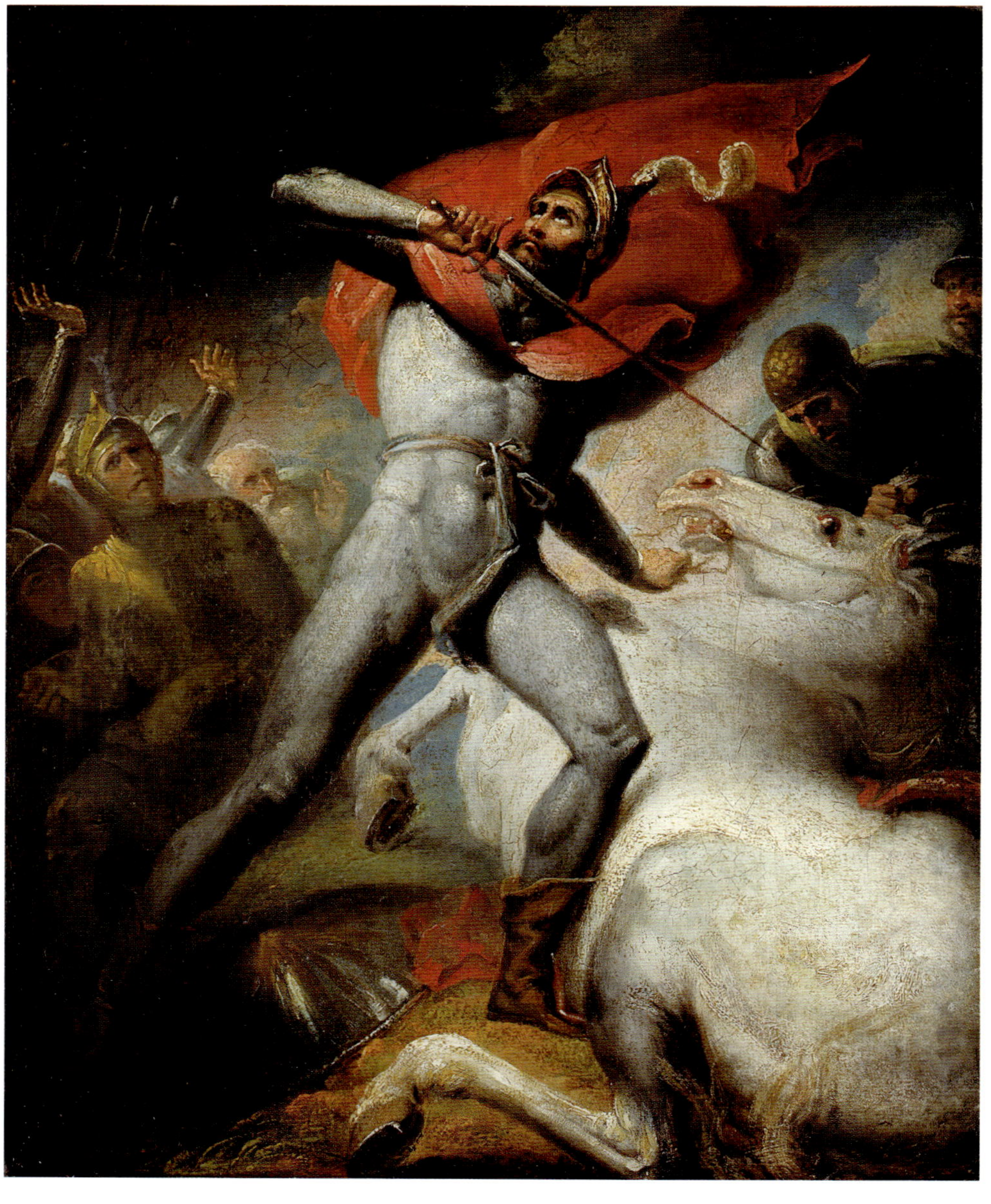

David Hume, History of England (1754–63)

The licence in which Queen Margaret had been obliged to indulge her troops, infused great terror and aversion in the city of London, and all the southern parts of the kingdom; and as she there expected an obstinate resistance, she had prudently retired northwards among her own partizans. The same licence, joined to the zeal of faction, soon brought great multitudes to her standard; and she was able, in a few days, to assemble an army, sixty thousand strong, in Yorkshire. The King and the Earl of Warwick hastened with an army of forty thousand men to check her progress; and when they reached Pomfret, they dispatched a body of troops, under the command of Lord Fitzwalter, to secure the passage of Ferrybridge over the river Ayre, which lay between them and the enemy. Fitzwalter took possession of the post assigned him, but was not able to maintain it against Lord Clifford, who attacked him with superior numbers. The Yorkists were chased back with great slaughter, and Lord Fitzwalter himself was slain in the action. The Earl of Warwick dreading the consequences of this disaster, at a time when a decisive action was every hour expected, immediately ordered his horse to be brought him, which he stabbed before the whole army, and kissing the hilt of his sword, swore, that he was determined to share the fate of the meanest soldier. And, to shew the greater security, a proclamation was at the same time issued, giving every one full liberty to retire; but menacing the severest punishment to those who should discover any symptoms of cowardice in the ensuing battle. Lord Falconberg was sent to recover the post which had been lost: he passed the river some miles above Ferrybridge, and falling unexpectedly on Lord Clifford, revenged the former disaster by the defeat of the party and the death of their leader.

(Hume 1983, II, pp.456–7)

49

Henry Fuseli 1741–1825
Siegfried Bathes in the Blood of the Dragon 1806
Pen, pencil and grey wash on paper
34.8 x 23.7 cm
Auckland Art Gallery Toi o Tāmaki.
Purchased 1965
[Illustrated on p.96]

By the light of the moon, the German hero Siegfried bathes in the blood of the dragon he has slain, making him invincible but for a spot between his shoulder blades. The subject derives from a fleeting reference to this scene from the German medieval epic the *Nibelungenlied*, although there was a wide literary tradition relating to the theme (Flood 1998). The drawing is inscribed with a phrase from Christoph Heinrich Myller's German edition (1782) included in the lines: 'The hero slew a dragon and bathed in its blood, from which its skin grew so horny so that no weapon will bite it' (Book III, line 104, Hatto 1969, p.28).

Fuseli frequently drew and painted scenes from the *Nibelungenlied* in the later part of his career (see no.27). He also returned to such themes in his own poetry. The last lines of his *Chriemhilds Klage um Sivrit* (c.1802–10) refer to this scene:

> May darkness veil the moonlit night
> when you slew the dragon; may the
> linden forests
> eternally splinter, in whose depths you
> bathed in the blood of the dragon.
> (see Tomory 1979, no.19)

The idea of a hero invulnerable but for one weak-spot links the northern hero Siegfried to the Greek Achilles in an obvious way (the latter was invincible but for his heel). Fuseli conceives of his Siegfried in an overtly classicising fashion: the smooth limbs and perfected physique evoke ancient sculptures, the appreciation of which involved an erotic dynamic that involved subjective identification and objectification, 'masculine' and 'feminine' desires (see Potts 1994). Both are brought fully into play by our artist with the presence of the enormous, inescapably phallic, snake, on the one hand, and the feminine elegance of his figure and the elaborate coiffure reminiscent of Fuseli's designs of femmes fatales, on the other.

50

Henry Fuseli 1741–1825
Siegfried and Kriemhild 1807
Pen and watercolour on paper 48 x 36 cm
Auckland Art Gallery Toi o Tāmaki.
Purchased 1965
[Illustrated on p.97]

Like no.49 this drawing, dated to January 1807, depicts a scene from the medieval German epic the *Nibelungenlied*. The hero Siegfried is shown on his knees before Kriemhild, at the moment of their first meeting (Hatto 1969, pp.47–99; see Tomory 1979, no.20). The dominatrix-like heroine cups his head in her hands, gently perhaps, but also suggesting violence; the themes of sexual domination, erotic submission and cruelty are intertwined in the story.

Nos.49 and 50 are from the group of highly developed watercolours and drawings representing scenes from the *Nibelungenlied* created by Fuseli in around 1805–7 (Klemm 2005). Quite exceptionally, these were created before an English translation of the text was available; there is a pattern of Fuseli turning to a particular literary source only at the appearance of a new translation (see no.51 for an example). Although the original text of the *Nibelungenlied* remained obscure to British readers, Fuseli did present a number of canvases representing scenes from this source at the Royal Academy, first in 1807 and again between 1814 and 1820. Fuseli was unusually well-informed about German medieval epic in purely scholarly terms, but he also recognised the directly emotional appeal of northern themes among cultural publics growing in self-confidence and a sense of national – and perhaps ethnic – identity (see Mee 1992, pp.75–120; Smiles 1994; Trumpener 1997). In one of his 'Aphorisms on Art' prepared in manuscript from around 1788 through to about 1818, he wrote: 'We are more impressed by Gothic than by Greek mythology, because the bands are not yet rent which tie us to its magic: he has a powerful hold of us, who holds us by our superstitions or by a theory of honour' (Knowles 1831, III, p.102).

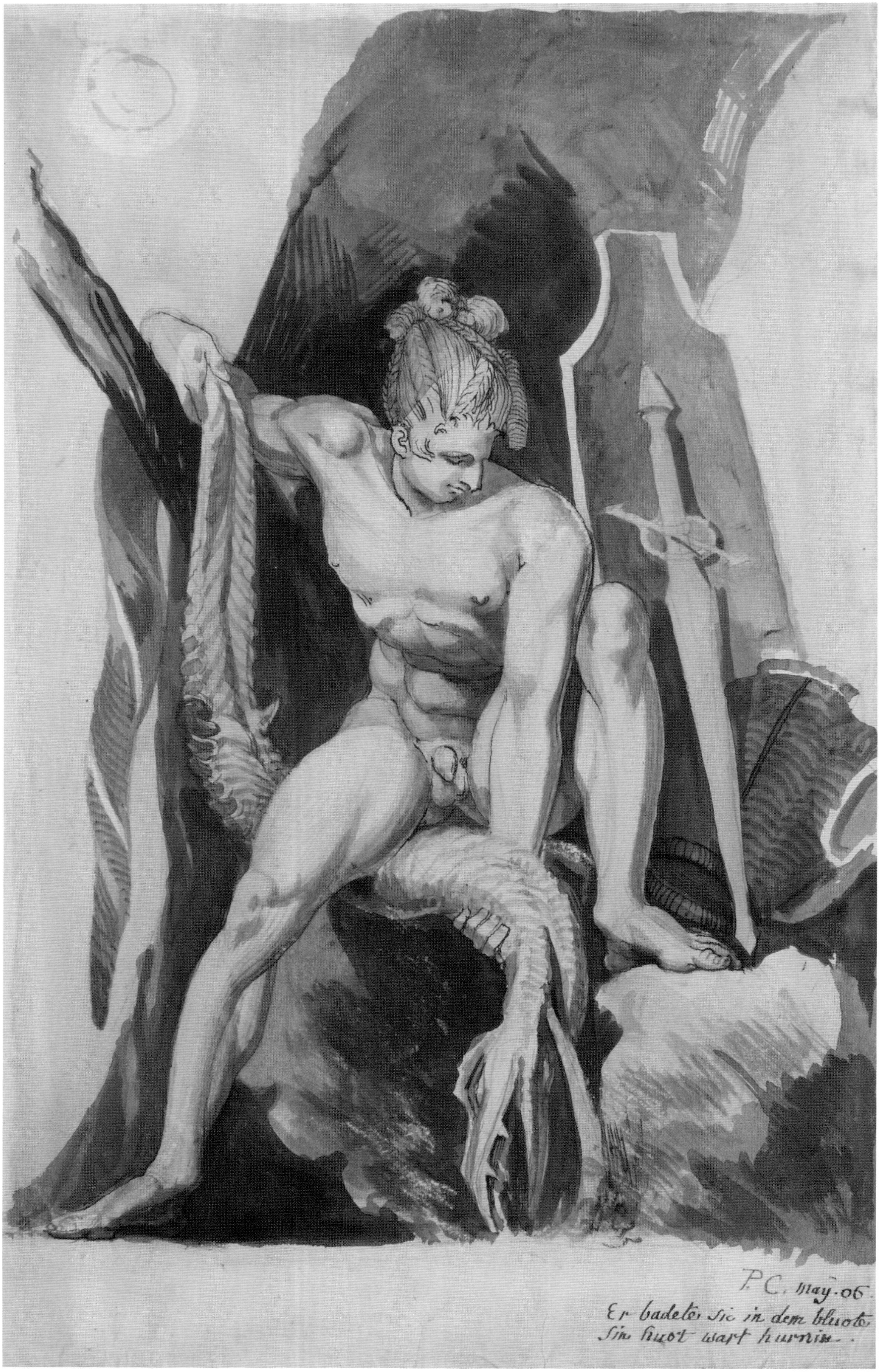
P.C. May. 06.
Er badete sic in dem bluote
Sin huot wart hurnin.

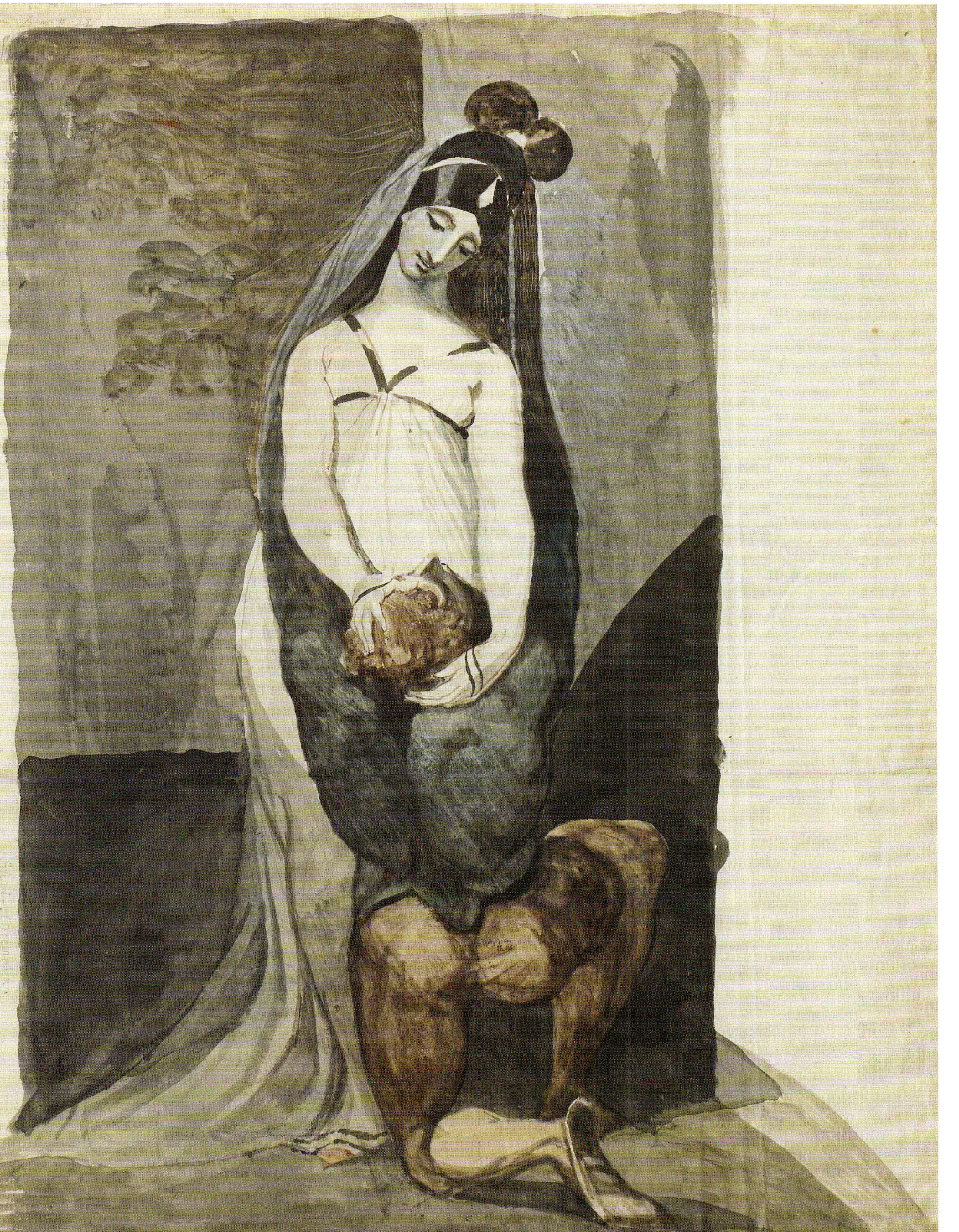

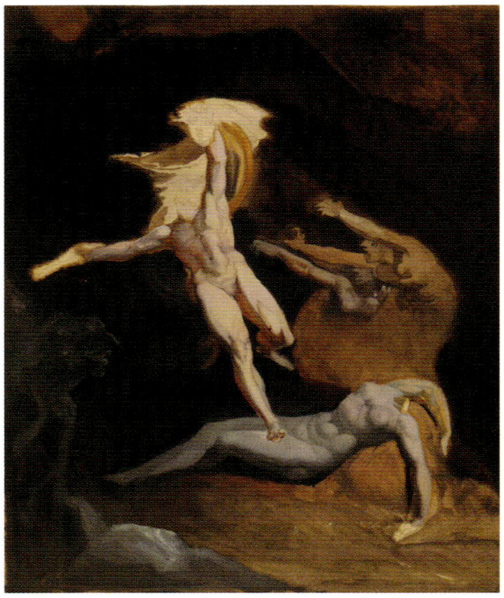

51

Henry Fuseli 1741–1825
Perseus Starting from the Cave of the Gorgons c.1816
Oil and oil wash over pencil and with touches of pen and black ink, on tan laid paper laid down on off-white Japanese paper 67.6 x 55.2 cm
Art Institute of Chicago. The Lenora Hall Gurley Memorial Collection (1980.1092)

The hero Perseus flies from the clutches of the Gorgons, the decapitated head of the foul snake-haired monster, the Medusa, in his hand. Her headless corpse lies across the lower portion of the design.

A now lost drawing of this composition is dated 1816 (Schiff 1973, no.1531) and is assumed to be the foundation of a painting exhibited in 1817 as 'Perseus Starting from the Cave of the Gorgons'. C.R. Leslie (1794–1859) saw Fuseli in his studio working on this: 'The figure of Medusa is very happily conceived, and he has contrived to hide all the disgusting part, – the stump of the neck and the blood, – very judiciously' (letter to Miss Eliza Leslie, 12 December 1816 in Weinglass 1982, p.429). The source, as indicated in the reference in the 1817 Academy catalogue, is Hesiod's 'Shield of Heracles', the Greek poet's extended evocation of the heroic and sublime scenes adorning that hero's shield. Fuseli's conception of the mid-air Perseus matches Hesiod's description of the almost magically crafted figure. The 'Shield' had featured in a new translation published in 1815, which may partly have prompted Fuseli's turning to this subject. The recreation of the more famous 'Shield of Achilles' described by Homer was the subject of a design by Flaxman (started c.1810, completed c.1818; see Bindman 1979, no.187 and Irwin 1979, pp.194–202).

The psychoanalytic possibilities of this image are rife. For theorists of sexuality, following Sigmund Freud's essay 'Medusa's Head' (1922), the story of the Medusa is a powerfully symbolic narrative (see Hertz 1985). Medusa is the exemplary phallically endowed woman, self-sufficient in sexual terms and therefore threatening and monstrous. Her decapitation may register a return to order, and her gaze, turning men to stone, an allegorisation of the male erection. Here we might want to attend particularly to the visual irony that sees Perseus himself headless – in the sense that his features are only lightly indicated – and the position of the hero's right foot jabbing the dead Medusa's pubic area.

Hesiod, The Shield of Hercules, trans. Charles Elton (1815)

There was the horseman, fair-hair'd Danaë's son,
Perseus: nor yet the buckler with his feet
Touch'd, nor yet distant hover'd: strange to think:
For nowhere on the surface of the shield
He rested: so the crippled artist-god
Illustrious framed him with his hands in gold.
Bound to his feet were sandals wing'd: a sword
Of brass with hilt of sable ebony
Hung round him from the shoulders by a thong:
Swift e'en as thought he flew. The visage grim
Of monstrous Gorgon all his back o'erspread:
And wrought in silver, wondrous to behold,
A veil was drawn around it, whence in gold
Hung glittering fringes: and the dreadful helm
Of Pluto clasp'd the temples of the prince,
Shedding a night of darkness. Thus outstretch'd
In air, he seem'd like one to trembling flight
Betaken. Close behind the Gorgons twain
Of nameless terror unapproachable
Came rushing: eagerly they stretch'd their arms
To seize him: from the pallid adamant,
Audibly as they rush'd. the clattering shield
Clank'd with a sharp shrill sound. Two grisly snakes
Hung from their girdles, and with forking tongues
Lick'd their inflected jaws; and violence gnash'd
Their fangs fell glaring: from around their heads
Those Gorgons grim a flickering horror cast
Through the wide air.

(Elton 1815, pp.226–7)

52

Henry Fuseli 1741–1825
Undine and Huldbrand c.1819–22
Watercolour on paper 48.1 x 31.9 cm
Auckland Art Gallery Toi o Tāmaki.
Purchased 1965

The subject is taken from the short tale *Undine*, by the German writer Friedrich de la Motte Fouqué (1777–1843), first published in 1811 and translated into English in 1818. His story is considered to be the masterwork of the early nineteenth-century German literary genre described as 'Kunstmärchen': 'artistic' fairy tales (see Tully 2000; also Zipes 2002, pp.43–103).

The story addresses themes of sexual desire, faithfulness and fate. A water-nymph, Undine, is taken in by two fisher-folk and brought up in the human community. She knows that to gain a soul and assume full human emotion she must marry a man who loves her as much as she loves him, and never betrays her; any fall from grace will mean she is reclaimed by the elements. She falls in love with the handsome Huldbrand and the two marry. It looks as if all will end well until the arrival of Bertalda, the true daughter of the fisher-folk who had been lost and adopted by wealthy parents. Huldbrand is torn between the two, and his divided passions, and the obscurely motivated interference of Undine's evil uncle Kühleborn, leads to tragedy (see also nos.109–10).

Fuseli created a group of at least ten drawings and paintings on subjects taken from *Undine* around 1819–22 (see Weinglass 1994, no.224A; Tomory 1979, no.34) suggested that the lines illustrated here relate to the moment when Undine warns Huldbrand of Kühleborn's threat, placing her love for him above her family:

> Huldbrand deeply felt the generosity of his lovely wife in thus earnestly shutting out her powerful protector, and doing the act of kindness to one who had so wantonly and ignorantly censured her for that very kindness. He pressed her affectionately to his bosom.
> (de la Motte Fouqué 1818, p.xx)

The lightly suggested figure in the distance would in this case be Bertalda. There may, however, be other incidents which might suggest themselves as potential sources, involving passionate embraces between the nymph and her husband.

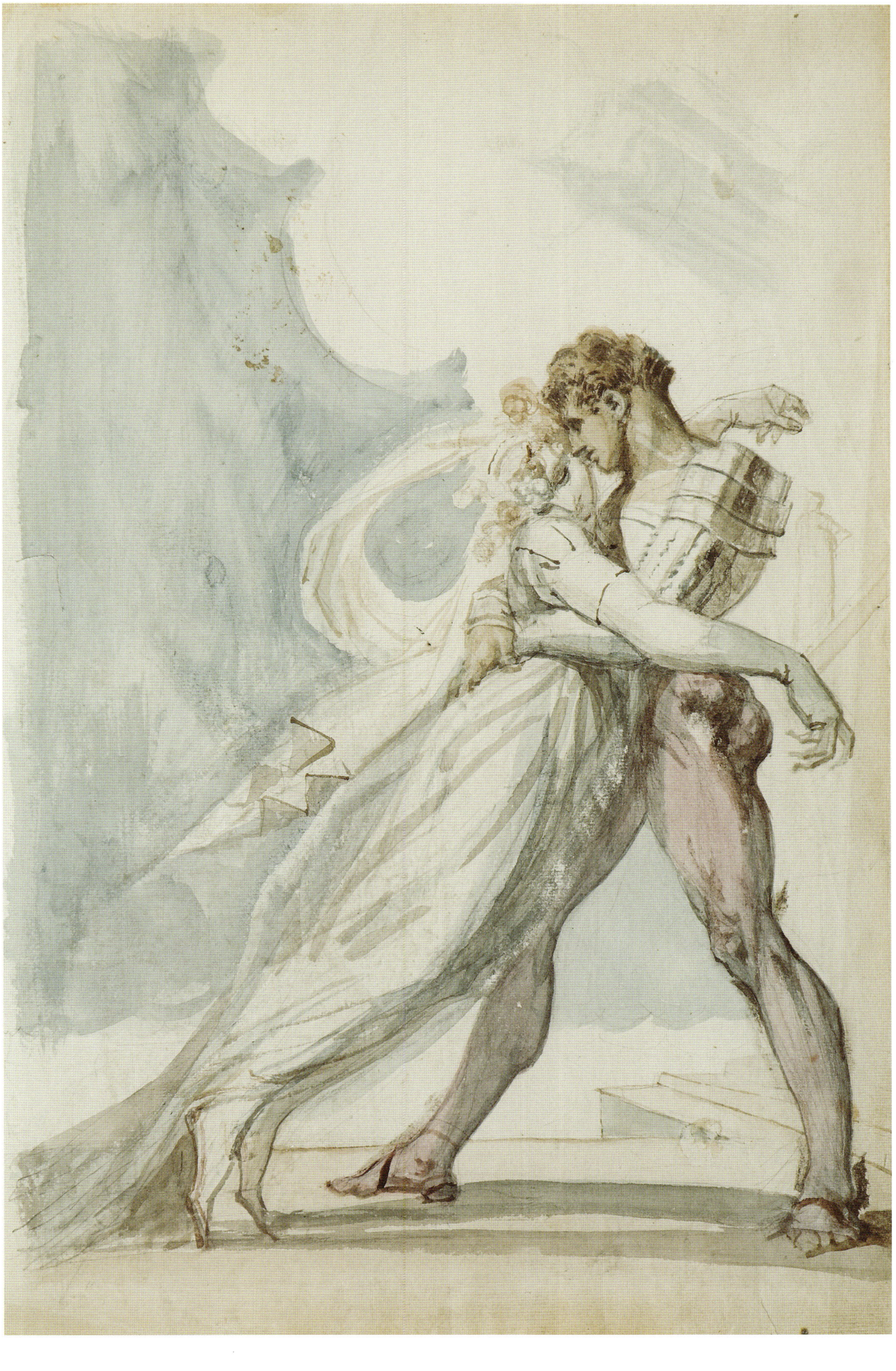

Gothic Gloomth

Castles and dungeons, blasted heaths and sepulchral cells, forests and storm-ravaged cliffs, maidens in distress, rugged heroes, alchemists, wizards, ghosts, rotting corpses, bleeding nuns, monks, mad priests and viragoes, distressed lovers and imprisoned virgins, overwrought widows, sex, death, madness, incest, infanticide, patricide, matricide, rape and torture ... these are the raw materials of the Gothic: sometimes genuinely shocking, more often extravagant, ridiculous, and laugh-out-loud silly.

The taste for Gothic horror and fantasy was *the* popular cultural phenomenon of the late eighteenth century. Originating in the reappraisal of medieval architecture and romance literature, the politically charged investigation of the ancient origins of the British state, and a new interest in Sublime themes of terror and the supernatural, the Gothic developed in the 1780s as the first form of trash literature, reaching a massive and socially diverse readership through cheap publication and circulating libraries.

The Gothic was a complex phenomenon, of central importance in late eighteenth- and early nineteenth-century literature, theatre, architecture and the visual arts. The term 'Gothic' had traditionally referred to the whole, vast historical period from the Romans to the Renaissance; it also referred to the aesthetic characteristics associated with that era – hardness, awkwardness and unnaturalness (Frank 1960; Sowerby 2000; Punter and Byron 2004, pp.32–8). It came into use as a general term of abuse for anything that displayed those characteristics, or simply lacked classical balance and order – from wigs to chairs to buildings.

Horace Walpole's (1717–1797) *Castle of Otranto* (1764) was the first novel we think of as 'Gothic', meaning that it dealt with themes that were supernatural, horrific or perverse and the damp, dank darkness evoked by that author's invented word, 'gloomth'. Indeed, the second edition carried the subtitle 'A Gothic Story'. It was, though, an isolated effort, until the later 1770s when the great outpouring of popular novels and stories dealing with 'Gothic' themes started to appear. Still, these tended to be called 'Romances', in recognition of their debt to medieval and Renaissance literature. In the 1790s, even more lurid and shocking subjects appeared in literature, notably with the translations of recent German novels and poems, and, particularly, Matthew Gregory Lewis's (1775–1818) vivid *The Monk* (1796). Ann Radcliffe's (1764–1923) hugely popular stories marked the highpoint of the Gothic as a literary phenomenon, and she achieved, almost uniquely, critical credibility as well.

Many editions of Gothic tales, across the market spectrum, featured illustrations, often deriving stylistically and for their motifs from the works of Fuseli. As a literary form associated with over-excited female readers and childish imaginations, Gothic literature was not, though, seen as an appropriate subject for high art. Although relatively few painters directly illustrated Gothic tales, many, and Fuseli most influentially, turned to supernatural and horrible subjects from more distinguished literary sources, mining the works of Greek playwrights and Shakespeare for the most shocking and bizarre themes. While such paintings played to the popular tastes of the day, they also claimed superior status as works of art.

The motivations and meanings of Gothic themes in literature and art have been the subject of much – and continuing – scholarly discussion. Resting so often on themes of sexual transgression and family ties, of memory and repression, psychological explanations have had much sway. But there is a general sense of agreement that Gothic responds to and represents anxieties beyond the personal. The historical traumas of the long international wars which loom over this period (1756–63, 1775–83 and 1793–1815) and the crises of Britain's empire (the loss of America in 1776 and the escalating criticism of the abuses of imperial authority and the slave trade) motivated collective fears. Further, long-repressed anxieties about the suppression of Catholicism and the ruination of the monasteries, and the associated worries about the legitimacy of the present Hanoverian dynasty haunt the Gothic. Meanwhile, concern about the apparent, disabling distance between modern life with its luxurious comforts, and the heroic past, the fractures and disjuncture within British society and between the constituent nations or ethnic identifications within the isles, and the transformations of gender relations with new ideas about sexuality and the rise of early forms of feminism were vital factors shaping the taste for romance and horror. Then there are the more materialist questions about the changing nature of cultural production, the accelerated reproduction of images and texts and the ascent of a culturally enfranchised middle rank of society.

Analysing the Gothic has been a particular preoccupation of literary history and cultural studies in America and Britain over the last couple of decades. Involving questions of gender and sexuality, definitions of high and low culture, forms of readership and production, and issues of transgression and cultural change, the Gothic seems to match many of the major concerns of contemporary scholarship. Moreover, the Gothic has reappeared in popular culture with a degree of vigour perhaps unknown since the 1790s. The Oscar success in 1992 of *Silence of the Lambs* (dir. Jonathan Demme, 1991) – a film whose dungeon aesthetics might have gratified 'Monk' Lewis – helped mark the ascent of the gory thrills of horror cinema into the mainstream, while previously denigrated genre efforts such as *Texas Chainsaw Massacre* (dir. Tobe Hooper, 1974) have been rediscovered as dynamic and powerful art. The huge international audience for *Buffy the Vampire Slayer* on television and the *Lord of the Rings* trilogy (dir. Peter Jackson, 2001–3) in cinemas, and the ubiquity of J.K. Rowling's *Harry Potter* series, have all pointed towards a mainstream acceptance of themes that were once the exclusive province of cultish enthusiasts. Contemporary writers such as Iain Banks and Patrick McGrath have achieved critical acclaim, while Gothic texts by Angela Carter and Toni Morrison have entered the canon. In the more rarefied field of the visual arts, Gothic motifs and themes have had a distinct presence in contemporary practice, as was demonstrated by the 1997 Boston Institute of Contemporary Art show, *Gothic* (Grunenberg 1997). As Carter announced, 'We live in Gothic times' (Carter 1995, p.460). What had been a relatively casual statement in 1974 has proved to be more astute than anyone could have realised.

53

Joseph Wright of Derby 1734–1797
A Philosopher by Lamp Light exh. 1769 at the Society of Artists
Oil on canvas 128.2 x 101.6 cm
Derby Museum and Art Gallery

An old man in the costume of a hermit or philosopher contemplates human bones in a lamp-lit cave, while two small men or boys dressed as pilgrims (the shells in the hats identify them as such) approach with trepidation.

The exact subject of this painting has been the source of some speculation (Nicolson 1968, no.196; Cummings 1970; Egerton 1990, no.41). Wright's picture evokes several literary sources, but the presence of the young men suggests a text by Lucian, 'The Lover of Lies, or The Doubter', which describes the philisopher Democritus as having shut himself up in a tomb with his studies, where boys discover him and attempt – unsuccessfully – to frighten him. A more modern literary source has been identified in a passage from Robert Burton's *The Anatomy of Melancholy*, first published as by 'Democritus junior' in 1621, which describes that philosopher in his garden, reading a book about 'melancholy and madness'. However, Wright himself was not entirely consistent. The picture was exhibited in 1769 under the title given here (presumably supplied by the artist), and was described in a review as 'a Philosopher contemplating the human Skeleton by the light of a Lamp' (*Lloyd's Evening Post*, 3–5 May 1769). It was engraved in 1770 by William Pether as 'An Hermit' (Egerton 1990, no.P.5). Wright refers to it in a letter of 12 February 1774 as 'Hermit Studying Anatomy'. The picture was listed in Wright's account book as 'The hermit' with a further reference to 'Galen for Ditto'. Does this suggest that at one time Wright meant the old man to be taken for that ancient anatomist?

Aside from the lack of exact clarity about the theme, the picture is all the more mystifying for its bizarre ambiguity of scale. Even if we accept that the two young men to the right are intended as children, they are diminutive in relation to the figure of the hermit They should be placed deep within the picture's space in order to be read in correct perspective. However, the boy to the left seems to rest his hand on a surface which is directly connected to the hermit's cave. Wright did sometimes struggle with perspective, as is evident in his drawing for the 'Captive King', where he turned for advice to his friend P.P. Burdett (no.55). But we might suggest that Wright's concern here is primarily atmosphere, and the eerie and disconcerting influence of this dislocation of scale, whether intended or not, enhances the overall effect of the painting. Such a disrupted space chimes with the complex and irrational spaces conceived within Gothic narratives.

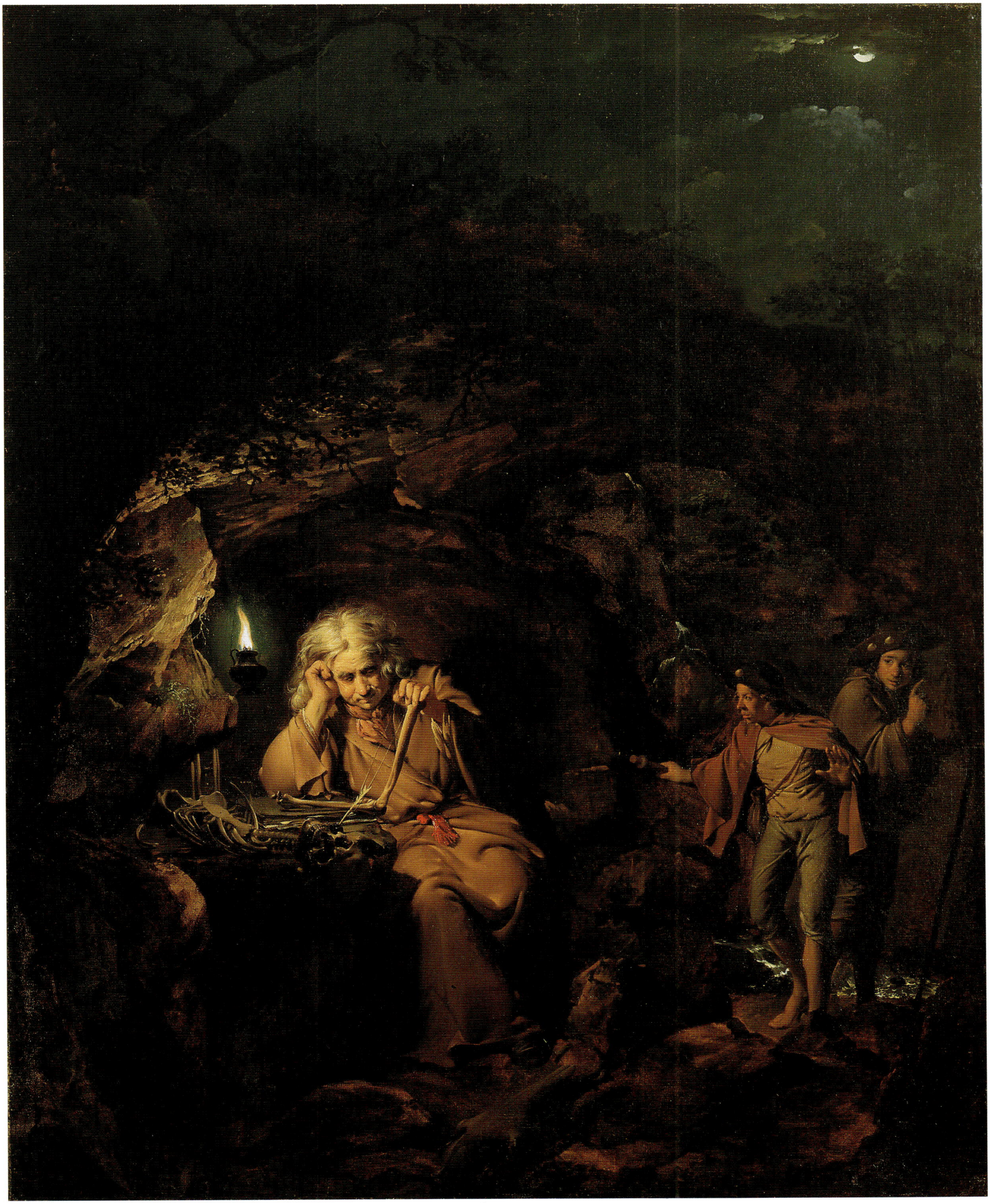

54

John Dixon fl.1767–1801
after Joshua Reynolds 1723–1792
Ugolino, published by John Boydell, 4 February 1774
Mezzotint 50 x 61 cm
The British Museum, London
(1893-5-16-112)

The story of the terrible imprisonment of Count Ugolino de Gherardeschi (d.1288) was the most celebrated episode in Dante's *Inferno*. Thrown into prison after a political intrigue, which had brought him temporarily to power in the city of Pisa, Ugolino was left to starve to death along with two of his sons and two grandchildren. The painting represents the moment at which he hears the door being permanently sealed, and he is suddenly awakened to his dreadful fate. Recounted in awful detail by Dante, Ugolino will be overcome by hunger and transformed into an anthropophagus beast.

The mezzotint reproduces the original painting, exhibited at the Royal Academy in 1773 (National Trust, Knole; Mannings 2000, no.2173; Postle 1995, pp.138–56). The print itself was shown at the rival Society of Artists in 1774. The composition incorporates a number of knowing art-historical references, to Michelangelo, Charles Le Brun and Annibale Carracci, though Ugolino's features are based on those of the much-employed artist's model, George White.

Dante's *Ugolino* was the one section of the *Divine Comedy* that was widely translated into English in the eighteenth century (see Yates 1951). A relief of the subject, thought then to be by Michelangelo and in the Casa Gheradesca (now Ashmolean, Oxford) was known by a cast brought to England in the early eighteenth century and commented upon by the Dante scholars Jonathan Richardson (1667–1745) and Joseph Warton (1722–1800) (Penny 1992, no.72). Richardson's translation of this episode was probably Reynolds's immediate source. According to an early commentator (*Quarterly Review*, vol.28 [January 1823]), the revival of interest in Dante began not with literary translations, but with this picture, a claim which is now seen as exaggerated but not wholly untrue. The picture was widely acclaimed at the time of its exhibition, and the publication of this print secured its enduring reputation.

The print technique used here, mezzotint, was generally only used for portraits, to which the velvety texture and subtle tones seem particularly suited. History painting was thought properly reproduced by line engraving, the most difficult, time consuming, and therefore prestigious and expensive medium. Narrative images of horror and the supernatural seemed to require something else. This print was important in affirming the singular suitability of the mezzotint for Gothic subjects. It was similarly used in reproductions of Mortimer's witchcraft scene (no.76), and the later mezzotint prints published after Fuseli's works (no.60).

55

Joseph Wright of Derby 1734–1797
Study for *The Captive King* c.1772–3
Pen and wash on paper 33.7 x 39.7 cm
Derby Museums and Art Gallery

Reclining on straw in a lamplit medieval castle, a prisoner takes up a pose indicative of melancholy contemplation.

In 1773 Wright exhibited a picture under the title *The Captive King*. Little is known of this work, early commentators remarking when it was displayed again in Wright's one-man show in 1785 that it was uncharacteristic of the artist in its execution (*Morning Post*, 20 April 1785 and *General Evening Post*, 28–30 April 1785). Nicolson has linked the painting and the present drawing to entries in Wright's account book describing a picture of 'Guy de Lusignan in Prison' (Nicolson 1968, nos.314–15). The detail of the crucifix leaning against the pillar suggests a setting in the Crusades. Guy de Lusignan (c.1150–94) was a Frankish king defeated by the Saracens on a crusade in 1187 and taken prisoner by them. The reference was, though, initially simply to 'The Captive', and we cannot be absolutely certain that the identification of the present canvas with Wright's 'Guy de Lusignan' is correct.

Guy, King of Jerusalem in 1186–92, had been condemned as cowardly by historians (see Mills 1820, I, pp.427–8n). However, his reputation as a hero was established by Voltaire's (1694–1778) loosely historical play, *Zaïre, tragédie* (1732). This had been adapted into English as *The Tragedy of Zara* by Aaron Hill (1685–1750), performed in London in 1735, and revived in 1751 after which date it was repeatedly staged until the 1780s (see Jacobs 1988; Hill 1981). This is most likely Wright's source. Although the text of the play does not feature a scene set within Guy's cell, the vision of his tragic imprisonment is conjured by one of the main characters and his release (Act II, scene 1) is the pivotal moment of the drama; is this episode suggested by the upward gaze of Wright's prisoner, and the open door at the top of the staircase? The composition, featuring a sketchy, relatively diminutive figure in a more carefully conceived architectural setting, is reminiscent of eighteenth-century stage designs.

This drawing is notable for the addition of notes marking the intended scale of the image, and the 'vanishing point' that would dictate the perspective of the architecture. The drawing is folded, as it was sent by post to Wright's friend P.P. Burdett (1735–93). On the back is a note returned to Wright by Burdett, giving advice on perspective in another picture.

54

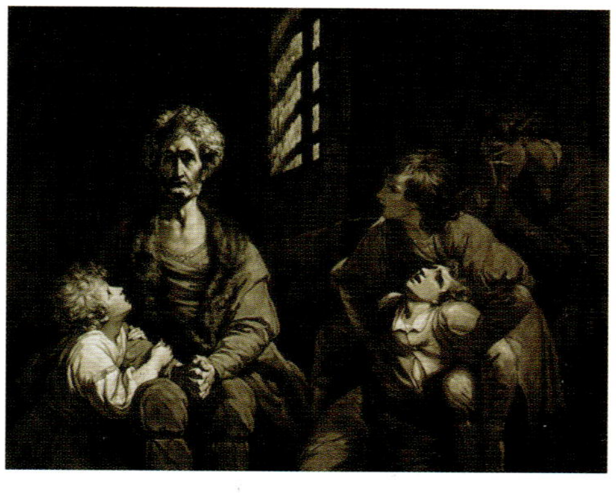

55

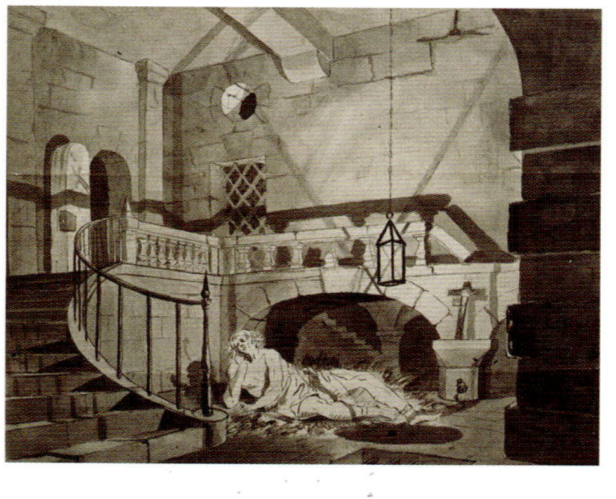

56

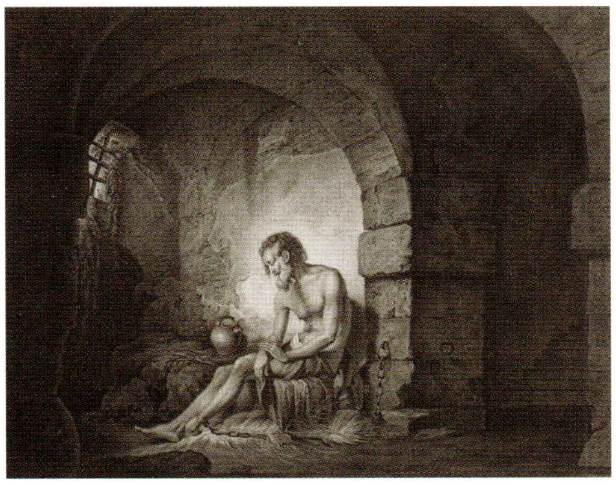

57

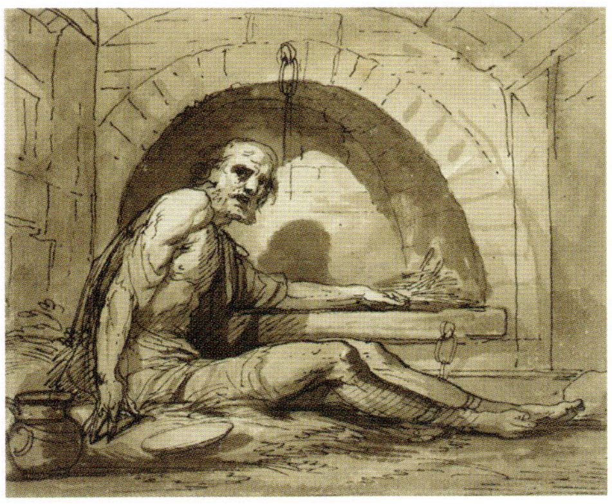

56

Thomas Ryder 1746–1810 after
Joseph Wright of Derby 1734–1797
The Captive, published by John and Josiah Boydell, 1 October 1786
Stipple engraving 43 x 50 cm
Derby Museums and Art Gallery

57

John Hamilton Mortimer 1740–1779
The Captive c.1770–4
Pencil, pen and ink, and watercolour on paper
10 x 12.8 cm
Tate. Purchased as part of the Oppé Collection with assistance from the National Lottery through the Heritage Lottery Fund 1996

Laurence Sterne's *A Sentimental Journey* (1768) comprises the encounters and reflections of the sensitive traveller Yorick, manifesting his character as a 'man of feeling'. In Paris, threatened with arrest because he lacks the proper passport, he reflects upon the terrors of the Bastille, in a section titled 'The Captive'. By focusing imaginatively on a single, suffering prisoner, Yorick is able to conjure the deepest sympathetic feelings, which the reader is invited to share.

A Sentimental Journey was one of the great popular novels of the time. Several of its scenes of sentiment were taken up by visual artists. The episode concerning Maria, a French girl abandoned by her lover and discovered by Yorick by the roadside, was a particular favourite, painted by Wright of Derby as well as featuring in many prints and decorative designs. Wright painted two large versions of the theme of 'The Captive'; the present print reproduces the canvas of 1774 in Vancouver Art Gallery (Nicolson 1968, no.216; Egerton 1990, no.53 and P.28). Mortimer's design is dated to around the same period, when he was working closely with Wright. Mortimer's captive is the more animated, his head turned to catch our attention (Sunderland 1986, no.89a). Wright's composition is, as John Bender has discussed, in the 'absorptive' mode, the prisoner seemingly consumed by his own thoughts and therefore, paradoxically, of the greater interest to the viewer (Bender 1987, pp.233–6). The appeal of both 'Maria' and 'The Captive' seems to have been their episodic quality as texts, their focus on the effort to 'figure' a profound emotional state, which was already pictorial in character and seemed therefore peculiarly suited to being put into visual form.

Laurence Sterne, <u>A Sentimental Journey through France and Italy by Mr Yorick</u> (1768)

THE CAPTIVE
PARIS

The bird in the cage pursued me into my room; I sat down close to my table, and leaning my head upon my hand, I began to figure to myself the miseries of confinement. I was in a right frame for it, and so I gave full scope to my imagination.

In was going to begin with the millions of my fellow creatures born to no inheritance but slavery; but finding, however affecting the picture was, that I could not bring it near me, and that the multitude of sad groups in it did but distract me. —

— I took a single captive, and having first shut him up in his dungeon, I then look'd through the twilight of his grated door to take his picture.

I beheld his body half wasted away with long expectation and confinement, and felt what kind of sickness of the heart it was which arises from hope deferr'd. Upon looking nearer I saw him pale and feverish: in thirty years the western breeze had not once fann'd his blood — he had seen no sun, no moon in all that time — nor had the voice of friend or kinsmen breathed through his lattice — his children —

— But here my heart began to bleed — and I was forced to go on with another part of the portrait.

He was sitting upon the ground upon a little straw, in the furthest corner of the dungeon, which was alternately his chair and bed: a little calender of small sticks were laid at the head notch'd all over with the dismal days and nights he had pass'd there — he had one of these little sticks in his hand, and with a rusty nail he was etching another day of misery to add to the heap. As I darkened the little light he had, he lifted up a hopeless eye towards the door, then cast it down — shook his head, and went on with the work of affliction. I heard his chains upon his legs, as he turn'd his body to lay his little stick upon the bundle — He gave a deep sigh — I saw the iron enter into his soul — I burst into tears — I could not sustain the picture of confinement which my fancy had drawn — I startled up from my chair …

(Sterne 2003, p.61)

58

John Downman 1750–1824
Robert, Duke of Normandy in Prison 1779
Oil on copper 23 x 19.1 cm
Paul Mellon Collection, Yale Center for British Art, New Haven

This painting shows Robert Curthose, Duke of Normandy (c.1050–1134), eldest son of William the Conquerer, imprisoned in Cardiff Castle. The discarded helmet and sword, and the tabard bearing a red cross must allude to his legendarily heroic role in the Crusades in 1096–1100. He had supposedly been offered the crown of Jerusalem, but had turned this down in expectation of attaining to the throne of England. However, his estrangement from his father led to disappointment and, according to legend, a horrible fate. His younger brother, Henry (c.1068–1135), became king in 1100. After defeating Robert's army at the battle of Tinchebrai (1106), Henry ordered that Robert be thrown into prison and (the early chronicles would have it) blinded by having red-hot metal bowls pushed into his eye sockets. Robert remained incarcerated until his death in 1134. The bright red tunic he wears in this painting may allude to the story of the scarlet robe. This recounted that Henry sent his brother a cast-off vestment of that colour, which was too small for him to wear. When Robert felt a tear in the tunic, where Henry had tried to squeeze into it, and discovered the source of the garment, he was inspired to lament his terrible lot.

Robert Curthose's achievements, adventures and sufferings had long been amplified by legend (see David 1920, pp.190–202). Eighteenth-century historians were generally more sceptical about such stories. But like Wright in no.55, Downman here plays to the public appetite for myths and legends associated with the Crusades and the darker aspects of the medieval past.

58

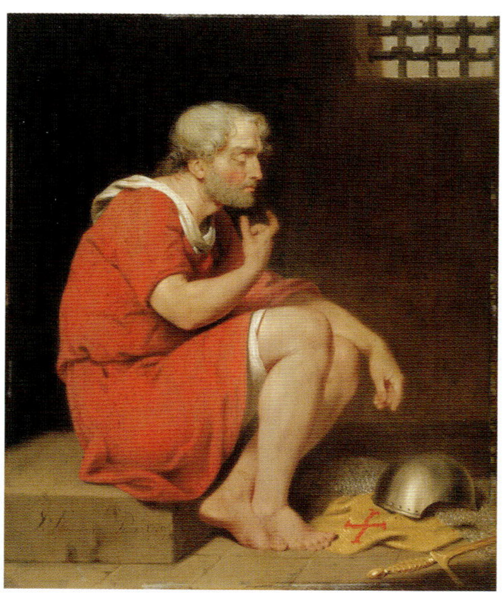

59

William Blake 1757–1827
Lear and Cordelia in Prison c.1779
Pen and watercolour on paper 12.3 x 17.5 cm
Tate. Bequeathed by Miss Alice G.E. Carthew 1940

The ageing British king Lear lies sleeping on his daughter Cordelia's lap while in prison. Lear's wilfulness has split the kingdom, and Cordelia laments the fate of her father and of the nation.

David Bindman has proposed that the drawing fits into a group of designs by Blake depicting scenes from British history (see Bindman 1973; Butlin 1981, p.16 and nos.51–70). He has suggested that the source for this scene is actually John Milton's *History of Britain* (1670). There, Lear appeared as the last in line from the Trojan Brutus, the great grandson of Aeneas, linking by blood Britain's history to the esteemed classical past. However, without suggesting that the drawing needs to be detached from that series, there is little foundation for proposing that the present design illustrates Milton's text, whether we interpret Blake's design as representing the reconciliation of the British king and his daughter, or her general lament over him. In Milton's text, Cordelia's lament over the fallen state of her father occurs only when she receives a letter; their reconciliation takes place in splendour rather than in the meagre surroundings of a prison cell (Milton 1971, pp.22–5). Instead, Blake's design more certainly follows Nahum Tate's adaptation (1681) of Shakespeare's *King Lear*, which was the only form in which the tragedy was performed in Britain in the eighteenth century (Maguire 1991). In Tate's play, Lear's imprisonment, only glancingly referred to in the original text, occupied a whole scene on stage. Blake has attended closely to the stage direction in his positioning of the figures and his conception of Lear.

59

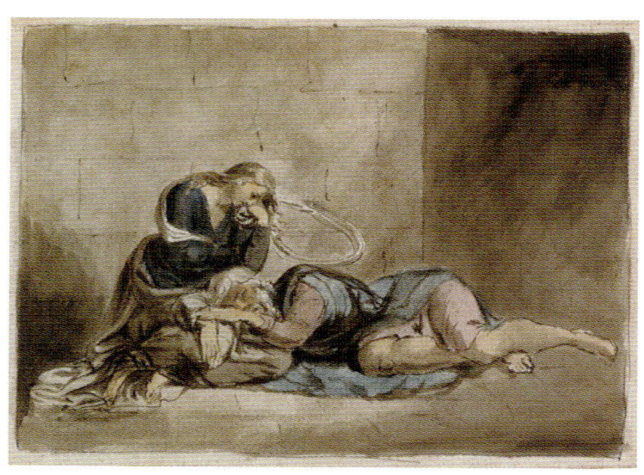

Oliver Goldsmith, The History of England (1771)

Henry, unmindful of his brother's former magnanimity with regard to him, detained him a prisoner during the remainder of his life, which was no less than twenty-eight years; and he died in the castle of Cardiff, in Glamorganshire. It is even said by some, that he was deprived of the sight by a red-hot copper bason applied to his eyes; while his brother attempted to stifle the reproaches of conscience, by founding the abbey of Reading, which was then considered as a sufficient atonement for every degree of barbarity.

(Goldsmith 1771, I, p.193)

Nahum Tate, The History of King Lear (1681), Act V, scene 6

Scene, a Prison
Lear asleep, with his head on Cordelia's lap.

CORDELIA. *What toils, thou wretched kind,*
hast thou endured
To make thee draw, in chains, a sleep so sound?
Thy better angel charm thy ravished mind
With fancied freedom. Peace is used to lodge
On cottage straw; thou hast the beggar's bed,
Therefore shouldst have the beggar's careless thought.
And now, my Edgar, I remember thee.
What fate has seized thee in this general wreck
I know now, but I know thou must be wretched
Because Cordelia holds thee dear.
O Gods! a sudden gloom o'erwhelms me, and
the image
Of death o'erspreads the place. Ha! who are these

Enter Captain and Officers with cords.

(Tate 1976, p.89)

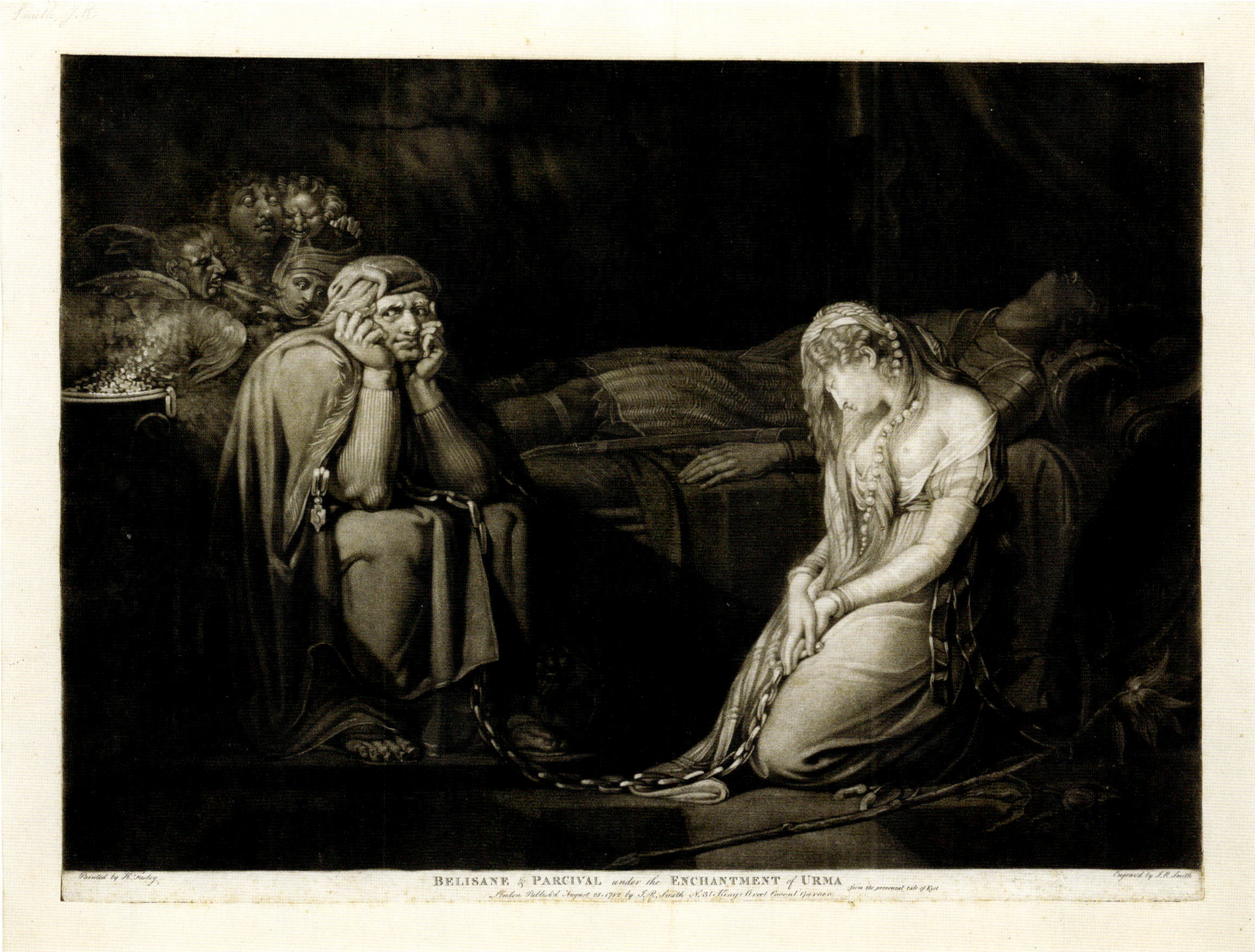

60

John Raphael Smith 1752–1812
after Henry Fuseli 1741–1825
Belisane and Parcival under the Enchantment of Urma from the Provenzal Tale of Kyot,
published by John Raphael Smith,
25 August 1782
Mezzotint 43.5 x 55.1 cm
Kunsthaus, Zurich, Grafische Sammlung

This print reproduces a lost painting, and represents a Gothic scene of Fuseli's invention. An evil witch or wizard, Urma, sulkily watches over an imprisoned maiden (Belisane) and an enchanted knight (Percival) in a tower or dungeon.

Although it has been suggested that the print represents the painting on this theme exhibited by Fuseli at the Royal Academy in 1783 (Weinglass 1994, no.70), the description of the exhibited painting in *Public Advertiser* (10 May 1783) confirms that it was actually the Tate picture (no.41) that was put on show that year.

As other examples here demonstrate (nos.54, 76) the velvety gloomth of mezzotint was seen as peculiarly appropriate to Gothic subjects of this sort. The present print comes from a succession of mezzotints published by John Raphael Smith after paintings by Fuseli in the years 1781–5 (D'Oench 1999, pp.81–5). These included *Ezzelin Musing over the Body of his Wife Meduna* (1781), *Lady Macbeth Walking in her Sleep* (1784), *Lear Wakes to Find Cordelia Beside his Bed* (1784) and *The Weird Sisters* (1785; see no.80). It was also in these years that Smith published Thomas Burke's stipple engraving of *The Nightmare* (no.4).

61

Philippe Jacques de Loutherbourg 1740–1812
A Philosopher in a Moonlit Churchyard 1790
Oil on canvas 86.3 x 68.5 cm
Paul Mellon Collection, Yale Center for British Art, New Haven

A study in mood and atmosphere: a figure in vaguely historical costume stands in the overgrown ruins of an abbey, contemplating the remnants of an old painting on the shattered wall showing the Resurrection. Above the figure of Christ a sundial throws a long moonlight shadow, suggesting the imminence of death and the possibility of salvation.

The ruin at the rear of the composition is identifiable as the exterior of the north transept of Tintern Abbey in the Wye Valley (Joppien 1964). This was one of the most visited tourist sites of the late eighteenth century, favoured because of its emotive historical associations with the Reformation. De Loutherbourg had visited and sketched the ruins in 1786, although the architecture in the foreground of this picture does not derive from actual topography. Rudiger Joppien has suggested that the painting alludes specifically to a section of Edward Young's *Night Thoughts* (1747; Part IV) where the narrator reflects upon death and upon the role of Christ as offering salvation. Whether or not this specific literary reference is intended, ruins were a recurring theme in eighteenth-century poetry, facilitating meditations upon the passage of history, the fate of civilisation and the fragile nature of humanity – all important ideas organising the historiography and cultural thought of the era. In the last third of the century the depiction of ruins became increasingly popular as part of the interrelated rise of the Gothic and of Picturesque ideals. In the 1790s, poetry, criticism, antiquarian research and artistic practice coincided around the image of the religious ruin as a symbol of a common cultural heritage. The landscape theorist William Gilpin (1813–94) mused: 'abbeys … being naturalized to the soil, might indeed, without much impropriety, be classed among its natural beauties … where popery prevails, the abbey is still inhabited, and of course less adapted to landscape' (Gilpin 1786, I, pp.12–13).

Recent scholarship has emphasised the importance of religious feeling in the Gothic: 'Whether responding with religious awe, curiosity, or anti-Catholicism, people found in ruined abbeys an image of a religious past to be addressed in the present' (Kennedy 2001, p.504). It has been argued that the ruined abbey stood as a symbol of the anxiety – even guilt – regarding the brutality of the Reformation and the suppression of the monasteries in the sixteenth and seventeenth centuries, and it was the associated guilty fears about superstition and Catholicism which underpinned the revival of the Gothic in its various manifestations in the later eighteenth century (Charlesworth 1994 and 2002). Recommending the picture's purchase to the collector Paul Mellon in 1974, the architectural historian John Harris noted that 'to my mind it epitomizes the whole aspect of the Gothic novel' (John Harris to Paul Mellon, 22 February 1974; letter on file at the Yale Center for British Art, New Haven).

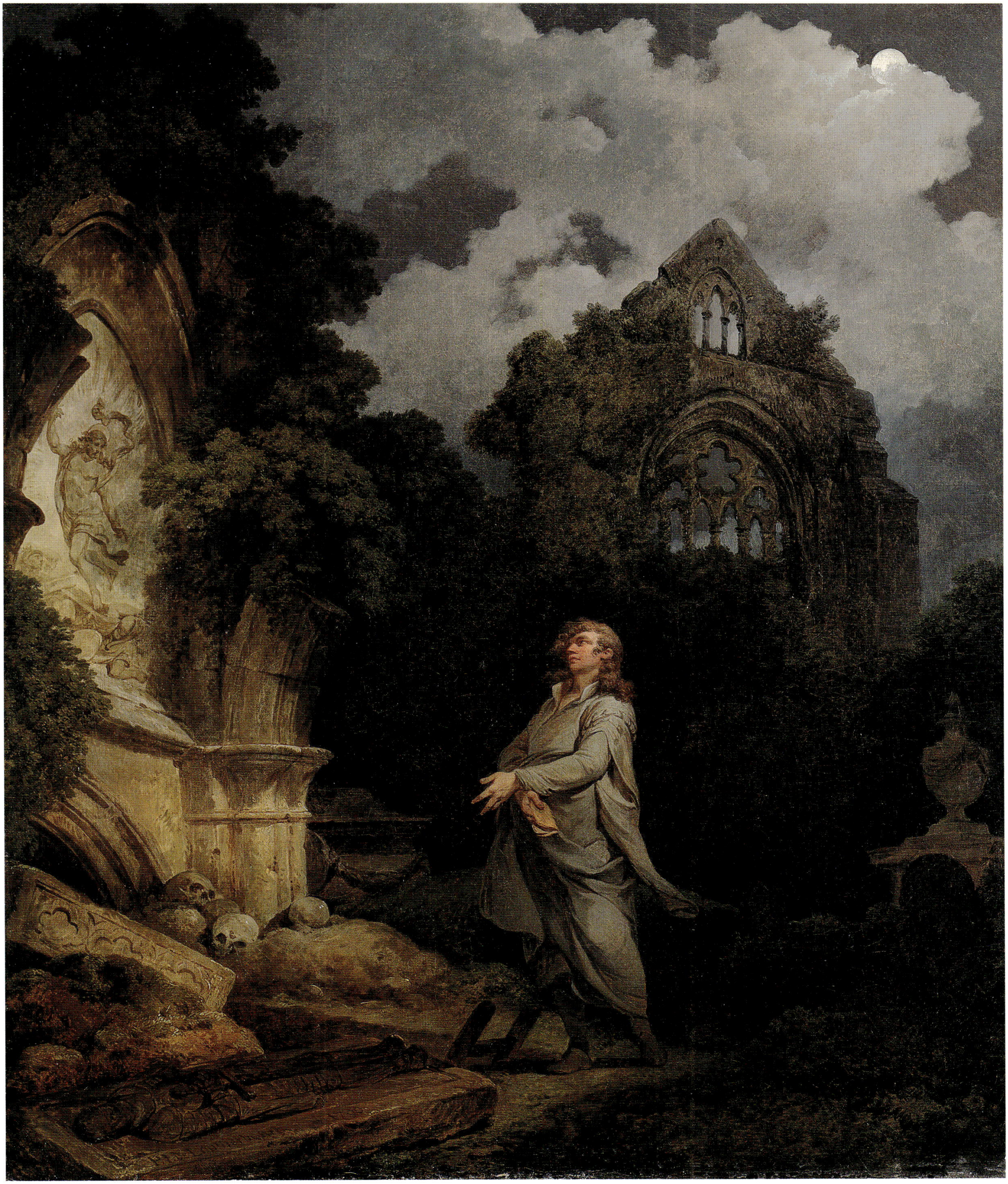

62

Thomas Robinson fl.1770–d.1810
The Hermit of Warkworth 1793
Oil on canvas 124 x 98 cm
Sir Robert Goff

The subject, previously unidentified, is from Thomas Percy's poem *The Hermit of Warkworth: A Northumberland Ballad in Three Fits* or *Cantos* (London 1771). The Hermit weeps as he tells the tragic tale of Sir Bertram and the 'beauteous maid' Isabel Widdrington to a pair of eloped lovers, Henry Percy, the son of Henry Hotspur who had died in the rebellion against Henry IV, and Eleanor Neville, the half-sister of the king. Henry wears the costume of a hunter, the profession he had taken up in his exile, and Eleanor is dressed in the flimsy costume in which she made her hasty escape. In the background, Sir Bertram mourns by the side of Isabel, the women he loved but who died accidentally by his sword, while the Hermit recites a narrative that will climax in the revelation that he was that ill-fated hero, now living in penance as a Benedictine monk.

Percy's poem claimed its subject from a sculpture in the chapel of the rock-hewn fourteenth-century Hermitage of Warkworth Castle, Northumberland. Although in a ruinous state even in Percy's time, the poet asserted the identity of these sculpted figures, taking the animal's head at the feet of the effigy as a bull's, the emblem of the Widdrington family. A modern description notes, by contrast, that all that remains of the sculpture are 'two much weather-worn lumps of rock' which require considerable imaginative efforts to be recognised as figures at all, and then, perhaps, as part of a Nativity group rather than a romantic memorial (Blair and Honeymoon 1981, p.5). Robinson's painting renders this scene ambiguously, so it may be read either as a spectral vision evoked by the Hermit's emotive words, as an imaginative reinvention of the original sculpture, or as the spectre of Sir Bertram visiting a sculpted tomb.

Thomas Percy (1729–1811) had been the chaplain of his namesake, Hugh Percy, the duke of Northumberland (to whom *The Hermit* was dedicated); he first visited the Hermitage when at the duke's nearby castle, Alnwick, in 1765. As an editor of old texts, Percy exercised a profound influence on contemporary taste. His compilation of old ballads, *Reliques of Ancient English Poetry* (1765), was the major scholarly document in the revival of earlier English literature, and an important source for artists (see nos.82, 96, 107). *The Hermit of Warkworth* was an extended pastiche of the old Northumbrian ballads Percy had previously compiled, a heady tale of storm-blasted Northern landscapes, castles and towers, knights in armour and Scottish bandits, dynastic feuding, passionate love and unbearable tragedy. It went through two editions in 1771, and continued to be republished through the nineteenth century. The scene painted here had been represented on the title-page of the first edition, in an engraving designed by Samuel Wale (Percy 1771).

The English artist Thomas Robinson worked in Ulster from around 1793, where he was extensively employed by Percy, who had become Bishop of Dromore, Co. Down, in 1782. The present canvas appears to have belonged to Robinson's son, Thomas Romney Robinson (1792–1882), whose precocious literary talents were cultivated by Percy. In the biography of the young Thomas Romney prefacing his *Juvenile Poems* (1806), it was said that:

> When his son was about two years old, Mr Robinson having drawn two pictures from the Hermit of Warkworth, was in the habit of reading aloud some pathetic passages of that beautiful poem. The child used to listen with fixed attention, watch with anxiety the variations of expression in his father's countenance and shed tears as he observed him affected.
> (Robinson 1806, p.iii)

A large-scale version of this composition appears in the background to Robinson's painting of a gathering at the Bishop's Palace at Dromore (Castleward, National Trust), although that house fell into ruin in the late nineteenth century and it is not clear whether this is mere fancy, or whether such a large painting did once exist. According to an early twentieth-century report, the dining room, which Robinson shows adorned with his large painting of the *Hermit of Warkworth*, had been converted into a chapel (Gaussen 1908, p.205).

Thomas Percy, The Hermit of Warkworth (1771)

Beside the altar rose a Tomb
All in the living stone;
On which a young and beauteous Maid
In goodly sculpture shone.

A kneeling Angel fairly carv'd
Lean'd hovering o'er her breast;
A weeping Warrior at her feet'
*And near to these her Crest**

The cliff, the vault, but chief the tomb,
Attract the wondering pair:
Eager they ask, What hapless dame
Lies sculptured here so fair?

The Hermit sigh'd, the Hermit wept,
For sorrow scarce could speak:
At length he wip'd the trickling tears
That all bedewed his cheek:

Alas! my children, human life
Is but a vale of woe;
And very mournful is the tale,
Which ye so fain would know …

** This is a Bull's Head, the crest of the WIDDRINGTON family. All the Figures, &c. here described are still visible; only somewhat effaced with length of time.*

(Percy 1771, pp.17–18)

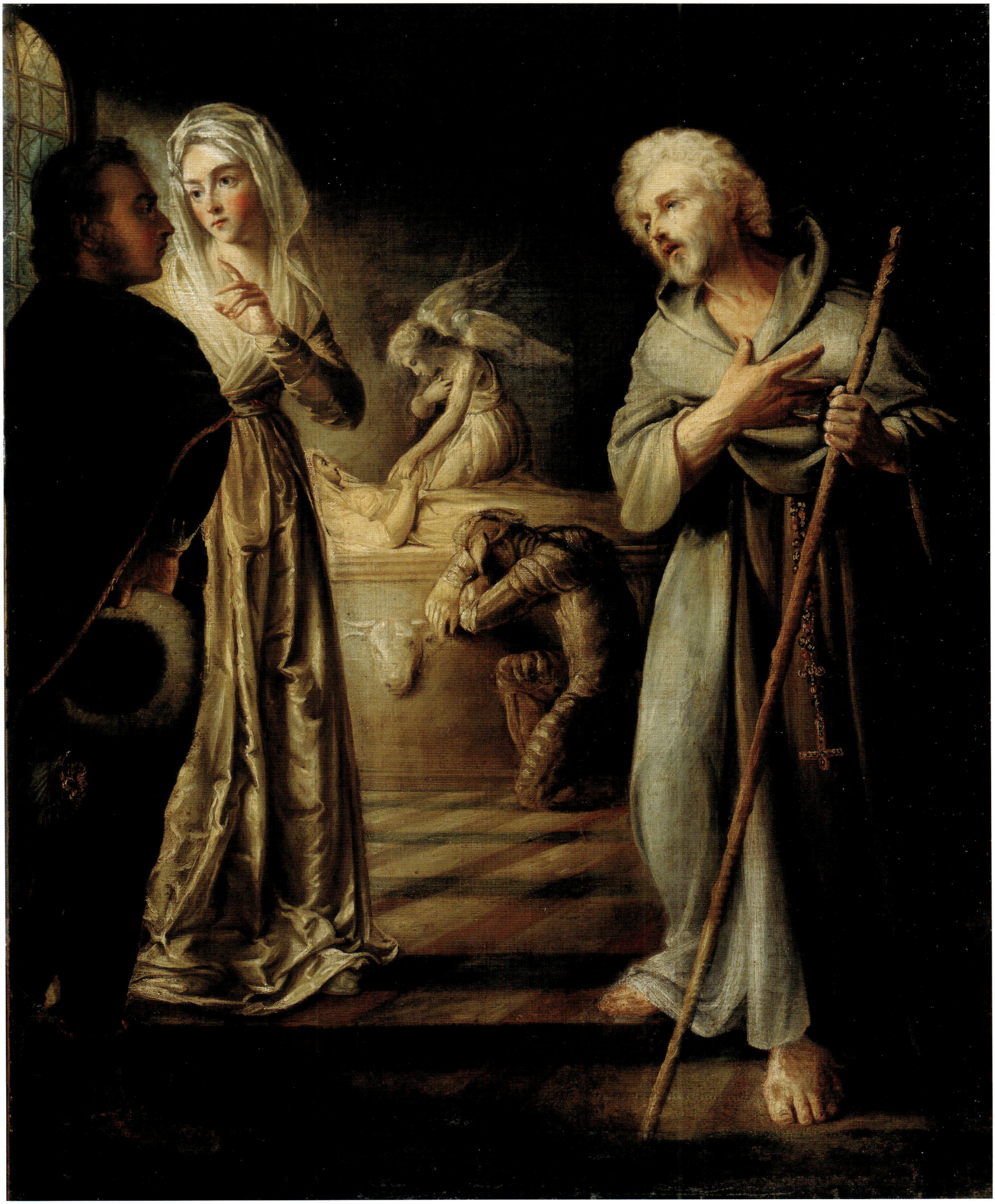

63

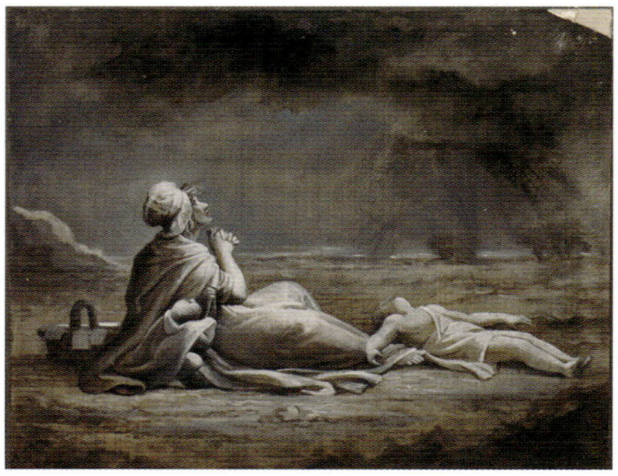

64

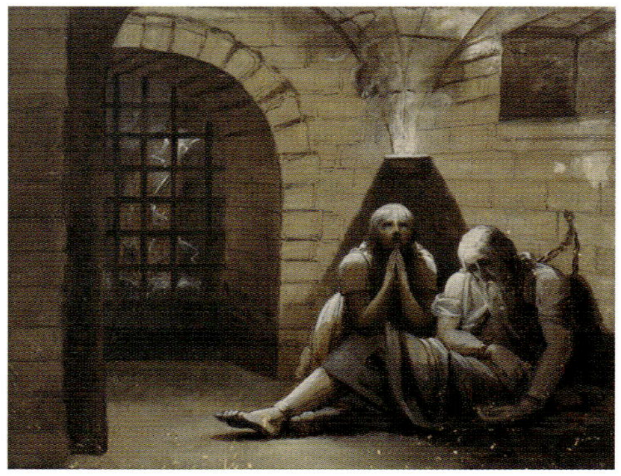

63

Maria Cosway 1760–1838
Night scene, woman with two children, one apparently dead at seashore (study for *The Wintry Day*, plate no.2) 1800
Brown ink and wash, heightened with white, on paper 22.5 x 28.1 cm
Print Collection, Miriam and Ira D. Wallach Division of Art, Prints and Photographs, The New York Public Library, Astor, Lenox and Tilden Foundations

64

Maria Cosway 1760–1838
Prison scene (study for *The Wintry Day*, plate no.6) 1800
Brown ink and wash, heightened in white, on paper 22 x 28.1 cm
Print Collection, Miriam and Ira D. Wallach Division of Art, Prints and Photographs, The New York Public Library, Astor, Lenox and Tilden Foundations

These drawings are from a group of designs created by Maria Cosway to illustrate the poem *The Wintry Day* by Mary Robinson (1758–1800), first published in 1800 (Barnett 1995, pp.147–8; Robinson 2000, p.16). Once a celebrated society beauty and mistress to the rich and famous, Robinson's last years were blighted by poverty and neglect, and the publication of these prints was meant charitably. Robinson had received a note from Cosway saying that they were completed in September 1800, but in the event she died before their publication, engraved by Caroline Watson (1758–1814) in 1804. The poem contrasts the fates of the rich and the poor. While the former drink, dance and are generally merry in luxurious and warm interiors, the latter undergo a variety of Gothic travails in damp hovels, on 'bleak and barren heath' (no.63) or on 'the prison's flinty floor' (no.64).

Robinson's literary productions were full of ripe emotional drama. She produced a number of Gothic novels, and the theme of imprisonment (which as a debtor she had experienced at first hand) recurs in her poems; but even in dealing with domestic themes – not least her own dramatic life in her *Memoirs* – the heightened feelings and sensitivities tended towards extravagance (Close 2004). The pictorial quality of her approach was highlighted in a series published as 'Poetical Pictures' in the *Morning Post* (1798–1800), evoking scenes of 'The Monk', 'The Cell of the Atheist' and 'The Dungeon', 'which it would require the best artists of Somerset House to execute' (*Morning Post*, 12 May 1798 in Robinson 2000, p.307). Still, in his introduction to his publication of the prints in 1804, Rudolph Ackermann wrote rather apologetically of the over-the-top nature of the accompanying designs created by Cosway, turning to the claims of 'original genius' as an alibi:

> Mrs Cosways designs, it must be admitted, are sometimes eccentric, but it is the eccentricity of *genius* ... we prefer the artist who rather overcharges his figure, to him who touches the canvas with a timid feeble pencil, and leaves the imagination of the spectator to supply what he cannot or dare not express.
> (Quoted in Barnett 1995, p.147)

From Mary Robinson, The Wintry Day (1800)

Is it in mansions rich and gay,
On downy beds, or couches warm,
That Nature owns the wintry day,
And shrinks to hear the howling storm?
Ah! No!

'Tis on the bleak and barren heath,
Where Mis'ry feels the ice of death,
As to the dark and freezing grave
Her children, not a friend to save,
Unheeded go!

...

Is it to flaunt in warm attire,
To laugh, to feast, and dance, and sing;
To crowd around the blazing fire,
And make the roof with revels ring?
Ah! No!

'Tis on the prison's flinty floor,
'Tis where the deaf'ning whirlwinds roar;
'Tis when the Sea-boy, on the mast,
Hears the wave bounding to the blast,
And looks below!

Robinson 2000, pp.340–2

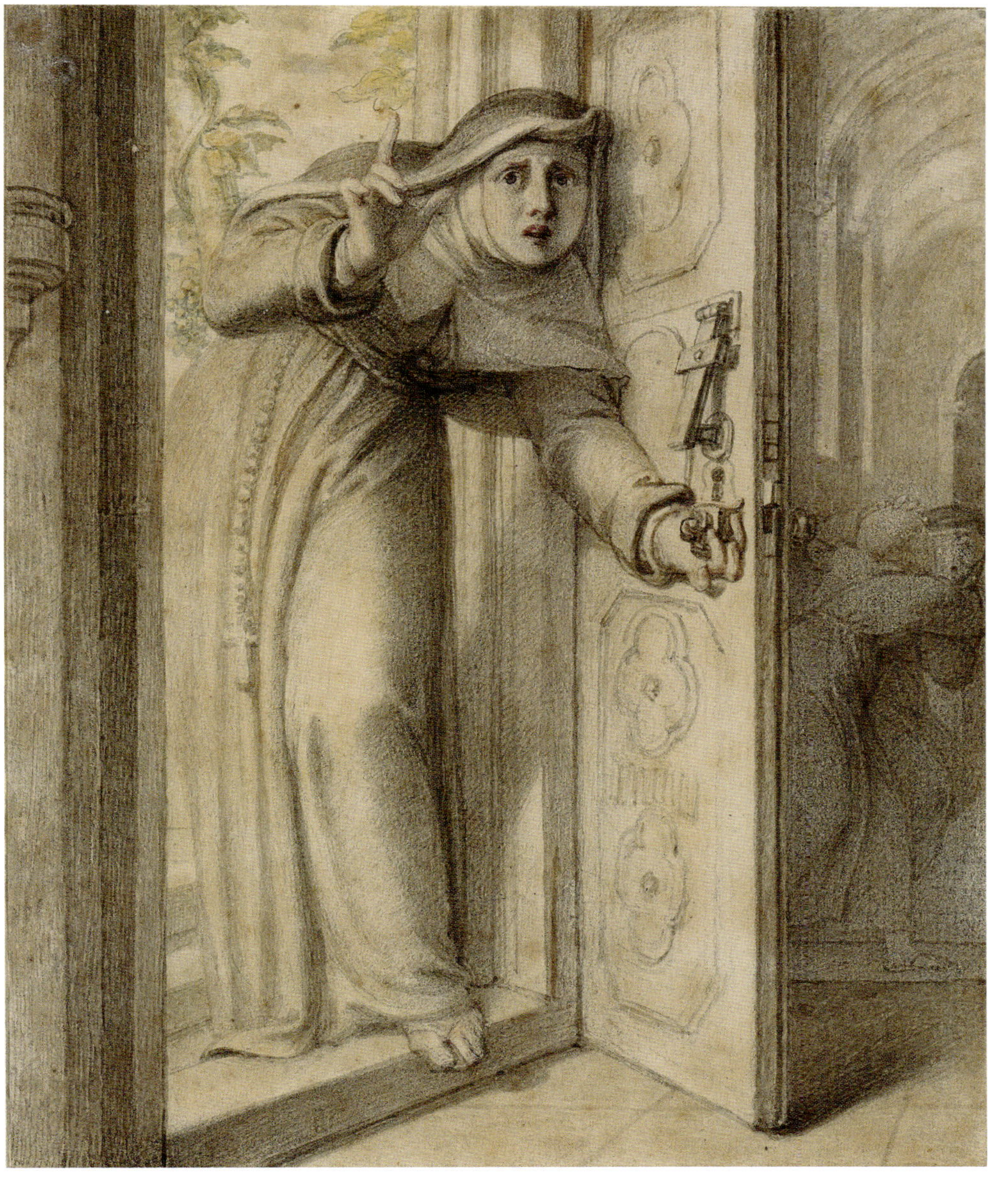

65

Richard Cosway 1742–1821
Nun Surprising a Monk Kissing another Nun in a Church Interior c.1790–1800
Pen and watercolour on paper 19.9 x 16.2 cm
Print Collection, Miriam and Ira D. Wallach Division of Art, Prints and Photographs, The New York Public Library, Astor, Lenox and Tilden Foundations

A gentle example of 'Nunsploitation'. In a medieval convent, a sister opens a door into a corridor, in the relative gloom of which a monk tussles with another nun. His intentions are, patently, sexual.

Nuns feature heavily in the erotic and pornographic literature of the eighteenth century, drawing from a tradition that can be traced back to Aretino and beyond (Wagner 1991). For readers in the Protestant world, Catholicism evoked a world of superstition, the supernatural and perversity that was as titillating as it was morally reprehensible. Gothic novelists from Horace Walpole onwards made the most of such associations by returning repeatedly to medieval and Renaissance Italy as a setting for their tales (see Tarr 1946; Miles 1999).

Nuns feature heavily in Lewis's *The Monk* (1796), where they are subject to rape, violence, torture and imprisonment. The gesture of the nun in the foreground in this design suggests she is revealing or commenting on the scene for our benefit, perhaps in the character of a narrator. Yet no specific literary source is evident. Randy monks and brazen nuns are a stock feature of visual erotica as well, with the refined and delicate productions of French book illustrators leading the field (see Wagner 1991, p.187). This titillating scene is executed in the characteristically delicate manner of Richard Cosway, and evokes this tradition of illustration.

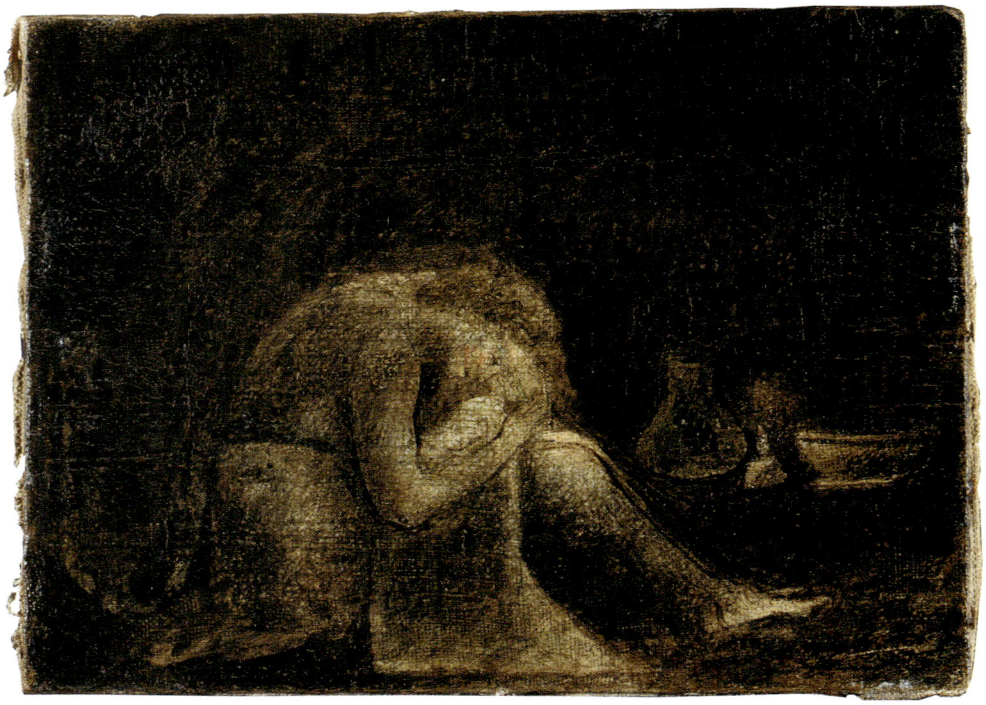

66

Catherine Blake 1762–1831
Agnes c.1800
Tempera on canvas 13.7 x 18.1 cm
The Syndics of the Fitzwilliam Museum, Cambridge, by whom acquired 1953 through the National Art Collections Fund

Believed dead but in fact drugged, the pregnant nun Agnes has been imprisoned in a sepulchral cell by the evil prioress. Surrounded by filth and rotten corpses, she eventually gives birth to a short-lived child. She is shown here embracing the corpse of that infant.

The source of this scene, Matthew Lewis's novel *The Monk* (1796), was a literary sensation, a shocker that pushed the bounds of taste and propriety to their limit and beyond (Parraux 1960; Macdonald 2000; Lewis 2004) With their author now a public figure (he became a Member of Parliament in 1797), a new edition was issued with cuts to the most offensive materials, although reputedly full, pirate versions were to be had in Dublin, with the most shocking passages underlined for ease of use. The story of Agnes was part of a relatively self-contained tale. It had a life separate from the main novel, being issued as a romance on its own terms, and forming the basis of a pantomime performed in 1797 (Lewis 2004, pp.418–22). Still, the choice of this subject remains shocking; if scenes from modern Gothic novels were only rarely painted by artists, still more rarely was such a graphic image of horror depicted. Nevertheless, as revealed in an inscription on the back of the canvas, the painting was given by the artist to the wife of William Blake's long-time patron Thomas Butts (1757–1845), 'in Gratitude and Friendship' (Butlin 1981, no.C1).

Packed full of perversion, incest, gore, ghosts and rotting flesh, and two personal appearances from Satan, Lewis's novel set a benchmark of horror which has hardly been equalled and betrays the anachronistic nature of arguments that would oppose the 'tasteful', 'literary' traditions of the Gothic to modern 'trash' or 'exploitation'. As Stephen King has remarked of this scene: 'It would be over a century and a half before another such parade of physical horrors would shock the eyes and sensibilities of young readers; these were the EC "shock comics" ... of the early 1950s. Matthew Lewis would have fit in perfectly as a staff writer' (Lewis 2002, p.viii).

From Matthew Lewis, The Monk (1796)

A full hour elapsed, before I was sufficiently myself to examine the surrounding objects. When I did examine them, what terror filled my bosom! I found myself extended upon a sort of wicker couch. It had six handles to it, which doubtless had served the nuns to convey me to my grave. I was covered with a linen cloth: several faded flowers were strown over me. On one side lay a small wooden crucifix; on the other, a rosary of large beads. Four low narrow walls confined me. The top was also covered, and in it was practised a small grated door; through this was admitted the little air that circulated in this miserable place. A faint glimmering of light, which streamed through the bars, permitted me to distinguish the surrounding horrors. I was oppressed by a noisome suffocating small; and perceiving that the grated door was unfastened, I thought that I might possibly effect my escape. As I raised myself with this design, my hand rested on something soft: I grasped it, and advanced toward the light. Almighty God! what was my disgust! my consternation! In spite of its putridity, and the worms which preyed upon it, I perceived a corrupted human head, and recognised the features of a nun who had died some months before. I threw it from me, and sank almost lifeless upon my bier.

...

My mental anguish, and the dreadful scenes in which I had been an Actress, advanced the period of my labour. In solitude and misery, abandoned by all, unassisted by art, uncomforted by friendship, with pangs which if witnessed would have touched the hardest heart, was I delivered of my wretched burthen. It came alive into the world; but I knew not how to treat it, or by what means to preserve its existence. I could only bathe it with tears, warm it in my bosom, and offer up prayers for its safety. I was soon deprived of this mournful employment: the want of proper attendance, my ignorance how to nurse it, the bitter cold of the dungeon, and the unwholesome air which inflated its lungs, terminated my sweet babe's short and painful existence. It expired a few hours after its birth, and I witnessed its death with agonies that beggar all description. But my grief was unavailing. My infant was no more; nor could all my sighs impart to its tender frame the breath of a moment. I rent my winding-sheet, and wrapped in it my lovely child. I placed it on my bosom, its soft arm folded round my neck, and its pale cold cheek resting upon mine. Thus did its lifeless limbs repose, while I covered it with kisses, talked to it, wept, and moaned over it without remission day or night.

(Lewis 2004, pp.335, 341)

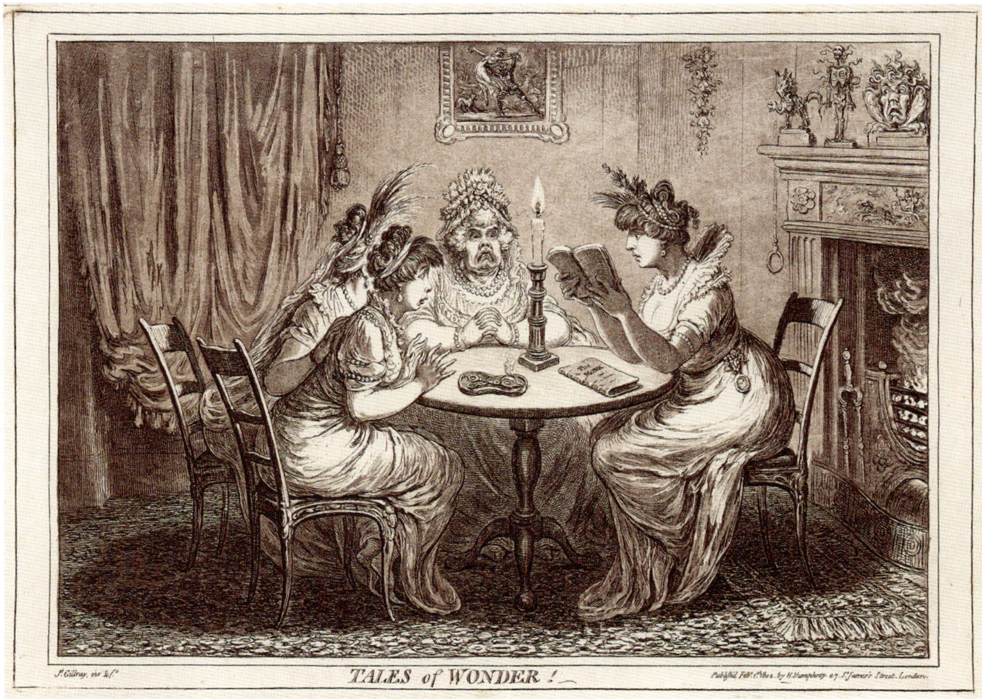

67

James Gillray 1756–1815
Tales of Wonder! published by Hannah Humphrey, 1 February 1802
Etching and aquatint 25.5 x 35.4 cm
Andrew Edmunds, London

Tales of Wonder was a collection of poems brought together by Matthew Gregory Lewis (1775–1818), which became the literary sensation of 1801 (Macdonald 2000, pp.141–53). In this famous print by Gillray (George 1935–54, no.9932), a group of women are shown reading from Lewis's most famous and famously lurid novel, *The Monk* (1796). A review of *The Monk* appearing in 1802 summed up the morally righteous view of the book: 'all the faults and immoralities ascribed to novels will be found realized in the Monk: murders, incest, and all the horrible and aggravated crimes which is it possible to conceive, appear in every chapter, and are dwelt on with seeming complacency' (*Scots Magazine*, vol.64 [1802], p.547). Gillray's print mocks the taste for such salacious and violent materials among the pampered bourgeoisie. These plump and finely dressed ladies are up well past their bedtime – the watch on the waist of the reader states 1.45 – and the smoking wick-trimmer on the table suggests that they have been keeping the candle alight through the night. The ornaments on the mantelpiece are ludicrous grotesques, and the carving below represents the theme of classical rape, with Pluto carrying off Persephone in his chariot. The painting on the wall at the rear is most telling: its style is distinctly Fuselian (cf. nos.40 and 48), the subject apparently medieval, with an armoured hero lifting up a limp maiden, either saving her from wickedness or capturing her for his own vile uses.

The 1790s had seen the introduction of more shocking and explicit Gothic literature, a phenomenon greeted with attacks and mockery from many critics, and outright condemnation by the self-appointed moral guardians like the satirical critic T.J. Mathias. His *Pursuit of Literature* (1797–8) claimed that the author of *The Monk* could actually be taken to court for obsenity. It was around 1798–1803 that Jane Austen (1775–1817) first composed the text of what became her famous satirical novel *Northanger Abbey* (1818), which features several comical scenes directed at the current taste for Gothic sensation, including this exchange:

> '... when you have finished Udolpho, we will read the Italian together; and I have made out a list of ten or twelve more of the same kind for you.'
> 'Have you indeed! How glad I am! – What are they all?'
> 'I will read you their names directly; here they are, in my pocket book. Castle of Wolfenbach, Clermont, Mysterious Warnings, Necromancer of the Black Forest, Midnight Bell, Orphan of the Rhine, and Horrid Mysteries. Those will last us some time.'
> 'Yes, pretty well; but are they all horrid, are you sure they are all horrid?'
> (Austen 2004, pp.24–5).

Jane Austen's text may appear dismissive of the girlish superficiality of the readers of Gothic literature, but modern commentators would stress the complexity and subtlety of her comments on the modern novel, contemporary taste, and gender stereotypes. She appears to have recognised the Gothic as a lively creative form, and was not, as Gillray may be, flatly condemning 'feminine' reading habits.

Notably, it has been argued that the perception that readers of Gothic were predominantly female was fallacious, and perhaps malicious. Work on library subscription lists may suggest that men read modern Gothic novels as much as women (cf. Jacobs 1995). Although such arguments are not conclusive, there is more secure evidence that would allow us to construct particular case-studies which would demonstrate a male readership. For instance, the teenage Thomas de Quincy (1785–1859) was an avid consumer of the most shocking Gothic literature, his reading in 1803 including translations of Friedrich Schiller's *The Ghost-Seer, or Apparitionist* (1795) and Karl Grosse's *The Dagger* (1795), Ann Radcliffe's *The Castles of Athlin and Dunbayne* (1789), Sophia Lee's *The Recess* (1783–5), Mary Pilkington's *The Accusing Spirit, or: De Courcy and Eglantine* (1802), Clara Reeve's *Memoirs of Sir Roger de Clarendon* (1793), Anne Bannerman's *Tales of Superstition and Chivalry* (1802) and, of course, Lewis's *Tales of Wonder* (see Bridgwater 2004, pp.20–7). Accordingly, it is important to understand that the idea that reading such novels was a woman's occupation, and was, as Gillray proposes here, to be mocked or condemned as such, was not a simple statement of fact, but rather a way of categorising forms of literature that were distant from the high-minded and exclusive Classics that were drummed into the public schoolboys who made up the old social establishment.

68

Henry Fuseli 1741-1825
Huon and Amanda with the Dead Alphonso
1804
Oil on canvas 60 x 44 cm
The Barrett Collection, Dallas

The romantic hero Huon comforts his lover, Amanda, when they discover the body of the goodly hermit Alphonso who had, eerily, predicted his own death.

Fuseli painted this scene (Schiff 1973, no.1788) as one of a series of twelve canvases commissioned by the publisher Caddell & Davis as the models for engraved illustrations to a new English edition of Christoph Martin Wieland's (1733-1813) epic German poem *Oberon* (1780). The paintings were probably initiated by the spring of 1804 (when Fuseli dined with the translator William Sotheby [1757-1833]) and all twelve were seen completed by Joseph Farington in November of that year (Weinglass 1982, p.297; Farington 1978-98, VI, p.2454). The engraving of the present design was paid for in May 1805, although the illustrated edition was not published until August 1806 (Weinglass 1994, nos.244-55).

The poem focuses on the adventures of Huon of Bourdeaux, sent on a mission to a fantasy Baghdad by the emperor Charlemagne, and incorporates Gothic romance, Orientalism and fairy-tale elements, pirates, monsters, the fairy queen Titania, Gandolf, a tyrannical Caliph and the titular Oberon, and a miscellany of hermits and wild men. Crazy and entertaining as it is, the narrative touches on themes of sexual liberty that were more pertinent to contemporary life. The scene depicted here follows a shipwreck sent as punishment by Oberon after Huon and Amanda have consummated their love. Alphonso takes the stranded lovers into his care, a liberal gesture in the context of an uncomprehending and unsympathetic world. The old hermit's death stirs Huon with a spirit of virtue and courage (which he will need all the more given the forbidding challenges awaiting him). Fuseli's illumination of his hero's features with the light that falls from a hidden window would seem to allude to this theme.

Wieland, Oberon, A Poem (1780), trans. William Sotheby (1805)

She comes — pale Huon meets her — neither speak,
Both inly boding with the same intent
Hiding the fears that spoke some dread event,
The hermit's hallow'd cell in silence seek —
How throbb'd their heart with unaccustom'd fear,
Mute as they come his noiseless cavern near!
Breathless he lies, his hands across his heart,
A deadly paleness marks each mortal part,
Yet, on each feature peace and heav'n seal'd
hope appear.

'Hush! he but sleeps,' Amanda softly says.
And on his hand hers so lightly prest,
As if she fear'd to interrupt his rest;
But when his clay-cold flesh no life displays,
And still his heart, and sunk his bloodless veins,
On his pale corse with agonizing pains
At once she sinks — the tears that bathe his cheek,
Her soul's unutterable anguish speak —
'Ah! father! thou art gone! no hope on earth
remains!'

Then up she starts, and sinks on Huon's breast:
Both on their knees before the mortal shrine
That held so long the purest soul divine,
By awful silence solemn who exprest;
And satiate sad the bitter sweet desire
To weep; and oft resolving to retire,
Press the last debt of love upon his hand;
Yet o'er his form, as fixt by magick, stand,
And thrill with pangs unknown, and woes that
never tire.

It seems, that in his features they behold
The twilight dawn of new existence beam,
And that from heaven a bright reflected gleam
Round his pale brow its living lustre roll'd;
Rays of supernal light already shine
That change the mortal substance to divine,
And a scarce visible celestial smile
Play'd hovering o'er his lips, that seem'd the while
In a last blessing clos'd his spirit to resign.

(Wieland 1805, pp.107–9)

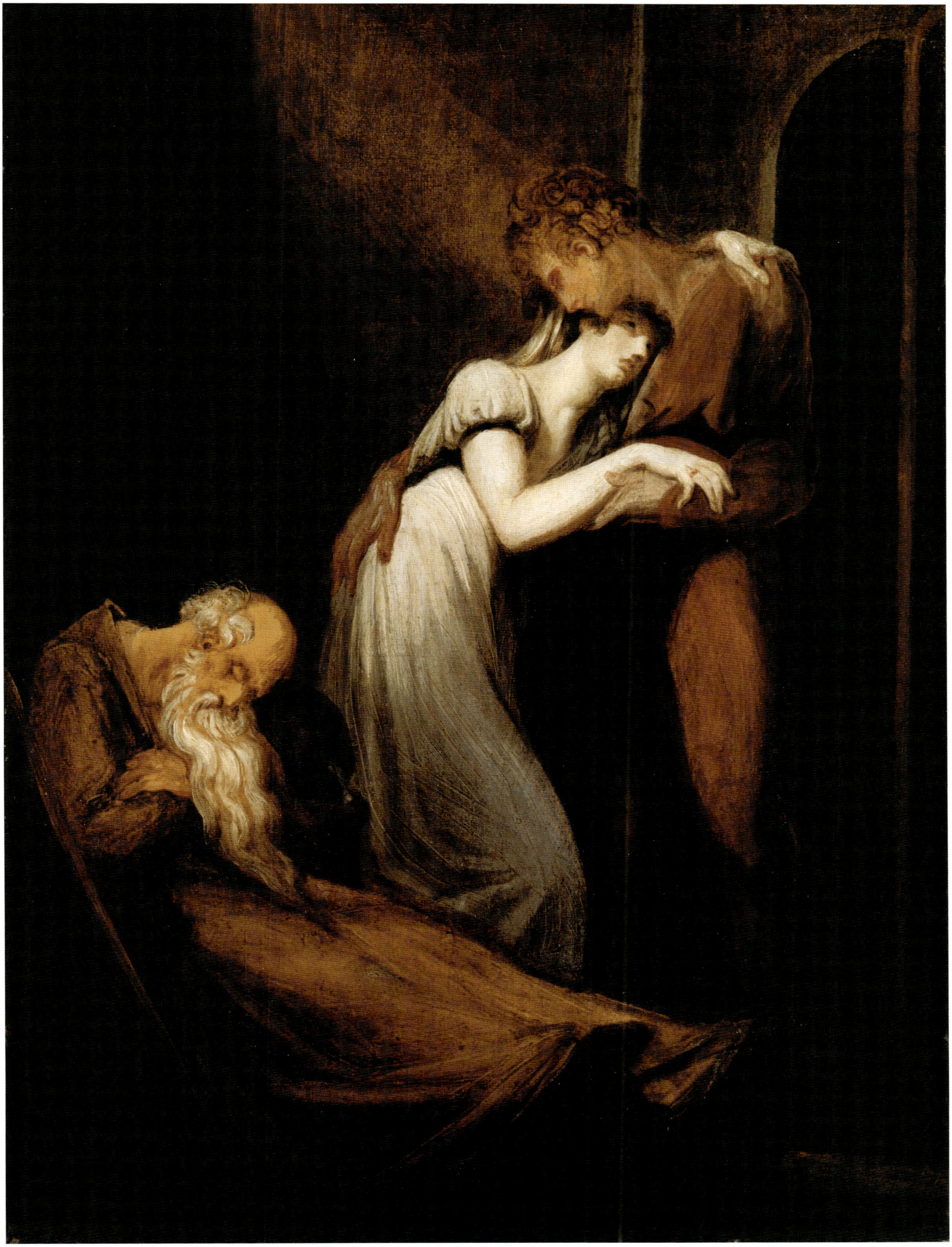

69

William Blake 1757–1827
Churchyard Spectres Frightening a Schoolboy 1805
Watercolour on paper 28.1 x 21.6 cm
Collection of Robert N. Essick

70

William Blake 1757–1827
A Widow Embracing the Turf of her Husband's Grave 1805
Pen and brush and black ink and watercolour on paper 15.4 x 20.8 cm
Paul Mellon Collection, Yale Center for British Art, New Haven

These two watercolours illustrate adjacent passages in Robert Blair's (1699–1746) poem *The Grave* (1743). In no.69 a schoolboy, satchel in hand, runs, terrified, from a female ghost who flies towards him before a gravestone. To the right, a bearded ghost stands in the pointed Gothic porchway; in his right hand he holds a flaming birch, while he points with his left, suggesting a schoolmasterly character. In no.70 a young woman has thrown herself onto the newly filled grave of her husband. A pair of elegant youths walking by look pityingly towards her.

These watercolours were prepared as part of a series of designs commissioned by the publisher Robert Cromek (1771–1812), who was planning a new edition of this famous poem which would have engaged Blake's talents as an original artist and as a printmaker. In the event, the compositions by Blake that were published were engraved by Louis Schiavonetti (1765–1810), much to the English artist's distress (Bentley 2004, pp.207–21, 225–81; Essick and Paley 1982; also Butlin 2002).

The Grave consists of melancholic reflections upon mortality. Both the present designs are unusual in Blake's output, and even in the context of his designs for *The Grave*, in featuring figures in modern-looking costumes. The subject of no.70 was advertised in the first prospectus issued by Cromek, but was not among the compositions engraved by Louis Schiavoretti. It therefore certainly belongs among Blake's original designs for *The Grave* rejected by the publisher or by the artist himself. It has been disputed whether no.69 should be associated with the same project (see Christie's, 8 June 1999, lot 123), although it is hard to imagine to what other purpose this unusual design would have been put. The very literal and rather comical treatment of the spectres – which brings Blake here close to Richard Newton or George Woodward (see nos.92–5) – sits well with the relatively whimsical quality of this part of Blair's text, which implies that the schoolboy has been prey only to the phantoms of an overexcited imagination.

Robert Blair, The Grave (1808), ll.56–87

Oft in the lone church-year at night I've seen,
By glimpse of moon-shine, chequering through the trees,
The school-boy, with his satchel in his hand,
Whistling aloud to bear his courage up,
And lightly tripping o'er the long flat stones
(with nettles skirted, and with moss o'ergrown)
That tell in homely phrase who lies below.
Sudden he starts! and hears, or thinks he hears,
The sound of something purring at his heels.
Full first he flies, and dares not look behind him,
Till out of breath he overtakes his fellows;
Who gather round, and wonder at the tale
Of horrid apparition, tall and ghastly,
That walks at dead of night, or takes his stand
O'er some new open'd grave; and, strange to tell,
Evanishes at crowing of the cock!
The new-made widow I've sometimes spied
(sad sight!) slow moving o'er the prostate dead:
Listless she crawls along: – doleful black,
While bursts of sorrow gush from either eye,
Fast falling down her now untested cheek.
Prone on the lowly grave of the dead man
She drops; while busy meddling memory,
In barbarous succession, musters up
The past endearments of their softer hours,
Tenacious of it's theme. Still, still she thinks
She seems him, and, indulging the fond thought,
Clings, yet more closely to the senseless turf,
Nor heeds the passenger who looks that way.

(Blair 1808, pp.3–4)

69

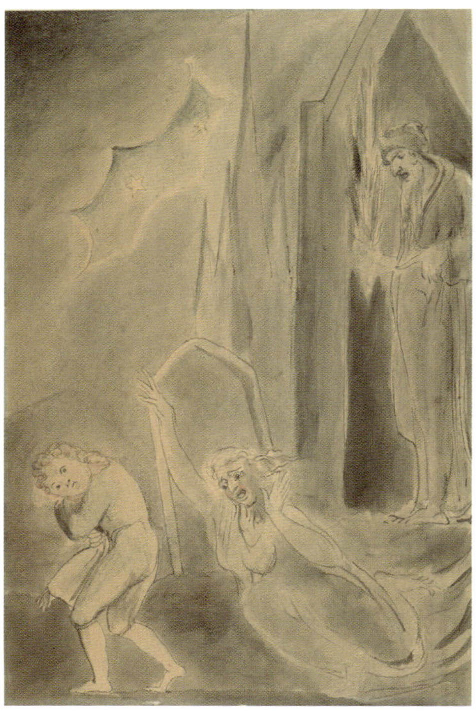

70

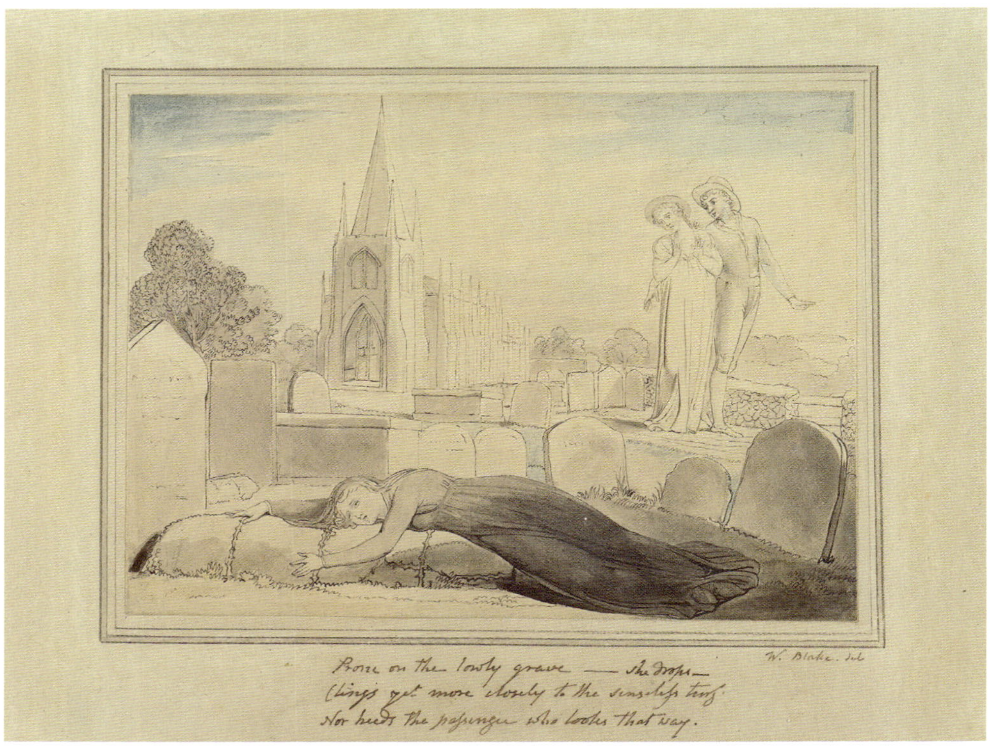

71

Henry Fuseli 1741–1825
Mad Kate c.1806–7
Oil on canvas 91 x 71 cm
Frankfurter Goethe-Museum, Frankfurt am Main

Kate is a serving maid who has been driven mad with grief over the death of her lover, a sailor. The subject is taken from William Cowper's (1731–1800) poem, *The Task* (1785), and was painted to be engraved as an illustration for a new edition of the poet's works published by Joseph Johnson in 1807.

Like Sterne's *The Captive* (see nos.56–7), Cowper presents a vivid episode, using a detailed description to prompt strong, sympathetic feelings in the reader. *The Task* recounts the travails and challenges of modern life. Cowper's personal melancholia aggravated his perceptions of the degenerate nature of the age. *The Task*, created in the wake of years of economic depression and hard winters, the Gordon Riots, and the vast, bloody, regrettable war with America, and dubious imperial policies in eastern and western colonies, embodied his feelings of gloom and despair.

Fuseli had an important, although indirect, connection with Cowper (King 1983). He had been an adviser on and reviser of the poet's translations of Homer, and for a brief period there was a plan to create an illustrated edition of Milton edited by Cowper in association with Fuseli's Milton Gallery (see nos.47, 91).

Fuseli painted eight pictures to illustrate Joseph Johnson's edition of Cowper's poems (Weinglass 1994, nos.267–74). These show Fuseli at his most varied, ranging from sentimental modern-life themes through fairy-painting and Gothic images like this. This depiction of female insanity may have been informed by Fuseli's direct knowledge: the painter told the diarist Joseph Farington of a doctor at Bedlam telling him that of the various types interned there, the most prominent were 'Woemen in love' (Farington 1978–98, VI, p.2288). Fuseli's vivid image of Kate's insanity matches Cowper's conception where, as Andrew Elfenbein notes, she represents 'a dark side of the feminine ... she raises the haunting fear that femininity may not be an escape from madness but a path to it' (Elfenbein 1989, p.8).

71

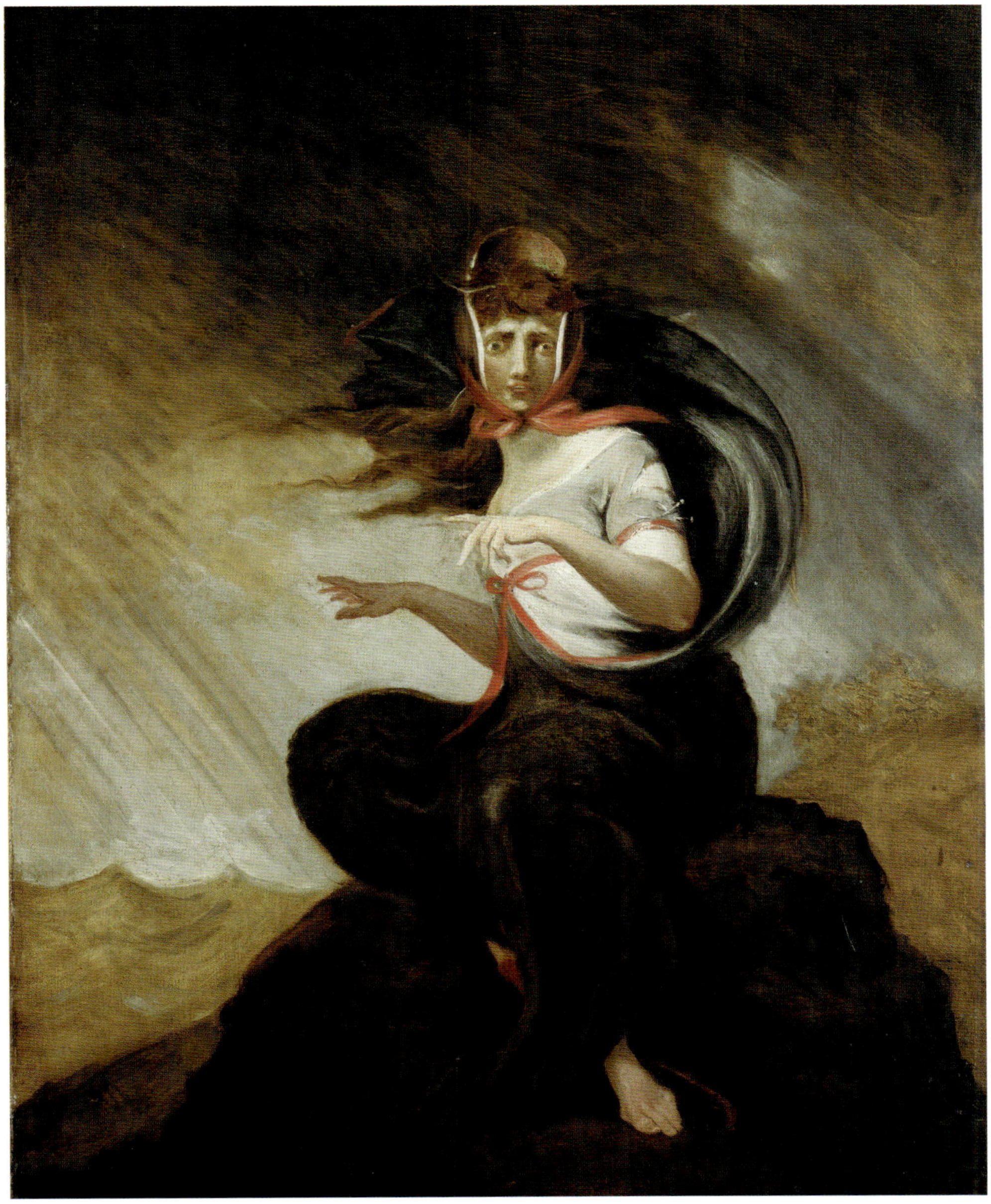

William Cowper, The Task (1785), Book I, ll.534–56

There often wanders one, whom better days
Saw better clad, in cloak of satin trimm'd
With lace, and hat with splendid ribbon bound.
A serving-maid was she, and fell in love
With one who left her, went to sea, and died.
Her fancy followed him through foaming waves
To distant shores, and she would sit and weep
At what a sailor suffers; fancy too
Delusive most where warmest wishes are
Would oft anticipate his glad return
And dream of transports she was not to know.
She heard the doleful tidings of his death
And never smil'd again. And now she roams
The dreary waste; there spends the livelong day,
And there, unless when charity forbids,
The livelong night. A tattered apron hides,
Worn as a cloak, and hardly hides a gown
More tatter'd still; and both but ill conceal
A bosom heaved with never-ceasing sighs.
She begs an idle pin of all she meets,
And hoards them in her sleeve; but needful food,
Though press'd with hunger oft, or comelier cloaths,
Though pinch'd with cold, asks never. – Kate is craz'd.

(Cowper 1980–95, II, pp.130–1)

72

Henry Fuseli 1741–1825
Wolfram Introducing Bertrand of Navarre to the Place where he Had Confined his Wife, with the Skeleton of her Lover c.1812–20
Oil on canvas 90 x 70 cm
Georg Schäfer Museum, Schweinfurt

The lord of a castle shows an unseen visitor his faithless wife, secreted in a sepulchral chamber, embracing, with horrible affection, the headless, skeletal remains of her lover.

This painting (Schiff 1973, no.1493) is a repetition or variation of an image exhibited in 1790 and based on a tale in Margaret, Queen of Navarre's (1492–1549) *The Heptameron*, novella 23 (first published in 1558). The text was widely available in French editions, and would in this form have been accessible to most educated British readers. Fuseli's original painting was later overpainted, but Frederica Lock recorded in a long letter how, when visiting the Lock family home in December 1789, the artist referred to the story:

> At breakfast Fuseli mentioned a picture which he had just sketched from an ancient German Ballad and promised at night to relate the Story – for he said it must be at night – 'I can only tell it at night'.
> (Frederica Lock to Frances Burney, 15–21 December 1789, in Weinglass 1982, pp.49–50)

William Lock reported that 'The point of time he [Fuseli] has chosen is the moment of the Barons throwing open the door of the Sepulchre and what the Knight then saw' (ibid., p.51). Fuseli's claiming the story as his own, taken from 'an ancient German Ballad' rather than Margaret of Navarre, might have been disingenuous, although we should remember how such tales might have been viewed as being in the public realm. In the 'Postscript' to his shocking Gothic incest play *The Mysterious Mother* (1768) Horace Walpole claimed that it was only after completing the outline that he 'accidentally discovered the origin of the tradition in the novels of the queen of Navarre' (Charlesworth 2002, I, pp.436–7).

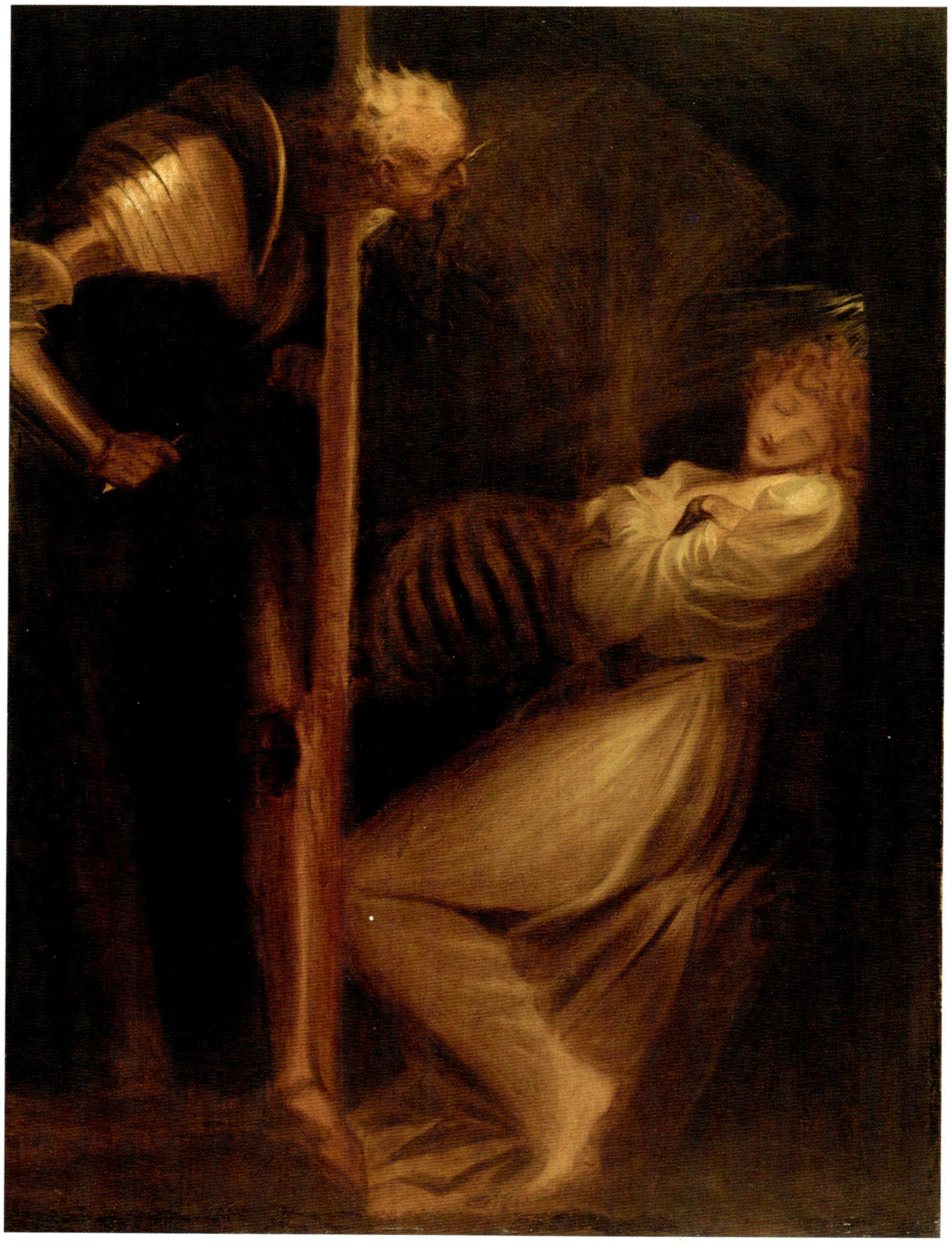

73

Theodor von Holst 1810–1844
Sketchbook c.1830–40
Pencil on paper 22.5 x 17 cm
(approx. sheet size)
Private collection
[open at f.6 verso and f.7]

This sketchbook of over fifty pages is filled with drawings by von Holst and was probably used by him in the 1830s. The range of subjects appearing on these sheets exemplifies the romantic and supernatural themes that preoccupied this artist, including figures in ecclesiastical and medieval costume; scenes from Goethe's *Faust* (1808), Friedrich de la Motte Fouqué's *Undine* (1811), and from Dante's *Divine Comedy* (1319–21); grotesques and devils, angels, monsters and heroes. There are also written notes, including a sheet of proposed 'Night Sketches' making the tantalising suggestions of 'Opium', 'the Vampyre', 'Punch Orgies' and 'the untrue lovers last Dream' as subjects for art, all of which would strengthen Dante Gabriel Rossetti's (1878–82) suggestion that von Holst should be considered 'the Edgar Poe of painting' (quoted in Schiff 1963b, p.32).

The pages illustrated here demonstrate von Holst's confident draughtsmanship, deeply indebted to Fuseli, and his supernatural interests. The right-hand page contains character studies for the types of figures that inhabit the artist's medieval and Renaissance subjects. The left-hand sheet features a skeleton-bride, a generic Gothic motif. Christopher Frayling has suggested (in personal correspondence) that it may represent, more specifically, the bride in Gottfried August Bürger's (1747–94) 'Lenore' (1773), or the vampire of Johann Wolfgang Goethe's (1749–1832) 'Die Braut von Corinth' (1797). Coming from a German-speaking family, von Holst could have known these works at first hand, and he was, importantly, the first British artist to draw from Goethe's works extensively (see Schiff 1963b; Browne 1994). Bürger's poem was translated into English by Thomas Taylor (1758-1835) in 1796, and latterly (1844) by Rossetti. It was also loosely adapted by Matthew Lewis as 'Alonzo the Brave and Fair Imogine' which featured in *The Monk* (1796) (see Lewis 2004, pp.271–3). The skeletal bride's features are, intriguingly, traced through from the preceding sheet, showing a monk with a skull's face (fig.26). Seen in juxtaposition, we may be reminded of the characteristic effects of the Phantasmagoria, which often featured faces turning to skulls and sudden appearances of skeletons (see below, p.146).

The sketchbook originally belonged to the sculptor Alexander Munro (1825–71), and presumably came from von Holst's studio via their mutual friend the artist Patric Park (1811–55), himself an associate of Rossetti, whose admiration for von Holst is well documented (see Browne 1994, pp.31–43). Information on the provenance of this sketchbook has been kindly supplied by Max Browne (personal correspondence).

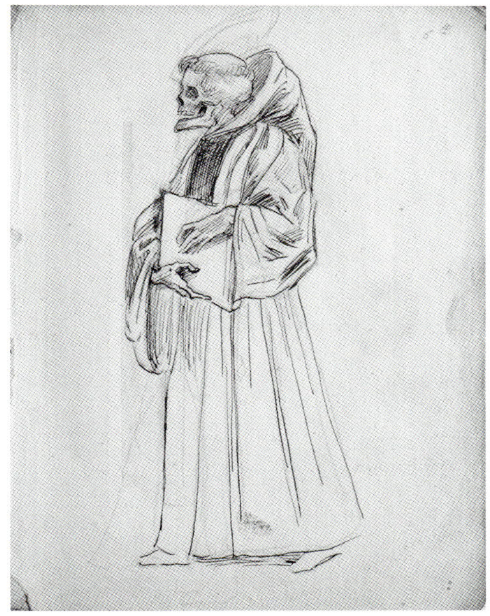

fig.26 Pencil and ink drawing on recto of f.6

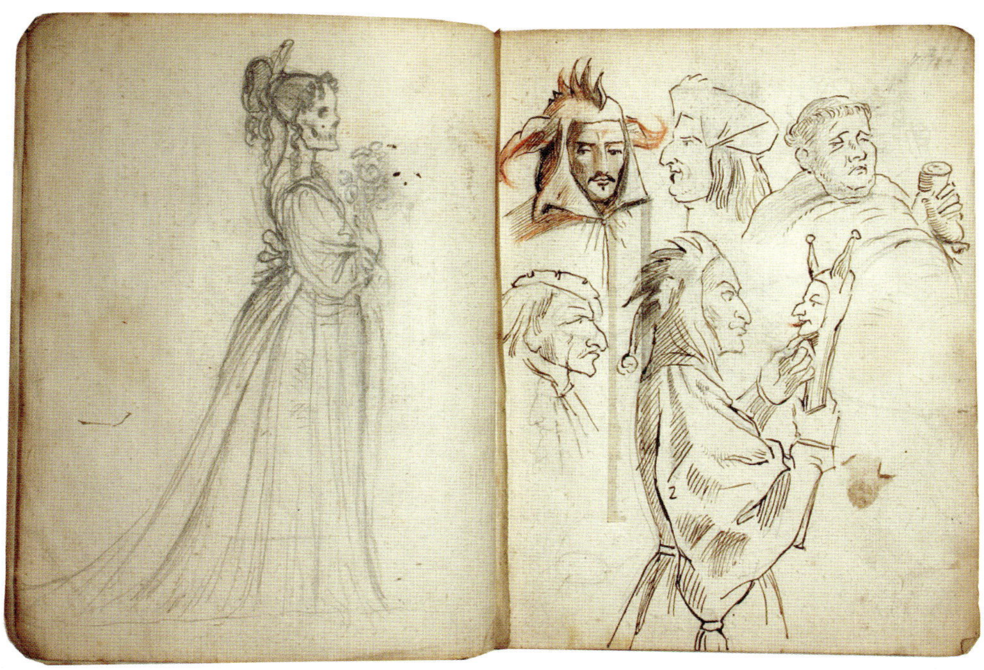

Witches and Apparitions

By the eighteenth century the great majority of people had ceased sincerely believing in witches and ghosts, or at least, tended more than ever to refrain from expressing such beliefs in public. The dominance of Protestantism, which rejected the liminal state of Purgatory and direct interventions in the material world by God, and the sceptical attitude which prevailed in modern science and philosophical 'enlightenment', combined to make a belief in the supernatural completely marginal among the educated sectors of society. Only children or simple country folk, it seemed, now believed in spectres and the powers of magic. A widespread belief in the supernatural was instead firmly associated with foreign, Catholic countries, or Britain's own Catholic past, when men 'loved to astonish themselves with the apprehensions of witchcraft, prodigies, charms and enchantments' (*Spectator*, 1 July 1712). After their terrible heyday in the sixteenth and early seventeenth centuries, witch trials became much rarer after the Civil War. The last death sentence for witchcraft was carried out in 1682; the last sentence passed by a jury was in 1712, and the last witch-trial occurred in 1717. In 1736 the Witchcraft Act was revoked, meaning that it was now an offence to pretend to use witchcraft or magic, rather than to actually try to exercise supernatural influence of this kind (Gijswijt-Hofstra, Levack and Porter 1999, pp.141–51).

Witchcraft and magic did not simply disappear with these developments. Superstitious beliefs continued, but now the stigma attached to their open expression grew so strong that such thinking was kept private (Davies and de Blécourt 2004). Paradoxically, the supernatural had, accordingly, a curiously enhanced allure in this materialist, rationalist age (Clery 1995; Gijswijt-Hofstra, Levack and Porter 1999, pp.245–50; also Geary 1987). The aesthetics of the Sublime, the revaluation of medieval and romance literature, and a novel emphasis on the creative imagination conspired in the late eighteenth century to give artists a licence to explore themes of witchcraft and magic. While the supernatural presence in even the most esteemed literature, notably Shakespeare, had troubled earlier commentators and illustrators, now such themes were tackled with abandon. Witches, apparitions and fantasy creatures both enticing and monstrous abound in painting and the graphic arts, and provided satirists with an incisive means of attacking the perceived deceptions and delusions of modern politics. Mocking the pretensions of high art, James Gillray developed a sophisticated visual vocabulary that drew on the extravagance and shock-tactics associated with the Gothic. Magic and illusion, meanwhile, were centrally important metaphors for the creative act; Fuseli, in particular, had a reputation as the 'Wizard Painter' from early in his public career. This was given literal demonstration when he dressed as a wizard during a Gothic theatrical organised in his honour by Brooke Boothby in 1782 (Myrone 2005, pp.227–32). Boothby, notably, was the original owner of *The Nightmare* (no.1; see Glover 1831–2, II, p.42).

There were rich resources of literary tradition and folklore to which artists could turn. Witches and ghosts feature prominently in Greek tragedy and in Shakespeare. Such associations lent dignity to the treatment of supernatural themes in art, even as the most shocking and sensational pictorial effects were being explored – and exploited. Paintings of supernatural themes occupy the same fissure within the emerging bourgeois and capitalist British culture as the Gothic novel – a fissure which marks the uncertain distinctions between high and low tastes, exultation and exploitation. While the artists who produced such images received some critical acclaim, and achieved wider public recognition through the sale of prints and the display of their paintings, there were still those among their contemporaries who felt that these developments were undermining the hierarchies of good taste and sound sense that had supposedly made Britain great.

Horace Walpole, 'Miscellany' (1786–95)

If a Man were now to say that he is Inspired, he woud not be believed — Inspiration is therefore like Witchcraft, which ceased to be pretended as soon as it ceased to be believed.

(Walpole 1978, pp.70–1)

Mark Akenside, Pleasures of the Imagination (1744)

... Hence by Night
The Village Matron, round the blazing Hearth,
Suspends the Infant Audience with her Tales,
Breathing Astonishment! Of witching Rhymes,
And evil Spirits: of the Death-Bed Call
To him who robb'd the Widow, and devour'd
The Orphan's Portion: Of unquiet Souls
Ris'n from the Grave to ease the heavy Guilt
Of Deeds in Life conceal'd: Of Shapes that walk
At Dead of Night, and clank their Chains and wave
The Torch of Hell around the Murd'rer's Bed.
At ev'ry solemn Pause the Cause recoil,
Gazing each other speechless, and congeal'd
With shiv'ring Sighs; till eager for th'Event,
Around the Bedlame all erect they hand,
Each trembling Heart with grateful Terrors quell'd!

(Akenside 1744, p.24)

74

John Runciman 1744–1768
The Three Witches c.1767–8
Ink and body colour on paper 23.5 x 24.8 cm
National Gallery of Scotland, Edinburgh

This vivid, apparently rapidly executed drawing has previously been catalogued as 'Three Satyrs', a title presumably suggested by the pointed ears and the arguably masculine appearance of the figures. But the clustering of these heads together, and their very mannishness, make it more likely that this is a representation of the three witches from *Macbeth*. The huddled heads, and the position of the right-hand witch's head, recall Albrecht Dürer's (1471–1528) engraving of *The Four Witches* (1493). The witches in Shakepeare's play are decidedly masculine (see nos.80–1).

John Runciman made a profound impression on his contemporaries during his tragically short life. With his brother Alexander (see no.75) he was among the first artists to treat Shakespeare as the source of heroic and supernatural subjects, presenting scenes and characters freed from the trappings of stage presentations.

William Shakespeare, Macbeth (1606), Act IV, scene 1, ll.1–38

1 WITCH. *Thrice the brinded cat hath mew'd.*
2 WITCH. *Thrice, and once the hedge-pig whin'd.*
3 WITCH. *Harpier cries ''Tis time, 'tis time.'*
1 WITCH. *Round about the cauldron go;*
In the poison'd entrails throw.
Toad, that under cold stone
Days and nights has thirty-one
Swelt'red venom sleeping got,
Boil thou first i' th' charmed pot.
ALL. *Double, double toil and trouble;*
Fire burn, and cauldron bubble.
2 WITCH. *Fillet of a fenny snake,*
In the cauldron boil and bake;
Eye of newt and toe of frog,
Wool of bat and tongue of dog,
Adder's fork and blind-worm's sting,
Lizard's leg and howlet's wing,
For a charm of pow'rful trouble,
Like a hell-broth boil and bubble.
ALL. *Double, double, toil and trouble;*
Fire burn and cauldron bubble.
3 WITCH. *Scale of dragon, tooth of wolf,*
Witches' mummy, maw and gulf
Of the ravin'd salt-sea shark,
Root of hemlock digg'd i' the dark,
Liver of blaspheming Jew,
Gall of goat, and slips of yew
Silver'd in the moon's eclipse,
Nose of Turk and Tartar's lips,
Finger of birth-strangled babe
Ditch-deliver'd by a drab,
Make the gruel thick and slab.
Add thereto a tiger's chawdron,
For th' ingredients of our caul'ron.
ALL. *Double, double, toil and trouble;*
Fire burn, and cauldron bubble.
2 WITCH. *Cool it with a baboon's blood,*
Then the charm is firm and good.

(Shakespeare 1997, p.1377)

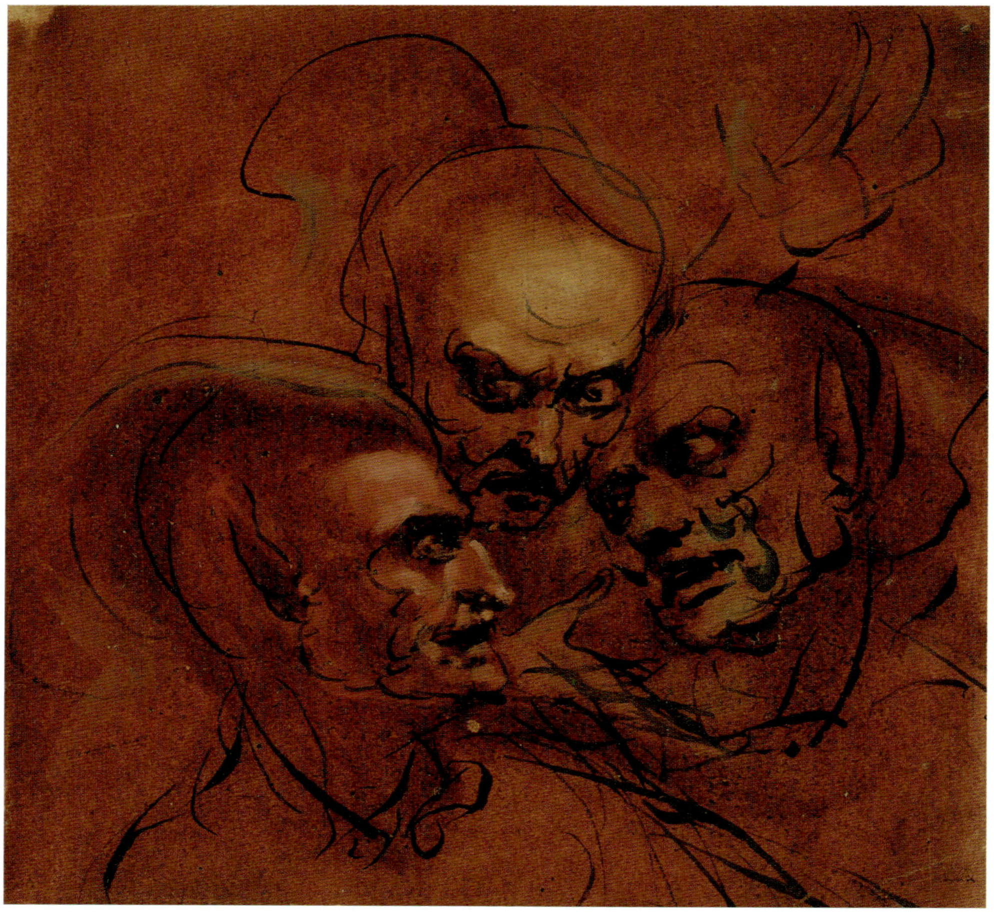

75

Alexander Runciman 1736–1795
The Witches Show Macbeth the Apparitions
c.1771–2
Pen and brown ink over pencil on paper
60.3 x 48 cm
National Gallery of Scotland, Edinburgh

The tragic Scottish king Macbeth is subjected to the alarming sight of the three witches and the goddess Hecate casting the spells that will conjure prophetic visions. This drawing seems to compress the images created by the famous spell of the three witches – 'Double, double, toil and trouble' – culminating with the dance around the cauldron 'Like elves and fairies in a ring', and the first of the visions, that of the armed head, presented to Macbeth. The content may in fact be rather muddled: the two figures throwing toads into the cauldron are presumably the witches, though the further, hooded figures behind and opposite them also fit the bill. The emaciated, demonic figure flying upwards is presumably Hecate.

Rather than elucidating the narrative, Runciman seems more interested in cramming as much gruesome detail as possible into his design, clearly on the famed model of Salvator Rosa's *Saul and the Witch of Endor* (c.1668; fig.27). Indeed, by comparison with contemporaneous depictions of witchcraft scenes by Mortimer and Fuseli (nos.76, 33), Runciman's design appears rather old fashioned, gaining its effect from an amassing of supernatural apparatus rather than the creation of atmosphere.

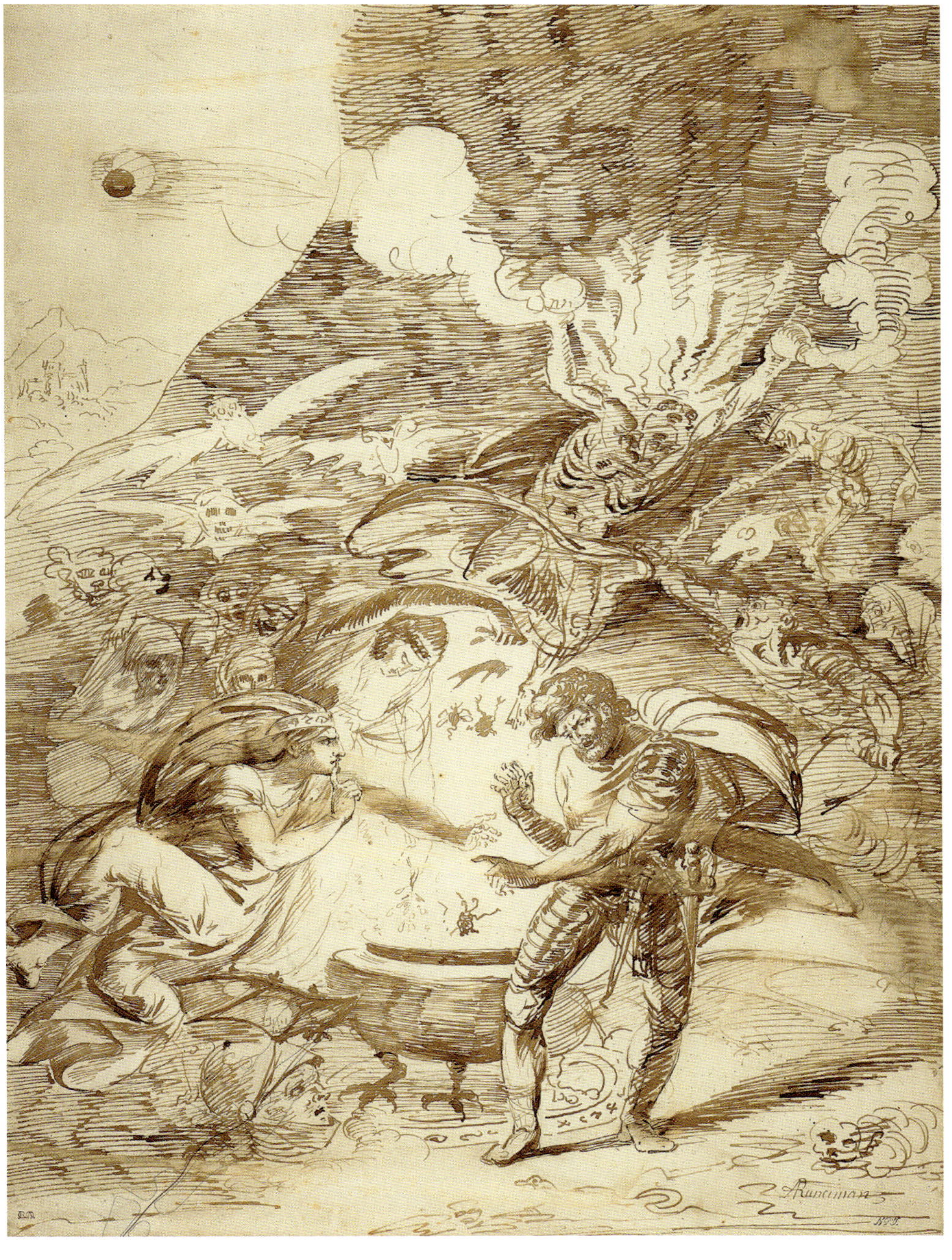

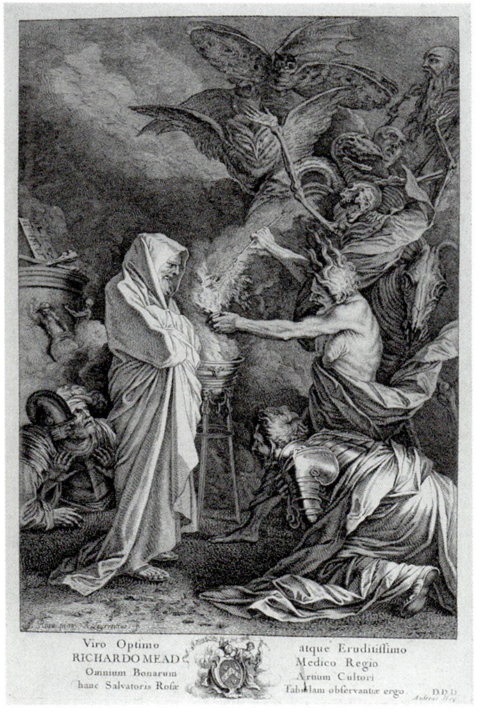

fig.27 A. Laurentius after Salvator Rosa (1615–73), *Saul and the Witch of Endor*, c.1740, engraving 42.6 x 31.7 cm. The Wellcome Library, London

76

John Dixon c.1740–c.1801 after John Hamilton Mortimer 1740–1779
An Incantation, published by John Boydell, 20 July 1773
Mezzotint 60.3 x 48 cm
The British Museum, London (1868-8-2638)

In the gloomth of a primitive cave, a witch casts a mysterious spell while her young female acolyte or prisoner reels back in horror.

This large mezzotint reproduces a painting exhibited by Mortimer at the Society of Artists in 1770, but lost in a fire (Sunderland 1986, no.36). It has been suggested that the subject is taken from Richard Glover's play *Medea* which had been performed in London in 1767. However, the iconography incorporates stock elements of witch-lore manifested in a long tradition of prints and textual description: the aged, haggard witch; the younger acolyte (perhaps her daughter); the magic circle with strange runes. Mortimer brings these clichéd elements together in a simple, bold composition which, in its treatment of the seated female figure in particular, aspires to the grand tradition of elevated pictorial representation rather than the more caricatured treatment characteristic of earlier works on this theme. Mortimer's combination of grotesque and supernatural subject matter with a heroic pictorial style made an important impression upon contemporary artists and critics. Works like this one, no.38 and no.131 precipitated several important developments in late eighteenth-century British art, though Mortimer's personal contribution was cut short by his untimely death.

Mortimer's art also inspired a number of poetic tributes. The original owner of the painting of *An Incantation* asked William Julius Mickle (1735–88) to write a poem around it, which led to the creation of his full-blooded Gothic 'The Sorceress of Wolfwold and Ulla'. Written in 'imitation of the ancient heroic ballad', of the sort that was gaining a wider readership at this point through such publications as Thomas Percy's *Reliques of English Poetry* (1765), 'The Sorceress' casts Mortimer's painting into Anglo-Saxon history, elaborating a narrative of separated lovers, war and tragic death in the setting of bleak and embattled Northumbria (see also no.62). The young woman is a Saxon princess, Ulla, who seeks information about the fate of her lover, Wolfwold, who is fighting the Danes. The skeleton is the spectre of Wolfwold's father, conjured by the aged witch. As this spectre has foretold a gloomy end for the young hero, the sorceress attempts a second premonition, conjuring a flame which if red will suggest the Wolfwold will live, and if blue, that he will die. Mickle imagines that Mortimer has painted the appearance of the tragic blue flame, with Ulla transfixed in terror at the sight.

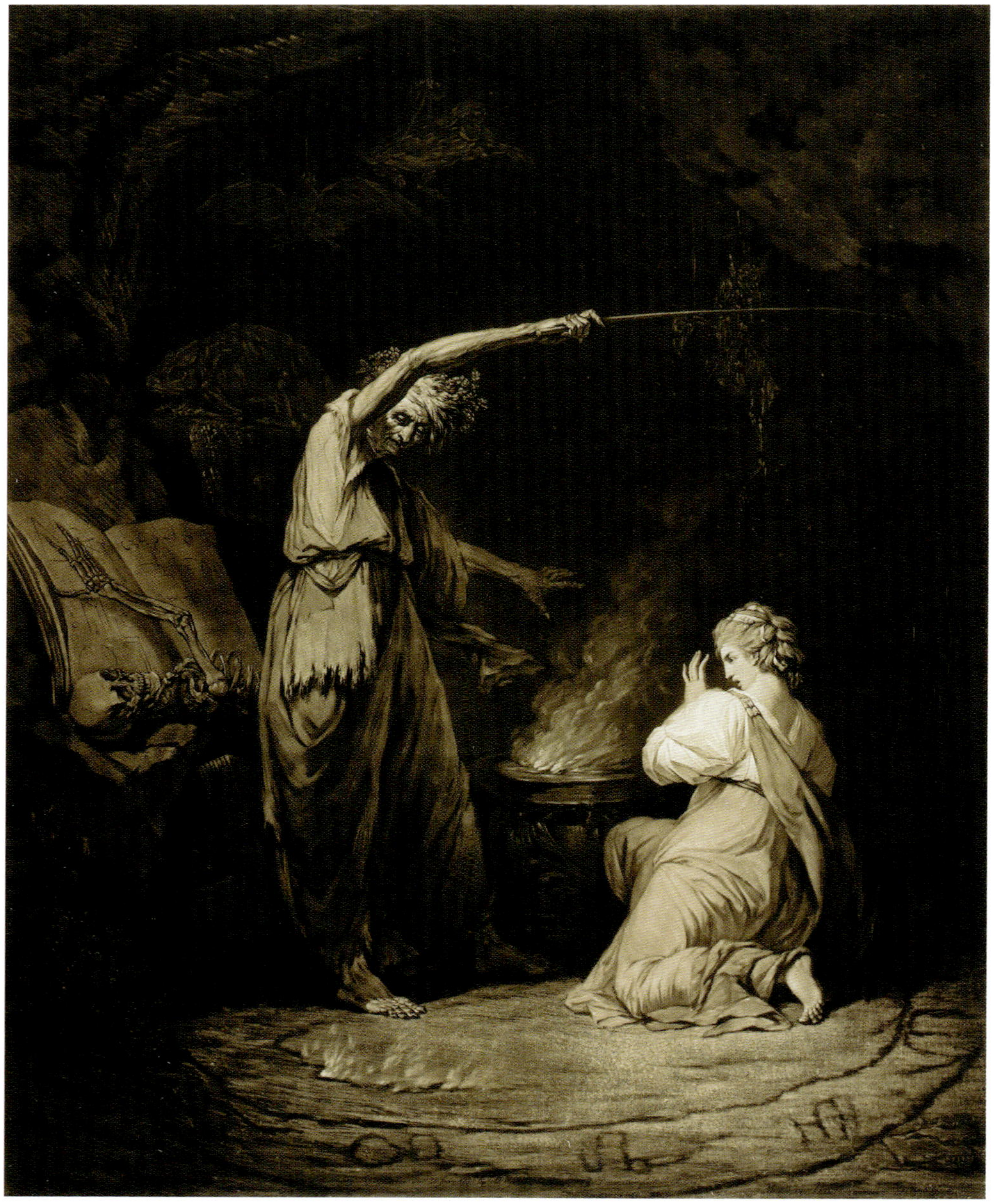

William Julius Mickle, 'The Sorceress of Wolfwold and Ulla' (c.1770)

The witch then rais'd her haggard arm,
And wav'd her hand on high;
And, while she spoke the mutter'd charm.
Dark lightning fill'd her eye.

Fair Ulla's knee swift smote the ground;
Her hands aloft were spread,
And every joint, as marble bound,
Felt horror's darkest dread.

Her lips, ere while so like the rose.
Were now as vi'let pale,
And, trembling in convulsive throes,
Exprest o'erwhelming ail.

Her eyes, ere while so starry bright.
Where living lustre shone,
Were now transform's to sightless white,
Like eyes of lifeless stone.

And soon the dreadful spell was o'er,
And glimmering to the view,
The quivering flame rose thro' the floor,
A flame of ghastly blue ...

(Mickle 1806, pp.118–19)

77

George Romney 1734–1802
The Ghost of Darius Appearing to Atossa
c.1777–9
Black chalk on nine sheets of laid paper
101 x 127 cm
National Museums Liverpool, The Walker

The defeated Persians suffer at the hands of the conquering Greeks. The lamenting Chorus is suddenly interrupted by the ghost of the former Persian king, Darius, who rises from the grave to tell his people and his widow, Atossa, that they can no longer fight the enemy (Potter 1777, pp.496–7).

This scene of bleak supernatural warning is one of two large designs by Romney illustrating Aeschylus's drama, *The Persians*. The other (also in The Walker) shows *Atossa's Dream*, where Atossa is visited by his ghost and a vision of their son's death. Both come from the same group of large-scale 'cartoons' showing supernatural and dramatic scenes executed by Romney around the end of the 1770s. Robert Potter (1721–1804) sat to Romney in 1778–9, and it is assumed that the two would have talked about the possibilities of the Greek tragedy. In a note to this scene, Potter wrote:

> The ghost of Darius here rises suddenly, and interrupts the unfinished hymn. The appearance of this royal shade, the servile prostration of the affrighted satraps, the grief and the tears of Atossa, present us with one of the finest subjects for picture that ever employed the pencil of a painter; indeed Æschylus abounds with picturesque images arising from the most vivid imagination marked with the most precise expression. The excellent Mr Romney gave a strong instance of his good sense and fine taste, when he called Æschylus 'the painter's poet:' the public may expect to see this scene, and some others, designed by him in the genuine spirit of Æschylus; so that the translator will have this merit, if he has no other, to have given rise to some paintings that will do honour to our country.
> (Potter 1777, p.599)

Aside from the Sublime potential of the subject matter, we might speculate on the contemporary resonance of this subject. Potter's translation, and Romney's design, appeared during the gruelling war with America, which to many in Britain seemed a hopeless and self-destructive endeavour.

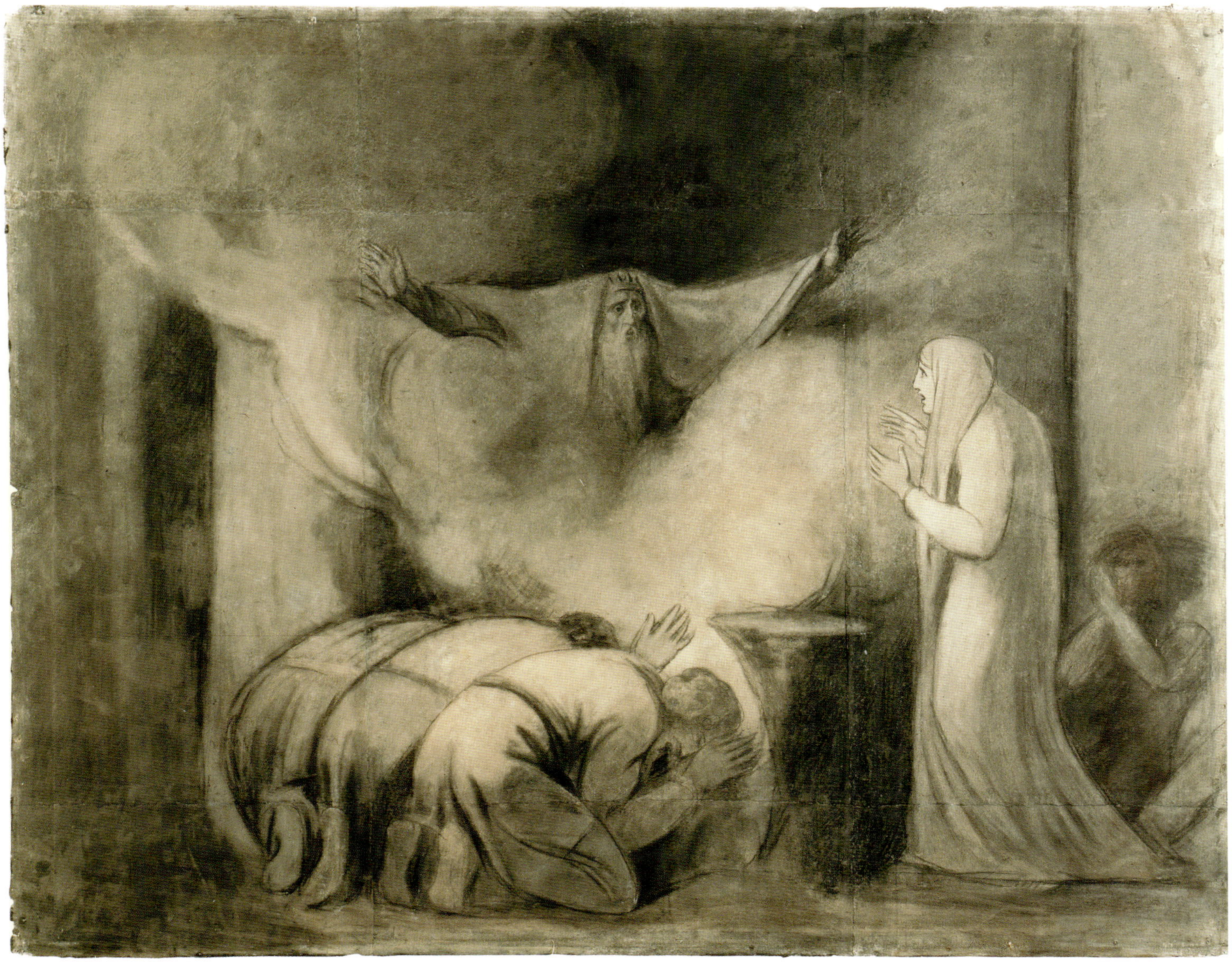

78

Henry Fuseli 1741–1825
Samuel Appears to Saul in the Presence of the Witch of Endor c.1777
Pencil and watercolour on paper
30.2 x 40.2 cm
Kunsthaus, Zurich (on loan from the Gottfried Keller Foundation)

This is a biblical scene. The armies of the Philistines are gathering to attack Israel; the prophet Samuel is dead, and Saul has driven out 'those that had familiar spirits, and the wizards'. But seeing the Philistine enemy, Saul becomes fearful. Feeling abandoned by God, he goes in disguise to seek, hypocritically, advice from the witch at Endor. She, deceived by his disguise and his blasphemous assurances, conjures the spirit of Samuel, who foretells of the death of Saul and the defeat of the kingdom.

Like the other artists who treated this theme, Fuseli must have had in mind Salvator Rosa's well-known version (see fig.27 on p.125). But where Salvator took the opportunity to crowd in spectral figures, Fuseli's design is notable for its stark, sparse formality. The striking, stiff-legged posture of Saul is a motif which appears in the work of Fuseli and his circle quite frequently. This pictorial rigor mortis arguably serves to give form to the physical effects of Sublime shock and horror, as described most influentially by Edmund Burke (1729–97). What Saul is experiencing is, after all, only what readers of Gothic tales, or the viewers of Fuseli's paintings, might be expected to feel. Fuseli's design was engraved as an illustration to the French edition of his friend Johann Caspar Lavater's (1741–1801) *Essai sur la physiognomies* (1781–6). Lavater's treatise was an attempt to elaborate, on quasi-scientific terms, the precise means by which the inner thoughts, feelings and characteristics of people are manifested in physical form.

J.C. Lavater, Essays on Pysiognomy, trans. Henry Hunter (1789–98)

The Witch of Endor. Her face presents a mixture of greatness and littleness, of originality and caricature. Her attitude expresses energy and astonishment.

The figure which represents the Spirit of Samuel is in every respect admirable.

That of Saul equally merits the highest praise, and is perfectly suitable to a Hero whom we see fainting in the arms of a Soldier inured to dreadful scenes.

(Lavater 1789–98, II, p.259)

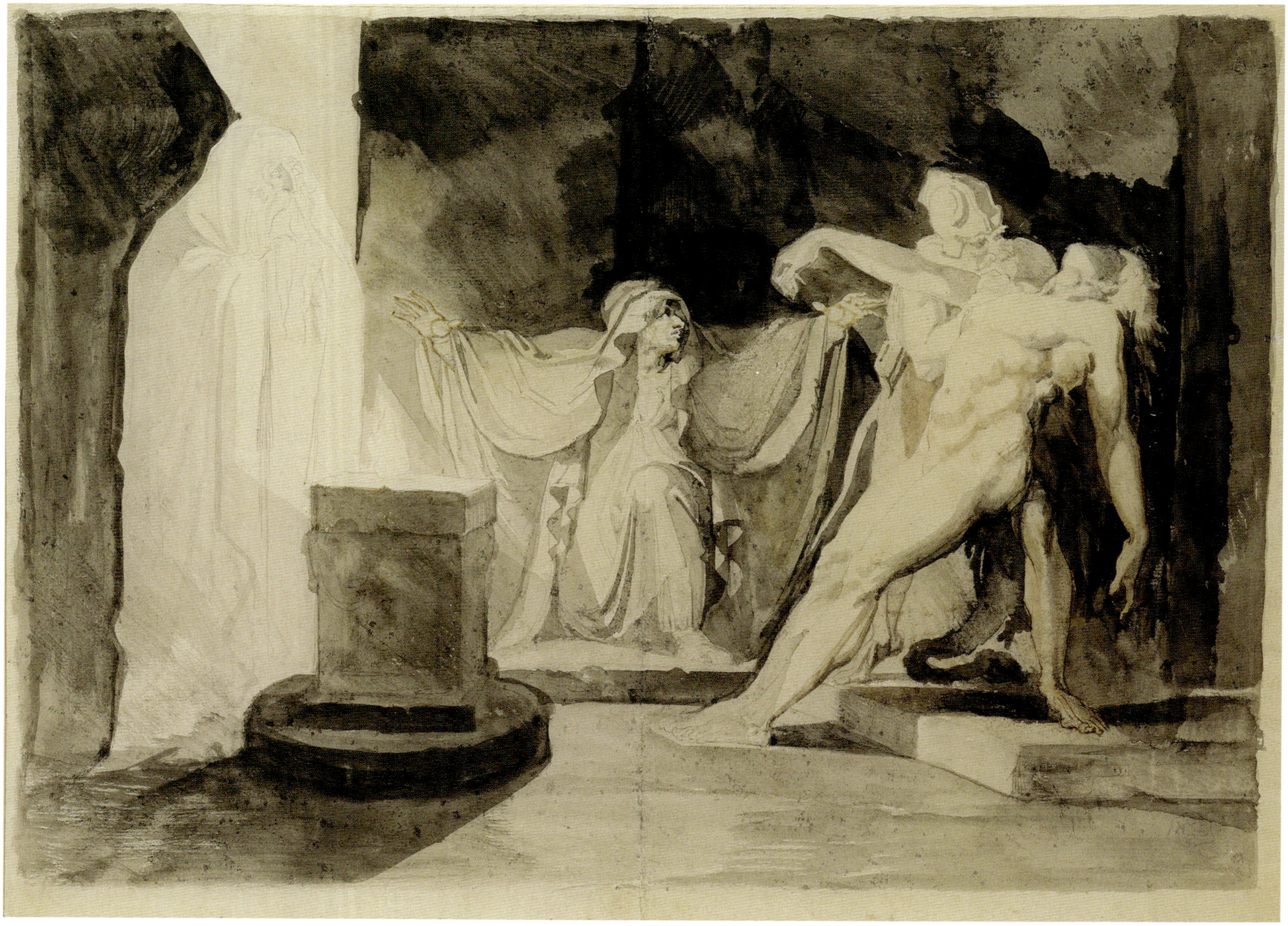

79

William Blake 1757-1927
The Witch of Endor Raising the Spirit of Samuel 1783
Pen and watercolour on paper
28.3 x 42.3 cm
Print Collection, Miriam and Ira D. Wallach Division of Art, Prints and Photographs, The New York Public Library, Astor, Lenox and Tilden Foundations

Blake's subject here is the same as Fuseli's in no.78.

This watercolour (Butlin 1981, no.78) is in the style of the more conventional narrative works that Blake created in the late 1770s and earlier 1780s, when he still entertained hopes of pursuing a career as an historical painter. He had treated this subject before and was to return to the theme again later. Given its straightforward style and its level of finish, it has been suggested that the work may have been submitted for exhibition, but rejected (Bindman 1982, no.11).

The appeal of this subject for British artists at this point – Benjamin West (1738-1820) undertook a version of this theme as well as Blake and Fuseli – remains to be fully explored. Its Sublime potential, and narrative economy, must have been important. But like Romney's *Ghost of Darius* (no.77), the subject deals with a gloomy premonition that might resonate with Britain's political situation at the time. This biblical narrative's status as a test-case of credulity may also have been important. By seeming to represent a direct, supernatural intervention into human affairs by God, the story of Saul and the witch of Endor was traditionally a rather awkward and embarrassing matter for Protestant commentators. The philosopher Thomas Hobbes (1588-1679) had provided a way out by saying that the purpose of the spectral apparition was only to frighten Saul, thus reducing this divinely inspired prophecy to a charade (Hobbes 1996, pp.291-2; see Gibbons 2004, pp.25-32).

The First Book of Samuel otherwise called The First Book of Kings 28:7–20

Then said Saul unto his servants, Seek me a woman that hath a familiar spirit, that I may go to her, and inquire of her. And his servants said to him, Behold, there is a woman that hath a familiar spirit at Endor.
And Saul disguised himself, and put on other raiment, and he went, and two men with him, and they came to the woman by night: and he said, I pray thee, divine unto me by the familiar spirit, and bring me him up, whom I shall name unto thee.
And the woman said unto him, Behold, thou knowest what Saul hath done, how he hath cut off those that have familiar spirits, and the wizards, out of the land: wherefore then layest thou a snare for my life, to cause me to die?
And Saul sware to her by the LORD, saying, As the LORD liveth, there shall be no punishment happen to thee for this thing.
Then said the woman, Whome shall I bring up unto thee? And he said, Bring me up Samuel.
And when the woman saw Samuel, she cried with a loud voice: and the woman spake to Saul, saying, Why hast thou deceived me? for thou art Saul.
And the king said unto her, Be not afraid: for what sawest thou? And the woman said unto Saul, I saw gods ascending out of the earth.
And he said unto her, What form is he of? And she said, An old man cometh up; and he is covered with a mantle. And Saul perceived that it was Samuel, and he stooped with his face to the ground, and bowed himself.
And Samuel said to Saul, Why hast thou disquieted me, to bring me up? And Saul answered, I am sore distressed; for the Philistines make war against me, and God is departed from me, and answereth me no more, neither by prophets, nor by dreams: therefore I have called thee, that thou mayest make known unto me what I shall do.
Then said Samuel, Wherefore then dost thou ask of me, seeing the LORD is departed from thee, and is become thine enemy?
And the LORD hath done to him, as he spake by me: for the LORD hath rent the kingdom out of thine hand, and given it to thy neighbour, even to David:
Because thou obeyedst not the voice of the LORD, nor executedst his fierce wrath upon Amalek, therefore hath the LORD done this thing unto thee this day.
Moreover the LORD will also deliver Israel with thee into the hand of the Philistines: and to morrow shalt thou and thy sons be with me: the LORD also shall deliver the host of Israel into the hand of the Philistines.
Then Saul fell straightaway all along on the earth, and was sore afraid, because of the words of Samuel: and there was no strength in him: for he had eaten no bread all the day, nor all the night.

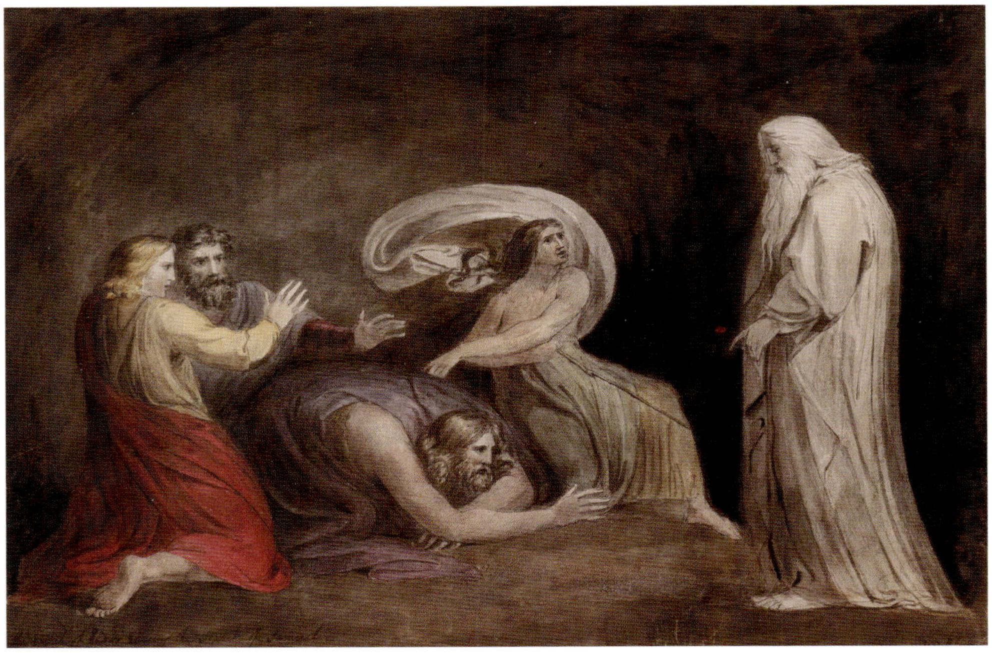

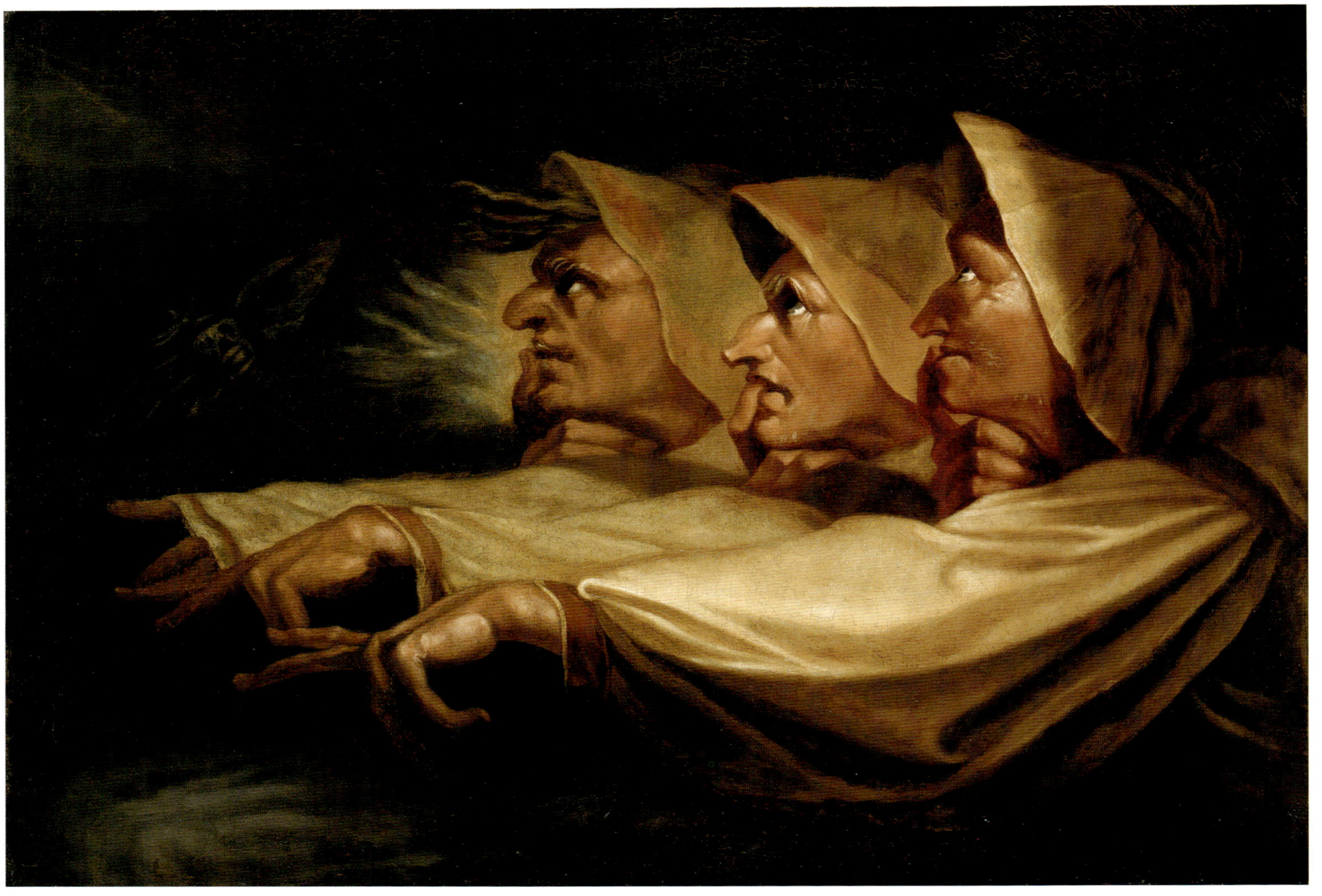

80

Henry Fuseli 1741–1825
The Weird Sisters or *The Three Witches*
exh. RA 1783
Oil in canvas 65 x 91.5 cm
Kunsthaus, Zurich. Gift of the City of Zurich

In one of his best-known compositions, Fuseli presents a dramatically stylised portrayal of the three witches from Shakespeare's *Macbeth*. When the official print of this composition was published by John Raphael Smith (1752–1812) in 1785, it was accompanied by these lines from the play (Act I, scene 3, ll.44–5): '– each at once her choppy finger / laying upon her skinny Lips.'

This composition (Schiff 1973, no.733) was repeated numerous times by the artist. Further versions of the picture in oils are to be found in the Picture Gallery and Museum of the Royal Shakespeare Theatre in Stratford-upon-Avon, in North Carolina Museum of Art and in a private collection in Rome (Schiff 1973, nos.734–6); a further version is in private hands (sold Christie's, 4 May 1995, lot 51). This last has an inscription on the frame and on the back of the relined canvas taken from Aeschylus's *Eumenides*, which translates as 'yet not women, But Gorgons rather'. These visible texts are assumed to derive from a now obscured inscription by the artist. As with no.49, Fuseli thus links Gothic and Greek mythology, the Northern and the Classical.

Commenting on this picture, the following remark appeared in the *Public Advertiser* (1 May 1783):

> Mr Fuseli's Weird Sisters are like every Thing else of Mr Fusili's, in the "extravagant and erring Spirit" – He draws correctly, but his Imagination, impetuous but not full, is the most incorrect Thing imaginable! – With some Abatement, as to Beauty of Fancy, Fuseli may be considered in Painting, as Nat. Lee was in Poetry, a mad Professor!

Horace Walpole was, by his standards, unusually generous towards the artist, noting in his catalogue: 'not bad, but more like old men than old Women'. However, the androgynous appearance of the figures fits with the allusion to Aeschylus, and Shakespeare's lines 'They should be Women! – and yet their beards forbid us to interpret, – that they are so' picked up by Gillray when he lampooned this design (no.81).

Another critic (*Morning Chronicle*, 9 May 1783) suggested that Fuseli had lifted his characterisation of the witches from Raphael. The source is in fact to be found among Leonardo da Vinci's drawings of grotesque heads (Royal Library, Windsor Castle) or, more exactly, Wenceslaus Hollar's (1607–77) etched reproductions of those heads, which re-arranges the designs so that the profiles overlap in the manner taken up by Fuseli (see Lambert 1987, no.7).

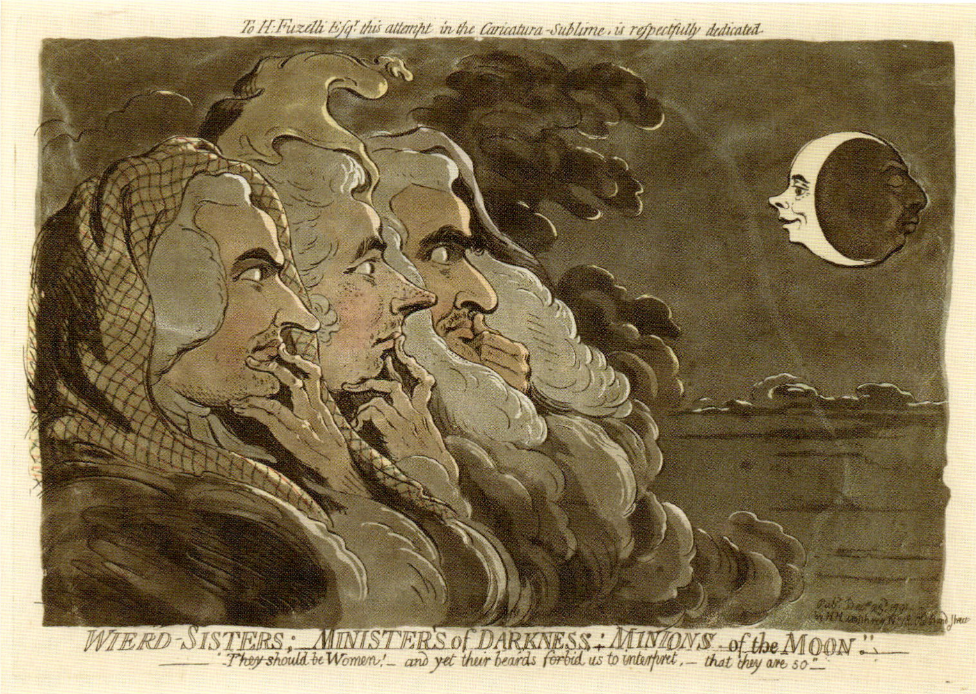

81

James Gillray 1756–1815
Wierd-Sisters; Ministers of Darkness: Minions of the Moon published by Hannah Humphrey, 23 December 1791
Coloured etching 24.7 x 34.9 cm
The British Museum, London (J.3-66)

The Home Secretary Lord Dundas, William Pitt, the prime minister, and Lord Thurlow, the Lord Chancellor, are cast as Fuseli's three witches from no.80 (George 1935–54, no.7937). The moon is made up of the distinctive profiles of George III and Queen Charlotte. It has been suggested that Gillray's depiction of the lunar monarchs alludes to the 'Minions of the moon' in Shakespeare's *Henry IV Part 1* (Bate 1986, pp.209–10).The inscription below is taken from *Macbeth*; that above reads: 'To H: Fuzelli Esqr this attempt in the Caricatura-Sublime, is respectfully dedicated'. Fuseli's composition was published as a mezzotint in 1785, and Gillray follows that artist's composition fairly closely.

The *Morning Chronicle* of 3 January 1792 referred to this as Gillray's 'Chef d'Œuvre', exhibiting 'more genius and skill than any jeu d'esprit of the kind ... unfortunately for the country there is biting truth in it'. On 8 June 1791 Dundas had been provisionally appointed Home Secretary. Thurlow and Pitt distrusted one another, and Pitt eventually secured Thurlow's resignation in May 1792. The joke, then, is not only that these men are dressed as comically grotesque women, but also in their contrariness and unease with one another. Their union is as unnatural and disturbing as the witches' union of masculine and feminine appearances and their supernaturalism.

This is one of the half-dozen occasions when Gillray directly lifted a composition from Fuseli, though the reference to 'Caricatura-Sublime' suggests, mockingly, that a whole genre of images in this vein could exist. The proximity of the comic and horrific, the Sublime and the ridiculous, caricature and high art – ostensibly always antithetical and mutually exclusive – is discussed more fully above (pp.34–9).

The idiosyncratic spelling of 'Wierd' may be incidental, although it is worth noting that Scots dialect has this variation, meaning 'troublesome' or 'mischievous' in a non-supernatural sense. As Gillray's father was Scottish it may be possible, then, that this deflatory allusion was intended.

William Shakespeare, Macbeth (1606), Act I, scene 3, ll.39–47

BANQUO. *What are these*
So wither'd and so wild in their attire,
That look not like th' inhabitants o' th' earth,
And yet are on't? Live you? or are you aught
That man may question? You seem to understand me,
By each at once her choppy finger laying
Upon her skinny lips. You should be women,
And yet your beards forbid me to interpret
That you are so.

(Shakespeare 1997, p.1362)

82

Henry Fuseli 1741–1825
The Mandrake: A Charm exh. RA 1785
Oil on canvas 63.5 x 74.9 cm
Paul Mellon Collection, Yale Center for British Art, New Haven

83a

Henry Fuseli 1741–1825
The Mandrake: A Charm c.1812
Pencil over indications of red chalk on paper
42.6 x 54.5 cm
Ashmolean Museum, Oxford. Bequeathed by Francis Douce, 1834

83b

Henry Fuseli (1741–1825)
The Witch and the Mandrake c.1812
Pencil over indications of red chalk on paper
42.8 x 54.5 cm
Ashmolean Museum, Oxford. Bequeathed by Francis Douce, 1834

The mandrake (*Mandragora officinarum*) is a flowering plant with a long, white fleshy root said by tradition to resemble a human torso. It was known to have sedative properties, and was still in use as an analgesic in the eighteenth century. More important were its rich diabolical and sexual associations, current since Classical times and a recurring feature of folklore and literary fantasy (Brunel 1992, s.v. 'Mandrake'; Thompson 1934). The trade in fake mandrakes and 'mannikins' (humanoid dolls fashioned from plants, usually imported from Germany) was still rife in Fuseli's time, although scientific opinion had generally moved against the idea of the root having any magical, aphrodisiac or even narcotic properties.

The painting, no.82, dates from 1785, while nos.83a and 83b are drawings that were presumably made in around 1812 as preparation for a pair of autograph etchings printed in that year, or may be copies after the prints. One of the prints is based on the painting from the 1780s, the other on a picture exhibited in 1812 (see Brown 1979; Brown 1982, nos.670–1; Weinglass 1994, nos.291–2).

Fuseli's images here are based on Ben Jonson's (1572–1637) 'Witches Song' in

82

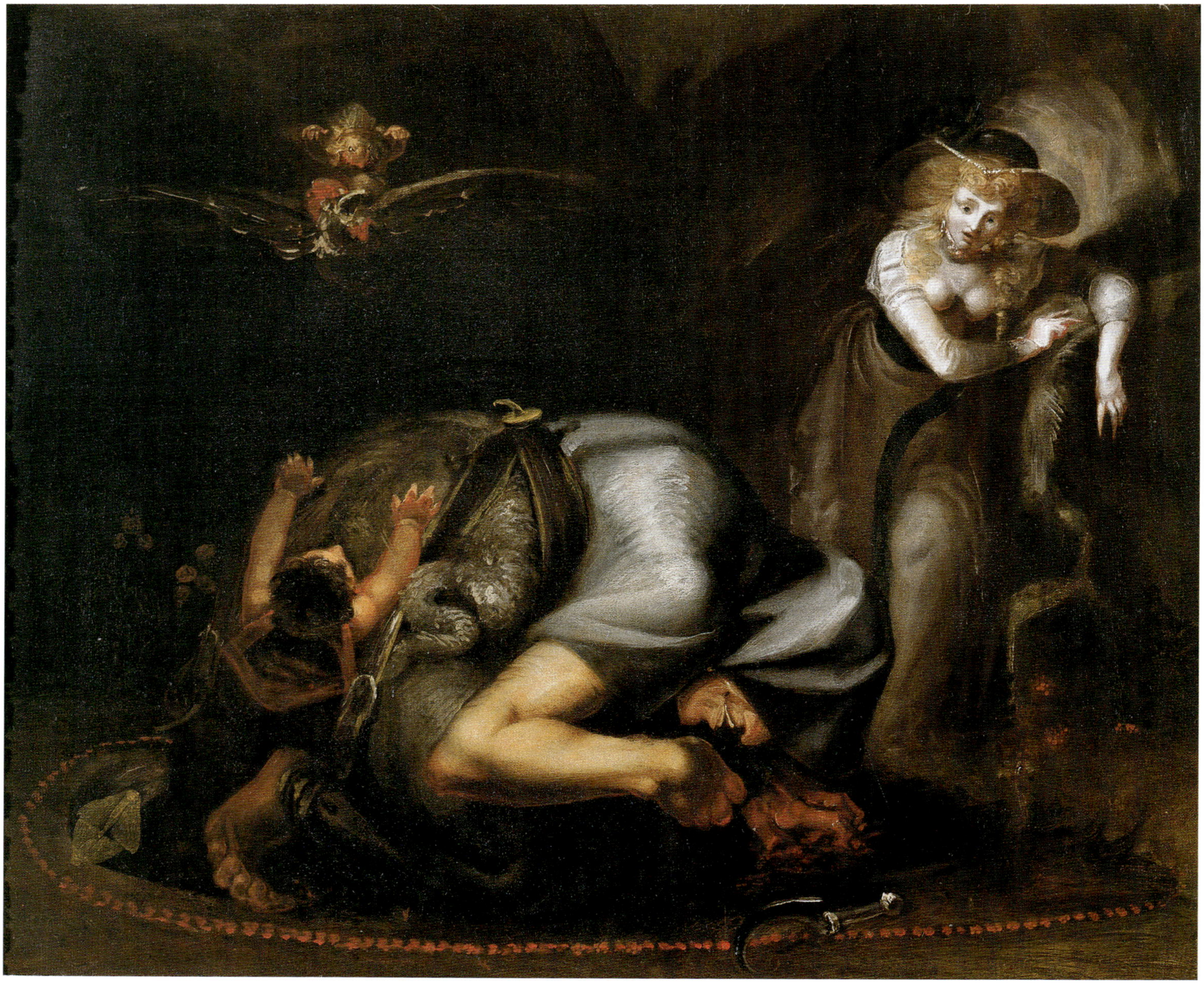

Masque of Queens (1609), the source identified when no.82 was shown at the Royal Academy in 1785:

> I, last night, lay all alone
> O' the ground, to heare the Mandrake grone;
> And pluck'd him up, though he grew full low,
> And as I had done, the cock did crow.
> (Tomson 1979, p.325)

Like the textual source for no.107, Jonson's 'Witches Song' had been printed as a separate piece in Percy's *Reliques of Antient English Poetry* (Percy 1765, III, pp.198–201). Such evocative imagery can, however, be found throughout Jacobean witchcraft literature, and also in Thomas Shadwell's satire *The Lancashire Witches* (1682) which is comically overloaded with (carefully documented) witchery:

> … And I
> Dug up a Mandrake which did cry;
> Three Circles I made, and the wind was good
> And looking to the west I stood.
> (Shadwell 1991, p.124)

Fuseli's painting attends carefully to the lore surrounding the mandrake: the idea that one needed to be in a magic circle in order to draw the plant from the ground comes from Classical sources.

It has been claimed that the painting, exhibited as 'The Mandrake: A Charm' in 1785, was lost and the missing composition repeated in 1812 (Schiff 1973, no.1497; Butlin 1990, p.100). In fact, the presence of the curved blade, which reappears in that 1812 painting, and the crouched position of the witch within a magic circle, suggests that the theme is of a mandrake being harvested, so we may suggest that no.82 was in fact the painting exhibited in 1785. The glimpse of what is presumably daylight in the cave opening at top right would presumably refer, then, to the lines of the crow of the cock once the mandrake was pulled from the ground.

This suggestion that the work included here was exhibited in 1785 is confirmed by details given in the review in the *Morning Post* (5 May 1785):

> We have frequently had occasion to admire the enthusiasm and eccentricity of this artist's imagination; but here it is genius run mad. Painters have various objects. If that of Mr *Fuseli*, in the present picture, was to excite disgust, he has completely attained it; yet, however strange his witches, their daughters appear to be more *fashionable* beings, as appears from the hat and *figaro fecthers* of the young woman in the back ground.

No such fashionably dressed figure appears in the 1812 canvas, and in Fuseli's drawn and etched version of this composition the woman is rendered in less ostentatious costume. The 1780s saw women's headwear grow to enormous and elaborate proportions, prompting an essayist in *The Lounger* (1786) to exclaim: 'What an opinion our great grandchildren might be led to form of the ladies' heads towards the close of the eighteenth century, if any of the fashionable hats should happen to be preserved.'

The 1785 report further confirms the suggestion that the young woman in nos.82 and 83a should be interpreted as the witch's daughter, probably of human birth, who is shocked by her mother's supernatural activities. By tradition, the awful smell or humanlike shriek that accompanied the pulling of the mandrake out of the ground would have deadly effects. The baby in 82 is presumably a further child, begotten with the devil. These motifs recur in Fuseli's *Titania and Bottom* (no.105). The motif of a mandrake being plucked by a witch occurs in his *Shepherd's Dream* (no.101).

No.82 was presumably one of the canvases that the reporter for the *Universal Daily Register* (2 May 1785) had in mind when he commented that 'Gypsies, Witches, and flying Devils seem to have engrossed the attention of many artists'. Walpole was blunter: 'Shockingly mad'. This picture, and Maria Cosway's visionary subjects also exhibited in that year, prompted a number of commentators to reflect on this trend, and on Fuseli's tendencies in this area. The same reporter noted of Fuseli's picture in the *Universal Daily Register* (3 May 1785):

> Beauty and Grace are the objects held out for the contemplation of genius; the investigation of *la belle nature* is the proper province of the pencil; but surely to croud into a bit of canvas every thing that is beastly and diabolical, seems to be Fuseli's object in this piece.

83a

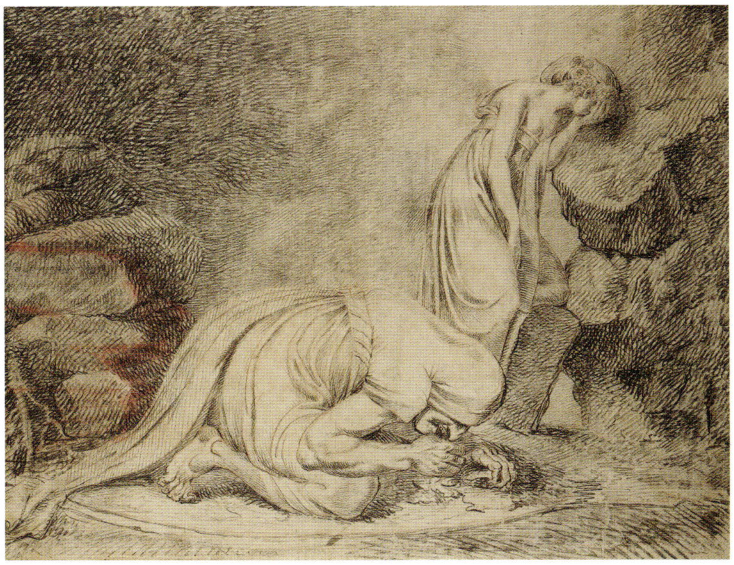

83b

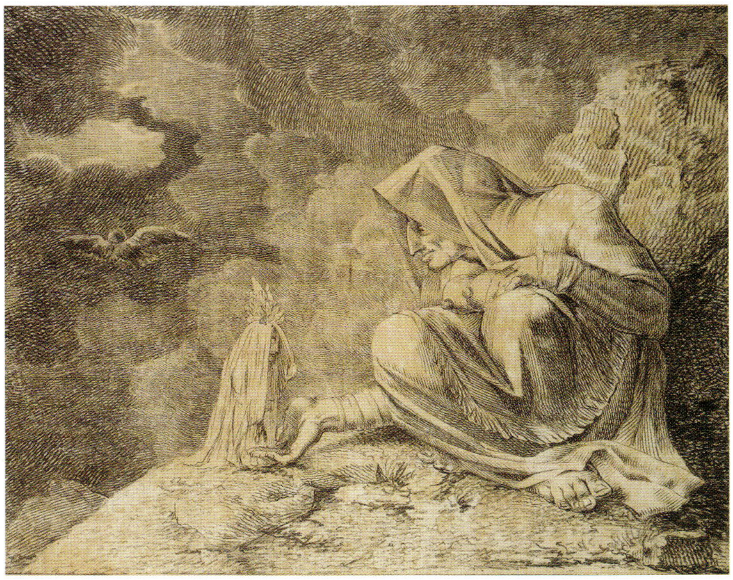

84

John Downman c.1750–1824
The Ghost of Clytemnestra Awakening the Furies 1781, exh. RA 1782
Oil on panel 50.8 x 64.8 cm
Paul Mellon Collection, Yale Center for British Art, New haven

The subject is from the Greek tragedy *The Furies* (or *Eumenides*) by Aeschylus, published in translation by Robert Potter in 1777.

Here the ghost of the wicked Clytemnestra, the faithless wife of Agamemnon, king of Argos, arouses the demonic 'Furies' to pursue her murderer, Orestes. Clytemnestra was of supernatural birth and an evil nature, and had murdered her husband on his return from the Trojan wars. Orestes, Agamemnon's son, had avenged his father's death by murdering Clytemnestra. He is eventually acquitted of any punishment, and the Furies raised by Clytemnestra are appeased. They are then called the 'Eumenides', meaning 'the benevolent ones'.

John Downman was primarily a portrait artist, and this work was not well received when it was exhibited at the Academy in 1782. Horace Walpole dismissed the painting as 'Distracted & disgusting', and the *Morning Chronicle* (9 May 1782) concurred:

> Another proof how artists sometimes loose themselves, and mistake their talents, we have, in two small pictures near No.119 and No.132, from Sophocles, and Æschylus, but these are rocks above water, and warning rather than examples. Nor is it easy to believe, that the finest sketches in the exhibition, No.368 and 369, &c. and the vilest history, should come from the same hand, yet both are marked J. Downman. The first you return to with admiration, you hang over them with satisfaction, and part with them with regret; but the latter you avoid with disgust or behold them to ridicule or condemn.'

As mentioned here, at the Royal Academy exhibition in 1782 Downman also exhibited *The Return of Orestes*, based on another Greek play, Sophocles' *Electra*. It is tempting to consider the paintings as a pair, as the writer in the *Morning Chronicle* did, in which case an intriguing question emerges, for that other painting represents identifiable contemporary figures in the roles of Sophocles' characters, most certainly and clearly Charles James Fox (1749–1806). This painting, and other pictures by Downman, put his sitters in character; amateur theatricals were a popular entertainment among the upper classes. *The Furies* may not be an obvious choice for an amateur performance, and the characters and actions are neither flattering nor decidedly 'theatrical', but private plays and masquerades could become quite elaborate, with costumes and special effects, and the features of the figures here are decidedly caricatural.

85

John Flaxman 1755–1826
The Ghost of Clytemnestra Arousing the Furies 1794
Pen and ink over pencil on paper
21.4 x 32.3 cm
Royal Academy of Arts, London

The subject is the same as no.84 – the ghost of the evil murderess Clytemnestra is rousing the Furies, who will pursue her murderer, Orestes: 'Awake, arise, rouse her as I rouse thee'.

This is a further design from the series of line illustrations that Flaxman created in 1794 for Georgiana, Countess Spencer (1736–1814). As with his designs for *Prometheus Bound* (nos.23–4), the sculptor returns to a theme treated by other artists and either purifies or enervates it, depending on one's point of view, through the use of a purely linear style. In contrast to the treatment of the same theme by John Downman (no.84), Flaxman deals with his supernatural materials with the greatest visual economy. The Ghost is reduced to a kind of architectural element, mimicking the form of a classical term. As Sarah Symmons has noted, Flaxman's point of reference for this composition is surely Romney's *Ghost of Darius*, which we know the artist admired (no.77; Symmons 1984, p.54).

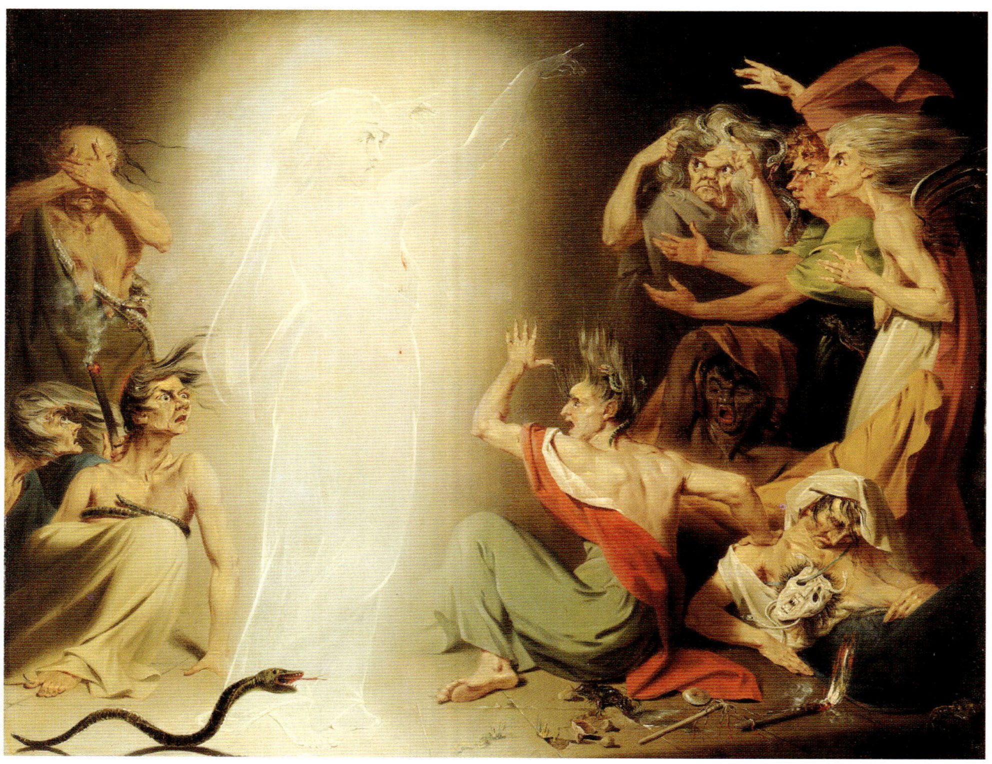

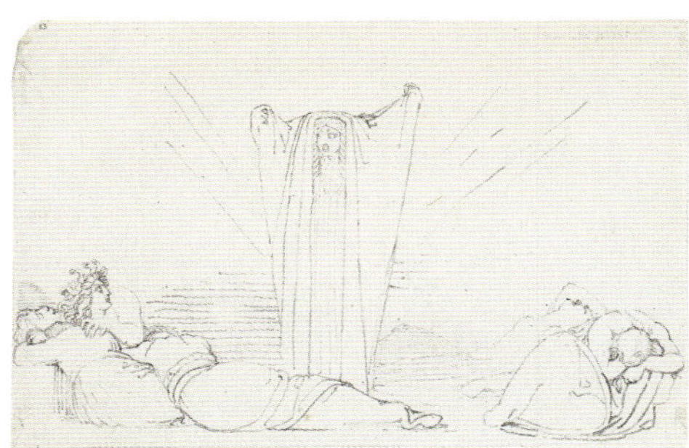

86

William Blake 1757–1827
Hecate c.1795
Colour print finished in pen and ink and watercolour 43.9 x 58.1 cm
Tate. Presented by W. Graham Robertson 1939

A witch, stripped naked to the waist, lays her left hand on a magic book. Two naked, youthful figures, apparently a boy and a girl, lean against her back, hiding their faces. Above their heads we can see the silhouette of a bat in the gloomth, and a weird, furry-faced bat-winged creature. Among the rocks to the left are a wide-eyed owl, a newt or toad, and an ass.

The subject of this print has been much discussed. It was traditionally called 'Hecate', after the title first provided by William Rossetti as late as 1863, and the subject related to Shakespeare's *A Midsummer Night's Dream*, Act III, scene 5 or Act IV, scene 1, or *Macbeth*, Act V, scene 1, l.391. It seemed, then, to be a personal elaboration by Blake of a slight literary reference (Butlin 1990, no.31). However, the treatment of Hecate does not correspond with traditional interpretations of this figure, nor is there any close correspondence between the present image and these literary allusions.

More recently, the composition has been explained by Gert Schiff with reference to Blake's idiosyncratic mythology, as set out in incomplete and contradictory ways in his poetry and various illuminated books (Schiff 2002). The seated female figure is now described as Enitharmon, Blake's invented character who in a 'night of joy' sets out her false, divisive principles. In this interpretation, the book she points to represents her oppressive laws, the two figures split apart by her body the male and female, divided from one another and damned to a joyless existence. But this interpretation is not definitive. Jean H. Hagstrum (Hagstrum 1965) has suggested that the witch figure is the personification of Jealousy, dividing Los and Enitharmon. Christopher Heppner argues that the image represents Medea contemplating the murder of her children (Heppner 1995, pp.120–31). This would require us to accept that Blake reworked the narrative to have Medea taking recourse to magic to kill her children, rather than attacking them with a knife, and that he aged those youngsters to enhance the erotic charge of the narrative. The story of this child-killer was, though, a potent subject and treated by artists Blake admired (Barry, Romney and Fuseli; see nos.120–1).

Whatever the subject, the print draws on the established resources of witchcraft images: the owl, bat and snake, toad or newt that peers out from behind a rock are stock elements in such designs, and bring Blake close to Fuseli and other contemporaries. In the drawing for this print (Butlin 1981, no.319), there are four regular bats in addition to the fuzzy-faced beastie, and the creature looking out from behind the rock is obviously a frog or toad.

Although it has been suggested that this image would have influenced Fuseli's treatment of *The Mandrake* (no.82; Butlin 1990, p.100), the relationship with what is affirmed here as a painting exhibited in 1785 suggests that in this case the influence, such as there is, went the other way. In fact, the weird-faced bat-creature with outstretched wings can be found, also, in Alexander Runciman's rather earlier drawing of Macbeth and the witches (no.75). The youthful figures hiding their faces are, furthermore, equivalents to the shocked younger figures who accompany witches in traditional lore, often as her children, and who featured as characters in Mortimer's influential composition (no.76) and in Fuseli's (nos.82, 83a). Given the currency of Elizabethan and Jacobean witchcraft literature demonstrated here, these sources may merit further investigation. The imagery of the work certainly chimes, to some extent, with that of the source alluded to by Fuseli, Jonson's *The Masque of Queens* (1609), or Thomas Shadwell's comical *The Lancashire Witches* (1682) (see no.82).

This, like nos.45 and 127b, is one of the series of twelve 'large colour prints' that Blake produced around 1795. These compositions incorporate a range of literary and mythological references that leave them open to conflicting interpretations.

Ben Jonson, The Masque of Queens (1609)

The owl is abroad, the bat and the toad,
And so is the cat-a-mountain;
The ant and the mole both sit in a hole.
And frog peeps out of the fountain.

(Jonson 1979, p.323)

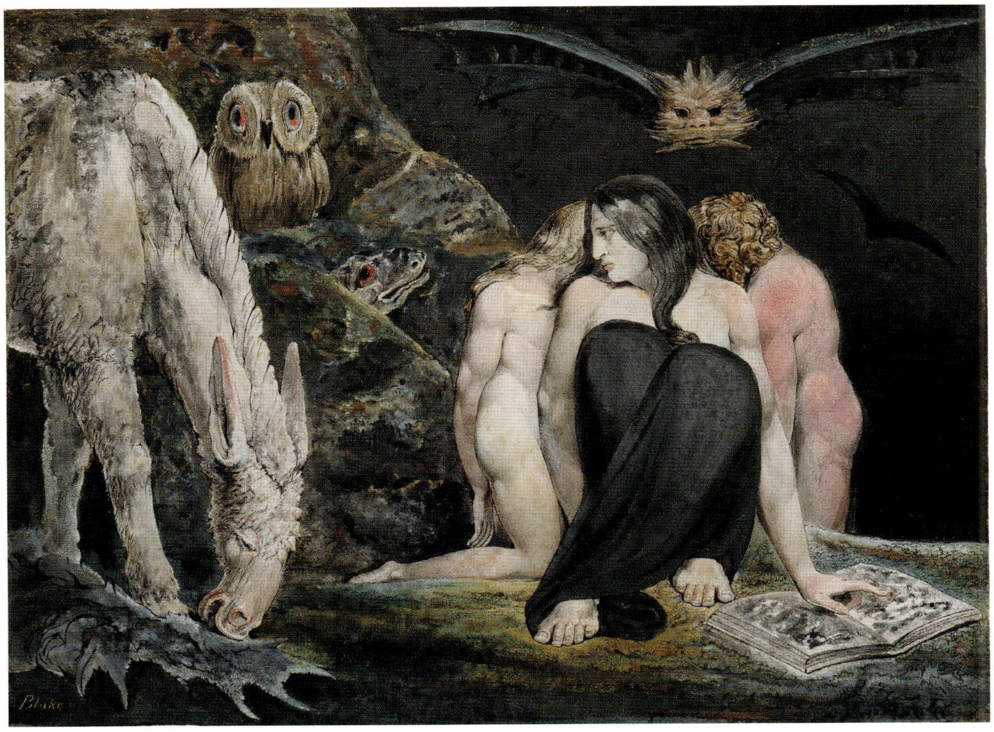

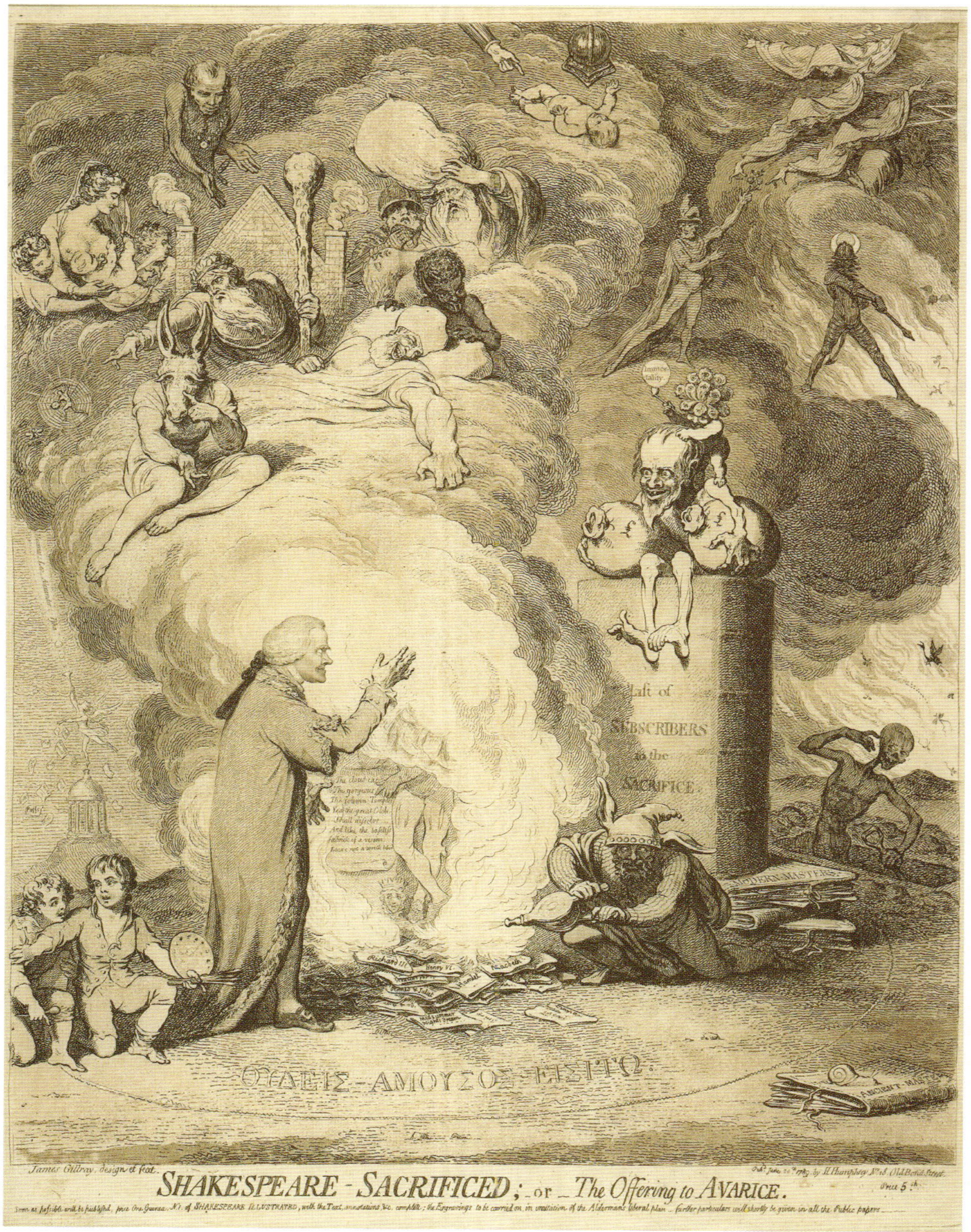

87

James Gillray 1756–1815
Shakespeare Sacrificed; – Or – The Offering to Avarice published by Hannah Humphrey, 20 June 1789
Etching 50.5 x 38.5 cm
The British Museum, London (1868-8-8-5870)

A satire on John Boydell's Shakespeare Gallery which had opened in Pall Mall in London on 4 May 1789. The project had been surreptitiously promoted and publicised for the previous two years, and expectations were high that this group of commissioned paintings on Shakespearean themes by leading British artists would lead to a revival of the arts. Gillray's print seeks to deflate these elevated hopes by exposing the cynical and venal motives behind Boydell's project, and lampooning the paintings that had been created for it.

The dense imagery of this print has been explored in detail by several authorities (George 1935–54, no.7584; Bate 1986, pp.200–2; Unverfehrt 1996; Godfrey 2001, no.41b). Boydell himself, wearing his Alderman's robes, is recognisable as the wizard, standing in a magic circle. He throws Shakespeare's works into a sacrificial flame and conjures visions of his characters from the smoke. The point of the satire is that he does this for money, rather than out of respect for the Bard or any truly patriotic motive: Roubiliac's famous statue of the playwright from Westminster Abbey is obscured by smoke, while an evil-looking imp holding vast money bags sits atop a monolith of a subscription book. On top of the temple to Fame in the distance on the left an allegorical figure of Fama calls the names of the great cultural patrons of the past – 'Maecenas! Leo! Alexander! Psha!' – while throwing out papers inscribed 'Puffs, Puffs, Puffs', 'Morning Herald', 'World' (the names of London's newspapers). The 'address line' (giving publication details) extends the satire:

> Soon as possible will be published, price One Guinea, N. I of Shakespeare Illustrated, with the Text, annotations, &c complete; the Engravings to be carried on, in imitation of the Aldermans liberal plan – further particulars will shortly be given in all the Public Papers

The characters appearing in the smoke are all derived from specific paintings in the Shakespeare Gallery. Fuseli's Peasebottom scratches the head of Avarice (cf. no.105) and his ghost of Hamlet's father can be seen on a cloud to the right (cf. no.88). The words within the magic circle are the Greek inscription 'Let none but men of taste enter here', which appeared above the door into the Great Room of the Royal Academy at Somerset House where the annual art exhibition was held. The two children to the left represent the arts of Painting and Engraving, with the former excluding the latter from entry – as engravers could not become members of the Royal Academy.

88

Robert Thew 1758–1802
after Henry Fuseli 1741–1825
Hamlet, Horatio, Marcellus and the Ghost
published by John and Josiah Boydell,
29 September 1796
Engraving 44.1 x 59.6 cm
Kunsthaus, Zurich, Grafische Sammlung

In a moonlit scene at the castle of Elsinor, the troubled Danish prince Hamlet breaks from his friend Horatio's hold and thrusts himself in the direction of the mysterious apparition of his dead father, who beckons him forward.

This engraving reproduces a large original painting (now lost) created by Fuseli for Boydell's Shakespeare Gallery (Schiff 1973, no.731; Weinglass 1994, no.124). This was one of the painter's most famous images. The treatment of the ghost, back-lit by the halo-like moon and standing precariously at the very edge of the platform before the churning water, was particularly admired for seeming to match the sense of danger and mystery evoked in the words of the play. In turn, Fuseli's figure was used as the model for a staged ghost in 1794 (Reno 1984).

As soon as the original painting was completed, stories of its masterly qualities circulated: 'If it in any degree approaches to the excellence attributed to it by the best judges, it is a masterpiece of perfection' (*Morning Post*, 3 September 1788). The completion date is confirmed by a notice (anonymously by the artist himself) of the Boydell Shakespeare Gallery in the *Analytical Review* (quoted in Mason 1951, p.290). The painting was generally well received when it was exhibited from 1789, and the publication of this print secured its international reputation. The American painter Charles Robert Leslie (1794–1859) recalled seeing the print as a boy, in a shop window in his native Philadelphia, as did Washington Allston (1779–1843) while he was in South Carolina around 1800 (Leslie 1860, I, p.67; Flagg 1893, p.38). The English artist Benjamin Robert Haydon (1786–1846), erstwhile acolyte of the Swiss painter, called it 'The finest conception of a ghost that ever was painted' (quoted in Weinglass 1994, no.124). Not everyone was so impressed, however, and the distinctive silhouette of the ghost of old Hamlet had a prominent place in Gillray's *Shakespeare Sacrificed* (no.87).

William Shakespeare, Hamlet (c.1600), Act I, scene 4, ll.58–86

HORATIO. *It beckons you to go away with it,*
As if some impartment did desire
To you alone.
MARCELLUS. *Look, with what courteous action*
It waves you to a more removed ground,
But do not go with it.
HORATIO. *No, by no means.*
HAMLET. *It will not speak, then I will follow it.*
HORATIO. *Do not, my lord.*
HAMLET. *Why, what should be the fear?*
I do not set my life at a pin's fee,
And for my soul, what can it do to that,
Being a thing immortal as itself?
It waves me forth again, I'll follow it.
HORATIO. *What if it tempt you toward the flood, my lord,*
Or to the dreadful summit of the cliff
That beetles o'er his base into the sea,
And there assume some other horrible form
Which might deprive your sovereignty of reason,
And draw you into madness? Think of it.
The very place puts toys of desperation,
Without more motive, into every brain
That looks so many fadoms to the sea,
And hears it roar beneath.
HAMLET. *It waves me still. –*
Go on, I'll follow thee.
MARCELLUS. *You shall not go, my lord.*
HAMLET. *Hold off your hands.*
HORATIO. *Be rul'd, you shall not go.*
HAMLET. *My fate cries out,*
And makes each petty artere of this body
As hardy as the Nemean lion's nerve.
Still am I call'd. Unhand me, gentlemen;
By heaven, I'll make a ghost of him that lets me!—
I say, away! Go on, I'll follow thee.

(Shakespeare 1997, pp.1196–7)

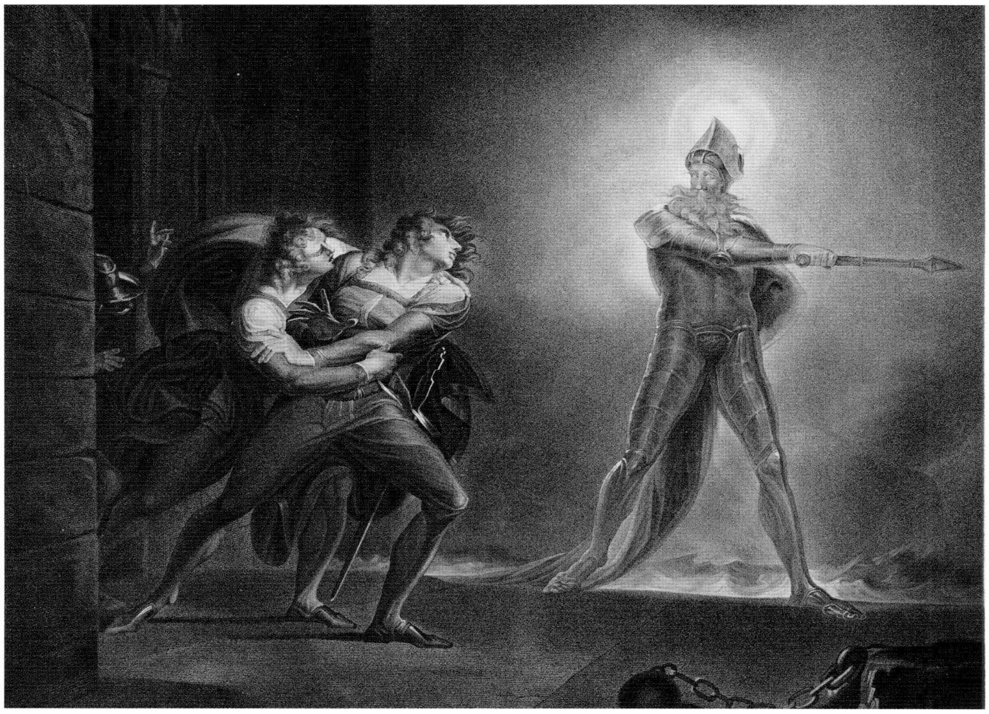

89

George Romney 1734–1802
Margery Jourdain and Bolingbroke Conjuring Up the Fiend c.1787–9
Pen and grey ink and grey watercolour wash over pencil on paper 38.2 x 56.2 cm
The Syndics of the Fitzwilliam Museum, Cambridge

A scene of diabolical conjuration from Shakespeare's *Henry VI Part 2*, Act I, scene 4, ll.10–11. Bolingbroke the sorcerer has been employed by the ambitious Duchess of Gloucester to discover whether her husband will become king. Here, Bolingbroke and the priest, Southwell, meet with Margery (or 'Mother') Jourdain in the Duke of Gloucester's garden; they raise the fiend and question him about the future.

This is one of the large number of drawn studies and experiments which Romney created for the pictures intended for the Shakespeare Gallery (Jaffé 1977, no.78; Dixon 1998, pp.61–4 and nos.42–4; Cross 2000, pp.143–9). Romney was claimed (by his son) to have been the originator of the scheme, but he became disillusioned, not least when the younger artist John Opie (1761–1807) took the initiative and completed a version of this subject. Romney contributed an allegorical painting, *The Infant Shakespeare Attended by Nature and the Passions* (c.1792), and an enormous canvas of *The Tempest* (c.1790), but this was not particularly well received – to the extent that Thomas Macklin was warned off using the painter for his Poet's Gallery (Farington 1978–98, I, p.215). Romney's unfinished painting of Margery Jourdain was abandoned and was destroyed along with other works when it was left exposed to the weather while the artist was away from his studio.

Shakespeare's Henry plays were extensively illustrated for the Shakespeare Gallery, rather out of proportion to the esteem or even popularity of these works. An explanation can be found in the comments of one reviewer responding to Opie's version of this subject:

> An ill-natured snarler has remarked upon the great number of subjects taken from these, certainly not the best Plays of SHAKESPEARE. – They should be told that a Painter looks at a Poet with one view, and an Actor with another – it is not the finest Writing, but the most powerful *Action*, he selects for his pencil
> (*The Oracle*, 30 March 1792)

It has been suggested that Romney's design 'plays against his own private demons' (Kidson 2002, cat.123). But as a commentator on Boydell's scheme noted: 'In the choice of their subjects the painters of the Gallery have been naturally led to adopt the excesses of horror, extravagance, vulgarity, and absurdity which are the characteristic defects of the author whose works were their model' (Walker's *Hibernian Magazine* [1791], quoted in Vickers 1974, VI, p.510).

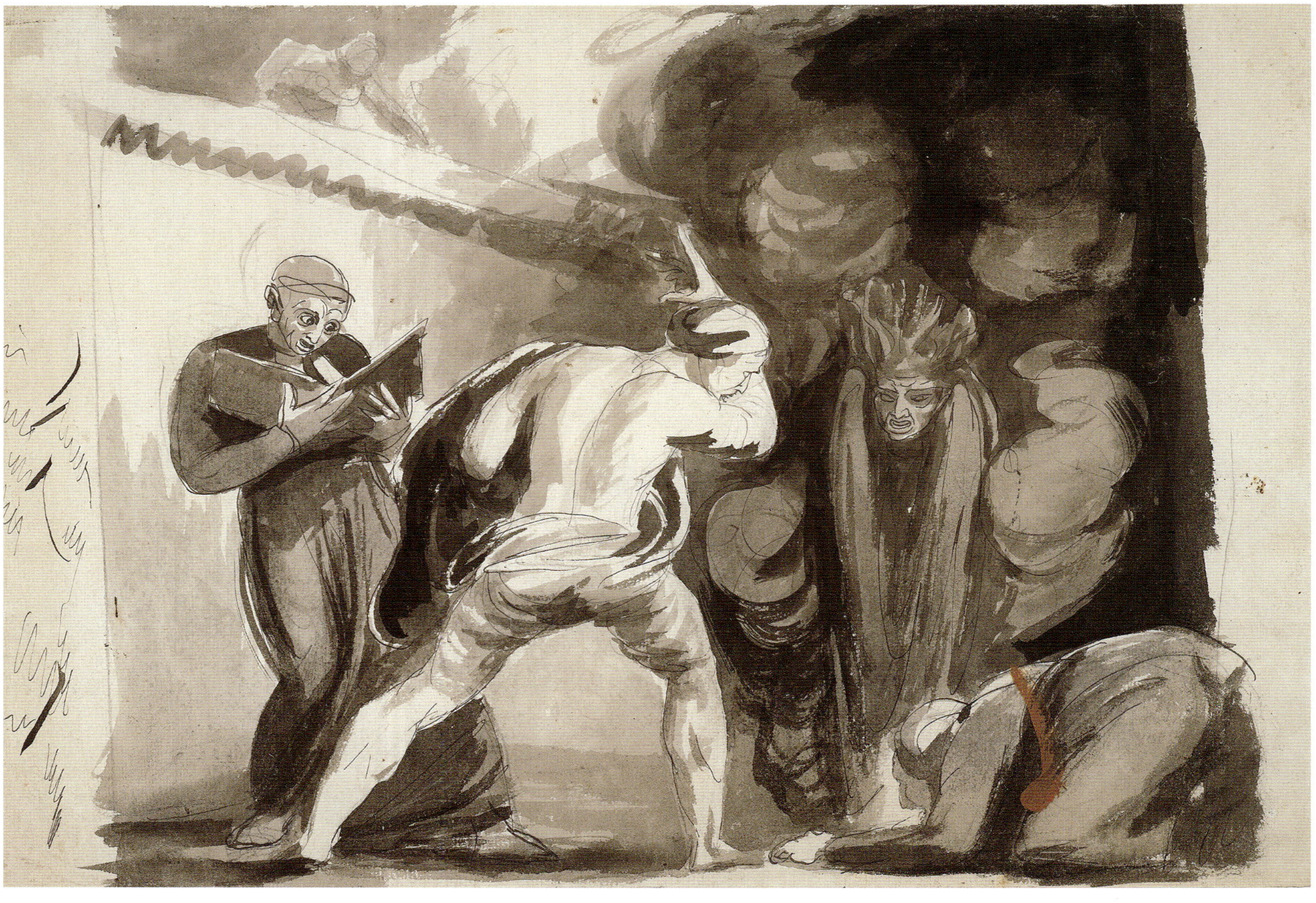

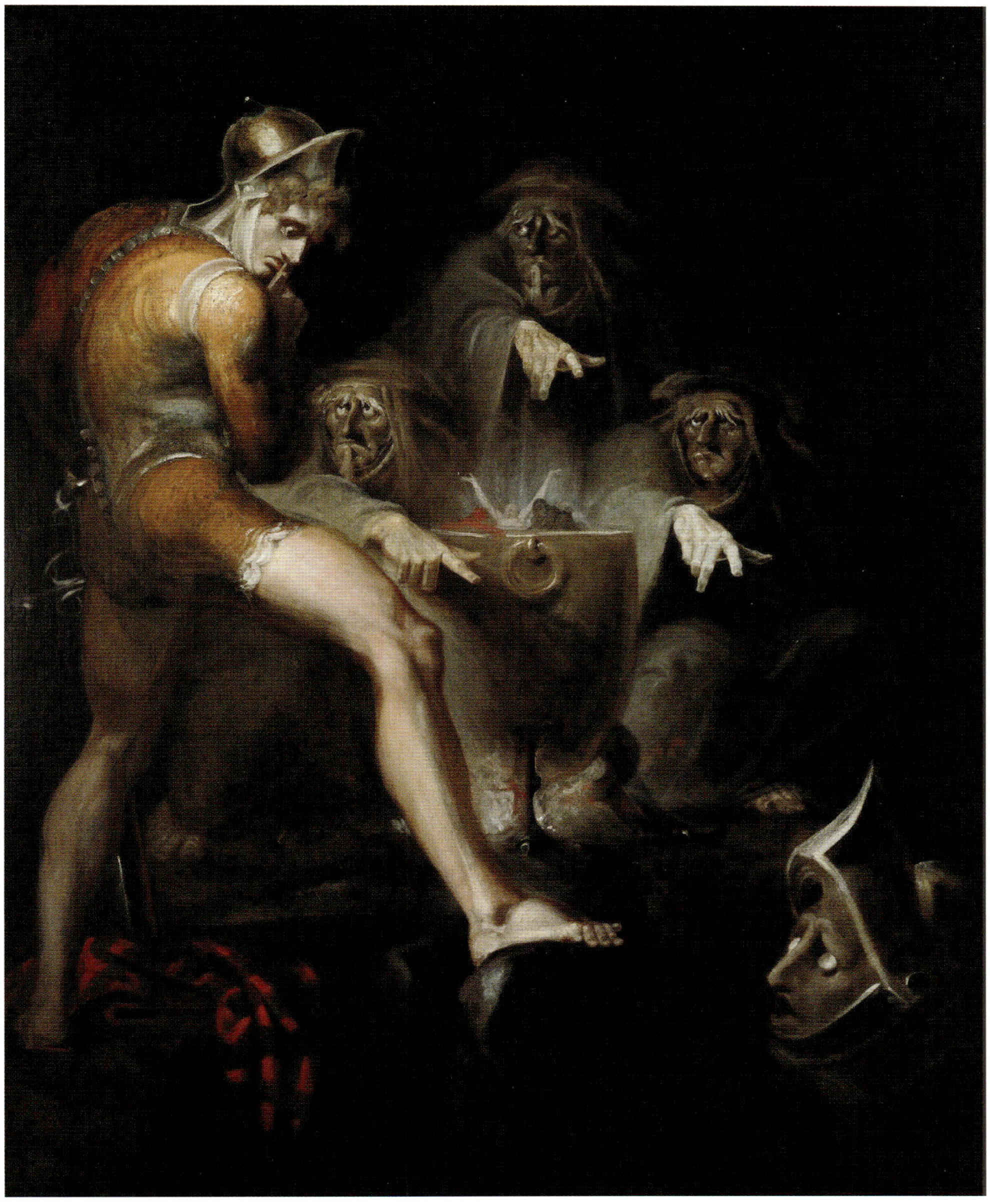

90

Henry Fuseli 1741–1825
Macbeth Consulting the Vision of the Armed Head first exh. Woodmason's Shakespeare Gallery, Dublin 1793
Oil on canvas 167.7 x 134.3 cm
Folger Shakespeare Library

A supernatural scene from Shakespeare's *Macbeth*, Act IV, scene 1. The Scottish prince Macbeth has asked the 'Weird Sisters' to see into the future and predict whether he will become king. The first of the troubling visions presented to him is of an armed head who warns 'Macbeth! Macbeth! Macbeth! Beware Macduff', referring to his political rival. These visions precipitate the horrific bloodshed that Macbeth unleashes in the rest of the play.

This canvas (Schiff 1973, no.881; Pressly 1993, no.24) was painted by Fuseli for the Shakespeare Gallery set up by the English stationer James Woodmason (d.1831) in Dublin in 1793 (Hamlyn 1978). Fuseli contributed four other pictures to this scheme. It reopened as 'The New Shakespeare Gallery' in London in 1794 but was not successful in either city. Still, a contemporary called this canvas of Fuseli's 'perhaps the very best picture he had ever painted' (*St James's Chronicle*, 28–30 January 1794). It was eventually sold to Fuseli's biographer, John Knowles (1781–1841). He recorded the painter's comments:

> You have another of my best poetical conceptions. When Macbeth meets with the witches on the heath, it is terrible, because he did not expect the supernatural visitation; but when he goes to the cave to ascertain his fate, it is no longer a subject of terror: hence I have endeavoured to supply what is deficient in the poetry. To say nothing of the general arrangement of my picture, which in composition is altogether triangular, (and the triangle is a mystical figure,) I have endeavoured to shew a colossal head rising out of the abyss, and that head Macbeth's likeness. What, I would ask, would be a greater object to you, if, some night on going home, you were to find yourself sitting at your own table, either writing, reading, or otherwise employed? would not this make a powerful impression on your mind? (Knowles 1831, I, pp.189–90)

The vertical format of this work was forced on the painter by Woodmason, who wanted images that could readily be transferred into printed form to be bound into a book. Characteristically, Fuseli complained about the restrictions of size as well: 'Fuseli always complained of not being able to effect all he wished in these pictures, in consequence of being limited to shape and size, as was stipulated by Woodmason, that those painted for his gallery should be 5 feet 6 inches high, by 4 feet 6 inches broad' (Knowles 1831, I, p.190).

91

Henry Fuseli 1741–1825
The Night-hag Visiting Lapland Witches or *Lapland Orgies* c.1794–6, first exh. at The Milton Gallery 1799
Oil on canvas 101.6 x 126.4 cm
Metropolitan Museum of Art, New York. Purchase, Bequest of Lillian S. Timken, by exchange, and Victor Wilbour Memorial, The Alfred N. Punnett Endowment, Marquand and Charles B. Curtis Funds, 1980 (1980.411)

A scene of diabolical wickedness: in the foreground, a bare-breasted witch squats next to a stolen child laid on a stone slab, momentarily distracted by the arrival of the 'night hag' – the distant horserider surrounded by a weird glow and accompanied by a pack of hounds. Below, witches dance wildly. The two most prominent of these figures, to the right, have winged or horned hoods, suggestive of medieval fools' caps or classical repesentations of the Medusa (see Feingold 1984, pp.52–3). They are celebrating the imminent sacrifice of the child, signalled here by the pair of hands appearing at the bottom of the canvas, one holding a murderous-looking knife.

As in his painting of *The Shepherd's Dream* (no.101), Fuseli here realises in visual form a literary simile from Milton's *Paradise Lost*. A contemporary reviewer noted that it was with such subject matter, derived indirectly from Milton's similes, rather from his descriptive passages, that Fuseli could give expression to his 'most fervid imagination' (*London Packet*, 22–24 May 1799, cited in Calè, forthcoming). Fuseli is alluding to the lines (Book II, ll.662–6) in which the hellhounds surrounding Sin are compared to those who:

> … follow the Night-Hag when call'd,
> In secret, riding through the Air she comes
> Lur'd with the smell of infant blood, to
> dance
> With *Lapland* Witches, while the labouring
> moon
> Eclipses at their charms.
> (Milton 1998, pp.400–1)

As with no.101, Fuseli's image draws on a wider fund of motifs than is provided directly in this slight textual reference. We could find further resonance with Elizabethan and Jacobean witchcraft literature; the child is a changeling, and thus the subject connects with *The Nightmare* (no.1) and the range of references that painting mobilised. Lapland, the distant northern territory invoked by Milton, was traditionally considered the realm of demonic forces, cannibalism and magic.

The picture was included in Fuseli's Milton Gallery, opened in 1799, under the title 'Lapland Orgies'. As Luisa Calè discusses, in an important new study of the Milton Gallery (Calè, forthcoming; also Calè 2003), this published title is more appropriate than its present designation, which derives from an earlier reference by the painter. Certainly, the Night-hag is only a detail and the picture is dominated instead by the grotesque orgy of dancing and violence. Fuseli has effectively appropriated the source-matter, and remade it on his own terms. Calè detects a rich range of subversive political, philosophical and theological reference in this work, centred on its display of a horrific blood-sacrifice in mockery of the Catholic liturgy.

This picture was among the canvases that could be seen at Fuseli's house in 1794, when he was trying to build up more support for the project (Fuseli to Roscoe, 30 April 1794, in Weinglass 1982, pp.116–17). He referred to it at that point as 'The Night-hag visiting Lapland Witches'. The picture was completed by the summer of 1796 (Fuseli to Roscoe, 9 August 1796, in Weinglass 1982, p.155). The Milton Gallery was Fuseli's attempt to emulate the initial successes of John Boydell's Shakespeare Gallery (first opened 1789) and Thomas Macklin's Poets Gallery (opened 1788). Unlike those schemes, however, Fuseli's Gallery was thought of primarily as a display of paintings, with the plan to publish a new edition of Milton with plates engraved from the paintings coinciding with rather than driving the project (Schiff 1963a; Becker 1997; Calè forthcoming).

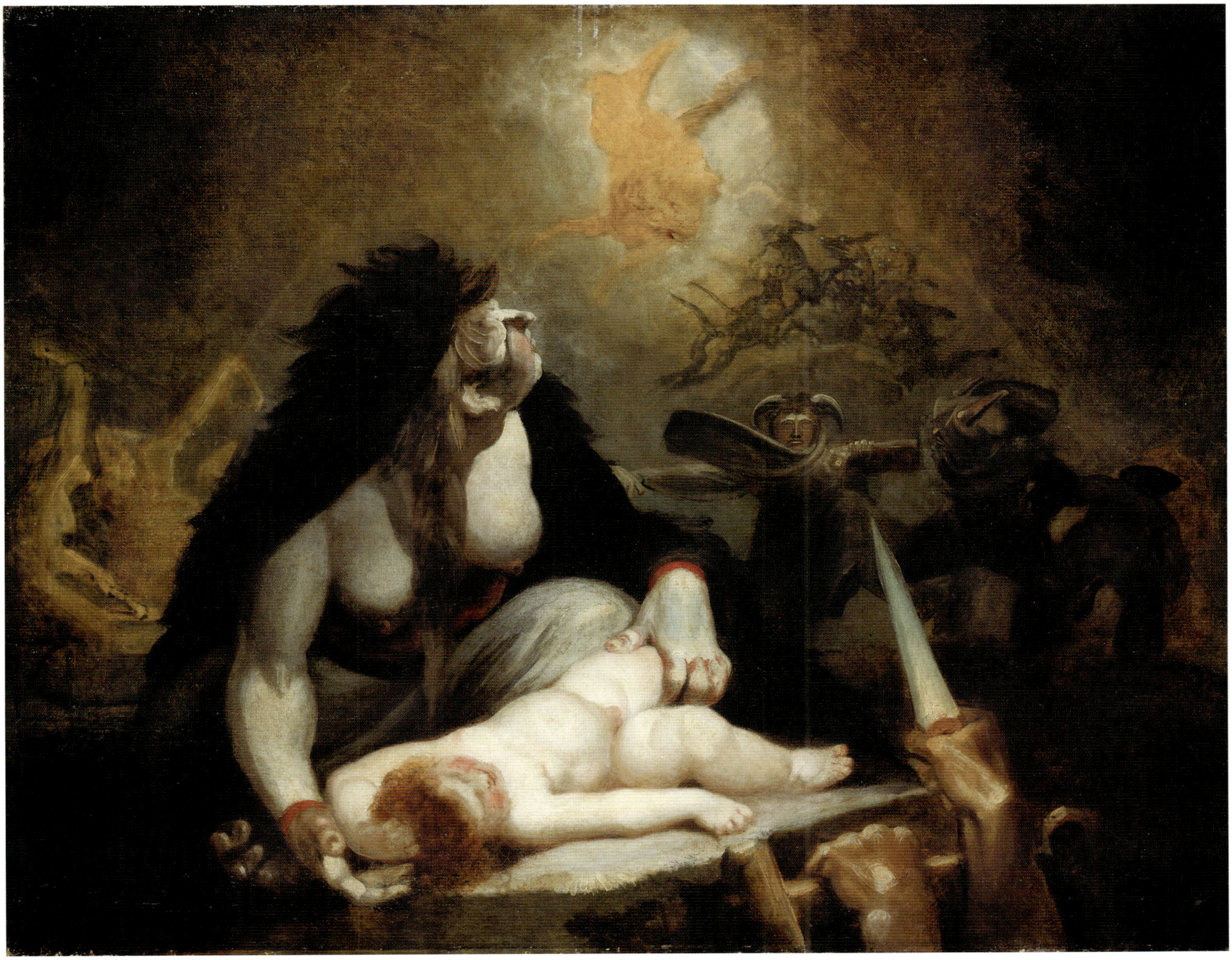

92

Richard Newton 1777–1798 after
George Murgatroyd Woodward c.1760–1809
Laying a Ghost!! 1 October 1792
Handcoloured etching and aquatint
35.7 x 24.5 cm
The British Museum, London (2001-5-20-37)

93

George Murgatroyd Woodward c.1760–1809
Gravedigger and a Ghost c.1790–2
Pen and watercolour on paper 25.7 x 22 cm
Derbyshire Record Office, Derbyshire
County Council

94

George Murgatroyd Woodward c.1760–1809
Gravedigger and Monster c.1790–2
Pen and watercolour on paper 12.6 x 17.1 cm
Derbyshire Record Office, Derbyshire
County Council

95

Richard Newton 1777–1798, with aquatint
by John Hassell d.1825
One too Many published by William Holland,
10 November 1792
Handcoloured etching with aquatint
35.5 x 47 cm
The British Museum, London (2001-5-20-17)

92

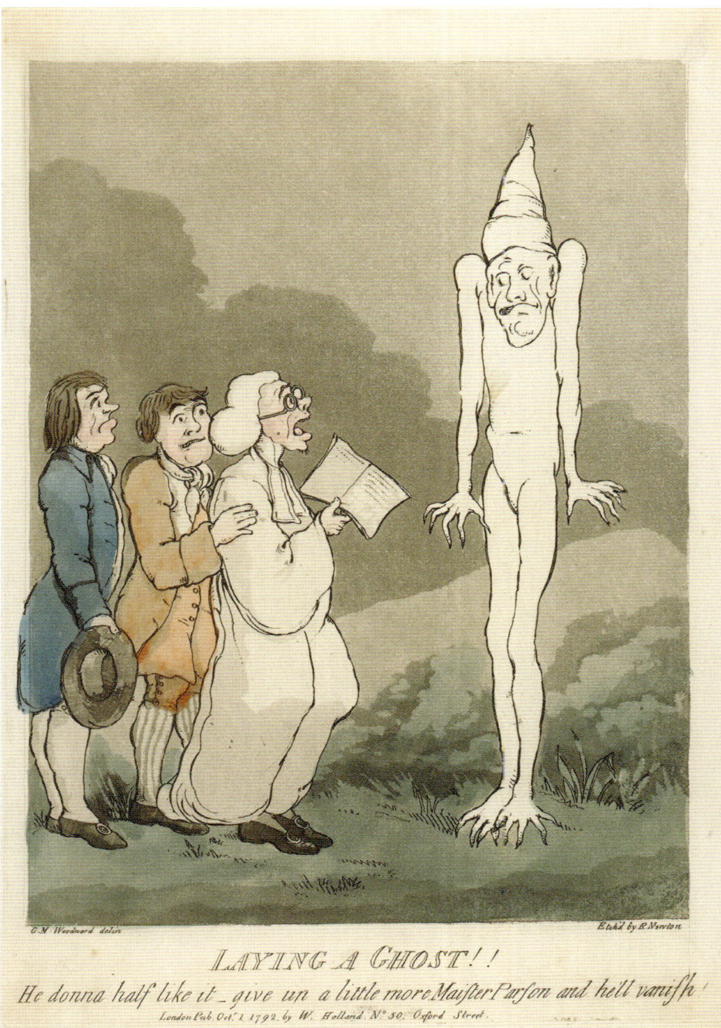

93

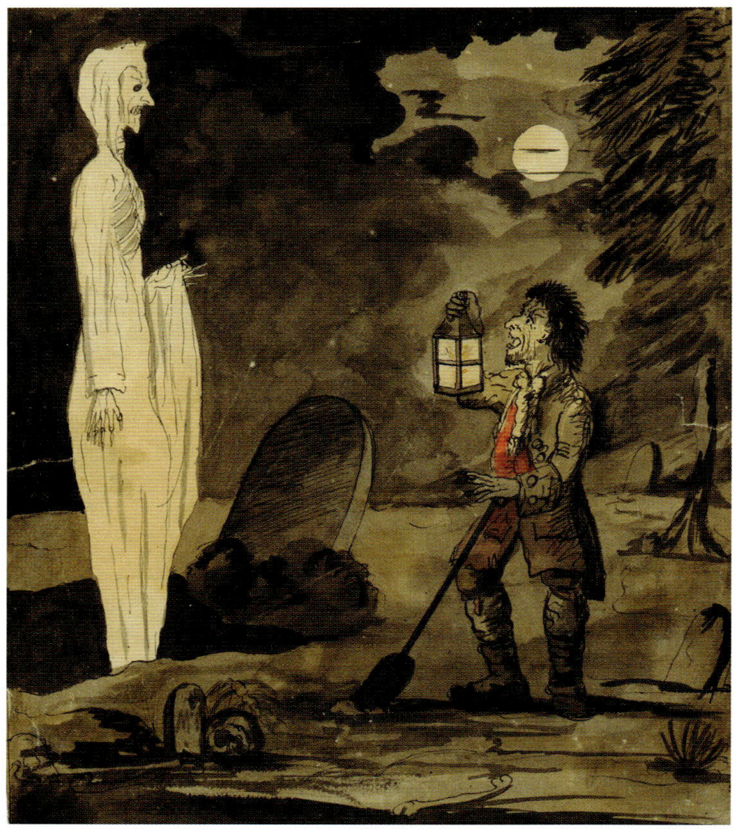

In the mid-1790s, Richard Newton produced a host of comic images featuring ghosts and monsters, often collaborating with the caricature designer George Murgatroyd Woodward (Alexander 1998). While supernatural themes provided a useful vehicle for political and social comment, in the case of these designs the point appears to be only to create a broadly humorous effect, poking fun at the stupidity and credulity of simpler country folk, or those from among the more sophisticated who have made themselves simple with drink. By the late eighteenth century a belief in ghosts was firmly associated with rural idiocy or childishness.

In no.92 a parson tries to exorcise a comically skinny ghost. One of the lumpen peasants accompanying him urges him on: 'He donna half like it – give up a little more Maister Parson and he'll vanish!' The power of exorcism was associated with Catholicism, and was viewed as crudely superstitious. The order of service of an exorcism was even printed in the eighteenth century as an outlandish curiosity (Bourne 1725). No.95 (Alexander 1998, no.9; George 1935–54, no.8209) has a ghost in armour joining an inebriated group of men (their costumes identifying them as naval officers) in a wine cellar; the knock-kneed, google-eyed terror this prompts is apparent, too, in the designs by George Woodward (nos.93–4).

The presence of the designs by Woodward is a reminder of the collaborative nature of the art of caricature in the eighteenth century. Caricaturists would often take instructions or ideas from their publishers or from customers, amateurs and associates. Woodward himself came from a well-established background in the Derbyshire landowning class, and drawings such as this suggest that any artistic training he received would have been rather rudimentary (Alexander 1998, pp.23–4). He was forced (perhaps because of his own profligacy) to sell such designs for money, blurring the distinction between the wealthy amateurs and the professional artists who might be involved in the creation of graphic satires. He had started working for the print publisher William Holland (1757–1815) in 1790; Newton joined Holland as a designer and printmaker the following year. The older man exerted a considerable influence over the still-teenaged artist, particularly in the execution of supernatural themes. The two drawings here probably date from around the time that Woodward and Newton collaborated. Although the design of no.95 is assigned to Newton by the inscription, it is one of numerous compositions that resembles Woodward's conceptions closely enough for us to suspect a verbal or visual prompt from him was involved. Notably, this print is a pendant to one identified as designed by Woodward, *The Haunted Cellar* (Alexander 1998, p.33). Like a number of Newton's prints published with William Holland at this time, the print also incorporates extensive aquatint and therefore a further collaborator, John Hassell (d.1825).

94

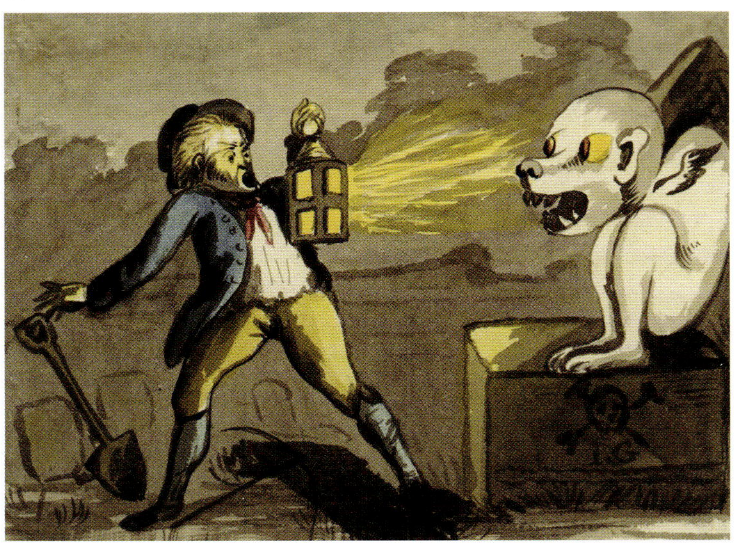

95

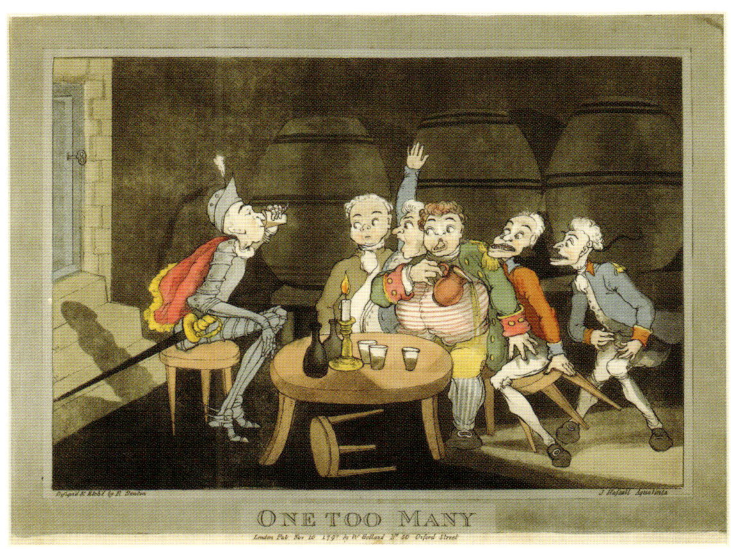

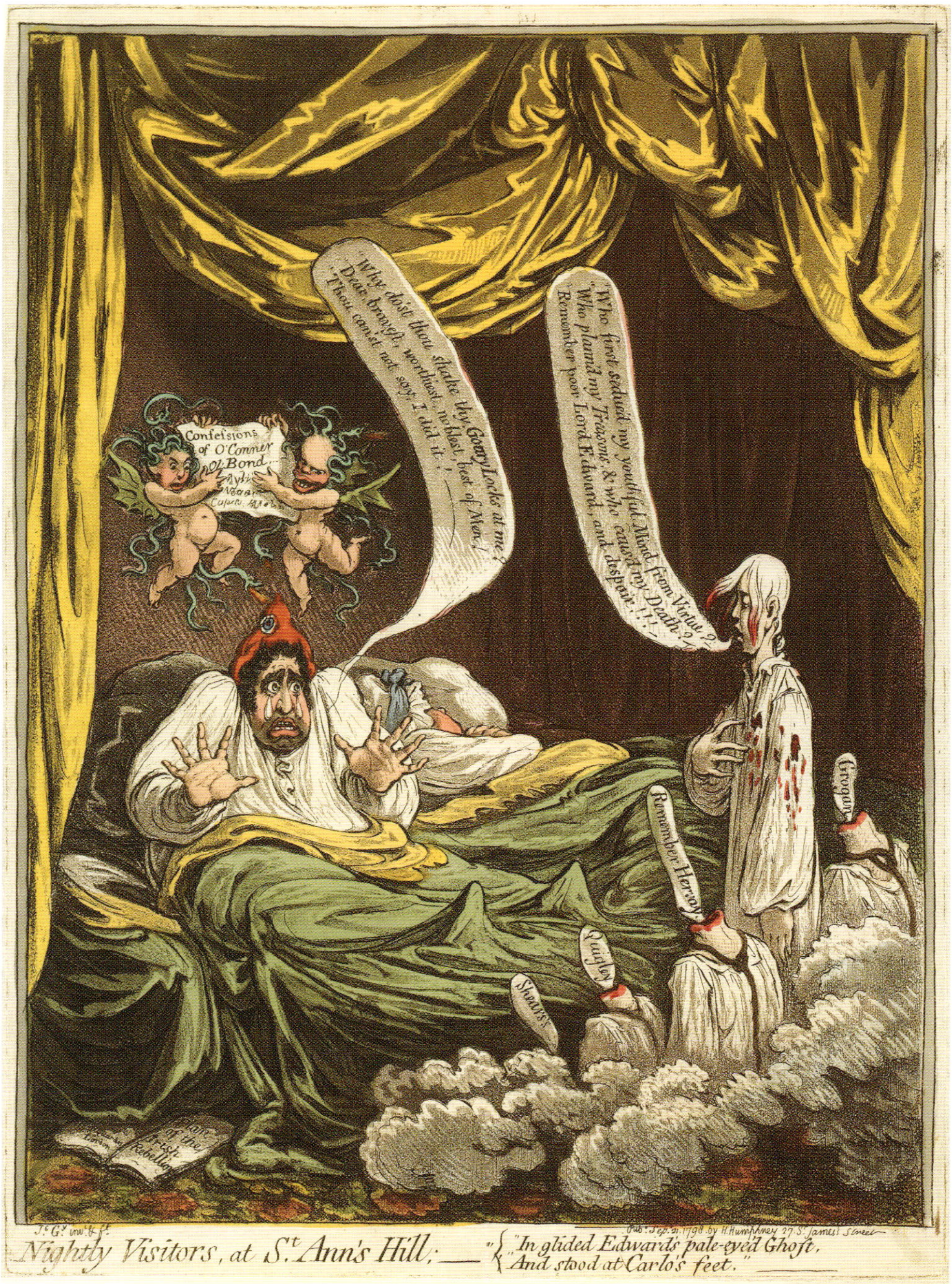

96

James Gillray 1756–1815
Nightly Visitors, at St Ann's Hill published by Hannah Humphrey, 12 September 1798
Coloured etching with aquatint 36.3 x 25.9 cm
The British Museum, London (1868-8-8-6767)

Charles James Fox (1749–1806), in bed, is assailed by a group of headless ghosts, fronted by the spectre of Irish revolutionary Lord Edward Fitzgerald (1763–98), who asks

> Who first seduc'd my youthful Mind from Virtue? –
> Who plann'd my Treasons, & who caus'd my Death? –
> Remember poor Lord Edward, and despair!!! –

Fox replies, with words adapted from *Macbeth* (Act III, scene IV, ll.49–50)

> Why dos't thou shake thy Goary Locks at me?
> Dear, bravest, worthiest, noblest, best of Men!
> Thou can'st not say, I did it!

The inscription at the bottom is adapted from David Mallet's (1702–65) version (1723) of the traditional Scottish ballad, 'Fair Margaret and Sweet William': 'In glided Margaret's grimly ghost, / And stood at William's feet'. This had been reprinted in Percy's *Reliques of Antient English Poetry* (Percy 1765, III, p.311).

The print (George 1935–54, no.9244) is an attack on Fox for his support of the Irish cause. The French had landed in Ireland in August 1798, and a bloody rebellion had followed. The headless ghosts are identified as various executed and otherwise dead Irish rebels, Cornelius Grogan, Bagenal Harvey, James Quigley, John and Henry Sheares. Fitzgerald himself had died of wounds when he had resisted arrest for his part in the rebellion. Above Fox, creatures hold up a paper inscribed 'Confessions of O'Conner O'Bond'. Bond had died in prison in September 1798. St Ann's Hill was Fox's home, and was identified as the seat of attempted secession from government. Ghosts crop up frequently in political satire, evoking powerfully the themes of memory, guilt and revenge: the appropriateness of Gothic motifs for articulating the fraught politics of Anglo-Irish political relations has drawn extensive comment (see Gibbons 2004).

97

William Blake 1757–1827
Richard III and the Ghosts c.1806
Pen and black ink, and grey wash, with watercolour on paper 30.8 x 19 cm
The British Museum, London
(1954-11-13.1 [21])

98

William Blake 1757–1827
Hamlet and his Father's Ghost 1806
Pen and grey ink, and grey wash, with watercolour on paper 30.6 x 18.5 cm
The British Museum, London
(1954-11-13.1 [27])

Two Shakespearean ghosts are illustrated here in a relatively conventional manner by Blake. No.98 represents the spectre of Hamlet's father, in the scene succeeding that famously painted by Fuseli (see no.88 and Baine 1976) where he tells his son the gloomy truth about the incestuous and dreadful plots surrounding him. In no.97 Richard III is assailed by the ghosts of the many victims of his plotting and violence. To the left, the ghost of Henry VI leads one group of spectres; to the right, Lady Anne, the dead wife of Richard, leads another. The spirits of the two murdered princes, the sons of Edward IV, arise at the legs of Richard III.

Blake produced six watercolours, dated 1806 and 1809, to illustrate a copy of a folio edition of Shakespeare's plays for the Revd Joseph Thomas (d.1811) (Butlin 1981, no.547; Merchant 1973, p.250). A regular patron of Blake, around these years Thomas employed a number of other artists to make the other thirty-two illustrations included in his copy of the folio edition. Thomas directed Blake as to the plays to be illustrated (though Blake did not follow this instruction) and the exact size and dimensions of the pieces (see Allentuck 1972).

97

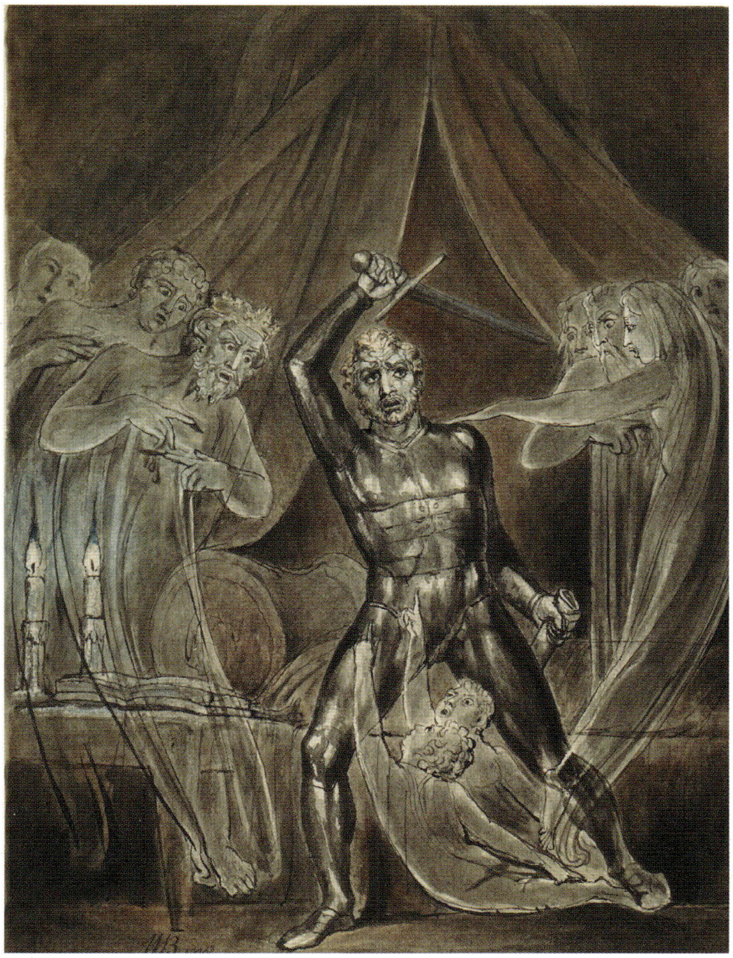

98

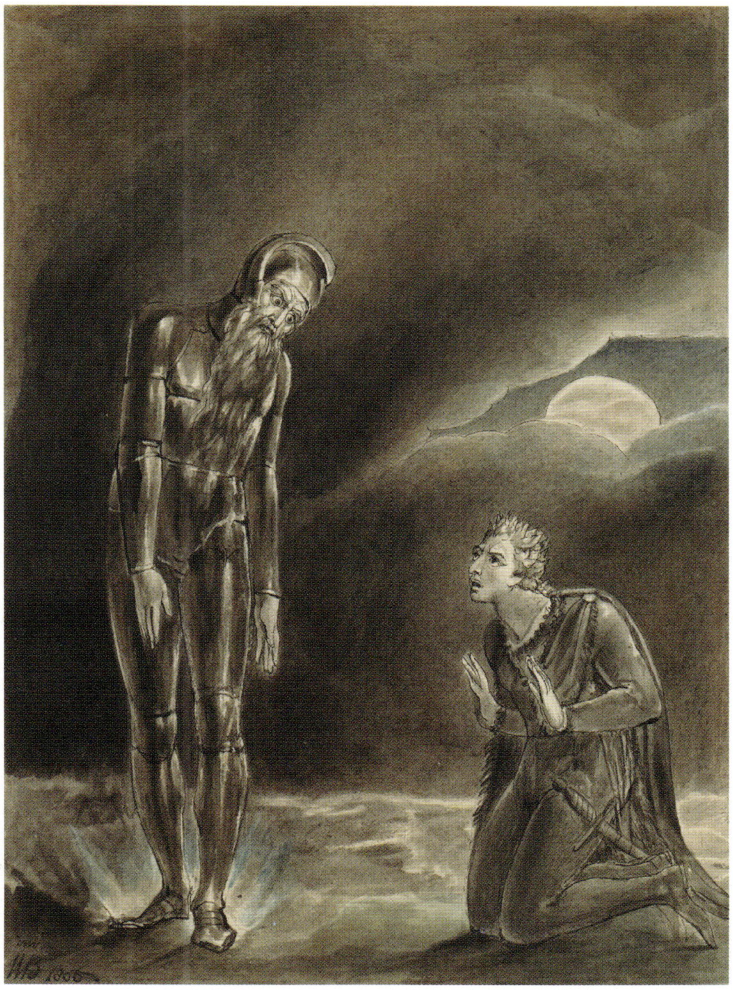

THE PHANTASMAGORIA

Martin Myrone and Mervyn Heard

The spectral and the modern spectator met head-on in the phenomenon of the Phantasmagoria. This form of animated slide-show enjoyed enormous popularity during the period considered by this exhibition, and often incorporated shocking and sensationalist Gothic images. Scenes of hauntings, horror and even Fuseli's *Nightmare* were made into slides and animated for an audience hungry for new sensations. In turn, the Phantasmagoria became a motif within satire, and an emblem of the spectral nature of the self in modern consumer society (Castle 1995).

Primitive forms of projectors were in use by the middle of the seventeenth century; the first magic lantern in England is recorded in the diary of Samuel Pepys in 1666. Magic lanterns came into wide use across Europe in the eighteenth century. Travelling conjurers and necromancers would generate startling visions of spectres using this simple projecting device, sometimes for fun and money, and sometimes also incorporating elements of mysticism and magic. In the 1760s, such spectacles were put on a more formal footing when the Leipzig coffee-shop owner Johann Shröpfer converted his billiard room into a seance chamber. His shows incorporated sound, smoke, electric shocks and smells to create a disconcerting experience for his audience. News of his spectacular shows spread, helping to inspire a new kind of theatrical entertainment – the Phantasmagoria (see Heard forthcoming).

The Phantasmagoria appears to have been christened by the magician Paul de Philipsthal or Philidor, the concept gradually evolving from his stage performances in Berlin (1790), Vienna (1791) and most significantly in Paris in 1792–3. The Phantasmagoria shows were based around a series of projections of supernatural, shocking or comical figures, accompanied by aural effects, ingenious lighting, music and commentary. By combining and moving slides and other special effects, figures were animated, magnified and shrunk to surprising effect. The form was perfected by the Belgian showman Etienne Gaspard Robertson, whose Phantasmagoria first appeared in Paris in 1797 staged, spectacularly, in the ruinous Convent des Capuchines, and then toured to Russia, Spain and eventually America. In the wake of Robertson's shows, new Phantasmagoria displays sprung up around Europe, and Philipsthal was tempted to resurrect his own show and bring it to London in 1801. Philipsthal's show was staged in the Lyceum in the Strand, originally built as the exhibition hall of the Society of Artists, a rival group to the Royal Academy.

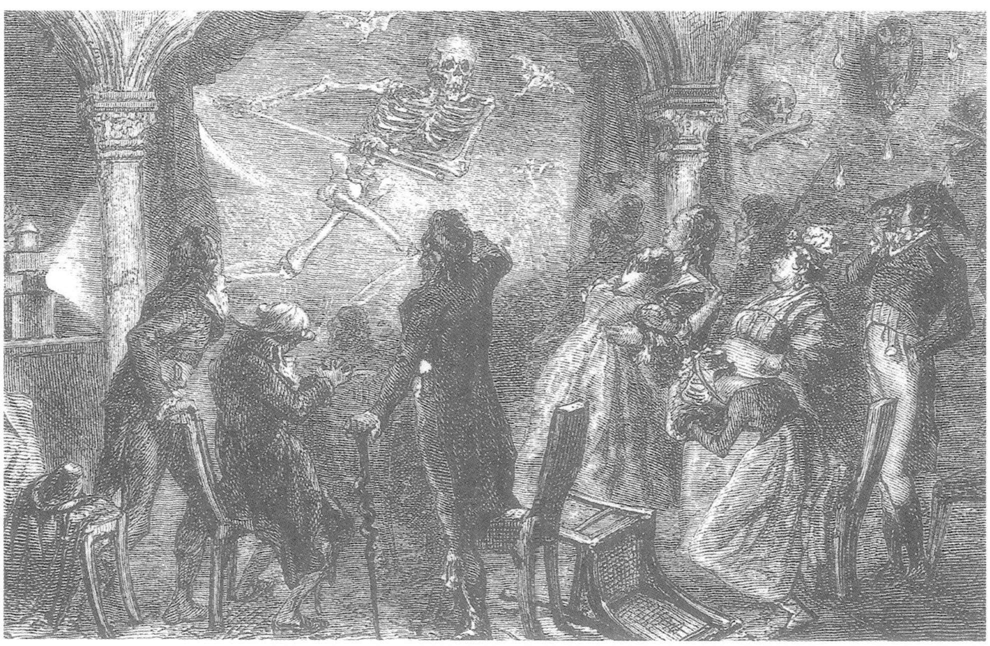

fig.28 Engraved view of a Phantasmagoria show, c.1800

The Phantasmagoria spans the realms of high culture and popular entertainment. Supernatural subjects and shock effects were of obvious appeal as fun forms of entertainment; but there were those who felt there was a serious, spiritual side to these experiences, and the artistry – and artistic references – of the makers of the slides should not be overlooked. Although often discussed as a precursor of cinema, the Phantasmagoria had a distinct aesthetic and existed as a form of theatrical entertainment with its own historically specific conventions. Indeed, The technology used to create Phantasmagoria effects was quickly superseded; by the 1820s it was largely out of fashion, displaced by the more sedate and tasteful 'dissolving views'.

The impact of the Phantasmagoria on the other visual arts has yet to be fully appreciated. While it is easy to see the shared iconographical ground, the deeper connections (in terms of narrative structures, visual effect and style) are only beginning to be explored (see Bird 2004). The airy visions of Blake, in poetry and image, would in particular seem somehow connected with the mechanics and poetics of Phantasmagorical projection. Neither, perhaps, is the wider legacy of the Phantasmagoria properly understood. Arguably, the true heirs of the Phantasmagoria showmen are not the Spielbergs and Lucases of today's effects-driven cinema, but those artists who have taken to slides because of the archaic, crafted feel they convey, the uncertain cultural values surrounding the medium of projection and the evocative associations of projected light. As a recent commentator on artistic enthusiasm for slides remarks, in a comment which appears curiously pertinent in this context: 'Slides have, for much of their history, occupied a place in the marketing and entertainment industries – highly visible outlets, to be sure, but distinct from the traditional realms of art. But when the hierarchies of art came under attack … these high/low divisions dissipated, making room for new formats and ideas previously excluded from artistic practice' (Alexander 2005, p.xix).

Henry Lemoine, 'The Phantasmagoria', The Gentleman's Magazine, no.72 (1802)

PHANTASMAGORIA

Mr URBAN, *June 30, 1801*
The popularity of the above subject, the taste for terror, and the long train of terrific romances or novels of late years published, I hope may plead for an excuse for troubling you with the following lines, particularly when it is now known, that a great French wit has busied himself with a long poem upon La Lanthorne Magique, from which however I have not borrowed, for I have never yet seen it.

HOW sweep the forms which magic fears impart,
Dismay and trembling to the doubtful heart!
Ah! e'en to those whom Death could ne'er appall,
Before the polish'd steel or cannon ball.
Nocturnal fear, we know, has cowards made
Of heroes that no dread had e'er betray'd.
What time when Pheobus in the West retires,
To gild remoter climes with vivid fires:
When fable eve, array'd in vesture grey,
Arrives to close the busy scenes of day;
When pale Lucerna combats with the gloom,
And Fancy follows phantoms from the tomb;
Behold expand the mimic scenes that show
Transparent objects from the realms below,
Whose fleeting forms, invisible by light,
Delusive on our optics steal at night;
So steals the Sorceress from her mystic cell,
Calling forth Spectres, and invoking Hell;
But when the fable curtain is withdrawn,
Fled is the vision with th' approach of morn.
See thro' the gloom the fiery splendour rise,
Affect the glare that Sol's bright face supplies,
When, swift as lightning passing o'er the hills,
Unnumber'd figures every corner fills;
As when the silver light of Cyntha steams,
Reluctant, thro' the clouds with dubious beams,
And circling Fairies dance their airy round,
With nimble footsteps o'er th'enchanted ground.
Of various forms an undistinguish'd train
Swim in array and crowd the pictur'd plain;
Crown'd with wild roses Sylvan bands advance,
Sport for a minute, vanish in a dance;
To these with stern grimace a set succeed,
Horrific grin at death as they proceed.
Next, to divert our melancholy, rise
A group the most grotesque that can suprise,
Laughing like lawyers at a Crim. Con. case,
Gambado's sons in ev'ry brother's face;
Their frolics o'er, another scene fills up
With Harry's Queen, the dagger and the cup.
In Woodstock's bower whilst next we take a peep,
Who can forbear at Rosamond to weep?
There courtly maids, suffus'd in grief, lament
The fatal rage that wrought the dire event.
And here, ye Fair, who grace this motley sight,
Learn to despise false notions from to-night;
Be wise in time, nor like the lonely dame,
That nods delirious o'er th' expiring flame,
When dimly blue her taper seems to burn,
And distant sounds proclaim the morn's return,
Faints with the haunted notions of her mind,
And half expires at whistling of the wind;
Nor too astonish'd at the subtle skill,
As Saul who call'd up Samuel at his will.
Here scepter'd monarchs strut their hour away,
Courtiers and priests, and monks, and friars pray,
Like Father Paul behind the scenes unite
Wine with devotion after prayer at night.
To these succeed in wild vindictive rage
A ghostly group, of spectres that engage
Fierce as the knights in chivalry of yore,
Or Milton's fallen spirits long before.
Appall'd with fear, see killing Death pursue,
E'en the sad victims of his silent crew,
'Till, sinking in a flood of liquid fire,
The vanquish'd and victorious both retire.
To other shapes these spectral warriors yield,
And shapes of love retake the purple field.
As waves on waves succeed in circles round,
And as the race of men on earth is found,
Quick in succession magic shades invite
Alternatively to torment or delight.
An awful sound proclaims a spectre near,
And full in sight behold it now appear;
Down from her head the mournful shroud depends,
Beneath her feet the winding garment ends;
Her lucid form a ghastly paleness wears,
Her trembling hand a livid taper bears,
In rueful order fun'ral torches pass,
Reflected through the Abbey's painted glass.
Retire, ye timid virgins, quickly fly,
Far from the deceitful scene avert your eye:
Lest, when in soft repose the Ghost should seem,
To haunt your slumbers, and revive in dream;
Resolv'd from what you see to take no fright,
Nor dread the lengthen'd horrors of the night.
Such are the forms Phantasmagoria shows,
And such the dread which round about us glows,
As when the weary limps repose in sleep,
What wild fantastic forms their vigils keep,
Men, Devils, Angels, unconnected train,
Compose the motley visions of the brain,
Until the purple blush of day appears,
And chaces from our brows nocturnal fears,
The busy scenes from their usual brightness wear,
And the false dream dissolves in shapeless air.
So fleet the golden dreams of human joys,
And vain delusion ev'ry hope destroys.

99

James Gillray 1756–1815
A Phantasmagoria: – Scene – Conjuring-up an Armed-Skeleton published by James Gillray, 5 January 1803
Handcoloured aquatint 33.4 x 24.7 cm
With permission of the Warden and Scholars of New College, Oxford

Three witches, Henry Addington (ladling the pot), Lord Hawkesbury (crouching) and Charles James Fox (the fat old woman), with the further, dwarfen, figure of William Wilberforce, conjure up a vision of Britannia as a skeleton. The print criticises the Peace of Amiens (1802), which was perceived as sacrificing Britain's interests in order to placate the great enemy, France, and its emperor, Napoleon (see George 1935–54, no.9962; Grainger 2004).

Phantasmagoric effects were used metaphorically in such satires, suggesting layers of illusion, deceit and confusion in politics. The feigned oval infers that the whole scene may be a phantasmagorical projection, although the 'phantasmagoria' of the title is presumably also intended to allude to the horrible visions being conjured within the scene.

This is one of a number of satirical prints using imagery from *Macbeth*, Act IV, scene 1, without necessarily referring to specific pictorial precedent (Bate 1986, pp.207, 210). The inscription 'Conjuring-up an Armed-Skeleton' necessarily invokes the witches' conjuring of the vision of the armed head (painted by Fuseli and drawn by Runciman, nos.90, 75).

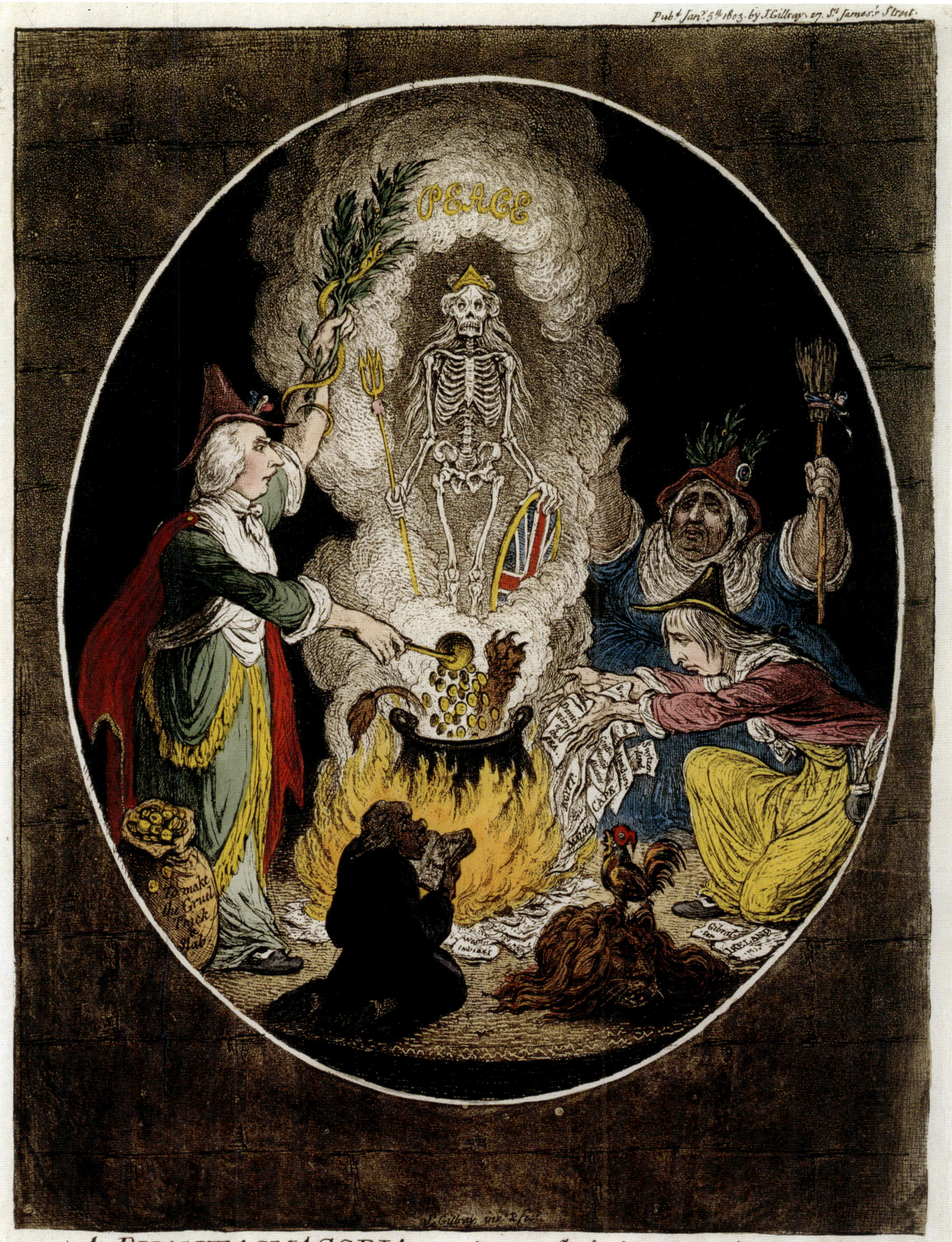

A PHANTASMAGORIA; — Scene — Conjuring-up an Armed-Skeleton.

Fairies and Fatal Women

This section brings together images of fairies and fantasy women. Although we might imagine that the sexually adult and childlike worlds represented by these figures are quite separate, they were in fact closely intertwined in the art, literature and popular culture of the eighteenth century.

Along with ghosts and witches, fairies were by the late eighteenth century cast as properly the province only of children and simple country folk. Almost no one in educated society would admit to believing in them. They could be reconciled neither to empirical science, nor to the Protestant faith. As manifestations of the spirit world, whose existence was generally dismissed by eighteenth-century British scientists and philosophers, fairies were tainted with associations of Catholic superstition. Antiquarians proposed that a belief in fairies prevailed 'in the benighted Ages of Popery ... when the Ignorance and Superstition of the *Romish* Church, had filled the World with *Apparitions* and *Ghosts*' (Brand 1777, pp.108–9). Thomas Hobbes (1588–1679) had famously concluded his *Leviathan* (1651) by damning the whole structure of the Catholic church as being like a fairy-world (Hobbes 1996, p.482). Indulging fantasies of fairy folk was not, then, just to give reign to the imagination, but was also to succumb to the temptations of a suppressed religious supernaturalism (Duffy 1989; Warner 1994; Zipes 2000; Zipes 2002; Brewer 2003). Yet fairy tales persisted, and with Fuseli, and latterly Blake, and the poet Samuel Taylor Coleridge (1772–1834) took on a dynamic new imaginative life (Adlard 1972; Watson 1990).

The literary traditions of fairy tales, the complex psychology and symbolism of their narratives and the folkloric dimensions of their historical survival are rich areas of enquiry (Duffy 1989; Warner 1994; Bown 2001; see also Haase 2000). In an eighteenth-century context, fairies potently represent the return of the repressed, as it might be described by psychoanalysts. Fairies offered guilty, even titillating pleasures, and the sexual dimensions of fairy-lore were deeply-rooted: 'To dream of elves and fairies, means that you will be teased a little by your lover' (*The Wizard, Or the Whole Art of Divining Dreams*, Derby 1816, p.27). The traditional colour of fairies – green – was associated with prostitutes, while the name of Shakespeare's figure 'Queen Mab' who 'gallops night by night / Through lover's brains' was a punning allusion to slang terms for sluttish woman (*Romeo and Juliet*, Act 1, scene 4, ll.53, 70–1; Shakespeare 1997, pp.1110–11). Partly because of Shakespeare's use of this character, Mab was established as the ruler of the realm of dreams, as well as queen of the fairies. She was, as a populist source from the early nineteenth century put it, 'fancy's midwife' (*The Wizard*, p.22). That variant reading of Shakespeare's reference to Mab as 'the fairies midwife' had been proposed by the scholar William Warburton (1698–1779) and though discredited maintained its appeal, capturing her role as the source of loose, perhaps saucy, imaginings.

Fuseli was universally acknowledged as the master painter of the fairy. His images are all the more interesting for the sexual politics and sense of dangerous femininity that run through them. As Nicola Bown has argued, his fairy works articulate anxieties around the concept of imagination, its transforming effects upon the subject, the body, and gender relations (Bown 2001). His conception of Shakespeare's fairy world puts female characters in charge – beautiful, long-limbed creatures of perfection contrasted with squat, grotesque, simple men. Titania appears as a kind of femme-fatale, dominating the guileless Bottom. Fuseli's private drawings of pornographic scenes present the intermingling of sex, death and power more directly, with sexy women torturing boys, suffocating men with their bodies, teasing haughtily. These images pose unresolved questions about sexuality and desire: do these fantasies of power and submission simply reaffirm the social reality of gender inequality, or do they open the door to a liberated imagination in which the economy of pleasure is radically transformed? (see Carter 1979).

<u>The Universal Fortune Teller: Or, Mrs Bridget's (commonly called the Norwood Gypsy) Golden Treasury Explained</u>, London (c.1770)

To dream of seeing strange apparitions,
As devils, hobgoblins, and such visions,
Does show thy love, or thy sweetheart,
Hath a fair face but devil's heart.

Henry Fuseli, 'Aphorisms on Art' (c.1788–1818)

Reality teems with disappointment for him whose sources of enjoyment spring in the elysium of fancy.

(Knowles 1831, III, p.68)

Henry Fuseli, 'Aphorisms on Art' (c.1788–1818)

Female affection is ever in proportion to the impression of superiority in the object. Woman fondles, pities, despises and forgets what is below her; she values, bears and wrangles with her equal; she adores what is above her.

(Mason 1951, p.145)

Willliam Blake, <u>Descriptive Catalogue</u> (18090

Shakespeare's Fairies also are the rulers of the vegetable world.

(Blake 1978, II, p.837)

100

Henry Fuseli 1741–1825
Queen Katherine's Dream exh. RA 1781
Oil on canvas 151.1 x 212.1 cm
Flyde Borough Council

In a scene from Shakespeare's *King Henry VIII* (1613) Queen Katherine dreams on her deathbed of eternal happiness. As the 'spirits of peace' depart from her, she raises her arms in joy, only to die in the morning.

Katherine of Aragon (1485–1536) was the Catholic wife of Henry VIII from 1501 until their divorce in 1533, the event that caused the break from Rome and allowed Henry to marry Ann Boleyn. The source of the deathbed vision given to her by Shakespeare is uncertain; a modern proposal is that it derives from the vision attributed to Margaret of Angoulême, Queen of Navarre (1492–1549), just before her death (Duncan-Jones 1961).

Like no.37, this was one of the seven canvases commissioned from Fuseli by Sir Robert Smyth, Bart (1744–1802) (see Weinglass 1982, pp.575–6; Licht, Rizzetti and Weinglass 1997, no.17). The painting was first exhibited at the Royal Academy in 1781. Fuseli's contributions to that show were highly strategic. His version of *The Death of Dido* (fig.2 on p.10) was designed as a direct challenge to the artistic authority of Sir Joshua Reynolds, whose own version of that theme Fuseli had seen in preparation for this show (see above, p.10). Accordingly, most commentators paid greater attention to the comparison between these canvases – and most found that Fuseli had the upper hand in terms of draughtsmanship, invention and composition. While that was a bloody and tragic classical subject, *Queen Katherine's Dream* showed Fuseli as a delicate fantasist and interpreter of Shakespeare at his most poetic. Samuel Johnson reckoned this scene 'above any other part of *Shakespeare*'s tragedies, and perhaps above any other scene of any other poet' (Vickers 1974, V, p.134). However, another contemporary dismissed Shakespeare's 'Vision of Angels' as a 'little pantomime ... fitter to tempt an audience to mirth and ridicule than to serious attention' (Thomas Davies, *Dramatic Miscellanies* [1784], in Vickers 1974, VI, p.374). Fuseli's painting was, though, generally well approved of. One pamphleteer remarked that the picture was 'A dream' (Lowe 1781). Another newspaper critic wrote: 'This composition is capital. There is a display of the most elegant figures imaginable, grouped with the best judgment and taste. This is, indeed, the particular excellence of this ingenious artist – we could wish, however, that he would attend more to the colouring' (*Gazetteer*, 12 May 1781). In fact, in its present appearance, this is one of the most simply attractive of Fuseli's paintings. It is painted in unusually clear tones, and the visionary personages are finished in a style quite uncharacteristic of the artist.

William Shakespeare, King Henry VIII (1613), Act IV, scene 2, ll.81–4

GRIFFITH. *She is asleep. Good wench, let's sit down quiet,*
For fear we wake her. Softly, gentle Patience.
THE VISION. *Enter, solemnly tripping one after another, six Personages, clad in white robes, wearing on their heads garlands of bays, and golden vizards on their faces, branches of bays or palms in their hands. They first congé unto her, then dance; and at certain changes, the first two hold a spare garland over her head, at which the other four make reverend curtsies. Then the two that held the garland deliver the same to the other next two, who observe the same order in their changes and holding the garland over her head. Which done, they deliver the same garland to the last two, who likewise observe the same order. At which (as it were by inspiration) she makes in her sleep signs of rejoicing and holdeth up her hands to heaven. And so, in their dancing, vanish, carrying the garland with them. The music continues.*
KATHERINE. *Spirits of peace, where are ye? Are ye all done*
And leave me here in wretchedness behind ye?

(Shakespeare 1997, p.1054)

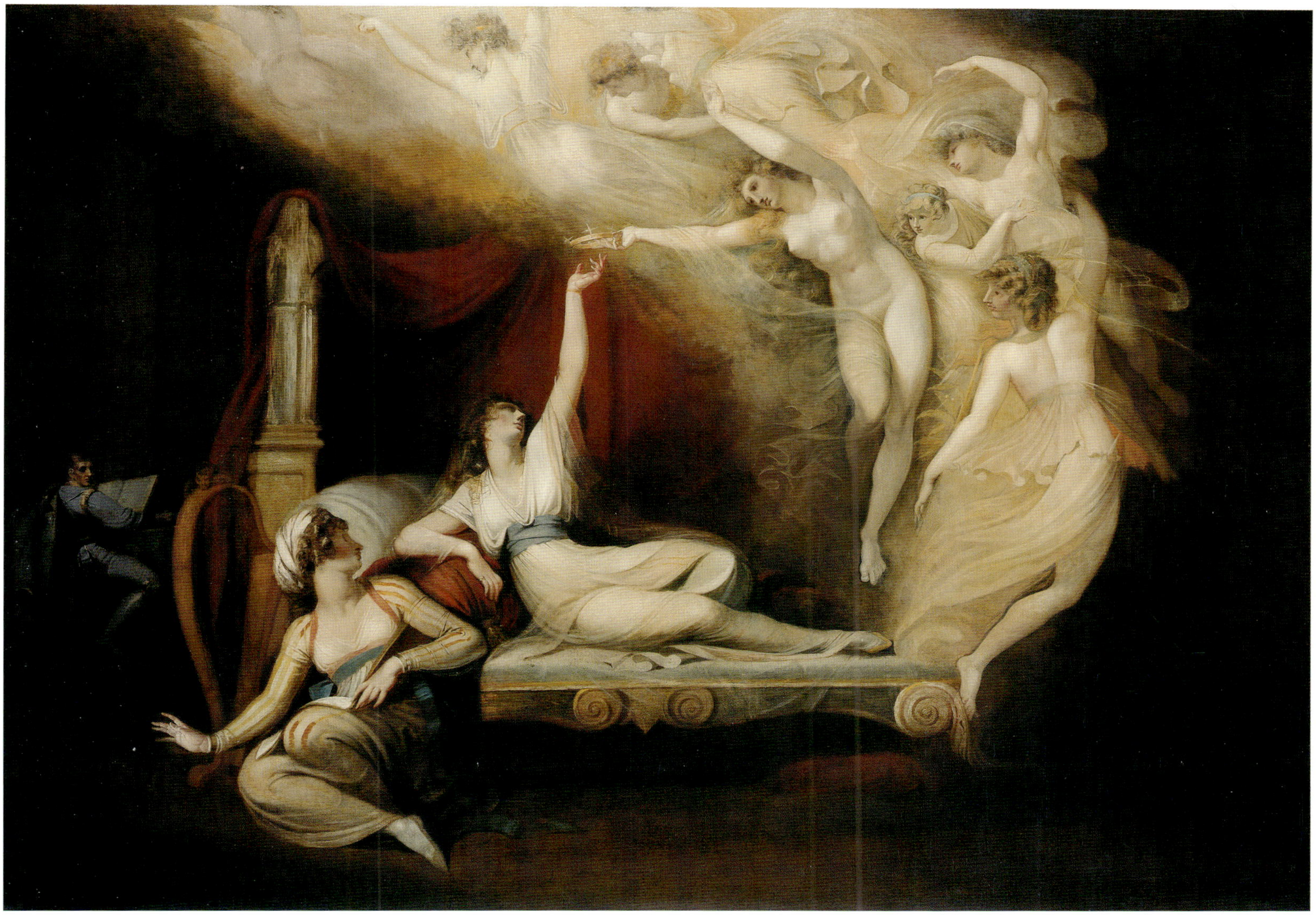

101

Henry Fuseli 1741–1825
The Shepherd's Dream probably c.1784–5, exh. RA 1786
Oil on canvas 154 x 215 cm
Tate. Purchased 1966

A shepherd rests while tending his sheep. Wrapped in his cloak, with his dog taking watch, he is visited by a parade of imps, fairies and elves who circle over him.

Such a fairy visitation had been evoked by Shakespeare's *A Midsummer Night's Dream* (Act II, scene 1), and the subject was elaborated in a poem printed in William Warner's *Albion's England* (1612). The vision of the shepherd was taken as a simile by John Milton in a passage at the end of Book I of *Paradise Lost*, where Hell is overflowing so the lower ranks of the fallen angels shrink to make more room. It was this text that Fuseli referred to when he first exhibited this painting.

The fairies in Fuseli's painting are drawn from that same cast of characters that do Titania's bidding in no.105 (Schiff 1973, no.1762); Robin Goodfellow (Puck) is hovering in front of the moon; Ariel rides a bat; a witch pulls a mandrake from the ground to the left; Queen Mab is seated on the steps in the right corner. The naked fairy combing her hair derives, according to Schiff, from Shropshire folklore. The building is either a temple of Diana (who in medieval folklore was transformed into a demon and led a troupe of witches through the sky at night), or the temple of Isis (in Swiss folklore), or the ivory portal through which dreams emerge in Homer and Virgil.

It has previously been assumed that this painting was the work included in Fuseli's ill-fated Milton Gallery, as 'Picture IV'. That canvas is mentioned as among those Fuseli had 'finished during the Course of the Last Year' in a letter of February 1795 (Fuseli to Roscoe, 16 February 1795, in Weinglass 1982, pp.126–7). However, here he refers unequivocally to this work as among the 'smaller' paintings he had created. This was noted by Schiff when he first catalogued the Milton Gallery (Schiff 1963a, p.142), but this evidence has latterly been overlooked.

Fuseli lists the 'Simile of the Peasant in the first book' alongside the Fairy Mab (70 x 91 cm; see no.107) and 'Milton Dictating to his Daughters' (121.2 x 118.7 cm; Art Institute of Chicago), which may give an indication of the size of this version of *The Shepherd's Dream*. It would be curious to refer to such an ambitious canvas as this so cursorily; notably, it is not among the subjects mentioned by Fuseli to Roscoe on 30 April 1794, nor does it appear on the longer list given to the same correspondent in 9 August 1796 (Weinglass 1982, pp.154–6). It seems possible that the design exhibited in the Milton Gallery was the smaller, simpler composition known from a drawing and a print of 1821, reproducing an otherwise undocumented painting (Schiff 1973, no. 1762b; Weinglass 1994, no.262; see also Becker 1997, no.24).

Instead, the present canvas is to be identified as the big picture mentioned in a letter to Fuseli's patron Brooke Boothby (1743–1824) early in 1785: 'As I was put into a train by Your pictures, I am now giving the last hand to the large Fairie Scene of the Sleeping Shepherd – the drawing, which I believe, You Saw, is now in Bartolozzi's hands' (Fuseli to Boothby, 22 January 1785, in Weinglass 1982, p.26). The drawing mentioned here is presumably the highly finished design (Schiff 1973, no.829) of which a version is squared up in preparation for reproduction as a print (Schiff 1973, no.1762a). This, however, seems never to have been published, although Francesco Bartolozzi (1727–1815) did engrave a comparable scene by Fuseli in his reproduction in 1788 of *Queen Katherine's Dream* for the Macklin Gallery (Weinglass 1994, no.77). It may be worth noting Fuseli's displeasure with the resulting print, expressed in his anonymous review of the Gallery published in the *Analytical Review*, and the fact that he did not employ this distinguished printmaker again (see Allentuck 1976).

The drawings follow this composition closely, with variations among some of the smaller figures. Although it has been suggested that it was a drawing that was exhibited at the Royal Academy in 1786, the evidence of the catalogue and contemporary reviews confirm that the work shown there was an oil painting (*Public Advertiser*, 4 May 1786; *Public Advertiser*, 22 May 1786).

The simile of the Shepherd's Dream, from John Milton, Paradise Lost (1667; 2nd ed., 1674), Book I, ll.777–89

So thick the aerie crowd
Swarm'd and were straitn'd; till the signal giv'n
Behold a wonder! they but now who seemd
In bigness to surpass Earths Giant Sons
Now less than smallest Dwarfs, in narrow room
Throng numberless, like that Pigmean Race
Beyond the Indian *Mount, or Fairie Elves,*
Whose midnight Revels, by a Forrest side
Or Fountain some belated Peasant sees,
Or dreams he sees, while over-head the Moon
Sits Arbitress, and neerer to the Earth
Wheels her pale course; they on their mirth and dance
Intent, with jocund Music charm his ear;
At once with joy and fear his heart rebounds.

(Milton 1998, p.378)

'A Tale of Robin-goodfellow' in William Warner, Albion's England (1612), p.367

A Shepheard, whilst his Flock did feede, him in his Cloke did wrap,
Bids Patch his Dog stand Sentenell, both to secure a nap,
And lest his Bagpipe, Shephooke, Shrop, and Bottell (most his wealth)
By vagrants (more then many now) might suffer of their stealth.
As he twixt sleepe and waking lay against a greene Banks side,
A Round of Fairie-Elves, and Larrs of other kind, he spide:
Who in their dancing him so charm'd, that though he wakt he slept,
Now Pincht they him, anticky about, and on, and off him lept.

(Warner 1612, p.367)

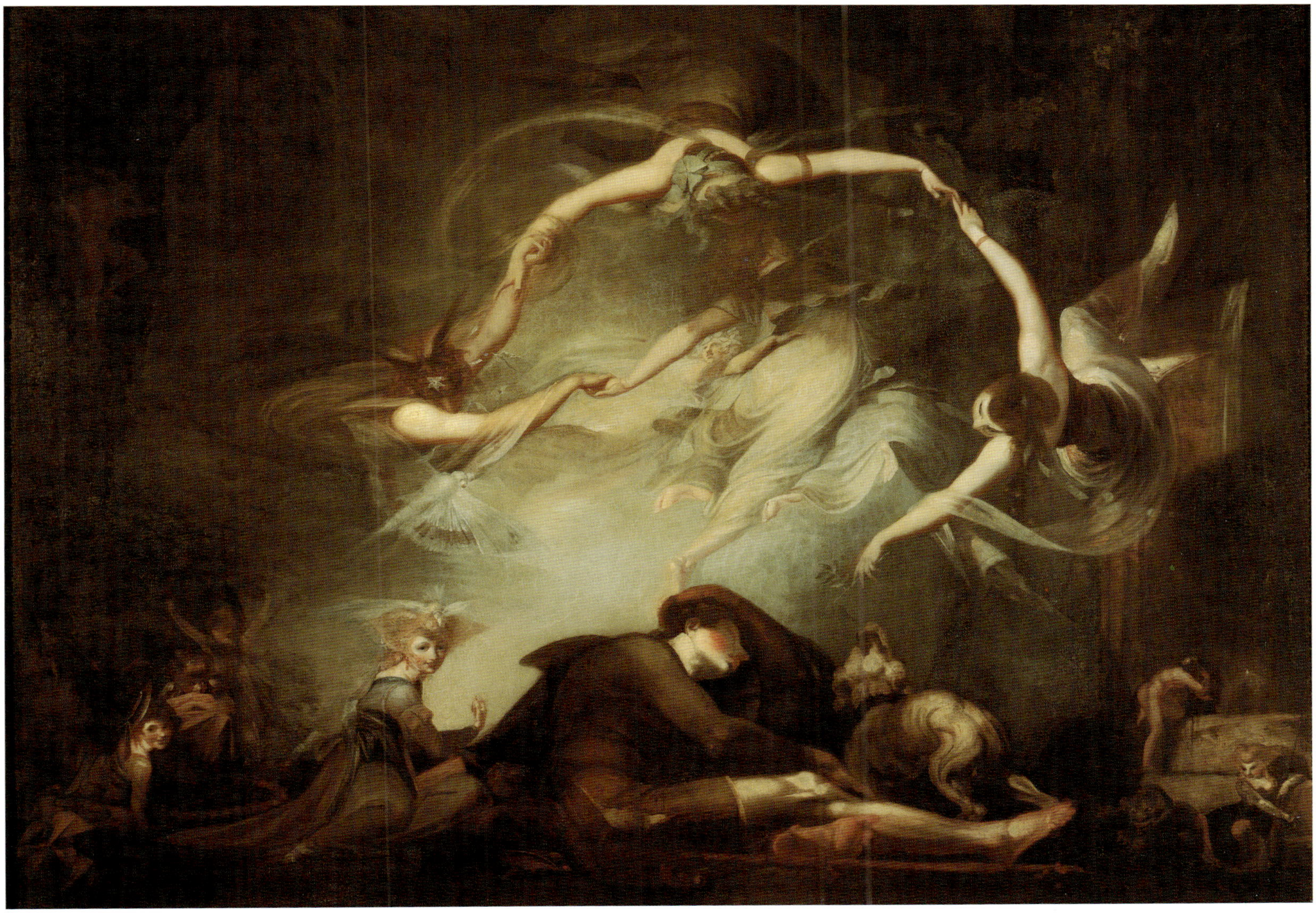

102

William Blake 1757–1827
Oberon, Titania and Puck with Fairies Dancing
mid-1780s
Pencil and watercolour on paper
47.5 x 62.5 cm
Tate. Presented by Alfred A. de Pass in memory of his wife Ethel 1910

103

William Blake 1757–1827
Queen Katherine's Dream mid-1780s
Pen, Indian ink, grey wash and watercolour over some pencil on paper 20.3 x 16.1 cm
The Syndics of the Fitzwilliam Museum, Cambridge

No.102 represents the closing scene of *A Midsummer Night's Dream*: the king and queen of the fairies, Oberon and Titania, embrace to the left, reunited at last after the separation which had set in motion the comic action of the preceding evening. Puck prances playfully next to them, his upraised arms and pointed ears recalling classical treatments of Bacchus or Satyrs. To the right a circle of fairies dance energetically, lifting from the ground as they spin, hand-in-hand.

The design (Butlin 1990, no.5) dates from around the time of Fuseli's most expansive explorations of the fairy world – *The Shepherd's Dream* and the two canvases from *A Midsummer Night's Dream* (nos.101, 105–6). But while Fuseli's images play on vast distortions of scale and disjuncture, putting into play therefore a cruel parody of sexual manners, Blake's figures are hearty, healthy figures all of a size (see Bindman 1982, nos.16, 23).

The scene in no.103 is the same as in no.100. Henry VIII's queen is visited by spectral apparitions, on the night before her sudden death. Blake is here clearly indebted to Fuseli's large composition, exhibited in 1781, and perhaps also his *Shepherd's Dream*, now redated as the painting exhibited in 1786 (see no.101). Although the dating of the present work has been disputed, it seems to date from the mid or late 1780s (Bindman 1970, no.2; Butlin 1981, no. 247).

While Milton, Dante and the Bible all drew sustained series of illustrations from Blake, the artist returned to Shakespeare more sporadically (see Merchant 1959, pp.81–6; Merchant 1973). There are several Shakespeare designs by Blake from around this date, and we might speculate whether these might have been stimulated by news of John Boydell's grand Shakespeare Gallery scheme, announced in 1786 (Butlin 1981, nos.245–50). Blake had hoped to find employment with Boydell, but in the end was employed to engrave only one small plate. He was further rebuffed by the proprietors of the other great commercial engraving schemes of the age, Thomas Macklin and Robert Bowyer.

102

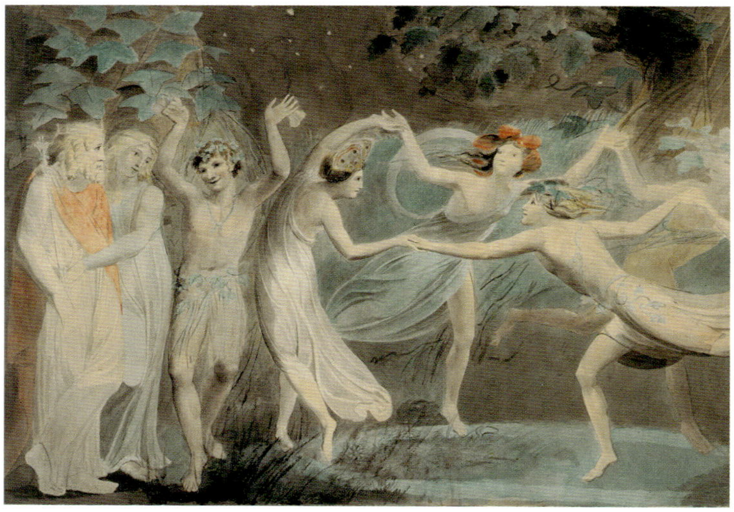

103

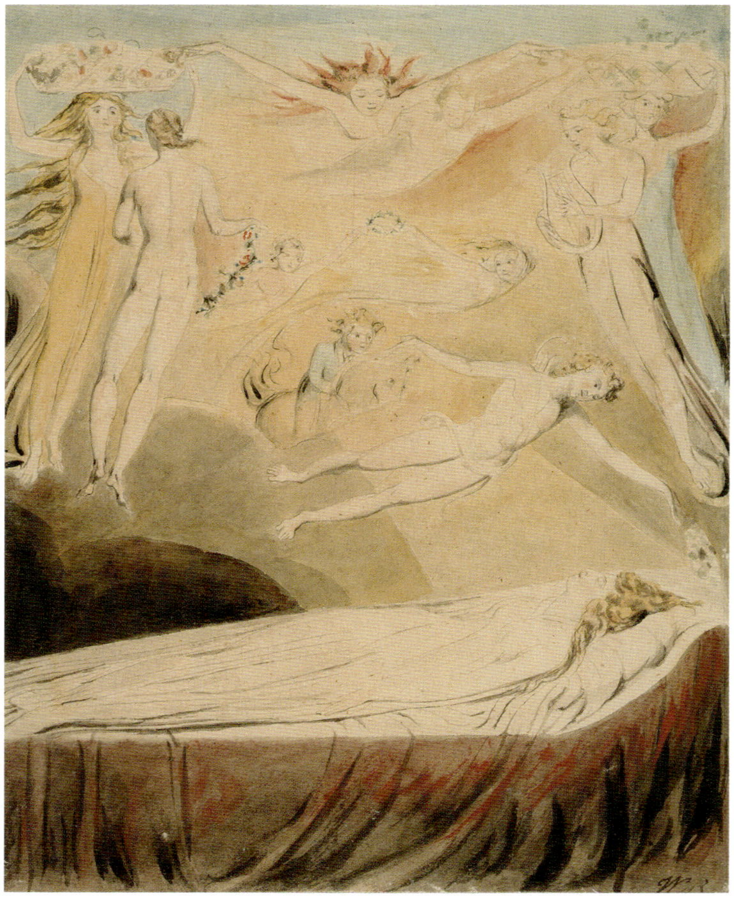

104

James Gillray 1756–1815
The Lover's Dream published by Hannah Humphrey, 24 January 1795
Etching and aquatint 32.1 x 42.6 cm
The British Museum, London
(1868-8-8-13651)

This etching is a sarcastic comment on the forthcoming marriage of the Prince of Wales to Caroline of Brunswick. The Prince was still romantically involved with Lady Jersey and the marriage with Caroline was arranged purely for diplomatic and financial reasons. Here, the dreaming prince imagines the loveliness of his new wife, and the treasures the marriage will bring him by way of money (offered by George III), an heir (his mother holds a copy of a book called 'The Art of Getting Pretty Children'), and thus long-lost parental approval. His various vices are shown retreating to the left: Lady Jersey, his extant, Catholic and thus illegitimate wife, Mrs Fitzherbert (see also no.122), and a serving girl (another lover?) skulk away; Charles James Fox, his political ally and gambling mate, cowers, along with Richard Brinsley Sheridan caricatured as a Jew; Lord Derby, in the form of a plump baby, sits astride a barrel of port.

The print (George 1935–54, no.8610; Godfrey 2001, no.157) invites us to laugh at the transparent absurdity of the prince's fantasy. The sheer sophistication and delicacy of the print technique extends the comedy, suggesting the most fancy of mythological or visionary prints. The inscription is adapted from Milton's *Comus* (1634), ll.453–8 :

> So dear to Heav'n is Saintly chastity,
> That when a soul is found sincerely so,
> A thousand liveried Angels lacky her,
> Driving off each thing of sin and guilt,
> And in cleer dream, and solemn vision
> Tells her of things that no gross ear can hear.
> (Milton 1998, p.144)

As a visual model, Gillray must certainly have had in mind Fuseli's *Queen Katherine's Dream*, either the painting shown in 1781 (no.100) or the version produced for Macklin which was engraved, with the greatest delicacy of effect, by Bartolozzi in 1788 (Weinglass 1994, no.77).

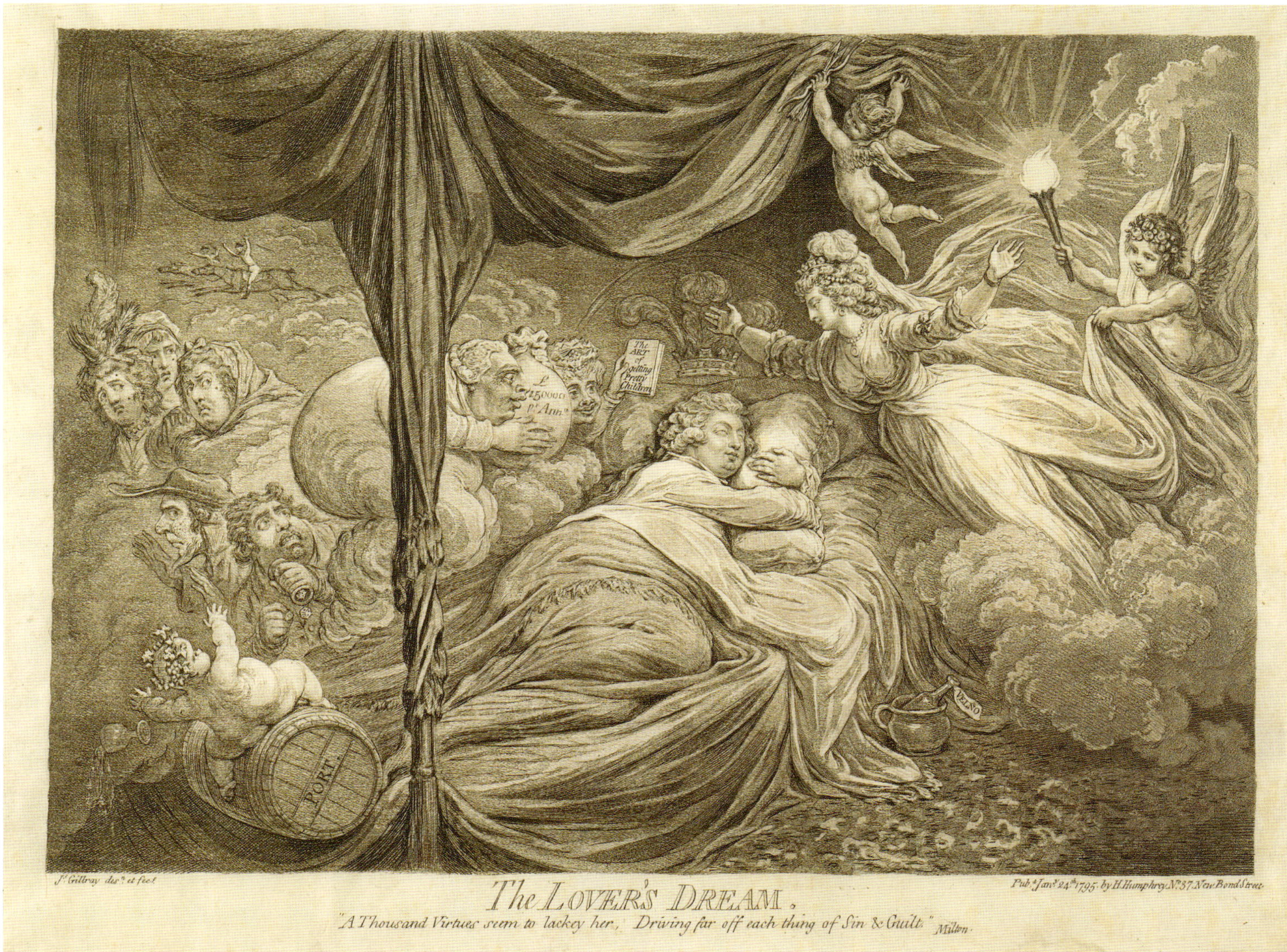

105

Henry Fuseli 1741–1825
Titania and Bottom with the Ass's Head
1788–9, first exh. Shakespeare Gallery 1789
Oil on canvas 216 x 274 cm
Tate. Presented by Miss Julia Carrrick Moore in accordance with the wishes of her sister 1887

Titania, the Queen of the Fairies, has been made by her jealous husband Oberon to fall in love with a simpleton, whose head has been magically transformed into that of an ass. That fool, Bottom, orders her fairies to serve his whims, which are now, naturally, ass-like: Peaseblossom scratches his head; Mustardseed, standing on Bottom's outstretched hand, reaches up to rub his nose; Cobweb, on the far left, kills a bumblebee. To the left and right of Titania are two 'Maids of Honour' in which characters the critic and writer on landscape Humphry Repton (1752–1818) claimed 'we may trace the native contrast of a coquette and prude'. That writer continued his description (Repton 1789, p.23):

> to the right of the Queen are two attendants who seem of more consequence than maids of honour; and on the left is a female figure, to whom Age seems subject, though she herself is subjected to Flattery. At the back of her is *Puck* or *Robin Goodfellow*, the treacherous elf who is the cause of all this confusion, and who seems to enjoy this mischief, and point out the consequences with his fingers. There is also a delightful laughing French-faced girl offering strawberries; and in the foreground, amongst a variety of elves and fairies, are Moth and a little Chrysalis her progeny: but here seems also the little Indian Child, which has no business in the scene, because, since the Queen's unnatural love, that object of contention had been given up.

The painting (Schiff 1973, no.753) was commissioned by the print publisher and entrepreneur John Boydell for the first showing of his Shakespeare Gallery (see no.87). Although sometimes dated as early as 1786, contemporary reports indicate that he had only just begun the subject by September 1788. See the *Morning Post* (3 September 1788) and a report by Fuseli himself in the *Analytical Review* (2, p.235 [October 1788]). The finished picture was enthusiastically received by the press. *The Gazetteer* (8 May 1789) opined: 'Beings, which "*melted into air, into thin air*," are now embodied upon the canvas; and the group of tiny elves, fairies, and fays, which gambol in the Midsummer Night's Dream, bring to our recollection the mythology of our childhood.' This last reference draws attention ot Fuseli's particular achievement in the integration of such personal or folkloric references with a knowingly Old Masterish presentation which evokes, in the poses and treatment of the various figures, Raphael and Leonardo, Michelangelo and Singorelli.

As Nicola Bown has discussed, the painting's treatment of the fairy realm represents a world turned upside down in gender terms. Titania's gesture and position suggests her sovereignty over the enchanted scene (though we should remember that the narrative of the play would have it that it is she who has been enchanted). Her figure is nearest to life-size, while the human peasant Bottom appears gigantic, his crunched-up pose emphasising his awkwardness. Most telling, for Bown, is the tiny male figure perched on Bottom's hand, a character who 'graphically represents the displacement of the male by a perversely dominant femininity' (Bown 1999, p.319; see also Bown 2001, pp.12–38).

William Shakespeare, A Midsummer's Night's Dream (1595–6), Act IV, scene 1, ll.1–39

TITANIA. *Come, sit thee down upon this flow'ry bed,*
While I thy amiable cheeks do coy,
And stick musk-roses in thy sleek smooth head,
And kiss thy fair large ears, my gentle joy.
BOTTOM. *Where's Peaseblossom?*
PEASEBLOSSOM. *Ready.*
BOTTOM. *Scratch my head, Peaseblossom. Where's Mounsieur Cobweb?*
COBWEB. *Ready.*
BOTTOM. *Monsieur Cobweb, good monsieur, get you your weapons in your hand, and kill me a red-hipp'd humble-bee on the top of a thistle; and, good mounsieur, bring me the honey-bag. Do not fret yourself too much in the action, mounsieur; and, good mounsieur, have a care the honey-bag break not; I would be loath to have you overflowen with a honey-bag, signior. Where's Monsieur Mustard-seed?*
MUSTARD. *Ready.*
BOTTOM. *Give me your neaf, Moonsieur Mustardseed. Pray you, leave your curtsy, good mounsieur.*
MUSTARD. *What's your will?*
BOTTOM. *Nothing, good mounsieur, but to help Cavalery Cobwb to scratch. I must to the barber's, mounsieur; for methinks I am marvail's hairy about the face; and I am such a tender ass, if my hair do but tickle me, I must scratch.*
TITANIA. *What, wilt thou hear some music, my sweet love?*
BOTTOM. *I have a reasonable good ear in musick. Let's have the tongs and the bones.*

Music. Tongs. Rural Music

TITANIA. *Or say, sweet love, what thou desirest to eat.*
BOTTOM. *Truly, a peck of provender; I could much your good dry oats. Methinks I have a great desire to a bottle of hay. Good hay, sweet hay, hath no fellow.*
TITANIA. *I have a venturous fairy that shall seek*
The squirrel's hoard, and fetch thee new nuts.
BOTTOM. *I had rather have a handful or two of dried peas. But, I pray you, let none of your people stir me; I have an exposition of sleep come upon me.*

(Shakespeare 1997, pp.272–3)

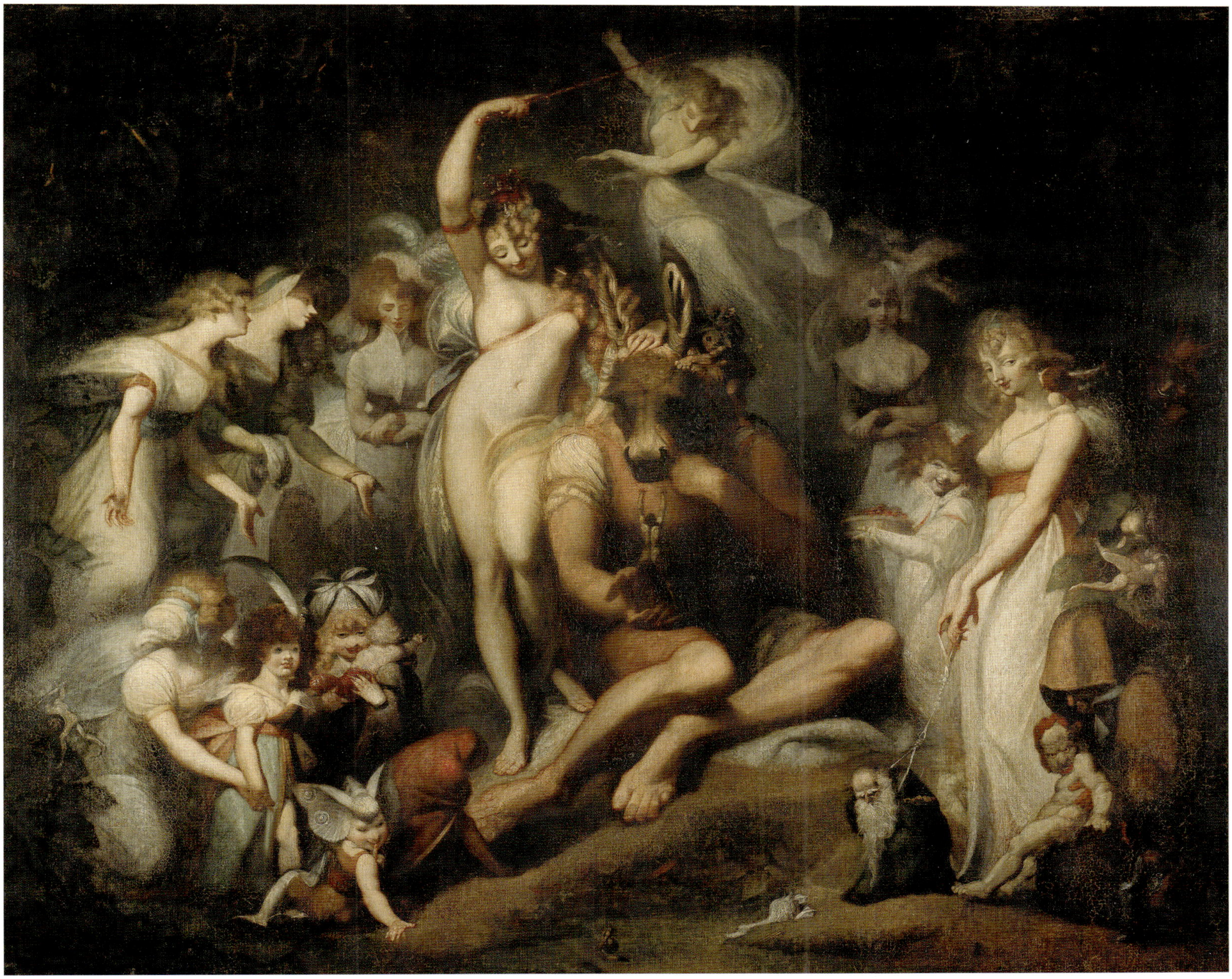

106

Henry Fuseli 1741–1825
Titania Awakening c.1789–91, first exh. Shakespeare Gallery 1791
Oil on canvas 222 x 280 cm
Kunstmuseum, Winterthur. Presented by George Reinhart 1946

This scene from Shakespeare's *A Midsummer Night's Dream* follows on from that shown in no.105 (Schiff 1973, no.754). Titania has just woken from her enchantment and tells Oberon of what she believes was a dream in which she was in love with an ass. Oberon points to Bottom asleep beside her and orders Puck to remove his ass's head (it appears at the top centre of this canvas), thus revealing that her dream had been an enchanted reality. The cloaked elf between Oberon and Titania is claimed by Schiff to represent the herb that destroyed the magic spell. A group of good fairies occupy the left side of the composition, with the personification of laughter and a dwarfish figure playing a small (perhaps phallic) bagpipe. Ballerina-like fairies ascend into the blackness here. To the right, Schiff identifies wicked figures, surrounding the huge form of Bottom. Above the sleeping peasant's head, recalling *The Nightmare* (no.1) and related subjects, a hobgoblin (Incubus?) rides a wild-looking horse. Three youthfully attired witches and their brood line up beside Bottom; one holds a goblin that, we can suspect, was born of her intercourse with the devil; her daughter kneels on the ground before her, perhaps an initiate into her evil cult (as in no.82). Below, an imp bares his arse as he rummages under the witch's skirt. In the foreground, some tiny fairies use Bottom's wooden clog as a boat to sail across a puddle.

Although a number of contributors to the Shakespeare Gallery were able to explore a single subject over two or more canvases, this painting shows, in effect, the same trick being played twice. It seems probable that Fuseli had not begun the canvas until the completion of that other work, and it is unlikely that Boydell would have initially have ordered two such similar subjects, until the immediate renown of the first canvas persuaded him otherwise. Fuseli was certainly at work on it by the end of November 1789, and the picture first featured in the gallery in 1791 (Fuseli to William Roscoe, 25 November 1789; Weinglass 1982, p.47 also pp.62–3).

William Shakespeare, A Mid-summer Night's Dream (1595–6), Act IV, scene 1, ll.46–90

OBERON. *Welcome, good Robin. See'st thou this sweet sight?*
Her dotage now I do begin to pity.
For meeting her of late behind the wood,
Seeking sweet favors for this hateful fool,
I did upbraid her, and fall out with her.
For she his hairy temples then had rounded
With coronet of fresh and fragrant flowers;
And that same dew, which sometime on the buds
Was wont to swell like round and orient pearls,
Stood now within the pretty flouriet's eyes,
Like tears, that did their own disgrace bewail.
When I had, at my pleasure, taunted her,
And she in mild terms begg'd my patience,
I then did ask of her changeling child;
Which straight she gave me, and her fairy sent
To bear him to my bower in fairy land.
And now I have the boy, I will undo
This hateful imperfection of her eyes.
And, gentle Puck, take this transformed scalp
From the head of this Athenian swain,
That he, awaking when the others do,
May all to Athens back again repair,
And think no more of this night's accidents
But as the fierce vexation of a dream.
But first I will release the Fairy Queen;
[Touching her eyes]
Be as thou wast wont to be;
See, as thou wast wont to see:
Dian's bud o'er Cupid's flower
Hath such force and blessed power.
Now, my Titania, wake you, my sweet queen.
TITANIA. *My Oberon, what visions have I seen!*
Methought, I was enamor'd of an ass.
OBERON. *There lies your love.*
TITANIA. *How came these things to pass?*
O, how mine eyes do loath his visage now!
OBERON. *Silence, a while. Robin, take off this head.*
Titania, music call; and strike more dead
Than common sleep, of all these five the sense.
TITANIA. *Music, ho, music, such as charmeth sleep!*
PUCK. *Now when thou wak'st, with thine own fool's eyes peep*
OBERON. *Sound, music!* [Louder music]
Come, my queen, take hands with me,
And rock the ground whereon these sleepers be.
Now thou and I are new in amity;
And will, to-morrow midnight solemnly,
Dance in Duke Theseus' house triumphantly,
And bless it to all fair prosperity:

(Shakespeare 1997, p.273)

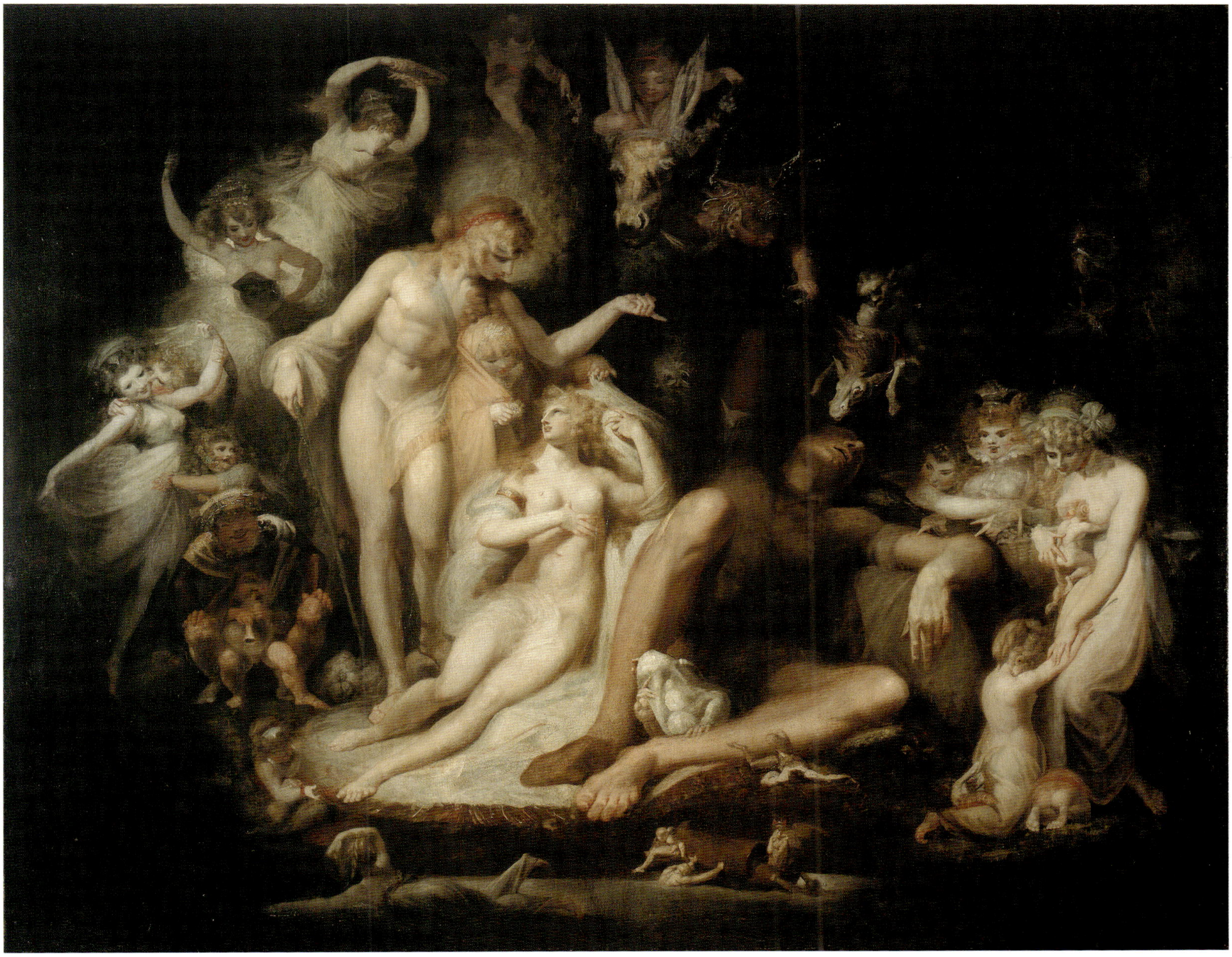

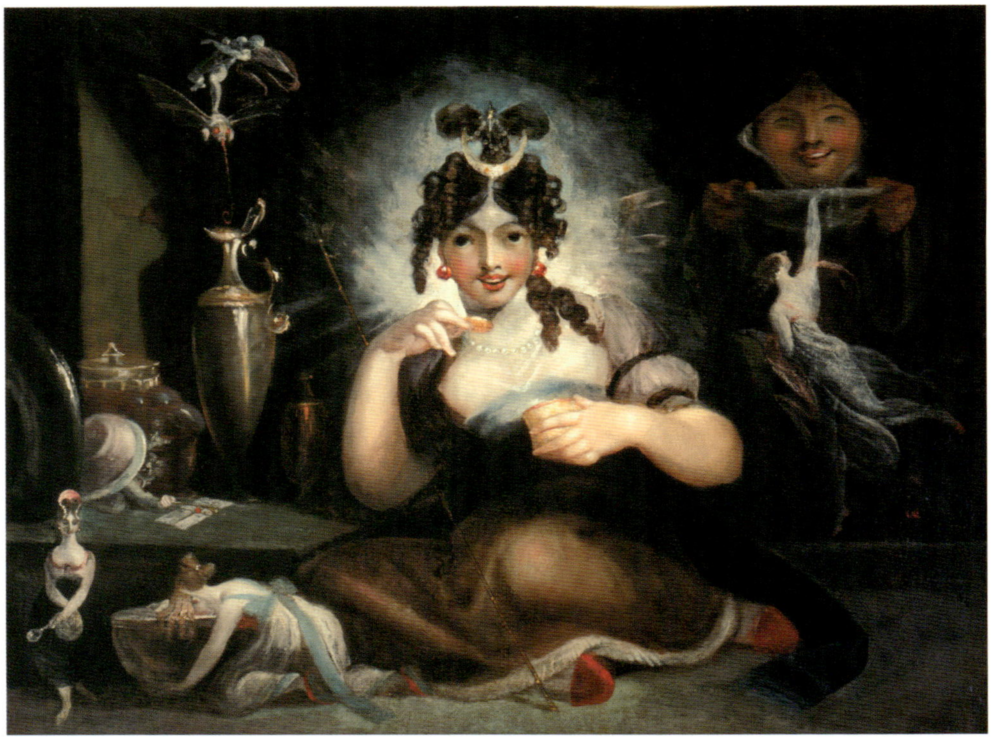

107

Henry Fuseli 1741–1825
Fairy Mab c.1815–20
Oil on canvas 70 x 90 cm
Folger Shakespeare Library, Washington DC

Mab is the generally good-natured chief female fairy in folklore, referred to in literary contexts by Shakespeare, Ben Jonson and Milton. The source of Fuseli's treatment of this figure is the description of peasant storytelling in Milton's poem *L'Allegro* (c.1630). As with the textual source for no.82, this section of Milton's poem had been republished separately within Thomas Percy's popular *Reliques of Antient English Poetry* (Percy 1765, III, p.201). Fuseli had painted two comparable versions of the subject in the 1790s, the first of which had featured in his Milton Gallery (Schiff 1973, nos.909 and 910). The painter's specific reference was to Milton's line 'How *Faery Mab* the junkets eat', and these were the words cited by Fuseli when he wrote to William Roscoe about the second version of this painting, being completed at the end of 1795 (Schiff 1973, no.910; see Weinglass 1982, pp.141–2). The painter claimed that with this picture he was attempting to express 'female Nature' in an abstracted or ideal form.

Mab was originally a rural character, associated particularly with the success or failure of dairy produce ('junket' is sweetened and flavoured cream-cheese, traditionally left out at night for the fairies in order to win their favours). So Jonson referred to her thus in 'The Satyres Verses' from *The Entertainment at Althorp* (Donaldson 1975, p.375):

> ... the mistress-fairy,
> That doth nightly rob the dairy,
> And can hurt, or help, the churning,
> As she please, without discerning.

The present painting (Schiff 1973, no.1498; Pressly 1993, no.20) was the most detailed of Fuseli's pictures on this theme, the one most clearly to depart from the rural associations of this subject and the version to emphasise sexual content most emphatically. Mab herself is provocatively attired, making a enticing display of pallid flesh, while her black hair is elaborately dressed (and bears a lunar crescent, associating her with the classical goddess, Diana). As Christoph Becker notes, 'she reminds one of the uncrowned queens of London's high-society balls' (Becker 2005, p.124). The diminutive fairies that surround her are dressed as young madams. One, posing daintily on the left, holds a bowl over her lap with her right hand, and a spoon in her left, obvious symbols of the female and male genitals; another plunges her face into a bowl of junket voraciously, embracing the great bowl with a passion which may recall the sexual hunger displayed in Fuseli's erotic designs. To the left, at the top, a male spirit rides the back of a dragonfly with supernatural agility, the tongue of the insect-mount dipping suggestively into a pitcher. The moonishly round face at top right may be interpreted as either that of a dwarfish brownie (another type of rural fairy), or perhaps the tanned features of the country girl who tells of Mab in Milton's poem, in order to cover up her own gluttonous junket-eating. A male fairy (on the table to the left, emerging from under an upturned bowl) holds a quill over a letter, associated by William Pressly with the love-epistle whose appearance in earlier paintings by Fuseli heralds the beginning of a seduction (Pressly 1993, no.29). With all these motifs, we can see Fuseli representing 'female Nature' as tending always to rapaciousness, sensuality and self-indulgence; the creamy qualities of Fuseli's paint, and the relatively rich colour palette, enhance this sentiment. In a sense, Mab represents a powerfully self-possessed revision of the victim in *The Nightmare* (no.1), each equally surrounded by the trappings of luxury, the one oppressed by forces beyond her control, the other a resplendent monarch in the realm of sensual desire.

John Milton, L'Allegro (c.1630), ll.97–116

...young and old com forth to play
On a Sunshine Holyday,
Till the live-long day-light fail,
Then to the Spicy Nut-brown Ale,
With stories told of many a feat,
How Faery Mab *the junkets eat,*
She was pincht, and pull'd she sed,
And he by Friars Lanthorn led
Tells how the drudging Goblin *swet,*
To ern his Cream-bowle duly set,
When in one night, ere glimps of morn,
His shadowy Flale hath thresh'd the Corn
That ten day-labourers could not end,
Then lies him down the Lubbar Fend.
And stretch'd out all the Chimney's strength;
And Crop-full out of dores he flings
Ere the first Cock his Mattin rings.
Thus don the Tales, to bed they creep,
By whispering Winds soon lull'd asleep.

(Milton 1998, pp.70–1)

108

Georgina North 1798–1835
The Shepherd's Dream after 1816
Pen and light brown wash on paper
75.5 x 54.5 cm
Art Institute of Chicago. The Leonora Hall Gurley Memorial Collection (1976.1291)

The subject is the same as that of no.101 and demonstrates a knowledge of Fuseli's works and, perhaps, Blake's.

Georgina North was the daughter of the Countess of Guildford, one of Fuseli's most important patrons later in life. According to John Knowles, 'he had for Lady Georgina, that affection which a master usually feels towards an amiable, accomplished, and highly promising pupil. This young lady had devoted much time to the study of the Fine Arts, and, assisted by the occasional hints and instructions of Fuseli, has arrived at eminence in the highest branch, that of historical design' (Knowles 1831, I, p.341). North not only created original designs in Fuseli's idiom, she appears to have directly copied his work. Mary Balmanno, in an important memoir of the artist (Balmanno 1858, p.208) recalls seeing her 'excellent copies' of his works in the painter's own house. There is the possibility that her canvases, originals and copies after the older artist, are now catalogued as works by Fuseli.

This drawing was among the designs purchased by the Chicago collector William F.E. Gurley in the 1920s as by Fuseli (see McCullagh 1997). Various attributions have been suggested subsequently, though comparison with her known illustrations for Alexander Pope's *Rape of the Lock* indicate that the present identification proposed by David Weinglass is definitive (cf. Halsband 1980, pp.58–63). The design is presumed to date from the period when Fuseli was a visitor to the North family country house at Putney Hill, during the last decade of his life. The watermark gives the date of 1816, so the drawing must be from after that year.

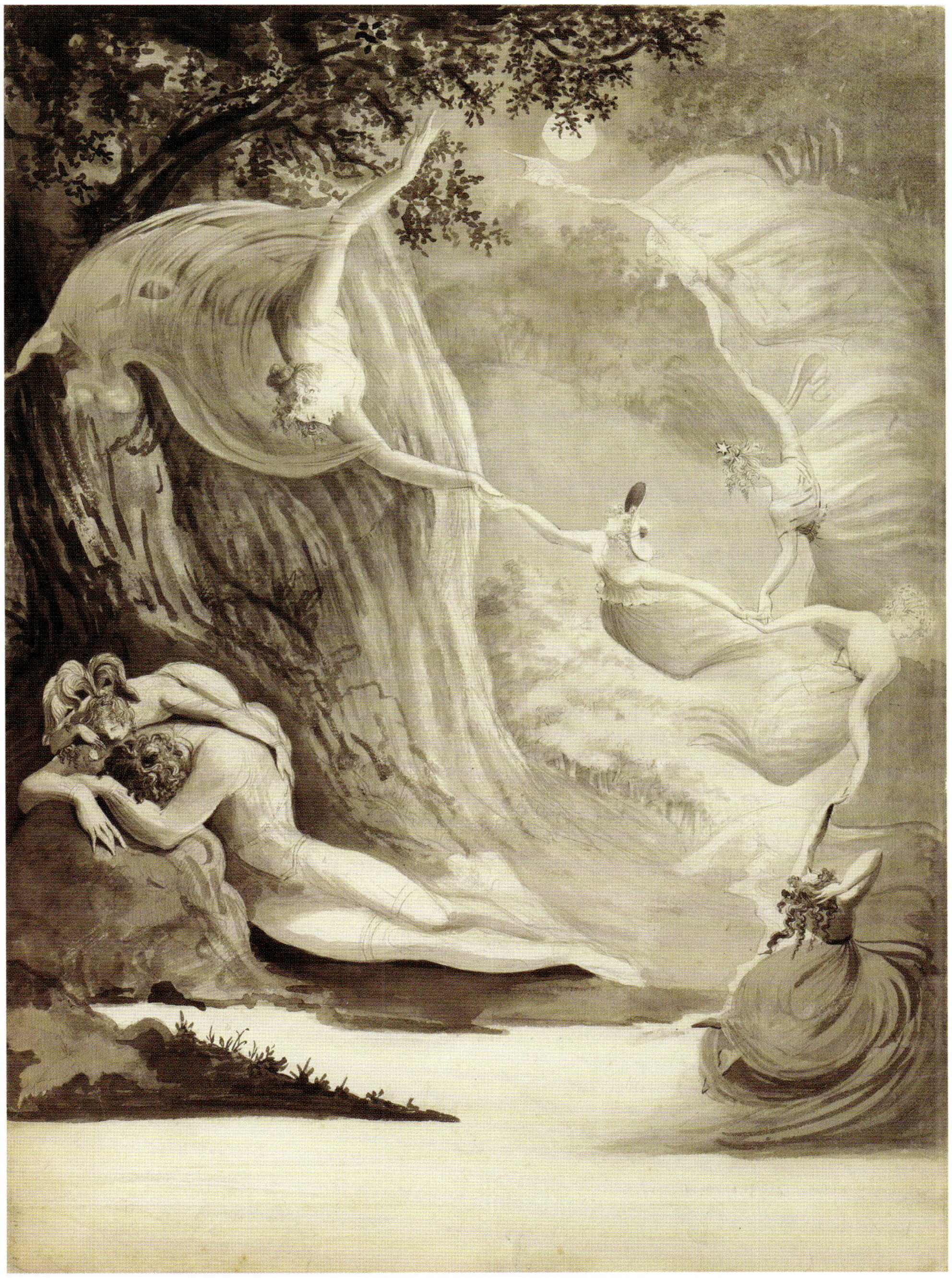

109

Theodor von Holst 1810–1844
Bertalda Frightened by Apparitions 1830–5
Oil on canvas 79.5 x 61.5 cm
Cheltenham Art Gallery and Museum / Holst Birthplace Museum (with assistance from the National Art Collections Fund, the MLA and V&A Purchase Grant Fund and with the support of the National Lottery through the Heritage Lottery Fund)

110

Theodor von Holst 1810–1844
Bertalda Frightened by Apparitions 1830
Oil on canvas 151.7 x 91.5 cm
Zurcher Kunstgesellschaft

Like no.52, these paintings illustrate de la Motte Fouqué's romantic fairy tale *Undine*. Bertalda, the beautiful daughter of simple fisher-folk, has entered the happy household of Huldbrand and the water-nymph Undine. The nymph's evil uncle, Kühleborn, intent on keeping the marriage between Undine and Huldbrand intact, tortures Bertalda mentally, haunting her with evil spirits (see Browne 1994, nos.60–1).

The original text provides a rather slight foundation for a painting, making a fleeting reference to 'strange spirits' and 'wrathful menaces' (de la Motte Fouqué 1818, pp.133–4). Still, the haunting and tormenting of Bertalda is replete with psychological and narrative weight. The tale's focus is, after all, on an (unconsummated) ménage à trois, and the tale pivots on unexpressed feelings and desires. Kühleborn's motives in his vengeful actions against Bertalda remain obscure, and we may be tempted to interpret the spectres attributed to him in the narrative as being expressions of Undine's repressed feelings of anxiety and vengeance against Bertalda, despite her conscious efforts to treat her mortal rival well: 'The poor Undine was sorely troubled … Bertalda particularly fancied that she found traces of the injured and jealous wife in the slightest deviation from her wishes'.

Drawing on the familiar motifs of Fuseli's fairy paintings, von Holst develops a claustrophobic atmosphere of threat. This subject was treated by Fuseli in a painting which von Holst must have known, given the similarities of composition and approach (Sotheby's, 9 March 1988, lot 91).

The suggestion (Butlin 1994) that no.110 should be attributed to Thomas Griffiths Wainewright (1794–1852), because of the marked differences between it and no.109, has not been generally accepted. Instead, Max Browne has proposed (in personal correspondence) that no.110 was the painting purchased from von Holst by their mutual friend, the novelist Edward Bulwer Lytton (1803–73) in 1832, and hung by him as a partner to *The Drinking Scene from Faust* by the same painter (see Browne 1994, p.24). The high finish of this canvas does suggest that it was intended for private sale, and it does not appear to have been exhibited by the artist.

109

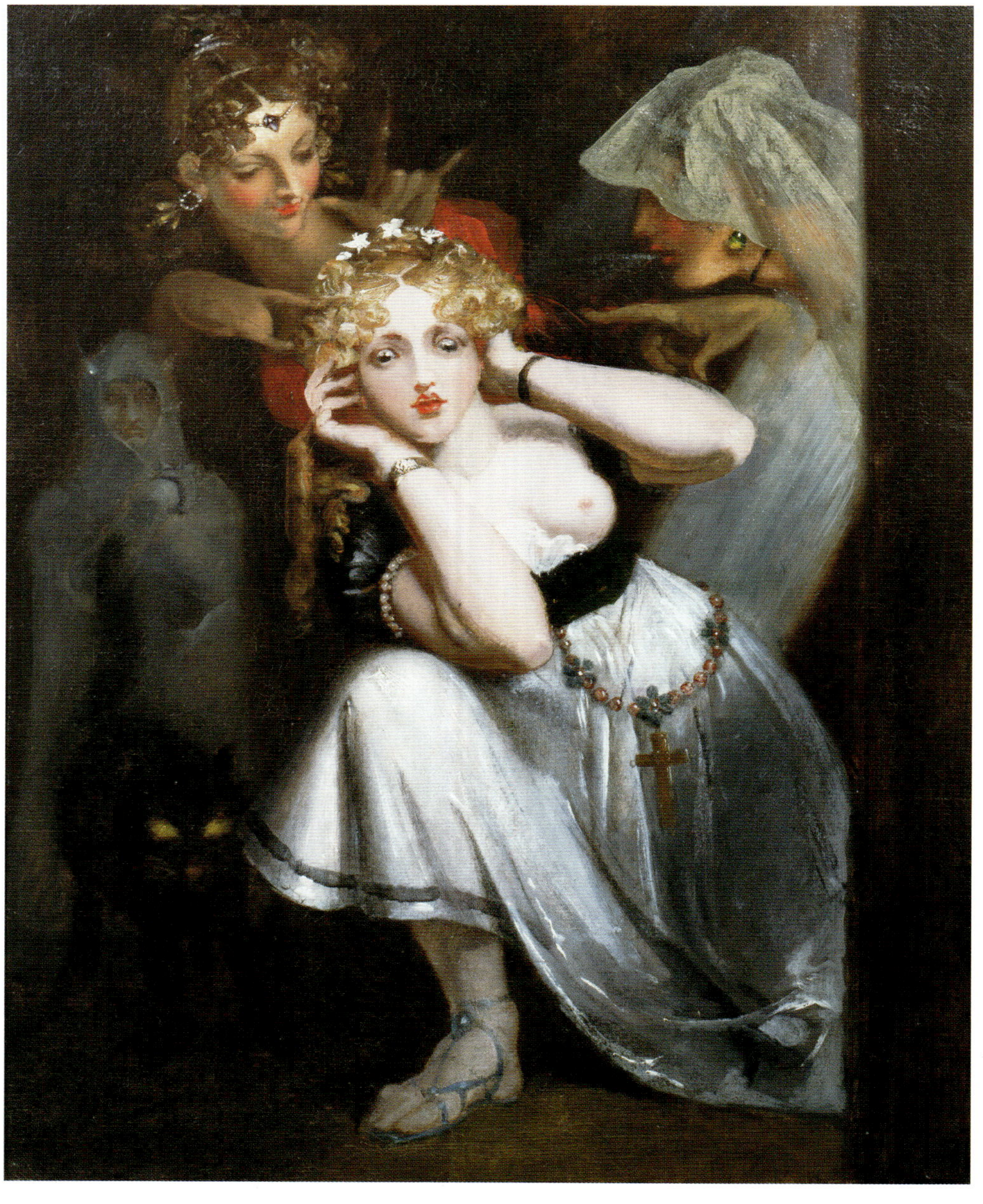

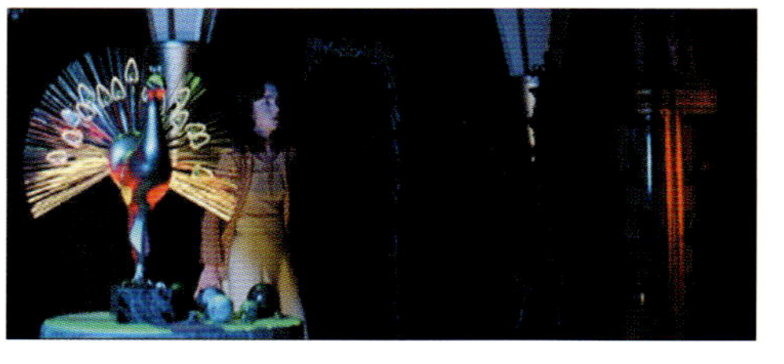

fig.29 A beautiful young woman is assailed by supernatural forces … Still from *Suspiria* (dir. Dario Argento, Italy/ Germany 1977)

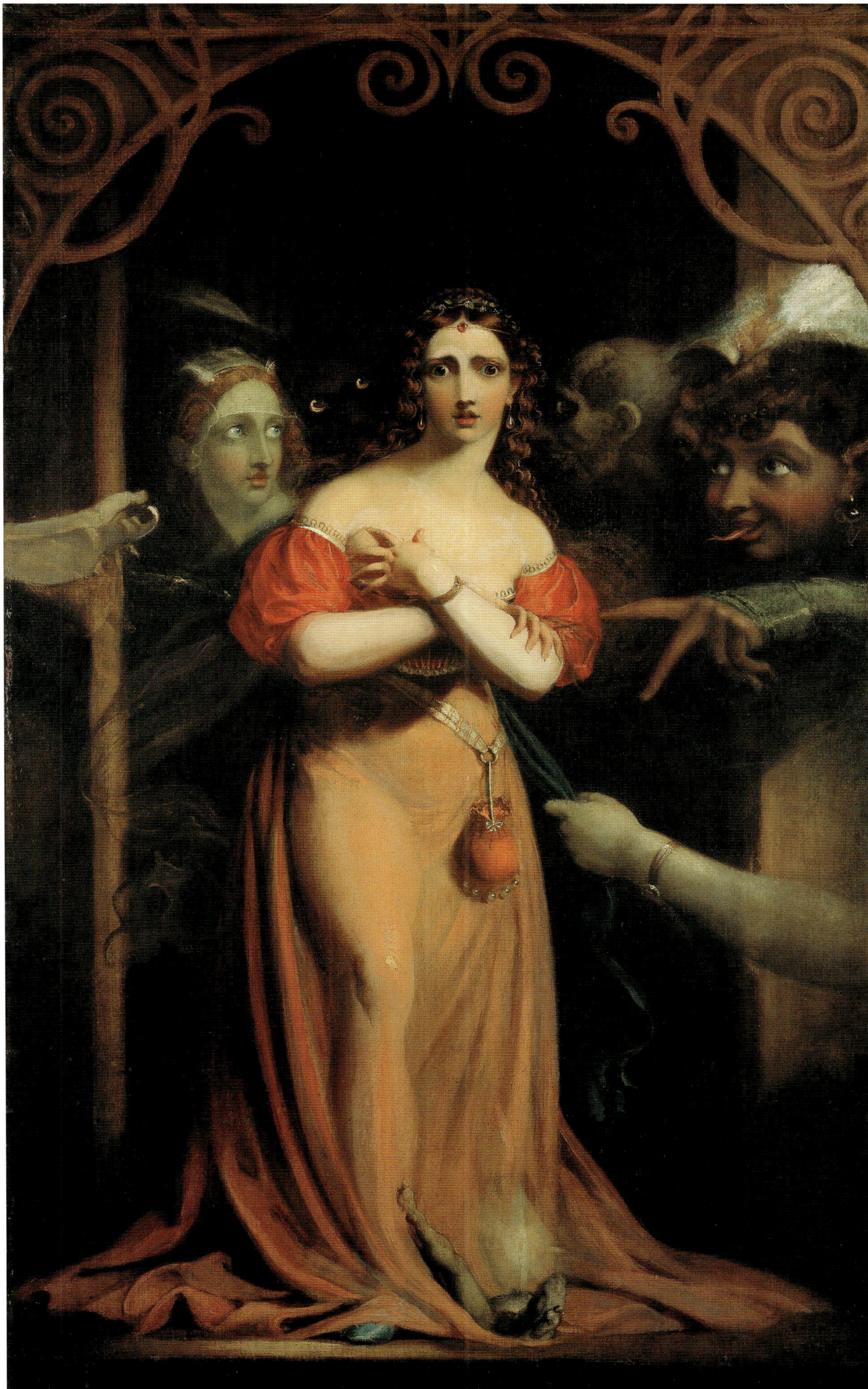

111

Henry Fuseli 1741–1825
Erotic scene with a man and a woman before a priapic term c.1770–8
Pen and grey wash on paper 26.1 x 37.6 cm
Museo Horne, Florence

112

Henry Fuseli 1741–1825
Erotic scene with a man and two women at the Foot of an Altar to Priapus c.1770–8
Grey wash, pen, and traces of black ink on paper 26.8 x 33.3 cm
Museo Horne, Florence

These are two examples from a small group of explicitly sexual drawings executed by Fuseli while in Rome in the 1770s, and now in the collection of the Museo Horne, Florence. Each shows a heroically proportioned man sexually assaulted by, assaulting, or struggling with one or two women. The settings are suggestively classical; in no.111 (Schiff 1973, no.538) the man grasps the impressively tumescent phallus of a priapic term (a half-figure mounted on a pilaster) whilst penetrating a woman spread out on an altar. The implication may be that this is a rape scene. In no.112 (Schiff 1973, no.540), a man struggles with two women in a classically attired interior; his nipple is gently tweaked by one of his assailants, while he stretches back to engage her in a kiss; there is the promise of fellatio from the other woman, who wraps herself around his thighs. The Greek inscription in the background translates as 'Grow large, male progenitor'.

The status of such drawings as these remains somewhat mysterious. The technical sophistication and care of the designs would rather obviate their interpretation as simple aids to masturbation (and therefore, in the baldest sense, pornography), but they are sexually frank and clearly intended to amuse and arouse. Were these elegant productions simply for private consumption or for common use? We might assume they were completely personal (see Wagner 1988, pp.289–91). But the evidence (shrouded by a history of obfuscation and wilful misinterpretation) is that middle-class and elite men could be openly sexually expressive in each other's company in the late eighteenth century, as indicated by literary and visual records of gatherings with prostitutes and dancers, as well as evidence relating to initiation rites in male clubs (Morgan 1995; Stevenson 2001; Harvey 2004, pp.68–77). There was certainly a high level of conviviality between Fuseli and his international circle of male artist-friends in Rome, and there is little doubt that they would have enjoyed what the city had to offer in the way of sexual intrigues, brothels and parties (Schiff 1973, pp.113–14; Andersen 1989). In fact, Fuseli's friend, the Swedish sculptor Johan Tobias Sergel (1740–1814) sketched a scene so close to no.111 that it seems impossible that they had not shared these drawings with one another, or even drawn them together (see Andersen 1989, p.160).

There were, importantly, new intellectual frameworks that gave an additional charge to the erotic adventures traditionally enjoyed by young artists on their travels. The 1760s and 1770s saw sustained investigations into the phallic cults of the ancient world. Most notably the English connoisseur Richard Payne Knight (1751–1824) pursued research into the ancient cult of priapus and cultivated a wider-reaching idea of the erotic foundations of the (masculine) creative imagination (see Rousseau 1987; Ponte 1992; Bermingham 1995; Pointon 1997, pp.73–8). It seems certain that such ideas were current in Fuseli's circle in Rome; Knight himself was in the city twice in the 1770s. The phallic symbolism that crops up in drawings by Fuseli and his circle – both those directly sexual in content and others – can be related to this eroticised idea of male creativity. The drawings illustrated here are evidence of how the boundaries between legitimate ideals of personal liberty and libertinism – the reprehensibly selfish pursuit of pleasure – and between classical scholarship, art and pornography, were porous and mutable at this time.

Henry Fuseli, 'Aphorisms on Art' (c.1788–1818), no.226

In an age of luxury women have taste, decide and dictate; for in an age of luxury woman aspires to the functions of man, and man slides into the offices of woman. The epoch of eunuchs was ever the epoch of viragos.

(Knowles 1831, III, pp.144)

111

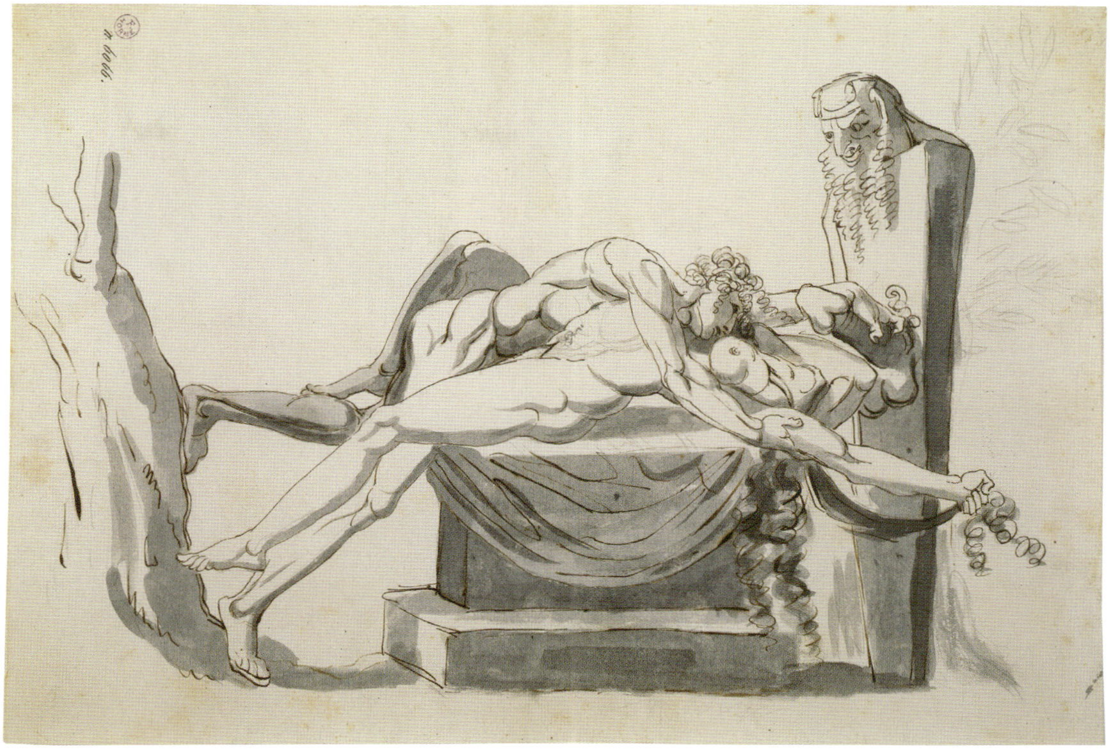

112

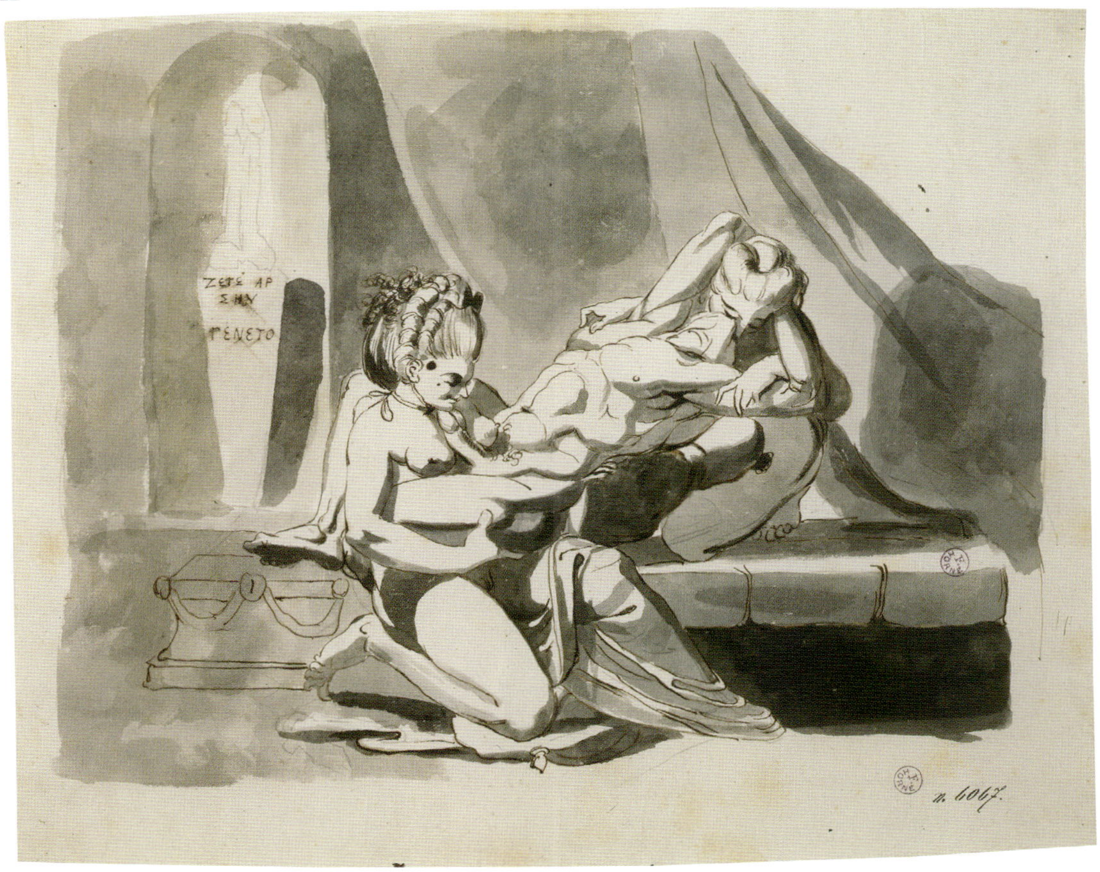

113

Henry Fuseli 1741–1825
The Debutante 1807
Pen and watercolour on paper 37 x 24 cm
Tate. Presented by Lady Holroyd in accordance with the wishes of the late Sir Charles Holroyd 1919

An image of perverted domesticity: three elaborately coiffed and dressed older women sit at a tea table, the stand of which has a weird, knobbly fleshiness to it. They look, perhaps leer, at a younger woman seated behind a screen, sewing, her neck fastened to the wall by a leather strap.

The title by which this work is now known was not of Fuseli's invention, although it does reflect a sense that the young woman is an initiate of some kind, presumably into a brothel (Sitwell 1943, pp.216–17). It has been suggested that the subject might be the scene in Samuel Richardson's (1689–1761) *Pamela* (1740), where Mrs Jewkes presents Pamela to the cook and maidservant at breakfast (Schiff 1973, no.1444; Weinglass 1991, p.308). Given the perverse undertones Fuseli could convey even in his ostensibly most conventional illustrations of modern literature, this is possible, although the details of Richardson's text are not apparent here (particularly that of the two keys on Mrs Jewkes's wrist, noted carefully by the novelist). Perhaps more suggestive would be a comparison with the claustrophobically imprisoned and systematically cruel communities that feature in the pornography of the Marquis de Sade (1740–1814): the women trapped at the Monastery of St-Mary-in-the-Wood in *Justine* (1791), or the epic cycle of abuse of *120 Days of Sodom* (written in 1785, but unpublished until the twentieth century). We might not be in a position to suggest that Fuseli is in any sense illustrating these texts, but we can remark upon a shared pornographic imagination. Compare, for instance, this cluster of women and de Sade's scrupulous, fetishistic description of the 'four wives' who with their husbands oversee the systematic sexual violence of the *120 Days of Sodom*. Might the two women in the middle be compared with Constance, whose 'eyes were large, black, and full of fire; her mouth extremely small and ornamented by the finest teeth imaginable', and Adelaide, 'twenty, small and slender, of an extremely slight and delicate build, of classic loveliness' with 'the finest blond hair to be seen'? The large woman might match Julie, large and tall, but dirty and with a 'stinking mouth ... a vast eater, she had a leaning toward drunkenness, little virtue, and I believe that had she dared try it, whoredom would have held little by way of terror for her'. The woman on the right might be imagined as Julie's young and simple sister, Aline, still a virgin (of sorts) at the opening of the novel and the least willing of the company: 'she had just become eighteen; she had a fetching, exuberantly healthy, and almost pert countenance; a little turned-up nose; brown eyes full of expression and vivacity; a delicious mouth; a most shapely though somewhat tall figure, well-fleshed; the skin a bit dark but soft and fine; the ass on the ample side but well-molded, a pair of the most voluptuous buttocks that ever a libertine eye may behold, the love mound brown-haired and pretty, the cunt a little low or, as they say, *à l'anglaise*, but as tight as one might wish' (see de Sade 1990, pp.211–17).

This is, necessarily, speculation. But it may be only in de Sade that we can find a comparable attention to physicality so intense it becomes in itself perverse, intrusive, and oddly forensic or decorative rather than simply arousing (cf. Klein 1991, p.285).

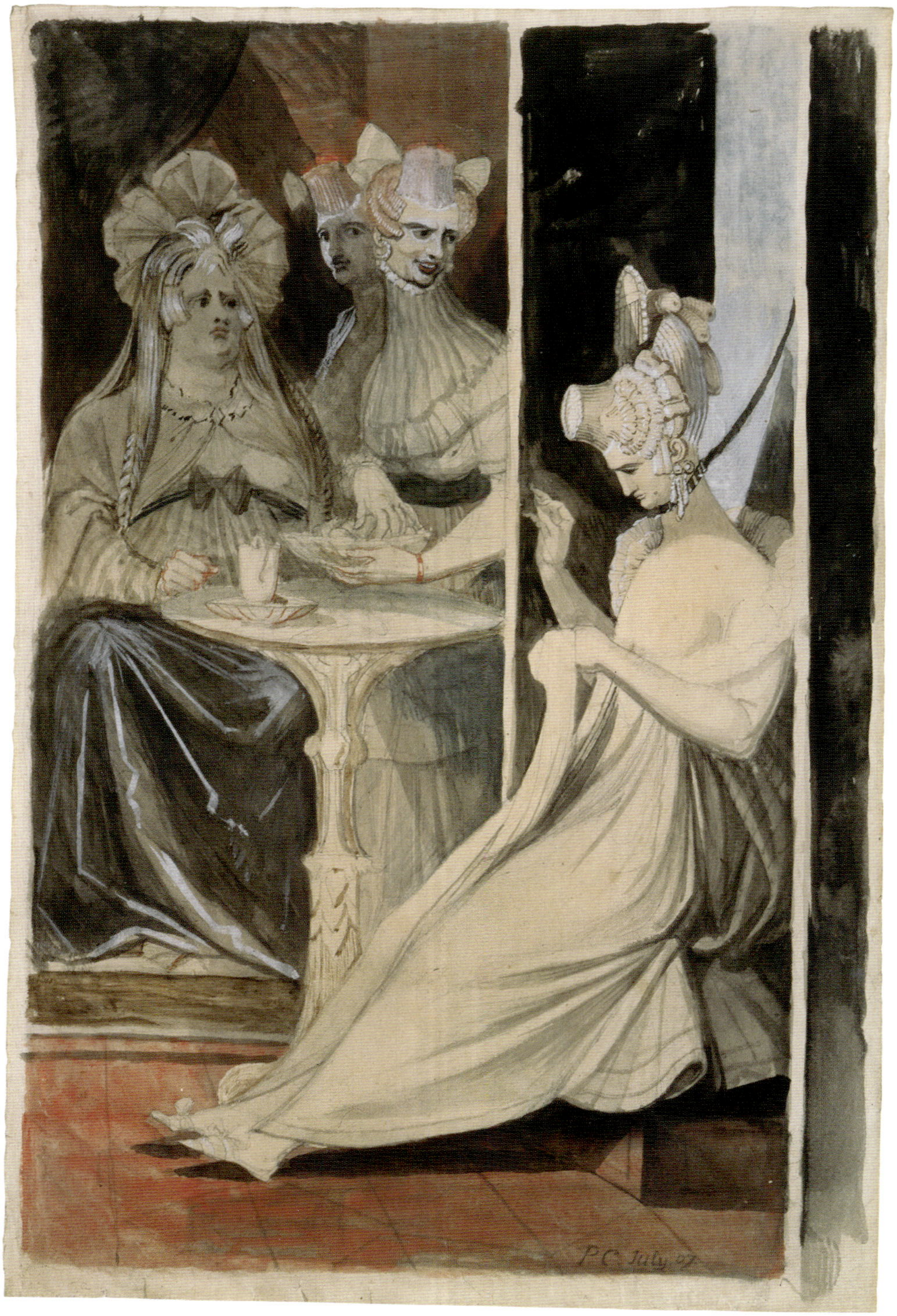

114

Henry Fuseli 1741–1825
Two courtesans with fantastic hairstyles and hats c. 1796
Pen and brown, pink and grey wash on paper
17.9 x 16.2 cm
Auckland Art Gallery Toi o Tāmaki.
Purchased 1965

115

Henry Fuseli 1741–1825
Courtesan with an elaborate headdress
c.1800–10
Pencil, ink and brush in grey, black and brown, grey and black wash and watercolour on paper
28.3 x 20 cm
Kunsthaus, Zurich (on loan from Gottfried Keller Foundation)

Fuseli drew numerous studies of women in weird and wonderful headdresses and elaborate coiffures, in more or less compromising positions and revealing costumes. Often remarkably delicate in their effects, they show him at his most technically virtuosic, yet also represent an apparently obsessive and highly sexualised vision of femininity.

The dating, purpose and content of such images remain disputed. They certainly appear in the later part of Fuseli's career, in the 1790s and 1800s, and also the 1810s. Their characteristic motifs appear in his domestic and narrative paintings of these years, but the drawings rarely appear to be preparatory studies for these works. They are usually indentified simply as 'women' or, more suggestively, 'courtesans', although many have been considered by Gert Schiff, and more completely by David Weinglass, as portraits of Fuseli's wife, Sophia Rawlins (1762/3–1832), whom he married in 1788 (Weinglass 1991, pp.304–5). However, any argument for identifying Fuseli's female fantasy figures with a living individual is essentially speculative. Mrs Fuseli, who was some years younger than the painter, was reportedly an artist's model; it may be quite possible to perceive among his fantasy women some similarity with her features, but whether that means that they should be considered generically as 'portraits' is another matter.

As noted above (no.113), Fuseli's attention to the details of costume and physique in such designs assumes a fetishistic or decorative quality which suggests a visual rejoinder of some kind to the perverse pornographic vision of the Marquis de Sade. His depiction of women prompts speculation about his own psychological tendencies, the wider gender politics of the time – with the emergence of foundational feminist ideals with Mary Woolstonecraft (1759–97), whose romantic attraction to Fuseli drew Mrs Fuseli's wrath – and the cultural symbolism of femininity. It might also lead us to reflect on the folkloric aspects of his work, more obviously – and self-consciously – apparent in his paintings of fairies, but in evidence here perhaps when we consider some of the old tales of alluring women and mysterious maidens (such as the story of 'Windows at which Ladies are Seen' recorded by Gervase of Tilbury c.1200). More prosaically, Fuseli's work may also reflect a society in which prostitution was a largely accepted fact of metropolitan life, and where among the upper classes the keeping of mistresses was a widely accepted practice. As noted in relation to nos.111–12, such ostensibly 'private' designs might be considered in the context of a society where bawdy and erotic discourse between men was an established activity.

Gervase of Tilbury, Otia Imperialia: Recreation for an Emperor (c.1200), III.43

Windows at which Ladies are Seen

Also in the kingdom of Arles, in the province of Aix, they say that there is a crag, on whose steep face, which is like a wall pierced with windows, two or more ladies appear to travellers when they are a long way ahead, conversing with each other, as they pretend, and clapping their hands at a shared joke. These women seem beautiful, charming, and alluring to people at a distance; but when they come closer, the vision utterly vanishes into illusion.

(Gervase of Tilbury 2002, p.641)

114

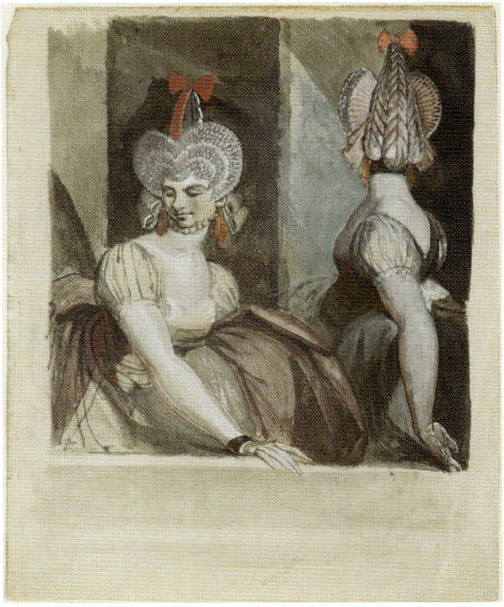

115

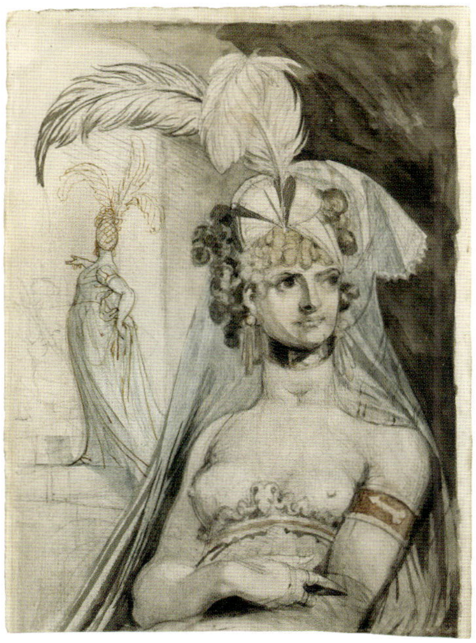

116

Henry Fuseli 1741–1825
The Inquisition 1806
Oil with touches of pencil on paper
53.7 x 44.8 cm
Art Institute of Chicago. The Leonora Hall Gurley Memorial Collection (1922.5686)

The Spanish Inquisition, personified as a powerful and gigantic woman, stands on top of a pyre, spreading her mantle and looking down upon a victim.

Fuseli's design illustrates lines from Book IV of Joel Barlow's *The Columbiad* (Barlow 1809, pp.117–18). In 1803, Barlow (1754–1812) commissioned a set of illustrations to his yet uncompleted *Columbiad* from John Vanderlyn (1775–1852) and Fuseli. The Swiss painter was given four subjects to illustrate, although after Vanderlyn abandoned the project the whole series was handed over to Robert Smirke (see Schiff 1973, no.883; Weinglass 1994, nos.256–9).

The Columbiad was written as an epic poem, but the author explained that its events were too recent in history to be treated in anything other than an allegorical fashion, were the vastness of the theme to be conveyed. Barlow meant the poem to have two aims: one 'to sooth and satisfy the desponding mind of Columbus' by showing that his labours, unrewarded in his lifetime, established a noble civilisation; the other to demonstrate the value of republicanism (Barlow 1809, pp.viii–ix). In Book IV, Columbus is presented with visions of the varied consequences of the discovery of America, including luxury, bigotry, ignorance, and seething violence, which triumph with the arrival of the Inquisition. It is characteristic of Fuseli that he reduces these enormous themes into a scene of sexualised violence.

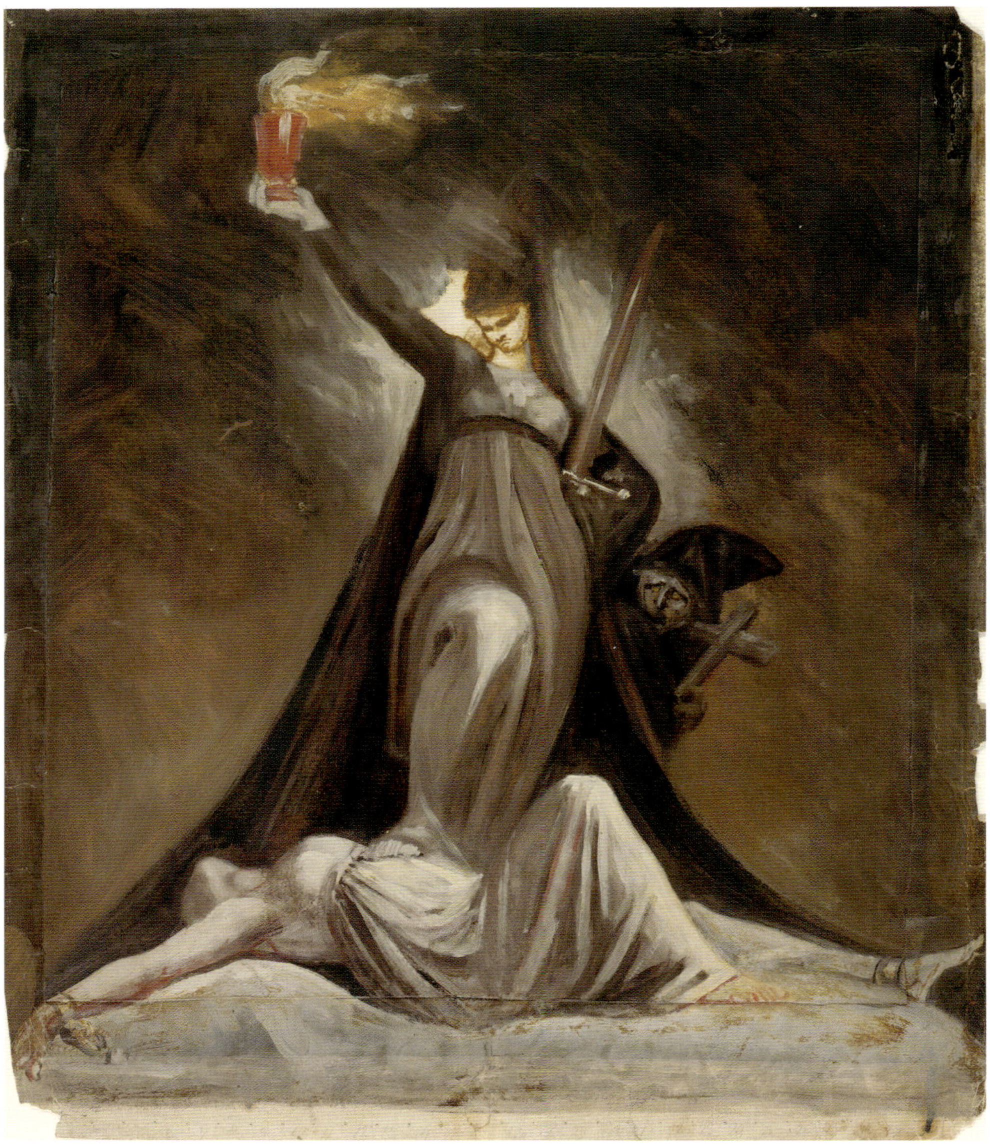

117

Henry Fuseli 1741–1825
The Great Father and Ancient Night c.1810
Pencil, grey wash and blue wash on paper
45 x 30 cm
Auckland Art Gallery Toi o Tāmaki. Purchased 1965

The subject of this drawing has been disputed. Gert Schiff (Schiff 1973, no.1804) asserted that this was an 'Allegory of Justice' c.1800–10, derived from Plato, *The Republic* (Book II, pp.359c–360b). In this account, Dike, the personification of Justice, stands at the edge an abyss; she is identified by the starry headdress and aura around her head – a reference to her ascent into the heavens as the constellation of Virgo. The giant arms reaching out of the abyss represent both good and bad being guided towards the light and offering rings to the two female figures accompanying Dike. Peter Tomory (Tomory 1972, p.123; Tomory 1979, no.28) proposed instead that the allegory is taken from *The Art of Preserving Health* (1744), a poem by Fuseli's friend John Armstrong (1709–79). In that case, the towering female figure is a personification of all-powerful Night; the male arms belong to the 'great Father' who reaches up 'thro' the lifeless gloom … to light another world, / And bid new planets roll by other laws' (Book II, lines 547–9). He now holds not rings but the seeds of new creation. The tiny figure rowing or flying to the left of the design would then be Charon, the boatman who rows damned souls to Hell.

Whatever the literary source and content, designs such as this, and nos.114–16, operate primarily as potent conceptions of a virile femininity. Fuseli's representation of women becomes thoroughly stylised, even hieratic in these compositions, the tendency to stark symmetry assisting in the sense of formal grandeur and, arguably, underscoring the phallic properties of such characters as Night/Justice.

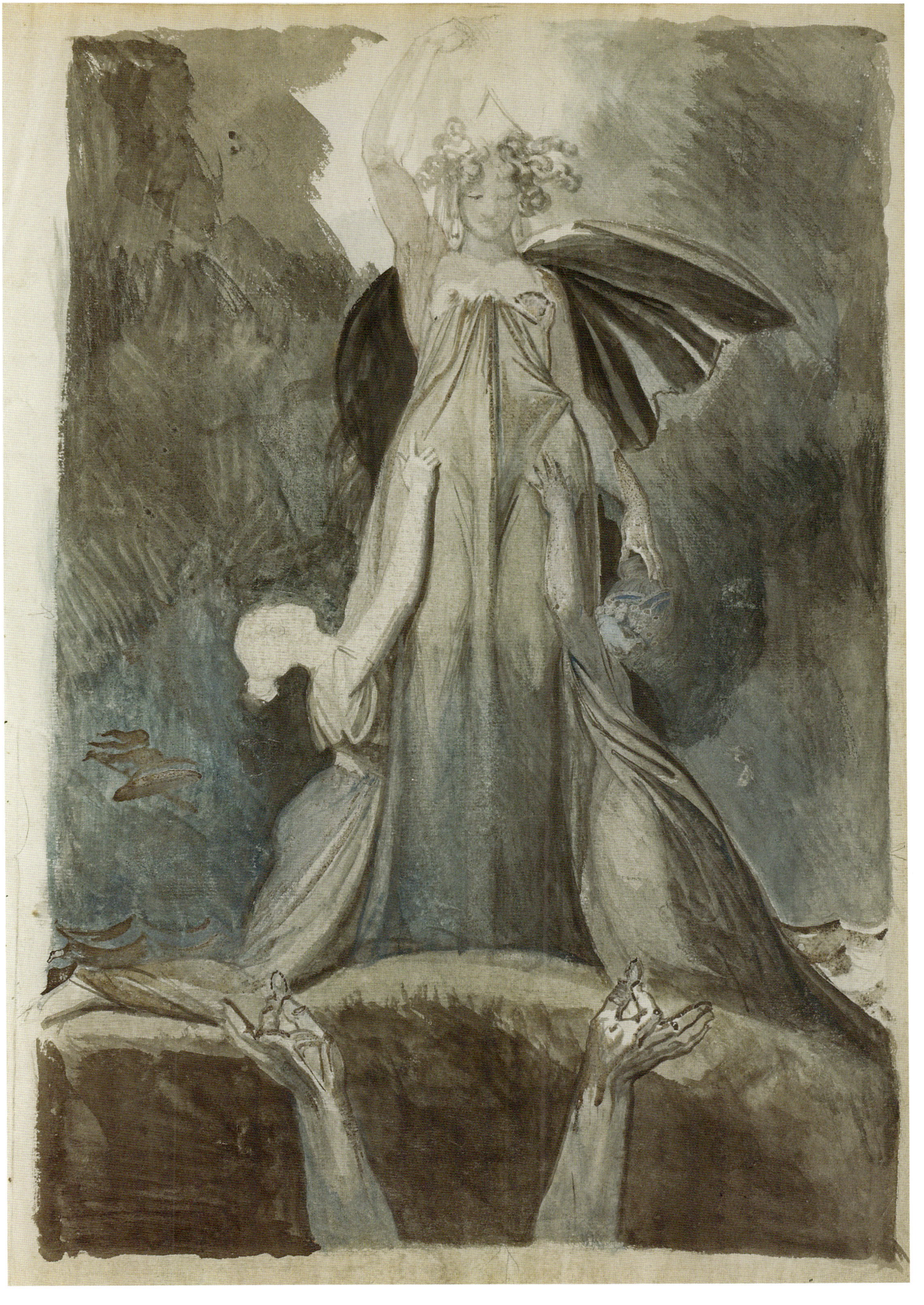

118

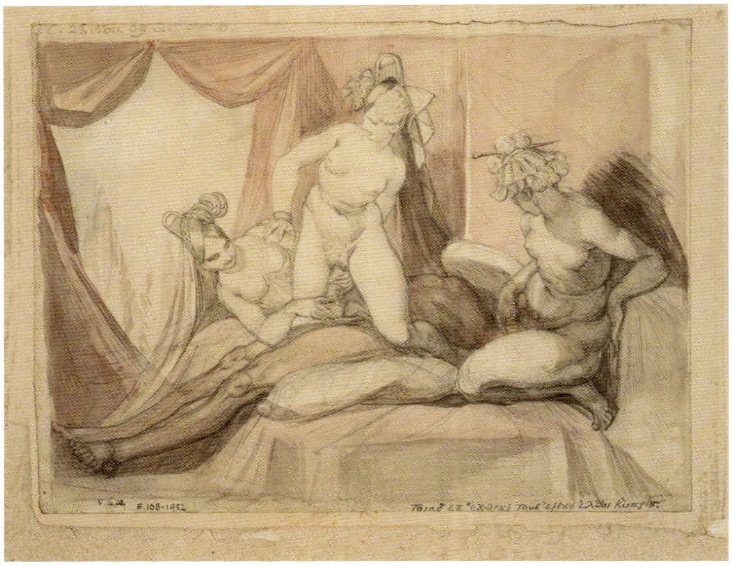

119

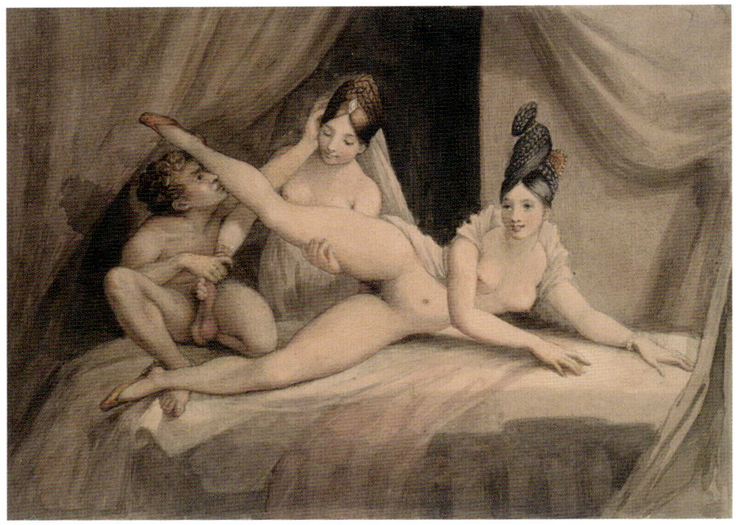

118

Henry Fuseli 1741–1825
Erotic scene with a man and three women
dated 1809 and 1810
Pencil with grey and pink wash on paper
18 x 24.5 cm
Victoria and Albert Museum, London

119

Theodor von Holst 1810–44
Erotic scene with a man and two women
c.1822–30
Pencil and watercolour on paper mounted on card 18.9 x 23 cm
Victoria and Albert Museum, London

These two drawings were first published, in suggestively fragmented form, among the details of pornographic designs in Ruthven Todd's *Tracks in the Snow* (1946), as both being by Fuseli (fig.30). No.119 is now attributed to Theodor von Holst (Browne 1994, no.25). It has also been suggested that this, with one further of the five drawings then owned by Todd, may be instead by Thomas Griffiths Wainewright (1794–1847), another direct imitator of Fuseli. All appear to have belonged first to Susan, Countess of Guildford (1771–1837), an assiduous collector of Fuseli's works and the mother of Georgina North (see no.108).

Todd saw these drawings as among Fuseli's very finest works, noting the 'static violence' and fetishism of the designs. He regretted that 'under our present dubious legal system' he was unable to reproduce them whole (Todd 1946, p.82). Even in 1975, Fuseli's drawing (Schiff 1973, no.1620) was included only as a rather discrete marginal illustration to the catalogue of the great Tate Gallery exhibition, rather than among the main selection of works (see Hoffman 1975, p.32).

No.118 is one of the drawings referred to by Gert Schiff, rather formally, as a 'symplegma', the technical term used to refer to classical statuettes or ceramics representing erotically intertwined figures. Fuseli invites an interpretation which would relate this design to ancient sources. The Greek inscription relays one of Prometheus's dramatic curses in Aeschylus's play (l.864). Prophesying the night when all but one of fifty virgins of Argos kill their hated, blood-related husbands in the nuptial bed, the bound hero exclaims: 'Thus fatal to my foes / Be Love' (Potter 1777, p.52). As with the Greek inscription on no.3, Fuseli brings sex and violence into a heady mixture.

Like the erotic designs from Fuseli's Roman years (nos.111–12), this drawing raises unresolved issues of status and intention. The sexual content is frank, even confrontational; the combination of athleticism and bored facial expressions, elaborate hairdos and physical struggle, creates, as Todd noted 'an extraordinary atmosphere' (Todd 1946, p.82) . They may not be as simply ingratiating as pornography, but neither, perhaps, can they be wholly removed to an 'elevated' realm of pure contemplation, confounding the modern demarcation of the private, bodily and sexual, and the public and intellectual.

The existence of direct copies or interpretations of such designs by Fuseli further complicate matters. According to an article in the magazine *The Art Union* in 1844, von Holst was actually commissioned in his youth by the painter Thomas Lawrence (1769–1830) to create such compositions for George IV (Browne 1994, pp.13–14). The truthfulness of this report remains moot. Certainly the design here shows a direct debt to Fuseli, and the relatively high level of finish might imply a commission rather than a work created for private pleasure.

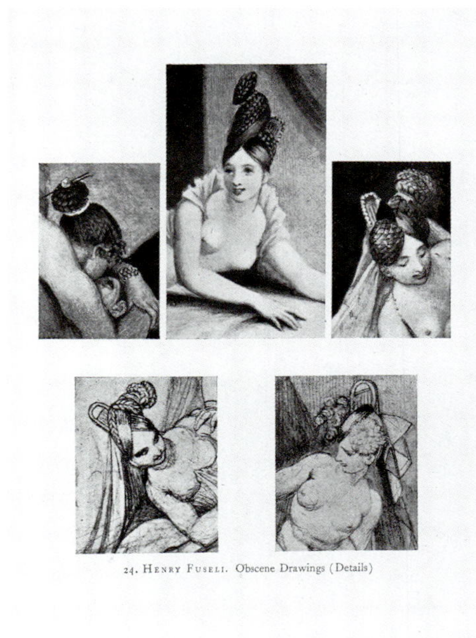

fig.30 Plate from Ruthven Todd, *Tracks in the Snow: Studies in English Science and Art*, London 1946, showing details from erotic drawings by Henry Fuseli and attributed to Theodor von Holst

120

Henry Fuseli 1741–1825
Study of a woman c.1815–20
Pencil, pen and brown ink on paper
16.2 x 10.5 cm
The Herbert, Coventry

121

Henry Fuseli 1741–1825
Woman torturing a child or small man
c.1815–20
Pencil, pen and sepia ink on paper
26 x 20.6 cm
Kunsthaus, Zurich, Grafische Sammlung

These two designs come from a group of drawings, and a mutilated painting (Petworth House, Sussex), apparently showing women in fashionable and revealing costumes more or less explicitly abusing, teasing or mutilating a small man or boy (Schiff 1973, p.384). One of these includes a date – 1821 – and an inscription in Greek meaning 'child murderess' which are taken as pertinent to the group as a whole (ibid., no.1603). Themes of infanticide appeared in a number of eminent classical and biblical stories, most notably that of Medea who in her madness murdered her children. James Barry (1741–1806) had, perhaps in his characteristically misguided way, painted a version of this horrific theme for submission as a Diploma Work when he was elected to the Royal Academy, and the subject appears among George Romney's large 'cartoons' created around 1779–80. As described above (no.86) it has been suggested that Blake's *Hecate* draws on the same motif. Fuseli's treatment of the theme is most striking in its juxtaposition of elaborate modern costumes with scenes of utter depravity. The details of such designs enhance the viewer's sense of unease, for example in no.121 the tool held by the woman resembles a chisel rather than a knife, and has been interpreted as a brush rather than any kind of blade (see Weinglass 1991, p.306 and note).

Such designs offer a case study in extreme sexual pathology. The women, empowered phallically with weapons and with their long hair, are at once attenuated symbols of highly sexualised femininity, and immediate threats to masculinity. The boy or small man is simultaneously the privileged object of their desires and attention, and destroyed by that attention. Fuseli's preoccupation with the intermingling of sex and death, of pain and pleasure, could be said to parallel the Gothic novel in the 'sense of ritualized play, or fantasy, that allows the voyeur-participant to vicariously experience the pleasures of both sadism and masochism' (see Gardiner-Scott 1997, p.48; also Klein 1991).

120

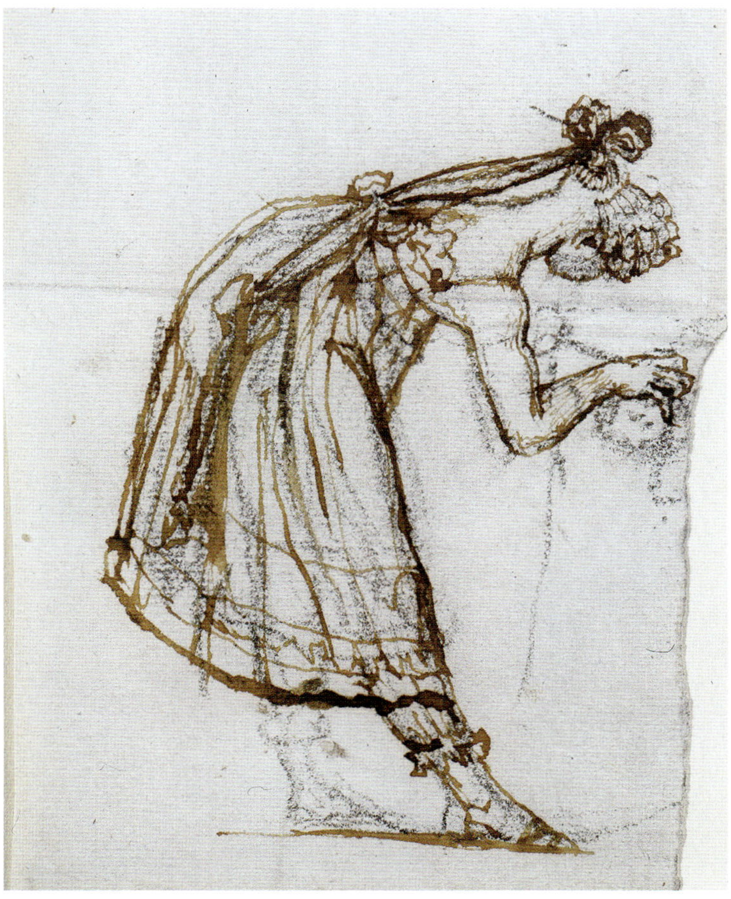

121

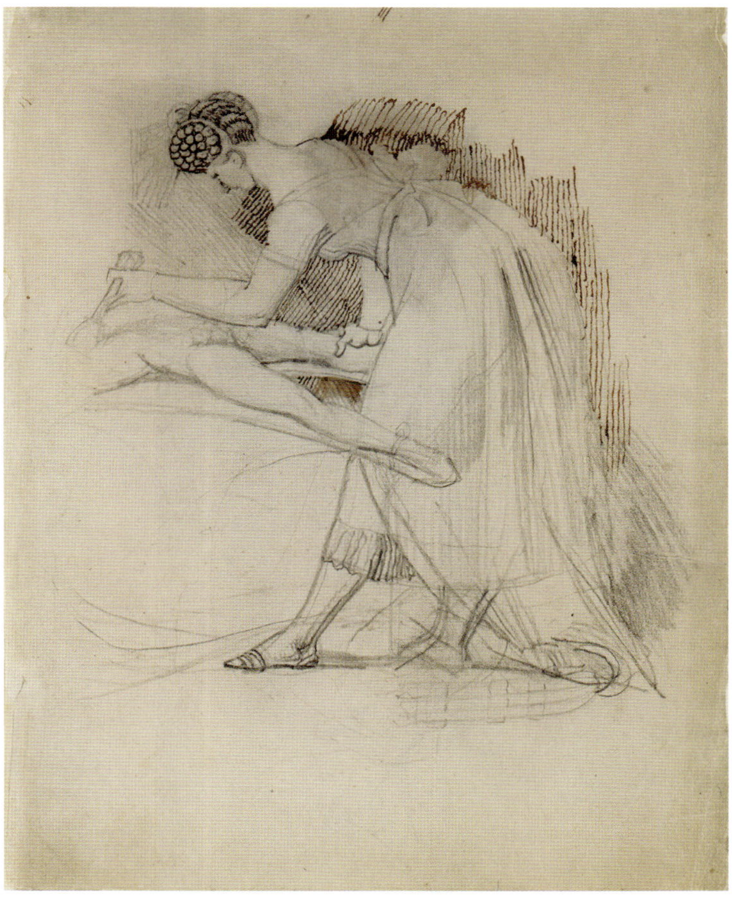

122

Theodor von Holst 1810–1844
Legs of a standing female figure c.1822–30
Pen and ink, watercolour and chalk on paper
12.2 x 8.8 cm
Courtauld Institute of Art Gallery, London

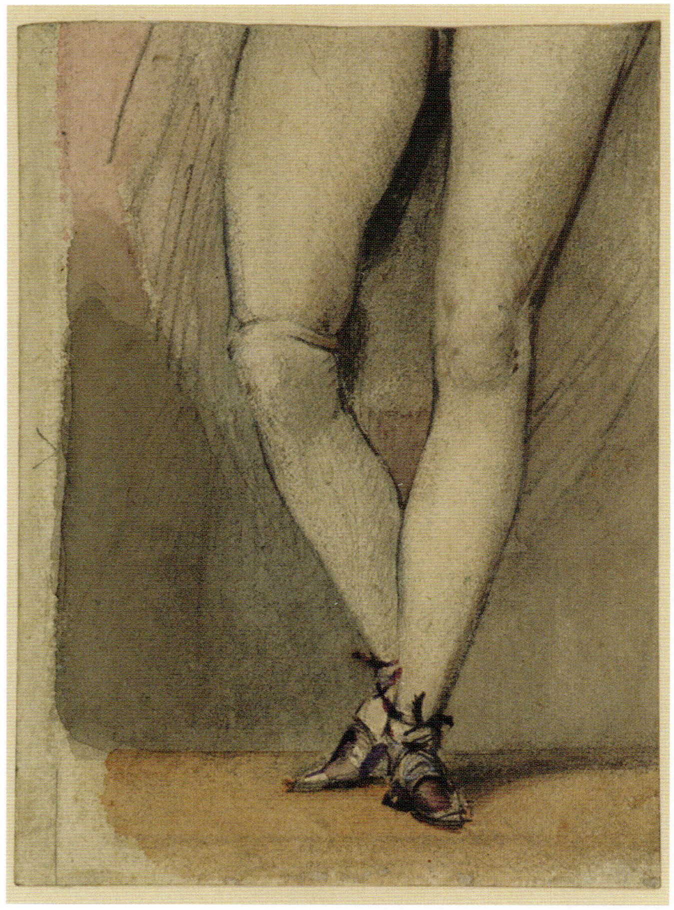

This is one of two drawings by von Holst showing the bare and shapely legs of a woman, truncated below the waist. In the other version (Paul Grinke collection) the upper margin of the sheet permits the presence of the woman's pubic hair (see Browne 1994, no.22). The present design (arguably an alternative rather than inferior version) remains more suggestive, particularly in the detail of the slipped stocking and in the extreme delicacy with which the feet are conceived.

Tradition has it that the legs are those of Maria Anne Fitzherbert (1756–1837), one of the lovers of George IV when Prince of Wales and (illegally, as she was a Catholic) his wife from 1785. As king, George was said to have commissioned a number of pornographic drawings. However, the description of these legs as literally Mrs Fitzherbert's is most likely fanciful, as they seem to be those of a much younger woman.

Aside from its immediate sensual appeal, the design is powerfully suggestive of the way in which a sexualised vision of the body can lead to the breakdown of that body in representation. The watercolour – and the very delicacy of its effects enhances this – effectively fetishises the body. For some critics and scholars such a dismemberment of the body represents a reprehensible objectification, removing sex from the realm of legitimate social exchange and individual expression (Mulvey 1975).

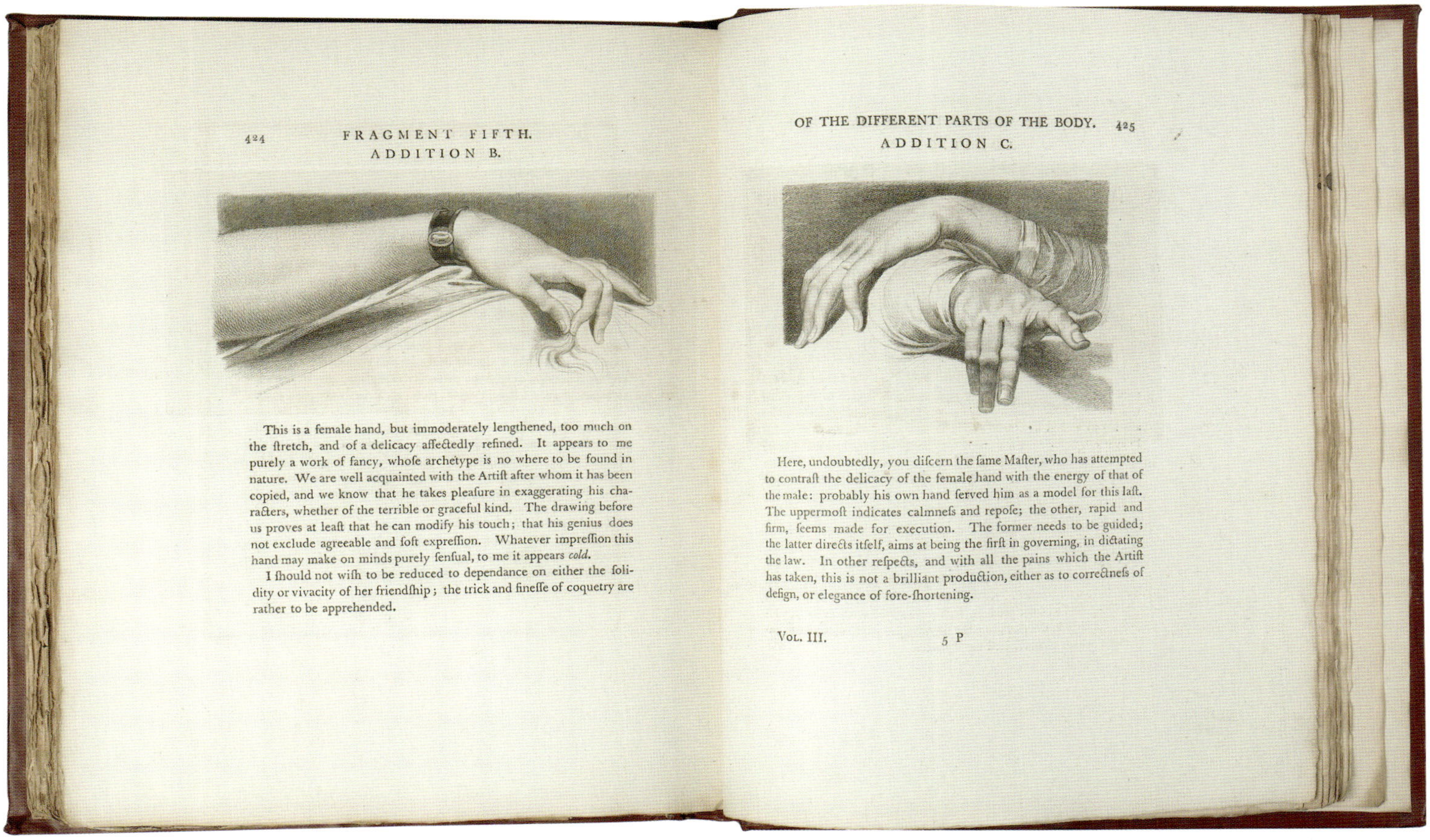

424 FRAGMENT FIFTH.

ADDITION B.

This is a female hand, but immoderately lengthened, too much on the ftretch, and of a delicacy affectedly refined. It appears to me purely a work of fancy, whofe archetype is no where to be found in nature. We are well acquainted with the Artift after whom it has been copied, and we know that he takes pleafure in exaggerating his characters, whether of the terrible or graceful kind. The drawing before us proves at leaft that he can modify his touch; that his genius does not exclude agreeable and foft expreffion. Whatever impreffion this hand may make on minds purely fenfual, to me it appears *cold*.

I fhould not wifh to be reduced to dependance on either the folidity or vivacity of her friendfhip; the trick and fineffe of coquetry are rather to be apprehended.

OF THE DIFFERENT PARTS OF THE BODY. 425

ADDITION C.

Here, undoubtedly, you difcern the fame Mafter, who has attempted to contraft the delicacy of the female hand with the energy of that of the male: probably his own hand ferved him as a model for this laft. The uppermoft indicates calmnefs and repofe; the other, rapid and firm, feems made for execution. The former needs to be guided; the latter directs itfelf, aims at being the firft in governing, in dictating the law. In other refpects, and with all the pains which the Artift has taken, this is not a brilliant production, either as to correctnefs of defign, or elegance of fore-fhortening.

Vol. III. 5 P

123

Thomas Holloway 1748–1827
after Henry Fuseli 1741–1825
Johann Casper Lavater, trans. Henry Hunter, *Essays on Physiognomy: Designed to Promote the Knowledge and the Love of Mankind*, 3 vols., London 1789–98, III, Part 2, open to pp.424–5 (Additions B & C)
Letterpress and engraved illustrations, plate marks 10.8 x 22.5 cm and 12 x 18.3 cm
The Wellcome Library, London

Two illustrations after drawings by Fuseli, included in the English edition of his old college-friend Johann Casper Lavater's influential *Essays on Physiognomy* (1789–98, translated from the French edition of 1781–6). In 'Addition B', a female hand lays lugubriously over a womanly hip, pinching the folds of her dress into suggestively labial forms. In the other image, a vigorous male hand is contrasted with a limp, ineffectual female.

The potential of a hand or foot to become powerful symbolic objects was vastly enhanced by the cult of physiognomy – the pseudo-science of interpreting personality and morals from physical appearances. In an era of shifting social identities – in which the poor might have access to fine clothes and the pretence of manners as much as the rich, and in which men were believed effeminated by luxury while women were made masculine by their claims to political rights and education – the idea that the essence of identity could be found in the physical traits of a personality won wide favour (Allentuck 1967; Graham 1979; Shookman 1993). Images such as these prints would seem to clear away such confusion: the manly hand is truly manly – bony, dramatically foreshortened – the female is graceful and lifeless. The cult of physiognomy matches the Gothic in intriguing ways: in both, gender identities tend to be caricatured, demonstrative, even hysterical (Myrone 2005, p.242; also Henderson 1992).

Fuseli's treatment of his male and female characters tended, as Lavater notes in his commentary on these designs, to extravagance. His sometime follower Benjamin Robert Haydon (1786–1846) noted, tellingly: 'His women are all whores, and men all banditti' (Haydon 1960–3, I, p.488). Lavater intimates 'a finesse of coquetry' to the sole female hand, which in its drawing together the folds of cloth evokes a whole tradition of more or less explicit images of women masturbating, a stock feature of pornographic frontispieces and prints (fig.20 on p.45). The ascent of print in the eighteenth century made possible more intimate, private cultural experiences by women, otherwise excluded from the realm of high culture. A proclivity to masturbation was seen as a danger attendant to female education, and the subject was susceptible to prurient treatments (Wagner 1988, pp.262–3).

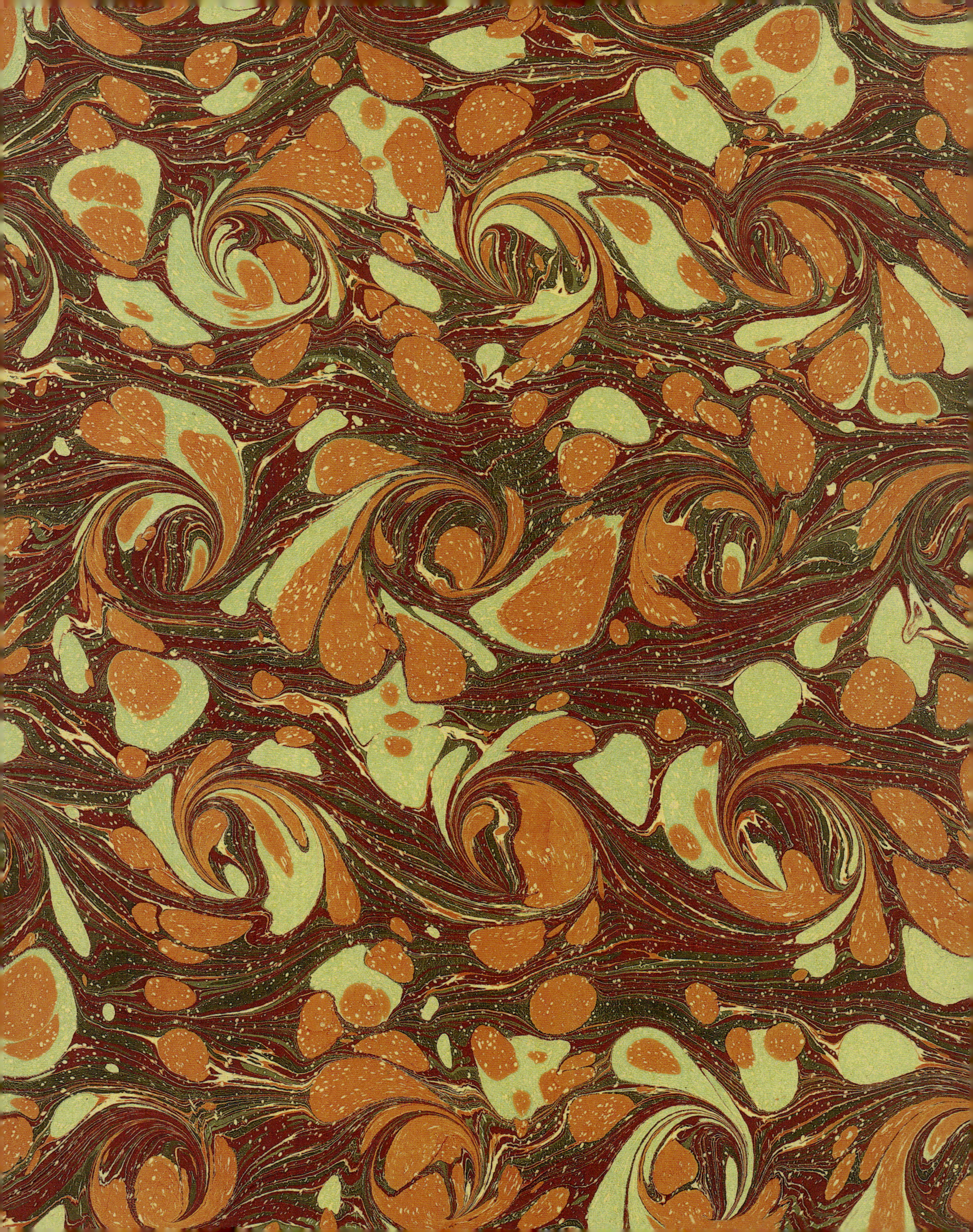

Revolution, Revelation and Apocalypse

Between the riots and political upheaval in Paris in 1789 that marked the opening shots of the French Revolution through to the Battle of Waterloo in 1815, which saw the defeat of Napoleon, Europe was transformed in ways that were not just unprecedented, but virtually unimagined. The fall of the infamous Bastille prison in July 1789, the rigorous pursuit of democratic principles in France, the imprisonment and execution of Louis XVI and the ascent of Napoleon as emperor marked the overhaul of the old material and symbolic structures, the rise of new ways of thinking about and experiencing the world, of brutal violence and painful optimism, impossible dreams of freedom and the bleakest terrorization of humanity. The world, it seemed, was to be made anew: either as a monstrous caricature, or as a utopia.

In Britain, the first stages of the French Revolution, from 1789 to the death of Louis and the proclamation of war with France in 1793, were warmly welcomed, especially among the liberal, intellectual class (Dickinson 1989; Crossley and Small 1989; Philp 1991; Andrews 2000). What happened in France might then appear to be only a just overthrowing of tyranny, broadly in line with the political transformations of the British state in the seventeenth century. But the publication of Edmund Burke's widely-read *Reflections on the Revolution in France* (1790) precipitated the emergence of virulent forms of conservatism which were to inform cultural discourse in decisive ways (Simpson 1993; Barrell 2000). Burke powerfully articulated a division between the naturalised, untheorised, conservative traditions that were supposedly native to Britain and the unbridled, unthinkingly rationalist principles of revolution pursued in France. Playing on long-established stereotypes about the national character, Burke established a set of deeply resilient terms for British conservatism, which rested on ideals of plain common sense and an unreflexive dedication to tradition - exemplified by the crusty Gothic castle. For radicals, the Gothic might represent, instead, the mysterious and mystifying dead weight of tradition that suffocated personal liberty and constricted individual expression, or, alternatively, a more radical national tradition of political freedoms that contested, rather than affirmed, the authority of the Crown. The motifs of darkness and light, of imprisonment and liberation, the classical temple and the castellated tower, rebounded between conservatives and radicals in a heated, prolonged debate which never resolved itself into a wholly predictable form.

Facing a fearful future, many Britons turned to extreme forms of religious enthusiasm or retreated into paranoid esotericism. An era that seemed, as Henry Fuseli put it, 'pregnant with the most gigantic efforts of character' witnessed the themes of apocalypse, gigantism and riot given elaborate and powerful visual form (Paulson 1983; Bindman 1989). The Book of Revelation had been treated sceptically, or at least coolly, in the earlier eighteenth century, but the revolutionary years saw it assume new importance, not as an historically distant allegory, but as a text of pressing importance: 'The mythical and the monstrous have now become a matter of contemporary public experience; they cannot so easily be bound in patterns of regular chronology or in a detached world of Gothic fantasy' (Burdon 1997, p.93). The prophetic and interpretive writings of the previous centuries were mobilised to support the idea that the millennium was arriving - that the war, famine and pestilence which were overwhelming Europe would bring a new era of peace and harmony.

More pragmatically, the war meant that a whole generation of artists was denied the opportunity to travel to Italy, the vital intellectual and social experience on which Fuseli, Romney, Barry and many others had founded their ambitions and staked their claims to greatness. The suffocating political paranoia of the era brought the faculty of imagination itself into question, as the potential source of rebellious tendencies, and artistic ambitions were materially curtailed. The cultural nationalism that became defined in the 1790s and 1800s turned the focus of critical attention away from the question of subject matter towards artistic techniques. Now, the painterly expressiveness of Constable and painters of genre could be dignified as expressions of a national character, despite (or perhaps because of) their rejection of the classical standards that had informed academic debate in earlier decades (see Kriz 1997). An artist like Fuseli now looked more decadent and irrelevant than ever, and his work was to slip into obscurity and myth after his death. The vital and dynamic exchange of high and low culture, of grand narrative and the grotesque, of shifting audiences and new critical voices, which had informed and motivated the visual Gothic became stultified, and a new era of bourgeois cultural conformity was ushered in.

Henry Fuseli in the Analytical Review (December 1789)

... an age pregnant with the most gigantic efforts of character, shaken with the convulsions of old, and the emersion of new empires

(Mason 1951, p.183)

Christopher Love (1651) quoted in Prophetic Conjectures on the French Revolution, and Other Recent and Shortly Expected Events, London 1793

Great earthquakes and commotions by sea shall come in the year of God 1779. —great wars in Germany and in AMERICA in 1780. — The destruction of popery, or BABYLON'S FALL, in the year 1790 — God will be known by many in the year 1795. This will produce a great man — The stars will wander, and the moon turn to blood in 1800 — Africa, Asia, and America will tremble in 1803 — A great earthquake over all the world, in 1805 — God will be universally known by all: then a general reformation, and peace for ever, when the people shall learn war no more — Happy is the man that liveth to see this day!

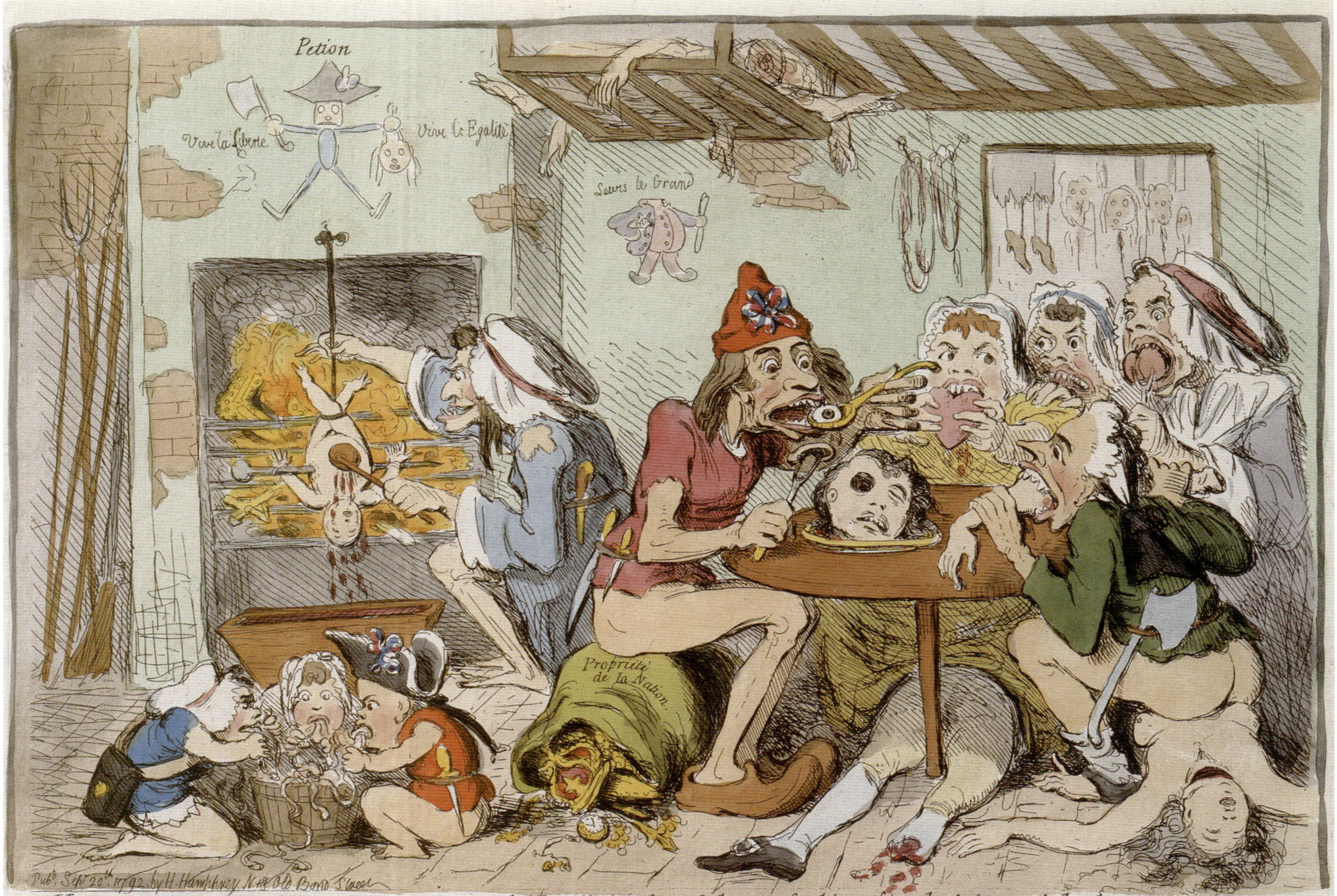

Un petit Souper, a la Parisienne: — or — A Family of Sans-Culotts refreshing, after the fatigues of the day.

Epigram extempore on seeing the above Print.

"Here as you see, and as 'tis known, —
"Frenchmen mere Cannibals are grown; —
"On Maigre Days each had his Dish
"Of Soup, or Sallad, Eggs, or Fish; –
"But now 'tis human Flesh they gnaw,
"And ev'ry Day is Mardi Gras.

124

James Gillray 1756–1815
Un Petit Souper, a la Parisienne: Or – A Family of Sans-Culotts Refreshing, after the Fatigues of the Day published by Hannah Humphrey, 20 September 1792
Handcoloured etching 24.8 x 35 cm, with the 'Epigram extempore' printed from a separate plate
With permission of the Warden and Scholars of New College, Oxford

A cannibal apocalypse: the subhuman depravity attributed to France's revolutionary 'sans-culottes' (referring to their rejection of aristocratic 'culottes' in favour of working-class dress) is manifested in a scene of bestial consumption. In a peasant cottage, an extended family is gathered to eat. A human head lies on the table, its right eye about to be popped into the mouth of an eager sans-culotte; three ravenous women chew on organs; another man, using a dead, naked woman as a seat, squashing her full breasts under his bare buttocks, chomps down on the raw stump of a forearm. To the left, three wicked children gobble down intestines from a tub. At the rear, an older woman bastes a spatch-cocked child before the open fire. More body parts decorate the rafters, and through the open door are signs of further carnage.

The print amplifies news of insurrection and massacres in revolutionary France. Reports condemning these would often refer to the revolutionaries as 'savages' or 'cannibals' (see Pressly 1999, pp.110, 151 for examples; also Nochlin 1994, p.15). At the same time, it draws on old stereotypes about the French. To cite the well-worn clichés, the common citizens of France were impoverished and lived on a meagre or even unnatural diet, even as its wealthy citizens set the standard of taste and fashion. The grotesque contrast between the explicit violence of the image and the affected delicacy of the title plays on these ideas. Apparently rapidly executed, the print nonetheless consciously incorporates recollections of an engraving of *The Poor Kitchen* after the 1563 painting by Pieter Breughel (1525–69) and, in the figure of the inverted child roasting in the fire, the etching by Jacques Callot (c.1593–1635) depicting the plunder of a farmhouse from his series *Miseries of War* (Godfrey 2001, nos.56–7; the Callot reference was kindly pointed out to me by Mary Kisler of the Auckland Art Gallery Toi o Tāmaki).

Gillray's print is rooted in a rich tradition of images of anthropophagy (people-eating). The religious and social upheavals of the sixteenth and seventeenth centuries brought accusations and counter-accusations of cannibalism between Protestants and Catholics (the Catholic liturgy being centred on the consumption of the transubstantiated flesh and blood of Christ), reported incidences of actual hunger cannibalism, and, vitally, accounts of cannibalism among the newly encountered peoples of the Americas (Zika 1997; Barker, Hulme and Iverson 1998; also Noble 2002). The historical reality of such practices among the 'primitive' peoples of the Americas and Pacific remains a contentious issue, but the images arising from such reports were seminal. Theodor de Bry's (1528–98) print entitled *Tupinamba Grilling Human Body Parts* first published in his *Americae Tertia Pars* (1592) is the classic example of this type (fig.31). It has been described, in terms that are equally pertinent here, as 'representing a cannibal society involving men, women and children; a complex narrative scenario, in which the viewer can experience the horrors of cannibalism repeatedly through each of the "savages" represented' (Zika 1997, p.89).

Stories of a cannibal families found an eighteenth-century apotheosis in the myth of the Scottish people-eater Sawney Bean, the influence of which persisted through to Tobe Hooper's film *The Texas Chainsaw Massacre* (fig.32), perhaps the only recent occasion on which the sheer claustrophobia and grisliness of Gillray's image has been effectively matched. Both represent what has properly been called a 'perverted fairy tale', a description that might further draw attention to the elements of perverse sexuality present here (Brottman 1996 and 2001). Gillray has translated the term 'sans-culottes' literally, to mean that his citizens are completely without trousers – and provocatively naked below the waist. The 'Petit Soupers' of the title were the meals served up in 'petits maisons' – brothels – which were said to be proliferating in Paris (see Bindman 1992, p.135).

The visionary intensity of this scene, as well as its thematic concern with the metaphors of cannibalism and consumption, have been related to William Blake's closely contemporary imagery on the theme of revolution (Behrendt 1987–8, pp.90–1).

Marquis de Sade, Reflections on the Novel (1800)

There was not a man alive who had not experienced in the short span of four or five years more misfortunes than the most celebrated novelist could portray in a century. Thus, to compose works of interest, one had to call upon the aid of hell itself, and to find in the world of make-believe things wherewith one was fully familiar merely by delving into man's daily life in this age of iron.

(de Sade 1990, p.109)

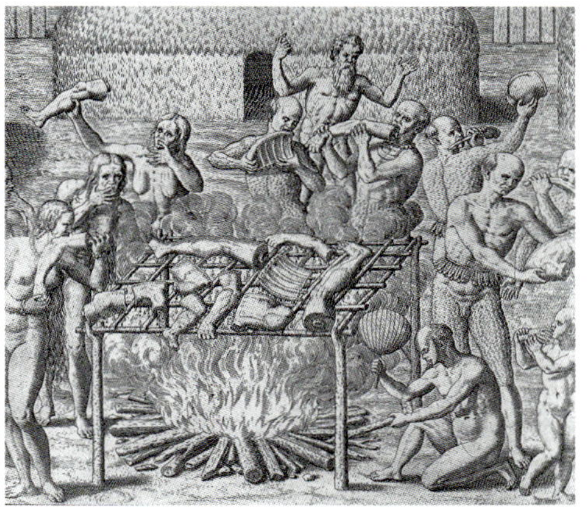

fig.31 Engraved illustration from Theodor de Bry (1528–98), *Newe Welt vnd americanische Historien*, Frankfurt 1655. The Wellcome Library, London

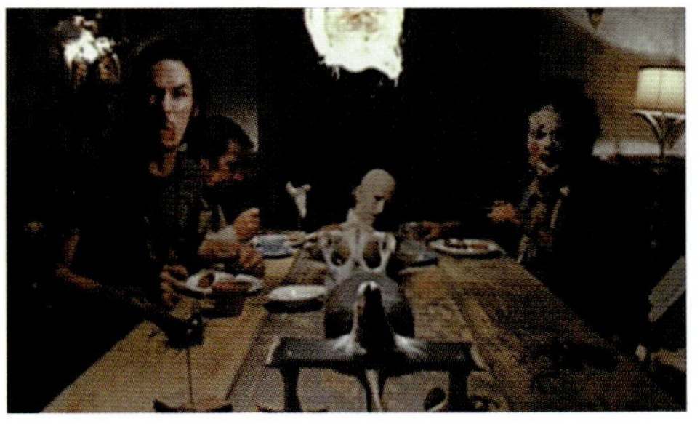

fig.32 Still from *The Texas Chainsaw Massacre* (dir. Tobe Hopper, USA 1974)

125

Henry Fuseli 1741–1825
Vision of the Lazar House perhaps c.1790–4
Pencil with some wash, heightened with white, on paper 56 x 66 cm
Zurich, Kunsthaus, Grafische Sammlung

The subject of this drawing is taken from John Milton's epic retelling of the biblical narrative, *Paradise Lost* (1667), and depicts the scene shown to Adam by the Archangel Michael, revealing the dreadful future of mankind, in suffering, madness and disease. Over the heads of suffering humanity looms the figure of Death, dart in hand and arms outstretched.

This uncharacteristically cautious drawing reproduces Fuseli's huge canvas on this subject (c.308 x 335 cm) completed by 1794, first exhibited at the Milton Gallery (see no.94) in 1799, and engraved by Moses Haughton in 1813 (see Weinglass 1994, no.293). This squared-drawing was probably done in preparation for this last, perhaps by Haughton rather than Fuseli. According to John Knowles, Fuseli's biographer (Knowles 1831, I, p.222),

> The Vision of the Lazar-house was justly considered by the best judges in the art, to be the *chef-d'œuvre* of the Gallery. It is a composition of seventeen figures, and parts of figures, in which the painter creates both terror and pity in the spectator, by judiciously excluding most of those objects represented by the poet as suffering under bodily diseases calculated to create disgust, and confining himself chiefly to the representation of the maladies of the mind, which are so forcibly described by the passage,
>
> 'Demoniac Phrensy, moping Melancholy,
> And moon-struck Madness ———'

As Knowles remarks, Fuseli represents a variety of clinical conditions – which he had observed at first hand on his trips to Bedlam Hospital (at that time still open for voyeuristic visits). The range of suffering types characterised by Fuseli, and his sources in physiognomy, medical theory and literature, has been extensively discussed by Matthias Vogel (Vogel 2001, pp.298–320). The central group of figures, restraining an energetically struggling man, is based on an earlier design of an incident that the artist witnessed at the Hospital of Santo Spirito in Rome; an engraving of this design prompted his friend Lavater's comment that 'Fury and force, an energy uniformly supported, and ever active – this is what distinguishes most of the figures and compositions of this masculine genius' (Schiff 1973, no.515; see above, no.9).

A visitor to Fuseli's studio in 1816 referred to the completed painting as 'one of the most appalling sights I ever beheld. The figures glare across the picture like a horrible dream' (C.R. Leslie to Eliza Leslie, 12 December 1816, in Weinglass 1982, p.429). Accordingly, the administration of the British Institution had hesitated when Fuseli sent the picture for exhibition there in 1806, 'considering the subject too terrible for the public eye' (Knowles 1831, I, p.289). Still, the painting was among those displayed around the walls of the room in the Royal Academy in which Fuseli's body was placed as part of his funeral ceremonies (ibid., p.343).

The visions of plague-houses crafted by Romney (no.128), Blake (no.127) and Fuseli in the 1790s can be located in a long history of visions of mass disease. From the seventeenth century, the still startling accounts of the plague of London of 1603 by dramatist Thomas Dekker (c.1570–1632) gave reportage a vivid, apocalyptic quality (see p.182). In the present age, the vision of communities decimated by disease and reinvented as undead, half-dead and cannibalistic has been distilled into a dystopian vision by a series of films in the 1970s and 1980s; the charnel-house, complete with winding-sheets, was given complete expression in an early scene in George A. Romero's remarkable *Dawn of the Dead* (1978; fig.33).

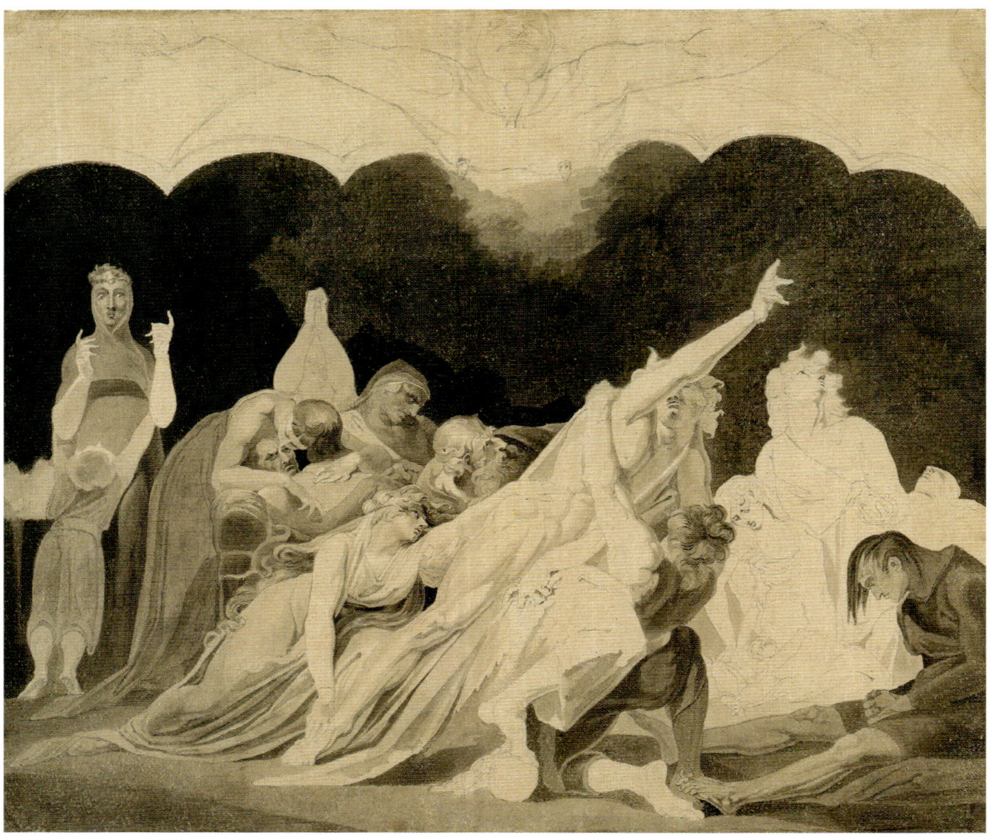

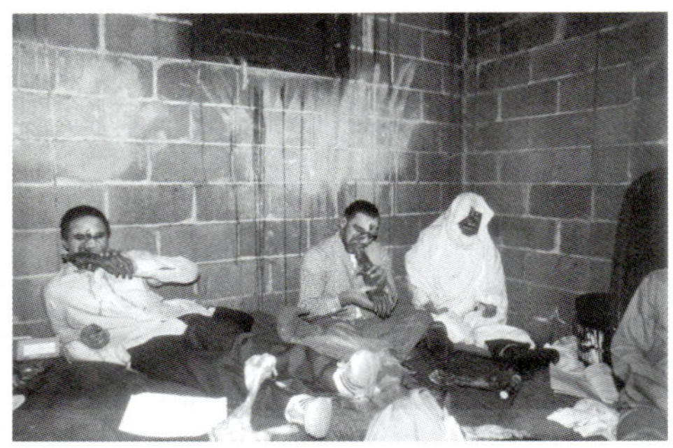

fig.33 Still from *Dawn of the Dead* (dir. George A. Romero, USA/Italy 1978)

126

William Blake 1757–1827
House of Death c.1790
Pencil, pen and wash on paper
31.8 x 45.1 cm
Tate. Bequeathed by Alice G.E. Carthew 1940

127

William Blake 1757–1827
House of Death 1795/1805
Colour print with ink and watercolour
48.5 x 61 cm
Tate. Presented by W. Graham Robertson 1939

The subject here is the same as in Fuseli's design of the same period, no.126: Death hovers over the plague-house, dart in hand, teasing his victims with the promise of eternal sleep but letting them suffer on.

No.126 (Butlin 1990, no.12) is considered to be a first attempt at composing this theme. It was once suggested that the drawing was actually by Fuseli, and it is certainly here that Blake's debt to the Swiss artist may be most explicit. However, the recumbent figures recall Blake's early studies of medieval sculpture at Westminster Abbey and the airborne figure of Death is typical of Blake's bearded figures. This drawing was damaged and repaired by its owner early in the twentieth century, before it came into the Tate collection.

No.127 (Butlin 1990, no.32) was listed in Blake's account with his patron, Thomas Butts, of 3 March 1806 as 'House of Death', but is also known as 'The Lazar House'. The print was one of the 'large colour prints' first produced by Blake around 1795. The position of Death, stretched across top of composition, contrasts with his earlier treatment of the theme and matches Fuseli's painting (completed in 1794). Frontally viewed figures with outstretched arms occur frequently in Blake's iconography. Here, the downturned palms might denote oppression or constriction, and have been linked with the gesture of the evil angel in his design of the good and evil angels struggling over a child (see no.45) (Warner 1984, pp.102–4). Blake's connection with Fuseli is further apparent in the schematically rendered figure, kneeling down and covering his ears with his hands to the right; this character assumes a posture like Fuseli's shepherd in the smaller version of *The Shepherd's Dream*, here proposed as that completed by the artist in 1794 for his Milton Gallery (see Schiff 1973, 1762b and above, no.101).

126

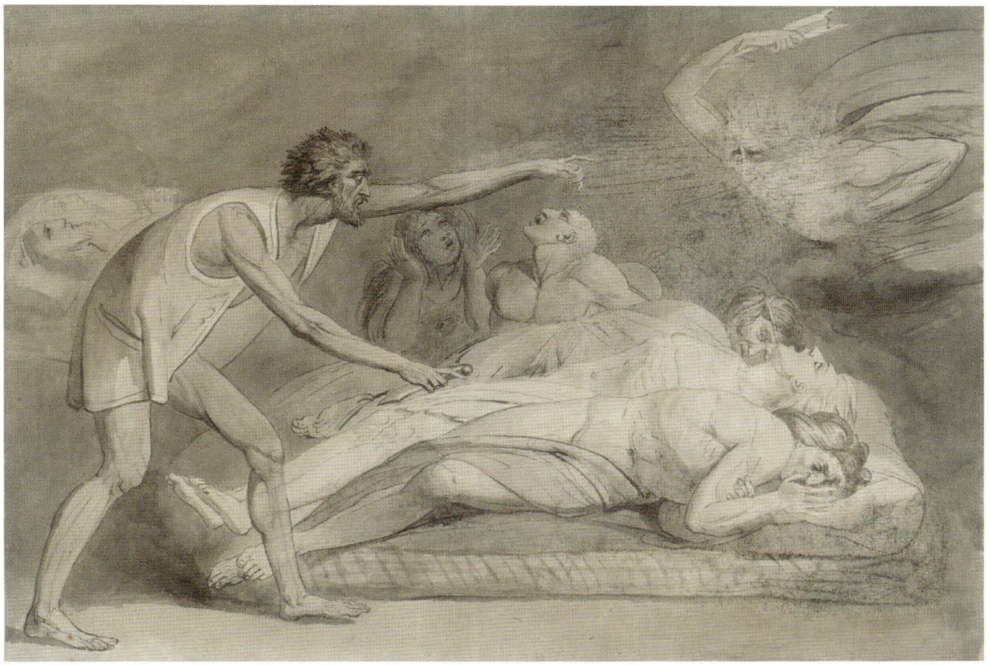

127

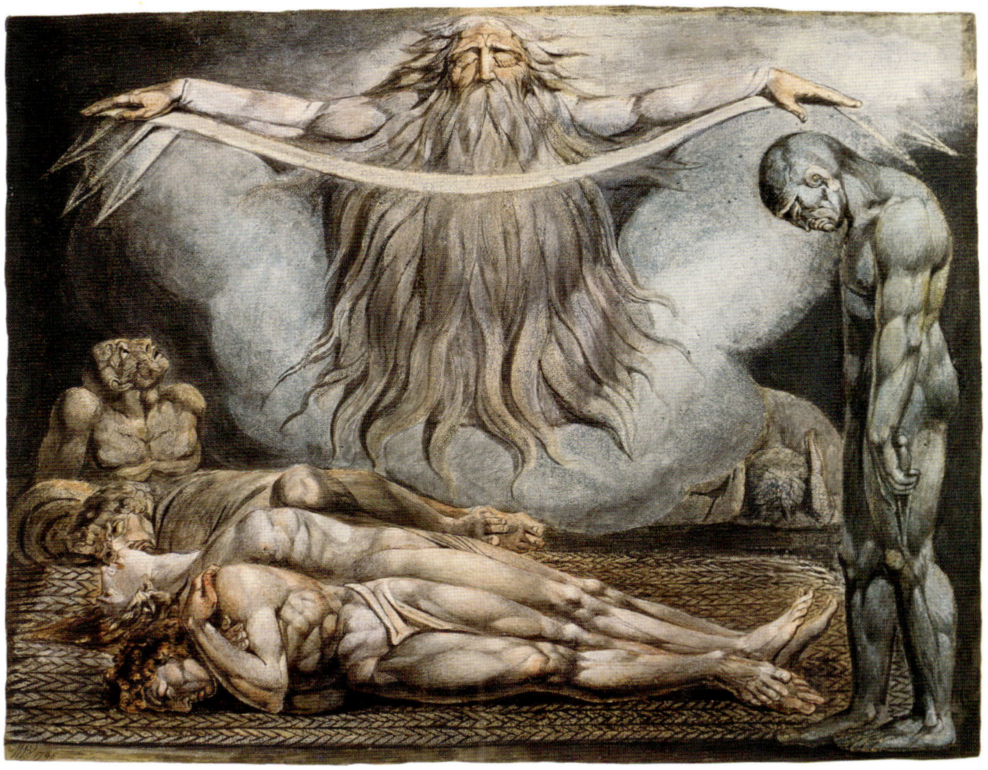

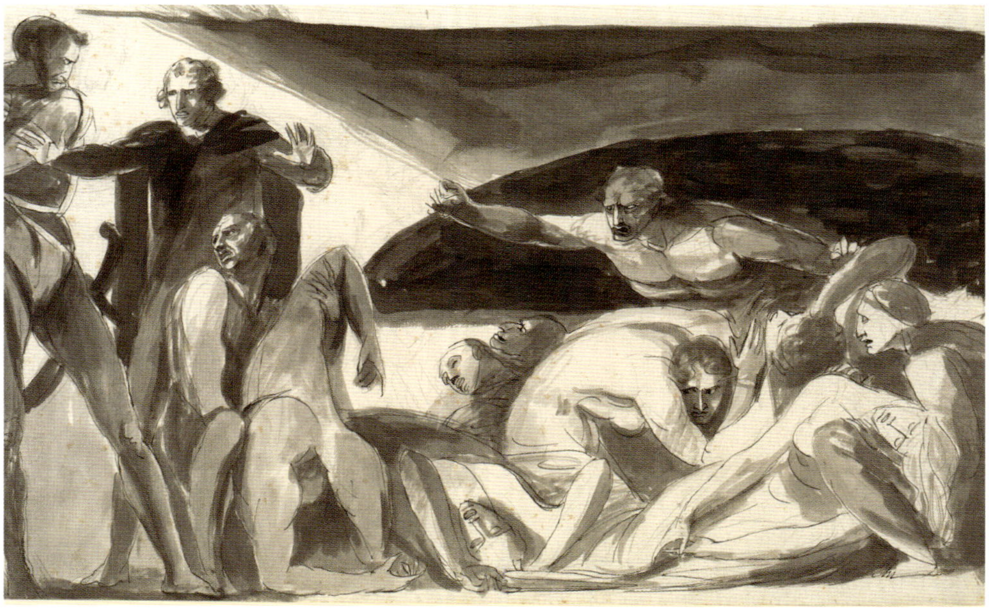

128

George Romney 1734–1802
John Howard Visiting a Lazaretto c.1790–4
Ink and wash over pencil on paper
33 x 52.5 cm
The Courtauld Institute of Art Gallery, London

The prison reformer John Howard (1726–90) is shown looking in horror upon a scene of human devastation inside a plague-house. Howard was a wealthy gentleman who pioneered the prison reform movement. In 1785 he began investigating conditions in the 'lazarettos' – buildings or ships kept aside for quarantining the diseased. A true investigative reporter, he submitted himself to trial a forty-two day quarantine in Venice. His observations were published as *An Account of the Principal Lazarettos in Europe* (1789).

Howard's heroic efforts won him public admiration, and his death in 1790 from disease contracted during his philanthropic endeavours triggered an outpouring of poems, prints and proposals for a public monument. The poet William Hayley (1745–1820) had suggested Howard to Romney as a subject as early as 1779, and it has been proposed that the artist may have been preparing studies during the 1780s, although these were not abandoned until around 1794 (see Kidson 2002, p.212; Cross 2000, pp.164–7). Howard famously never sat for his portrait, but Romney was one of several artists to attempt narrative subjects about him around this time (Ireland 1999). Francis Wheatley (1747–1801) exhibited an oil painting on the subject exhibited in 1788 under the rather uninspiring title of 'Mr Howard Offering Relief to Prisoners' (private collection), reproduced in an engraving advertised with the racier – even Miltonic – identification as 'Howard's Visit to the Cells of Wretchedness' (*The World*, 14 April 1788). James Gillray's print on the same theme, *The Triumph of Benevolence*, was advertised in the same year (*The World*, 19 May 1788) (Webster 1970, no.57 and p.68; Godfrey 2001, no.39).

Romney appears never to have attempted to commit this subject to canvas, even though his drawings for a composition on this theme are numerous. His visionary treatment of the subject draws on the rich resource of the Gothic and on the tradition of plague visions. Here he depicts Howard repelling a brutal-looking gaoler, a gigantic, long-legged figure. The distortion of the human form is particularly evident in the weird, shapelessly Lovecraftian conglomeration to the left-centre of the composition, held up by the squatting male figure whose head is turned sharply back over his shoulder. As Yvonne Romney Dixon has traced, this began life in other designs as a more composed female figure, but has by now 'been pushed to expressionistic extremes until it registers as an ideograph of human misery' (Dixon 1998, p.91).

John Milton, Paradise Lost (1667; 2nd ed. 1674), Book XI, ll.477–93

– Immediately a place
Before his eyes appeared, sad, noysom, dark,
A lazar-house it seemd, wherein were laid
Numbers of all diseas'd, all maladies
Of ghastly Spasm, or racking torture, qualmes
Of heart-sick Agonie, all feavorous kinds,
Convulsions, Epilepsies, fierce Catarrhs,
Intestin Stone and Ulcer, Colic pangs,
Daemoniac Phrenzies, moaping Melancholie,
And Moon-struck madness, pining Atrophie,
Marasmus, and wide-wasting Pestilence,
Dropsies, and Asthma's, and Joint-racking Rheums.
Dire was the tossing, deep the groans, despair
Tended the sick busiest from Couch to Couch;
And over them triumphant Death his Dart
Shook, but delaid to strike, though oft invok't
With vows, as thir chief good, and final hope.

(Milton 1998, p.675)

The Wonderfulle Yeare: Wherein Is Shewed the Picture of London, Lying Sicke of the Plague (1603)

What an unmatchable torment were it for a man to be bard vp euery night in a vast silent charnell-house? hung (to make it more hideous) with lamps dimly and slowly burning, in hollow and glimmering corners: where all the pauement should, in-stead of green rushes, be strewde with blasted rosemary, withered hyacinthes, fatall cipresse and ewe, thickly mingled with heapes of dead mens bones: the bare ribbes of a father that begat him, lying there: here the chaplesse hollow scull of a mother than bore him: round about him a thousand coarses, some standing bold vpright in their knotted winding sheetes: others half mouldred in rotten coffins, that should suddenly yawne wide open, filling his nostrils with noysome stench, and his eyes with the sight of nothng but crawling wormes. And to keep such a poore wretch waking, he should heare no noise but of toads croaking, screech-owles howling, mandrakes shriking: were not this an infernall prison? would not the strongest-hearted man (beset with such a ghastly horror) looke wilde? and run madde? and die?

(Morgan 1731, p.37)

129

William Blake 1757–1827
Plague c.1805
Pen and watercolour over pencil on paper
30.2 x 43 cm
Museum of Fine Arts, Boston. Gift by subscription

A view of a community torn apart by disease: a husband holds the lifeless body of his wife, their dead child on her lap; a daughter or wife looks, horrified, upon the body of a loved one carried, covered, on a stretcher. A man collapses, dropping the spade he has used to bury a man and a woman (his parents?). Behind, smoke billows from a funeral pyre, and we catch a glimpse of desperate worshippers raising their hands in pleading despair within the church.

This watercolour originally belonged to Thomas Butts, and is associated with a group of narrative disaster images, including and *War, Famine* and *Fire* (Butlin 1981, p.70 and nos.193–6). The content, sequencing and dating of these works has been the subject of some discussion (Bennett 1984–5; Viscomi 1994; Behrendt 2002). However, the present design is certainly from around 1805, when Butts paid for it, making it the final treatment of the theme of *Plague* to take this narrative form.

When it was first composed at the end of the 1770s the design may have been intended to represent the devastation of late seventeenth-century London, and to refer in some way to present-day travails (the war with America and her European allies and the grotesque anti-Catholic feeling that culminated in the Gordon Riots). Blake's treatment of the theme became more generalised over time. The compression of incidents, the timeless quality of the costumes, in combination with a recognisably medieval English town context, create a sense of unease and mystery, and would prompt speculation about the content of the narrative and the allegorical significance intended by the artist. Blake has recourse to a number of specific visual precedents here, each referring to biblical and classical sources which may have been in his mind. The narrative treatment of plague as a theme had been established by Raphael (1483–1520) in his drawing of *The Plague of Phrygia* (c.1512–13), which took Virgil's Aeneid as its source and was engraved as *Il Morbetto* by Marcantonio Raimondi (fig.34). This was the ultimate source of the motif of the dead mother with a child, either dead itself or clutching at her breast. It recurs in subsequent historic examples which may have informed Blake's treatment of the subject – including *The Plague of Ashdod* (1630) by Nicolas Poussin (1594–1665) and Pierre Mignard's (1612–95) scene of biblical plague, engraved under various titles (see Boeckl 2000, pp.62–3, 189–90 n.167). The last great plague in Europe had been the disastrous contagion which ravaged Marseilles in 1720, in part inspiring Daniel Defoe (1660–1731) to write his *Journal of the Plague Year* (1722) (see Defoe 1992). However, as metaphor – and as an actual threat – plague remained a potent source of terror, compounded by the biblical and classical incidences of plague evoked by this visual tradition (see Gordon 1997).

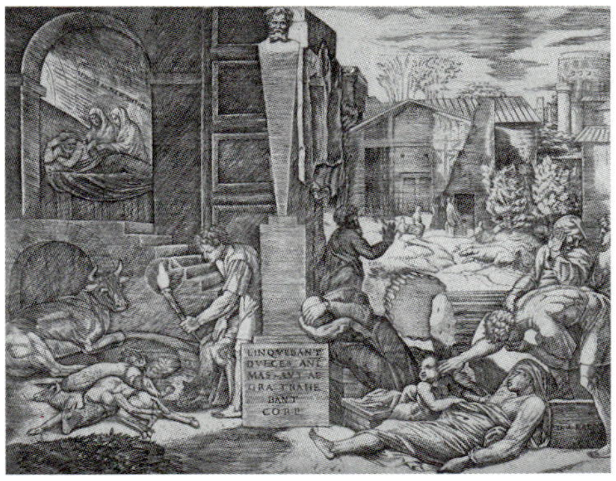

fig.34 Marcantonio Raimondi (c.1480–1534) after Raphael (1483–1520), *Il Morbetto (The Plague of Phrygia)* c.1512–13, printed 1773, etching 19.6 x 24.7 cm. The Wellcome Library, London

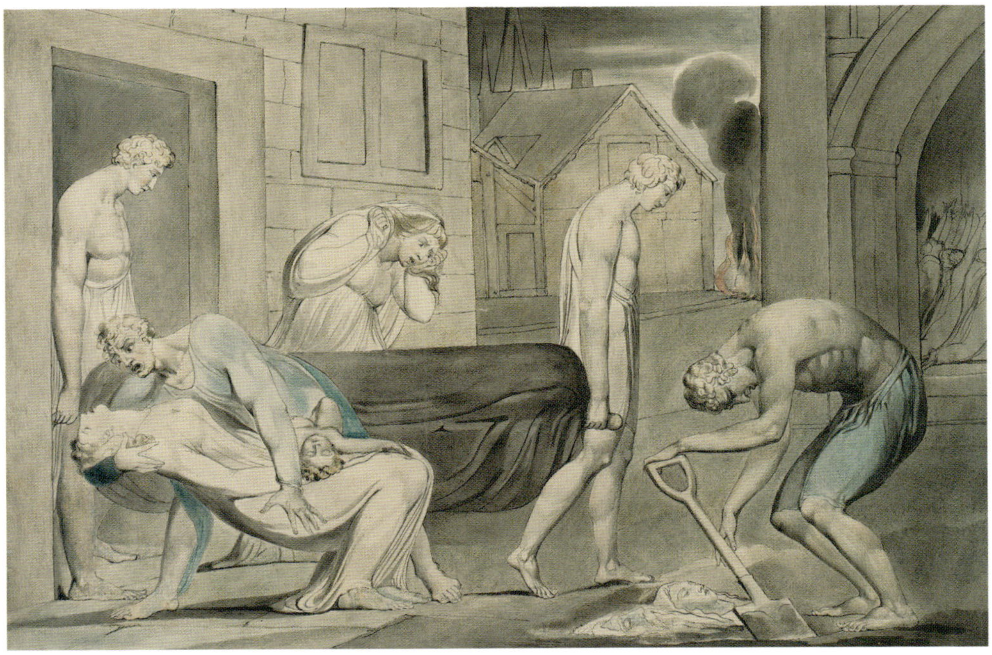

130

William Blake 1757–1827
Pestilence: The Death of the First-Born
c.1805
Pen and watercolour over pencil on paper
30.4 x 34.2 cm
Museum of Fine Arts, Boston. Gift by subscription

As with no.129, Blake represents the theme of disease, but here more certainly in the form of a biblical allegory, deriving from Exodus 12:21–3, 29–30 (Butlin 1981, no.442). The gigantic figure of Pestilence strides over Egypt, spreading the foul contagion over the land that will claim the lives of all the first-born. To the left and right his victims fall or throw their arms up in despair. Beneath his feet a woman mourns her dead child. The angel standing in the doorway presumably embodies Moses's promise of protection to the Jews who marked their doors with the blood of the Passover Lamb.

God's destructive will is embodied as a vast, scaly creature. Its form anticipates Blake's vampiric *Ghost of a Flea* (no.154) and may even recall Fuseli's imp from the *Nightmare* (no.1). The outstretched arms spreading destruction – indicated by action lines apparent even in the otherwise perfunctory pencil sketch of this composition (British Museum, London) – recall the figure of Death of Blake's lazar house (no.127) and perhaps his giant vampiric spectre in plate 33 of *Jerusalem* (no.7) and more generally Fuseli's striding heroes and villains (Blunt 1955, p.40). Such a gigantic characterisation of plague has a biblical precedent, in the various other comments to 'the destroyer', most notably in Psalm 91: 'Thou shalt not be afraid for the terror by night ... Nor for the pestilence that walketh in darkness'. It was this text that the narrator of Defoe's *Journal of the Plague Year* comes upon when seeking scriptural consolations (Defoe 1992, p.15). More speculatively, the figure's gigantic, bounding stride offers a visual rejoinder to Thomas Dekker's (c.1570–1632) 'ruffianly swaggerer (Death)' who strides cheerfully 'like a Spanish Leager, or rather like stalking *Tamberlaine*' (Morgan 1731, pp.42, 39). In that respect, we can further note the resemblance between this vast, monstrous Pestilence and the giant dancing goblin of Blake's illustration to *L'Allegro* (c.1816–20; Pierpont Morgan Library, New York).

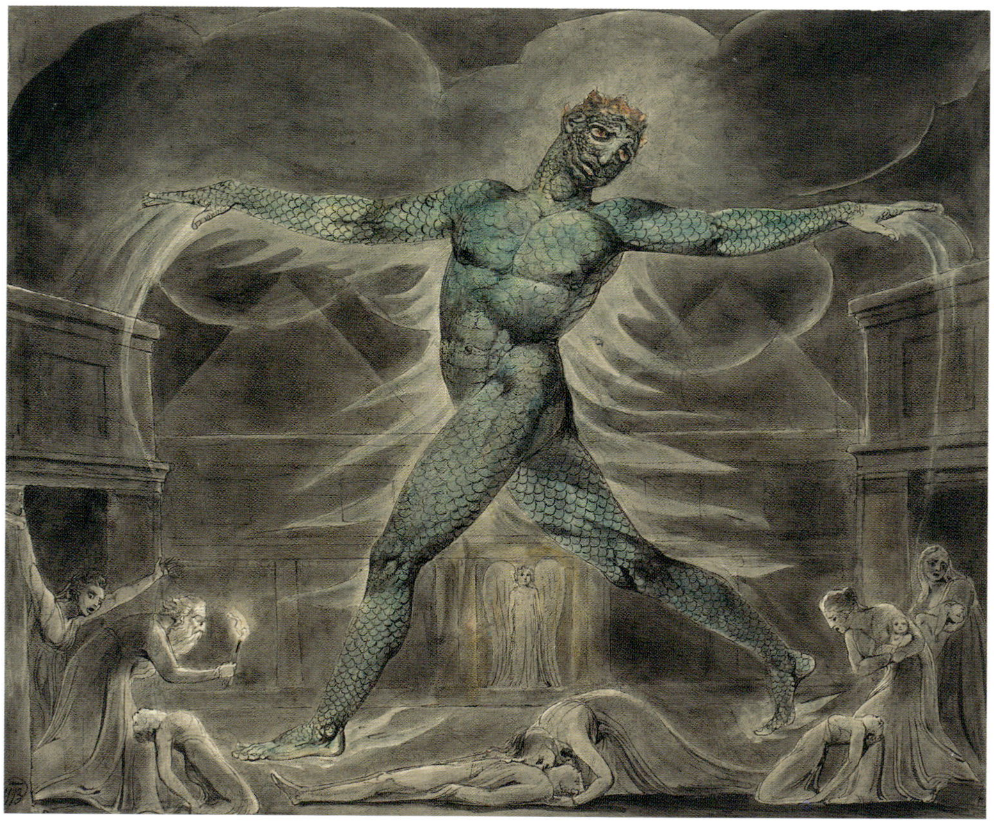

131

Joseph Haynes 1760–1829 after
John Hamilton Mortimer 1740–1779
Death on a Pale Horse published by
Jane Mortimer, 1 January 1784
Etching 68 x 46.5 cm
The British Museum, London
(1865-5-20-866)

This posthumously issued etching closely follows a large drawing (Yale Center for British Art, New Haven) which had been exhibited by Mortimer with the Society of Artists in 1775.

The subject is from Revelation chapter 6, where St John bears witness to a vision of the horsemen who will appear at the end of the world. The last of these is 'Death', riding on a 'pale horse'. In Mortimer's design, humanity is crushed under the hooves of his steed, or falls in terror; behind him fly a weird, monstrous snake, a bat-winged lizard and a toad. The basic visual format derives, ultimately, from Albrecht Dürer's famous *Four Horsemen of the Apocalypse* (see Carey 2000, p.133).

As with nos.13 and 38 , Mortimer precipitates a whole tendency in late eighteenth-century British art: here, the apocalyptic.

A newspaper critic commented that Mortimer's exhibits in 1775 were 'an additional proof of his unrivalled power in exciting the passions of fear and terror' (*London Chronicle*, 16–18 May 1775). West, Blake, de Loutherbourg and Gillray all lifted directly from his template (see nos.132–4, 136). The bold simplicity of Mortimer's composition, and the deliberately heroic proportions of the figures in what is (by the rationalist standards of the late eighteenth century) essentially a grotesque and ludicrous theme, offered a model of the balancing act that was required to negotiate between the Sublime and the ridiculous.

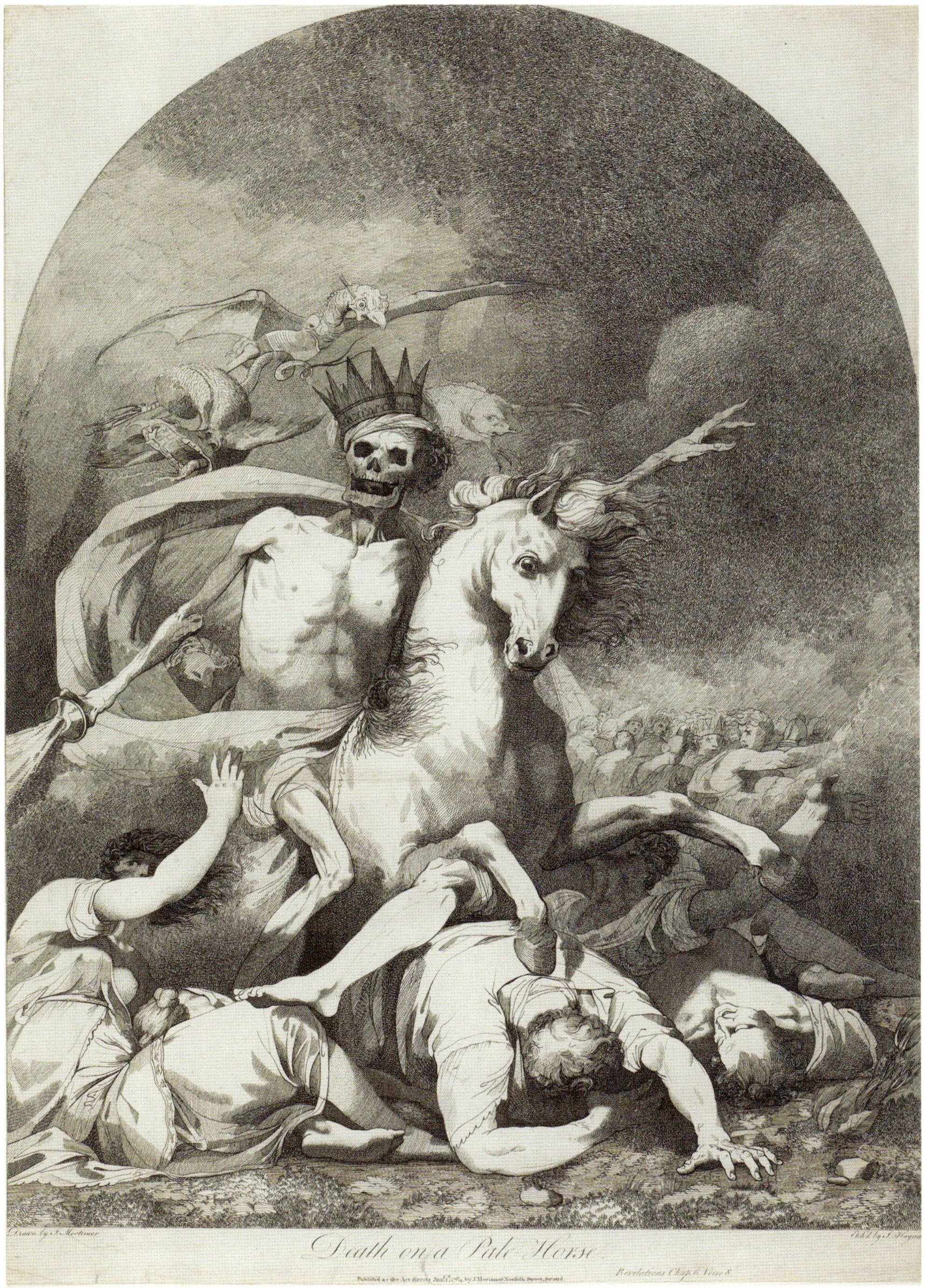

Revelation 6:1–8

AND I saw when the Lamb opened one of the seals, and I heard, as it were the noise of thunder, one of the four beasts saying, Come and see.
And I saw, and behold a white horse: and he that sat on him had a bow; and a crown was given unto him: and he went forth conquering, and to conquer.
And when he had opened the second seal, I heard the second beast say, Come and see.
And there went out another horse that was red: and power was given to him that sat thereon to take peace from the earth, and that they should kill one another: and there was given unto him a great sword.
And when he had opened the third seal, I heard the third beast come say, Come and see. And I beheld, and lo a black horse; and he that sat on him had a pair of balances in his hand.
And I heard a voice in the midst of the four beasts say, A measure of wheat for a penny, and three measures of barley for a penny; and see thou hurt not the oil and the wine.
And when he had opened the fourth seal, I heard the voice of the fourth beast say, Come and see.
And I looked, and behold a pale horse: and his name that sat on him was Death, and Hell followed with him. And power was given unto them over the fourth part of the earth, to kill with sword, and with hunger, and with death, and with the beasts of the earth.

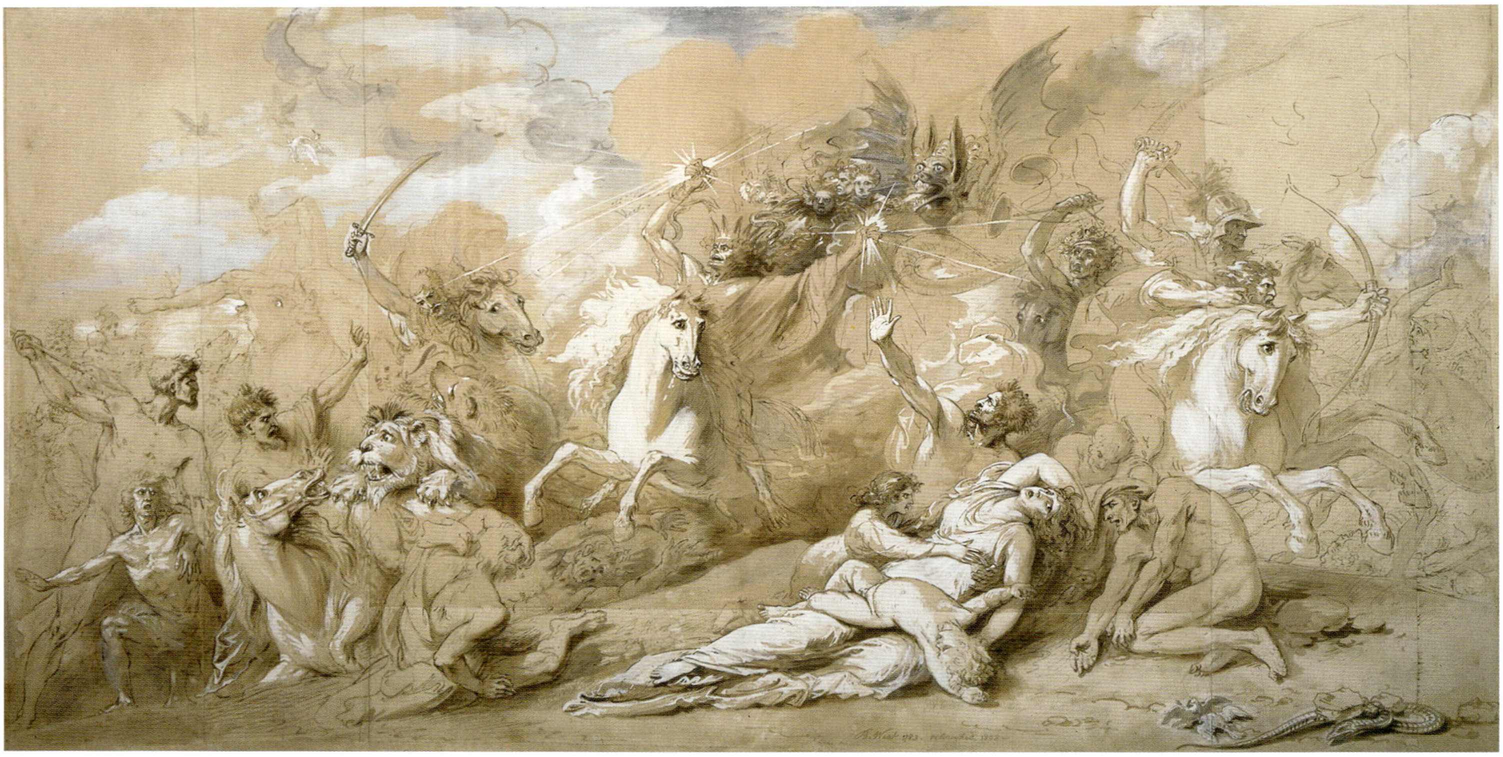

132

Benjamin West 1738–1820
Death on a Pale Horse dated 1783 and 1803, exh. RA 1784 as 'The triumph of Death, from the Revelations, a design for a picture in his Majesty's chapel at Windsor-castle'
Pen and brown ink and wash, heightened with white, on paper 57 x 112 cm
The Royal Academy of Arts, London

The image is based on Revelation 6:2–6. Death is the dominant figure at the centre, clutching lightning-bolts. The black horse of the Apocalypse is to the left, the white and red horses to the right.

The drawing was first exhibited at the Royal Academy in 1784. West returned to this image several times (Staley 1980; von Erffa and Staley 1985, nos.401–3). In 1796 he produced an oil painting (Detroit Institute of Arts), which follows this design quite closely. He later reworked this drawing – perhaps adding the white highlights – and added a new date, '1803'. In that year he also exhibited the 1796 oil painting at the annual Salon in Paris, during the temporary peace between Britain and France. It was only then that West used the more succinct title *Death on a Pale Horse*, by which these pictures are now customarily known. In 1817 he created a vast oil painting on the theme (Philadelphia Academy of Arts), developing the design in a number of ways.

Although originally designed, as his text in the exhibition catalogue of 1784 indicates, for the extensive scheme of decorations West was commissioned to create for George III's chapel at Windsor, the scheme eventually fell apart. West enjoyed a virtual monopoly on George III's patronage of history paintings, but by the beginning of the nineteenth century relations had become strained. When the painter drew up a list of proposed subjects for the scheme in 1801, he notably avoided including any apocalyptic subjects. George III had let it be known that he was displeased with the possibility of his illustrating 'Bedlamite scenes' – thus revealing the association of imaginative subjects with madness and rebellion in the post-revolutionary era, even when these were given licence by biblical references.

This design has been linked to the upheavals of the American and the French Revolutions by modern commentators. The fantastically wealthy and eccentric William Beckford (1760–1844), whose Gothic obsessions are well documented and who employed West to paint visionary subjects for his fantasy home, Fonthill, made precisely this link in a letter of 1810:

> For the future I discover only phantasms, stranger and more terrifying than those in the Apocalypse. Where is the mountains that will hide us from the wrath of a God justly angered by the massacres and ravages caused by our Cabinet, so coldly hypocritical and basely mercantile ... It will be West's Apocalypse, his Triumph of Death, painted in the same terrible colours, a mingling of mire and blood. (William Beckford to Gregorio Franchi, 10 November 1810, quoted in Paley 1986, p.31).

Richard Brothers, A Revealed Knowledge of Prophecies & Times (1794), p.69

I have said already that the SIXTH *Chapter of the Revelation was now fulfilling: the First Four Seals are opened, and the covering which has kept the meaning of the Prophecies a profound secret until the present time is removed*

(Brothers 1794, p.69)

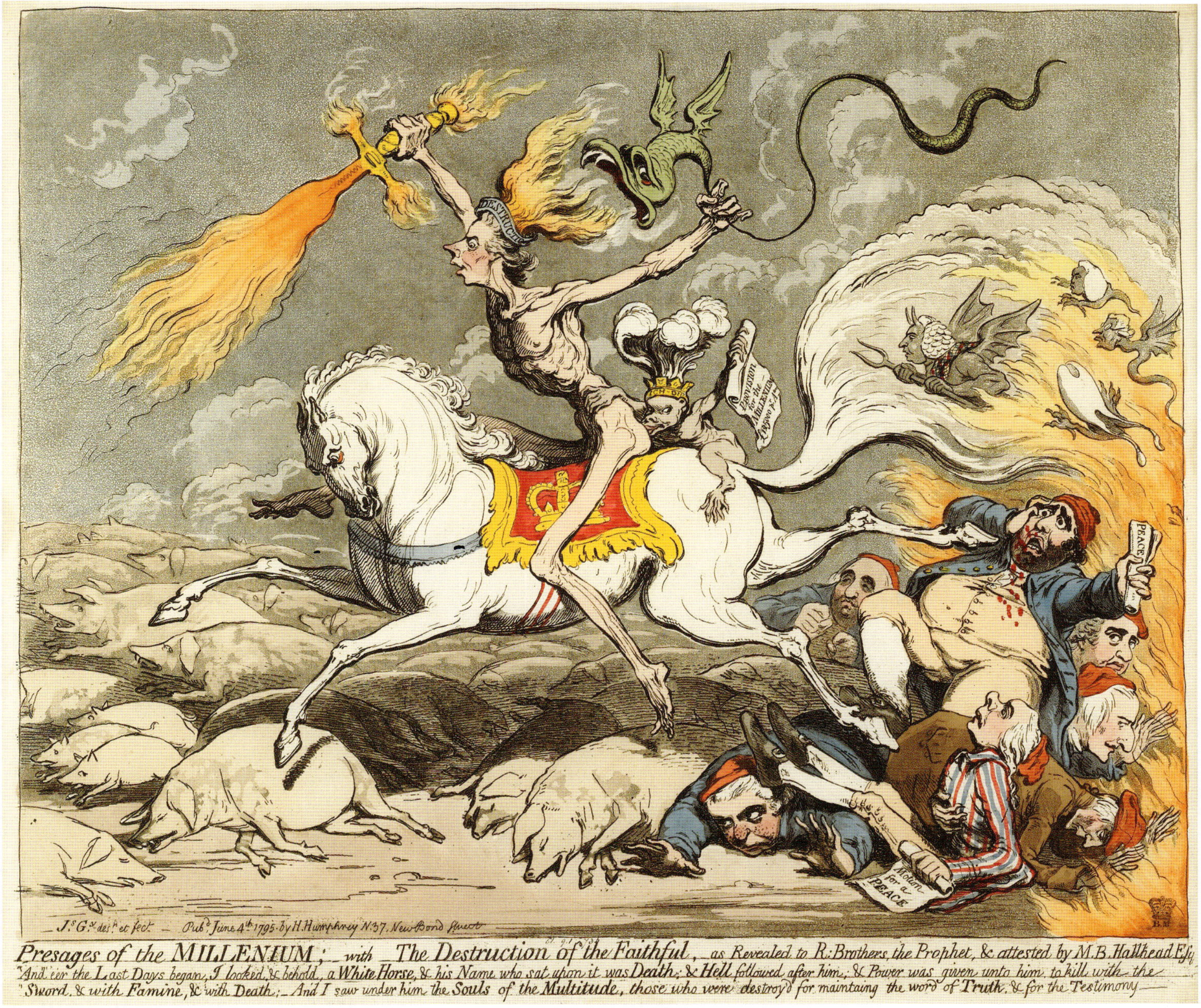

133

James Gillray 1756–1815
Presages of the Millenium; with the Destruction of the Faithful, as Revealed to R: Brothers, the Prophet, published by Hannah Humphrey, 4 June 1795
Handcoloured etching and aquatint
32.6 x 37.5 cm
The British Museum, London (1851-9-1-736)

The emaciated figure of William Pitt is shown astride a mighty white horse – the symbol of the house of Hanover as well as a biblical figure from Revelation 6 – charging through a scene of chaos, delivering death and casting his political foes into hell (George 1935–54, no.8655). The squat monkey seated behind him is the Prince of Wales (the three feathers identify this character), kissing his backside in gratitude. The reason for this obsequiousness is revealed on the paper, inscribed 'Provision for the Millenium £125,000 pr. An'. Pitt is trailed by a devilish Robert Dundas and three imps, identifiable as Lord Loughborough, Richard Pepper Arden and Edmund Burke, his distinctive profile atop a winged snake. To the right, Pitt's opponents, including Charles James Fox, are thrown into hell. The pigs are presumed to be a reference to Burke's dismissive comment about the 'Swinish Multitude' – the common people (Carey 2000, p.247).

The print satirises the prophecies of Richard Brothers (1757–1824), who had recently been arrested for treason. Brothers had announced that the apocalyptic prophecies of the Bible were coming true in the present age, and that he was the salvation of mankind and (most provocatively of all, perhaps) George III should hand the crown over to him. Revelation 6 represented to Brothers 'the present War – its progress – and consequences; and its destruction by the woeful, but just judgment of an offended God' (Brothers 1794, p.90). Aside from the political content, Gillray's target is, quite evidently, the visionary art which had been making a public appearance in recent years (Paley 1986, pp.184–6). The double-edged nature of his satire is in evidence here: while Pitt is cast as an heroic, saviour-like figure, his reckless destructiveness might attract censure, and his own bony figure looks absurd set atop the handsome white beast.

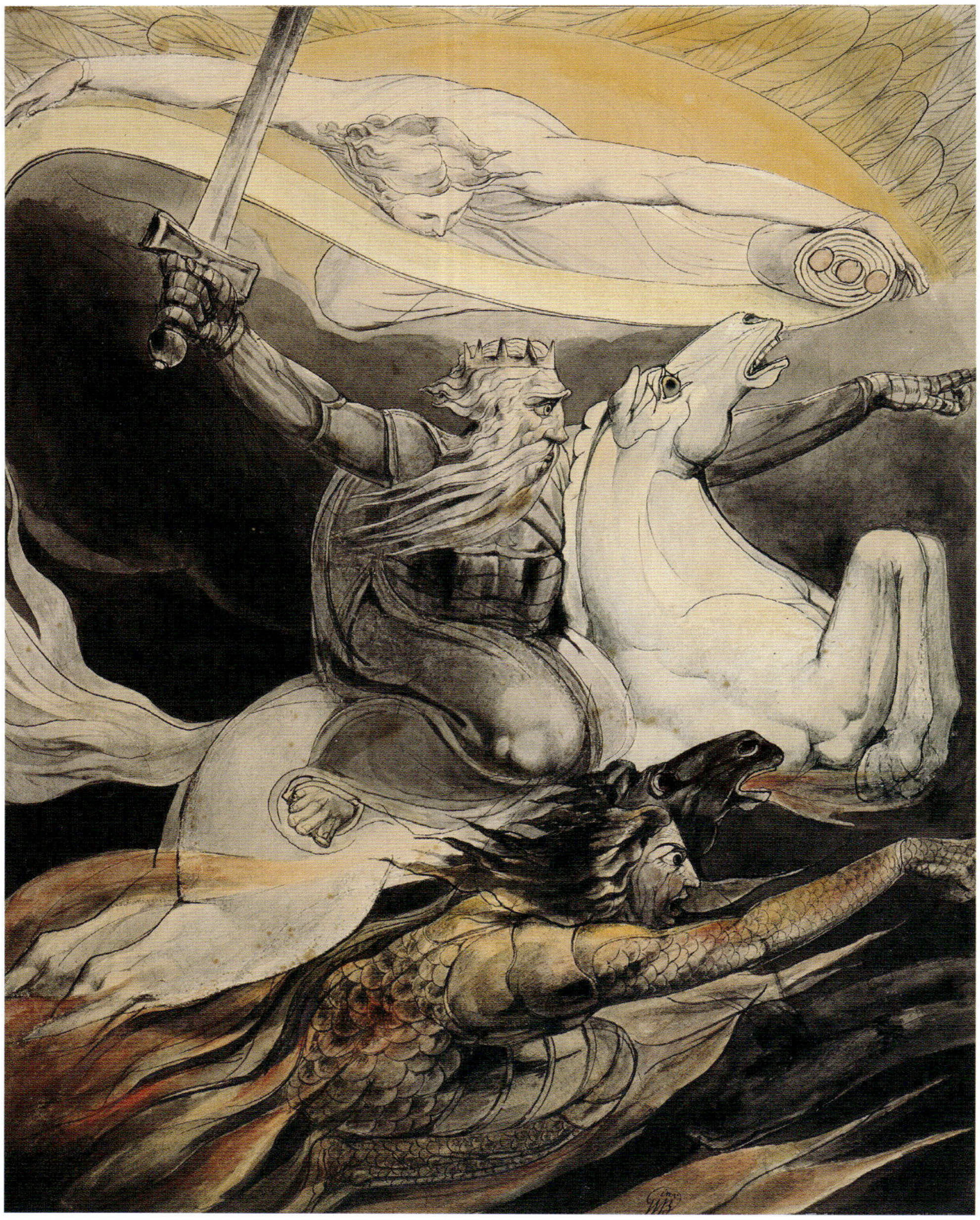

134

William Blake 1757–1827
Death on a Pale Horse c.1800
Pen, indian ink, grey wash and watercolour on paper 39.3 x 31.1 cm
The Syndics of the Fitzwilliam Museum, Cambridge

Like nos.131–3, this watercolour represents the vision at the opening of chapter 6 of the Book of Revelation. Blake depicts the final rider to appear to St John, Death, on a pale horse (Revelation 6:8), at the opening of the fourth seal (Butlin 1981, no.517). The remaining three seals can be seen on the unrolled scroll held by the angel at the top of the composition. The feathers above this figure probably refer to the image of divine protection pronounced in, for instance, Psalm 91:4 – 'He shall cover thee with his feathers, and under his wings shalt thou trust' (Paley 1986, p.83). The figure at the bottom must be the third rider, on a black horse, spreading famine, although it might also be considered as a personification of hell, as mentioned in the biblical text.

The presence of the scroll with three remaining seals, and of the black rider, should leave no doubt but that this does illustrate Revelation 6. However, Blake's characterisation of Death contrasts with the more traditional, emaciated figures conceived by Mortimer and West, conventionally armed with a fork or dart. Instead, the bulky, bearded and fierce figure evokes the crowned first rider, on a white horse, and the second horseman armed with 'a great sword'. The resemblance between Death and Blake's original conception of the warlike tyrant, Urizen, in his prophetic books of the 1790s, has also been noted (Bindman 1970, no.23). But there may be a further specific further biblical allusion. Given that de Loutherbourg's slightly earlier depiction of these figures was confused by Macklin with the vision of a white horse from Revelation 19 (see no.136), we might speculate that Blake intended some resonance with that later passage here. The rider of the white horse in the later section of Revelation is, rather than simply destructive, the harbinger of transformative war which heralds the imminent arrival of the millennium. He is a powerful and righteous figure whose mouth issues 'a sharp sword' (like Christ in St John's initial vision: see no.137). Blake's characterisation of Death in this more positive light, even as a Christ-like warrior, may suggest a more ambivalent treatment of the theme of war.

This is probably one of the first of the long series of watercolour illustrations to the Bible created by Blake for the civil servant Thomas Butts, one of his most important patrons (see no.26). David Bindman has suggested it may even have been intended as a frontispiece for the whole collection (Bindman 1970, no.23).

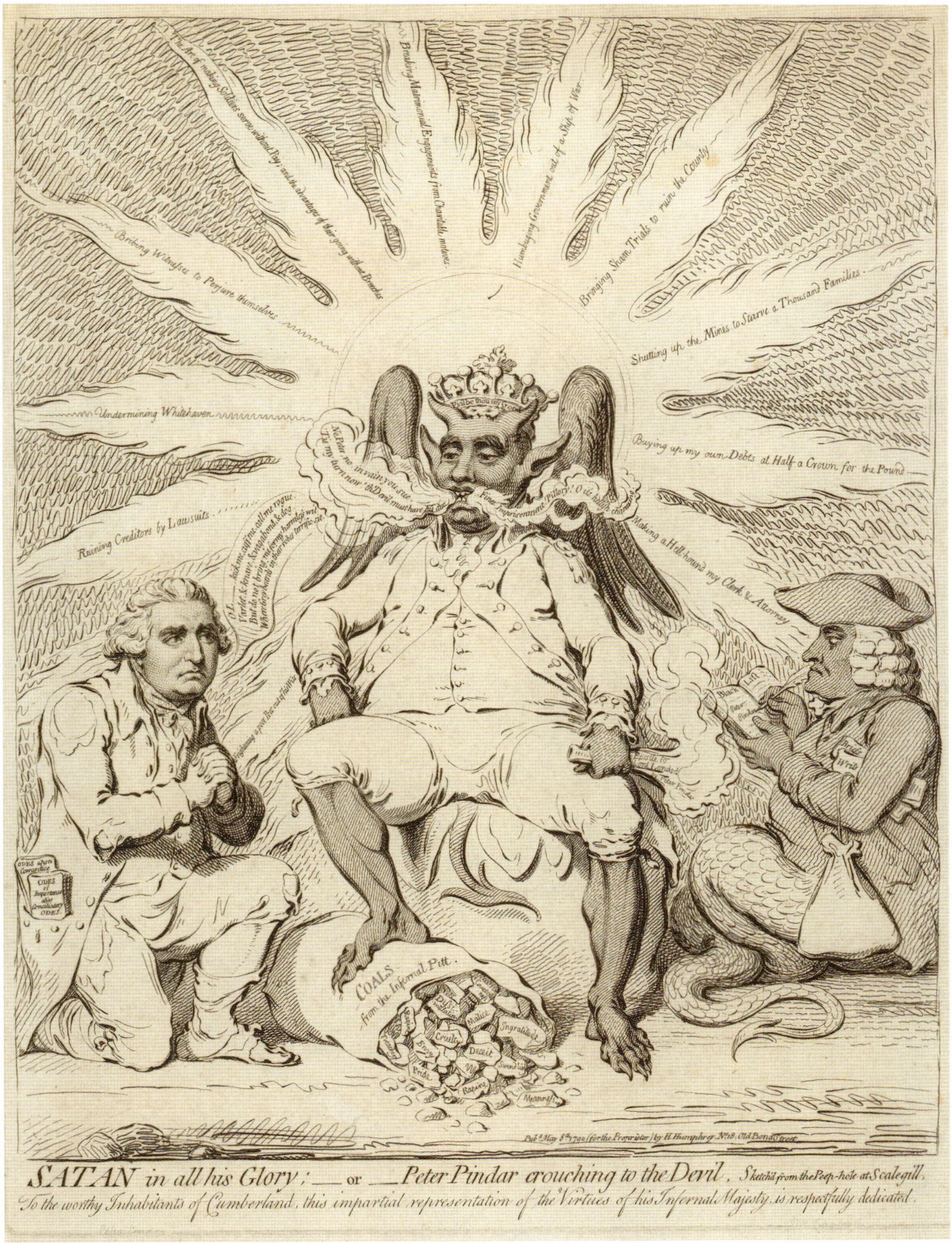

caused to local houses by the mines, to which event Lonsdale had responded by closing down his mines, promising to open them again only on the condition that he would not be held responsible for any damage to homes that they might be caused by his enterprises (see George 1935–54, no.8156).

As so often with Gillray more generally, but also with regard to the figure of Satan in the 1790s, the satire here is double-edged. This devil is a rather handsome and powerful figure; by contrast, Pindar, for whom Gillray had worked in providing illustrations for the offending publication, appears comically meek.

Richard Brothers, A Revealed Knowledge of the Prophecies & Times, London 1794

The very loud and unusual kind of Thunder that was heard in the beginning of January, 1791, was the voice of the Angel mentioned in the Eighteenth chapter of the Revelation, proclaiming the judgment of God and the fall of Babylon the great ... Read attentively the Eighteenth Chapter; and you will perceive described in it, the prodigious Wealth, Grandeur, and Commerce of London.

(Brothers 1794, pp.40, 46)

135

James Gillray 1756–1815
Satan in all his Glory; or – Peter Pindar Crouching to the Devil published by Hannah Humphreys, 8 May 1792
Etching and engraving 45.9 x 34.3 cm
The British Museum, London
(1868-8-8-10372)

The diabolical face of modern capitalism: the Earl of Lonsdale is represented as a Miltonic Satan, powerful, arrogant and gross. The words on his crown, 'Evil be thou my Good' are taken from *Paradise Lost* (Book IV, l.110). At his feet the satirical writer John Wolcot (1738–1819), who published as 'Peter Pindar', pleads for mercy. The figure with snakes instead of legs – like Milton's Sin – is a lawyer.

James Lowther, Earl of Lonsdale (1726–1802) was a notoriously foul and exploitative landowner. He accrued a huge fortune through his properties, and aggressively promoted and extended his colliery interests largely at the expense of his workers and tenants. He was remembered by a contemporary as 'more detested than any man alive ... truly a madman, though too rich to be confined' (Alexander Carlyle, *Autobiography* [1860], quoted in Beckett 2004). Wolcot had published satirical comments regarding Lonsdale's tyranny over the coalmines he owned in Cumberland. According to the satirist, a case had been won against Lonsdale regarding the damage

136

Philippe Jacques de Loutherbourg 1740–1812
Vision of the White Horse 1798
Oil on canvas 122.2 x 99.1 cm
Tate. Purchased 1969

Like Mortimer and West, de Loutherbourg illustrates Revelation 6:2–4, although he depicts only the first two riders revealed to St John, those riding the white and the red horses.

The painting was created for Thomas Macklin's Bible Gallery, a commercial gallery featuring paintings of biblical subjects that were latterly engraved (Boase 1963; Groom 1992). Following the example of John Boydell's Shakespeare Gallery (see no.87), Macklin established the scheme with the intention of publicising a new luxury edition of the Bible, incorporating large engraved plates and further illustrations. De Loutherbourg was the greatest single contributor to his Bible Gallery and, beside the twenty-two of the seventy-one main plates, engraved many of the headpieces. The project was admirably adapted to his highly theatrical approach and his rather esoteric spiritual interests (see Daniels 1992; MacCalman 2005).

When this painting was engraved by John Landseer (1769–1852) for Macklin in 1800, the print gave the biblical reference as Revelation 19:11–12, which describes the vision of 'a white horse' whose rider was 'Faithful and True, and in righteousness he doth judge and make war'. However, that figure, often identified as Christ in a martial role, leads the armies of God in their final triumph, heralding the millennium. The biblical rider has 'many crowns' on his head, a 'vesture dipped in blood' and a double-edged sword coming from his mouth (like Christ in no.137). The bow and crown of de Loutherbourg's figure, and the presence of a second rider, would make it certain that it is the earlier passage that is represented here. It is not known whether this was an honest misunderstanding on the part of Macklin, or an attempt to contrive a better distribution of images through the volumes than might otherwise be possible. Still, the title on that print, *The Vision of the White Horse* has become standard, compounding the error.

Revelation 19:11–12

And I saw heaven opened, and behold a white horse; and he that sat upon it was called Faithful and True, and in righteousness he doth judge and make war.
His eyes were as flames of fire, and on his head were many crowns; and he had a name written, that no man knew, but himself.

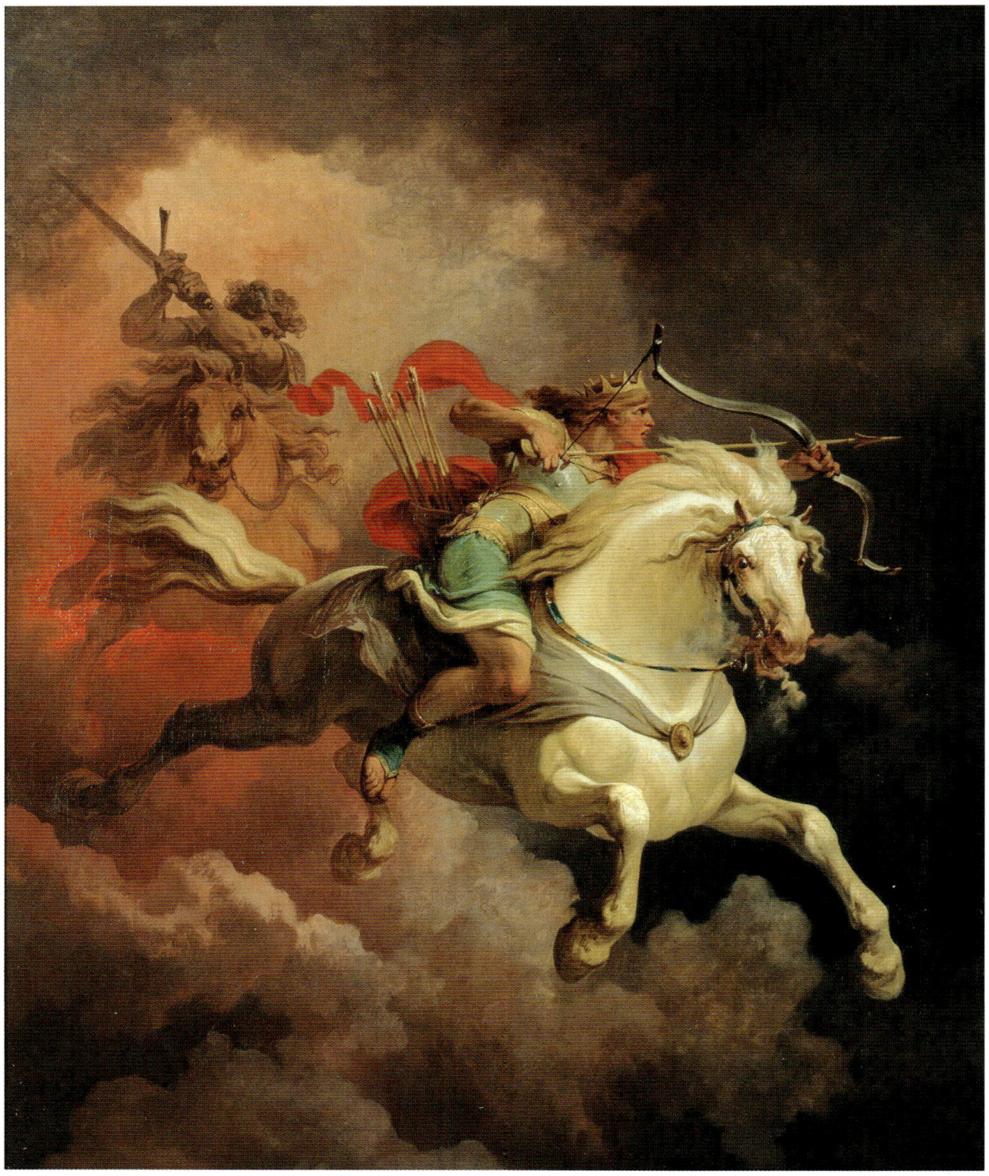

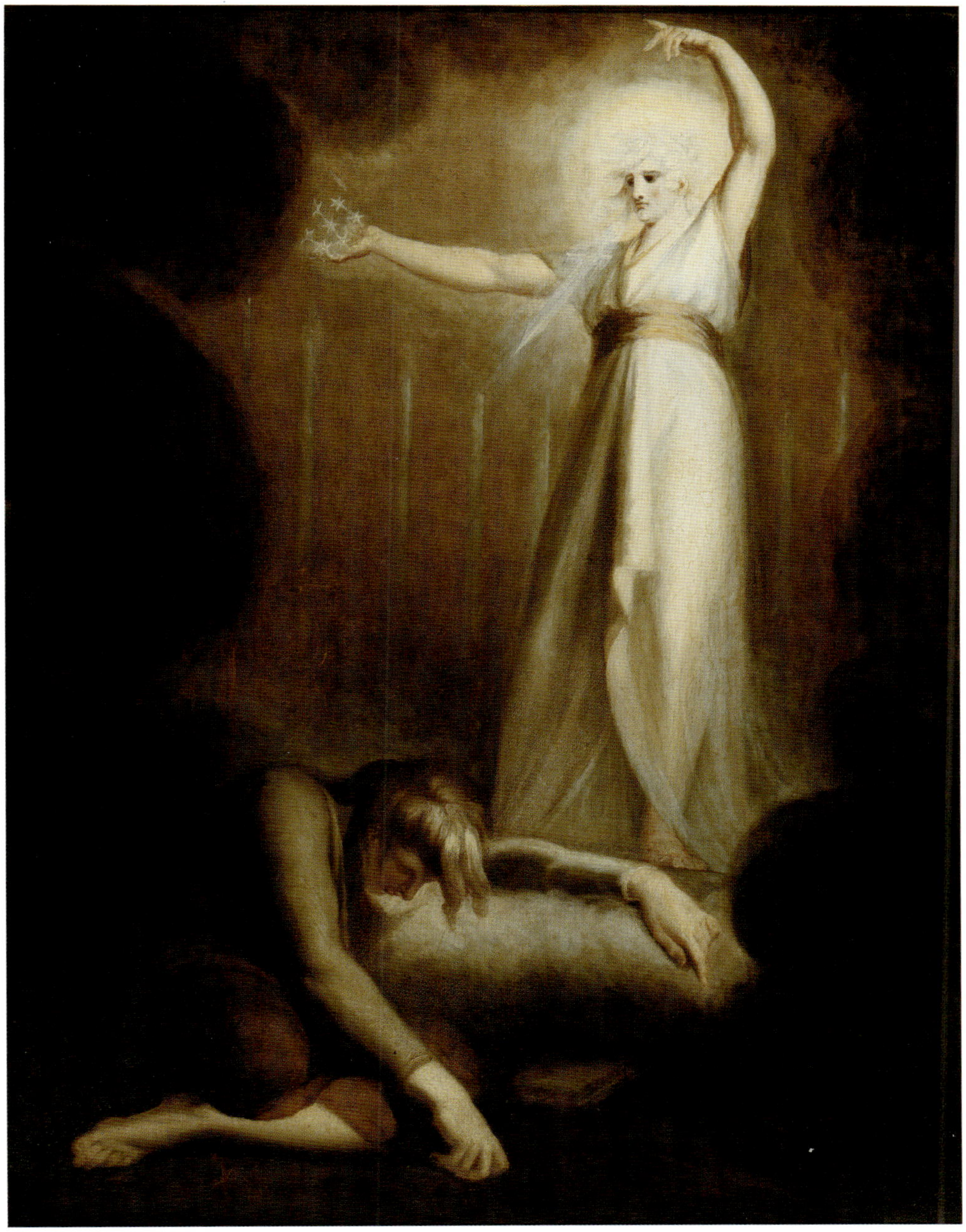

137

Henry Fuseli 1741–1825
St John's Vision of the Seven Candlesticks
1796
Oil on canvas 132 x 101 cm
Ivor Braka Ltd, London

At the beginning of the Book of Revelation, St John describes being struck down 'as if dead' by the vision of a white-clad Christ in the midst of seven golden candles. Fuseli's painting presents a literal visual interpretation of the scene.

Like de Loutherbourg's *Vision of the White Horse* (no.136), this painting was commissioned for Thomas Macklin's Bible Gallery. Fuseli was seeking a commission in the summer of 1795, but he knew that Macklin may be reluctant as he had worked so much more extensively for Boydell and the publisher suspected – apparently correctly – that he had published a negative review of his previous venture, the Poets Gallery (Henry Fuseli to William Roscoe, 14 August 1795, in Weinglass 1982, pp.137–9). By April 1796, with William Roscoe acting as broker, the commission looked likely, and Fuseli was proposing to paint 'the Seven candlesticks or the Pope Spitting frogs' (Henry Fuseli to William Roscoe, 5 April 1796, Weinglass 1982, p.147). The latter subject, interpreting Revelation in anti-Catholic terms (as was usual among Protestants), was discarded as a possibility, and though Fuseli quipped 'I am not in the habits of handling Candlesticks', he noted that John's vision 'offers a Very grand Subject and perhaps the grandest of all, M. has offered to the Public' (Henry Fuseli to William Roscoe, 15 April 1796, in Weinglass 1982, p.149). The present canvas was completed by August that year. However, Fuseli, always sensitive about the restrictions and unpredictable nature of such commissions, grew unhappy about the engraving of this work: he felt that the artist commissioned to execute the reproduction of this painting was inexperienced, and that in this Macklin was slighting him (see Weinglass 1994, no.141). And although he heard on the grapevine that Macklin was satisfied with his contribution, Fuseli was disappointed not to be further employed by him. For his part, Macklin had said that he was 'also afraid to employ Fuseli on acct. of the great inequality of his works' (Farington 1978–98, I, p.215).

The upright format, with a large figure of the deity occupying the upper portion of the composition and a slumped, seated or supine St John below, has been traced to an engraved illustration in Johann Rudolf Wirz's *Romae animale exemplum* (1677) or further to a woodcut of 1523 by Hans Burgkmair (1473–1531) (Schiff 1973, no.931; Sotheby's, 12 November 1997, no.120). Even that latter source may have referred back to Albrecht Dürer's woodcut of 1498, and that, in turn, to medieval sources (see Carey 2000, nos.7, 25, 27 and p.104, fig.2 for the Dürer and further examples). More pertinently, Fuseli's treatment compares closely with William Blake's of the same theme, included among his youthful illustrations for a commercially published Bible in 1782 (Essick 1991, no.III.5). This was claimed as an original composition, but in fact derives from a design by Bernard Picart (1673–1733). Fuseli's concern has evidently not been with compositional innovation, and is rather with the refinement of a pictorial formula to enhance its Sublime impact. His conception of a youthful, athletic Christ and the bizarre, heavy-limbed collapse of St John combine to economical physical drama, playing on a vivid contrast between the heavy, material body and the supreme grace of the deity. The low viewpoint and the high-waisted costume of Christ (perhaps suggestive of contemporary female costumes) further enhance this effect.

138

William Blake 1757–1827
The Whirlwind: Ezekiel's Vision of the Cherubim and Eyed Wheels c.1803–5
Pen and ink and watercolour on paper
39.5 x 29.5 cm
Museum of Fine Arts, Boston. Gift by subscription

139

William Blake 1757–1827
Satan in his Original Glory: 'Thou Wast Perfect Till Iniquity was found in Thee' c.1805
Pen and ink and watercolour on paper
42.9 x 33.9 cm
Tate. Presented by the executors of W. Graham Robertson through the National Art Collections Fund 1949

Two complex biblical allegories derived from the prophetic book of Ezekiel in the Old Testament. Both were painted for Thomas Butts as part of the extended sequence of watercolour illustrations to the Bible created for him by Blake. The Book of Ezekiel was of particular significance to Blake, representing an authentic prophetic vision and providing him with some of his most important motifs – particularly in the symbolism around the number four and its multiples (see Herrstrom 1981).

No.138 is dense with imagery and difficult to interpret (Butlin 1981, no.468; Grant 1972). The design alludes to the opening vision of the Book of Ezekiel. The diminutive figure at the bottom of the composition is the prophet, lying captive on the bank of the river Chebar, looking in awe as a whirlwind delivers the vision of a man, whose fourfold aspect – with four faces and four wings – anticipates the four Evangelists or the four Beasts of the Apocalypse, and Blake's 'Four Zoas' that underpin much of his imagery. As envisioned by Blake, this humanoid vision takes the form of a cherub – like Satan in his original glory – a guarding, protective angel. As the vision unfolds, Ezekiel witnesses a wheel 'full of eyes', hears the voice of God, and sees 'the likeness of a throne' and the 'likeness of a man' – a vision of 'the glory of the LORD'.

As David Bindman has noted, Blake's greatest triumph here would seem to be his ability to convey in visual terms the sense of overwhelming, ceaseless movement evoked by the biblical text (Bindman 1977, p.142). In this we might detect some political resonance as well. The editor of *Prophetic Conjectures on the French Revolution, and Other Recent and Shortly Expected Events* (London 1793) elaborated Ezekiel's vision of the wheel as an allegory of the bloody political upheaval that will herald the millennium: 'The wheel subsists by *revolutions* ... if the voice from heaven cry, "REVOLUTION!", in vain would all the powers upon earth attempt to arrest the motions of those wheels' (pp.62–3).

No.139 alludes to Ezekiel 28:11–19, where God describes to Ezekiel the 'king of Tyrus' – understood as an alternative name for, or embodiment of, Satan – in his former glorious state, standing on the 'mountain of God' (Butlin 1990, no.44; also Bindman 1970, p.142). The passage alluded to here is preceded by ten lines addressed to the 'prince of Tyrus', perhaps meant as an historical personage. The tiny, joyous figures may be taken as embodying the luminescent precious stones and beautifully crafted musical instruments mentioned in the biblical text. The stars and globes beneath the figure's feet could be interpreted as the 'stones of fire' that the king of Tyrus walks among; the

138

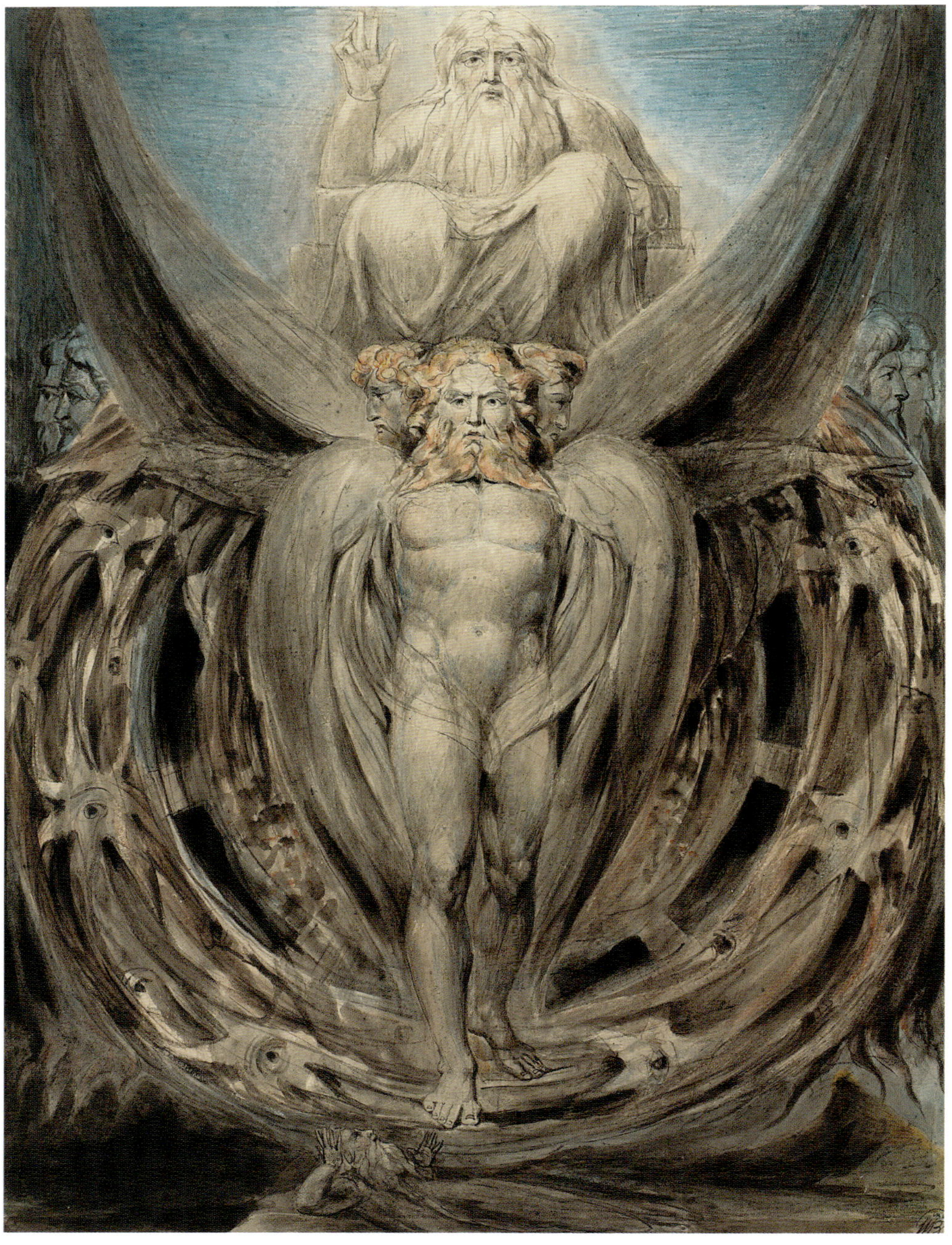

139

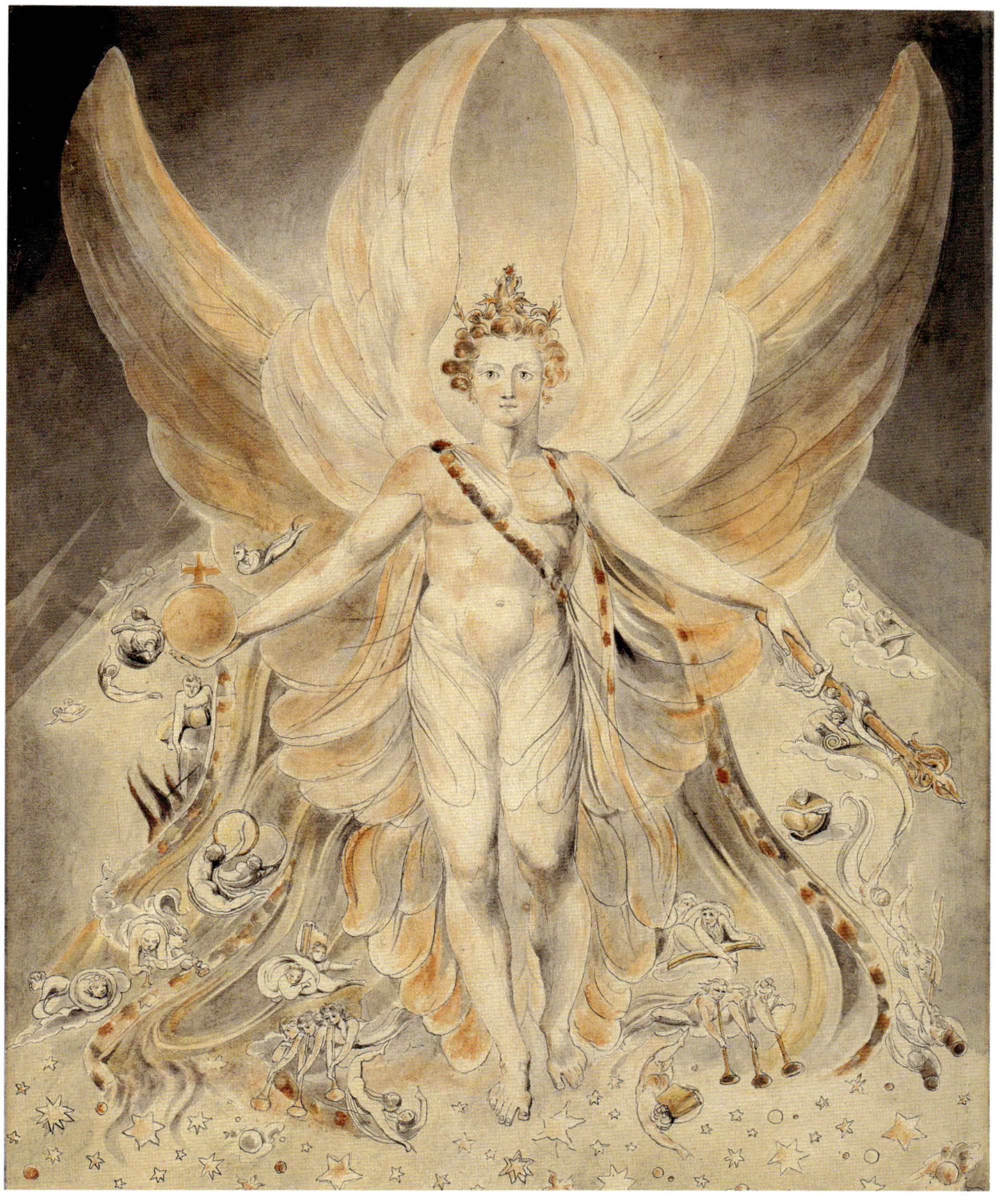

abstract forms of the background may indicate a mountaintop. The orb and sceptre are iconographic additions by Blake, perhaps alluding to Satan's assumption of tyrannical powers and regal status. This treatment of the 'king of Tyrus' is ostentatiously classical, evoking the ideal of the Apollo-like athleticism and beauty (Warner 1984, p.5). The large wings visualise Satan as 'the anointed cherub that covereth', using feathers as a symbol of divine protection, as in no.134. Blake's intention would seem to be to present an heroic version of Satan. This image has also been interpreted as an opposition to or parody of the goodly vision of no.138 (Herrstrom 1981, p.75 n.4).

Ezekiel 1:4–11

And I looked, and, behold, a whirlwind came out of the north, a great cloud, and a fire infolding itself, and a brightness was *about it, and out of the midst thereof as the colour of amber, out of the midst of the fire.*

Also out of the midst thereof came *the likeness of four living creatures. And this was their appearance; they had the likeness of a man.*

And every one had four faces, and every one had four wings.

And their feet were *straight feet; and the sole of their feet* was *like the sole of a calf's foot: and they sparkled like the colour of burnished brass.*

And they had *the hands of a man under their wings on their four sides; and they four had their faces and their wings.*

Their wings were *joined one to another; they turned not when they went; they went every one straight forward.*

As for the likenesses of their faces, they four had the face of a man, and the face of a lion, on the right side: and they four had the face of an ox on the left side; they four also had the face of an eagle.

Thus were *their faces: and their wings* were *stretched upward; two* wings *of every one* were *joined one to another, and two covered their bodies.*

Ezekiel 28:12–15

Son of man, take up a lamentation upon the king of Tyrus, and say unto him, Thus saith the Lord GOD; Thou sealest up the sum, full of wisdom, and perfect in beauty.

Thou hast been in Eden the garden of God; every precious stone was *thy covering, the sardius, topaz, and the diamond, the beryl, the onyx, and the jasper, the sapphire, the emerald, and the carbuncle, and gold: the workmanship of thy tabrets and of thy pipes was prepared in thee in the day that thou wast created.*

Thou art the anointed cherub that covereth; and I have set thee so: thou wast upon the hold mountain of God; thou wast upon the holy mountain of God; thou hast walked up and down in the midst of stones of fire.

Thou wast perfect in thy ways from that day that thou wast created, till iniquity was found in thee.

140

William Blake 1757–1827
David Delivered out of Many Waters c.1805
Pen and ink and watercolour on paper
41.5 x 34.8 cm
Tate. Presented by George Thomas Saul 1878

A complex and still elusive biblical allegory. At the top a youthful Christ descends in a golden glow, floating above a regimented group of angels, each with four wings which interlock in forms suggestive of Gothic architecture. At the bottom, in a black and churning sea, an old bearded man looks up at this heavenly vision, his arms tied back stiffly by ropes.

This watercolour has traditionally been taken to allude to the images of salvation in Psalms 18 (Butlin 1990, no.41). The prophet David, bound by ropes into the attitude of crucifixion and floating helpless in a black sea, is salved by the arrival of a divine spirit riding on the backs of 'a cherub': 'yea, but he did fly upon the wings of the wind' (Psalms 18:10). The cherub is elaborated by Blake into a vision which has been taken as representing the Four Ages of Man, drawn together to embody the Seven Eyes of God (Tolley 1972, pp.29–30). His introduction of a vision of Christ into an Old Testament scene fits with standard eighteenth-century Christian interpretations of the Hebrew Bible, which would see these earlier evocations of the divine as anticipations of the figure of Jesus.

However, this interpretation has never been wholly satisfactory. As Christopher Heppner notes, the proposal that Blake represents the Seven Eyes of God cannot be upheld, as we can see the hands of additional angels to the left and right, meaning that the artist wanted visibly to indicate the presence of nine, and perhaps to imply that there were many more (Heppner 1995, pp.190–2). Mary Lynn Johnson has proposed that the watercolour further alludes to Psalms 130 and 139, and most importantly to Psalm 69 (Johnson 1990), where an older and wiser David appeals for salvation from the 'deep waters, where the floods overflow me' (Psalm 69:2). She interprets this design as combining the imagery of Psalms 18 and 69, the former representing the youthful warrior David – who we might expect Blake to find misguided – the latter the wiser, more humble older man. Noting that the figure astray in the bleak sea is the same size as his deity, Johnson concludes that, in contrast to the overwhelming visions experienced by the diminutive prophets in nos.138 or 142, here 'Blake depicts the merciful and empathic response to the human situation of a deity conceived within the imagination of a sufferer who ... has transcended his own self-pity' (Johnson 1990, pp.129–30).

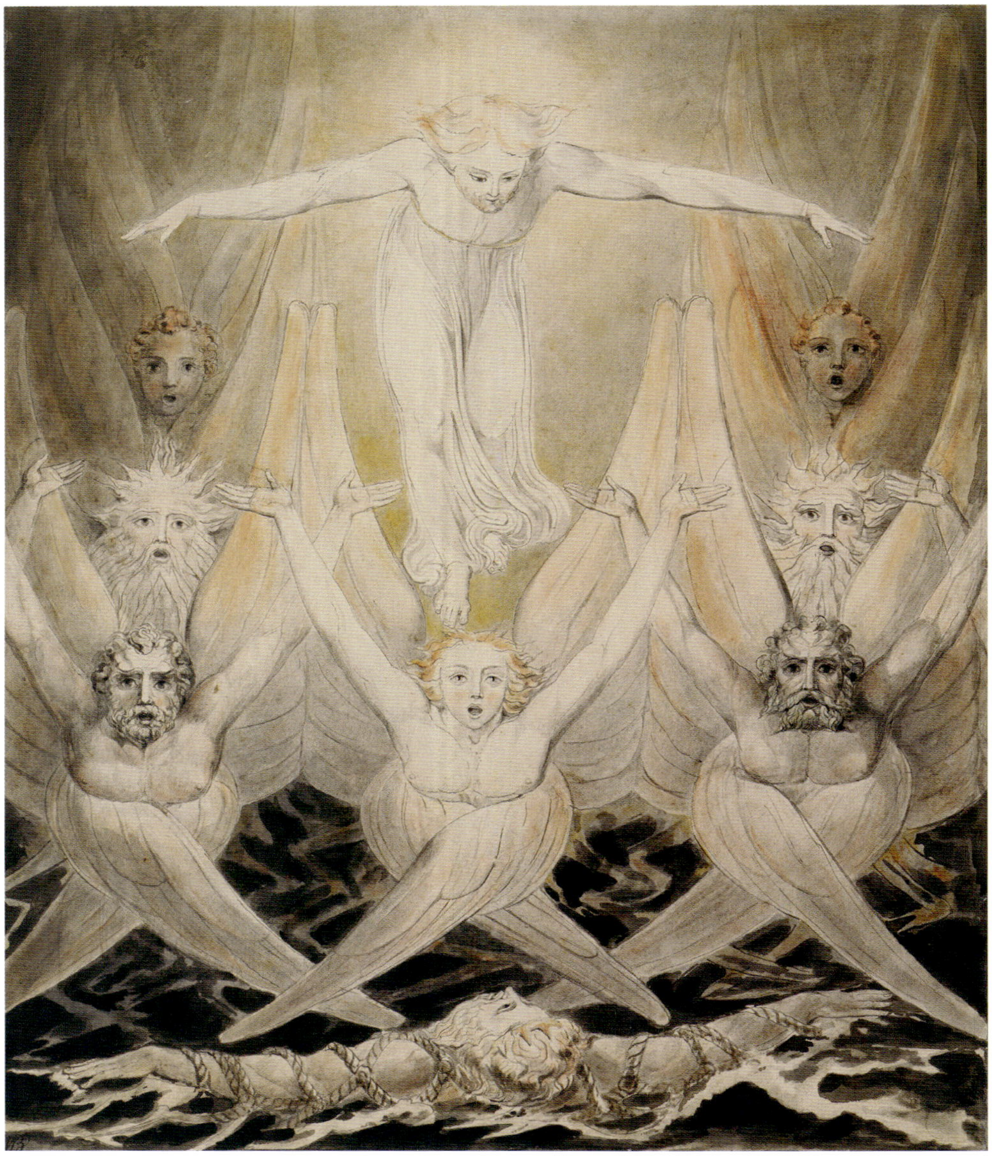

Psalm 69:14–20

Deliver me out of the mire, and let me not sink: let me be delivered from them that hate me, out of the deep waters.
Let not the waterflood overflow me: neither let the deep swallow me up, and let not the put shut her mouth upon me.
Hear me, O LORD; for thy loving-kindness is good: turn unto me according to the multitudes of thy tender mercies.
And hide not thy face from thy servant: for I am in trouble: hear me speedily.
Drew nigh unto my soul, and redeem it: deliver me because of mine enemies.
Thou hast known my reproach, and my shame, and my dishonour: mine adversaries are all before thee.
Reproach hath broken my heart; and I am full of heaviness: and I looked for some to take pity, but there was none; and for comforters, but I found none.

141

William Blake 1757–1827
The Four and Twenty Elders Casting their Crowns before the Divine Throne c.1805
Pencil and watercolour on paper
35.4 x 29.3 cm
Tate. Presented by the executors of W. Graham Robertson through the National Art Collections Fund 1949

This watercolour (Butlin 1990, no.51) is a further illustration of the Book of Revelation, in this case Chapters 4 and 5. St John witnesses the glorious vision of a bejewelled throne surrounded by a rainbow. Around the throne are twenty-four elders dressed in white, wearing golden crowns, and 'four beasts full of eyes before and behind' – an eagle, a beast with the face of a man, a calf and a lion. The elders, neatly lined up by Blake, cast down their crowns – the symbols of temporal power – before the greater authority of God. The deity, enthroned, holds in his right hand 'a book written within and on the backside, sealed with seven seals'. The opening of these seals will be described in Revelation 6 (and are illustrated here, in nos.131–4, 136). Before the throne is 'a Lamb, as it had been slain, having seven horns and seven eyes, which are the seven Spirits of God sent forth into all the earth'. The seven spikes rising from the back of the lamb might be taken as alluding to these 'horns', the seven cherubim as representing the 'Spirits of God' referred to here, and by the 'seven lamps of fire' of Revelation 4:5.

St John's vision elaborates and transforms Ezekiel's vision of the whirlwind, painted by Blake in no.138.

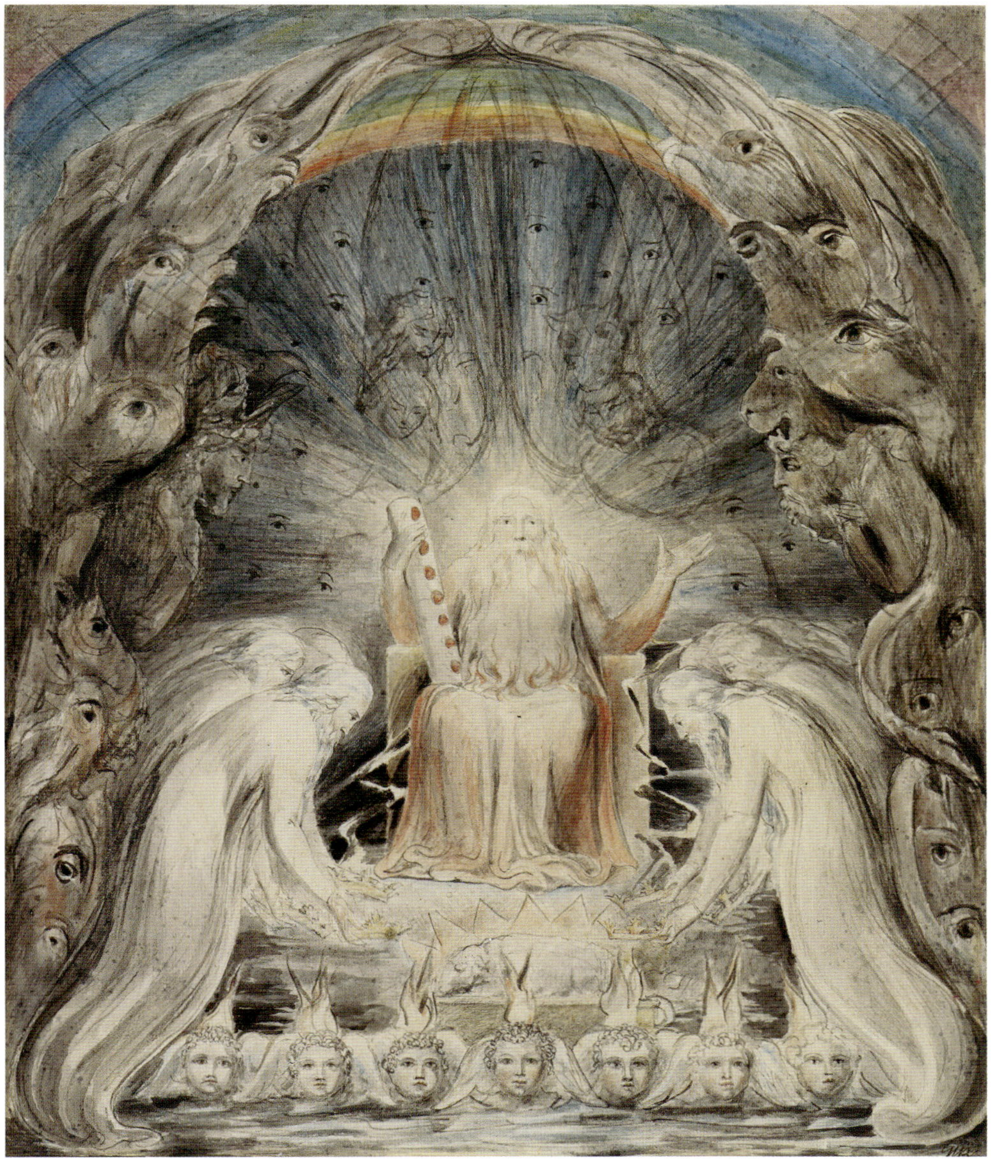

142

William Blake 1757–1827
God Writing on the Tables of the Covenant
c.1805
Pen and ink and watercolour on paper
40.6 x 33.2 cm
National Gallery of Scotland, Edinburgh

In a scene of fiery revelation Moses bows before God in abject submission as the deity inscribes the Law of the Commandments. Moses is shown as a comically diminutive figure, curled into an almost snail-like form at the bottom of the composition. God is a youthful, heroically muscular figure (see Butlin 1981, no.448).

The inscription on the original mount suggested that the specific text alluded to by Blake is from the Book of Deuteronomy (9:10):

> And the LORD delivered unto me two tables of stone written with the finger of God; and on them was written according to all the words, which the LORD spake with you in the mount out of the midst of the fire in the day of the assembly.

Blake's rejection of the laws set down in the historical books of the Old Testament is well documented. While the prophetic books, poetic, allusive and open-ended as they are, were a powerful resource for his writings and his art, for him the Mosaic Law was the subject of scorn. So, in contrast with the visions witnessed by Ezekiel and David in nos.138 and 140, Moses is here refused a sight of the deity's face. While their visions are full and honest, that of Moses is restricted and remote, and therefore potentially deceptive (see Johnson 1990, p.119).

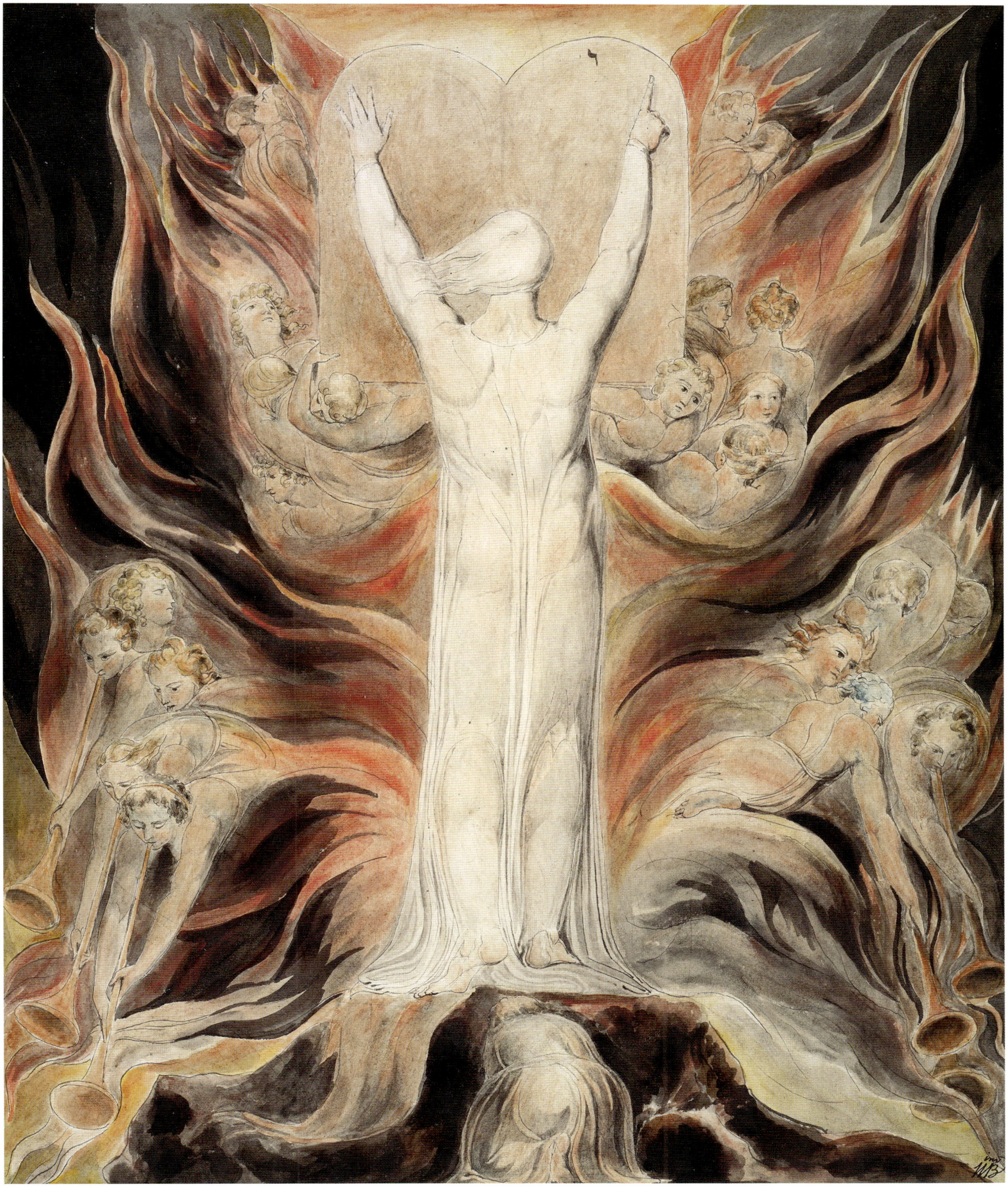

143a

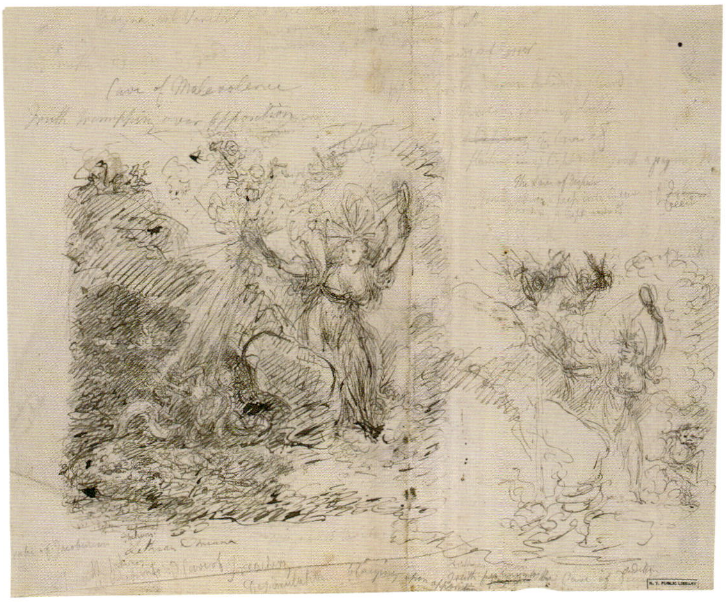

143b

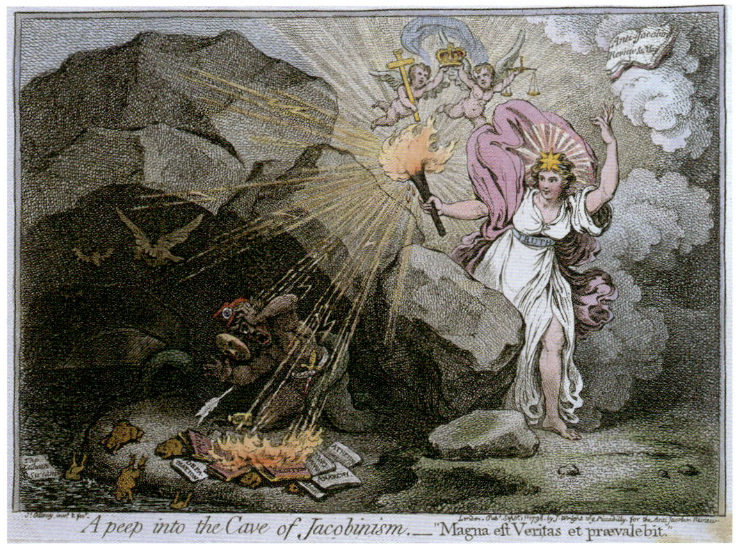

143a

James Gillray 1756–1815
Preparatory drawing for *A Peep into the Cave of Jacobinism* 1798
Pen and ink and pencil on paper 31.5 x 36.6 cm
Print Collection, Miriam and Ira D. Wallach Division of Art, Prints and Photographs, The New York Public Library, Astor, Lenox and Tilden Foundations

143b

James Gillray 1756–1815
A Peep into the Cave of Jacobinism
published by J. Wright for *The Anti-Jacobin Magazine and Review*, 1 September 1798
Handcoloured etching and engraving
19.4 x 26.2 cm
With permission of the Warden and Scholars of New College, Oxford

This (George 1935–54, no.9243) was the frontispiece for first volume of the reactionary periodical, *The Anti-Jacobin Magazine and Review*, published in 1798. The figure of Truth holds up a torch, illuminating the dark cave of political sedition from which emanates the Lethean Stream (the river of forgetfulness in classical myth). The pamphlets strewn on the ground read 'Libels', 'Defamation', 'Sedition', 'Ignorance', 'Anarchy' and 'Atheism' – the leading themes of revolutionary politics according to the conservative view. The Latin motto is that of *The Anti-Jacobin*: '*Magna est Veritas et prævalebit*' ('Truth is great and will prevail'; 1 Esdras 4: 41).

The Anti-Jacobin Magazine and Review was the long-lived successor to *The Anti-Jacobin, or Weekly Examiner*. While that publication had run only for a period of months between November 1797 and July 1798, the *Review* eventually ran for sixty-one volumes, the last being published in 1821. Both magazines featured commentaries, reviews and poetry directed against the (according to the editors) rampant tendency to social rebellion, moral corruption and sexual dissidence inspired by the French Revolution and associated with all kinds of free thinking. The often violent sentiments expressed in the pages of these publications helped shape a deep-rooted sense of conservatism that dominated British culture in these years.

Although his personal politics remain vague, Gillray was in the pay of the reactionary government around this time, producing prints that supported (although perhaps not unequivocally) William Pitt and his repressive brand of politics. However, such direct government support of scurrilous prints was a matter of considerable discretion; the original *Anti-Jacobin* was closed down at least in part because the identity of its authors – which included prominent members of the government – was becoming more widely-known.

Gillray's satire effectively inverts the associations of radical reason with enlightenment proffered in the symbolism of revolution and taken up by British sympathisers, such as this commentator from the mid-1790s: 'It is an enlightened age ... may we soon see all Europe imitating the example of France, likely erecting a throne in every land, Slavery skulking away to the dens and caves of the earth, and Superstition hiding her gloomy visage from the eyes of man' (editor's comment in Goodwin 1796, pp.52–3; see also Jordonova 1990).

Gillray's original drawing (no.143a) shows his characteristically vigorous, expressive draughtsmanship, and the very great efforts he went to in drafting and redrafting the possible textual elements of such prints. Among these notes can be found an indication of titles and ideas: 'Cave of Malevolence', 'Truth trampling over Opposition', 'Peep into the cave of Deceit', 'Clouds of Error', 'The Cave of Despair', 'Cave of Sedition', 'Shrinking from ye Light'. Such sheets as this are clearly working tools, though the frantic outpouring of thoughts and images is such that they may call to our minds the artist's approaching mental decline.

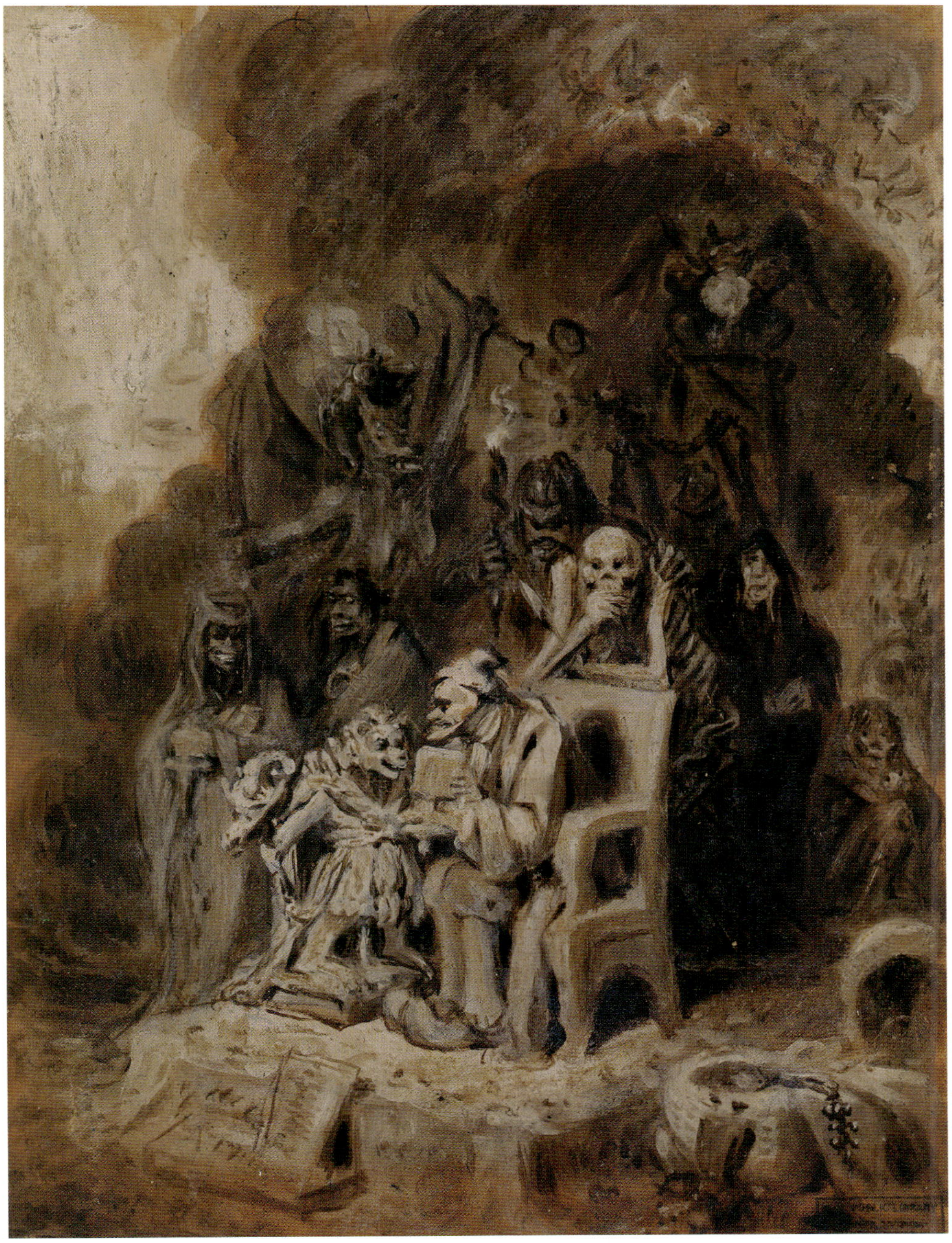

144

James Gillray 1756–1815
Voltaire Instructing the Infant Jacobinism
c.1800
Oil on paper 27.3 x 20.3 cm
Print Collection, Miriam and Ira D. Wallach Division of Art, Prints and Photographs, The New York Public Library, Astor, Lenox and Tilden Foundations

A monster-infant representing revolutionary democracy – the creed of Jacobinism – is shown receiving his education at the knee of the French philosopher Voltaire (1694–1778). Spectral and monstrous figures lurk in the shadows around them, embodying the various sins and misunderstandings being instilled into the youth by the old thinker.

Draper Hill has proposed that this painted sketch is meant to illustrate the 'Ode to Jacobinism', published by *The Anti-Jacobin or Weekly Examiner* and reissued in the collections of anti-Jacobin poetry published from 1799 (Hill 1965, pp.100–1; see also Godfrey 2001, no.72). We may be able to detect, beyond Voltaire and the infant Jacobinism, figures of Revenge (on the far left, smiling), Ingratitude (the next figure, 'With anxious eye wild glancing round'), Death (the skeleton) and Poverty (the figure crouching to the right). Injustice, Anguish, and the Destroyer further mentioned in the text, with their 'Fire, rapine, sword and chains', may be represented by the other figures gathered around Voltaire's chair. The white horse at the top of the composition might evoke the figure of Death on a pale horse (which Gillray had already lampooned, see no.133), perhaps the white horse of Hanover, or part of a group representing 'Domestic Virtue, Social Joy' who flee from encroaching Jacobinism in the 'Ode'.

As a rationalist, materialist and liberal, Voltaire was seen by British conservatives as the forerunner of the worst principles of the French Revolution – what Burke called, in a scathing perversion of the ideal of enlightenment, 'this new conquering empire of light and reason' (Burke 1987, p.67). He was, as the conservative newspaper *The Times* had put it 'the professed apostle of infidelity – whose writings make a mockery of every religious faith upon the face of the globe – who lived a blasphemer and died blaspheming' (5 July 1791, quoted in Ascherson 1975, p.50).

Like no.145, this sketch was created to illustrate a luxury edition of poetry drawn from *The Anti-Jacobin, or Weekly Examiner*, planned in 1800, but abandoned (Hill 1965, pp.88–102). On the evidence of the surviving designs, Gillray appears to have projected a scheme of Grand Manner-style illustration, using allegory and monstrosity to sublime effect, rather than caricature. While he was preparing these designs, his friend and supporter Revd John Sneyd (1763–1835), wrote to him: 'Pray don't forget Fuseli, for I think his mad taste will be very serviceable and essential to you' (Hill 1965, pp.89–90; part of Gillray's reply appears above, p.31).

From the 'Ode to Jacobinism', published in The Anti-Jacobin, or Weekly Examiner, 2 March 1798

When first to scourge the sons of earth,
Thy Sire his darling child design's,
Gallia received the monstrous birth –
Voltaire inform'd thy infant mind:
Well-chosen nurse! his sophist lore
He bade thee many year explore!
He mark'd thy progress, firm though slow,
And statesman, princes, leag'd with their
inveterate foe ...

(Rice-Oxley 1924, p.76)

145

James Gillray 1756–1815
Jacobin Grammar c.1800
Oil on paper 14 x 18 cm
Print Collection, Miriam and Ira D. Wallach Division of Art, Prints and Photographs, The New York Public Library, Astor, Lenox and Tilden Foundations

The retired opposition politician Charles James Fox (1749–1806) is haunted by a nightmarish vision of Alecto, one of the monstrous Furies. She leads the radical journalist and politician John Horne Tooke (1736–1812) and instructs Fox to give him lessons in sedition.

This sketch appears to illustrate the ironic 'Imitation' of the classical Greek poet of bucolic themes, Bion (fl. c.100 BC), which appeared in *The Anti-Jacobin* on 5 March 1798 (Hill 1965, pp.100–1). This was supposedly penned by Fox, at the house to which he had retired in 1797, St Ann's Hill. The point of the satire is to besmirch the name of Fox, placing him as the progenitor of the revolutionary radicalism which seemed to threaten the status quo in the 1790s. Having been inspired with the spirit of the Whig political reform described by Fox, Tooke is stirred to sing 'of treasons, deep and low, / Of rapine, prisons, scaffolds, blood, / Of war against the great and good'. Fox is then so impressed with the 'magic of his tongue' that he forgets his original – more moderate – political creed of reform.

From 'An Imitation of Bion', published in The Anti-Jacobin, or Weekly Examiner, 5 March 1798

Scarce had my eyes o'erspread,
Ere Alecto sought my bed;
In her left hand a torch she shook,
And in her right led John Horne Tooke.

O thou! Who well deserv'st the bays,
Teach him, she cried, Sedition's lays –
She said, and left us ...

(Rice-Oxley 1924, p.66)

146

James Gillray 1756–1815
Political Dreamings! – Visions of Peace! – Perspective Horrors! published Hannah Humphrey, 9 November 1801
Handcoloured etching and engraving
26 x 36 cm
The British Museum, London (J.3-34)

The violently reactionary war minister William Windham (1750–1810) is shown in bed, sleepless, and surrounded by the terrible parade of monstrosity and perversion which he feared would accompany the proposed peace with France (George 1935–54, no.9735). Above the headboard, a vulture weighs down an olive branch (the emblem of peace); to the left, a skeleton on stilts straddles a pile of discarded British trophies, wearing the revolutionary *bonnet rouge*. Justice, the diminutive female figure, slumps in despair by one side of the bed. On the other side, a fat demon recognisable as the democratic politician Charles James Fox plays and sings '*Ça ira, Ça ira*' – the folk tune of the revolutionaries. The decapitated figures gathering around the head of the bed include Louis XVI and Marie Antoinette. Opposition politicians appear as rat-headed figures gobbling up the mean pickings of 'Candle Ends' and 'Cheese Parings'. In the background, the Tower of London flies the French flag, the dome of St Paul's collapses in flame, and Bonaparte leads Britannia in chains to the guillotine.

The print was the subject of an extended analysis published in the German magazine *London und Paris*, noting the visionary excesses of Gillray's imagination – which in this case, however, matched the rhetoric of his subject. In Parliament, Windham had asked rhetorically of his prophecy of bloody disaster, 'are these idle dreams the phantoms of my disordered imagination?' (see Godfrey 2001, no.120). The German commentator called the scene as a whole a 'phantasmagoria', and was able to perceive a richly elaborate iconography which demanded a knowledge of Freemasonry, Milton, Egyptian and classical mythology, ancient literature, Shakespeare, and recent French and British history to even begin to interpret (see p.201).

145

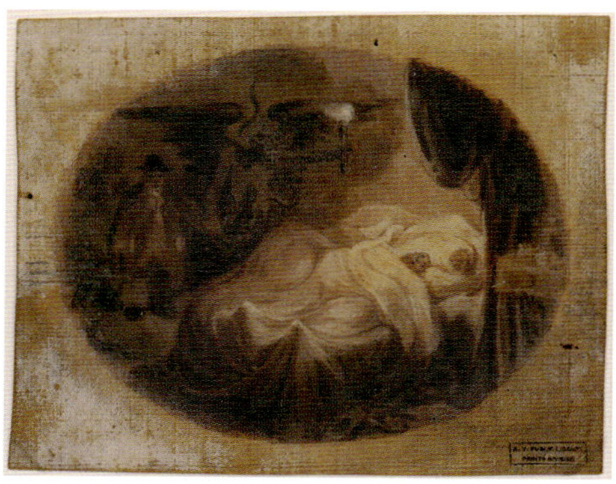

146

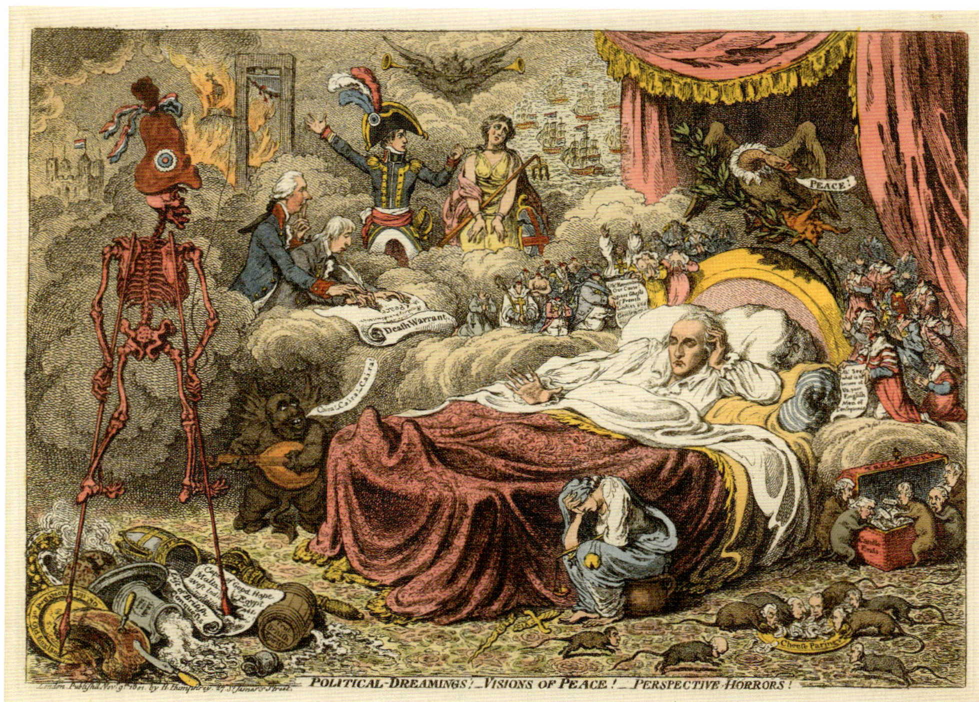

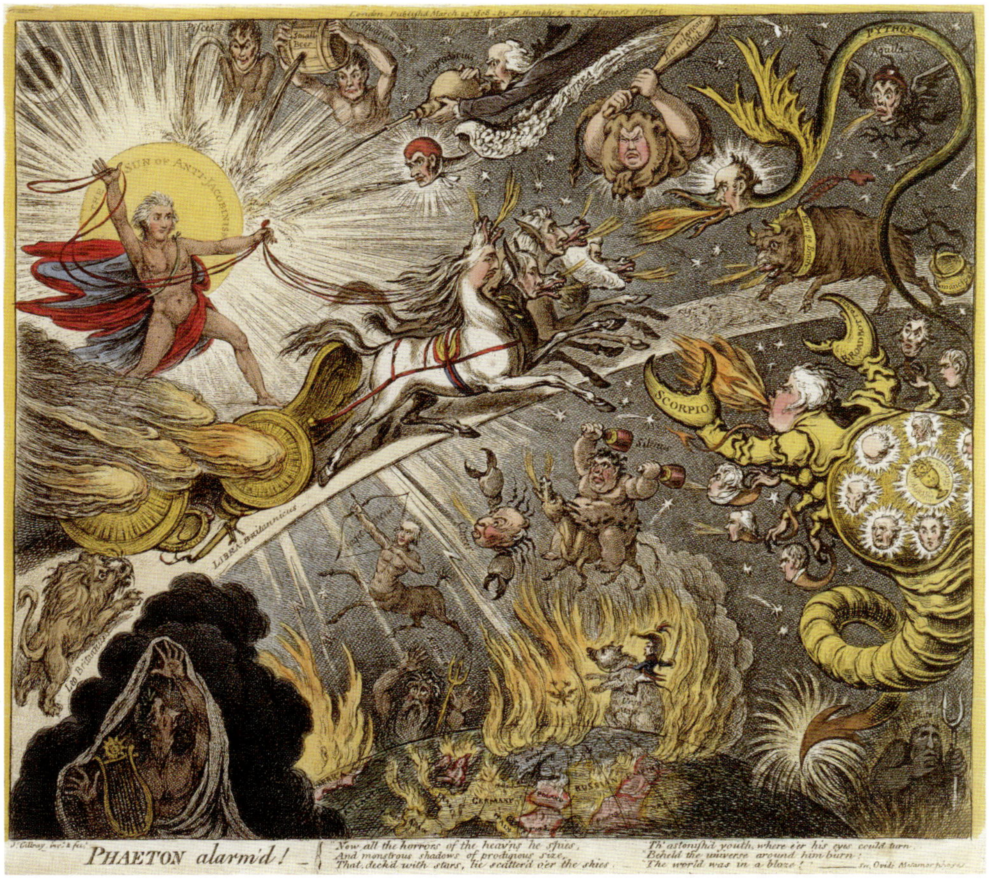

147

James Gillray 1756–1815
Phaeton Alarm'd! published by Hannah Humphrey, 22 March 1808
Handcoloured etching and aquatint
34.2 x 37.8 cm
With permission of the Warden and Scholars of New College, Oxford

In an extravagant cosmological phantasmagoria (George 1935–54, no.10972) the Foreign Secretary, George Canning (1770–1827), is cast as an over-ambitious Phaeton, driving his father's chariot across the sky and causing chaos in the constellations.

The horses are identifiable as Canning's political allies, Lord Hawkesbury, Spencer Perceval, Lord Castlereagh and Lord Eldon. The animated signs of the Zodiac represent his various political opponents and emblems of the troubled times. As the inscription, adapted from Addison's translation of Ovid's *Metamorphoses* (1704) describes:

> Now all the horrors of heav'n he spies
> And monstrous shadows of prodigious size,
> That, deck'd with stars, lie scatter'd o'er
> the skies.
> ...
> Th' astonish'd youth, where-e'er his eyes
> could turn,
> Beheld the universe about him burn:
> The world was in a blaze!
> ('The Fall of Phaeton', from Ovid's *Metamorphoses*, Book II, trans. J. Addison, ll.224–6, 265–8)

In Gillray's grotesque constellation, Taurus is the Irish bull, alluding to the issue of political independence; Scorpio is Richard Grenville; Sagittarius is William Windham; Silenus the famous drinker Richard Brinsley Sheridan; Pisces, taking a piss, is Henry Petty-Fitzmaurice, and Samuel Whitbread takes the role of Aquarius. To the bottom left, the ghost of Canning's mentor, William Pitt, looks on mournfully. At the bottom of the composition, the world is set in flames by the crazed but diminutive figure of Napoleon.

The satire is, characteristically of Gillray, ambiguous. If we follow the mythological narrative, we might conclude that Canning is as foolish as Phaeton and will similarly plummet to his destruction. However, he is here also the 'Sun of Anti-Jacobinism', occupying the same heroic role as that taken up by Pitt in an earlier engraving by Gillray, *Light Expelling Darkness* (published 30 April 1795; George 1935–54, no.8644) and in no.133.

'Political Dreamings' from <u>London und Paris</u>, no.8 (1801)

Not since Don Fransisco Quevedo Villegas dreamed his world-famous sueños, *or visions of the Last Judgement, hell and earth, has there been a more terrible and ridiculous fairy apparition than this – not even in the realm of Morpheus, that master of illusion and deceit. It represents the vision of ex-minister Windham, and created a stir even in London, where normally the most remarkable things hardly cause a stir ... William Windham, Secretary of State for War in Pitt's administration, distinguished himself in all his actions and parliamentary speeches as the most bitter adversary of the revolution, and the most vehement opponent of any measures which seemed even remotely to be aimed at Burke's 'regicide peace'. Those who are familiar with the events of the day will clearly remember the rhetorical thunderbolts which he hurled even at Lord Malmesbury's putative peace negotiations, despite the fact that he was utterly convinced that the whole thing was just a political charade. Thus, the actual signing of the Peace Preliminaries was for him like the glance of the mythic Gorgon. The anger he reined in for a full month burst out in the remarkable parliamentary debate of 3 and 4 November 1801 ... His opponents flatly accused him of being a mad visionary. Ah yes, exclaims his advocate Gillray in the print before us, the noble patriot has indeed been granted a vision: all hell is broken loose! Now you can see for yourselves the atrocities and horrors of this fine Peace, which have gathered around the deeply-troubled patriot's bed in the eerie witching hour!*

(Banerji and Donald 1999, pp.116–18)

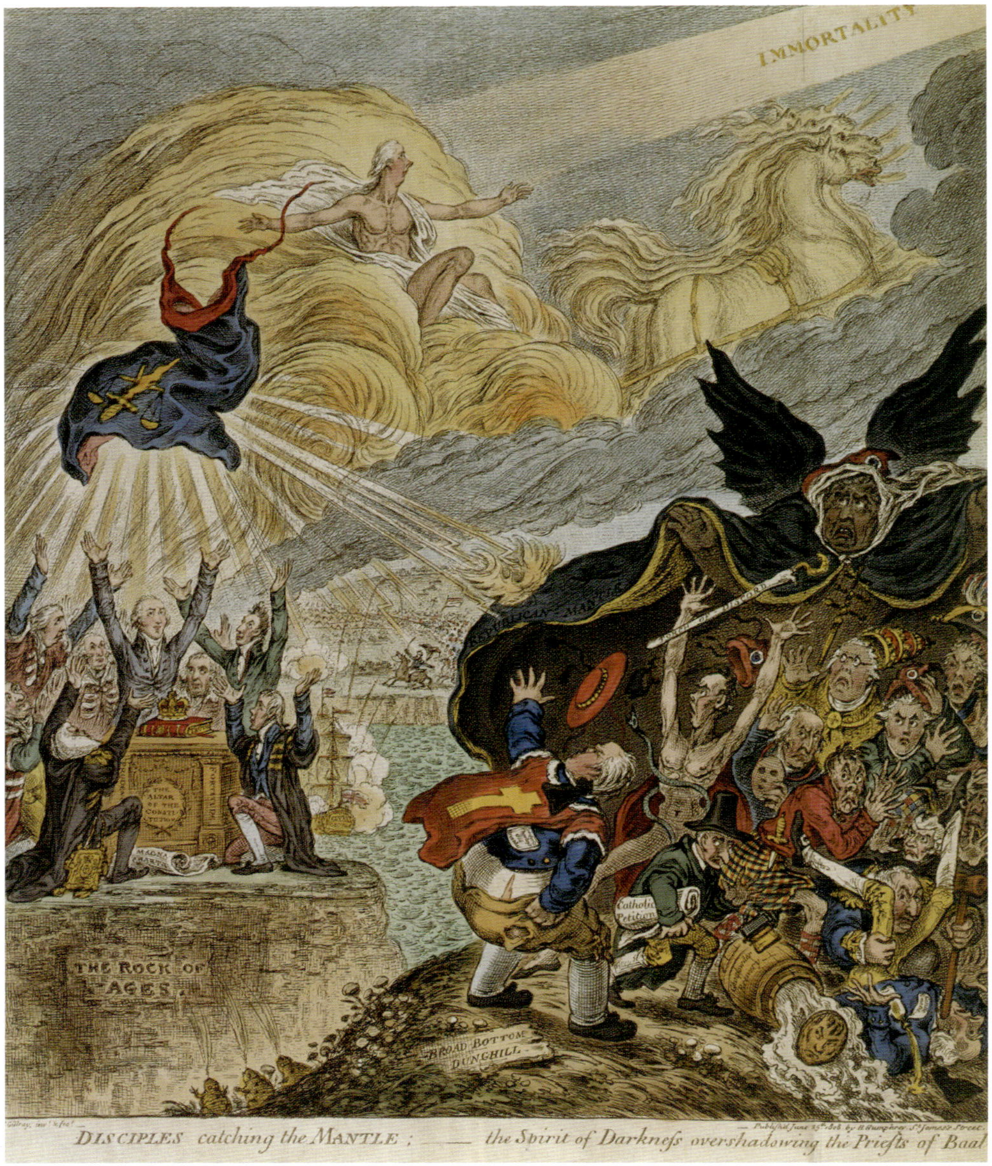

148

James Gillray 1756–1815
Disciples Catching the Mantle: The Spirit of Darkness Overshadowing the Priests of Baal
published by Hannah Humphrey, 25 June 1808
Handcoloured etching 39.8 x 33.9 cm
With permission of the Warden and Scholars of New College, Oxford

In a comically overblown scene of biblical spectacle (George 1935–54, no.10992), the late prime minister William Pitt is lauded as the prophet Elijah, ascending to heaven. Pitt is the heroically nude figure riding in a chariot pulled by four fire-breathing horses. As he flings his cloak to one side, his political followers, gathered on a rock, reach up to catch the garment. Each hopes to be the made successor to the prophet by the receipt of this mantle – as Elisha was made to suceed Elijah in the scriptures. On the right, Pitt's political opponents are cast as the pagan followers of Baal, blasted by righteous beams of light emanating from the cloak. The demonic spectre of Pitt's rival, Charles James Fox, throws out his dark cloak in an effort to protect them.

The theme, and overall composition, recalls de Loutherbourg's *Ascent of Elijah* painted for Macklin's Bible Gallery in 1791 (now lost) and engraved in 1800. Gillray is, though, targeting the overblown and theatrical language of contemporary religious art more generally. *Disciples Catching the Mantle* evokes the central incident in the story of Elijah, when he confronted the 450 pagan prophets of Baal on Mount Carmel. Having challenged the prophets to cook a slaughtered bull supernaturally by evoking the names of their false gods, Elijah successfully draws 'the fire of the Lord' upon his own 'burnt sacrifice'. So impressed are the people that they turn against the prophets of Baal, who are taken away and executed on the prophet's orders (1 Kings 18:1–40). Gillray's print alludes more particularly to Elijah's spectacular airborne departure, when Elisha is promoted to be his earthly successor (2 Kings 2). The Priests of Baal – long-dead, according to biblical narrative – are here resurrected to be impressed all over again by the supernatural powers of the prophet.

As Jean H. Hagstrum noted, it is with this image that Gillray is most completely an 'apocalyptic cartoonist', giving us 'a version of the Last Judgment as well as an ascent of Elijah – both eminently Blakean themes' (Hagstrum 1978, p.63).

2 Kings 2:11–15

And it came to pass, as they still went on, and talked, that, behold, there appeared a chariot of fire, and horses of fire, and parted them both asunder; and Elijah went up by the whirlwind into heaven.
And Elisha saw it, and he cried, My father, my father, the chariot of Israel, and the horsemen thereof. And he saw him no more: and he took hold of his own clothes, and rent them in two pieces.
He took up also the mantle of Elijah that fell from him, and went back, and stood by the bank of Jordan;
And he took the mantle of Elijah that fell from him, and smote the waters, and said, Where is *the* LORD *God of Elijah? and when he also had smitten the waters, they parted hither and thither: and Elisha went over.*
And when the sons of the prophets which were to view at Jericho saw him, they said, The spirit of Elijah doth rest on Elisha. And they came to meet him, and bowed themselves to the ground before him.

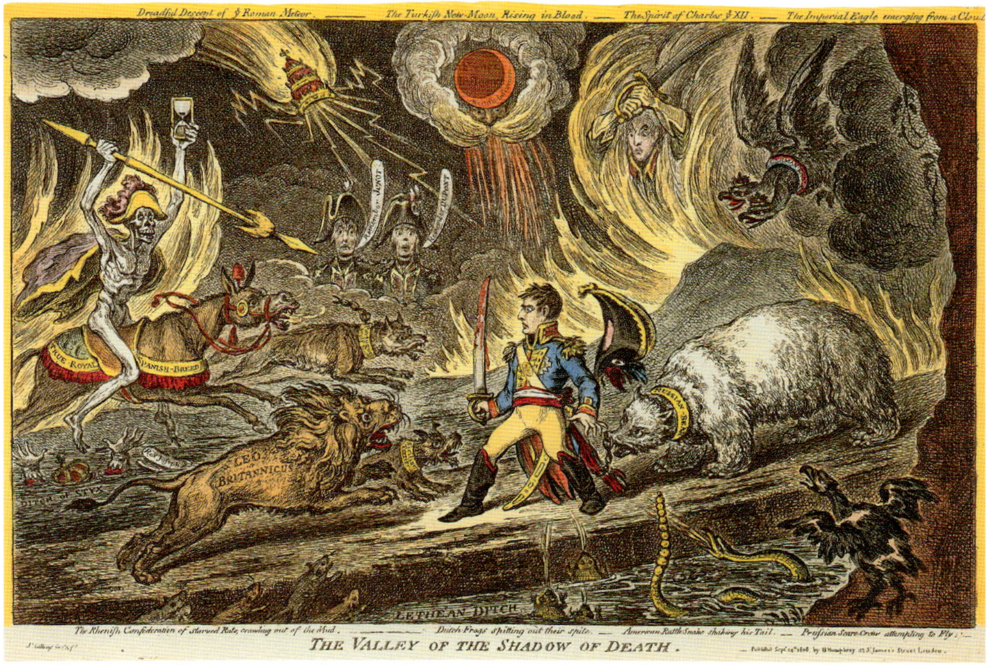

149

James Gillray 1756–1815
The Valley of the Shadow of Death published by Hannah Humphrey, 24 September 1808
Handcoloured etching and aquatint with engraving 26.6 x 39.1 cm
With permission of the Warden and Scholars of New College, Oxford

This is an allegory of the current European war (George 1935–54, no.11031). Napoleon is ironically cast as a Christian pilgrim, from John Bunyan's (1628–88) Protestant epic, *The Pilgrim's Progress* (1678), assailed on all sides by monstrous personifications in the Valley of the Shadow of Death, full of 'Hobgoblins, Satyrs, and Dragons of the Pit' overhung with 'the discouraging clouds of confusion' where 'Death also doth always spread his wings over it'. Napoleon might be interpreted as playing the part of the hero of the *Progress*, Christian, or, more likely, the soldier and guide, Mr Great-heart, who leads a succession of pilgrims through the dread Valley, shielding them from the horrors they encounter. Here, the British lion is on the attack, along with the Portuguese wolf and a Sicilian terrier dog. Death, holding up the hourglass which tells of the imminence of Napoleon's end, rides on the back of the Spanish mule. France's ally, Russia, is the bear who lumbers behind Napoleon. The papal tiara is in flames – 'Dreadful Descent of ye Roman Meteor' – and a Turkish new moon is bathed in blood. The 'Spirit of Charles XII' and the double-headed eagle of the Austrian Empire swoop down from the clouds. Further emblems of the allies – snakes, rats, frogs and a rough-looking crow – ascend from the lower edge of the composition.

Following a series of British victories in Spain and Portugal, it seemed that Napoleon was facing his doom. However, he was to turn his fortunes around and the wars with France were to continue for years yet.

Most commentators would agree that Gillray was past his peak by this point, and the more rigorous invention of his finest years had given way to a greater dependence on rather literal-minded allegory. Yet these crowded late compositions retain a visionary power, and are all the more interesting seen in relation to Blake's curious and exactly contemporary allegorical inventions.

John Bunyan, Pilgrim's Progress (1678)

When they had passed by this place, they came upon the Borders of the Shadow of Death, and this Valley was longer than the other, a place also most strangely haunted with evil things, as many are able to testifie. But these Women and Children went the better through it, because they had day-light, and because Mr. Great-Heart *was their Conductor.*

When they were enterd upon this Valley, they thought that they heard a groaning as of dead men: a very great groaning. They thought also they did hear Words of Lamentation spoken, as of some in extream Torment. These things made the Boys to quake; the Women also looked pale and wan; but their Guide bid them be of Good Comfort.

So they went on a little further, and they thought that they felt the Ground begin to shake under them, as if some hollow place was there; they heard also a kind of a hissing as of Serpents; but nothing as yet appeared. Then said the Boys, Are we not yet at the end of this doleful place? But the Guide also bid them be of good Courage, and look well to their Feet; Lest haply, said he, you be taken in some Snare.'

... They went therefore on, as being a little refreshed; but they had not gone far, before Mercie, looking behind her, saw, as she thought, something most like a Lion, and it came at a great padding pace after; and it had a hollow Voice of Roaring; and at every Roar that it gave, it made all the Valley eccho, and their Hearts to ake, save the Heart of him that was their Guide. So it came up, and Mr. Great-Heart *went behind, and put the pilgrims all before him. The lion also came on apace, and Mr.* Great-Heart *addressed himself to give him battle. But when he saw that it was determined that resistance should be made, he also drew back, and came no further.*

(Bunyan 1960, pp.240–2)

150

William Blake 1757–1827
The Spiritual Form of Nelson Guiding Leviathan, in whose Wreathings are infolded the Nations of the Earth c.1805–9; exh. at Blake's private exhibition 1809
Tempera on canvas 76.2 x 62.5 cm
Tate. Purchased (National Loan Exhibitions Fund) 1914

151

William Blake 1757–1827
The Spiritual Form of Pitt Guiding Behemoth; He Is that Angel who, Pleased to Perform the Almighty's Orders, Rides on the Whirlwind, Directing the Storms of War: He is Ordering the Reaper to Reap the Vine of the Earth, and the Plowman to Plow Up the Cities and Towers 1805; exh. at Blake's private exhibition 1809
Tempera heightened with gold on canvas 74 x 62.7 cm
Tate. Purchased by the National Gallery 1882; transferred to the Tate Gallery 1931

150

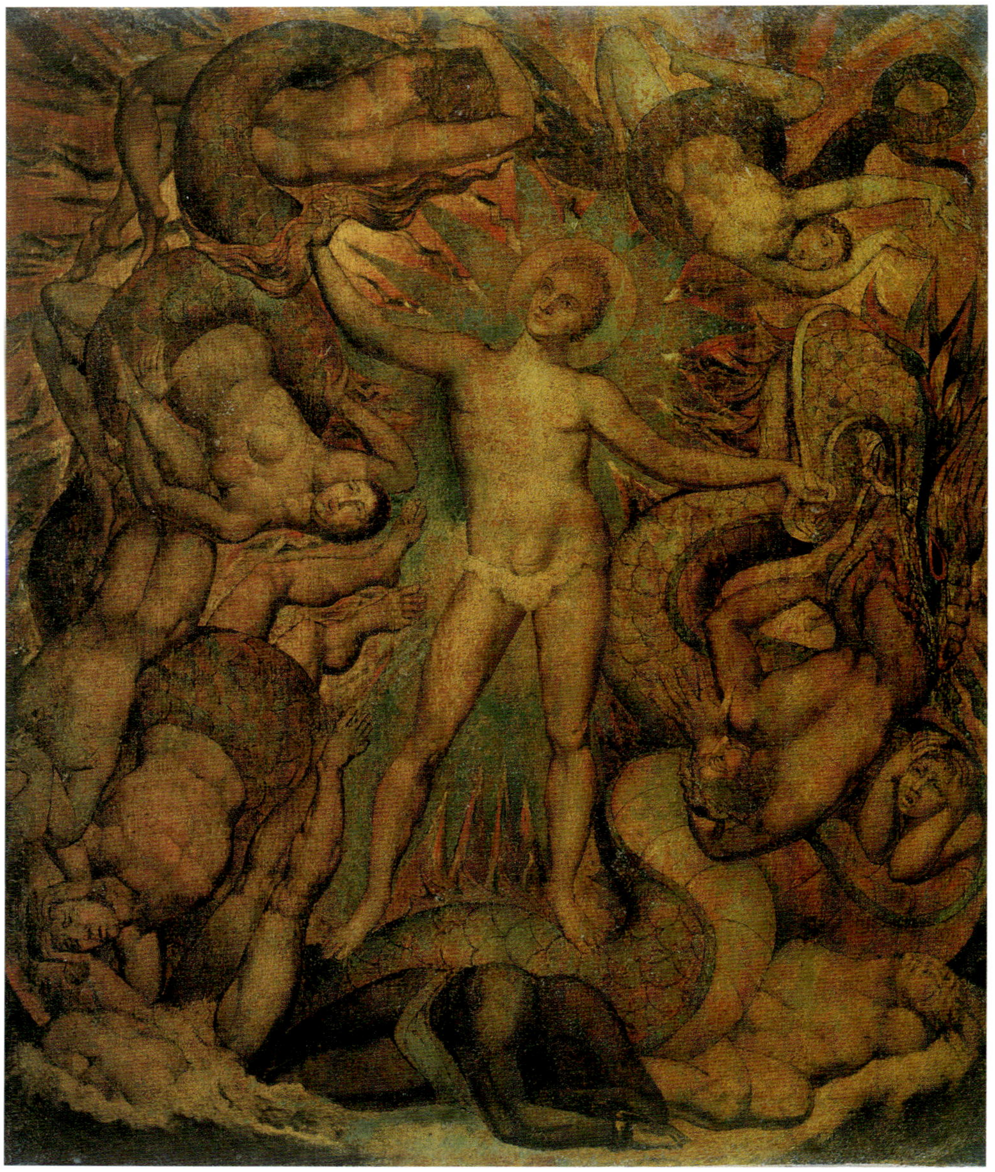

Two allegorical compositions dealing with the contemporary wars between Britain and France in their moral and political dimensions. In no.150, Nelson, in the form of a smooth-limbed young athlete modelled on ancient representations of Apollo, conducts the movements of the gigantic biblical beast Leviathan (from Job 41). This painting was badly damaged by the flood that hit the Tate Gallery in 1928, and what we see today is heavily restored and, in some details, altered (Butlin 1990, no.58). In no.151 (Butlin 1990, no.59), Pitt, in a costume that may recall images of Jesus, guides another destructive monster from scripture, Behemoth (Job 40). Both images are dense with allusions, yet to be fully explained. These paintings have been interpreted as apocalyptic visions of war, either as a perversion or as righteous.

These two pictures were shown as a pair in Blake's private exhibition of 1809, a show which secured his reputation as a madman (Bentley 2004, pp.281–7). As discussed in Blake's accompanying catalogue, these pictures were intended as emulations of a kind of visionary art from the most ancient times, 'where more is meant than meets the eye'. Important in this effort was his use of an invented medium which he called 'fresco'. Eschewing the easy and sensual effects of oil painting, Blake pursued a kind of watercolour painting which he argued carried greater moral weight and would bring the modern artist closer to the perfect masters of ancient times. His mission was to create a serious modern art that encompassed the contemporary and the visionary; the irony is that his message is still obscure. Moreover, Blake was acutely aware that his pursuit of idiosyncratic techniques meant that these paintings would not be exhibited on the walls of the main room of the Academy, the chief showcase for contemporary art, where only oil paintings were displayed. After being shown in 1809, the two pictures were also included in the 1812 exhibition of the Associated Painters in Watercolour, a body that set out to establish an alternative forum for the appreciation of the medium (Essick 1993; see also Smith 2002, pp.35–7, 211–14).

These two works represent contributions to the contemporary, competitive efforts to apotheosise Pitt and Nelson as national heroes. Benjamin West had painted a large narrative treatment of Nelson's death and shown this in his studio in 1806. Responding to the competition initiated in 1807 by the government sponsored 'Committee of Taste' to find the best way to memorialise the hero, West had also exhibited his painted proposal for an altar-like architectural assemblage featuring an allegorical 'Apotheosis of Nelson' at his house (Yale Center for British Art), and a sketch of the 'Apotheosis' itself (National Maritime Museum, London) at the Academy in 1807 (Von Erffa and Staley 1986, nos.108–11). John Flaxman began the large monument to Nelson for Westminster Abbey, proposed by the Committee, in 1808, and would continue to work on it until 1818 (Yarrington 1988 and 1983; Hoock 2003, pp.257–76). This features Nelson standing on a plinth while Britannia leads two young apprentice sailors to admire him; a fierce lion stands guard.

151

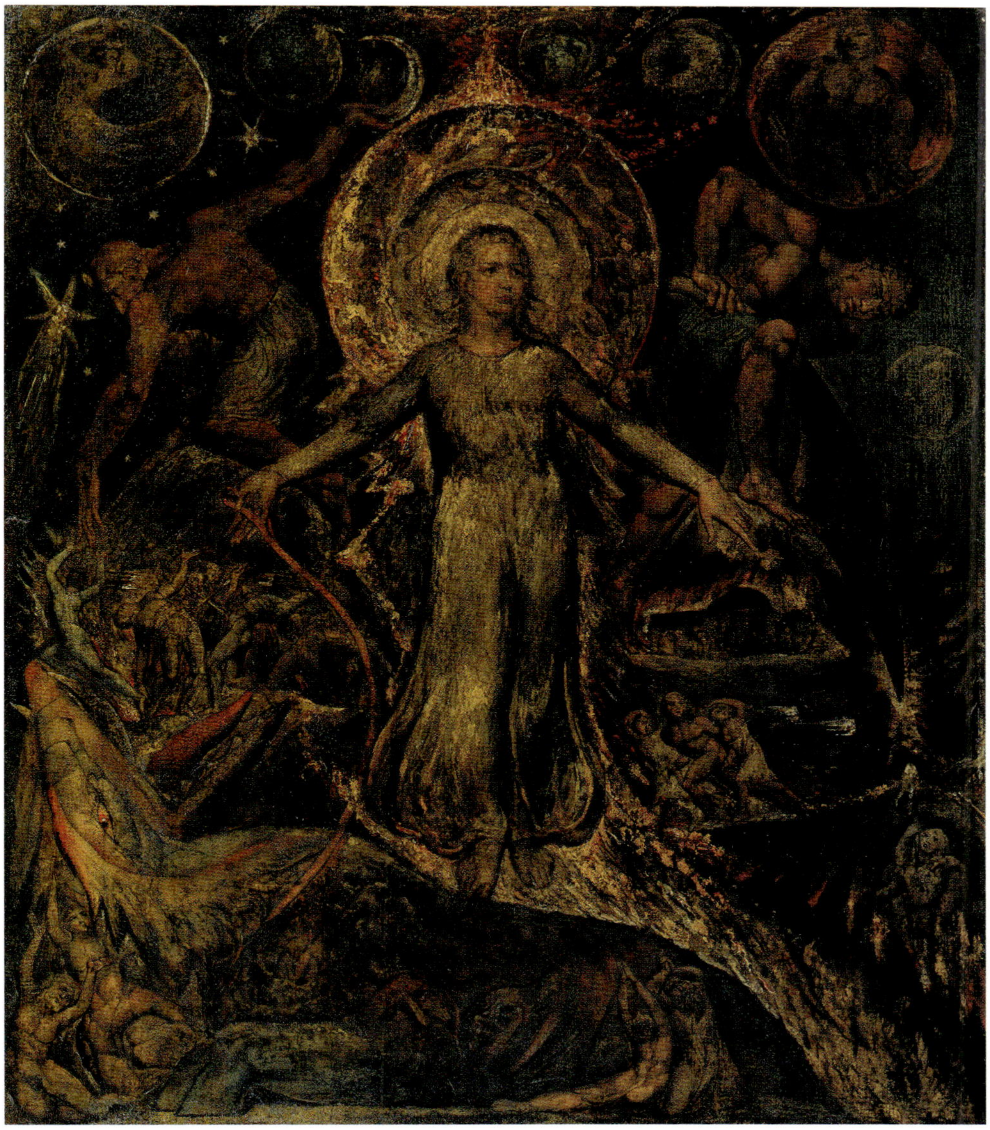

William Blake, A Descriptive Catalogue of Pictures, Poetical and Historical Inventions, London 1809

The two Pictures of Nelson and Pitt are compositions of a mythological cast, similar to those Apotheoses of Persian, Hindoo, and Egyptian Antiquity, which are still preserved on rude monuments, being copies from some stupendous originals now lost or perhaps buried till some happier age. The Artist having been taken in vision into the ancient republics, monarchies, and patriarchites of Asia, has seen those wonderful originals called in the Sacred Scriptures the Cherubim, which were sculptured and painted on walls of Temples, Towers, Cities, Palaces, and erected in the highly cultivated states of Egypt, Moab, Edom, Aram, and among the Rivers of Paradise, being originals from which the Greek and Hetrurians copied Hercules Farnese, Venus of Medicis, Apollo Belvidere, and all the grand works of ancient art. They were executed in a very superior style to those justly admired copied, being with their accompaniments terrific and grand in the highest degree. The Artist has endeavoured to emulate the grandeur of those seen in his vision, and to apply it to modern Heroes, on a smaller scale ...

Those wonderful originals seen in my visions, were some of them one hundred feet in height; some were painted as pictures, and some carved as basso relievos, and some as groups of statues, all containing mythological and recondite meaning, where more is meant than meets the eye ...

(Blake 1978, II, pp.829–31)

A further ambitious monument to Nelson was erected in the Guildhall between 1806 and 1811 by James Smith (1795–1815), at the same time as a monument to Pitt by James Bubb (c.1782–1853), commissioned in 1806 and unveiled in 1813 (Ward-Jackson 2003, pp.170–7). Both feature a range of allegorical and mythical figures: Nelson is accompanied by embodiments of the City, Britannia and Neptune, Pitt by Apollo, Mercury and Britannia riding on a hippogriff. Richard Westmacott's (1775–1856) monument to Pitt for Westminster Abbey was begun 1807 and completed in 1815 (Busco 1994, p.76). This features seated figures of Anarchy, in chains, and History. In the context of these various efforts, Blake's allegorical language may look a little less eccentric or wilful.

Ultimately, the closest parallel to these dense allegories of contemporary political and moral life might in fact be found in the later prints of James Gillray (nos.147–9). There is, in each, the mobilisation of a complex and ambiguous frame of reference that can encompass myth and legend, history, literature and scripture, strange shifts of scale and transitions between the temporal and the divine realms. Both Blake and Gillray took it as their task to interpret in an idiosyncratic fashion the current project to apotheosise the nation's heroes, a project that – in its authorised version – defined Britain's cultural identity in decisive ways (Colley 1992).

A third picture by Blake, of Napoleon, was known in the nineteenth century but is now lost (Butlin 1981, no.652). This was not exhibited in 1809 or 1812, and may have been painted only at Napoleon's death in 1822.

The Nightmare in Modern Culture

Christopher Frayling and Martin Myrone

It is fitting that Fuseli is recorded as at work on a final version of *The Nightmare* in the last weeks of his life (Weinglass 1994, p.57). That image, which had done so much to establish his reputation, had been resurrected, reworked and re-invented throughout his life. It had served to make him famous, infamous, and derided: and he must have known that it would ensure that the memory of his art lived on, long after his death, even after his name had slipped into obscurity – although this was to happen in ways that he could never have imagined.

The artistic progeny of *The Nightmare* are legion. This painting of Fuseli's continued to be reproduced in the nineteenth century and beyond; the stream of caricatures and pastiches continued unabated. The possibilities for the fantastic heralded by this single painting were explored more imaginatively by a few artists. Theodor von Holst pastiched Fuseli's work; what, we might speculate, would his design for 'The Vampyre', included as a projected subject among the 'Night Sketches' in one of his sketchbooks (no.73) have owed to that artist's famous creation? And surely when Blake invented his famous flea (no.154) a recollection of the Swiss artist's wicked imp was in his mind?

Yet even as he was occasionally recalled as the master of the weird in the nineteenth century, doubts were expressed about the limitations of his art. For Edgar Allan Poe it was the material literalness of Fuseli's painting which prevented it from being as seriously frightening as the 'pure abstractions' painted by Roderick the master of the House of Usher: these canvases exhibited in the setting of a melancholy mansion, instil 'an intolerable awe, no shadow of which felt I even yet in the contemplation of the certainly flowing yet too concrete reveries of Fuseli' (Poe 1967, pp.145–6). H.P. Lovecraft was later to make a similar judgement of the artist, measuring the painter by his own stringent standards of 'cosmic' horror (Lovecraft 1982, p.34).

Even by the time Poe wrote the first version of *The Fall of the House of Usher* in 1839 the literalness of Fuseli's image had become well established through the medium of book illustrations, especially in the Paris of the 1820s and early 1830s where horror stories were proving popular both on stage and on the page. *The Nightmare*'s dissemination, which began with prints and caricatures in the 1790s, now fused with the mythology of the vampire (Powell 1973, pp.80–96; Twitchell, p.21–30). The prolific French illustrator Tony Johannot adapted Fuseli's *The Nightmare* several times during this period, and in the process turned the *mara* into the by then obligatory figure of a bloodsucker (see Avila, Barraud and Bellanger 1977). In the pages of *Punch* later in the nineteenth century, we find several occasions where *The Nightmare* is reworked as a vampire scene, now alluding to the horrors of Anglo-Irish political relations (see Gibbons 2004, pp.77–87).

From thence to production design in films, as a way of organising the visual image within the frame. In Robert Wiene's *The Cabinet of Doctor Caligari* (1919), the somnambulist Cesare (Conrad Veidt) enters through the painted curtains and hovers over his sleeping victim with a knife, like a black-clad *mara* in human form: the design, like that of a number of later German films in the Weimar period revisits Romantic paintings through the prism of Expressionism (see fig.7 on p.19). Emigré Hollywood art directors from the late 1920s onwards – especially those working on horror films – often turned to Northern European visual sources, with a preference for German Romanticism and German Symbolism (Hollander 1991). The art department on each studio project would customarily compile a 'bible' of possible visual sources and in the case of horror films, Fuseli's celebrated painting must have been prominent among them. From James Whale's *Frankenstein* onwards, *The Nightmare* was to be transformed into countless gaudy variations on the theme of beauty and the beast, among the guilty pleasures of late night movies. More subtly, in Eric Rohmer's 1975 adaptation of Heinrich von Kleist's novella *The Marquise of O* (1811), the phantom pregnancy of Giulietta (Edith Borckhardt) is depicted as a direct transcription of Fuseli's *The Nightmare*, with the handsome Russian Count who is the real culprit standing in for the *mara* (fig.35). In the original novella, the rape of the Marquise is hidden within the words 'she fainted dead away. A little while after, when her terrified women appeared, he told them to call a doctor' (von Kleist 1963, p.43). In the film, instead of fainting the Marquise takes some opium tea (maybe *that* is what is on the bedside table in *The Nightmare*), and she appears in her bedroom to the Count – who is both angel and devil – in the likeness of a Gothic fantasy. The novella is set in 1799, and throughout *the Marquise of O*, Rohmer refers to paintings – Jacques-Louis David's portraits, Jean-Baptiste Greuze's domestic scenes, Jean-Honoré Fragonard for the morning after – which help him contrast classical order and romantic disorder: but for the pivotal moment in the story, Fuseli's *Nightmare* represents both (Dalle Vacche 1996, pp.81–106). Then again, in quite another sector of the market, when the distributors of the gory horror movie *Dream Demon* (dir. Harley Cokliss, GB 1988) wanted an alternative poster that would emphasise the artiness of the production, they turned to Fuseli's painting as a model (Conrich 2003, p.28).

Film references – from German Expressionism to Hollywood horror to recent costume dramas – have 'democratised' Fuseli's most famous painting to the point where it has long since moved beyond visual cliché. The image has proved both resilient and malleable. In a unique way, *The Nightmare* compounds, confounds and conflates high and low culture, the sensational and the high-minded, the aspirational and the debased, and in so doing provides a singular resource, seemingly inexhaustible, always reinvented, always breaking the stifling bonds of art history and undermining, even as it affirms, the value of art.

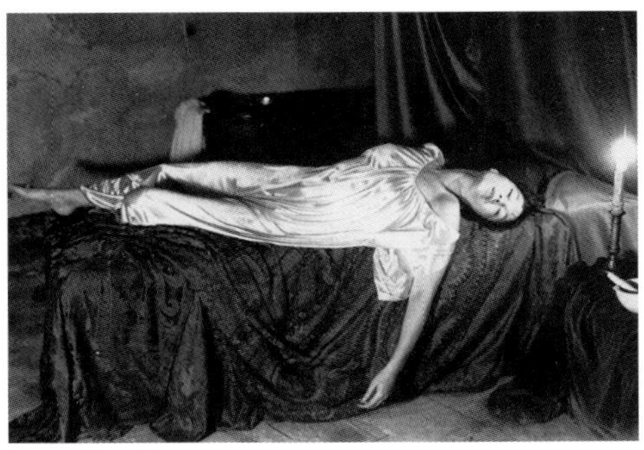

fig.35 Still from *The Marquise of O* (dir. Eric Rohmer, France 1976)

152

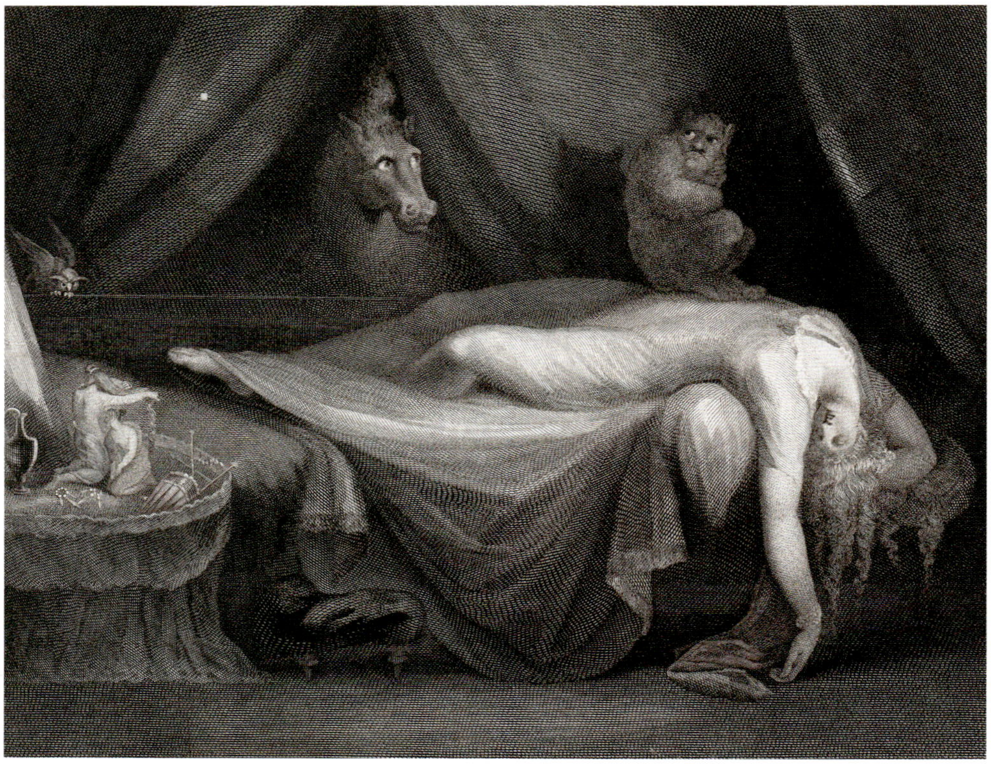

153

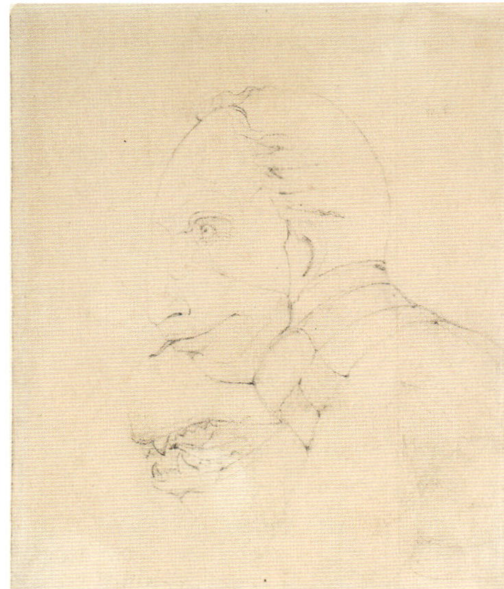

152

William Raddon fl.1816-62
after Henry Fuseli 1741-1825
The Nightmare, published by William Raddon, 20 April 1827
Proof engraving 18.4 x 23 cm
Victoria and Albert Museum, London

This print (Weinglass 1994, no.67D) reproduces the final version of *The Nightmare* created by Fuseli at the very end of his life. According to the inscription on the completed, published print, the painting was in the collection of Susan, Countess of Guildford (1771-1837), Fuseli's most important patron in the latter part of his life and the mother of Georgina North (see no.108).

The major elements of the original painting remain in place, though the imp or *mara* looks back over his shoulder towards the horse, whose features are rather more refined and handsome than in the original painting. The completed print was published with lines from Erasmus Darwin's 'The Loves of the Plants' (1789) from his *Botanic Garden* (1791), as was the original print of 1783 (no.4). There are, however, important visual additions, to the left of the composition. To the far left a bushy-browed owl flaps its wings. On the table top are two fairies, reminiscent of the little female creatures in Fairy Mab (no.107). One, with extravagantly long hair, preens herself, looking over her shoulder at, we might presume, her reflection, caught in the mirror that is propped up at the end of the bed. These add a certain note of whimsy to the scene, and we can further note that the imp itself is proportionally smaller, and sits much more lightly on the woman's body. He is placed rather further up her body, also. Whether these changes, which move the image in the direction of greater decorousness, were apparent in Fuseli's painting or were introduced in the course of the engraving cannot be ascertained.

153

William Blake 1757-1827
The Head of a Ghost of a Flea c.1819
Pencil on paper 18.9 x 15.3 cm
Tate. Bequeathed by Miss Alice G.E. Carthew 1940

154

William Blake 1757-1827
The Ghost of a Flea c.1819-20
Tempera heightened with gold on mahogany panel 21.4 x 16.2 cm
Tate. Bequeathed by W. Graham Robertson 1949

Like Fuseli's *The Nightmare* (no.1), Blake's *The Ghost of a Flea* incorporates elements of myth, folklore and private mythology. Both images have, retrospectively, been incorporated into 'Gothic' iconography, specifically the mythology of vampirism. The subject was referred to as early as 1827 as being a 'pernicious little *vampire*', and the painting itself was exhibited in the late nineteenth and early twentieth century under the title of 'A Vampire'.

The design appears to have originated among the drawings of 'Visionary Heads' that Blake was prompted to create by watercolour painter and astrologist John Varley (1788-1842) at Varley's house in around 1819-25 (see Burke 1964; Butlin 1969; Keynes 1971, pp.130–5; Butlin 1981, nos.692–768; Butlin 1990 p.153; Bentley 2002; Paley 2003, pp.300–4). These were claimed to document Blake's visions of figures from the spiritual realm, though the degree to which these were sincere or were created to humour the mystically inclined Varley is contested. Some of these drawings were subsequently engraved for Varley's *Treatise on Zodiacal Physiognomy* (1828), including the design representing the spirit of the flea. Varley's text commented:

> I felt convinced by his mode of proceeding, that he had a real image before him, for he left off, and began on another part of the paper, to make a separate drawing of the mouth of the Flea, which the spirit having opened, he was prevented from proceeding with the first sketch, till he had closed it. During the time occupied in completing the drawing, the Flea told him that all fleas were inhabited by the souls of such me, as were by nature blood-thirsty to excess.

The present drawing comes from the 'Small Blake-Varley Sketchbook' of around 1819, which was first used by Varley for landscape sketching and then by Blake for his visionary designs (Butlin 1969; Butlin 1990, no.63). The painting originally belonged to Varley (Butlin 1990, no.64).

A visual source for Blake's conception of this figure has been detected in Robert Hooke's *Micrographia, or Some Physiological Descriptions of Minute Bodies Being Made by Magnifying Glasses* (1665) (see Keynes 1960). The creature has a precedent in Blake's work with his personification of pestilence as 'the destroyer' (no.130), and may also carry memories of Fuseli's monstrous imp. Fleas also feature in folklore. The incubus-like 'little Pricke' who bites virgins 'like a Flea' in the night in *The Maydes Metamorphosis* (c.1600; see above, no.3) may be one point of reference, and there is the weird tale of 'The Flea' which featured such an insect swollen to the size of a sheep (this folk story was recorded in *The Pentamerone* of Giambattista Basile, first published in 1634).

Blake's ghost holds an acorn in his left hand, implying his incredibly diminutive proportions. Acorn-cups featured regularly in fairy-literature, for instance in Shakespeare's *Midsummer Night's Dream*, Act II, scene 1, ll.30–1. Its presence here may reinforce the idea that Blake has conceived of this figure as a wicked imp or incubus. The little curved spike in the figure's right hand is presumably meant to represent the bite or sting of the flea.

Literary Chronicle, 1 September 1827

The MAN FLEA. – Mr Blake had a conversation with a flea, which, on being related to us, naturally reminded us of the saying of the great Napoleon, 'that from the sublime to the ridiculous – was but a step.'

The flea communicated to Mr Blake what passed, as related to himself, at the Creation. *'It was first intended,' said he (the flea) 'to make me as big as a bullock; but then it was considered from my construction, so armed – and so powerful withal, that in proportion to my bulk, (mischievous as I now am) that I should have been a too mighty destroyer; it was determined to make me – no bigger than I am.'*

It must, in justice to the genius and professional renown of Mr Blake, be added, that he made a drawing, composed in a poetic mood, of this pernicious little vampire, enlarging it to the figure of a man, encased in armour, folded somewhat analogously to the rhinoceros-like coat of the flea, and denominated it – The Man Flea; and, to speak without hyperbole, it is indubitably the most ingenious, and able personification of a devil, or malignant and powerful fiend, that ever emanated from the inventive pencil of a painter.

(Bentley 2004, pp.469–70)

154

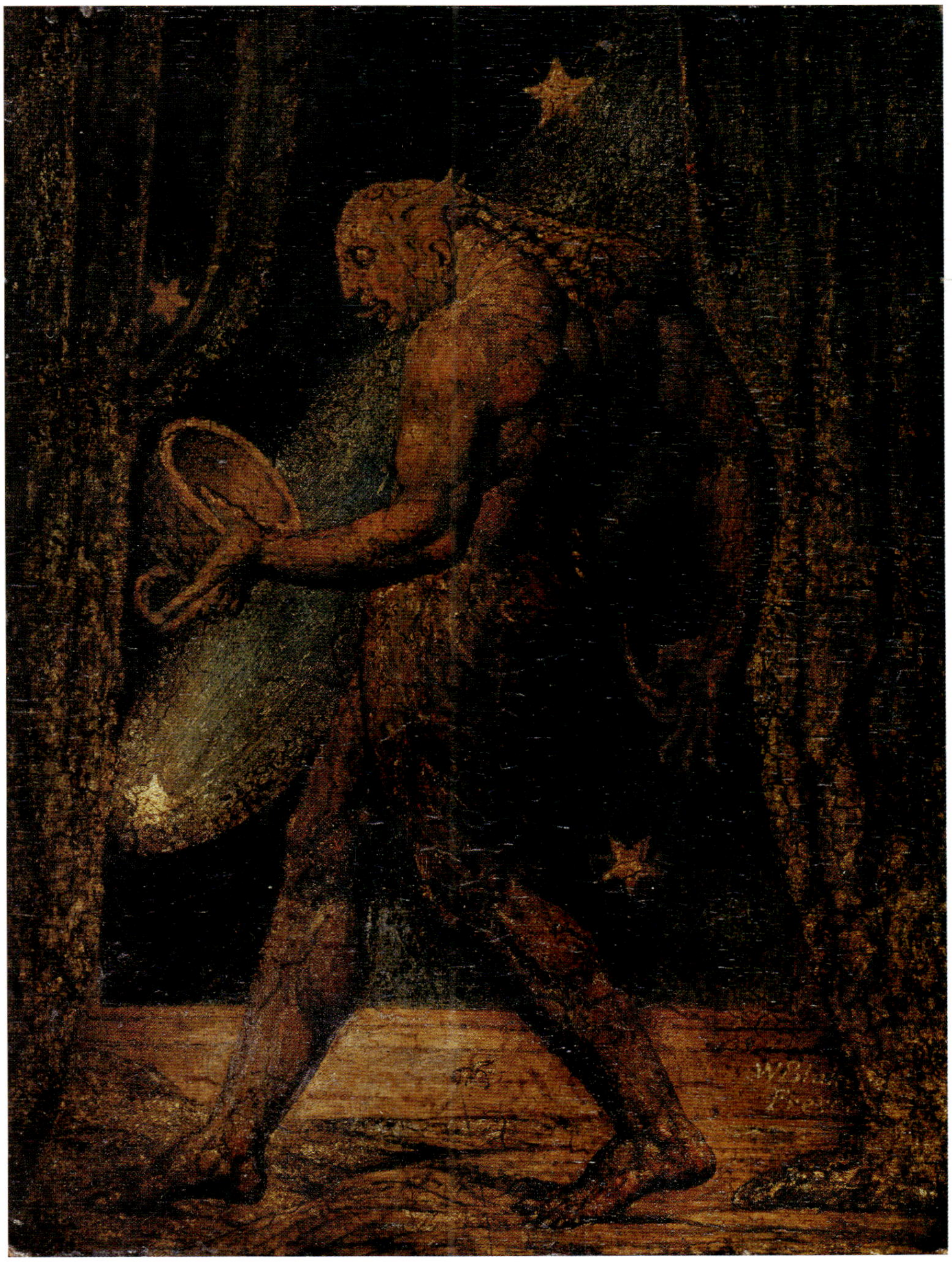

155

Nosferatu: A Symphony of Terror
Dir. Friedrich Wilhelm Murnau 1888–1931, Germany 1922

Murnau's *Nosferatu: A Symphony of Terror* was the first (unofficial) cinematic adaptation of Bram Stoker's *Dracula* (1897). Although the names of the protagonists were changed and the setting moved to early nineteenth-century Germany, the source of the story was unmistakable and, unluckily, announced in some of the publicity. Following legal advice, Stoker's widow, Florence took the producers to court and as a consequence of the complex case that followed all copies of the print were ordered to be destroyed. A pirate copy survived, and the film is now universally hailed as a masterwork of silent cinema, one of the major achievements of German Expressionism and a classic – perhaps the classic – horror film (see Frayling 2001).

Many of the visuals created by designer Albin Grau (d.1942) and Murnau were based on the landscape paintings of Caspar David Friedrich (1774–1840), supplemented with Biedermeier (folksy-bourgeois) domestic interiors (see Dalle Vacche 1996, pp.161–96). However, for the climatic sequence where the vampire finally enters the heroine Ellen's bedroom and she sacrifices herself to him (or does she fulfil her secret desires?), the visualisers turned to Fuseli. The production drawing by Grau for this scene seems to have been directly based on *The Nightmare*. The vampire, Count Orlok (played memorably by Max Schreck), stares hypnotically through the window at the restless heroine (Greta Schroeder) and, as dawn strikes, the Count's bald head – with its leathern ears and rodent teeth – becomes a substitute for the *mara*.

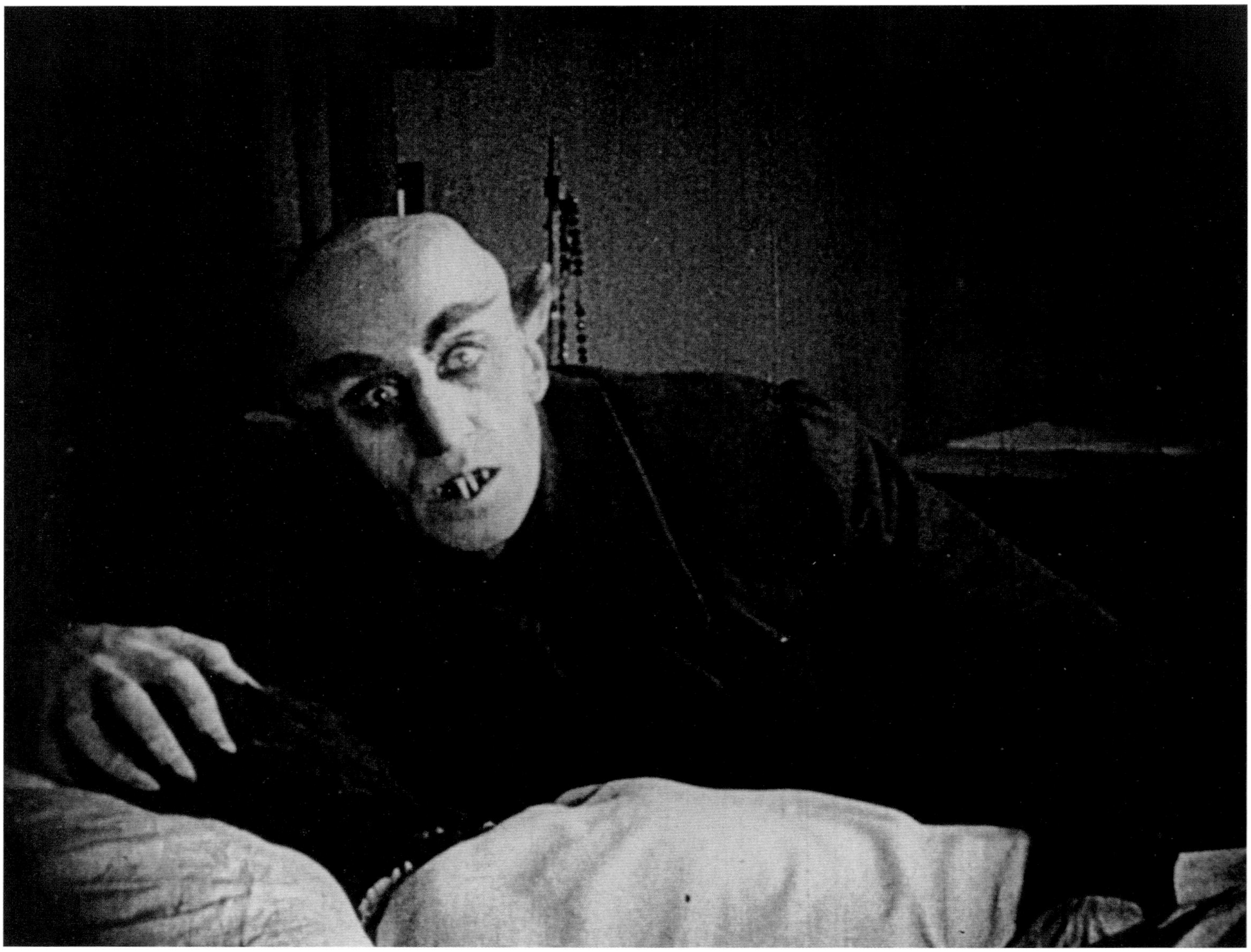

156

Frankenstein
Dir: James Whale 1889–1957, USA 1931

The 1931 Universal Studios film adaptation of *Frankenstein* remains for many people the most powerful realisation of Mary Shelley's story (although it owes little to the original text) and the high-point of horror-film history. Boris Karloff, as made up by Jack Pierce (1889–1968), provided the definitive modern version of the monster, and successive film-makers have struggled against – or exploited – the legacy of this image.

In the scene represented here, the monster created by Frankenstein has assaulted the misguided scientist's new wife, Elizabeth, on their wedding night. The composition of this scene – the only sequence in the entire film to be directly derived from Mary Shelley's book – is unmistakably based on *The Nightmare*, with Karloff standing at the window and actress Mae Clarke lying prone on the bridal bier in an exact replica of Fuseli's design. A lobby card of this moment was produced, and the pose appeared on some of the posters as well as on the tie-in book jacket. Fuseli's *Nightmare* had been reborn, once again.

The film sequence renders one of the climactic scenes of Mary Shelley's *Frankenstein* (vol.3, chap.6 of the 1818 edition, chap.23 of the revised 1831 version), which itself may have been based on a recollection of Fuseli's painting or a print after it. Shelley's description of the chilling scene of the creature fulfilling his prophecy ('I shall be with you on your wedding-night') directly echoes that image. Here, Elizabeth is the victim while the creature is the *mara* which visits her in the night. As in the painting, the scene is full of sexual tension, with Victor Frankenstein's suppressed desires (he has always seemed much more interested in his research work), his bride's released passions (she has up to now been 'regarded as his sister') and the creature's fury at being refused a handbuilt mate by his creator. When Victor looks up at the moonlit window of the inn at Evian he sees 'The shutters had been thrown back; and, with a sensation of horror not to be described, I saw at the open widow a figure the most hideous and abhorred. A grin was on the face of the monster; he seemed to jeer.' Do we need to ask where this monstrous expression could have come from? How the lumbering eight-foot creature reached the upper window is not explained; it may have had as much to do with Fuseli as with probability.

Mary Shelley, <u>Frankenstein</u> (1818), vol.3, chap.6

She left me, and I continued some time walking up and down the passages of the house, and inspecting every corner that might afford a retreat to my adversary. But I discovered no trace of him, and was beginning to conjecture that some fortunate chance had intervened to prevent the execution of his menaces; when suddenly I heard a shrill and dreadful scream. It came from the room into which Elizabeth had retired. As I heard it, the whole truth rushed into my mind, my arms dropped, the motion of every muscle and fibre was suspended; I could feel the blood trickling in my veins, and tingling in the extremities of my limbs. This state lasted but for an instant; the scream was repeated, and I rushed into the room.

Great God! why did I not then expire! Why am I here to relate the destruction of the best hope, and the purest creature of earth? She was there, lifeless and inanimate, thrown across the bed, her head hanging down, and her pale and distorted features half covered by her hair. Every where I turn I see the same figure—her bloodless arms and relaxed form flung by the murderer on its bridal bier. Could I behold this and live? Alas! life is obstinate and clings closest where it is most hated. For a moment only did I lose recollection; I fainted.

(Shelley 2003, p.278)

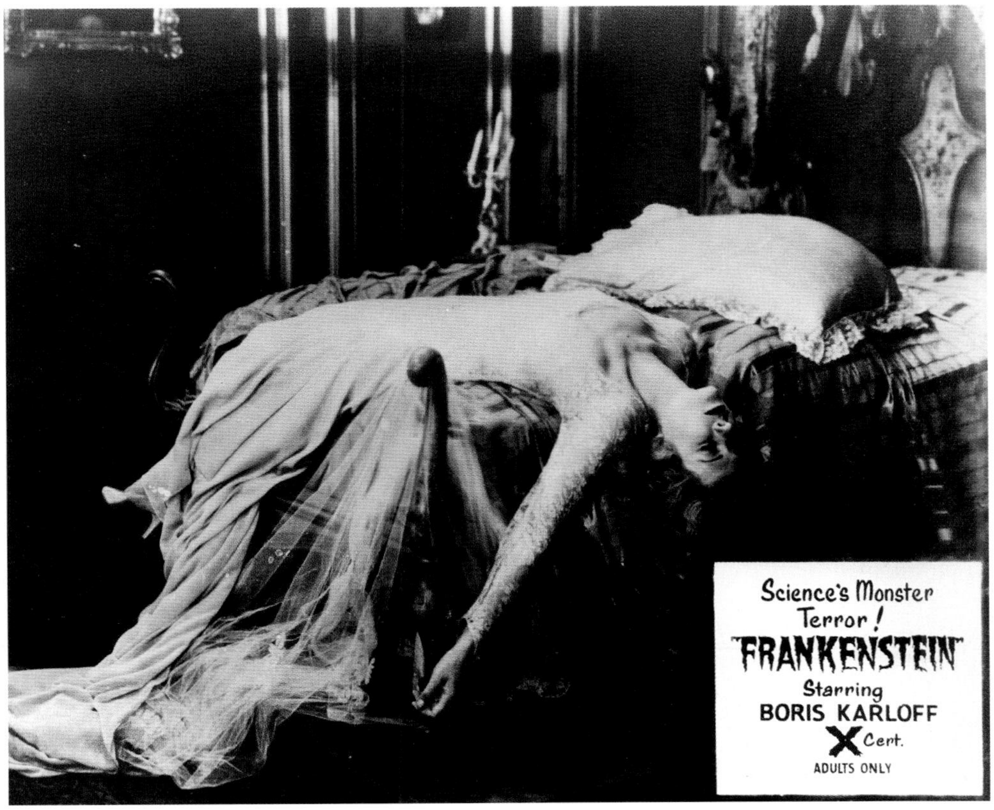

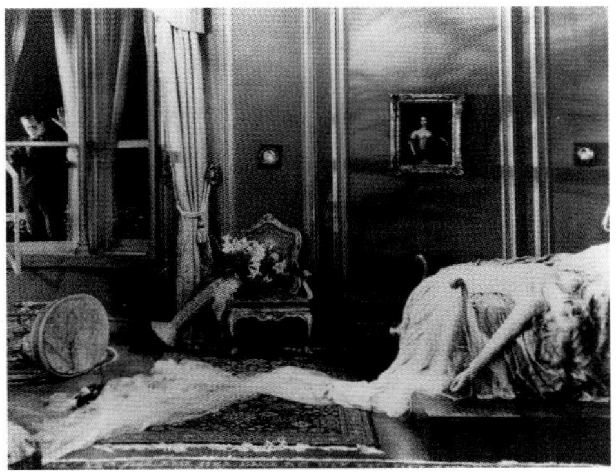

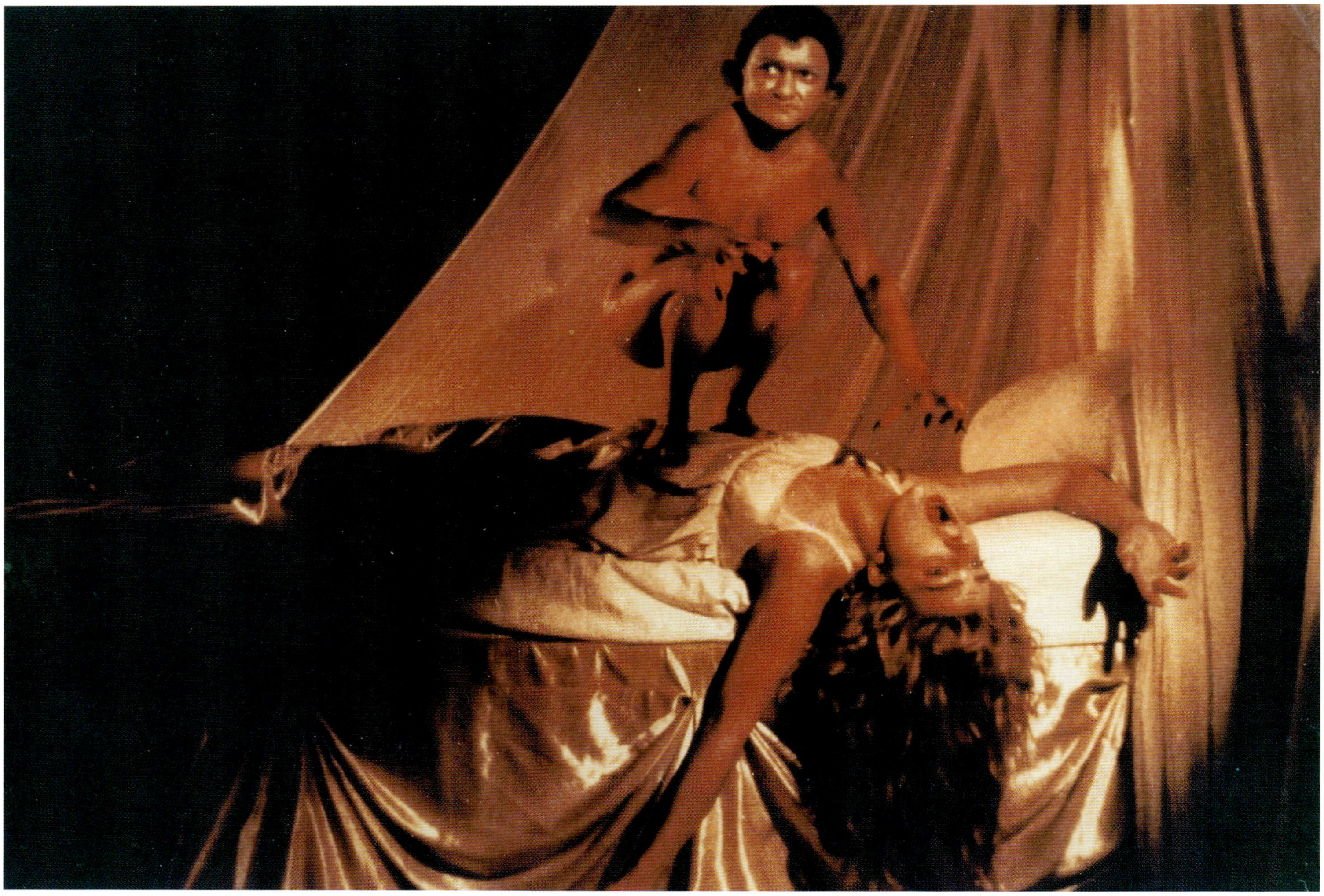

157

Gothic
Dir: Ken Russell (b.1927), GB 1986

Mainstream cinema has helped ensure that Fuseli's *The Nightmare* has become inextricably woven into accounts of the legendary story-telling session involving Byron, Mary Godwin (as Mary Shelley then was) and her half-sister, Claire, Percy Bysshe Shelley and John Polidori at the Villa Diodati on the shore of Lake Geneva, June 1816. Modern film-makers seem inevitably to feature the painting in their renditions of this famously overwrought and mythologised event, which had led to the creation of *Frankenstein* (1818) and Polidori's *The Vampyre* (1819). In Ivan Passer's *Haunted Summer* (USA, 1988), Lord Byron reveals the painting in the villa to his companions, and, although the film is set in 1816, there are discussions about its meaning which suggest they have all been reading Nicolas Powell's study of 1973 (Powell 1973). As illustrated here, Ken Russell's *Gothic* makes even more explicit the connection between Mary Godwin's waking dream and Fuseli's *Nightmare*: an oversized copy of the 1782 painting hangs above the fireplace in Percy and Mary's bedroom at the villa, and a viewing of it from her bed during a thunderstorm leads Mary (Natasha Richardson) to imagine the libidinous *mara* is squatting on her chest – a tableau which was to turn into the film's poster and video-cover. The *mara* in the film's copy of the painting has exaggerated pop-eyes, is smiling more suggestively and looks younger than in the original. Since this is supposed to be the first night of the famous short story competition of June 1816, it is clear that *Frankenstein* has been inspired by this leering version of the Fuseli original, illuminated by flashes of lightning. But, as Ken Russell recalls, the idea did not in fact come from art history:

> I'd known that Fuseli painting for some time. It was used as an album cover for a nineteenth century symphony by a composer so obscure I can't remember his name now – a painting of a horrible little dwarf perched on a sleeping woman's chest. He's inhuman and he's frightening. It was really fun to find a horrid little man two feet high and put him on this beautiful woman's breast. The painting inspired one of the most scary scenes in the film.
> (Frayling 2003)

From the Royal Academy, via prints and lampoons, pastiches and copies, through cinematic re-creations, derivations and allusions, illustration, commentary, book-covers and half-remembered record-sleeves, Fuseli's *Nightmare* finds here, in Russell's recollection, a singularly fitting context – simultaneously schlocky and artful.

Bibliography

Addison 1914: A.C. Guthkelch (ed.), *The Miscellaneous Works of Joseph Addison*, 2 vols., London 1914

Adlard 1972: John Adlard, *The Sports of Cruelty: Fairies, Folk-songs, Charms and Other Country Matters in the Work of William Blake*, London 1972

Akenside 1744: Mark Akenside, *The Pleasures of the Imagination: A Poem, in Three Books*, London 1744

Alexander 1998: David Alexander, *Richard Newton and English Caricature in the 1790s*, Manchester and New York 1998

Alexander 2005: Darsie Alexander et al., *Slide Show: Projected Images in Contemporary Art*, London 2005

Alexander and Godfrey 1980: David Alexander and Richard T. Godfrey, *Painters and Engraving: The Reproductive Print from Hogarth to Wilkie*, exh. cat., Yale Center for British Art, New Haven 1980

Allentuck 1967: Marcia Allentuck, 'Fuseli and Lavater: Physiognomical Theory and Enlightenment', *Studies on Voltaire and the Eighteenth Century*, 55 (1967), pp.89–112

Allentuck 1972: Marcia Allentuck, 'Blake, Flaxman and Thomas: A New Document', *Harvard Literary Bulletin*, 20 (1972), pp.318–19

Allentuck 1973: Marcia Allentuck, 'Henry Fuseli's Nightmare: Eroticism or Pornography?', in Thomas Hess and Linda Nochlin (eds.), *Woman as Sex Object*, London 1973, pp.33–41

Allentuck 1976: Marcia Allentuck, 'Henry Fuseli's "Queen Katherine's Dream" and Macklin's Poets Gallery: A New Critique', *Journal of the Warburg and Courtauld Institutes*, 39 (1976), pp.266–8

Andersen 1989: Jøregen Andersen, *De År i Rom: Abildgaard, Sergel, Füssli*, Copenhagen 1989

Anderson 1992: Perry Anderson, *English Questions*, London 1992

Andrews 2000: Stuart Andrews, *The British Periodical Press and the French Revolution, 1789–99*, Basingstoke 2000

Andrus 1995: Z. Dana Andrus, 'Some Implications for Another Reading of Henry Fuseli's *The Nightmare*', *Gazette des Beaux-Arts* 126 (1995), pp.235–52

Antal 1956: Frederick Antal, *Fuseli Studies*, London 1956

Armstrong 1744: John Armstrong, *The Art of Preserving Health: A Poem*, London 1744

Armstrong 1773: John Armstrong, *Medical Essays*, London 1773

Ascherson 1975: Neal Ascherson, *'The Times' Reports the French Revolution: Extracts from 'The Times', 1789–1794*, London 1975

Austen 2004: Jane Austen, *Northanger Abbey (1818)*, ed. Susan Fraiman, New York and London 2004

Avila, Barraud and Bellanger 1977: Avila, Barraud and Bellanger (eds.), *Tony Johannot 1803–1852*, Paris 1977

Ayrton 1946: Michael Ayrton, *British Drawings*, London 1946

Baine 1976: Rodney M. and Mary R. Baine, 'Blake's Sketch for *Hamlet*', *Blake Newsletter* 9 (1976), pp.117–19

Baine 1987: Rodney M. Baine, 'Blake's Dante in a Different Light', *Dante Studies* 15 (1987), pp.113–56

Bakhtin 1984: Mikhail Bakhtin, *Rabelais and his World*, trans. Helene Iswolsky, Bloomington, Indiana 1984

Baldick 1987: Chris Baldick, In *Frankenstein's Shadow: Myth, Monstrosity, and Nineteenth-Century Writing*, Oxford 1987

Balmanno 1858: Mary Balmanno, *Pen and Pencil*, New York 1858

Banerji and Donald 1999: Christiane Banerji and Diana Donald (trans. and eds.), *Gillray Observed: The Earliest Account of his Caricatures in London und Paris*, Cambridge 1999

Bann 1994: Stephen Bann (ed.), *Frankenstein: Creation and Monstrosity*, London 1994

Barkan 1999: Leonard Barkan, *Unearthing the Past: Archeology and Aesthetics in the Making of Renaissinace Culture*, New Haven and London 1999

Barker, Hulme and Inversen 1998: Francis Barker, Peter Hulme and Margaret Iversen (eds.), *Cannibalism and the Colonial World*, Cambridge 1998

Barlow 1809: Joel Barlow, *The Columbiad: A Poem*, London 1809

Barnett 1995: Gerald Barnett, *Richard and Maria Cosway: A Biography*, Tiverton 1995

Barrell 2000: John Barrell, *Imagining the King's Death: Figurative Treason, Fantasies of Regicide 1793–1796*, Oxford 2000

Bate 1986: Jonathan Bate, 'Shakespearean Allusion in English Caricature in the Age of Gillray', *Journal of the Warburg and Courtauld Institutes*, 49 (1986), pp.196–210

Becker 1997: Christoph Becker with Claudia Hattendorff, *Johann Heinrich Füssli: Das Verlorene Paradies*, exh. cat., Staatsgalerie, Stuttgart 1997

Becker 2005: Christoph Becker, 'Friar Puck and Fairy-Shot: The Spirits in Fuseli's Art', in Franziska Lentzsch et al., *Fuseli: The Wild Swiss*, Zurich 2005, pp.115–140

Beckett 2004: J.V. Beckett, 'Lowther, James, earl of Lonsdale (1736–1802)' in H.C.G. Matthew and Brian Harrison (eds.), *Oxford Dictionary of National Biography*, 61 vols., Oxford and New York 2004

Behrendt 1986: Stephen C. Behrendt, '"This Accursed Family": Blake's *America* and the American Revolution', *The Eighteenth Century: Theory and Interpretation* 27 (1986), pp.26–51

Behrendt 1987–8: Stephen C. Behrendt, '*Europe* 6: Plundering the Treasury', *Blake: An Illustrated Quarterly*, 21 (1987–8), pp.85–94

Behrendt 2002: Stephen C. Behrendt, 'The Evolution of Blake's *Pestilence*', in Alexander S. Gourlay (ed.), *Prophetic Character: Essays on William Blake in Honor of John E. Grant*, West Cornwall, Connecticut 2002, pp.3–26

Bell 1938: C.F. Bell, *Annals of Thomas Banks*, Cambridge 1938

Bender 1987: John Bender, *Imagining the Penitentiary: Fiction and the Architecture of Mind in Eighteenth Century England*, Chicago and London 1987

Bennett 1984–5: Shelley M. Bennett, 'A Newly Discovered Blake at the Huntington', *Blake: An Illustrated Quarterly*, 18 (1984–5), pp.132–9

Bentley 1964: G.E. Bentley, *The Early Engravings of Flaxman's Classical Designs: A Bibliographical Study*, New York 1964

Bentley 2004: G.E. Bentley (ed.), *Blake Records* (1968/1988), 2nd ed., New Haven and London 2004

Bermingham 1995: Ann Bermingham, 'Elegant Females and Gentleman Connoisseurs: The Commerce of Culture and Self-Image in Eighteenth-Century England', in Ann Bermingham and John Brewer (eds.), *The Consumption of Culture 1600–1800: Image, Object, Text*, London and New York 1995, pp.489–513

Bindman 1970: David Bindman, *William Blake: Catalogue of the Collection in the Fitzwilliam Museum, Cambridge*, Cambridge 1970

Bindman 1973: David Bindman, 'Blake's "Gothicised Imagination" and the History of England', in Morton D. Paley and Michael Phillips (eds.), *William Blake: Essays in Honour of Sir Geoffrey Keynes*, Oxford 1973, pp.29–39

Bindman 1977: David Bindman, *Blake as an Artist*, Oxford 1977

Bindman 1979: David Bindman ed., *John Flaxman*, exh. cat., Royal Academy of Arts, London 1979

Bindman 1982: David Bindman, *William Blake: His Art and Times*, exh. cat., Yale Center for British Art, New Haven 1982

Bindman 1989: David Bindman, *The Shadow of the Guillotine: Britain and the French Revolution*, exh. cat., The British Museum, London 1989

Bindman 1992: David Bindman, '"Revolution-Soup, dished up with human flesh and French Pot-Herbs": Burke's Reflections and the Visual Culture of Late Eighteenth-Century England', in Guilland Sutherland (ed.), *British Art 1740- 1820: Essays in Honor of Robert R. Wark*, San Marino 1992, pp.125–43

Bird 2004: Wendy Bird, 'Oh Monstrous Lamp! Special Effects in Goya's A Scene from El Hechizado por Fuerza in the National Gallery, London', *Apollo*, 159 (March 2004), pp.13–19

Blair 1808: Robert Blair, *The Grave* (1743), with notes by J. Evans, London 1808

Blair and Honeyman 1981: C.H. Hunter and H.L.H. Honeyman, *Warkworth Castle, Northumberland* (1954), London 1981

Blake 1978: G.E. Bentley (ed.),*William Blake's Writings*, 2 vols, Oxford 1978

Blunt 1955: Anthony Blunt, *The Art of William Blake*, London 1955

Boardman 2000: Andrew W. Boardman, *The Battle of Towton*, Stroud 2000

Boase 1947: T. S. R. Boase, 'Illustrations of Shakespeare's Plays in the Seventeenth and Eighteenth Centuries', in *Journal of the Warburg and Courtauld Institutes*, 10 (1947), pp.83-108

Boase 1963: T.S.R. Boase, 'Macklin and Bowyer', *Journal of the Warburg and Courtauld Institutes*, 26 (1963), pp.148–77

Bogan 1976: James Bogan, 'Vampire Bats & Blake's Spectre', *Blake Newsletter* 10 (1976), pp.32-33

de Bolla 1989: Peter de Bolla, *The Discourse of the Sublime. Readings in History, Aesthetics and the Subject*, Oxford 1989

Bond 1953: John Bond, *An Essay on the Incubus, or Night-Mare*, London 1753

Botting 1991: Fred Botting, *Making Monstrous: Frankenstein, Criticism, Theory*, Manchester 1991

Bourdieu 2000: Pierre Bourdieu, *Pascalian Meditations*, trans. Richard Nice, Cambridge 2000

Bourne 1725 Henry Bourne, *Antiquitates Vulgares; or, the Antiquities of the Common People, Giving an Account of Several of their Opinions and Ceremonies*, Newcastle 1725

Bown 1999: Nicola Bown, 'The Enchantments of Tradition: Men, Women and Fairies in the Late Eighteenth Century', *Women: A Cultural Review*, 10 (1999), pp.308–25

Bown 2001: Nicola Bown, *Fairies in Nineteenth-Century Art and Literature*, Cambridge 2001

Boyer 1994: Regis Boyer, 'Vikings, Sagas and Wasa Bread' in Andrew Wawn (ed.), *Northern Antiquity: The Post-Medieval Reception of Edda and Saga*, Enfield Lock, Middlesex 1994, pp.69–81

Brand 1777: John Brand, *Observations on Popular Antiquities: Including the Whole of Mr. Bourne's Antiquitates Vulgares, with Addenda to Every Chapter*, Newcastle 1777

Brewer 1997: John Brewer, *The Pleasures of the Imagination: English Culture in the Eighteenth Century*, London 1997

Brewer 2003: David Brewer, 'The Interpretation of Fairy Tales', in Hilda Ellis Davidson and Anna Chaudri (eds.), *A Companion to the Fairy Tale*, Cambridge 2003

Bridgwater 2004: Patrick Bridgwater, *De Quincy's Gothic Masquerade*, Amsterdam and New York 2000

Briggs 2002: Katharine Briggs, *The Fairies in Tradition and Literature* (1967), repr., London 2002

Bromley 1793-5: Robert Anthony Bromley, *A Philosophical and Critical History of the Fine Arts*, 2 vols, London 1793-5

Brothers 1794: Richard Brothers, *A Revealed Knowledge of Prophecies & Times, Book the Second*, London 1794

Brottman 1996: Mikita Brottman, 'Once Upon a Time in Texas: The Texas Chainsaw Massacre as Inverted Fairytale', in Andy Black (ed.), *Necromicon: The Journal of Horror and Erotic Cinema*, 1 (1996), pp.7-21

Brottman 2001: Mikita Brottman, *Meat is Murder!: An Illustrated Guide to Cannibal Culture*, London and New York 2001

Broughton 1968: Roger J. Broughton, 'Sleep Disorders: Disorders of Arousal?', *Science*, 159 (1968), pp.1070-8

Brown 1979: David Blayney Brown, 'Fuseli's Drawings for Ben Jonson's "Masque of Queenes"', *Burlington Magazine*, 121 (1979), pp.111-13

Brown 1982: David Blayney Brown, *Ashmolean Museum Oxford: Catalogue of the Collection of Drawings: Vol.4, Earlier British Drawings*, Oxford 1982

Browne 1994: Max Browne, *The Romantic Art of Theodor von Holst 1810-44*, exh. cat., Hazlitt Gooden & Fox, London, and Cheltenham Art Gallery and Museum 1994

Brownell 2001: Morris R. Brownell, *The Prime Minister of Taste: A Portrait of Horace Walpole*, New Haven and London 2001

Bruhm 1994: Steve Bruhm, *Gothic Bodies: The Politics of Pain in Romantic Fiction*, Philadelphia 1994

Brumoy 1759: Fr Pierre Brumoy, *The Greek Theatre of Father Brumoy*, trans. Charlotte Lennox, 3 vols., London 1759

Brunel 1992: Pierre Brunel (ed.), *Companion to Literary Myths, Heroes and Archetypes*, London 1992

De Bruyn 1987: Frans de Bruyn, 'Hooking the Leviathan: The Eclipse of the Heroic and the Emergence of the Sublime in Eighteenth-Century British Literature', *The Eighteenth Century: Theory and Interpretation* 28 (1987) pp.193-215

Bryant 2005: Julius Bryant, *Thomas Banks 1735-1805: Britain's First Modern Sculptor*, exh. cat., Sir John Soane's Museum, London 2005

Buffon 1766: Georges Louis Leclerc Buffon, *Histoire naturelle, générale et particulière*, Paris 1766

Bukatman 2003: Scott Bukatman, *Matters of Gravity: Special Effects and Supermen in the 20th Century*, Durham, North Carolina, and London 2003

Bullen 1882-5: A.H. Bullen (ed.), *A Collection of Old English Plays*, 4 vols., London 1882-5

Burdon 1997: Christopher Burdon, *The Apocalypse in England: Revelation Unravelling 1700-1834*, Basingstoke 1997

Burke 1964: Joseph Burke, 'The Eidetic and the Borrowed Image: An Interpretation of Blake's Theory and Practice of Art' (1964), reprinted in Robert N. Essick, *The Visionary Hand: Essays for the Study of William Blake's Art and Aesthetics*, Los Angeles 1973, pp.253-302

Bunyan 1960: John Bunyan, *The Pilgrim's Progress, From This World to That Which is to Come* (1678), ed. James Blanton Wharey (1928), 2nd ed., ed. Roger Sharrock, Oxford 1960

Busco 1994: Marie Busco, *Sir Richard Westmacott: Sculptor*, Cambridge 1994

Butler 1981: Alban Butler, *Butler's Lives of the Saints* (1956), 2nd ed. London 1981

Butlin 1969: Martin Butlin, *The Blake-Varley sketchbook of 1819 in the Collection of M. D. E. Clayton-Stamm*, London 1969

Butlin 1981: Martin Butlin, *The Paintings and Drawings of William Blake*, 2 vols., New Haven and London 1981

Butlin 1990: Martin Butlin, *William Blake 1757-1827 (Tate Gallery Collections: Volume Five)*, London 1990

Butlin 1994: Martin Butlin, review of exh. *The Romantic Art of Theodor von Holst*, in *Burlington Magazine*, 126 (1994), p.476

Butlin 2002: Martin Butlin, 'New Risen from the Grave: Nineteen Unknown Watercolours by William Blake', *Blake: An Illustrated Quarterly*, 35: 3 (2002), pp.68-73

Calè 2003: Luisa Calè, '"Lapland Orgies: The Hell-Hounds Round Sin": Réécriture et Invention dans la Galerie Miltonienne de J.H. Füssli', in Giovanni Bardazzi and Alain Grosrichard (eds.), *Dénouement des Lumières et Invention Romantique*, Geneva 2003

Calè (forthcoming): Luisa Calè, *Fuseli's Milton Gallery: 'Turning Readers into Spectators'*, Oxford, forthcoming

Carey 2000: Frances Carey (ed.), *The Apocalypse and the Shape of Things of Come*, exh. cat., The British Museum, London 2000

Carter 1979: Angela Carter, *The Sadeian Woman: An Exercise in Cultural History*, London 1979

Carter 1995: Angela Carter, *Burning Your Boats: Collected Short Stories*, London 1995

Castle 1995: Terry Castle, *The Female Thermometer: Eighteenth Century Culture and the Invention of the Uncanny*, New York and Oxford 1995

Von Chamisso 1824: Adelbert von Chamisso, *Peter Schlemihl* ('from the German of Lamotte Fouqué'), trans. J. Bowring, London 1824

Chappell 1986: Miles L. Chappell, 'Fuseli and the "Judicious Adoption" of the Antique in The Nightmare', *Burlington Magazine*, 128 (1986), pp.420-2

Chard 1999: Chloe Chard, *Pleasure and Guilt on the Grand Tour: Travel Writing and Imaginative Geography*, 1600-1830, Manchester 1999

Charlesworth 1994: Michael Charlesworth, 'The Ruined Abbey: Picturesque and Gothic Values', in Stephen Copley and Peter Garside (eds.), *The Politics of the Picturesque: Literature, Landscape and Aesthetics Since 1770*, Cambridge 1994, pp.62-80

Charlesworth 2002: Michael Charlesworth (ed.), *The Gothic Revival 1720-1870: Literary Sources and Documents*, 3 vols., Mountfield 2002

Chibnall and Petley 2002: Steve Chibnall and Julian Petley (eds.), *British Horror Cinema*, London and New York 2002

Cieszkowski 1990: Krzysztof Cieszkowski, 'The Formation of the Collection', in Butlin 1990, pp.11-16

Clayton 1997: Timothy Clayton, *The English Print, 1688-1802*, New Haven and London 1997

Clery 1995: E.J. Clery, *The Rise of Supernatural Fiction, 1762-1800*, Cambridge 1995

Clery 1996: E.J. Clery, 'The Pleasure of Terror: Paradox in Edmund Burke's Theory of the Sublime' in Roy Porter and Marie Mulvey Roberts, *Pleasure in the Eighteenth Century*, Basingstoke and London 1996, pp.164-81

Clery and Miles 2000: E.J. Clery and Robert Miles (eds.), *Gothic Documents: A Sourcebook 1700-1820*, Manchester 2000

Close 2004: Anne Close, 'Notorious: Mary Robinson and the Gothic', *Gothic Studies* 6 (2004), pp.172-91

Colley 1992: Linda Colley, *Britons: Forging the Nation 1707-1837*, London 1992

Conrich 2003: Ian Conrich, 'The Contemporary British Horror Film: Observations on Marketing, Distribution and Exhibition', in Harvey Fenton (ed.), *Flesh and Blood: Compendium*, Godalming 2003, pp.27-31

Cowper 1791: *The Iliad and Odyssey of Homer*, trans. William Cowper, 2 vols., London 1791

Cowper 1980-95: John D. Baird and Charles Ryskamp (eds.), *The Poems of William Cowper*, 3 vols., Oxford 1980-95

Coxe 1779: William Coxe, *Sketches of the Natural, Civil and Political State of Swisserland*, London 1779

Cross 2000: David A. Cross, *A Striking Likeness: The Life of George Romney*, Aldershot 2000

Crossley and Small 1989: Ceri Crossley and Ian Small (eds.), *The French Revolution and British Culture*, Oxford 1989

Crowley 2001: John E. Crowley, *The Invention of Comfort: Sensibilities & Design in Early Modern Britain & Early America*, Baltimore and London 2001

Cummings 1970: Frederick Cummings, 'Folly and Mutability in Two Romantic Paintings: *The Alchemist* and *Democritus* by Joseph Wright', *Art Quarterly*, 103 (1970), pp.247-75

Cunningham 1830-3: Allan Cunningham, *The Lives of the Most Eminent English Painters, Sculptors and Architects*, 2nd ed., 6 vols., London 1830-3

Daniels 1992: Stephen Daniels, 'Loutherbourg's Chemical Theatre: *Coalbrookdale by Night*', in John Barrell (ed.), *Painting and the Politics of Culture: New Essays on British Art, 1700-1850*, Oxford 1992, pp.195-230

Darwin 1791: Erasmus Darwin, *The Botanic Garden: A Poem, in Two Parts*, 2 vols., London 1791

David 1920: Charles Wendell David, *Robert Curthose, Duke of Normandy*, Cambridge 1920

Davidson and Fisher 1979-80: Hilda Ellis Davidson and Peter Fisher, *Saxo Grammaticus: The History of the Danes*, 2 vols., Cambridge 1979-80

Davies and Blécourt 2004: Owen Davies and Willem de Blécourt (eds.), *Beyond the Witch Trials: Witchcraft and Magic in Enlightenment Europe*, Manchester 2004

Dayes 1805: Edward Dayes, *The Works of Edward Dayes*, London 1805

Deutsch 1996: Phyllis Deutsch, 'Moral Trespass in Georgian London: Gaming, Gender, and Electoral Politics in the Age of George III', *Historical Journal*, 39 (1996), pp.637-56

Defoe 1992: Daniel Defoe, *A Journal of the Plague Year: Authoritative Text, Backgrounds, Contexts, Criticism*, ed. Paula R. Backscheider, New York and London 1992

Dickinson 1989: H.T. Dickinson (ed.), *Britain and the French Revolution*, 1789–1815, Basingstoke 1989

Dixon 1998: Yvonne Romney Dixon, *Designs from Fancy: George Romney's Shakespeare Drawings*, exh. cat., Folger Shakespeare Library, Washington DC 1998

Dobson 1999: Michael Dobson, *The Making of the National Poet: Shakespeare, Adaptation and Authorship, 1660–1769*, Oxford 1999

D'Oench 1999: Ellen G. D'Oench, *'Copper into Gold': Prints by John Raphael Smith 1751–1812*, New Haven and London 1999

Donald 1989: James Donald, 'The Fantastic, the Sublime and the Popular; Or, What's at Stake in Vampire Films?', in James Donald (ed.), *Fantasy and the Cinema*, London 1989, pp.233–51

Donald 1996: Diana Donald, *The Age of Caricature: Satirical Prints in the Age of George III*, New Haven and London 1996

Donaldson 1975: Ian Donaldson (ed.), *Ben Jonson: Poems*, Oxford 1975

Doody 1977: Margaret Anne Doody, 'Deserts, Ruins and Troubled Waters: Female Dreams in Fiction and the Development of the Gothic Novel', *Genre* 10 (1977), pp.529–72

Douglas 1966: Mary Douglas, *Purity and Danger: An Analysis of Concepts of Pollution and Taboo*, London 1966

Duffy 1989: Maureen Duffy, *The Erotic World of Faery* (1972), repr. Guernsey 1989

Duncan-Jones 1961: E.E. Duncan-Jones, 'Queen Katherine's Vision and Queen Margaret's Dream', *Notes & Queries*, 8 (1961), pp.142–3

Dunne 2005: Tom Dunne (ed.), *James Barry 1741–1806: 'The Great Historical Painter'*, exh. cat., Crawford Art Gallery, Cork 2005

Eaves 1992: Morris Eaves, *The Counter-Arts Conspiracy: Art and Industry in the Age of Blake*, Ithaca and London 1992

Edmundson 1997: Mark Edmundson, *Nightmare on Main Street: Angels, Sadomasochism, and the Culture of Gothic*, Cambridge, Massachusetts and London 1997

Egerton 1990: Judy Egerton, *Wright of Derby*, exh. cat., Tate Gallery, London 1990

Elfenbein 1989: Andrew Elfenbein, 'Cowper's *Task* and the Anxieties of Femininity', *Eighteenth-Century Life*, 13:3 (1989), pp.1–17

Elton 1815: Charles Abraham Elton, *The Remains of Hesiod the Ascræn, Including the Shield of Achilles, Translated into English Rhyme and Blank-verse: With a Dissertation on the Life and Æra*, rev. ed., London 1815

Erdman 1949: David V. Erdman, 'William Blake's Debt to James Gillray', *Art Quarterly* 12 (1949), pp.165–70

von Erffa and Staley 1986: Helmut von Erffa and Allen Staley, *The Paintings of Benjamin West*, New Haven and London 1986

Esche 1993: Edward J. Esche, *A Critical Edition of Thomas Middleton's The Witch*, New York and London 1993

Essick 1991: Robert N. Essick, *William Blake's Commercial Book Illustrations: A Catalogue and Study of the Plates Engraved by Blake after Designs by Other Artists*, Oxford 1991

Essick 1993: Robert N. Essick, 'Blake's 1812 Exhibition', *Blake: An Illustrated Quarterly*, 27:2 (1993), pp.36–42

Essick and Paley 1982: Robert N. Essick and Morton D. Paley, *Robert Blair's The Grave Illustrated by William Blake: A Study and Facsimile*, London 1982

Farington 1978–98: Joseph Farington, *The Diary of Joseph Farington*, ed. Kathryn Cave, Kenneth Garlick and Angus Macintyre, 16 vols., New Haven 1978–84, with index volume (1998) by Evelyn Newby

Feinberg and Woolf 1996: Larry J. Feinberg and Martha Wolff (eds.), *French and British Paintings from 1600 to 1800 in The Art Institute of Chicago: A Catalogue of the Collection*, Princeton 1996

Feingold 1984: Lawrence Feingold, 'Fuseli, Another Nightmare: The Night-Hag Visiting Lapland Witches', *The Metropolitan Museum Journal* 17 (1984), pp.49–61

Ferguson 1992: Frances Ferguson, *Solitude and the Sublime: Romanticism and the Aesthetics of Individuation*, New York and London 1992

Flagg 1893: Jared B. Flagg, *The Life and Letters of Washington Allston*, London 1893

Flood 1998: John L. Flood, 'Siegfried's Dragon-fight in German Literary Tradition', in Winder McConnell (ed.), *Companion to the Nibelungenlied*, Drawer 1998, pp.42–59

Folkenflik 1982: Robert Folkenflik (ed.), *The English Hero, 1660-1800*, Newark 1982

Ford 1998: Jennifer Ford, *Coleridge on Dreaming: Romanticism, Dreams and the Medical Imagination*, Cambridge 1998

Frankl 1960: Paul Frankl, *The Gothic: Literary Sources and Interpretations through Eight Centuries*, trans. Priscilla Silz, Princeton 1960

Frayling 1991: Christopher Frayling, *Vampyres: Lord Byron to Count Dracula*, London 1991

Frayling 2001: Christopher Frayling, *Nosferatu*. Documentary film: BFIVD520 (2001)

Frayling 2003: Christopher Frayling, *The Art of Film*. BBC Radio 3 documentary, dir. Stephen Hughes (2003)

Frayling and Wokler 1982: Christopher Frayling and Robert Wokler, 'From the Orang-utan to the Vampire: Towards and Anthropology of Rousseau', in R.A Leigh (ed.), *Rousseau after Two Hundred Years*, Cambridge 1982, pp.109–15

Friedman 1961: Albert B. Friedman, *The Ballad Revival: Studies in The Influence of Popular on Sophisticated Poetry*, Chicago and London 1961

Fryer 1809: Edward Fryer, *The Works of James Barry*, 2 vols., London 1809

Furniss 1993: Tom Furniss, *Edmund Burke's Aesthetic Ideology: Language, Gender, and Political Economy in Revolution*, Cambridge 1993

Fuseli 1960: Henry Fuseli, *Remarks on the Writings and Conduct of J.J. Rousseau* (1767), repr. as *Augustan Reprint Society*, vol.82, Los Angeles 1960

Gardiner-Scott 1997: Tanya Gardiner-Scott, 'Androgynous Architecture: Fantasies of Gender Bending in the British Gothic Novel', in Michael A. Morrison (ed.), *Trajectories of the Fantastic: Selected Essays from the Fourteenth International Conference on the Fantastic in the Arts*, Westport, Connecticutt, and London 1997, pp.47–54

Gattrell 1994: V.A.C. Gattrell, *The Hanging Tree: Execution and the English People 1770–1868*, Oxford 1994

Gaussen 1908: Alice Cecilia Caroline Gaussen, *Percy: Prelate and Poet*, London 1908

Geary 1987: Robert F. Geary, 'From Providence to Terror: The Supernatural in Gothic Fantasy', in Donald E. Morse (ed.), *The Fantastic in World Literature and the Arts: Selected Essays from the Fifth International Conference on the Fantastic in the Arts*, Westport, Connecticutt, and London 1987, pp.7–19

Gelder 2000: Ken Gelder, *The Horror Reader*, London and New York 2000

George 1935–54: M. Dorothy George, *Catalogue of Political and Personal Satires, Preserved in the Department of Prints and Drawings in the British Museum*, 6 vols. (vols.5–11), London 1935–54

Gervase of Tilbury 2002: *Gervase of Tilbury, Otia Imperialia: Recreation for an Emperor (c.1200)*, ed. and trans. S.E. Banks and J.W. Binns, Oxford 2002

Gipponi 1998: Tino Gipponi (ed.), *Maria e Richard Cosway*, Torino 1998

Gibbon 1956: J.E. Norton (ed.), *The Letters of Edward Gibbon*, 3 vols., London 1956

Gibbons 2004: Luke Gibbons, *Gaelic Gothic: Race, Colonization, and Irish Culture*, Galway 2004

Gibson-Wood 2000: Carol Gibson-Wood, *Jonathan Richardson: Art Theorist of the English Enlightenment*, New Haven and London 2000

Gijswijt-Hofstra, Levack and Porter 1999: Marijka Gijswkijt-Hofstra, Brian Levack and Roy Porter, *Witchcraft and Magic after the Witch Trials: The Eighteenth and Nineteenth Centuries*, London 1999

Gilpin 1786: William Gilpin, *Observations, Relative Chiefly to Picturesque Beauty, Made in the Year 1772 on Several Parts of England, Particularly the Mountains and Lakes of Cumberland and Westmoreland*, London 1786, facsimile edition, Poole 1996

Gizzi 1985: Corrado Gizzi, *Füssli e Dante*, exh. cat., Torre de' Passeri, Casa di Dante, Abruzzo 1985

Glover 1831–2: Stephen Glover, *The History and Gazetteer of the County of Derby*, ed. Thomas Noble, 2 vols., Derby 1831–2

Godfrey 1978: Richard T. Godfrey, *Printmaking in Britain: A General History from its Beginnings to the Present Day*, Oxford 1978

Godfrey 2001: Richard Godfrey, with Mark Hallett, *James Gillray: The Art of Caricature*, exh. cat., Tate Britain, London 2001

Goldsmith 1771: Oliver Goldsmith, *The History of England from the Earliest Times to the Death of George II*, 4 vols., London 1771

Godwin 1927: William Godwin, *Memoirs of Mary Wollstonecraft* (1798), ed. W. Clark Durant, London 1927

Goodwin 1796: Anon. (ed.), *The French Revolution Foreseen, in 1639: Extracts from an Exposition of the Revelation by an Eminent Divine* [Thomas Goodwin], London 1796

Gordon 1997: Daniel Gordon, 'The City and the Plague in the Age of Enlightenment', *Yale French Studies*, 92 (1997), pp.67–87

Graham 1979: John Graham, *Lavater's Essays on Physiognomy: A Study in the History of Ideas*, Bern 1979

Grainger 2004: John D. Grainger, *The Amiens Truce: Britain and Bonaparte 1801–1803*, Woodbridge 2004

Grant 1968: John E. Grant, 'You Can't Write About Blake's Pictures Like That', *Blake Studies* 1 (1968), pp.193–202

Grant 1972: John E. Grant, 'The Visionary Perspective of Ezekial', *Blake Studies*, 4 (1972), pp.153–7

Griffin 1986: Dustin H. Griffin, *Regaining Paradise: Milton and the Eighteenth Century*, Cambridge 1986

Grigson 1950: Geoffrey Grigson, 'Painters of the Abyss', *Architectural Review*, 108 (1950), pp.215–20

Gripsrud 1989: Jostein Gripsrud, '"High Culture" Revisited', *Cultural Studies*, 3 (1989), pp.194–207

Groom 1992: Gloria Groom, 'Art, Illustration, and Enterprise in Late Eighteenth-Century English Art: A Painting by Philippe James de Loutherbourg', *The Art Institute of Chicago: Museum Studies*, 18 (1992), pp.125–35

Grudin 1987: Peter D. Grudin, *The Demon-lover: The Theme of Demoniality in English and Continental Fiction of the Late Eighteenth and Early Nineteenth Centuries* (Ph.D. Dissertation, Harvard University 1971), pub. New York 1987

Grunenberg 1997: Christoph Grunenberg, *Gothic: Transmutations of Horror in Late Twentieth Century Art*, Cambridge, Massachusetts, and London 1997

Guest 1992: Harriet Guest, 'The Wanton Muse: Politics and Gender in Gothic Theory After 1760' in Stephen Copley and John Whale (eds.), *Beyond Romanticism: New Approaches to Texts and Contexts 1780–1832*, London and New York 1992, pp.118–39

Haase 2000: Donald Haase, 'Feminist Fairy-Tale Scholarship: A Critical Survey and Bibliography', *Marvels & Tales: Journal of Fairy-Tale Studies*, 14 (2000) pp.15–63

Hägin 1964: Peter Hägin, *The Epic Hero and the Decline of Heroic Poetry: A Study of the English Neoclassical Epic with Special Reference to Milton's 'Paradise Lost'*, Bern 1964

Hagstrum 1965: Jean H. Hagstrum, '"The Wroth of the Lamb": A Study of William Blake's Conversions', in Frederick W. Hilles and Harold Bloom (eds.), *From Sensibility to Romanticism: Essays Presented to Frederick A. Pottle*, New York 1965, pp.311–20

Hagstrum 1978: Jean H. Hagstrum, 'Blake and British Art: The Gifts of Grace and Terror', in Karl Kroeber and William Walling (eds.), *Images of Romanticism: Verbal and Visual Affinities*, New Haven and London 1978, pp.61–80

Hall 1985: Carol Louise Hall, *Blake and Fuseli: A Study in the Transmission of Ideas*, New York and London 1985

Hallett 1999: Mark Hallett, *The Spectacle of Difference: Graphic Satire in the Age of Hogarth*, New Haven and London 1999

Halsband 1980: Robert Halsband, *The Rape of the Lock and its Illustrations 1714–1896*, Oxford 1980

Hamlyn 1978: Robin Hamlyn, 'An Irish Shakespeare Gallery', in *Burlington Magazine*, 120 (1978), pp.515–29

Harvey 2004: Karen Harvey, *Reading Sex in the Eighteenth Century: Bodies and Gender in English Erotic Culture*, Cambridge 2004

Hatto 1969: A.T. Hatto (trans.), *The Nibelungenlied* (1965), 2nd ed., Harmondsworth 1969

Haut 2004: Asia Haut, 'Reading Flora: Erasmus Darwin's The Botanic Garden, Henry Fuseli's Illustrations, and Various Literary Responses', *Word & Image*, 20 (2004), pp.240–56

Hawkins 2000: Joan Hawkins, *Cutting Edge: Art-Horror and the Horrific Avant-Garde*, Minneapolis and London 2000

Haydon 1844–6: Benjamin Robert Haydon, *Lectures on Painting and Design*, 2 vols., London 1844–6

Haydon 1960–3: W.B. Pope (ed.), *The Diary of Benjamin Robert Haydon*, 5 vols., Cambridge, Massachusetts 1960–

Haydon 1993: Colin Haydon, *Anti-Catholicism in Eighteenth-Century England, c.1714–80: A Political and Social Study*, Manchester and New York 1993

Heard, forthcoming: Mervyn Heard, *Phantasmagoria: The Secret Life of the Magic Lantern*, forthcoming

Henderson 1996: Andrea K. Henderson, *Romantic Identities: Varieties of Subjectivity: 1774–1830*, Cambridge 1996

Heppner 1995: Christopher Heppner, *Reading Blake's Designs*, Cambridge 1995

Herrick 1915: Robert Herrick, *The Poetical Works*, ed. F.W. Moorman, Oxford 1915

Herrstrom 1981: David Sten Herrstrom, 'Blake's Transformation of Ezekial's Cherubim Vision in *Jerusalem*', *Blake: An Illustrated Quarterly*, 15:2 (1981), pp.64–77

Hertz 1985: Neil Hertz, 'Medusa's Head: Male Hysteria under Political Pressure', with responses by Catherine Gallagher and Joel Fineman, in *The End of the Line: Essays on Psychoanalysis and the Sublime*, New York 1985, pp.161–215

Hicks 1998: Michael Hicks, *Warwick the Kingmaker*, Oxford 1998

Hill 1965: Draper Hill, *Mr Gillray the Caricaturist*, London 1965

Hill 1981: Aaron Hill, *The Plays of Aaron Hill*, ed. Calhoun Winton, London and New York 1981

Hipple 1957: Walter J. Hipple, *The Beautiful, the Sublime, and the Picturesque*, Carbondale 1957

Hoare 1801: Prince Hoare, 'Biographical Sketch of Henry Fuseli, Esq., RA', *Monthly Mirror*, 11 (1801), pp.5–9

Hobbes 1996: Thomas Hobbes, *Leviathan* (1651), ed. Richard Tuck, Cambridge 1996

Hofmann 1975: Werner Hofmann, 'A Captive', in Schiff 1975, pp.29–37

Hofmann 1980: Werner Hofmann (ed.), *Goya: Das Zeitalter de Revolutionen Kunst um 1800*, exh. cat., Kunsthalle, Hamburg 1980

Hollander 1991: Anne Hollander, *Moving Pictures*, London 1991

Hogarth 1997: William Hogarth, *The Analysis of Beauty* (1753), ed. Ronald Paulson, New Haven and London 1997

Holmes 1974: Richard Holmes, *Shelley: The Pursuit*, London 1974

Hoock 2003: Holger Hoock, *The King's Artists: The Royal Academy of Arts and the Politics of British Culture 1760–1840*, Oxford 2003

Hordern House 2002: *Imaginary Voyages and Invented Worlds*, exh. cat., Hordern House, Sydney 2002

Hume 1983: David Hume, *The History of England from the Invasion of Caeser to the Revolution in 1688* (1754–63, rev. ed. 1778), 6 vols., Indianapolis 1983

Hunt 1993: Lynn Hunt (ed.), *The Invention of Pornography: Obscenity and the Origins of Modernity, 1500–1800*, New York and London 1993

Hunter 2001: Michael Hunter, *The Occult Laboratory: Magic, Science and Second Sight in Later Seventeenth-Century Scotland*, Woodbridge 2001

Hutton 1992: Richard Wetherill Hutton, 'Robert Bowyer and the Historic Gallery: A Study of the Creation of a Magnificent Work to Promote the Arts in England', Ph.D. Thesis, 6 vols., University of Chicago 1992

Ireland 1999: Richard W. Ireland, 'Howard and the Paparazzi: Painting Penal Reform in the Eighteenth Century', *Art, Antiquity and Law*, 4 (1999), pp.55–62

Irwin 1962: David Irwin, 'Gavin Hamilton: Archaeologist, Painter, and Dealer', *Art Bulletin*, 44 (1962), pp.87–102

Irwin 1966: David Irwin, *English Neoclassical Art: Studies in Inspiration and Taste*, London 1966

Irwin 1979: David Irwin, *John Flaxman 1755–1826: Sculptor, Illustrator, Designer*, London 1979

Jacobs 1988: Eva Jacobs, (ed.), 'Zaïre, tragédie', in *The Complete Works of Voltaire*, The Voltaire Foundation, Oxford 1980– , vol.8 (1988), pp.273–525

Jacobs 1995: Edward Jacobs, 'Anonymous Signatures: Circulating Libraries, Conventionality, and the Production of Gothic Romances', *ELH*, 62 (1995), pp.603–29

Jaffé 1977: Patricia Jaffé, *Drawings by George Romney*, exh. cat., Fitzwilliam Museum, Cambridge 1977

Johnson 1755: Samuel Johnson, *A Dictionary of the English Language*, 2 vols., London 1755

Johnson 1983: Mary Lynn Johnson, 'Blake's Judgment on the Book of Judges: The Watercolour Designs as Biblical Commentary', in Mary Lynn Johnson and Seraphia D. Leydon (eds.), *Reconciliations: Studies in Honour of Richard Harter Fogle*, Salzburg 1983, pp.41–71a

Johnson 1990: Mary Lynn Johnson, 'David's Recognition of the Human Face of God in Blake's Designs for the Book of Psalms', in David V. Erdman (ed.), *Blake and his Bibles*, West Cornwall, Connecticut 1990, pp.117–56

Joll 2002: Evelyn Joll, *Watercolours and Drawings: Cecil Higgins Art Gallery*, Bedford 2002

Jonson 1979: Robert M. Adams (ed.), *Ben Jonson's Plays and Masques*, New York and London 1979

Joppien 1964: Rudiger Joppien, 'A Visitor to a Ruined Churchyard – A Newly Discovered Painting by P.J. de Loutherbourg', *Apollo* 118 (1964), pp.294–301

Jordanova 1990: Ludmilla Jordanova, 'The Authoritarian Response', in Peter Hulme and Ludmilla Jordanova (eds.), *The Enlightenment and its Shadows*, London 1990, pp.202–16

Kalman 1971: Harold D. Kalman, 'Füssli, Pope and The Nightmare', *Pantheon*, 29 (1971), pp.226–36

Keightley 1910: Thomas Keightley, *The Fairy Mythology* (1828), London 1910

Kennedy 2001: Deborah Kennedy, 'The Ruined Abbey in the Eighteenth Century', *Philological Quarterly*, 80 (2001), pp.503–23

Keynes 1960: Geoffrey Keynes, 'Blake's Visionary Heads and the Ghost of the Flea', *Bulletin of the New York Public Library*, 64 (1960), pp.567–72

Keynes 1971: Geoffrey Keynes, Blake Studies: Essays on his Life and Work (1949), 2nd ed., Oxford 1971

Keynes 1979: Geoffrey Keynes, 'Blake's Spectre', *The Book Collector*, 28:1 (1979), pp.60–6

Kidson 2002: Alex Kidson, *George Romney*, exh. cat., National Portrait Gallery, London 2002

Kiessling 1977: Nicolas Kiessling, *The Incubus in English Literature: Provenance and Progeny*, Washington State University Press 1977

King 1983: James King, 'An Unlikely Alliance: Fuseli as Revisor of Cowper's Homer', *Neophilologus*, 67 (1983), pp.468–79

King-Hele 1989: Desmond King-Hele, 'A Twist in the Tale of "The Tyger"', *Blake: An Illustrated Quarterly*, 23 (1989), pp.104–6

Kirk 1976: Robert Kirk, *The Secret Common-wealth; and, A Short Treatise of Charms and Spells*, ed. Stewart Sanderson, Cambridge 1976

Kitson 2003: Peter J. Kitson, 'Milton: The Romantics and After', in Thomas A. Corns (ed.), *A Companion to Milton*, Oxford 2003, pp.463–80

Klein 1991: Jürgen Klein, 'Mathematics of Desire: On the Meanings of Darker Movements in English Eighteenth-Century Literature and the Fine Arts', in Peter Wagner (ed.), *Erotica and the Enlightenment*, Frankfurt 1991, pp.210–87

Klein 2005: Jürgen Klein, *Schwarze Romantik: Studien zur englischen Literatur im europäischen Kontext*, Frankfurt 2005

von Kleist 1963: Bernd Heinrich Wilhelm von Kleist, *The Marquise of O–, and Other Stories*, trans. Martin Greenberg, London 1963

Klemm 2005: Christian Klemm, 'Friedel's Love and Kriemheld's Revenge: Fuseli's Revels in the Kingdom of the Nibelungs', in Franziska Lentzsch et al., *Fuseli: The Wild Swiss*, Zurich 2005, pp.149–74

Klonsky 1980: Milton Klonsky, *Blake's Dante: The Complete Illustrations to the Divine Comedy*, London 1980

Knowles 1831: John Knowles, *The Life and Writings of Henry Fuseli*, 3 vols., London 1831

Koerner 1993: Joseph Leo Koerner, *The Moment of Self-Portraiture in German Renaissance Art*, Chicago and London 1993

Kriz 1997: Kay Dian Kriz, *The Idea of the English Landscape Painter: Genius as Alibi in the Early Nineteenth Century*, New Haven and London 1997

Lambert 1987: Susan Lambert, *The Image Multiplied: Five Centuries of Printed Reproductions of Painting and Drawings*, New York 1987

Lavater 1789–98: Johann Casper Lavater, trans. Henry Hunter, *Essays on Physiognomy. Designed to Promote the Knowledge and the Love of Mankind*, 3 vols., London 1789–98

Leigh 1965: Jean-Jacques Rousseau, *Correspondence Complète*, ed. R.A. Leigh, Geneva 1965–

Lempriere 1792: John Lempriere, *Bibliotheca Classica; or, a Classical Dictionary, containing a full account of all the proper names mentioned in antient authors, etc.*, 2nd ed., London 1792

Leslie 1863: Charles Robert Leslie, *Autobiographical Recollections*, ed. Tom Taylor, London 1863

Levine and Knoepflmacher 1979: George Levine and U.C. Knoepflmacher, *The Endurance of Frankenstein*, Berkeley and London 1979

Lewis 1937–83: W.S. Lewis (ed.), *Yale Edition of Horace Walpole's Correspondence*, 48 vols., Oxford and New Haven 1937–83

Lewis 1992: Linda M. Lewis, *The Promethean Politics of Milton, Blake, and Shelley*, Columbia, Missouri, and London 1992

Lewis 2002: Matthew Lewis, *The Monk* (1796), with an introduction by Stephen King, Oxford 2002

Lewis 2004: Matthew Lewis, *The Monk* (1796), ed. D.L. Macdonald and Kathleen Scherf, Peterborough, Ontario 2004

Licht, Pizzetti and Weinglass 1997: Fred Licht, Simona Tosini Pizzetti and David H. Weinglass, *Füssli pittore di Shakespeare*, exh. cat., Fondazione Magani Rocca Mamiano di Traversetolo, Parma 1997

Lindsay 1986: Suzanne G. Lindsay, 'Emblematic Aspects of Fuseli's "Artist in Despair"', *The Art Bulletin*, 68 (1986), pp.483–4

Lloyd 1995: Stephen Lloyd, Richard & Maria Cosway: *Regency Artists of Taste and Fashion*, exh. cat., Scottish National Portrait Gallery, Edinburgh 1995

Lovecraft 1982: H.P. Lovecraft, *The Best of H.P. Lovecraft: Bloodcurdling Tales of Horror and them Macabre*, New York 1982

Lowe 1781: Mauretius Lowe (attrib.), *The Ear-wig: Or an Old Womans Remarks on the Present Exhibition of Pictures of the Royal Academy*, London 1781

McCalman 2005: Ian McCalman, 'Magic, Spectacle, and the Art of de Loutherbourg's Eidophusikon', in Ann Bermingham (ed.), *Sensation & Sensibility: Viewing Gainsborough's 'Cottage Door'*, exh. cat., Yale Center for British Art, New Haven, and the Huntington Library, Art Collections & Botanical Gardens, San Marino 2005

McCreery 1993: Cindy McCreery, 'Satiric Images of Fox, Pitt and George III: The East India Bill Crisis 1783–84', *Word & Image*, 9 (1993), pp.163–85

McCullagh 1997: Suzanne Folds McCullagh, 'Introduction', in Suzanne Folds McCullagh and Laura M. Giles, *Italian Drawings before 1600 in the Art Institute of Chicago: A Catalogue of the Collection*, Princeton 1997, pp.ix–xi

Macdonald 2000: D.L. Macdonald, *Monk Lewis: A Critical Biography*, Toronto 2000

Macmillan 1978: Duncan Macmillan, '"Truly National Designs": Runciman's Scottish Themes at Penicuik', *Art History* 1 (1978), pp.90–8

Macpherson 1996: James Macpherson, *The Poems of Ossian and Related Works*, ed. Howard Gaskill, Edinburgh 1996

Maguire 1991: Nancy Klein Maguire, 'Nahum Tate's *King Lear*: "the king's blessed restoration"', in Jean I. Marsden (ed.), *The Appropriation of Shakespeare: Post-Renaissance Reconstructions of the Works and the Myth*, Hemel Hempstead 1991, pp.29–42

Mallett 1770: Paul Henri Mallet, *Northern Antiquities: Or, A Description of the Manners, Customs, Religion and Laws of the Ancient Danes, and Other Northern Nations ... With a Translation of the Edda, or System of Runic Mythology* (1755), trans. Thomas Percy, 2 vols., London 1770

Manlove 1990: Colin N. Manlove, 'The Elusiveness of Fantasy', in Olena H. Saciuk (ed.), *The Shape of the Fantastic: Selected Essays from the Seventh International Conference on the Fantastic in the Arts*, Westport, Connecticut, and London 1990, pp.53–65

Mannings 2000: David Mannings, with Martin Postle, *Sir Joshua Reynolds: A Complete Catalogue of his Paintings*, New Haven and London 2000

Marchand 1975: George Gordon, Lord Byron, *Byron's Letters and Journals*, ed. Leslie A. Marchand, 11 vols., London 1973–87

Martineau 2003: Jane Martineau et al., *Shakespeare in Art*, exh. cat. Dulwich Picture Gallery, London 2003

Mason 1951: Eudo C. Mason, *The Mind of Henry Fuseli: Selections from His Writings with an Introductory Essay*, London 1951

Mathias 1797–8: Thomas James Mathias, *The Pursuits of Literature: A Satirical Poem*, London 1797–8

Mee 1992: Jon Mee, *Dangerous Enthusiasm: William Blake and the Culture of Radicalism in the 1790s*, Oxford 1992

Meller 1996: Horst Meller, 'The Parricidal Imagination: Schiller, Blake, Fuseli and the Romantic Revolt against the Father', in Frederick Burwick and Jürgen Klein (eds.), *The Romantic Imagination: Literature and Art in England and Germany, Amsterdam and Atlanta*, Georgia 1996, pp.76–94

Merchant 1959: W. Moelwyn Merchant, *Shakespeare and the Artist*, London 1959

Merchant 1973: W. Moelwyn Merchant, 'Blake's Shakespeare' in Robert N. Essick (ed.), *The Visionary Hand: Essays in the Study of William Blake's Art and Aesthetics*, Los Angeles 1973, pp.233–52

Martineau 2003: Jane Martineau et al., *Shakespeare in Art*, exh. cat., Dulwich Picture Gallery, London 2003, pp.61–3

Michel 2001: Régis Michel, *La Peinture Comme Crime: Ou, La Part Maudite de la Modernité*, exh. cat., Louvre, Paris 2001

Mickle 1806: William Julius Mickle, *The Poetical Works*, ed. John Sim, London 1806

Miles 2002: Robert Miles, 'Europhobia: The Catholic Other in Horace Walpole and Charles Maturin' in Avril Horner (ed.), *European Gothic: A Spirited Exchange 1760–1960*, Manchester 2002, pp.84–103

Mills 1820: Charles Mills, *The History of the Crusades, for the Recovery and Possession of the Holy Land*, 2 vols., London 1820

Mills 1980: Alice Mills, 'The Spectral Bat in Blake's Illustrations to *Jerusalem*', *Blake Studies* 9 (1980), pp.87–99

Milton 1971: John Milton, 'The History of Britain' in *The Complete Prose Works of John Milton*, general editor Don M. Wolfe, London and New Haven 1959– , vol.V, part i (1971)

Milton 1993: John Milton, *Paradise Lost*, ed. Scott Elledge, New York and London 1993

Milton 1998: John Milton, *The Riverside Milton*, ed. Roy Flannagan, Boston and New York 1998

Moffitt 1990: John F. Moffitt, '*Malleus Maleficarum*: A Literary Context for Fuseli's Nightmare', *Gazette des Beaux-Arts*, 132 (1990), pp.241–8

Monk 1960: Samuel H. Monk, *The Sublime: A Study of Critical Theories in XVIII-Century England*, Michigan 1960

Monleón 1990: José B. Monleón, *A Specter Is Haunting Europe: A Sociological Approach to the Fantastic*, Princeton 1990

Moore 2003: Dafydd Moore, *Enlightenment and Romance in James Macpherson's The Poems of Ossian: Myth, Genre & Cultural Change*, Aldershot 2003

Morgan 1731: John Morgan, *Phoenix Britannicus: Being a Miscellaneous Collection of Scarce and Curious Tracts*, London 1731

Morgan 1995: Edwin Morgan, 'A Scottish Trawl', in Christopher Whyte, *Gendering the Nation: Studies in Modern Scottish Literature*, Edinburgh 1995, pp.205–22

Moskal 1991: Jeanne Moskal, 'Blake, Dante, and "Whatever Book is for Vengeance"', *Philological Quarterly* 70 (1991), pp.317–37

de la Motte-Fouqué 1818: Friedrich de la Motte Fouqué, trans. George Soane, *Undine: A Romance*, London 1818

Mulvey 1975: Laura Mulvey, Visual Pleasure and Narrative Cinema', *Screen* 16:3 (1975), pp.6–18

Murray 1924: *The Iliad of Homer*, trans. A.T. Murray, 2 vols., London and New York 1924–5

Myrone 2001a: Martin Myrone, 'The Sublime as Spectacle: The Transformation of Ideal Art at Somerset House', in Solkin 2001, pp.77–91

Myrone 2001b: Martin Myrone, *Henry Fuseli*, London 2001

Myrone 2005: Martin Myrone, *Bodybuilding: Reforming Masculinities in British Art, 1750–1810*, New Haven and London 2005

Newlyn 1993: Lucy Newlyn, *Paradise Lost and the Romantic Reader*, Oxford 1993

Nicholson 1985: John Nicholson, *The Great Liberty Riot of 1780: Being an Account of how the People Destroyed the Prisons of London and Set Free the Prisoners; Together with a Thorough Examination of how this Event has been Portrayed in History and Literature*, London 1985

Nicolson 1990: Benedict Nicolson, *Joseph Wright of Derby: Painter of Light*, 2 vols., London and New York 1968

Noble 2002: Louise Christine Noble, 'Corpus Salubre: Medicinal Cannibalism in Early Modern English Culture', Ph.D. Thesis, Queen's University, Kingston, Ontaria 2002

Nochlin 1994: Linda Nochlin, *The Body in Pieces: The Fragment as a Metaphor of Modernity*, London 1994

Norton 2000: Rictor Norton (ed.), *Gothic Readings: The First Wave, 1764–1840*, London and New York 2000

Ogborn 1998: Miles Ogborn, *Spaces of Modernity: London's Geographies, 1680–1780*, New York and London 1998

Omberg 1976: Margaet Omberg, *Scandinavian Themes in English Poetry, 1760–1800*, Uppsala and Stockholm 1976

Otto 2004: Peter Otto, 'James Graham as Spiritual Libertine' in Peter Cryle and Lisa O'Connell (eds.), *Libertine Enlightenment: Sex, Liberty and License in the Eighteenth Century*, Basingstoke 2004, pp.204–20

Paley 1986: Morton D. Paley, *The Apocalyptic Sublime*, New Haven and London 1986

Paley 1991: Morton D. Paley, *William Blake: Jerusalem The Emanation of the Giant Albion* (*Blake's Illuminated Books*, vol.1), London 1991

Paley 2003: Morton D. Paley, *The Traveller in the Evening: The Last Works of William Blake*, Oxford 2003

Pape and Burwick 1996: Walter Pape and Frederick Burwick (eds.), *The Boydell Shakespeare Gallery*, exh. cat., Bottrop 1996

Parraux 1960: André Parraux, *The Publication of The Monk: A Literary Event*, Paris 1960

Pasquin 1796: Anthony Pasquin (pseud. John Williams), *Memoirs of the Academicians: Being an Attempt to Improve the National Taste*, London 1796

Paulson 1983: Ronald Paulson, *Representations of Revolution (1789–1820)*, New Haven 1983

Paulson 1991–3: Ronald Paulson, *Hogarth*, 3 vols, New Brunswick and London 1991–3

Paulson 1996: Ronald Paulson, *The Beautiful, Novel and Strange: Aesthetics and Heterodoxy*, Baltimore and London 1996

Percy 1765: Thomas Percy, *Reliques of Ancient English Poetry*, 3 vols., London 1765 (facsimile ed. with introduction by Nick Groom, London 1996)

Percy 1771: Thomas Percy, *The Hermit of Warkworth: A Northumberland Ballad in Three Fits or Cantos*, London 1771

Penny 1972: Nicholas Penny, *Catalogue of European Sculpture in the Ashmolean Museum 1540 to the Present Day, Volume 1: Italian*, Oxford 1972

Phillips 2005: Michael Phillips, 'James Barry: Artist-Printmaker' in Dunne 2005, pp.141–7

Philp 1991: Mark Philp (ed.), *The French Revolution and British Popular Politics*, Cambridge 1991

Picart 2003: Caroline Joan S. Picart, *Remaking the Frankenstein Myth on Film: Between Laughter and Horror*, Albany 2003

Pinkerton 1782: John Pinkerton, *Rimes*, London 1782

Piper 1947: John Piper, *British Romantic Artists*, London 1947

Pirie 1973: David Pirie, *A Heritage of Horror: The English Gothic Cinema 1946–1972*, London 1973

Poe 1967: Edgar Allan Poe, *Selected writings of Edgar Allan Poe: Poems, Tales, Essays and Reviews*, ed. David Galloway, Harmondsworth 1967

Poe 1978: Edgar Allan Poe, *The Collected Works*, ed. T.O. Mabbott, 3 vols., Cambridge, Massachusetts, 1978

Pointon 1970: Marcia Pointon, *Milton & English Art*, Manchester 1970

Pointon 1997: Marcia Pointon, *Strategies for Showing: Women, Possession, and Representation in English Visual Culture, 1665–1800*, Oxford 1997

Ponte 1992: Allesandra Ponte, 'Architecture and Phallocentrism in Payne Knight's Theory', in Beatriz Colomine (ed.), *Sexuality & Space*, New York 1992, pp.273–305

Pope 1967: *The Iliad of Homer*, trans. Alexander Pope, ed. Maynard Mack, 2 vols., New Haven and London 1967

Porter 1982: Roy Porter, *English Society in the Eighteenth Century*, London 1982

Postle 1995: Martin Postle, *Sir Joshua Reynolds: The Subject Pictures*, Cambridge 1995

Potter 1777: Robert Potter, *The Tragedies of Æschylus Translated*, Norwich 1777

Potts 1994: Alex Potts, *Flesh and the Ideal: Winckelmann and the Origins of Art History*, New Haven and London 1994

Powell 1973: Nicolas Powell, *Fuseli: The Nightmare*, London 1973

Pressly 1977: Nancy L. Pressly, 'James Jefferys and the "Master of the Giants"', *Burlington Magazine*, 119 (1977), pp.280–4

Pressly 1979: Nancy L. Pressly, *The Fuseli Circle in Rome: Early Romantic Art of the 1770s*, exh. cat., Yale Center for British Art, New Haven 1979

Pressly 1981: William L. Pressly, *The Life and Art of James Barry*, New Haven and London 1981

Pressly 1993: William L. Pressly, *A Catalogue of Paintings in the Folger Shakespeare Library: 'As Imagination Bodies Forth'*, New Haven and London 1993

Pressly 1999: William L. Pressly, *The French Revolution as Blasphemy: Johan Zoffany's Paintings of the Massacre at Paris, August 10, 1792*, Berkeley, Los Angeles and London 1999

Pressly 2001: William L. Pressly, 'James Barry and the Print Market: A Painter-Etcher avant la lettre', in Elise Goodman, *Art and Culture in the Eighteenth Century*, Newark, Delaware 2001

Punter 2000: David Punter (ed.), *A Companion to the Gothic*, Oxford 2000

Punter and Byron 2004: David Punter and Glennis Byron, *The Gothic*, Oxford 2004

Radcliffe 1996: David Hill Radcliffe, *Edmund Spenser: A Reception History*, Columbia, South Carolina 1996

Rawson 2001: Claude Rawson, *God, Gulliver and Genocide: Barbarism and the European Imagination*, Oxford 2001

Reno 1984: Robert P. Reno, 'James Boaden's *Fontainville Forest* and Matthew G. Lewis' *The Castle Spectre*: Challenges of the Supernatural Ghost on the Late Eigtheenth-Century Stage', *Eighteenth-Century Life*, 9 (1984), pp.95–107

Repton 1789: Humphrey Repton, *The Bee*, London 1789

Reynolds 1826: Frederick Reynolds, *The Life and Times of Frederick Reynolds*, 2 vols., London 1826

Reynolds 1994: Richard Reynolds, *Superheroes: A Modern Mythology*, Jackson, Mississippi 1994

Rice-Oxley 1924: L. Rice-Oxley (ed.), *Poetry of the Anti-Jacobin*, Oxford 1924

Rigaud 1984: William L. Pressly (ed.), 'Facts and Recollections of the XVIIIth Century in a Memoir of John Francis Rigaud Esq., RA. by Stephen Francis Dutilh Rigaud', *Walpole Society*, 50 (1984), pp.1–164

Rigby 2004: Jonathan Rigby, *English Gothic: A Century of Horror Cinema*, 3rd ed., London 2004

Ritson 1783: Joseph Ritson (ed.), *A Select Collection of English Songs*, 3 vols., London 1783

Robinson 1806: Thomas Romney Robinson, *Juvenile Poems: To Which is Prefixed, A Short Account of the Author*, Belfast 1806

Robinson 2000: Judith Pascoe (ed.), *Mary Robinson: Selected Poems*, Peterborough, Ontario 2000

Roe 1953: A.S. Roe, *Blake's Illustrations to the Divine Comedy*, Princeton 1953

Rogers 1990: Nicholas Rogers, 'Crowd and People in the Gordon Riots' in Eckhart Hellmuth, *The Transformation of Political Culture: England and Germany in the Late Eighteenth Century*, Oxford 1990, pp.39–55

Rosenblum 1967: Robert Rosenblum, *Transformations in Late Eighteenth Century Art*, Princeton 1967

Rosenthal 1999: Michael Rosenthal, *Thomas Gainsborough: 'a little business for the eye'*, New Haven and London 1999

Rosenthal and Myrone 2002: Michael Rosenthal and Martin Myrone, 'Thomas Gainsborough: Art, Society, Sociability', in Michael Rosenthal and Martin Myrone (eds.), *Gainsborough*, exh. cat., Tate Britain, London 2002, pp.10–25

Ross 1773: Walter Ross (attrib.), *A Description of the Paintings in the Hall of Ossian at Pennycuik near Edinburgh*, Edinburgh 1773

Ross 1998: Margaret Clunies Ross, *The Norse Muse in Britain 1750–1820*, Trieste 1998

Rousseau 1964: Jean-Jacques Rousseau, *Oeuvres Complètes*, ed. Bernard Gagnebin and Marcel Raymond, vol.3, Paris 1964

Rousseau 1987: G.S. Rousseau, 'The Sorrows of Priapus: Anticlericalism, Homosocial Desires and Richard Payne Knight', in G.S. Rousseau and Roy Porter (eds.), *Sexual Underworlds of the Enlightenment*, Manchester 1987

Rubel 1978: Margaret Mary Rubel, *Savage and Barbarian: Historical Attitudes in the Criticism of Homer and Ossian in Britain, 1760–1800*, Amsterdam and Oxford 1978

Rudé 1970: George Rudé, *London and Paris in the Eighteenth Century: Studies in Popular Protest*, London 1970

de Sade 1990: The Marquis de Sade, *The 120 Days of Sodom and Other Writings*, compiled and trans. Austryn Wainhouse and Richard Seaver, London 1990

Said 1999: Edward W. Said, *Out of Place: A Memoir*, London 1999

Sancho 1994: Paul Edwards and Polly Rewt (eds.), *The Letters of Igantius Sancho*, Edinburgh 1994

Sayers 1965: Dorothy L. Sayers, 'The Art of Translating Dante', *Nottingham Mediaeval Studies*, 9 (1965), pp.15–31

Schenck 1969: M.D Schenck, 'Henry Fuseli, Nightmare and Sleep Paralysis', *Journal of the American Medical Association*, 207 (1969), pp.725–6

Schiff 1963a: Gert Schiff, *Johann Heinrich Füsslis Milton-Galerie*, Zurich and Stuttgart 1963

Schiff 1963b: Gert Schiff, 'Theodore Matthias von Holst', *Burlington Magazine*, 105 (1963), pp.23–32

Schiff 1973: Gert Schiff, *Johann Heinrich Füssli*, 2 vols., Zurich and Munich 1973

Schiff 1975: Gert Schiff, *Henry Fuseli 1741–1825*, exh. cat., Tate Gallery, London 1975

Schiff 2002: Gert Schiff, *'The Night of Enitharmon's Joy*: Catalogue Entry', *Blake: An Illustrated Quarterly*, 36 (2002), pp.38–9

Schiff and Viotto 1977: Gert Schiff and Paola Viotto, *L'Opera completa di Johann Heinrich Füssli*, Milan 1977

Sconce 1995: Jeffrey Sconce, '"Trashing" the Academy: Taste, Excess, and an Emerging Politics of Cinematic Style', *Screen* 36 (1995), pp.371–4

Shadwell 1991: Thomas Shadwell, *The Lancashire-Witches, and Tegue o Divelly the Irish Priest* (1682), ed. Judith Bailey Slagle, New York and London 1991

Shaftesbury 1999: Anthony Ashley Cooper, 3rd Earl of Shaftesbury, *Characteristics of Men, Manners, Opinions, Times* (1711), ed. Lawrence E. Klein, Cambridge 1999

Shakespeare 1997: William Shakespeare, *The Riverside Shakespeare* (1974), G. Blakemore Evans (ed.), 2nd ed., Boston and New York 1997

Shawcross 1972: John T. Shawcross (ed.), *Milton, 1732–1801: The Critical Heritage*, London 1972

Shelley 2003: Mary Shelley, *Frankenstein; Or, The Modern Prometheus* (1818), ed. D.L. Macdonald and Kathleen Scherf (1999), 2nd ed., Peterborough, Ontario 2003

Shookman 1993: Ellis Shookman (ed.), *The Faces of Physiognomy: Interdisciplinary Approaches to Johann Casper Lavater*, Drawer 1993

Siegel 2000: Jonah Siegel, *Desire and Excess: The Nineteenth Century Culture of Art*, Princeton and Oxford 2000

Silver and Ursini 2000: Alain Silver and James Ursini (eds.), *Horror Film Reader*, New York 2000

Simond 1817: Louis Simond, *Journal of a Tour & Residence in Great Britain, during the Years 1810 & 1811*, 2nd ed., Edinburgh 1817

Simonsuuri 1979: Kirsti Simonsuuri, *Homer's Original Genius: Eighteenth-century Notions of the Early Greek Epic (1688–1798)*, Cambridge 1979

Simpson 1993: David Simpson, *Romanticism, Nationalism and the Revolt against Theory*, Chicago and London 1993

Sinfield 1992: Alan Sinfield, *Faultlines: Cultural Materialism and the Politics of Dissident Reading*, Oxford 1992

Sitwell 1943: Sacheverell Sitwell, *Splendours and Miseries*, London 1943

Smiles 1994: Sam Smiles, *The Image of Antiquity: Ancient Britain and the Romantic Imagination*, New Haven and London 1994

Smith 2002: Greg Smith, *The Emergence of the Professional Watercolourist: Contentions and Alliances in the Artistic Domain, 1760–1824*, Aldershot 2002

Solkin 1993: David Solkin, *Painting for Money: The Visual Arts and the Public Sphere in Eighteenth-Century England*, New Haven and London 1993

Solkin 2001: David Solkin (ed.), *Art on the Line: The Royal Academy Exhibitions at Somerset House 1780–1836*, New Haven and London 2001

Sørensen 2002: Preben Meulengracht Sørensen, 'Thor's Fishing Expedition', in Paul Acker and Carolyne Larningham (eds.), *The Poetic Edda: Essays on Old Norse Mythology*, New York and London 2002, pp.119–37

Southey 1951: Robert Southey, *Letters from England*, ed. Jack Simmons, London 1951

Sowerby 2000: Robin Sowerby, 'The Goths in History and Pre-Gothic Gothic', in David Punter (ed.), *A Companion to the Gothic*, Oxford 2000, pp.15–26

Spenser 1977: Edmund Spenser, *The Faerie Queene* (1590–6), ed. A.C. Hamilton, London and New York 1977

Stafford 1988: Fiona J. Stafford, *The Sublime Savage: A Study of James Macpherson and the Poems of Ossian*, Edinburgh 1988

Staley 1980: Allen Staley, 'West's Death on the Pale Horse', *Bulletin of the Detroit Institute of Arts*, 58 (1980), pp.137–49

Stallybrass and White 1986: Peter Stallybrass and Allon White, *The Politics and Poetics of Transgression*, Ithaca 1986

Starobinksi 1974: Jean Starobinksi, 'La vision et al dormeuse', in *Trois fureurs*, Paris 1974, pp.129–62

Sterne 2003: Laurence Sterne, *A Sentimental Journey and Other Writings*, ed. Ian Jack and Tim Parnell, Oxford 2003

Stevens 1999: Adrian Stevens, 'Fiction, Plot, and Discourse: Wolfram's Parzival and Its Narrative Sources' in Will Hasty (ed.), *A Companion to Wolfram's Parzival*, Drawer 1999, pp.99–123

Stevenson 2001: David Stevenson, *The Beggar's Benison: Sex Clubs of Enlightenment Scotland and their Rituals*, East Linton 2001

Sumner 1938: B.H. Sumner, 'Michelangelo and Dante', *Italian Studies*, I (1938), pp.153–69

Sunderland 1986: John Sunderland, 'John Hamilton Mortimer: His Life and Works', *Walpole Society* 52 (1986)

Sweet 2005: Matthew Sweet, *Shepperton Babylon: The Lost Worlds of British Cinema*, London 2005

Swift 1996: Jonathan Swift, *Gulliver's Travels* (1726), ed. Paul Turner, Oxford 1996

Symmons 1984: Sarah Symmons, *Flaxman and Europe: The Outline Illustrations and their Influence* (Ph.D. Thesis, Courtauld Institute of Art, London 1979), pub. New York and London 1984

Tarr 1946: Sister Mary Muriel Tarr, *Catholicism in Gothic: A Study of the Nature and Function of Catholic Materials in Gothic Fiction in England (1762–1820)*, Washington DC 1946

Tate 1976: Nahum Tate, *The History of King Lear* (1681), ed. James Black, London 1976

Taylor 1968: Clyde R. Taylor, 'Iconographical Themes in William Blake', *Blake Studies* 1 (1968), pp.39–85

Taylor 1990: Gary Taylor, *Reinventing Shakespeare: A Cultural History from the Restoration to the Present*, London 1990

Taylor 1992: S.S.B. Taylor, 'Public Awareness of the Voltaire-Rousseau Quarrel: The Iconographical and Bibliographical Evidence', in Marian Hobson, J.T.A. Leigh and Robert Wokler (eds.), *Rousseau & The Eighteenth Century: Essays in Memory of R.A. Leigh*, Oxford 1992, pp.209–23

Thompson 1934: C.J.S. Thompson, *The Mystic Mandrake*, London 1934

Tille 1898: Alexander Tille (ed.), *Goethe's Satyros and Prometheus (Publications of the Glasgow Goethe Society*, 2), Glasgow 1898

Tinkler-Villani 1989: V. Tinkler-Villani, *Visions of Dante in English Poetry: Translations of the 'Commedia' from Jonathan Richardson to William Blake*, Amsterdam 1989

Tomalin 1994: Claire Tomalin, *Mrs Jordan's Profession: The Story of a Great Actress and a Future King*, London 1994

Tomory 1972: Peter Tomory, *The Life and Art of Henry Fuseli*, London 1972

Tomory 1979: Peter Tomory, *The Poetical Circle: Fuseli and the British*, exh. cat., Australian Gallery Directors' Council, Florence 1979

Todd 1946: Ruthven Todd, *Tracks in the Snow: Studies in English Science and Art*, London 1946

Tolley 1972: Michael J. Tolley, review of Martin Butlin, *William Blake: A Complete Catalogue of the Works in the Tate Gallery* (1971), *Blake Newsletter*, 6 (1972), pp.28–30

Trumpener 1997: Katie Trumpener, *Bardic Nationalism: The Romantic Novel and the British Empire*, Princeton 1997

Tully 2000: Carol Tully (trans. and ed.), *Romantic Fairy Tales*, London 2000

Turner 1999: Nicholas Turner with Rhoda Eitel-Porter, *Roman Baroque Drawings c.1620 to c.1700 (Italian Drawings in the Department of Prints and Drawings in the British Museum)*, 2 vols., London 1999

Turner 2001: Kathleen Turner, *British Travel Writers in Europe, 1750–1800: Authorship, Gender, and National Indentity*, Aldershot 2001

Twitchell 1985: James B. Twitchell, *Dreadful Pleasures: An Anatomy of Modern Horror*, New York and Oxford 1985

Tyson 1699: Edward Tyson, *Orang-outang*, London 1699

Unverfehrt 1996: Gerd Unverfehrt, 'Shakespeare Sacrificed: Boydell's Shakespeare Gallery in Gillray's Caricatures' in Pape and Burwick 1996, pp.161–74

dalle Vacche 1996: Angela dalle Vacche, *Cinema and Painting: How Art Is Used in Film*, London 1996

Vickers 1974: Brian Vickers, *Shakespeare: The Critical Heritage*, 6 vols., London 1974

Viscomi 1994: Joseph Viscomi, '*A Breach in a City the Morning after the Battle*: Lost or Found?', *Blake: An Illustrated Quarterly*, 28: 2 (1994), pp.44–61

Vogel 2001: Matthias Vogel, *Johann Heinrich Füssli: Darsteller der Leidenschaft*, Zurich 2001

Voltaire 1974: Voltaire, *Candide* (1759), trans. John Butt, London 1974

Wagner 1988: Peter Wagner, *Eros Revived: Erotica of the Enlightenment in England and America*, London 1988

Wagner 1991: 'Anticatholic Erotica in Eighteenth-Century England', in Peter Wagner (ed.), *Erotica and the Enlightenment*, Frankfurt 1991, pp.116–92

Walker 1986: John Walker, 'Maria Cosway, an Undervalued Artist', *Apollo*, 123 (1986), pp.318–24

Walpole 1978 Lars E. Troide (ed.), *Horace Walpole's 'Miscellany' 1786–1795*, New Haven and London 1978

Ward 1999: Aileen Ward, 'Romantic Castles and Real Prisons: Wordsworth, Blake, and Revolution', *The Wordsworth Circle*, 30 (1999), pp.3–15

Ward 2000: Maryanne C. Ward, 'A Painting of the Unspeakable: Henry Fuseli's *The Nightmare* and the Creation of Mary Shelley's *Frankenstein*', *The Journal of the Midwest Modern Languages Association*, 33 (2000), pp.20–31

Ward-Jackson 2003: Philip Ward-Jackson, *Public Sculpture of the City of London*, Liverpool 2003

Wardropper 1976: Bruce W. Wardropper, 'The Epic Hero Superseded', in Norman T. Burns and Christopher Reagan (eds.), *Concepts of the Hero in the Middle Ages and the Renaissance*, London 1976, pp.197–221

Warner 1612: William Warner, *Albion's England*, new ed., London 1612

Warner 1984: Janet A. Warner, *Blake and the Language of Art*, Kingston, Ontario 1984

Warner 1994: Marina Warner, *From the Beast to the Blonde: On Fairy Tales and their Tellers*, London 1994

Warner 1998: Marina Warner, *No Go the Bogeyman: Scaring, Lulling, and Making Mock*, London 1998

Warren 1999: Samuel Warren, 'The Spectre-Smitten' (1831) in Chris Baldick (ed.), *Tales of Terror from Blackwood's Magazine*, Oxford 1999

Watson 1990: Jeanie Watson, *Risking Enchantment: Coleridge's Symbolic World of Faery*, Lincoln, Nebraska, and London 1990

Watson 1997: Paul Watson, 'There's No Accounting for Taste: Exploitation Cinema and the Limits of Film Theory', in Deborah Cartmell et al. (eds.), *Trash Aesthetics: Popular Culture and its Audience*, London 1997, pp.66–83

Watt 1999: James Watt, *Contesting the Gothic: Fiction, Genre and Cultural Conflict, 1764–1832*, Cambridge 1999

Webster 1970: Mary D. Webster, *Francis Wheatley*, London 1970

Weinglass 1982: David H. Weinglass (ed.), *The Collected English Letters of Henry Fuseli*, New York 1982

Weinglass 1991: David H. Weinglass, '"The Elysium of Fancy": Aspects of Henry Fuseli's Erotic Arts', in Peter Wagner (ed.), *Erotica and the Enlightenment*, Frankfurt 1991, pp.294–315

Weinglass 1994: David H. Weinglass, *Prints and Engraved Illustrations by and after Henry Fuseli: A Catalogue Raisonné*, Aldershot 1994

Westfahl, Slusser and Plummer 2002: Gary Westfahl, George Slusser and Kathleen Church Plummer, *Unearthly Visions: Approaches to Science Fiction and Fantasy Art*, Westport, Connecticut, and London 2002

Whitlark 1988: James Whitlark, *Illuminated Fantasy: From Blake's Visions to Recent Graphic Visions*, London and Toronto 1988

Whitley 1915: William T. Whitley, *Thomas Gainsborough*, London 1915

Whytt 1765: Robert Whytt, *Observations on the Nature, Causes and Cure of Nervous Disorders*, 2nd ed., London 1765

Wieland 1805: Christoph Martin Wieland, *Oberon, a Poem* (1780), trans. William Sotheby, 2nd ed., London 1805

Williams 1999: Linda Williams, 'Film Bodies: Gender, Genre, and Excess' (1991) in Leo Braudy and Marshall Cohen (eds.), *Film Theory and Criticism: Introductory Readings* (1974), 5th ed., New York and Oxford 1999, pp.701–15

Winther 1989: Bert Winther, 'A Knight Rescues a Maiden from a Giant: An Iconographic Study of a Drawing by Henry Fuseli', unpublished paper, New York University, June 1989

Wrigley 1996: Richard Wrigley, 'Infectious Enthusiasms: Influence, Contagion, and the Experience of Rome', Chloe Chard and Helen Langdon (eds.), *Transports: Travel, Pleasure, and Imaginative Geography, 1600–1830*, New Haven and London 1996

Wutrich 1995: Timothy Richard Wutrich, *Prometheus and Faust: Promethean Revolt in Drama from Classical Antiquity to Goethe*, Greenwood, Connecticut 1995

Yarrington 1983: Alison Yarrington, 'Nelson the Citizen Hero: State and Public Patronage of Monumental Sculpture 1805–18', *Art History* 6 (1983), pp.315–29

Yarrington 1988: Alison Yarrington, *The Commemoration of the Hero 1800–1864: Monuments to the British Victors of the Napoleonic Wars* (Ph.D. Thesis, University of Cambridge 1980), published New York and London 1988

Zika 1997: Charles Zika, 'Cannibalism and Witchcraft in Early Modern Europe: Reading the Visual Images', *History Workshop Journal* 44 (1997), pp.77–105

Zimmermann 1778: Eberhard Zimmermann, *Geographische Geschichte des Menschen*, Leipzig 1778

Zipes 1983: Jack Zipes, *Fairy Tales and the Art of Subversion: The Classical Genre for Children and the Process of Civlization*, London 1983

Zipes 2000: Jack Zipes (ed.), *The Oxford Companion to Fairy Tales*, Oxford 2000

Zipes 2002: Jack Zipes, *Breaking the Magic Spell: Radical Theories of Folk and Fairy Tales* (1979), rev. ed., Lexington, Kentucky 2002

Lenders

Public Collections

Auckland Art Gallery Toi o Tāmaki 28, 49, 50, 52, 114, 117
Basel, Kunstmuseum 14
Bedford, Cecil Higgins Art Gallery 40, 45a
Birmingham City Museums and Art Gallery 31, 42
Boston, Museum of Fine Arts 129, 130, 138
Cambridge, Fitzwilliam Museum 66, 89, 103, 134
Cheltenham Art Gallery and Museum/Holst Birthplace Museum 109
Chicago, Art Institute of Chicago 51, 108, 116
Coventry, Herbert Read Gallery 120
Derby Museum and Art Gallery 53, 55, 56
Detroit Institute of Arts 1
Edinburgh, National Gallery of Scotland 11, 34, 74, 75, 142
Florence, Museo Horne 111, 112
Flyde Borough Council 100
Frankfurt am Main, Frankfurter Goethe-Museum 71
Liverpool, National Museums on Merseyside, The Walker Art Gallery 17, 77
London, The British Museum 4, 6, 7, 12, 13, 22, 35, 36, 46, 54, 76, 81, 87, 104, 131, 133, 135, 146
London, Courtauld Institute of Art 122, 128
London, The Guildhall Library 8
London, National Portrait Gallery 9
London, Royal Academy of Arts 21, 23, 24, 43, 44, 85, 132
London, Tate 25, 26, 29, 38, 41, 45b, 57, 59, 86, 101, 102, 105, 113, 126, 127, 136, 139, 140, 141, 150, 151, 153, 154
London, Victoria and Albert Museum 19, 118, 119, 152
London, The Wellcome Library 123
London, City of Westminster Archive Centre 5a, 5b
Manchester Art Gallery 48
New Haven, Yale Center for British Art 58, 61, 70, 82, 84
New York, Metropolitan Museum of Art 91
New York Public Library 20, 63, 64, 65, 79, 143a, 145
Nottingham City Museums and Galleries 27
Oxford, Ashmolean Museum 16, 83a, 83b
Schweinfurt, Georg Schäfer Museum 72
Stuttgart, Staatsgalerie 37
Washington DC, Folger Shakespeare Library 90, 107
Winterthur, Kunstmuseum 106
Zurich, Kunsthaus 2, 3, 10, 14, 15, 33, 39, 60, 78, 80, 88, 110, 115, 121, 125

Private collections

The Barrett Collection, Dallas 68
Ivor Braka Ltd, London 137
Andrew Edmunds 67
Robert N. Essick 69
Sir Robert Goff 62
Oxford, New College 99, 124, 143b, 147, 148, 149
Private collections 30, 47, 73
Private collection, courtesy Andrew Wyld 18
Private collection, courtesy Aroldo Zevi Limited, London 32

Photographic Credits

Figure Illustrations

Unless otherwise stated, copyright in the photograph is as given in the caption

Barry Batchelor © AP/EMPICS fig.24
Max Browne fig.26
Guildhall Library, Corporation of London / Geremy Butler Photography figs.14, 15
John Moore © AP/EMPICS fig.25
Trustees of Sir John Soane's Museum fig.16

Catalogue Illustrations

Unless otherwise stated, copyright in the photograph is as given in the lender credit

Cheltenham Art Gallery and Museum/ Bridgeman Art Library 109
Tate Photography / Rodney Tidnam / Andrew Dunkley / Marcus Leith / Joanna Fernandes 25, 26, 29, 38, 41, 45b, 57, 59, 86, 101, 102, 105, 113, 126, 127, 136, 139, 140, 141, 150, 151, 153, 154
Davison & Associates 62
Derby Museum & Art Gallery / W.W. Winter Ltd 53, 55, 56
Kunsthaus, Zurich / Cécile Brunner 2, 3, 10, 14, 15, 33, 39, 60, 78, 80, 88, 110, 115, 121, 125
Frankfurter Goethe-Museum / Ursula Edelmann 71
Guildhall Library, Corporation of London 8
Kunstmuseum Basel / Martin Bühler 14
Max Browne 73
The Bridgeman Art Library Courtesy of the Warden and Scholars of New College, Oxford 145, 143b, 147, 148, 149
Royal Academy of Arts, London / Paul Highnam / J. Hammond / Prudence Cuming Associates 21, 23, 24, 43, 44, 85, 132
The V&A Picture Library 19, 118, 119, 152

Index